36th Congress, 2d Session. } SENATE. { Ex. Doc. No. 10.

MESSAGE

FROM THE

PRESIDENT OF THE UNITED STATES,

COMMUNICATING,

In compliance with resolutions of the Senate, information upon the subject of the Aves Island.

February 25, 1861.—Read, and ordered to be printed.
March 2, 1861.—*Ordered,* That 2,500 extra copies of the message of the President of the United States, communicating, in compliance with resolutions of the Senate of the 17th and 18th February, 1858, correspondence relative to the Aves Island, be printed for the use of the Senate.

To the Senate of the United States:

In compliance with the resolutions of the Senate of the 17th and 18th February, 1858, requesting information upon the subject of the Aves island, I transmit a report from the Secretary of State, and the documents which accompanied it.

JAMES BUCHANAN.

Washington, *February* 23, 1861.

Department of State,
Washington, February 23, 1861.

The Secretary of State, to whom was referred the resolution of the Senate of the 17th February, 1858, requesting the President, "if not incompatible with the public interests, to cause to be furnished to the Senate all the correspondence, papers, and documents on file in the Department of State, in original or in copy, in the case of Philo S. Shelton and Sampson & Tappan, respecting 'Shelton's' or 'Aves' island, not heretofore furnished by said department to the Senate;" and the supplementary resolution of the 18th February, requesting, in addition, to be furnished with "all the correspondence, papers, and documents on file in the Department of State, in original or copy, relative to the cases of Lang & Delano, and Wheelwright & Cobb, respecting the island of Aves, in the Caribbean sea, not heretofore furnished by said department," has the honor to lay before the President the papers mentioned in the subjoined list.

Respectfully submitted.

J. S. BLACK.

The President.

List of documents.

Mr. Marcy to Mr. Sanford, July 7, 1856.
Mr. Thomas to same, July 8, 1856.
Mr. Sanford to Mr. Thomas, July 11, 1856.
Same to Mr. Marcy, July 15, 1856.
Mr. Marcy to Mr. Sanford, July 21, 1856.
Sampson & Tappan and Shelton to Mr. Marcy, July 21, 1856.
Mr. Sanford to the same, (inclosure,) August 11, 1856.
Mr. Eames to same (inclosure,) October 9, 1856.
Mr. Sanford to the President, December 14, 1856.
Same to Mr. Marcy, December 16, 1856.
Mr. Marcy to Mr. Sanford, December 23, 1856.
Mr. Sanford to Mr. Marcy, December 27, 1856.
Mr. Eames to same, (inclosure,) January 7, 1857.
Mr. Marcy to Mr. Sanford, January 9, 1857.
Mr. Sanford to Mr. Marcy, January 10, 1857.
Same to same, (inclosure,) January 22, 1857.
Same to same, (inclosure,) January 26, 1857.
Mr. Shelton to Mr. Marcy, January 31, 1857.
Mr. Marcy to Mr. Shelton, February 3, 1857.
Same to Mr. Sanford, February 3, 1857.
Same to Mr. Eames, (inclosure,) February 3, 1857.
Mr. Eames to Mr. Marcy, February 28, 1857.
Mr. Cass to Mr. Eames, April 1, 1857.
Mr. Eames to Mr. Cass, (inclosure,) April 1, 1857.
Mr. Cass to Mr. Shelton, April 3, 1857.
Same to Mr. Eames, April 3, 1857.
Mr. Cass to Mr. Eames, May 25, 1857.
Mr. Eames to Mr. Cass, (inclosure,) June 12, 1857.
Mr. Sanford to same, (inclosure,) August 10, 1857.
Same to same, (inclosure,) August 16, 1857.
Mr. Cass to Mr. Eames, August 31, 1857.
Mr. Sanford to Mr. Cass, (inclosure,) August 31, 1857.
Mr. Appleton to Mr. Sanford, September 4, 1857.
Mr. Cass to Mr. Eames, September 4, 1857.
Mr. Ribas to Mr. Cass, September 4, 1857.
Mr. Cass to Mr. Ribas, September 11, 1857.
Mr. Ribas to Mr. Cass, September 18, 1857.
Mr. Gutierrez to same, September 21, 1857.
Mr. Sanford to same, September 29, 1857.
Mr. Cass to Mr. Eames, October 6, 1857.
Mr. Eames to Mr. Cass, (inclosure,) October 31, 1857.
Mr. Gutierrez to same, (inclosure,) October 31, 1857.
Mr. Eames to same, (inclosure,) November 3, 1857.
Mr. Cass to Mr. Gutierrez, November 12, 1857.
Mr. Eames to Mr. Cass, (inclosures,) December 3, 1857.
Mr. Cass to Mr. Eames, December 15, 1857.
Mr. Shelton to Mr. Cass, December 17, 1857.
Mr. Cass to Mr. Briceño, February 22, 1858.
Mr. Briceño to Mr. Cass, February 24, 1858.
Mr. Eames to same, (inclosure,) February 24, 1858.
Mr. Cass to Briceño, February 26, 1858.

Messrs. Sampson & Tappan and Shelton to Mr. Marcy.

BOSTON, *January* 15, 1855.

SIR: The undersigned, merchants of Boston, beg to call your attention to an outrage which seems to us unprecedented, committed upon our rights by the government of Venezuela.

The circumstances are as follows: In the month of March last, 1854, the undersigned fitted out the brig J. R. Dow, Captain N. P. Gibbs, to search for guano deposits on the small island of Aves or Bird Island, and others in that portion of the Caribbean sea. Captain Gibbs found guano on Aves Island, and in June following was fitted out with a force of twenty-five men, and took possession of the island in July, fencing in that portion containing guano. Captain Gibbs has remained in quiet possession of the island, although visited by English, French, and Danish vessels of war, until about the 13th of December last, he was visited by a small schooner under Venezuelan colors, claiming to be a national vessel of the government of Venezuela, commanded by Domingo Dias, who styles himself Captain de Navio, and second in command of the naval force of the government of Venezuela. This officer claimed the island in the name of his government, and landed troops with arms, and took possession of the island, hoisted the flag of Venezuela, and notified Captain Gibbs he could only remain on sufferance until such time as they saw fit to eject him. About the 21st of December a second armed vessel of the Venezuelan government called there and landed twenty more troops. They now hold possession, and Captain Gibbs writes he may be ejected by force any day. We address ourselves to you, sir, with the request that you will lay the matter before the President, and in the name of the undersigned solicit his aid, with that of the government of the United States, to protect us in our rights so far as the government of Venezuela is concerned, as that government has not a shadow of a title to this island, for the following reasons:

First. Aves or Bird Island is in north latitude 15° 50′, and longitude 63° 43′ west from Greenwich; is a small barren island of only about one mile in circumference; has been known to exist for over 200 years, and never inhabited. It is at least 600 miles from the coast of Venezuela; it is not over 90 to 100 miles from the British colony of Dominica and the French colony of Guadaloupe.

Second. If Venezuela claims it as having belonged to Spain by priority of discovery, she must fail, as the Spanish colony of Puerto Rico being only about one half the distance from it, or some 300 miles nearer than Venezuela; and if any such claim were recognized, Spain, and not Venezuela, would have it.

Third. We maintain that no nation has any title, as it has remained uninhabited for 200 years, until we took possession and built domicils for our laborers and fenced in what we claim as our possessions.

Fourth. We think we have good reasons for believing that the government of Venezuela has, *for a consideration*, undertaken to eject us, to allow other parties to avail of the value of our discoveries under the shadow of protection of that government, who are really irresponsible as to any just pecuniary claims, and therefore indifferent to them. The undersigned believe this to be a case where simple justice requires the interference of this government to protect the interests of her citizens which are trampled upon in this outrageous manner by a foreign power without shadow of right. They do not ask the island to be protected as a national territory, but that the Venezuelan government *be made* to relinquish a possession to which they can show not even the semblance of a title.

All the foregoing is respectfully submitted, and the protection of the government solicited.

SAMPSON & TAPPAN.
PHILO S. SHELTON.

Hon. W. L. MARCY,
Secretary of State for the United States.

Messrs. Sampson & Tappan and Shelton to Mr. Marcy.

BOSTON, *January* 29, 1855.

SIR: Under date of 15th January current the undersigned addressed you a representation of the aggression committed upon them by the government of Venezuela, taking forcible possession of the Islas Aves, or Bird Island, held by their agent and men under him in the employ of the undersigned, now beg to inform you that their agents and men have been *forcibly* ejected from the island by the force of Venezuela sent for that purpose. The undersigned have suffered large losses in consequence of this summary ejection, by the loss of their establishment and appliances for loading guano, placed there at heavy expense, and by false freights on various ships that have to return without cargoes, and these losses are positive. Further, they consider themselves entitled to the sum of damages for the loss of the profit they could have realized by collecting, shipping, and selling the guano on said island, of which they have been so unjustifiably forced to relinquish by Venezuela.

The undersigned inclose a statement of such damages, and implore the aid of the executive department of government to exact the same from the Venezuelan government, believing it to be just and reasonable that they should pay the undersigned the damages they have sustained by the illegal acts of said government.

SAMPSON & TAPPAN,
PHILO S. SHELTON.

Hon. W. L. MARCY,
Secretary of State of the United States.

BOSTON, *January* 29, 1855.

SIR: The undersigned claim from the government of Venezuela for damages in consequence of the forcible ejection from Islas Aves, or Bird Island, of their agent and his men by an armed force from Venezuela acting under orders of that government.

For the guano on said island, estimated as a minimum at 25,000 tons, (probably 50,000 tons,) which, under the management of the subscribers, would have produced a net profit of $12 50 per ton, which on 25,000 tons is......	$312,500
For false freights on vessels under charter to load guano, that this ejection prevented loading, whereby false freights and damages have to be paid on several thousand tons capacity of vessels, say......	20,000
For loss in fixtures, launches, houses, wharves, &c., which have cost the proprietors a large sum of money, rendered quite worthless by this interruption......	8,500
	$341,000

SAMPSON & TAPPAN.
PHILO S. SHELTON.

Hon. WM. L. MARCY,
Secretary of State of the United States.

Mr. Marcy to Messrs. Sampson & Tappan and Philo S. Shelton.

DEPARTMENT OF STATE,
Washington, January 31, 1855.

GENTLEMEN: I have to acknowledge the receipt of your letter of the 29th instant, inclosing a statement of your claim against the government of Venezuela for the alleged losses you have sustained in consequence of the ejection of your agents and men from the Aves Islands.

This claim will, at the proper time, receive the attention of this department.

I am, gentlemen, &c.,

W. L. MARCY.

MESSRS. SAMPSON & TAPPAN AND PHILO S. SHELTON, *Boston.*

Mr. Shelton to Mr. Marcy, on Bird Island.

WASHINGTON, D. C., *February* 26, 1855.

SIR: I present herewith copy of a license or permit (1) signed by Domingo Dias, commander of the Venezuelan vessel of war sent to take possession of Aves or Bird Island by that government.

This document styles the island as the "Windward Bird Island," thus showing that the pretext set up that they made a mistake and took the wrong Bird Islands is a mere *evasion*. This license of the Commander Dias says they may remain until the pleasure of the supreme government is known. This is on the 13th December; on the 24th or 25th (the vessel having gone back to Venezuela) a second expedition arrives bringing more troops. Sufficient time having elapsed since the departure of the first vessel for Venezuela for her to arrive and the second to be dispatched by order of government, showing conclusively the government were acting understandingly, this second vessel communicated with St. Thomas, after landing the troops, and on her return thence ordered our men to quit the island within twenty-four hours, refusing to allow them to remove the buildings they had erected, but took possession of them for their own residences; and the same with regard to the wharf we had placed there which they required for their use, only allowing us to take off our provisions on condition of a part being given up to them.

There is no question that the *act* was deliberately done by the government of Venezuela. They fully understood what they were doing, as they about the same time *ejected* from the *Leeward* Bird Island near their own coast another party of men gathering guano there with whom we had no connection.

It is evident from subsequent developments the government of Venezuela agreed to take the island and hold it for the benefit of a company who had contracted with them to do so, and were to pay them a large sum of money so soon as the arrangement was completed.

Prior to the taking of the island a Danish sloop-of-war came up from St. Thomas and stated to our agent, Captain Gibbs, that the Danish government had been urged to take the island, but they had declined, and that he was bound to Venezuela to inform that government that the Danish government would not claim it, and that they should not object to Venezuela's doing so.

Captain Nickels, of the ship James N. Cooper, who arrived there after Captain Gibbs and his men had been ejected, states that the officer in command informed him that the island had been taken by the Venezuelan government at the instigation of the Venezuelan consul at St. Thomas, and that no vessels would be allowed to load except those bringing permits from the company who had contracted with that government.

All this shows clearly and conclusively that the Venezuelan government acted with a perfect understanding as to what they were doing, and that right or wrong they would take the island in consideration of the large sum of money they were to receive.

We ask from our government that damages—and I hope they may be exemplary damages—should be exacted from the government of Venezuela for this act of robbery. If the claim we have put is deemed excessive, we are willing it should be somewhat modified; but we urge upon this government the propriety of its protecting our rights by its insisting upon indemnity being paid us in this case.

With much respect,

PHILO S. SHELTON,
Acting for self and others interested.

Hon. W. L. MARCY.
Secretary of State.

(No. 1.)

Domingo Dias, capitan de navió, 2° jefe de la escuadra Venezolana y comisionada por el gobierno supremo de la republica, para celar las antillas deciertas que le pertenecen en el mar caribe; he veni do convenir, siempre que mi gobierno lo aprueve, en que los SS. Charles H. Lang, (agente por la compañiá Lang y Delano, de Boston,) y Nathan P. Gibbs, (agente por la de Sampson & Tappan y P. S. Shelton, tambien de Boston,) á quienes he encontrado estraiendo el huano de esta ista en que:

1°. Continuen cargando los tres buques que hay á la carga;

2°. Que continuen cargándolo hta. tanto que llegue la compañiá con quien el gobierno ha hecho contrata, ó que llegue a esta isla la aprobacion ó desaprobacion del S. gobierno;

3°. Y nosotros Charles H. Lang y Nathan P. Gibbs nos compremetemos á prestar los aucilios que necesitare la guarnicion de esta ilsa;

4°. Y al efecto ponemos nuestras pzas. de artilleria y armamento á las ordenes y bajo el pabellon Venezolano á quien pertenece la isla y;

5°. Yo Domingo Dias, 2° jefe de la escuadra ordeno á los SS. comandantes de los buques de guerra que crusan en las antillas que respeten esta convencion hta. tanto que el gobierno disponga otra cosa.

Ysla de Aves de Barlovento el trece de Diciembre de mil ochocientos cincuenta y cuatro.

DOMINGO DIAS.

Mr. Marcy to Mr. Shelton.

DEPARTMENT OF STATE,
Washington, March 2, 1855.

SIR: I have to acknowledge the receipt of your letter of the 26th ultimo, inclosing copy of a certain license granted by the commander of the Venezuelan man-of-war at the Aves Islands, to the parties therein named, to take guano from those islands. This paper will receive proper attention in the consideration of the subject.

I am, &c.,

W. L. MARCY.

PHILO S. SHELTON, Esq., *Washington*.

Mr. French to Mr. Marcy.

WASHINGTON, *May* 5, 1855.

SIR: I inclose a copy of the memorandum about the Aves Islands, to which I referred during our interview yesterday.

With much respect,

HENRY F. FRENCH.

Hon. WILLIAM L. MARCY,
Secretary of State.

March 17, 1835.—Her Majesty's ship Race Horse landed men on Aves Island. They found a party of Danes gathering eggs. The Danes collect them twice a day, and sell them at St. Thomas.

A hut for egg collectors was found. A tomb was in the center of the island. "The governor, a person at the head of a party of egg collectors, having died, was buried there."

The form of the island, oval; length, about 830 paces; width, 116 paces. Can be seen only about six miles. Latitude, 15° 40′ 56″.

No mention of any other occupants or visitors.

See the Nautical Magazine, vol. 7, *p.* 12, *Library of Congress.*

See, also, Blunt's American Coast Pilot, p. 476, "*Aves.*"

Mr. French to Mr. Marcy.

WASHINGTON, D. C., *May* 12, 1855.

SIR: I send herewith evidence of the claim of Wheelwright & Cobb for damages for the loss of the voyage of the brig Panola, by the illegal conduct of an officer of the Venezuelan government at Aves Island.

It is stated in the English papers by the Hermann, just arrived at New York, that the question of the title of the British government to this island has recently been discussed in Parliament, and that it is conceded that the British government has no right of sovereignty over it, but may claim equal right with other nations to take the guano.

If this be so the right of our citizens is clear, and the only question remaining is, whether our government can and will procure for them compensation for their loss.

With much respect,

HENRY F. FRENCH,
Attorney for Wheelright & Cobb.

Hon. WILLIAM L. MARCY,
Secretary of State.

BOSTON, *March* 2, 1855.

DEAR SIR: We take this method of informing you of a serious loss which we have recently incurred through the occupation of Aves Island, situated in the Caribbean sea, by the Venezuelan government, who had, a few days previous to the arrival of our vessel at that island, forced the occupants of the same, Messrs. Lang & Delano, of Boston, or their representatives, to leave the island. That you may come to a full understanding of the facts of the case, we beg leave to make the following statement, and also present for your perusal several affidavits, marked severally A., B., C., D., duly executed by parties who visited the aforementioned island as our agents in the prosecution of the voyage to and from that place:

In November last we made an agreement with Messrs. Lang & Delano, of this city, for the purchase of a cargo of guano, to be delivered alongside a vessel at the aforementioned Aves island. We accordingly chartered a vessel, the brig Panola, of New York, commanded by Warren Wass, for a voyage to the said Aves Island, there to take on board a full cargo of guano, to be brought to Baltimore or Philadelphia. This vessel sailed upon the voyage aforesaid from this port, on the twenty-seventh day of November, 1854, and as it appears from statements made by Captain Wass, also, our agent on board, Mr. J. H. McClennen, and the first officer, and boy, which you have herewith, upon reaching Aves Island they found the same occupied by the Venezuelan government, the representative of which informed our agent that his government had taken possession and forced the former occupants of the said island to leave. This officer in charge, however, agreed to furnish our agent a cargo of guano upon the payment of a stipulated sum of money, whereupon our agent, not being in possession of the requisite funds, proceeded with the vessel to St. Thomas to procure the same, being fully assured by the said officer in charge, that upon his return to the island with the required amount the guano would be in readiness for immediate shipment.

However, after going to St. Thomas, procuring the money under great disadvantage, and returning to the island with the same, the guano was then refused our agent, who tendered the stipulated amount in gold. Our agent, captain, and crew were driven from the island under repeated threats of violence at the hands of the occupants, so that our vessel, after cruising in vain for some two and a half months, was forced to return in ballast, after an unsuccessful and very expensive cruise.

We may add that port charges, or rather anchorage dues, were exacted of our agent by the officer in charge.

We have thus given you an outline of this unfortunate expedition, but for the detail of all the incidents relating to the same, we would respectfully ask your attention to the accompanying statements, duly certified and executed.

The loss incurred by us in consequence of the course taken by the Venezuelan government in occupying Aves Island as aforementioned, is a serious matter to us, amounting, in round numbers, to some fifteen thousand dollars, and if we have a legal claim against that government, as we are constrained to believe, we trust you will be willing to take the necessary steps in our behalf to enforce it.

Asking your early attention to this matter, we are, dear sir, very respectfully, your obedient servants,

WHEELWRIGHT & COBB.

Hon. W. L. MARCY,
Secretary of State.

A further certificate, signed by the captain and mate of this vessel, has already been forwarded and placed on file in the State Department.

A.

NEW YORK, *March*, 1855.

I, Warren Wass, master and agent for the owners of the brig Panola, of New York, certify that on the eighteenth day of November, A. D. 1854, I chartered said brig to Messrs. Wheelwright & Cobb, merchants of Boston, for a voyage to the "Aves or Bird Island," to procure a cargo of guano, thence to Philadelphia or Baltimore, United States of America. Said Wheelwright & Cobb put on said brig a number of extra men to assist in loading said vessel, as also extra provisions, tools, and implements for the same. They also sent on board their agent, Mr. John H. McClennen, of said Boston, under whose orders I was to act. We sailed from the port of Boston, accompanied by said McClennen and extra men, &c., in said brig, with ballast, and proceeded on our voyage. We arrived at the "Aves Island" on the second day of January, A. D. 1855, and anchored. I proceeded on shore with said Mr. McClennen, in order to procure a cargo of guano, in accordance with a permit or order on the agent of Messrs. Lang & Delano, of Boston.

Upon getting on shore, found the island in possession of an armed band of men, commanded by one Nicholas Peraro, who demanded of us port charges, stating that the island had been constituted a port of entry by authority of the Colombian or Venezuelan government. We paid the said charges according to his demand. He further informed us that Messrs. Lang & Delano's agent and men had left the island by orders of the above-named government a few days previous to our arrival. In consideration of the circumstances, Mr. McClennen stipulated with him for a full cargo of guano for the sum of $400, the same to be paid him in gold on delivery of said cargo within reach of said brig's tackles.

He further agreed to collect the same (and we left our tools and implements for that purpose) with his own men and at his own expense. It was further stipulated that we should proceed to the island of St. Thomas to procure the necessary funds, as we had not the amount on board the vessel. We sailed for St. Thomas and procured the stipulated amount and returned to the island and anchored as before. Upon going on shore we learned, to our surprise, that nothing had been done towards collecting the cargo. We then offered to collect it with our own men, at our own expense, and pay the stipulated price. He refused, and with many threats ordered us to get our vessel under weigh and leave the island within the hour. This we did, and were obliged to return to the United States, in ballast, *via* St. Thomas, at which place we hoped to obtain a freight or charter, to save some portion of the loss.

We arrived at St. Thomas, and found many vessels there, and no freights to be had, neither charters, and consequently were obliged to return to the United States as above, thereby totally defeating the voyage, and entailing great loss and disappointment.

WARREN WASS.

City and County of New York, *ss:*

Before me, A. B. Vanolinda, a public notary in and for said city and county, personally came and appeared Warren Wass, who, being by me duly sworn, doth depose and say that the annexed certificate by him subscribed is correct and true in all and every particular.

[L. S.] In testimony whereof, I have hereunto set my hand and affixed my seal of office, this first day of March, A. D. 1855.

A. B. VANOLINDA,
Notary Public.

B.

New York, *March* 1, 1855.

To whom it may concern:

I, John Wass, seaman on board the brig Panola, of New York, Warren Wass master, on a voyage from Boston to the Aves or Bird Island for a cargo of guano, thence to a port of discharge in the United States, do hereby certify that I sailed on board said vessel on said voyage. On arrival at the above-named island I was called upon to act as interpreter between Mr. John H. McClennen, the agent or supercargo of the brig, and Captain Wass and one Nicholas Peraro, the officer in command of an armed band of Venezuelan soldiers, who held possession of said island. I hereby certify that the statement marked A, subscribed by Captain Wass, is true and correct in every particular, the same having been this day read and exhibited to me.

JOHN WASS.

Witness: A. B. Vanolinda.

City and County of New York, *ss:*

Before me, A. B. Vanolinda, a public notary in and for said city and county, personally came and appeared John Wass, who, being by me duly sworn, doth depose and say that the annexed certificate, by him subscribed, is correct and true in every and all particulars.

[L. S.] In testimony whereof, I have hereunto set my hand and affixed my seal of office, this first day of March, A. D. 1855.

A. B. VANOLINDA,
Notary Public.

C.

To whom it may concern:

I, Luther White, of the city of Boston and Commonwealth of Massachusetts, mariner, certify that on the twenty-seventh day of November, A. D. 1854, I sailed from said Boston in the brig Panola as mate, on her voyage from that port to the "Aves" or Bird Island, for a cargo of guano, and thence to the United States via St. Thomas, West Indies, and that the statements of Mr. John H. McClennan, marked D., also of Captain Warren Wass, master of said brig Panola, marked A., also of John Wass, seaman on board said brig, marked B., are true and correct in every particular, the same having been inspected by me personally.

LUTHER WHITE,
Mate of brig Panola.

Commonwealth of Massachusetts, *Suffolk County*, } *ss:*

Then personally appeared the above named Luther White, and made oath that the above statement signed by him is true.

Before me,

GEORGE MORRILL,
Justice of the Peace.

March 2, 1855.

D.

Boston, *March* 2, 1855.

I, John H. McClennen, of the city of Boston and Commonwealth of Massachusetts, merchant, certify that on the twenty-seventh day of November, A. D. 1854, I sailed from the said city of Boston in the brig Panola of New York, Warren Wass, master, as the authorized agent of Messrs. Wheelwright & Cobb, of said Boston, merchants, bound to the Aves or Bird Island, situated in latitude 15° 39′, longitude 63° 38′, for the purpose of obtaining a cargo of guano. I arrived at said Aves Island, with said brig Panola, on the second day of January, A. D. 1855, having a permit or order for a full cargo of guano in my possession, signed by Messrs. Lang & Delano, of said Boston, merchants, who had legal possession of said island at the date of said permit, and date of my departure from the United States on said voyage. On my arrival at Aves Island, and the vessel anchored, I proceeded on shore, accompanied by Captain Wass, above named, for the purpose of presenting the aforesaid order or permit, and obtaining a cargo in accordance with my instructions, and of said order or permit, and found that the said Aves Island had, a few days previously, been taken forcible possession of and held by an armed band of Venezuelans, under authority of the Colombian or Venezuelan government, and that the agent and men employed by Messrs. Lang & Delano had been driven by them from the Island, and by orders from the said Colombian or Venezuelan government. Having an interpreter on board the said brig Panola, I entered into communication with Nicholas Peraro, the authorized agent of said government, informing him of the circumstances under which I had come to the Aves Island. He declined to attend to my case until I had first acceded to a demand made by him for port charges, which he alleged was due his government, as he had constituted it a port of entry under their instructions. I acceded to his demand by paying him the sum required; when he offered to collect a full cargo of guano and deliver the same within reach of the vessel's tackles, provided I would pay him the sum of four hundred dollars in doubloons, and to deliver the said cargo at once, on payment of the above sum. Not having the specie on board the vessel, we stipulated an agreement between us to the effect that I should sail with said brig Panola for the Island of St. Thomas, there to obtain said funds and return to said Aves Island. It was further agreed that I should furthermore loan him sundry tools and implements to collect said cargo of guano, and he agreed to collect and pile the same on the beach during my absence. I delivered him the tools and sailed for St. Thomas on the third day of January, A. D. 1855, and arrived on the 7th day of the said month. On my arrival, I negotiated a bill of exchange on Boston, United States, procured the necessary funds and sailed again for the Aves Island. We arrived at said island the second time on the 10th of January, A. D. 1855; anchored the vessel and proceeded on shore with the said specie to pay for the aforesaid cargo. To my surprise he disclaimed any intention of fulfilling his agreement, and would not allow me to take cargo myself with my own men, although I offered to load the vessel myself, without expense or trouble to him; and also agreed to pay him the stipulated price for the cargo, but with many threats to sink the vessel by pointing a loaded cannon, as she lay at anchor, and threatening to take our lives if we did not get under weigh and leave the island within the hour, he drove us from the island, in consequence of which we were obliged to return to the United States in ballast. I would also certify that we had a number of extra men on board the said brig

Panola, with extra provisions and equipments for said voyage, which very materially increased our loss by the voyage.

We arrived at Wilmington, North Carolina, on the 1st day of February, A. D. 1855, having been absent on the voyage sixty-seven days, and the objects of which totally defeated, having gone out and returned in ballast, thereby entailing a severe damage to the charterers.

All of which is respectfully submitted.

JOHN H. McCLENNEN.

COMMONWEALTH OF MASSACHUSETTS, *Suffolk County*, } *ss:*

Then personally appeared the above named John H. McClennen, and made oath that the above statement signed by him is true.

Before me,

GEORGE MORRILL,
Justice of the Peace.

MARCH 2, 1855.

Mr. Shelton to Mr. Marcy.

BOSTON, *May* 14, 1855.

SIR: Insomuch as we remain entirely unacquainted in respect to any decisive action having been taken by the executive branch of the federal government of the United States towards obtaining just and speedy reparation from the State of Venezuela, for the wrongs and injuries received by us from its authorities, we deem it not improper to again solicit your early attention, and, through you, the notice of his excellency, President Pierce, to the facts and principles of international law and justice upon which our claim for full indemnity and for effectual measures, if need be by force, to obtain that redress, is founded. The honor and dignity and rights of our country are not, we know, in our keeping. If it was our privilege, it is not our duty, to make any suggestions on such topics to the Chief Magistrate of the United States, or to you, with whom is placed that high trust, except in so far as our individual and personal rights as citizens are directly involved. And, possessed of that confidence, the declarations of the President on assuming the responsibilities of his exalted station were so well calculated to inspire, as well as the evidences since exhibited, in more than one instance, of his firm resolution, and that of yourself, to "submit to nothing that is wrong," we have no motive for thrusting our opinion on that subject before you, either in the form of counsel or admonition. We desire to *confine* ourselves to the taking care of "our own affairs," and this is, in the *first* place, what we would respectfully urge upon our government it should constrain the Venezuelan government to do. Our government will not, in acceding to this request, "ask anything that is not clearly right;" for such is the duty of nations as well as individuals. And, in the *second* place, we desire that our government should require of Venezuela full and prompt reparation for the wrongs and injuries done to us, and of which we have heretofore complained.

And now, sir, we would respectfully ask you to reperuse the letter and remonstrance of the undersigned, addressed to you officially, dated Boston, January 15, 1855, on the files of your department.

That letter, you will perceive, states the principal facts in relation to the discovery in March, 1854, and the taking peaceable possession of, and the actual occupation in a few weeks subsequently by our agents, in merchant vessels of the United States, bearing its flag, with a company of seamen and laborers, of the *Isla de Aves*, or "Bird Island." These islands, as they are called, are merely barren rocks, situated in the Caribbean sea, in about 15° 40′ north latitude, and 63° 38′ west longitude from Greenwich. The principal isle (SHELTON'S ISLE) is about a mile in circumference; had not in March, 1854, any soil, or land, or houses, or trees, or herbage of any kind upon it, and was never inhabited by man before our agents landed on it. The others near it are still smaller. Our agents discovered a deposit of guano on the principal isle, before then unknown, and the presence of which gives the chief, if not sole, value to the island. On being informed of this, we fitted out from the United States, for the express object of procuring cargoes of that article, as merchandise, several vessels with extra crews and laborers, and at no trifling expense. We made contracts for the supply of that article at prices which would, if we could have carried them out, yielded us a handsome profit. We shipped materials for houses, and provisions thither for our laborers; and we provided barrows, implements, and tools, launches and other conveniences, wherewith to gather and lade the vessels with it. We sent materials for wharves and landing places to be erected on the edge of the rock, so that our vessels could come near to it. We intended to establish there a permanent settlement, and purposed the transportation of soil thither by our vessels on their outward voyages from the United States, wherewith to make gardens, and plant shrubs and trees.

Who, we ask, had any right to complain of this, much less to prohibit us from so doing; or after our arrival there and commencement of operations and continuance thereof for several months, to eject us by force from the island, seize our property carried thither, and forbid our return? Doubtless the *existence* of this desolate rock has been known for nearly two centuries, and perhaps longer. It is not improbable that French, English, Danish, Dutch, Spanish, and Portuguese and American merchantmen, and also men-of-war, likewise the noted pirates that formerly infested those parts, have often visited *Shelton's Isle;* but it is not believed any government or individuals ever thought of it as a *possession*, and certainly none ever *occupied* it till last year, when we planted the stars and stripes upon it. Mere discovery, unless it is followed by occupation, confers no right upon a government or upon an individual, either to an *island* or to a barren *rock* in the ocean, or to the *shore* of a continent, whether inhabited by idolatrous savages or utterly uninhabited. The merely *seeing* an island or other land, or a rock at sea, though before unknown, and landing thereon, and leaving it again,—in other words, mere temporary occupation, without the *animus revertendi*, cannot confer any right. Discovery must be followed by occupation. And *constructive* possession will not answer for a series of years, much less for a century and a half, or two centuries after discovery! It is not contended that *actual and uninterruptedly continued* occupation or possession *de facto* from the time of the first discovery is necessary, and it is conceded that *reasonable allowance* may be made. We insist, however, that the law is, that positive possession, *pedis possessio*, or "actual occupation," must be had at *some period*, and there must be some acts of ownership exercised, or at least asserted, or "continental claim" of ownership and jurisdiction made, or a general acknowledgment of right by other nations, in order to confer any right of dominion over a newly-discovered island upon the government of the *first* discoverer. All the legal authorities, we are told, show this to be the true principle. Our counsel has furnished us with the following references, which you can appreciate better than we, for we are no lawyers, though we can perceive they are entirely consistent with common sense: Grotius, *Jur. Bel. ac Pac.* L. 2., chap. 4. Puffendorff, *Jur. Nat. et Gen.* L. 4., c. 12, and also page 413, and *Jur. Nat.*, vol. 1, c. 1, § 51. Vattel, *Droit des gens*, vol. 1, lib. 2, c. 11, and p. 99, c. 18, § 207 of translation. Rutherford, *Int. Nat. Law*, vol. 1, c. 8, vol. 2, c. 9, § 3, 6. Klüber, § 126. Savigny, *Das Recht des Besitzes*, § 1–9, &c. Dr. Phillimore, *Int. Law*, vol. 1, pp. 213, 236, 237, 238, 242, 247, 263, *ut passim.* 8 Wheat. Rep. S. C. U. S. 571, 605, *Johnson vs. McIntosh.* 5 Robinson's *Ad. Rep.*, (Lord Stowell,) p. 385; *The Anna.* Wheat., *Elm. Int. Law*, c. 4, § 5, &c., p. 209, *et seq.* to 237, &c.*

Admitting Spain, the antecessor of Venezuela, *first* discovered the existence of Shelton's Isle, never having taken formal possession of it, never having exercised any acts of ownership of any kind in relation to it, the claim of title by Venezuela is preposterous. The idea of her claiming it on the score of its being contiguous or appurtenant to her shores, is simply ridiculous. Whilst it is conceded that it is not necessary upon the discovery of land before unknown to the civilized world, in order to acquire possession, that *all parts* of the newly discovered region should be actually occupied, and that the occupation of the principal and commanding or controlling points will suffice as to

*In these authorities the *jus usucapio* is treated of fully. Possession by intervals signifies nothing. Non-possession for a long time destroys right, though without any opposing appropriation and occupation. So, if the thing is deserted. Must be actual corporeal retention and intention to retain. Discovery gives *inchoate* title merely. Discovery and settlement are necessary ingredients of a title by occupation. Original acquisition must be followed by possession—that is, use and settlement are essential ingredients of that occupation necessary to constitute a valid title to national acquisitions. Islands formed by accretions near a river belong to the country from which the river flows. Not to be called "*no man's land*," like islands far in the sea, not possessing soil of sufficient consistency or in sufficient quantity to support the purposes of life and uninhabited, and only resorted to for purposes of shooting or fishing, or for taking bird's nests, and the like. If islands are near the coast ownership may be claimed upon the principle of alluvium and increments, or upon the principle of contiguity and being appurtenant and geographically dependent, and actual and continual possession or occupation of such island is not necessary to give title. So the discovery, conquest, and colonization or settlement, or long and uninterrupted possession gives title, because of the natural utility tending to promote the general welfare of mankind. Heathen barbarians were formerly held by popes and princes to be lawful prey and spoil of Christian conquerors. Alexander VI, in 1493, allotted by a Bull all the Americas to Spain and Portugal; and Henry VII, of England, by patent gave to Cabot a commission to discover, adjacent, contiguous, and appurtenant country, naturally tributary to them, yet no respectable authority can be found to warrant Venezuela, as the successor of any Spanish discoverers, in laying claim to a barren rock at least 500 miles from any part of her coasts, and totally dissevered and disconnected from them. Why, it is much nearer the Island of Dominica and Guadaloupe; and, in fact, Puerto Rico is but half as far from *Isla Aves* as is the Venezuelan coast. How the authorities of Venezuela came to put forth the claim they have, and enforce it as they did against us, can only be accounted for on the supposition that they were deceived and misled by third parties seeking to make a speculation for themselves in the premises regardless of law or right.

It is out of the question to admit that a State may, after discovery by her flag, or the flag of her antecessors, abandon such island, neglect to use it for any purpose, cultivation, fishing, hunting, or wooding, leave it *derelict* for a series of years; nay, even since landing on it, if they ever did land on it, and then when other people, with greater enterprise, seek to use it for beneficial purposes, drag forth from the oblivion of centuries the dormant *claim* of discovery. Such claim is not merely dormant, it is DEAD! Especially when such claim is urged on the flimsy ground of *constructive* right merely, as an *appurtenance* to main land separated by the ocean from it, and 500 miles distant; should it be disregarded? [*Vide* authorities before cited: "Facility with which adjacent vacant land may be reached in a short time, and settled and cultivated and defended, or as compared with the probability and facility of the same things from another quarter," is an important consideration. The Russian right to the possession of the desolate country *north* of Sitka, uncontested and peaceful for many years, is founded on this principle. An island "must be a natural appendage to the coast," "geographically appurtenant and tributary" to it, to justify the possession of the coast "reaching it," and making such possessory title valid without "actual occupation of such island."]

We learn that England, as usual in such cases, has put in her claim to this rock. *That* was to be expected. She is famous, and always was, for "finding things," and is doubtless well sustained with all sorts of muniments of title and proofs of title, made exactly to suit the case. As there never has been an Indian on the *Isla de Aves* out of which

---

subdue, and occupy and possess lands in America, and the right of the Indian was held to be subordinate to that of the Christian discoverers and occupiers. The possession necessary to be exercised is personal action on the land and excluding action of others, full of permanent control or power over it, and intention of appropriation to claimant's own use; all this must be united to constitute possession. Occupation is *pedis possessio*, with power of excluding others at pleasure; it is *de facto*, and not constructive possession, that is necessary. Intent to occupy and hold must be manifested by outward and external acts of a positive character. By the common consent of nations these acts are, in discovered countries, use and settlement. Continuous use is an indispensable element of occupation. The possession must be real, must form settlement, practical use. It must not be unreasonably delayed. Monuments, hoisting flags, making land-marks, firing salutes, and erecting crosses, and the like, are empty ceremonies if unaccompanied by continued occupation. So are mere surveys. On the voluntary desertion or abandonment of first discoverers of lands, and especially of a barren and uninhabited rock in the high seas, the same becomes thereby derelict, or "*no man's land*," and the next discoverer may occupy and hold it. The right to Nootka Sound, in dispute last century between England and Spain, is an example of this, and there are many others.

The terms employed in this note are extracted from authorities cited in the text and others employed in them.

to manufacture a king for them, and as, in fact, nothing ever lived there until 1854, except *aquatic birds*, we are informed that she founded her claim on the assertion that an officer of the British navy once made a survey of it. This kind of title might as well be preferred by the British to about half of our uninhabited Florida Keys, and to the Alacranes in the Gulf of Mexico; for she has been *surveying* in that region for a quarter of a century past. And she may likewise just as well claim several islands off of the coast of California and in the Gulf of California on the same ground. It would not be at all surprising if she proved that the red cross of St. George was formally raised on SHELTON'S ISLE, and loyally saluted by a salvo of cannon and small arms, drinking the health of its sovereign, and singing "Britannia rules the waves," &c., as acts of sovereignty. The Dutch, we learn, have also put forth their claim, and have, since our ejection, driven Venezuela off by force, or the latter has allowed and admitted their right; which the Danish, it seems, had conceded Venezuela possessed. Spain, doubtless, will claim also, and Portugal and Denmark, as contiguous to some place or other; and it is quite likely France, if not alone, in partnership with England, will set up like pretensions, as their alliance, it is said, extends over all creation, and the guardianship of all creation, and the cultivation of "*ideas*" over all creation.

We have one answer to all these "people," and that is, whoever discovered *Isla de Aves*, or SHELTON'S ISLE, 200 or 250 years ago, is of no consequence; forasmuch as no positive acts of ownership, no exercise of sovereignty, no possession or occupation, actual or constructive, was ever had or attempted by any body, Spanish or Dutch, Portuguese, French, Venezuelan, or English, or Yankees, till 1854; and when we took possession and occupied it, it was uninhabited and vacant, abandoned and *derelict*. It is too late for any of these people to hunt up old papers and surveys, and the like, and to trace back to history to discover who first discovered it. These things are out of date, and do not deserve consideration in this practical age—the age that Napoleon III calls the age of "*ideas*," and that we call the "*age of progress*."

There is no land, nor earth, nor, properly speaking, soil, on *Shelton's Isle*. It, and the trifling isles near it, are, as before said, barren, desolate, naked, vacant rocks, elevated but a few feet above the ocean. The survey we had made of it in 1854, a copy of which we send you, we will vouch is superior to the alleged British survey, manufactured, we doubt not, since. Until we discovered *guano* there, no possible inducement or motive could exist for any individual to occupy it. It is most desirable that this country should possess this island on account of the great advantage to our agriculturists of the Atlantic States, given by that best of all newly discovered fertilizers, of which there is a deposit on it, and it is due to that branch of our industry that some exertions should be made to prevent the odious monopolies existing on the other side of this continent in that article, and which it is sought to perpetuate there, and also here, at the expense of our farmers. Except upon the Alacranes, on the gulf coast of Yucatan, *Shelton's Isle* is the first discovery on the eastern side of the continent having such deposit. It is not doubted there are other barren and desolate and *derelict* rocks containing it (of as good, if not better, quality than the *Pacific* guano, and that can be furnished to our agriculturists at one third the cost of the other) to be found in the American seas, south of 25° north latitude. Acquiescence, without remonstrance and effective action in the proceedings that have been had in this case, may establish a precedent highly injurious to our country in this respect.

The largest rock, (SHELTON'S ISLE,) possibly, may be made, with some outlay, important to our commerce passing near it, by erecting a lighthouse upon it, by constructing a martello tower for defense there, boring deep wells to obtain water, and by having deposits of coal there for our steamers in the merchant service and in the Navy. But in all this we are not *directly* and *immediately* interested; nor in the fact that it would constitute an admirable outpost or picket guard for our interests, present and ultimate, in all that region.

We look to the deposit of guano as the only present means of rendering the island valuable to us as individuals, by bringing to market for our farmers at a small advance on cost this rich fertilizer; and we are entirely willing to transfer all our rights to our government, (*reserving the guano*,) without charge or compensation, and if the government decides that said course is desirable, we will do so promptly. We have heard that some exceedingly squeamish and strict constructionists say that the federal government has not the "faculty of acquisition" of a foreign country, by the discovery and occupation of its citizens under its flag, because the case is not *in terms* provided for in the federal Constitution. And so, too, by purchase, or a free transfer, such as we propose; and particularly, that the Executive cannot so act without a law of Congress authorizing it, or the concurrence or direction of Congress otherwise given. So, at the commencement of this century, was it objected that the executive and legislative branches *together* had no power to annex Louisiana, and yet the most important function of the federal government from that day to this has been to provide and regulate annexation by purchase, by conquest in open war, and otherwise. And the Executive has more than once arranged for naval depots and yards, &c., at Port Mahon, in Minorca, and Spezzia, in Sardinia, and elsewhere, at different times, and the concurrence of Congress has *only* been asked to furnish the necessary funds. In this case, as no money is requisite, no *such* concurrence is necessary. We presume, therefore, there can be no difficulty on this point. If the United States has no faculty of acquisition of newly discovered and primarily possessed and occupied islands, this attribute of sovereignty must revert to the State of our allegiance, *Massachusetts*, or to *ourselves*. This sovereignty cannot be in *abeyance, and it cannot die*. It exists somewhere, and if not delegated to the federal government, it is "reserved to the States" and to "the people." (Art. X Fed. Const. Amend.

Our first letter to you, dated January 15, 1855, above mentioned, states to you the facts as to our discovery and taking possession, in the spring of 1854, of the chief isle, and of our quiet, peaceful, and undisturbed possession of it for several months, and until the middle of December, 1854, with our workmen, and that we had several vessels there lading guano.

On December 13, 1854, a personage styling himself Don Domingo

Dias, "*capitan de navio, second jefe de la esquadra Venezuela,*" came there in a schooner of the Venezuela navy, armed and equipped and manned, and having also regular troops of that State on board, and claimed the isles as belonging to Venezuela, stating that he acted by the express authority and command of the government of that power, and notifying our seamen and laborers of his commission, and that the vessel under his command was a government vessel. He landed some troops, and hoisted and saluted the Venezuelan flag, (upon the isle,) and warned us that we could not stay any longer than he saw fit. He then went to Laguira to procure more troops, and on December 24th another Venezuelan vessel arrived and landed more troops, and in a short time we were informed that we must leave the isle within twenty-four hours, or they would drive us away by the soldiery. During the time that had elapsed from their first arrival, our workmen had been prevented from progressing advantageously in the lading of the guano, and now a *prohibition* was not only backed by the presence of an armed force and threats of personal violence to our men therefrom, and *demonstrations actually made,* but they were dispossessed of the materials, tools, &c., sent thither, and their houses taken from them by the soldiers by force.

The said Dias, on December 13, had drawn up and signed a paper in Spanish, (on file in your department,) and which our agent, Captain Gibbs, was *constrained* under the circumstances to take, and which Dias styled his "*permit!*"

In conformity with a peremptory order, doubtless intended when Dias issued that paper, our employés and our vessels left the island and returned to the United States. Charges were exacted by Captain Dias of some of the American vessels at the isles. You will perceive from documents on file at the department, that other Boston merchants have preferred claims somewhat analagous to ours, but in relation thereto it is not necessary, and indeed it would not be proper, for us in this communication to say one word. Every man should attend to his own business only, and not interfere with that of others.

We invoked, in the letter above mentioned, the protection of the government of the United States, and its interposition to obtain just redress for us.

In addition to the letter of January 15, 1855, on the 29th of the same month we addressed you again. That letter is on file, and we respectfully solicit your reperusal of it. We refer in it to our first letter, and respectfully reiterate the request it makes for protection and redress. We state the heavy losses that we had sustained by the illegal interference in our legitimate business and the outrage on our rights, and we give to you the particulars of our losses, and we ask their prosecution by the government against Venezuela. We had some reasons to hope that a vessel of war of the United States would have been dispatched with the demand for redress.

On February 26, 1855, we wrote to you a third time, reiterating like requests, and communicated additional information to that before given to you. We stated that Captain Dias, after his first visit to Shelton's Isle, and before his command to us to quit, had visited the Danish island of St. Thomas and had communications with the shore, and that information had been received from a Danish man-of-war that came from St. Thomas, that the Danish authorities had been approached by certain parties to procure them to claim the isle and drive us off, which suggestion was not favorably received by the Danish authorities, and the man-of-war in question was sent to Venezuela with information that they (the said authorities) would not interpose any objection to the government of Venezuela claiming the isle, thus showing that the Venezuelan authorities *knew they had no right*, and that their interference was instigated by parties wishing to speculate upon the government, or *with* it, in respect of the guano. Some of these parties are indicated in the last letter, amongst them *the Venezuelan consul at St. Thomas*. Another and an important fact indicated in the last letter, of February 26, is that between Dias's first visit and the last ample time had elapsed for the Venezuelan government to have revoked a hasty or mistaken order, and that, therefore, the order for expulsion, as to Venezuela, was deliberate and well weighed. It cannot be excused or palliated on the ground of mistake, or inadvertance, or haste. Right or wrong, her course was adopted knowingly, and if procured to be done by *subsidiary* means, it only heightens the enormity of the outrage.

We have also made personal applications, since the last mentioned letter, to your department, through friends, for some action.

We regret to be informed no vessel of war of the United States has, as we hoped and expected, been sent to Venezuela with instructions to our able and patriotic minister there to insist upon justice being done to us, by promptly paying us our just damages. We hope this will yet be done, and as speedily as practicable. It seems to us that it would not involve any great expense or trouble to send one of the vessels composing the squadron of Commodore McCauley, off Cuba, to Venezuela for the purpose indicated. We presume that by this time the vessel might be spared from the squadron sent to Cuba, to resist the pretended right set up by the Spaniards to discover whether a vessel rightfully bears our flag or not, by firing towards her to bring her to and by visiting her, and that it is quite as important that the actual outrage on the American flag, *known* to be rightfully borne, in the case of our vessels, perpetrated five months since, should be atoned for.

It has been contended that we admitted the right of the Venezuelan government to *Shelton's Isle*, and the right of Captain Dias to drive us off; in other words, that we were trespassers; and this, too, in the paper given by Dias to Captain Gibbs. How perfectly idle and worse than idle is such pretense. We might have resisted Dias and his soldiers with some loss of human life on both sides; we ought, perhaps, to have done so. We believe we could easily have chastised and captured his whole force, vessel and soldiers included, if we had resorted to arms and bloodshed; but we preferred relying on the protection of our country. We submitted to Dias's commands, because he was an officer of a sister American republic with whom our country was at peace, and was acting by its authority with its public force. We submit, sir, to you and the President that our forbearance was commendable. The orders and conduct of Captain Dias were unnecessarily harsh. Our tools and implements, materials and provisions, were seized in part by his soldiers, and our houses were taken from our workmen. The loss sustained thereby amounts to many thousand dollars. We were prevented from lading guano prepared to put on board our ship, and constrained, by military force, to abandon the isle with no cargoes for some vessels and with but part cargoes for others. Our heavy contracts for furnishing guano are by consequence unfulfilled, and heavy damages incurred by us. The wages of our numerous workmen, who were rendered valueless to us by his illegal and unwarranted interference, reach, in the aggregate, a large sum. Our whole outlay for the business is a dead loss. We have had to pay for false freights and demurrage and damage, and besides all this, the consequences directly resulting to us from this outrage have been such as can readily be anticipated by any commercial man. They are embarrassments, and well nigh ruin unless redress is promptly afforded us. We solicit your consideration of all this, and trust it may induce to immediate action in our behalf.

How can Venezuela justify her course in the face of her acts, seeking the Danish authorities of St. Thomas to interfere, thus admitting *she* had no right? How can she have the face to do so since her relinquishment of the isle to the Dutch? Suppose the Dutch have a title, or the English, or French, or Spanish, or Portuguese; can she, a *tort feasor*, set up any title *in them* in defense of her tortious acts towards us?

And now, sir, we trust you will not regard it as unreasonable for us to ask that you will, besides sending a United States vessel of war to Venezuela, send *another* to convoy such vessels as we may desire to dispatch to Shelton's Isle for guano, and resume the lawful possession from which we were forcibly ousted; protect us in our rights there. And we respectfully ask to be informed if this request can be accorded. If it cannot be, we then ask whether the federal government will allow *us*, at our own expense, to fit out and arm vessels and man them with sufficient force of armed men to enable us to recover our possession against all who may contest it? The peremptory demand for redress and its prompt enforcement we conceive, as American citizens, we are entitled to. If any additional proofs are wanting of the facts we have stated, we ask to be informed thereof at an early period, that we may obtain them whilst the witnesses are at hand. And if the President and yourself are of opinion that both convoy and protection and also permission to fit out an armed expedition of ourselves as suggested should be denied by our government, we respectfully request that you will advise us thereof as soon as practicable, as we have reason to believe that we cannot make a profitable transfer of *our* right to the isle and guano to some English and French merchants here and in New York and Philadelphia who feel assured of the protection of their government. We are particularly solicitous that if the government of the United States has the slightest desire to obtain a transfer from us, *without cost*, (we reserving the guano of Shelton's Isle, &c.,) it should be indicated to us as early as possible. The reasonableness of this request you can readily appreciate, as it regulates our decision upon the disposition to foreigners to which we have referred, and in relation to which we also particularly desire an answer from you. Unless speedy action is had, the guano deposits on the Shelton's Isle, worth, if properly managed, hundreds of thousands of dollars, will be abstracted, and though we shall demand pay for every ton from the Venezuelan government (that so illegally and wrongfully ejected us) as well as of those guilty of the *asportation*, and intend likewise to claim damages for the detention of the isle *till it is restored*, we know well that in such matters "an ounce of prevention is worth a pound of cure." Neither the Venezuelan nor Dutch government is celebrated as good paymasters. The former has perhaps the excuse of inability; the latter has not; and the case of Mr. Seely, of New York, in the Crown Diamond case is by no means creditable to it. We trust that if justice is earnestly insisted upon by our government in our case, it will be yielded with less delay.

We are, very respectfully, your fellow citizens and obedient servants,

PHILO S. SHELTON,
For self and others interested.

Hon. WILLIAM L. MARCY,
Secretary of State.

Mr. Marcy to Mr. Shelton.

DEPARTMENT OF STATE,
Washington, June 14, 1855.

SIR: I have to acknowledge the receipt, in due time, of your communication of the 14th ultimo, in relation to the forcible ejectment of your agents and laborers from the Aves Islands by the Venezuelan government.

In that communication the following paragraph occurs:

"The said Dias, on the 13th December, had drawn up and signed a paper, in Spanish, (on file in your department,) which our agent, Captain Gibbs, was *constrained*, under the circumstances, to take, and which Dias styled his "permit."

Upon reference to your former correspondence upon this subject, I find a letter from you of the 26th February, ultimo, transmitting a "copy of a license or permit, signed by Domingo Dias, commander of the Venezuelan vessel of war sent to take possession of Aves or Bird Island by that government; and the fourth article of this license or permit is translated in the following words:

4th. And to that effect, we [Nathan P. Gibbs, agent of Philo S. Shelton *et als.*, and Carles H. Lang, agent for Lang & Delano,] place our piece of artillery and armament at the orders and under the flag of Venezuela, to whom the island belongs."

The department cannot discover any expression in your letter, transmitting this agreement, which indicates that it was not a voluntary proceeding on the part of your agent, or that it was signed under duress; it is further to be remarked that, in your letter of the 15th January, setting forth the grounds of your claim against Venezuela, no reference is made to this agreement of the 13th December, although your statement of events is brought down to the 21st of that month; nor does it appear that any allusion to this agreement is made in your correspondence until it was transmitted on the 26th February, one month after the instruction on the subject had been forwarded from the department to the minister resident of the United States.

When, therefore, Mr. Eames, under that instruction, made an application in your behalf, he was met at the first step by a reference to this agreement, the original of which is in the hands of the Venezuelan government.

You cannot fail to perceive how the fact of the existence of this document complicates the business.

It is my duty, therefore, to inform you, that before proceeding further, the department must be satisfied that this agreement was made under duress; for, if that should not be the fact, your failure to disavow or protest against the concessions and acknowledgment of your agent will, at least, seriously impair your claim to indemnification.

I am, sir, &c.,

W. L. MARCY.

PHILO S. SHELTON, Esq.,
Boston.

Mr. Shelton to Mr. Marcy.

BOSTON, *June* 20, 1855.

SIR: We acknowledge the honor of having on the 18th instant received your official communication, dated the 14th instant. Before it came to hand, we had written a communication to be sent to you, soliciting a reply to the inquiries and requests made in ours of the 14th May, which we withhold till we have answered yours, the receipt of which is above noted.

The terms of your letter seem to indicate *suspicions* entertained by you that do us great injustice. If so, we can only attribute them to misconceptions of facts on your part, or the misrepresentations of others interested adversely to our claims and rights; and also to the mistake by you, quite apparent from your letter, of confounding together matters essentially distinct and different from each other; as we are quite confident you will be satisfied, after you have received our explanation, and reëxamined carefully the papers on file in your department.

In the *first* place, your letter intimates a suspicion, (and, indeed, it well nigh assumes an accusation,) that in our two letters of the 15*th and* 29*th of January last*, we purposely avoided or suppressed all reference or "allusion" to a paper which we designate as the "Dias *license*, *permit*, or *notice*," dated December 13, 1854. The motive for such suppression or purposed concealment (as we conceive inferable from your letter) was supposed by you to be apprehension by us that this paper might injuriously affect our claims and rights.

In reply to this we respectfully submit to you that, in order to subject us to such imputation, it is necessary that we should have had, *at the time those letters were written*, some information of the existence of that paper. Your presumption that this was *the fact*, (as we conceive apparent from your letter,) is an entire misconception.

When we wrote to you on the 15th and 29th January we had no idea of any such paper, or of any other, referring to Shelton's Isle, and the transactions there having been signed or given by any person there. Aware that our agent had not the shadow of authority from us, express or implied, to do any act whatever *destroying*, *relinquishing*, or in any degree *impairing* the rights he was *deputed to maintain and protect*, and knowing that such an act, whatever its form, would be utterly void and null, as a preposterous violation of those universal principles of justice and law, that are respected in every country, and that operate upon governments as well as individuals, we were not stimulated by an apprehension of our rights and interests having been jeoparded, or by any distrust of the fidelity of our agent to any special inquiries in this regard. An eagerness or even a willingness (in the absence of express impeachment by some person) to *suspect* our agent, either on the score of fidelity or intelligence, which only could have prompted such inquiry, would have been gratuitous, unbecoming, and unwarrantable on our part.

We had learned when we wrote to you on the 15th of January that Dias had intruded with an armed Venezuelan force upon the island and taken possession of it, and had threatened the expulsion of our employés and vessels from it. We stated that the Venezuelans, on the 13th of December, after taking such forcible possession, had "*notified*" Captain Gibbs that "*he could only remain on sufferance until such time as they saw fit to eject him*;" and that on the 21st they had landed more troops, and that "*Captain Gibbs writes he may be ejected by force any day.*" We communicated to you all that we had then learned. Messrs. Lang and Delano, of this city, on the same day (as we are informed,) also addressed you, giving similar information to that contained in our letter, but more circumstantial in details; and we learn it is also silent (for similar causes, it is presumed,) as to any paper having been signed, or given by any person connected with the transactions.

When we wrote to you on the 29th of January, we had been informed that (as we *anticipated* in our letter of the 15th,) our agents had been "*unjustifiably forced to relinquish*" the collecting and shipping the guano on the island; and that all of our employés and vessels had been *driven away*, and our implements and materials, houses, wharf, &c., wrested from us by Dias and his Venezuelan soldiery. This "*forcible ejection by an armed force*," as then characterized by us, took place on the 28th of December, three days after the time, to which you observe, "our statement of events is brought down," in our previous letter. We freely concede that these statements do not appear entirely consistent with that voluntary, unconstrained, peaceful and willing exodus from an abandonment of Shelton's Isle by our employés and vessels; and in pursuance of an unconstrained, ultroneous "*agreement*," previously volunteered, with full knowledge by our agent, expressly acknowledging the isle to "*belong*" to Venezuela; and in atonement for our illegal intrusion upon it, placing our pieces of artillery and armament at the orders and under the flag of Venezuela, and engaging to "lend their aid" to the Venezuelan "garrison" at the isle; which, it seems from your letter, the Venezuelan officials now represent the departure of our vessels and employés from the isle to have been! But we aver our statements in those letters to be strictly correct, and we can maintain them by full and incontestible proof, and in addition to what is already on file in your department, so soon as circumstances will enable us, we will transmit other testimony, more in detail, and utterly refuting the ridiculous and fraudulent defense thus set up by Venezuela.

But this has little bearing on the imputation against us as to an attempted *suppressio veri* in our letters above referred to. We have stated that we had not *then* any information as to the Dias "*permit or notice.*" In verification of this, we are entirely willing to submit to your personal inspection all our correspondence with our agents and others respecting the occurrences at Shelton's Isle, though it contains matters not pertinent to this case, or proper to be placed on the departmental file.

It should be borne in mind that when we wrote these letters our agents and employés, &c., had not yet returned to this city, and our information was of course chiefly derived from our correspondence; and an inspection of it will satisfy you that *all* we had then received in any respect material, was set forth fully in those letters, though they do not profess to state minute occurrences, circumstantially and in detail.

You will notice also in that of the 15th of January, we positively *deny*, in no less than four separate clauses, that Venezuela has a shadow of title to Shelton's Isle, and give reasons for our denunciations of her claim as unfounded; and in both letters we remonstrate against her tortious, forcible, and unjustifiable outrage in taking possession of the isle, effected by an armed force, after we had been several months in its peaceful occupation; and in that, our first letter, we appeal to our government to compel Venezuela to relinquish a possession to which she had not a "semblance of title." We had not then heard of our employés and vessels being driven off the isle on the 24th of December.

In that of the 29th of January, we represent that Dias and his armed soldiery and naval force, followed up their wrongful intrusion by threats and acts of hostility, by their forcible expulsion of our agent and employés and vessels, and the taking of our houses and implements, structures, &c., and by the use of our stores, &c., for all of which we claim indemnity.

To presume that we were cognizant of the *Dias license*, *permit*, or notice, and purposely avoided reference or allusion to it, and sought to suppress it under an apprehension that peradventure it might possibly have a destructive effect, or might militate against or impair the validity of our claims for indemnification, and our rights respecting Shelton's Isle, would be to write us down not only as being arrant knaves, but also egregious asses; the former for adopting the dishonest mean of the *suppressio veri* for any purpose, and the latter for resorting to a shallow and useless artifice in a case in which speedy detection and exposure was certain, and likewise for not perceiving that such paper as that *permit*, or *license*, or *notice*, when brought forth, could not justly complicate the business.

We think it ought rather to have been presumed that if we were not devoid of common sense and common intelligence, and had any knowledge of such paper, and anticipated the probability of our adversaries (the Venezuelan officials and the speculators combined with them) seeking to urge it against us, we would have noticed it in the outset, and sought to meet and overcome it. If it is fancied that we may have hoped Dias kept no copy, or that if he did he may have lost it, the case is not altered, insomuch as most men of moderate intelligence are aware that the *leges gentium* contains no provisions relating to such license, permit, or notice similar to those in the British and American statutes of frauds and perjuries invalidating it, if not in *writing, and signed, &c.*, and that therefore its efficacy could not depend on the fact whether it was written and signed, or merely verbal; and likewise, that if written, and either lost or mislaid or *suppressed*, its contents could be established by parole testimony. No sensible motive can therefore be reasonably assigned for such *suppression* by us, if we had known of its ever having been in existence, and if, in fact, we purposely sought to surpress it in January last, what could have induced us to transmit it to the department in February, so soon as it came to our hands; and what induced Messrs. Lang and Delano to insert in the Boston *Evening Gazette*, of the 24th of February, a translation of the duplicate they had, and to send that publication and a copy of the Spanish permit to you early in March?

The facts are proved by the papers in your files.

We shall hereafter, in another communication, suggest several distinct grounds, in addition to that already intimated, upon which we insist that this "*permit*," "*license*," or "*notice*," placed by us on the files of your department, and to which your attention was called by our letter of the 26th February, cannot possibly militate against or impair in any degree the claims for indemnity, or the right to the isle we are contending for, nor in any degree absolve our government from the duty of promptly enforcing those claims, and maintaining those rights in our behalf. Nay, sir, we hope to satisfy you that this paper, and *also the other* (unlike this in respect to the signatures affixed to it) with which the Venezuelian officials have met Mr. Eames, and the production of it by those officials as the sole foundation of their claim, and as the sole justification for their outrages, and *especially* when the circumstances connected with those papers, and attendant upon all their proceedings at Shelton's Isle and *since*, are considered, so far from weakening or impairing, do materially STRENGTHEN and FORTIFY our claims and rights; and as to our government, superadd to the incentive of protecting its citizens against violence and outrage, that of exposing, correcting, and rebuking attempted rascality and fraud to sustain a trumped up and baseless claim, preferred for the benefit of knavish speculators in Venezuela and in the United States who have combined to wrong us. At present, however, the foregoing suggestions have been made merely to dispel *your suspicions* of unworthy conduct on our part, in reference to which we confess we feel as every honest man, jealous of everything that appears to impeach his character for dealing fairly and aboveboard with his fellow men, ought to feel.

It appears from your letter that it is inferred or considered at the department that when we wrote our letter, dated Washington, February 26, transmitting the Dias "permit," or "license," or "notice," (styled by you "*this agreement*,") we tacitly confirmed it and acquiesced in it *as an "agreement"* by our agent, insomuch "*as the department cannot discover in that letter any expression indicating that it was not a voluntary proceeding of your* [*our*] *agents, or that it was signed under duress*," and insomuch, also, as we "*failed to disavow or protest against the concession or acknowledgments of your* [*our*] *agents*."

In answer to this we would observe, that in inclosing that paper we designated it as a "*license*," or "*permit*," signed by Domingo Dias, commander, &c.; we could not properly style it "*an agreement*." *It was not signed by any person but Dias.* We transmitted the *original* given to Captain Gibbs by Dias, having Dias's signature affixed to it, and no other. It would have been absurd to have impeached Dias's *signature* as having been "*signed under duress*," or for any other cause; and the necessity or propriety of expressions indicating that that paper was not a "voluntary proceeding of our agents," or of disavowing and protesting against any concessions or acknowledgments of our agents therein or thereby made, is not yet discovered by us. Indeed, as we think it is patent on the face of *that* paper that it was exclusively a proceeding of Dias, and did not purport to be anything else, and as our agents had not signed it or concurred in it, or thereby and therein made any "concessions or acknowledgments whatever," such "expressions," "disavowal," and "protest" would have been simply ridiculous. We regarded the paper as an *ex parte* production, drafted in Spanish by Dias solely, agreed to and signed by himself alone, and according to his own fancy, as a sort of military or naval proclamation or *pronunciamento*, or bulletin of his acts and doings and purposes, announcing also in military and naval style the terms he felt disposed in his generosity to extend to our agent and the line of operations he proposed to pursue in respect of our employés and property on the island. Mark! the first that is heard in this case of the *other* paper, asserted to be dated the same 13th of December at the same "*Isla de Aves de Barlovento*," and to be signed by Gibbs as well as by Dias, and also by C. H. Lang, is in your letter of the 14th instant, which states that it has been produced by the Venezuelan officials to meet Mr. Eames, in which, however, it is quite evident the two papers are confounded as one and the same.

What we gather from your letter of the character of this paper, called by you "this agreement," and from the account of a friend who has examined the *copy* transmitted to your department, it appears to be a regular *military or naval capitulation*, or surrender by Gibbs as agent for Sampson & Tappan and Philo S. Shelton, of Boston, and by C. H. Lang, as agent for Lang & Delano, of Boston, to Dias, of the isle, and all their artillery, armaments, &c., thereon, signed and executed by all three—the agents in behalf of their respective "companies," and Dias in behalf of the "supreme government of the republic of Venezuela, as captain of its navy and second chief of its squadron, and commissioner to watch over the desert Antilles of the Caribbean sea," in due form according to the LAWS OF WAR! And in this capitulation, too, the Yankee troops are not only denied the honors of war, but a sort of enlistment *pro hoc vice* of the captives under the flag of the supreme government of the Venezuelan republic is stipulated and agreed to! To that part of your letter stating the necessity of satisfying the department that "*this agreement*" was "signed under duress," and of the difficulty that will arise if "*that should not be the fact*," we may, we think, not impertinently suggest here, that as to this asserted "agreement" Venezuela is stopped from denying (*whatever the fact may be*) that it was given under *duress* of the strongest character. She cannot gainsay the acts of her commissioned officer acting under her express orders. She has expressly adopted and confirmed the acts of her military "commissioner," set forth in this document by the production of it in her defense, and she must abide the consequences. She cannot be permitted to deny its recitals, and they are irrefragably conclusive against her on this point. An inspection of this paper is alone all sufficient to establish the fact of *duress*, and that not merely threats and menaces and belligerent manifestations, but positive acts offered by her military or naval officers, with a public vessel of war and an armed military and naval force were the means of such *duress*. This is manifest from the tenor and character of the paper. The fact is recorded in it. Why, sir, it is quite apparent that it was expressly intended by Commander Dias to herald the heroic exploits of himself and comrades in the guano war of Shelton's Isle. It is obvious that it was drawn up by him to be used as legal and formal evidence "*in perpetuam rei memoriam*" of the vigilance and valor displayed by that illustrious warrior and his army, and of the triumph they achieved, and the glory they won by their descent upon Shelton's Isle, wresting it from the Yankee intruders, hauling down the flag of the United States, and, after reducing our agents and employés to submission, making prize of our vessels and property, compelling the prisoners of war to enter the Venezuelan service, and pledge their fealty and allegiance to the "supreme government" of that republic whilst remaining on the island, and finally by driving them and our vessels away—having also taken our cannon and armaments as *trophies of victory!*

There is little doubt that Dias would display amazement and indignation, even if affected, if told that any body imagined this agreement was volunteered by Gibbs and Lang. He would scout the idea that it sprung from a deliberate conviction by them that the claim of Venezuela was just, derived from historical research, and an investigation of the principles of law governing the case, as laid down by publicists, which, it seems, she would now fain pretend. She puts it forth as conclusive, as if Gibbs and Lang were fully empowered and unquestionably competent to decide the whole matter, and that they had so decided it in writing, and irrevocably, and that no appeal can be had from their *decree*, whatever the fraud practiced to procure their signature, however palpable the mistake or error they committed, and notwithstanding the judges may have been under military duress in regard to this very matter. Suppose the agents to collect and ship guano did come to the conclusion that the isle "pertained" or "belonged" to

Venezuela, and that as honest and consciencious men, constrained by nothing except the dictates of justice, and wholly uninfluenced by awe of Dias's potential authority and might, or dread of his military force, ought to yield it up to her representative, and even to "lend their aid" to him in sustaining her rights, and to yield to him also our personal property, carried thither from this city, without authority *from us* so to do, such acts cannot prejudice our rights, and much less can their acts affect the rights of the United States. And further, the participation by Venezuela and her officers in such course, by those agents, who are not public officers, in derogation of their duty as agents, *manifestly* exceeding their authority, is of itself a fraud upon us, and an insult to the United States, meriting cogent and efficacious rebuke. The incompatibility of the suppositious *decision* adverted to with the tenor and character of the paper produced, the testimony this paper gives as to the circumstances of the case, otherwise notorious, the significant dissimilarity between the signatures to the two papers, not only destroy the defense of Venezuela to our claim, but place her in a position in which she cannot creditably advance any other. She is forced to encounter the *dilemma* presented on the one hand of relying on this alleged agreement or capitulation, and to admit the "*duress*" stamped on its face; or, on the other, that of abandoning it, confessing that it was procured by disreputable deceit and fraud, to maintain a claim as false as the surreptitious testimony by which *exclusively* she has sought to oppose it.

We fully admit that we did not in our letter of the 26th February, bestow more extended notice upon the *other* paper, the "license, permit, or notice," signed by Dias alone, solely because we did not regard it as of sufficient importance to merit much comment. Our immediate object in transmitting it, as our letter shows, was to furnish all the facts as well as exhibit the *false pretenses* resorted to by Venezuela for her officers despoiling us of our property and committing outrages upon our rights as citizens of the United States, which are briefly alluded to in the same letter. We did not anticipate that the mere *taking* by our agent into his keeping of a paper written in a foreign language, not understood by him, and signed and presented by another person, would prejudice us in the manner you intimate, and we did not deem it necessary to suggest that it was probably received, in part, because a refusal to "take" it would probably have excited angry feelings, led to hostilities, have occasioned recourse to harsh measures, and, perhaps, the belligerent collision of armed men, and the sacrifice of human life. Nor did we refer, in our letter of the 26th February, to the fact that our instructions to our agent emphatically forbade resistance by arms to the authorities of Venezuela, if they should claim and seek to assume possession of the isle; whilst in the same instructions, we expressly denied that any nation had "*any just right to dispossess us.*" If we erred in not extending the length and enlarging the scope of that letter, and including those facts, it was because we attached no consequence to the "permit, license, or notice," therewith transmitted, or its contents, except as then intimated, and did not anticipate any possible use that it could be applied to rendering these facts material. It is our misfortune that we did not regard it of the importance that you seem to, and we are constrained to abide by its effects, whatever they may be. Had the other paper, the asserted "agreement," signed by Gibbs and Lang, been under consideration by us when we wrote that letter, we should have said it was the bounden duty of our agents to preserve the peace, and it would have been inexcusable for them not to have exerted themselves to that end; and that of *signing* such document was the *only* means, or the *best* means, in their judgment, to prevent outbreak and the probable effusion of blood on either side, such course was *excusable*, though the unauthorized act to which the agents would have been "*constrained*" by such circumstances could have had no effect or force on our rights; and we should have so said, without reference to the direct falsehood and fraud, which we are *now* satisfied were practiced by Dias to procure it, and which utterly vitiates it, *even without such "constraint."*

And now that we have arrived, in regular order of time, to our letter of the 14th ultimo, we proceed to notice what is said in your communication respecting *its* contents. In referring in that letter to the Dias "permit, license, or notice," we say that "*Dias, on December* 13, *had drawn up and signed a paper in Spanish, (on file in your department,) and which our agent, Captain Gibbs, was constrained under the circumstances to take, and which Dias styled his 'permit.'*" You extract and quote this sentence in your communication. A careful reperusal of the papers on file in your department must, however, satisfy you that, as before suggested, there is in the *first* place, a misconception of fact as to the particular paper we specially referred to, and that it was *confounded* with the asserted "*agreement*" with which Mr. Eames was "met" at Caraccas, which we did not and could not refer to, insomuch as the existence of *that* paper had not then been suggested in any of the papers filed in the case. This misconception is not unimportant, for the character of the two papers are not identical. And in the *second* place, there is a misconception of the *purport* of our remarks above quoted in relation to the paper, *that we did so refer to.* This will be quite apparent by a reperusal of those remarks and of your letter. As we have already observed, we did not intend to convey the impression that *that* paper styled a "permit" by "Dias," drawn up in Spanish by him, and *signed by him* and *by no one else*, was so signed (by Dias) under *duress*, or that *it* was not a "voluntary proceeding" by him. We did not refer to any paper as having been "*signed*" by Gibbs, either voluntarily or under "*duress*," and in respect of the "permit," the remark made by us that he was "constrained" under the circumstances to "take" (not "sign") it, appears by your letter to have been misinterpreted by you in another particular. We state, in the last paragraph but two of our letter, containing the remark just quoted, as follows:

"It has been contended that we admitted the right of the Venezuelan government to Shelton's Isle, and the right of Captain Dias to drive us off! In other words, that we were trespassers, and this, too, in the paper given by Dias to Captain Gibbs. How perfectly idle, and worse than idle, is such pretense. We might have resisted Dias and his soldiers with some loss of human life on both sides. We ought, perhaps, to have done so. We believe *we could have easily chastised and captured his whole force, vessels and soldiers included, if we had resorted to arms and bloodshed. But we preferred relying upon the protection of our country. We submitted to Dias's commands because he was an officer of a sister American republic with whom our country was at peace, and was acting by its authority with its public force.* We submit, sir, to you and the President that our forbearance was commendable. The orders and conduct of Captain Dias were unnecessarily harsh; our tools and implements, materials and provisions were seized in part by his soldiers, and our houses taken from our workmen. The loss sustained thereby amounts to many thousand dollars. We were prevented from lading guano prepared to be put on board our ships, and constrained by military force to abandon the isle with no cargoes for some vessels and with part cargoes for others. Our heavy contracts for furnishing guano are by consequence unfulfilled, and heavy damages incurred by us; the wages of our numerous workmen, who were rendered valueless to us by his illegal and unwarranted interference, reach, in the aggregate, a large sum. Our whole outlay for the business is a dead loss. We have had to pay for false freight and demurrages and damages. And besides all this, the consequences directly resulting to us from this outrage have been such as can readily be anticipated by any commercial man They are embarrassments and well nigh ruin, unless redress is promptly afforded us. We solicit your consideration of all this, and trust it may induce to immediate action in our behalf."

Not only was this overlooked by you, but it is also apparent that you did not recollect that Messrs. Lang & Delano, in their letter to you on the 15th January said, in reference to Dias and his soldiers, "*we could easily have kept possession by force had we seen fit so to do.*" We cannot imagine that, if you had adverted to these two extracts, you would have so misconceived the expression used by us in our letter of the 14th ultimo, "*constrained under the circumstances to take,*" as to construe it to imply that Captain Gibbs was *scared* by Dias into taking it, as your employment of the common law term "*duress,*" without qualification, implies you supposed. We did not mean to insinuate he *took* it under fright. We frankly say to you that as to *that* paper, whether styled a "permit" or "license" or "notice," or given any other name, and as to its being taken by Gibbs, we shall not urge as a defense (whatever the consequence to our claim, or whatever the effect upon our rights) anything inconsistent with the declarations of ourselves and Messrs. Lang & Delano, just quoted, for they *are the veritable truth.* You inform us that the department must be "*satisfied this agreement was made under duress.*" Whether you refer to the "permit," "notice," or "license," or allude to the other alleged paper, is immaterial. We do not imagine that your meaning was, that we must furnish proofs that our agent was in a state of bodily fear, paralyzed in mind by apprehensions of impending personal danger, terror stricken from threats and menaces, or hostile demonstrations or belligerent acts of Dias and his soldiers, though some of the common law cases, as to contracts between individuals, advance doctrines that would require proof of a state of mind akin to a condition of panic to constitute "*duress*" as necessary to nullify the contract. Lest we may possibly err as to the extent of your requisition, we are constrained by a regard for truth and candor to concede that we do not believe we can comply with such requisition. Unless, as heretofore hinted, the character and terms of the alleged agreement, *per illud*, afford such presumption, we are at present unaware of any testimony tending to the establishment of a *duress* of which such personal panic was an element. We are confident, however, that, as to both papers, without recourse to such defense, there is amply sufficient in the circumstances under which Captain Gibbs *took* the one or (if his signature is not similated, which we do not at present charge) *signed* the other, and in the character of the alleged concessions, acknowledgments deduced from either, to render both documents, or any others Venezuela may bring forth, worse than worthless in defense or justification or palliation of *her conduct*. And there is nothing in them which should impair *our* claims or affect our rights or the rights of the United States, or that should cause any abatement of vigilance and firmness in the prosecution of the demand on that government for prompt atonement and indemnification.

An imputation of cowardice against our fellow citizens who were at Shelton's Isle would be a calumny that we scorn to intimate in any mode or for any object. We know your feelings of patriotic pride would revolt at the idea of presenting such ground to the Venezuelan officials. Why, sir, we reiterate that there was not, at any time during the fortnight our employés were on the isle with Dias and his soldiers, either before or after his reinforcements, that Gibbs and Lang and their companions, if they had not been peaceful and forbearing, could not have tied the representatives of the "supreme government" of the republic, and every one of his half starved ragamuffin corps, hand and foot, and pitched them heels over head into the Caribbean sea, and if they had dared to attempt resistance, *exterminated* them on the rock, and this too without any serious peril to themselves. The example given by the military bungling of Dias's soldiers in blowing out the brains of one of themselves whilst attempting to salute their flag, shows that little danger was to be apprehended from them. It is probable Dias would not, on the 13th December, been able to land on the isle but for the assistance of some of the Bostonians there, who in charity loaned him boats and volunteered to aid his lubbers to manage them. After they had thus got on the rock, commiseration for their miserable condition "constrained" our people to provide them with food and water and to share our shelters with them. No forcible resistance was made to their hoisting the Venezuelan flag on the isle, nor to their demands made after they had landed, because they came there under the authority and orders of their *government*, but we feel bound to repel any supposition that craven fear of personal harm or other unhappy personal consequences resulting from a hostile conflict with the Venezuelan legion could have restrained our agents and employés from opposing them to all extremities, or *constrained* them or influenced their course in any respect. In fine, sir, we insist that the documents manufactured by Dias add to the enormity of the outrage upon the American settlers at Shelton's Isle by Venezuela, and to the unjustifiable character of her spoliation of our property, and they also aggravate her insults to our national flag. Full proof of the circumstances referred to shall be furnished the department so soon as we can obtain it. Captain Gibbs is now on a voyage to Marseilles in France, and most of the other witnesses are scattered, but the utmost diligence shall be used. Captain Gibbs is entirely ignorant of Spanish, necessarily he must have had to rely on others as to the purport of papers *written in that language.* We can readily imagine that fraudulent misrepresentations or mistakes occurred in this respect. The tenor and character of the papers exhibited justify such conclusions. No translation of them in writing was dared to be made by Dias and given to Captain Gibbs. The object and purpose of Dias's "descent on Shelton's Isle in a vessel of war and with troops," was avowedly to take possession of it, *vi et armis*, in behalf of Venezuela, and as "belonging" to her, and to expel Captain Gibbs and others therefrom. If Venezuela really had any valid claim to the isle susceptable of proof, wherefore the necessity or propriety of the manufacturing these papers? Truly he must have had strong doubts of the rightfulness of her claim to feel "*constrained*" thus to endeavor to bolster it up by such bungling contrivance, so discreditable to his government and to himself, and which, if not as devoid of intelligence as of honesty, *he* must have known would be utterly futile. It is absurd to imagine that admissions of Gibbs and Lang, not of particular facts or incidents peculiarly within their knowledge, but of a general character, as to the isle "pertaining" to Venezuela, can create a title for her or benefit her in any degree. Her title depended upon the *facts* as to the discovery and actual occupation of the isle by antecessors or by herself, and upon her continued possession of it and upon the law of nations, and not upon any admission of individuals who may be on the isle when they are made, though they may be reduced to writing and signed. Her abandonment of the isle long antecedent to our discovery and occupation of it, extinguished any former right she may have had, and Messrs. Gibbs and Lang could not by any admission or concession *destroy this fact.* They were not competent to decide as to these different questions either in respect of any peculiar means of information possessed by them, or in virtue of any authority delegated to them either by the United States or by us, to determine them, and whilst at the isle, on the 13th December, from whence, or from whom, except Dias could they, *there* and *then*, received the new special proofs that so enlightened them as to the validity of the title of Venezuela? Why is it that these proofs, if any exist, are now withheld by her? Why, instead of honestly producing and relying upon *them*, does she resort to such paltry muniments as the second hand *opinion* of an agent (not empowered to decide the right) even if attested by his signature to a paper written by *her* agent in a language the *signer* could not read and did not understand. And further, a presumption of the fairness of the paper produced is inconsistent with its stipulations. After the warning that they must evacuate the isle, and that Dias came there to expel them, there could not be any reasonable motive for making the concessions it purports to make. A permission dependent on contingencies and subject to revocation by him, or by his government, *at will*, "to continue loading with guano the three vessels then taking cargo," surely will not be regarded as being a fair consideration for the absolute and unqualified relinquishment of the right of the United States and of our right to the island and to *all the guano on it*. And if, without any other constituents of *covin*, this was a case between individuals, such arrangement would be set aside and nullified by a court of equity, not only as a usurpation of authority by the agent in illegal violation of the principals' rights, but as an "*unconscionable*" exaction by the other party. Why, if Dias had any right to the artillery and armament, &c., was it *stipulated* that he might take possession of it, and if he had no right, wherefore was it yielded up in such form without any equivalent therefor? Why, also, were they bound to "lend their aid to the garrison of the island with such auxiliaries as they might require," and subject themselves to the "orders" and place themselves "*under the flag of Venezuela?*" If Gibbs and Lang did, in fact, voluntarily "*sign*" this alleged agreement produced by Venezuela, we are convinced, from its purport alone, that it was misrepresented to them, or at least to *him*. They probably either supposed it to be a mere acknowledgment of the service of the notice or receipt of the permit Dias had given him, and of which it is nearly a copy, and regarded it as of no moment except to serve Dias with his government as proof of his having given it. When the stipulations we have adverted to are well considered no other reasonable conclusion can be made consistent with his fidelity to us, (that we do not doubt,) and consistent with his knowledge of the rights we claimed and which he was specially deputed to maintain and protect, except it be that the paper was extorted by force.

Messrs Lang and Delano sent you, on the 15th of January last, an extract from their instructions to their agent, enjoining him "not to make forcible resistence to any government," and in ours, dated June 21, 1854, we say, "we don't wish you to resist the armed force of any government, although we feel confident the island does not belong to any nation whatever; yet there may be claims of this kind we don't know of, and we do not wish to place yourself, by any chance, in a false position by resisting any government force that may be sent there." Our *second* instructions, dated June 22, 1854, are somewhat different. In them we say: "No government has any better claim than we have, and this you can insist upon. Don't mind any threats, because there is nothing they can or dare do to injure you. The probability is, if anybody comes under English, French, Dutch, or Danish flags they will say they are by order of government; but resist all attention to their orders, and insist they must take you all as prisoners and make prizes of your vessels before you will go, and leave it for your government to settle the matter with them. I am sure they will not move you, but will frighten you if they can. Against other comers you must take your chance and drive them off." Copies of these instructions, retained by us, are inclosed herewith for the inspection and satisfaction of the President and yourself; but as there are private matters alluded to in them, of no public interest, we desire, after your examination of them, they may be returned to us.

If it is inquired why we specified four nations to be resisted and did not name *Venezuela*, we answer that these four nations have unquestionable ability to protect themselves, and are precisely the four of all others that we would not at any time yield an inch to, unless in a case of unquestionable right on their side; and we claim the prerogative of indulging such fancy (as some will perhaps regard it) without affording just cause for censure from any. We did not include Venezuela, as we did not anticipate any intermeddling by her; and, besides, even if we had anticipated that her officials could have lent themselves to the gang of speculators that have inveigled her into this scrape, insomuch as she is a sister American republic, poor and weak, and likely to be kept so by bad men, we would probably have expressly excepted her from the list, given in the last letter, of those to be resisted. Our anxiety to give no ground for any accusation of *fillibustering* on neighbors less powerful than ourselves, which of late years has been so freely imputed to citizens of the United States, and for which our country is so much reproached, would also have prompted to such exception. We did not wish to involve our government in any trouble on our account with any foreign power, but, if unavoidable, we preferred a "foeman worthy of our steel." It was this desire that influenced us in writing our letter of January 15 to you, to say (whilst we earnestly insisted that Venezuela had not a shadow or semblance of right, and protested against her unjustifiable proceedings,) we did not then "ask the island to be protected as a national territory" of the United States, and limited our application for your interposition to demand from Venezuela indemnity for having "trampled in an outrageous manner" upon our rights and interests as individual citizens, and for her spoliation of our property. We left the questions of redress for the violation of the national rights of our country in respect to this isle, and of atonement for her insults to the flag of the United States (as it became us to do) entirely to the President and yourself, on whom the laws devolved them. You, and not we, had them in charge. Some persons have attributed our difficulties in this case to what they choose to characterize as a want of spirit and an overstock of prudence, and that our troubles with the *fillibusters* of Venezuela are but another exemplification of the unprofitableness of that "most rascally virtue." We are confident, however, that the President and yourself, and the considerate portion of our countrymen, will appreciate our motives and commend them. And we are equally confident *they* will not cause any relaxation of efforts to effect just redress for our wrongs.

If, as is possible, we have misconceived your letter, and that, in the employment of the word *duress*, you adopted it as sometimes loosely used in common parlance, and not in reference to its technical common law signification; and likewise, that in your reference to such defense of *duress* only you did not mean to *exclude* those of mistake, misrepresentation, or fraud, or a compound of one or of all, with duress or constraint, to overthrow the admissions, &c., in the alleged agreement. Hoping this may be so, we have, since the receipt of your letter, sought for authentic information from all sources available to us, and we expect to forward to you, if not with this letter by the mail after, conclusive proof of misrepresentation and fraud practiced to effect its being signed by Captain Gibbs, (if that produced is the one he did sign,) and who, when he did sign, believed it was an entirely different document, and utterly refused to make any acknowledgment of the title of Venezuela, or to do any act compromitting our claims. We hope to procure the deposition of a respectable and impartial witness, who, we understand, was present when Gibbs was solicited by Dias to sign the paper he did sign. We shall forward also other proofs so soon as we can have them prepared in proper form.

In the the meantime, and upon this the first opportunity we could appropriately take, since advised by you of the production by Venezuela of this alleged "agreement," we do most unequivocally and emphatically and solemnly disavow the same, and protest against the same, and all and singular the concessions, acknowledgments, or admissions and relinquishments in general and in particular therein made, as unauthorized and as untrue, and do aver that said alleged paper is a "false, foul, flagrant, and flagitious fraud," and utterly null and void for the causes above suggested, and others that we shall expose in another communication to you. That other communication will contain citations to works on the laws of nations and on the civil law and on the common law and of diplomatic history, where the principles controlling the questions presented in this case may be at once referred to.

The present communication, as stated in its commencement, is intended as a defense of ourselves against the suspicion we supposed, from your letter, you entertained of a want of candor and fairness in our former letters. We have sought to correct the misapprehensions of fact and misconstructions of those letters that gave rise to these suspicions. We have made explanations to exonerate ourselves from censure. If in performing this duty to ourselves we have appeared to be in any degree hypercritical, we trust you will not attribute to us any feeling or motive inconsistent with high regard for yourself and high respect for the great ability you have brought to the administration of your important office. The only object not heretofore stated that we could have in referring to any of those unavoidable omissions, inaccuracies, or mistakes or errors caused by the pressure of official business, and of which no resonable man will complain, would be to plead them when asking a liberal indulgence in respect to our own.

We have the honor to be, sir, with great respect, your obedient servants and follow citizens,

PHILO S. SHELTON,
For self and others.

Hon. WILLIAM L. MARCY,
Secretary of State.

Mr. French to Mr. Marcy.

EXETER, N. H., *June* 22, 1855.

SIR: Having been employed by Lang & Delano, of Boston, as their attorney in the matter of their claim for indemnity of the Venezuelan government for damages in being driven from the "Aves Island," I desire to be informed, as far as proper, of the state of the negotiation by our government and that of Venezuela on the subject.

Please communicate with my brother, Hon. B. B. French, who will be at liberty, now that he has resigned his office, to act for me at Washington.

With much respect,

HENRY F. FRENCH,

Care of Hon. B. B. French, Washington, D. C.

Hon. WILLIAM L. MARCY,
Secretary of State.

Mr. Shelton to Mr. Marcy.

WASHINGTON CITY, *June* 24, 1855.

SIR: The accompanying memoranda are submitted to your consideration in connection with our former letters, and the following testimony herewith inclosed:

A. Deposition of Captain Joshua F. Safford as to FRAUD of Dias with respect to "agreement" and *hauling down the United States flag by Dias*, dated June 20, 1855, &c.

B. Deposition of Captain J. Wheeler, June 8, 1855, discovery of guano on Shelton's Isle *by Captain Gibbs, &c.*

C. Deposition of Captain J. Wheeler, June 15, 1855, as to the United States flag being hoisted and kept flying on Shelton's Isle, and as to declaration of British commander of her Britannic Majesty's ship Devastation as to our rights, &c.

D. Letter of Captain N. P. Gibbs to P. S. Shelton, received about January 29, 1855.

E. Certificate by Nathan P. Gibbs, in his handwriting, made in January, 1855, and given to P. S. Shelton.

F. Letter of N. P. Gibbs to P. S. Shelton, received January 15 via St. Thomas. (Landing of second company of Venzuelans.)

G. Letter of Captain N. P. Gibbs to P. S. Shelton, received in January, 1855.

H. Protest of *George W. Nickels*, master, Henry C. Dearborn, mate, and Patrick Scollan, second mate of ship James N. Cooper, New York, February 20, 1855.

I. Extract from N. P. Gibbs's report to P. S. Shelton, dated Aves Island, April 6, 1854: (discovery of said island.)

We have confidence that our letter of the 20th instant has satisfied the President and yourself that we have not had any desire to suppress any fact or to withhold any information in our possession respecting this case, and especially that our statement that Captain Gibbs was "*constrained* under the circumstances to take" the Dias permit was a correct version of the facts stated in *proper* terms in such language as the facts justified, and that that language was not used to mislead in any wise the department. We are particularly anxious to convince you that the statement as to *constraint* was not an afterthought put forth to explain any concealment in our letters of the 15th and 29th of January last, or to obviate any injurious effect by the transmission of that permit on the 27th of February. If you desire further proof on this point, and of our want of knowledge of all the circumstances when our first letters were written, we will furnish it so soon as Captain Gibbs returns. If not deemed objectionable by you, we would wish to lay this case before Congress at its next session, by memorial, to sanction by express law the equitable right we conceive we have to the island and guano thereon, subordinate to that of eminent domain and property of the United States, in virtue of our discovery and occupation.

We would respectfully ask of you to indicate to us, if proper, what course the department may probably pursue in this case, and also what is expected of us, and, if according to rule, that the requests made in our letter of the 14th ultimo may be complied with as information on those points will regulate our conduct.

We would respectfully request the department to ask Mr. Eames to procure, if practicable, a copy of Dias's official report.

On the return of the undersigned to Boston, or perhaps in New York, on the way to Boston, we will address you again, and in special reference to another part of this case not yet sufficiently alluded to. We are apprehensive that possibly our rights and interests may be prejudiced by the inadvertent action of our government, which it is reported (on the authority of persons concerned in the combination of speculators heretofore alluded to, located Philadelphia, Caraccas, and St. Thomas) it has taken, or it is about to take, in behalf of those speculators. We think we understand all who are concerned and the designs of the managing parties. They have sought to swindle Venezuela by misrepresentations, and they seek to complicate the United States without regard to the interests or the preservation of the honor of its government, and their scheme is in disregard of our just and honest rights, and they are striving to carry it out to our injury, and any favorable notice the officers of this government may bestow them will be used at Caraccas to satisfy the officials there that the President and yourself are disposed to back them. An indisposition to do any person injustice, or to accuse any one before full investigation, constrains us to withhold at present a statement of facts, partly prepared, which facts, we are informed, exist with reference to the parties concerned in the combination, and are of a character, when fully known to you, that will save us the trouble of any express remonstrance by us against the government of the United States encouraging it by any words, or in any manner, or to any extent. A different course will be certain to lead the government into difficulties, and to embarrass, if not compromit, the enforcement of our just claims.

We are apprehensive that the fair prospect of the arrangement of this unpleasant business so as to save ourselves harmlessly a sale and transfer of our rights in Shelton's Isle, with the permission of our government to certain English and French merchants, (who feel satisfied they would have the protection of their government,) is destroyed by our being without any reply to our request on that subject, in our letter of the 14th ultimo. Indeed, from our not having any signification of the consent of the government, the offer is regarded as withdrawn. This, sir, is extremely hard in its effects upon us, who have done nothing wrong. Though our prospect for the sale of our rights in Shelton's Isle, as above indicated, is no longer favorable, we still desire your *sanction* or *dissent*, in the event of application by other parties.

We have the honor to be, very respectfully, your fellow-citizens and obedient servants,

PHILO S. SHELTON,
For self and others interested.

Hon. WILLIAM L. MARCY,
Secretary of State.

Mr. Shelton to Mr. Marcy.

HEADS OF MEMORANDA FOR HON. MR. MARCY.

I. Fact of discovery.

II. Description of Shelton's Isle.

III. Fact of our occupation.

IV. Discovery, of itself, gives no title.

V. Asserted claims of discovery by Spain and by Venezuela as her successor.

VI. Title claimed by Venezuela from *contiguity, &c.*

VII. The possession and occupation must be actual use and settlement.

VIII. Such possession and occupation must be continued.

IX. Abandonment of occupation and use destroys claim.

X. Faculty of acquisition by the United States of such isle by discovery.

XI. If faculty is not in the United States, it remains in state of discoverer.

XII. Executive may enforce and maintain public and private rights resulting from discovery and occupation without action of Congress.

XIII. The non-existence of any restraining or directory law leaves plenary power with the President.

XIV. Discovery by private citizens vests rights in the United States.

XV. Rights and interests of citizen discoverers.

XVI. Extent of our rights in the present case.

XVII. A discoverer has no right or power to alienate rights of his State, or his own, to foreign powers, and admissions by him to such effect are of no force.

XVIII. Misrepresentation and fraud vitiate all contracts.

XIX. Mistake or error vitiates contracts, if material.

XX. Misrepresentation and fraud by a government in transactions with individuals vitiate contracts.

XXI. Constraint or coercion by menace or threats of a government, or its officers, destroys contract with an individual.

XXII. Admissions by agents.

XXIII. Captain Gibbs's agency.

XXIV. The Dias capitulation obtained by the compound means of misrepresentation and fraud and constraint, or force or duress.

XXV. *Onus probandi* as to title rests on Venezuela.

XXVI. Venezuela bound by the consequences of the fraud and mal-conduct of her officers, and, having avowed them, cannot hereafter change the issue.

XXVII. Form of relinquishment by agent immaterial.

XXVIII. Insults to the United States by Venezuela and outrages upon our persons and property in this case a just *casus belli.*

XXIX. Damages and indemnity.

Memoranda by Philo S. Shelton, in his case, for State Department, June, 1855.

I. FACT OF DISCOVERY.

Captain N. P. GIBBS, in command of the brig John R. Dow, in our employ, whilst on a cruise, expressly for *discovery of guano* on desert islands in the Caribbean sea, about last of March, 1854, or first of April, discovered "AVES ISLANDS," in latitude 15° 40′ north, longitude west 63° 38′. The principal one is named "SHELTON'S ISLE." He personally landed on it, and assumed possession, having found guano, of which he was in search, upon it, [vide extracts from his letter or report to us, dated April 6, 1854, marked I, inclosed.] He returned to the United States to get vessels to go back and take possession of the guano and island, with a competent force, as soon as possible. His formal affidavit will be procured of these facts as early as practicable. We did not think it essential to procure and send it to you, insomuch as the consummation (of the *inchoate* right thereby acquired) by occupation, in a few weeks subsequently, is the most material. But Captain JAMES WHEELER's deposition (now filed, B) proves conclusively the *discovery* of the guano, &c., as stated. WHEELER was at that time in our employ, and then engaged in shipping guano for us from the Gulf of Mexico; and whilst in the Gulf, Captain GIBBS told him of the discovery he had recently made, and on his (W.) visiting Boston in May, he (W.) communicated the facts to Lang & Delano.

II. DESCRIPTION OF SHELTON'S ISLE.

See map heretofore submitted, and that now sent, (I.) The isle is about 4,000 feet long, and about 350 feet wide. *It is a desert uninhabited rock.* It has, however, become *inhabited.* When he discovered it, it was not susceptible of being inhabited, unless great artificial improvements were made by sending tenements and soil thither; and also by carrying provisions and water there, till the latter could be procured by deep boring in the rock. The pretence that before we took possession it was ever inhabited or occupied by any human being for any considerable length of time is utterly false. Its appearance then showed this conclusively.

We have learned that it was visited in March, 1835, by her British Majesty's ship Race Horse, and that then, and formerly, some stragglers from St. Thomas occasionally visited it, and gathered eggs there; and in a publication, in a pamphlet called the "Nautical Magazine," stated to be an account of the island, it is said there was an "egg collector's" hut there *then*, "and a tomb in the center of the island," being that of "the governor of the egg collectors;" but the description of the form of the isle, and its length and width, &c., do not correspond with the fact. No appearance of any tomb, or of any hut ever having been there, existed in 1854, when GIBBS first landed. The Magazine account is, therefore, more or less *fancy*. The latitude stated nearly agrees with ours, but no longitude is given.

The Danes, (if the occasional visits of the St. Thomas egg collectors can be regarded as actual permanent use and occupation,) may have had some right in 1835. But this was abandoned; and, in 1851 and in 1854, it was *uninhabited* and "DERELICT."

"Johnston's Gazeteer," published in London in 1851, says: "Aves or Bird Island is a small group of islands in the Dutch West Indies, southeast of the Island of Buen Ayre—so called from the vast number of birds which frequent there; the only inhabitants are a few Dutch fishers;" [those are latitude 12° north, longitude 67° 40′ west, more than 180 miles further south, and 240 miles further west than SHELTON'S ISLE.] "II. An uninhabited island, 147 mile west of Dominica, latitude 16° 40′ north, longitude 63° 38′ west." The Islands of Guadaloupe and St. Thomas are nearest SHELTON'S ISLE. (See Wyld's and Johnson's atlas. See *Bouillet's Dict. Univer. d' Hist. et de Geog.*, as to Aves Island being near Curaçao, and claimed by the Dutch. These are not Shelton's Isle.

III. FACTS OF OUR OCCUPATION.

In June, 1854, we dispatched several vessels to SHELTON'S ISLE to occupy it and procure the guano. We did not *delay* after Captain GIBBS' return and the report of his discovery. We dispatched them forthwith, and continued to do so, up to the 15th January, 1855, when we *first heard of* the isle being invaded by DIAS, and of GIBBS being ordered off, &c. *Our occupation of it was notorious during all that time.* LANG & DELANO, upon WHEELER's disclosure to *them*, sent vessels also in June. *Our* vessels were the brig J. R. Dow, N. P. GIBBS, master, (brought home by the mate, Smith;) brig Cronstadt, HOWLAND, master, (who died at the isle, and also some of his crew;) ship Junius, ERSKINE master; ship James N. Cooper, NICKELS master; bark Carlo Maurin, Safford master, (dispatched from Liverpool;) bark Amazon, ——— master; brig Viator, ——— master; brig Mary Pearce, ——— master, and others, whose names we cannot here remember, not having papers to refer to. They were all vessels of the *United States*, and manned "as required by law" by American citizens.

As stated in Captain Wheeler's first affidavit, (marked B,)our first vessel arrived nearly about the same time (early in July) as he did, in one of Lang & Delano's; and all commenced taking guano. Our taking possession of it was undisputed, and of course peaceful. We continued this occupation, with many employés, *uninterruptedly and without molestation*, until the month of December, (13th,) 1854, though several vessels of other flags and *some public vessels of war* visited the isle during that time. The proofs of discovery and of assuming the occupation peacefully, and peaceful use and possession for several months, if deemed imperfect, will be rendered complete. The fact that several foreign vessels, and amongst them ships-of-war, as above stated, visited the isle, is partly proved by Wheeler's second affidavit (marked C.) But other proof will be furnished.

As to our intention of permanent possession of "Shelton's Isle," we will show that we sent out and placed on the isle several *houses*, wharves, &c., &c., and carried out at different times water, provissions, &c.; even "*American soil*" went out as ballast to be left there, and also American females, (wives of some of our employés,) went out in some of our vessels.

We feel assured that if our company had staid there some time longer, and the question of citizenship had been raised as to persons *born* there, our government would not have deemed them *native citizens of Venezuela*. We purposed to make the isle *a place of rendezvous* for our guano vessels, and for supplies of coal, water, wood, &c.

IV. DISCOVERY OF ITSELF GIVES NO TITLE.

As is shown in our letter of the 14th May, by the *jus gentium*, the mere discovery of vacant isles in the high seas does not vest in the individual discoverer, or in the State to which he belongs, any right except that of taking within a reasonable time the actual occupation and possession of the isle; and that if such right is neglected to be exercised, any subsequent discoverer acquires such right equally as the first. We refer you to the authorities cited in that letter.—(Vattel, *Droit des Gens*, Am. ed., 1854, p. 98, &c., §§ 207–8–9; 1 Phill. *Int. Law*, p. 242, §224; 1 Kent, p. 177, *jus in re, jus in rem*, as to cessions; Wheaton's *Int. Law*, ed. of 1855, pp. 217, 218; Puffendorf, l. 4, c. 6, §3; ibid, l. 4, c. 6, §1, p. 1; ibid, 4, 12, 6, 8; Grotius, 2, 3, 4; ib., l. 2, c. 2, §2, 5; 3 Kent, p. 462; Klüber, Bynkershoek, D. M. 1.)

V. ASSERTED CLAIM TO DISCOVERY BY SPAIN AND OF VENEZUELA AS HER SUCCESSOR.

It is not pretended by Venezuela that she is the first discoverer; but it is said *Spain* was, and that Spain is her antecessor. Whether either of these assertions are fact or not is wholly immaterial; for neither *Spain* nor *Venezuela* ever took possession, or if they did, they abandoned it long since. *Venezuela* has not produced any proof as to the first discovery, which she should be required to do.—(See 1 Phill., §267, p. 288; § 274, p. 298; Grotius, l. 2, c. 9, § 8, &c., § 260, p. 280; 1 Kent's Com., VI., p. 25; see Wheat. *Elm. Int. Law*, 40–41–42; Puff., lib. 4, c. 9, l. 8, c. 12, §§ 1, 2, 3; Vatt. § 98, p. 170; see the "Fama," 5 Rob. Ad. Rep., p. 114.)

Spain is no more *her* antecessor, and she is no more the inheritor, than Mexico and the other States, formerly provinces of Spain; and Shelton's Isle no more "pertains" to Venezuela than it does to Cuba or Puerto Rico.

VI. TITLE CLAIMED BY VENEZUELA FROM CONTIGUITY, ETC.

Shelton's Isle is separated by several hundred miles of open sea from her shores. She has no possessions near it. As before stated, it is nearer those of at least three other nations, and in fact the Dutch have possessions between it and the Venezuelan coasts.—(See maps and charts generally.)

The locality of this isle, we conceive, destroys the probability that as to it Spain was her antecessor as to "*discovery*" and as to occupation, or that either Spain or she ever exercised any jurisdiction over it.

The claim on the ground of contiguity is clearly preposterous, as on the score of natural "*increments*" no right "*pertains*" to her on either score.—(See 1 Phill., §§ 234–235, p. 248, § 239, p. 255; Vat., p. 128, &c., §§ 289, 290; 5 Rob. Rep., 573, the *Anna*, Puff., Grotius, *de Jure Bel. ac Pac*, lib. 2, c. 3, § 10; Vattel, lib. 1, c. 23, §§ 288, 296, p. 127, &c.; see Bynk., *Quæst. Jur. Pub.*, lib. 1, cap. 8; *De dom mar.*, cap. 2.

VII. POSSESSION AND OCCUPATION MUST BE ACTUAL USE AND SETTLEMENT.

It must be *pedis possessio*, and coupled with positive exercise of actual jurisdiction; merely hoisting national flag, planting crosses, and such like ceremonies or surveys are of little moment.

And the *possession* and *occupation* must be *notorious;* other nations must have knowledge of the claim.—(See 1 Phill., § 241, p. 259; ib., § 247, p. 263; § 248, p. 263; § 230, p. 246–7; Klüber, § 126; Vattel, §§ 141 to 146, pp. 187 to 190; ib., § 208–9, p. 100; Wallace's Pamph. on the Oregon Question; Bynk., *de dom. mar.*, vol. 4, c. 1, p. 360; Eug. Ortolan, *dom. Int.*, p. 37; 8 Wheat., p. 573.

VIII. SUCH POSSESSION AND OCCUPATION MUST BE CONTINUAL.

It is not only true that discovery alone of such uninhabited isle vests no title, (but an *inchoate* right to acquire one,) and that occupation by the discoverer is absolutely necessary, but it *must be continued*, in order to maintain any title in the discoverer, or the State to which he belongs, and the right of sovereignty or eminent domain in such State, is inseparable from and dependent upon such actual occupation.—(See 1 Phill., § 230, p. 246, § 283, p. 207; Grotius, lib. 2, c. 9, lib. 3, c. 9, § 9; Bynk., *de dom. mar;* Eug. Ortolan, *dom. Int.*, Vattel, §§ 241 to 246, pp. 187 to 190.)

IX. ABANDONMENT OF OCCUPATION AND USE DESTROYS CLAIM.

Of course this means a voluntary abandonment. The authorities show that if the occupation or possession is abandoned by the first discoverer, or the exercise of jurisdiction discontinued by a State, any subsequent discoverer may occupy and possess the abandoned and *derelict* isle, and the rights of proprietary in him, and of sovereignty or eminent domain in his State, vests from commencement of *his* occupancy.—(See Vattel, supra, and other authorities last cited. 1 Phill., §§ 259, 260, pp. 279, 280, the case of the island *St. Lucie*, in 1754.)

In this case the English had abandoned the island, they said, through violence. The French said the abandonment was *amino et facti* and *sine spe redeundi*, and therefore France had taken possession of it. It was regarded as a case of voluntary dereliction, and the possession returned to the class of vacant and unowned territories.—(See 1 Phill., p. 307, § 284.)

X. FACULTY OF ACQUISITION BY THE UNITED STATES OF SUCH ISLE BY DISCOVERY, ETC.

The federal government of the United States possess this faculty as an inherent power necessary to it, and an attribute of every sovereign State, and it possesses it equally and fully as any other sovereign power.

The Constitution contains no prohibition against the exercise of such power. It is appropriate to it, and in the distribution of the various powers between it and the State governments, unless it is impliedly excluded, it is to be considered as possessed by the United States.—(See U. S. *vs.* Canter, &c., 1 Peters, S. C. R., p. 542, &c.; Vattel, § 4, p. 2, § 13, p. 3; Elliott's Debates, vol. 4, p. 207; Wheat., p. 45, *Elm. Int. Law*, Ib., p. 210. Ib., p. 78, note; Story *on the Constitution*, vol. 3, p. 156, and the cases therein cited: New edition, § 1282 to 1289, § 1339.)

The acquisition of Louisiana, Florida, Texas, California, New Mexico, and the Messilla valley, can only be sustained as constitutional on such ground. The treaty-making power and the war-making power were invoked to sustain these acquisitions, and it was contended they were included in the legitimate exercise of those powers.

The legitimate exercise of those powers, thus construed, involves the admission that the faculty of acquisition in any other mode, not forbidden by the laws of nations, or by the federal Constitution, is equally possessed by the United States. No one will contend that there is any illegality in the act of discovery or occupation by the United States, of vacant lands, or a desert island, with *respect to other nations*, that have no right thereto.

The question, therefore, comes back to the consideration whether there is any prohibition in the federal Constitution.

And the power to regulate the intercourse with foreign nations, commerce, navigation, &c., and to maintain and provide a navy, &c., may be invoked with equal force to sustain the faculty of acquisition, by discovery, in the exercise of those powers, as the treaty and war making power can be appealed to, to uphold an acquisition by purchase and cession, or by conquest.

So can the power to admit new States be invoked, and there is no distinction in the Constitution between new States formed out of Territories *ultra mare*, on an isle or island on the high seas, and such states created out of adjoining portions of this continent. The power can be exercised as legitimately with respect to all the Antilles, or the Sandwich Islands, as with respect to Canada, or Mexico, or New Albion.

Besides, the federal government of the United States, in its dispute with Great Britain respecting the possessions claimed by both on the Pacific, (Oregon,) presented and urged in the diplomatic correspondence, in executive documents, and in the debates in Congress, our prior discovery by Captain Gray, master of a merchant vessel of Boston in 1792, and Lewis and Clarke's explorations in 1805–6, and occupation under them of that region.

And in no American document on that subject, nor in any speech in Congress, has any denial of this power of acquisition by discovery been found.—(See Wheat. *Int. Law*, p. 229 ; Greenhow's *Oregon*, pp. 418, 427, 449, 466, app ; I Phill., p. 250, § 233, Ib., p. 247 ; *British State Papers*, vol. xiii, pp. 506 to 509 ; *Cong. Doc.*, 1st sess. 20th Cong., No. 189.)

Voyages and expeditions for discovery have been several times undertaken by the federal government ; sometimes by previous authority of Congress, by special appropriations for such objects, and sometimes by the executive department alone, in the exercise of its authority over the Army and Navy, without the previous express sanction of Congress. Amongst them may be mentioned Lewis and Clarke's expedition to the Columbia river ; Pike's expedition ; and Colonel S. H. Long's expeditions ; and Colonel Frémont's expeditions ; Lynch's expedition to the Dead Sea ; Strain's expedition ; Herndon's and Gibbon's expeditions ; and Wilke's exploring expedition ; Ringgold's surveying and exploring expedition ; and Commodore Perry's expedition ; and the aid afforded by the government to different expeditions to the north pole region. The history of our government is replete with such examples.

Some of these expeditions were essentially voyages for discovery or exploration out of the limits of the United States.

It is absurd to concede to the executive government constitutional power to undertake them, and that such prerogative is a mere naked, impotent or barren right, which can be productive of no results, beget no direct advantages, and which is utterly barren of any fruits beyond the credit of making such discoveries for the benefit of some other nation.

The framers of our glorious Constitution did not certainly, in our humble judgment, intend thus to emasculate the federal government, and make us the only *eunuch nation* on the face of the earth.

History furnishes some rare examples, such as in China and Japan, and the Germanic confederation, of the abnegation of sovereign rights, but Vattel says "that a nation ought to act agreeably to its nature," &c., p. 3, §§ 13, 14, *et seq.* (*Droit des Gens.*)

XI. IF FACULTY NOT IN THE UNITED STATES, IT REMAINS IN THE STATE OF DISCOVERER.

If this faculty is not in the United States it must remain in the State of discoverer, which in this case is Massachusetts.

The full attributes of sovereignty possessed by every independent State are possessed either by the federal government or by the respective States, for they cannot die, or be extinguished or alienated, without the consent of the respective States, either impliedly or expressly given. The States possessed them originally. (See Vattel, p. 30, §§ 60, 271; 1 Phil., p. 147, § 125; 4 Cranch, 212, McIllvane *vs.* Coxe.)

It would not be appropriate to the functions of a State government *now* to possess them. It would be inconsistent with other powers delegated to the federal government for each State to possess them. To allow a State to acquire territory in any mode would not be in harmony with the principles upon which the federal Constitution was based. It might be a mode by which the clause respecting the admission of new States could be evaded. For instance, Texas might find it convenient to annex Tamaulipas; Maine, New Brunswick; Michigan or New York, Canada; and Florida, the Bahamas and Cuba; and, if the government and people of those countries assented thereto, this might possibly be done *by a mere act of the State legislatures*, without contravening that provision of the Constitution prohibiting the States from making treaties and compacts, &c., with foreign nations and among themselves, and thus extend their limits without restriction.

Article X of the amendments to the federal Constitution declares that "the powers not delegated to the United States by this Constitution, nor prohibited in it to the States, are reserved to the States respectively, or to the people."

If, therefore, the faculty and power in question has not been delegated to the federal government, as contended, it is yet possessed by each State, *and the power to enlarge its boundaries ad libitum, in the mode suggested, is still possessed by each*, and in this case is possessed by the State of Massachusetts, to which we, as well as Captain Gibbs, belong.

This argument is used to show the effect and result of denying to the federal government the faculty and power referred to.

But this is a question as respects our own laws, and with which no foreign government can interfere. It is none of their business. We can settle this question among ourselves and by ourselves. Whenever any difficulty arises, and even if a State has the right referred to, when the claim of a foreign power is interposed, it is a constitutional function, and it is the duty of the federal government to enforce such right.—(See Vattel, lib. 1, c. 3, §§ 36, 37.) This authority is indisputable.

VII. EXECUTIVE MAY ENFORCE AND MAINTAIN PUBLIC AND PRIVATE RIGHTS RESULTING FROM DISCOVERY AND OCCUPATION WITHOUT ACTION OF CONGRESS.

The faculty of acquisition by discovery being so possessed by the federal government, no special act of Congress is necessary to enable the Executive to exercise the acts necessary to give effect to such faculty, or to entitle the United States to the benefits, or to reap the fruits of such discovery. It is appropriately an executive function and power, and from its nature and character does not call for previous legislation.—(Attorneys General Opinions, vol. 1, cited, 1 Phill., p. 243.)

If diplomatic action, or any measures (except actual *war*) as to a foreign State, is necessarily required for the maintenance and protection of the rights of the United States, or of a State, or of any citizen thereof, (whether they result from discovery and occupation of an isle in the high seas,) and in all cases the preliminary proceedings are an executive function. The regulation of our foreign intercourse, and all diplomacy, is a constitutional executive function, and not a legislative duty.—(See Kennett *vs.* Chambers, 14 Howard, p. 38; Wheat. Int. Law, p. 35.)

Congress may not rightfully interfere with it, except by express law, and cannot control it even then beyond certain limits. The Senate may refuse to ratify a treaty, and both houses or either house may refuse to vote appropriations; and in some cases it might be proper for Congress to adopt advisory or directory resolutions, and in others condemnatory resolutions; but in these last cases such action is not constitutionally imperative in the Executive, and the constitutional propriety of withholding appropriations by the House has been strongly questioned.

The laws of nations are a part of the laws of the United States, which the President has sworn to see are "*faithfully executed.*"—(Wheat. Int. Law, p. 514.)

The rights of the United States, and of the discoverer who belongs to her, in virtue of such discovery and occupation of a vacant isle, are founded upon the laws of nations, and the Executive is as much bound to enforce and maintain them as he is to enforce and maintain the exemption of our vessels on the high seas from visit and search, which is also guarantied by the *jus gentium.*—(Vattel, book 2, c. 6, § 71, p. 161; Ib., lib. 1, § 17, p. 5; Ib. p., 392, § 205.)

XIII. THE NON-EXISTENCE OF ANY RESTRAINING OR DIRECTORY LAW LEAVES PLENARY POWER WITH THE PRESIDENT.

The absence of any statutory prohibition or direction as to the course to be pursued by the Executive is an implication that Congress intended to let the rights of the United States and of its citizens, resulting from the discovery and occupation of a vacant isle, in virtue of the laws of nations, to stand upon the laws of nations, and that the executive maintenance and protection of those rights should be according to the principles of international law. Any fetter or restraint upon the executive powers (admitting that Congress can impose it) must not be implied. The intention to do so must be manifested by express law enacted in due form.—(As to President's power, see 5 Wheat., app., Marshall's speech; 1 Gallison's Rep., p. 563; 3d vol. Opinions Attorneys General, p. 28; 7 Howard, 1; 13 Peters, 498; 12 Wheat., 19; 9 Cranch, 126.)

XIV. DISCOVERY BY PRIVATE CITIZEN VESTS RIGHTS IN THE UNITED STATES.

It is entirely immaterial whether such discoverer is a *private citizen or subject*, or a commissioned officer of a State. The same rights, in either case, vest in the State to which he belongs. Vattel only refers to discoverers furnished with a commission from their sovereign; and this was the British argument in the Oregon case; but the United States do not hold to such opinion, and Great Britain has not always held it. There are two cases of discovery and occupation by private citizens or subjects, in merchant vessels, that are now recollected as having been contended for as the foundation of right, one by Great Britain and the other by the United States.

The first is the celebrated case respecting Nootka Sound, in 1790, in which a Mr. Mears, a half-pay lieutenant in the British navy, out of service, and sailing a Portuguese merchantman on a private adventure, sailed to and occupied Nootka Sound, which, it was said, as well from his discovery and occupation as from prior British discoveries, belonged to Great Britain.

It will be seen by an examination of the Nootka Sound case, that it resembles the present closely. The place had been discovered and was known when Mears occupied it. Spain had been its actual occupant, but it had been abandoned. Some time after Mears settled there, a Spanish vessel-of-war captured his vessels, and drove him away. The vessels were, however, subsequently restored by the viceroy of Mexico. Mears appealed to the British government for redress, and it was rendered forthwith.

The promptness and energy of the British government in that case affords a wise example for all other nations that have the ability and disposition to maintain their rights. (See British An. Reg., 1790, pp. 185, 305; Ib. 1791, pp. 208 to 227; "Gentleman's Magazine," 1790; Greenhow's Oregon, p. 446, and app.)

The other case was the discovery, by Captain Gray, in 1792, of the mouth of the Columbia river, he being master of a whale ship. He was a citizen of the United States, and his vessel was an American vessel, and upon his discovery and occupation, and upon continued occupation by Mr. Astor's employés and others, citizens of the United States, the United States based its right to all that region of country.

It is true it contended for the right upon other grounds also, but this specific ground was maintained, and Great Britain, then remembering to forget the *Mears case*, and many other similar cases, questioned the principle, that the uncommissioned Yankee skipper of a private merchant vessel could lay the foundation of such a right, and Dr. Phillimore observes with no little naiveté, (vol. 1, p. 251,) "If the circumstances had been these, viz: that an actual settlement had been grafted upon a discovery made by an authorized public officer of a nation at the mouth of a river, the law would not have been unreasonably applied." § 236.

Other authors and statesmen have maintained the principle, that upon a discovery by a private citizen or subject, the same rights enure to his State as if he was a commissioned officer, and no one has questioned the principle, that if adopted by his government by occupation, under its authority, such rights enured as if the discovery was by an officer. Even Dr. Phillimore acknowledges that adoption by a State, on discovery by a private citizen,* (1, p. 242, § 224,) and he also admits that the *"individual" has a natural title to be undisturbed in the possession of the territory which he occupies, as against all third powers.*—(Ibid., p. 242.)

And if such discovery was of a vacant, uninhabited island, the occupation and possession by such private citizen or subject, being necessarily peaceful and unopposed, is to be considered that of his government. And it is entitled to the same rights of sovereignty and eminent domain. from the inception of his occupation, as if it was by express authority and commission.—(See authority above cited; Vattel, §§ 203 to 209; Ibid., lib. 2, c. 7, §§ 96, 97, 98.)

The cases upon the subject of captures by private subjects or citizens of a Sthte, in time of war, of an enemy's property, on land or on the sea, wherein such private citizens or subjects are not expressly commissioned, nor otherwise expressly authorized to make such captures, are pertinent to the point now under consideration.

By some eminent jurists it is held, that the public declaration of waa is a sufficient commission and authority to every citizen or subject of the power making it to capture the enemy's property wherever found, in the name of and for his government, and that his personal interest therein is dependent upon the prize or booty acts of his State. (See 8 Cranch's Reports, p. 210, U. S. *vs.* Brown; Vattel, lib. 3, c. 15, §§ 223 to 228; Ibid. § 164, p. 365, and § 202, p. 391, citing French Law; Klüber, *Droit des gens*, § 267; Wheat. Int. Law, p. 430, § 8; 2 Wheat's Rep. app., note 1, p. 7.)

The question as to his private interest in the proceeds of the captured property is one of local and domestic law merely, and if allowed no share, it neither impairs the right of his government nor the legality or validity of the capture. The right of the government enures equally as if he were a commissioned officer, and the prize courts that have denied his interest in certain cases, unless allowed by express acts, have, nevertheless, maintained that of his government.—(See Vattel, lib. 2, c. 2, §§ 96 to 98, p. 170; 13 Johnston's Rep., p. 276; 1 Gall. Rep., p. 563; 2 Wheat., 76; 5 Ib., 338; 6 Ib., 1; 10 Wheat., 306.)

XV. RIGHTS AND INTERESTS OF CITIZEN DISCOVERERS.

When the discoverer is a commissioned officer of the State, ordinarily, no *private rights* result to *him*, personally, from the discovery; but when he is not such officer, but a mere private citizen or subject, he acquires a right of preëntry into property in the territory and appurtenances *paramount* over that of any other subject or citizen of the same State, and *excluding positively* all claims of any *foreign* subject or citizen of any *foreign State*.

We admit his personal right is subject to such general regulations and restrictions as the *laws of his State*, then in force, or such special regulations and limitations as his State may prescribe in respect thereof;

*6 Rob. Rep., 364, *The Rolla*—a case of adoption of a blockade.

but without either such general or special regulations, his right of possession of the land discovered by him, in a small and uninhabited isle in the high seas, extends over the entire island so discovered, and its appurtenances.

This is, however, a question between him and his own government, and in this case Venezuela has no right to meddle in it.

In this very case the records of the department will show that it has recognized and adopted the doctrine that the discovery and occupation by a citizen vests title; and it declared that "*if the authorities of any foreign government should attempt to prevent or interfere with a discoverer* (though a citizen) *in taking guano from the Aves Island, they will be expected to assign sufficient reason therefor.*" This declaration, though made to parties not discoverers, settles two points: First, the doctrine now contended for as to citizens; and, second, the adoption of such discovery by the government—by the act of the Executive.

XVI. EXTENT OF OUR RIGHTS IN THE PRESENT CASE.

Insomuch as no restrictions or limitations exist by any law of the United States as to our rights in this case, they extend to the whole isle, and the guano upon it; and until the declaration or establishment of limitations of such right by *law of the United States*, duly enacted, or at least by executive authority, the federal government is to be deemed as *acquiescing* and *confirming* them to their entire extent. This is, however, a question in which Venezuela has no concern. (See Vattel, lib. 2, c. 4, § 54.)

XVII. A DISCOVERER HAS NO RIGHT OR POWER TO ALIENATE RIGHTS OF HIS STATE, OR HIS OWN, TO FOREIGN POWERS, AND ADMISSIONS BY HIM TO SUCH EFFECT ARE OF NO FORCE.

A discoverer has no right or power to alienate, or transfer, by his personal act, the rights of sovereignty or eminent domain acquired by his State, and vested in it by his discovery and cccupation, and such act is illegal and utterly void.

And *à fortiori*, no admission, or connection, or compromise by such citizen or subject can affect the rights of his State, so acquired, and vested by his discovery and occupation as aforesaid; and that, without express authority of his government, he is incompetent to relinquish his own rights and possession (those of his State being based upon them) to any *foreign government* whatever. (See Bard., p. 239.) Individuals cannot prejudice rights of States by their acts. (Vattel, lib. 1, c. 21, § 260, p. 117; Ib. lib. 1, c. 21, § 261; 2 Phill., p. 52, § 49; 1 Ibid., pp. 145–6, §§ 122–3; Bynk., p. 223, § 239.) *Individual has no power to alienate or impair in any mode public property or rights.* (Puff. lib. 3, c. 7, ar. 11, p. 334.) "Subjects cannot contract, either among themselves or with others, and prejudice the duty and allegiance they owe to their lawful sovereign." (Note in supra from Grammond's Hist. Gal., l. 5.)

As to *admissions*, three cases are recollected that are somewhat pertinent. On the 25th of December, 1814, Mr. Gallatin, United States commissioner at Ghent, wrote to the Secretary of State, making admissions against the title of the State of Massachusetts to territory on her northeastern boundary. His letter was published, and the British government afterwards brought it up against the United States in the arbitration before the King of the Netherlands. (See letter, p. 24, British statement, note; and see also Mr. Gallatin's reply, in the most sarcastic style and severest terms, pp. 94–5, Am. statement.)

It is worthy of note, also, that in this reply Mr. Gallatin denies the right of the federal government to cede any portion of the territory of a State. (See Northeastern Boundary Document, cited above.)

Another case was when Mr. Pinckney, our minister to Spain, in 179–, made an admission with respect to the boundary of Louisiana and West Florida, which Mr. Pizarro, Spanish Secretary of State, cited to Mr. Erving, our minister, in 180–. Mr. Erving replied that the admission was of no validity, being his own opinion merely, not authorized by the government to be made, except upon terms of adjustment then proposed and not accepted, and therefore was of no force.

The third case was that of Mr. Andrew Ellicott, United States commissioner to run the boundary between us and the Spanish provinces under the treaty of 1795. He made an admission respecting the same boundary between Louisiana and West Florida, which was also cited against us by the Spanish government; the reply to which was, that he was not authorized to make any such admissions, and that it was his mere private opinion, and was of no consequence. (See Am. State Papers, Tit. *Foreign Relations*, vol. 3, p. 520, &c.; Bynk. as to *Sponsio*, p. 223, and Wheat. *Int. Law*, p. 322, &c., and p. 329, (citing Ulpian;) Wheat. p. 473, § 24. Even in time of war the commander of a fort cannot stipulate for its surrender and perpetual cession—Vattel, lib. 5, § 156, p. 193; Klüber, § 142.)

We have a statute prohibiting a citizen from negotiating, corresponding, &c., with foreign governments on diplomatic subjects. (Act of June 30, 1799, 1 Statutes at Large, p. 603.)

VXIII. MISREPRESENTATION AND FRAUD VITIATE ALL CONTRACTS, ETC.

Misrepresentations and fraud in all cases, either between individuals or between an individual and a government, vitiate contracts, agreements, &c., and destroy the effect of acts or admissions procured from an individual thereby. (See Vattel, lib. 2, c. 12, §§ 157–8–9; Klüber, § 143; Schmalz, *Eurp. Volks R.* v. pp. 53, 54; Grotius, lib. 2, c. 17, §§ 18, 19.)

Signature to a written promise or agreement, written in a foreign language, and obtained by misrepresentation of its purport, is void, in all cases.

"Consent must not have been given in error, or produced by deceit, either by misrepresentation (*suggestio falsi*) or by concealment of important facts, (*suppressio veri.*") 2 Phill. § 49, p. 62. (See Puff., p. 22, lib. 7, tit. 6; Ibid., p. 30, lib. 3, § 13; S. 2, p. 227, lib. 3, c. 6, § 6, 7; Ibid., p. 280, §§ 7, 8, p. 281, notes 1 & 2; Story's *Comm. on Eq.*, § 201, citing several cases.)

XIX. MISTAKE OR ERROR VITIATES CONTRACTS, ETC., IF MATERIAL.

If the "agreement" is not void on the ground of fraud by Dias in obtaining it, it should be disregarded, and the admissions of Gibbs and Lang thereon made should be disregarded as of no force, on the ground of mistake or error by them, as well in respect of the admission of their authority as agents to make such admissions or agreements, as also with respect to the title of Venezuela, and their relinquishment of the isle, guano, and other property to her.—(Rep. Temp. Hard., pp. 281–3–4–9, Gray and Baker.)

XX. MISREPRESENTATION AND FRAUD BY A GOVERNMENT IN TRANSACTIONS WITH INDIVIDUALS, VITIATES CONTRACTS.

In cases of fraud, governments or princes are no exemption from the general rule. The misrepresentation and fraud is, of course, in every case of such character, practiced by their officers and agents, for whose conduct the government is responsible.—(See authorities above cited.)

Fraud is a canker that affects the contract and vitiates it, whoever the party perpetrating it upon the defrauded party. It destroys the contract, and makes it a *nude pact*, or no obligation or promise. Whatsoever it touches it kills.

XXI. CONSTRAINT OR COERCION BY MENACE OR THREATS OF A GOVERNMENT OR ITS OFFICERS DESTROYS CONTRACT OF AN INDIVIDUAL.

The rules of common law as to "duress," in contracts between individuals, apply with greater force to those made with governments. (See Phill., last above cited, and other authorities sup.)

Admissions, relinquishments, concessions, or other acts, or a declaration of consent obtained by a government or its officers, from an individual by coercion, or constraint, or by menace or threats of such government, or its officer, is, in no case, valid. The idea that fraud, coercion, or constraint, is not to be imputed to a government founded upon the false maxim of monarchists "the king can do no wrong," is not admitted to be law, The *fact* is unquestionably the reverse.

Kings and governments are not exempted from the effect of the fall of man. Both are mere human institutions, and "man is prone to error as the sparks fly upwards."—(See Job v, 7; see history of all usurpations and wars from the time of David down to Louis Napoleon.)

Contracts made under duress are void, because they are not voluntary.—(See Roll. *Abr.* p. 688, Black.'s *Comm.;* Pothier *on Contracts*, Story *on Equity*, § 201, and cases there cited.)

Duress, as defined by the common law, especially in the early cases, was being in fear of bodily harm, imprisonment, and the like, from threats or menaces, or being then imprisoned; and apprehension of loss of property merely was not sufficient.—(See cases above cited.) In case of treaty, personal fear of actual violence by the representative of a State negotiating it, voids the treaty.—(Phill., p. 63, § 49; Wheat. *Int Law*, 331.)

This strict rule, as just observed, is not adhered to in modern cases, but it is now generally held both by the civil and common law that any undue constraint operating upon the mind and will of a prudent man, though he may not be put in bodily fear, renders the act not voluntary, and vitiates it.—(See Kent's *Comm.*, part 5, § 39, and cases cited; 16 Vesey, p. 159; 1 Ibid., jr., p. 22; 16 Vesey, p. 159; 11 Ibid., p. 649; 1 Jacob and Walker, p. 96; 14 Vesey, p. 289; 2 Coke's Inst., 5 Rep., p. 149.)

In the case of a government the rules should be still more extended, by reason of the fact that the very demand by a government, made through its officers, carries with it, to all law-observing men, the *constraint* of obedience. When such demand is imperative, backed by an armed naval and military force, commanded by a military and naval officer, and accompanied by threats and menaces, stated to be by order of the government, an act, agreement, contract, concession, relinquishment, or admission obtained thereby from the citizen or subject of another government, is void and of no force, as being given under duress. The law of individual contract applies to it, though it cannot be asserted as a well settled principle that a nation can plead duress.—(See Wheat., p. 324; Klüber, § 142.)

It is sufficient if the party is constrained by apprehensions of the power of such government being exerted to the injury of his rights or his interests, in respect of property, the subject of contest, though such apprehension may not extend to bodily harm to himself.—(See Puff., lib. 3, c. 6, § 9, p. 281; § 10, note 3, p. 285, cites Plato.)

If he is constrained by apprehension or well founded belief of collision between such armed force and himself, or individuals associated with him, and that personal injury may result to any or either side, or that he may have imposed upon him the necessity of forcible resistence to such governmental authority and officers, and military force under the command of such officers, and may be obliged to overcome and capture such force, to do which he possesses the ability; even such constraint nullifies his acts of concession and his admissions, as not being voluntary.—(See Puff., lib. 22, &c., before cited, and *ut passim.*)

Besides, it is the duty of every law-abiding subject or citizen, enjoined by the principles of the laws of nations, ordinarily in such cases to yield to the demands of such foreign government, and if he is wronged, to appeal to his own government to obtain him redress.

It is upon this principle that it has been held that the hostile rescue by a neutral crew of a neutral vessel, captured in time of war by one of the belligerents, though the vessel may not be a good prize, if retaken again by captors of the same power, it is liable to confiscation for such recapture by the court of the belligerent power.—(See Wheat. *Int. Law*, p. 455.)

The neutral resists at his peril, and such resistance has been held to divest him of his immunity from capture as a neutral. This is at least the British doctrine, though it may be questioned.

In this case, the intrusion of Venezuela by an armed force, and our on was in time of profound peace between the two governments. By resistance our employés could, doubtless, at the risk of bloodshed, have overcome and made prisoners Dias, his vessel, and his whole force. By refusing the provisions and water, in a few days we could have starved them out, in all probability; but we were not only not bound to adopt any such means of resistance, but, on the contrary, it was our duty to limit our opposition to remonstrance and protest.

Vattel says, § 223, p. 399, that the unexpected attack of foreigners may be repelled on the ground of self-defense; but they are advised not to commit hostilities, even in time of war, without a commission.

And if to keep the peace, prevent probable bloodshed, or injury to our rights and interests, either with respect to our vessels, their cargoes, the isle, the guano thereon, or our other property there, or the welfare and safety of our employés, our agents were constrained to yield, as they did, their acts do not impair, or compromise, or weaken, or prejudice, or militate against our original rights because of such restraint. (See Vattel, § 325, p. 275; 9 Cranch, 55.)

The intended effect of Dias's acts and the legal effect of his acts are the same—constraint of Gibbs, &c., and thereby his concessions were not voluntary.

XXII. ADMISSIONS BY AGENTS.

Admissions or agreements of an agent beyond the scope of his authority and its objects, and also sale, transfer, or relinquishment, or an extinguishment, or concession, or admission by an agent, cannot be allowed to destroy his principal's right to property intrusted to his care and management; and acts destroying or relinquishing such right or compromising it upon inequitable terms, are *prima facie* to be regarded as made without authority of his principal, and do not bind him. (See 2 Phill., p. 63, § 49, citing Vattel, lib. 2, c. 12, § 158; Wheaton, p., 332, § 8, citing Ed. Review, No. 154, ar. 1; Grotius *De Jure Bel.*, lib. 2, 14, §§ 4, 12; Martens *Précis*, lib. 2, c. §§ 50, 52; Lee *vs.* Munroe, 7 Cranch, p. 366; Wilson *vs.* Turner, 1 Taunton, p. 398; Puff., lib. 3, c. 7, ar. 11, p. 304; U. S. *vs.* Gooding, 12 Wheat., p. 460.)

No admission by an individual of a thing, of the truth of which he is not necessarily cognizant, and as to which he has no peculiar means of knowledge, though he be an agent, is not conclusive in any case, and if incorrect—as is the fact in this case—it is of no force or effect whatever. (See General Ins. Co. *vs* Ruggles, 12 Wheat., p. 408; 1 Domat, p. 425, ch. 3, ar. 1, § 1186 to 1192; Ibid., p. 427, § 1146, § 1154.)

And this is so, whether as respects his own rights, or the rights of others. With regard to the rights of others, if of matters of fact, such admissions are considered as mere hearsay. They are never noticed; are not competent testimony either by the civil or common law, and whether oral or in writing; and if matters of law, or matters of fact and law mixed, as in this case, they are of no weight whatever.

If such agent knows any facts, he must be adduced as a witness by the party claiming under his acts, or seeking the advantage of his admissions. This is the law in cases between individuals, and it applies to governments. (See 10 Vesey, pp. 128, 763; 1 Taunton, p. 398, Wilson *vs.* Turner.)

The power of a proxy or agent must be limited by reasonable presumption of principle and objects. (Domat, article 1186, 1146, &c. General power not sufficient for alienation.)

If a party, whether a State or an individual, claims under acts or admissions by one said to be the agent of an adverse party, he must give distinct and unequivocal proof of the authority to do the act, or make the admission; and such authority is never to be implied. (See STORY *on Agencies*, § 116; SMITH *on Contracts*, p. 347.)

Especially is this the law in a case of total alienation or relinquishment by an agent, of the property of his principal to such claimant, or as to admissions of a general character going to destroy his principal's rights, as such acts and admissions are inconsistent with the general delegation to use the property beneficially for his principal, and are ordinarily deemed invalid for want of authority, if full and special authority is not proved; and if in any degree inequitable, or made without equivalent received for his principal, will be deemed collusive and fraudulent, and void on that account. (See SMITH *on Contracts,* by RAWLE, p. 347 [249] citing many cases; see also Patterson *vs.* Tash, 2 STRANGE, p. 1178; Daubigney *vs.* Duval, 5 Term, 604; Martini *vs.* Coles, 1 Man., &c., p. 140–493; Graham *vs.* Dyster, 6 *id.*, p. 114; Quioroz *vs.* Freeman; 3 BARN. & CRESS., 343; Fielding *vs.* Kymer; 2 BROD. & BING., 639. Such is recognized as the rule on this side of the Atlantic. See cases cited in SMITH, supra.)

In this case there was no equivalent or consideration for the alleged agreement. The pretended consideration or permission to stay as long as Dias or his government would allow them was a mockery. (See 2 Phill., p. 63, § 49.)

The agreement shows that it is a clear case of *lesion,* as well as constraint, and not reciprocal.

The permission to load these vessels was equally trifling, and its value depended upon the title of Venezuela, which is denied; and besides, these vessels did not load, and could not load, before they were ordered off peremptorily upon a few hours' notice.

These facts show that the "agreement" was not only in the inception, but in the end, a trick and fraud, "made to delude, and purposed to deceive."

The power and authority must be exercised according to the intention of the constituent. General procuration or agency is not sufficient for alienation of property the agent was to preserve, nor for a recission of contract he was to execute. (*Corp. Jur.* lib. 25, lib. 60, *D. de Procur.* lib. 63, eo.; Master of vessel restrained to incidental power relating to ordinary employment of ships; Story *on Agency*, p. 35.)

XXIII.—CAPTAIN GIBBS' AGENCY.

He went out as master of the brig J. R. Dow, and staid out on the isle as general agent to gather and ship guano from thence. (See instructions.)

He was not, whilst there, master of any of our vessels. As such general agent as aforesaid, he had no authority to relinquish or alienate the isle or guano, or to impair, or destroy, or weaken our title thereto, in any wise.

He was expressly prohibited from so doing, and instructed to resist certain anticipated intrusion by certain governments, specifically named, by force; and with respect to others not named, among which was Venezuela, he was instructed not to yield possession till they resorted to actual force, and made prizes of his vessels; and that he must resist to the extent of imposing such necessity upon them before he allowed them to evict him. (See instructions in letter of 20th June.

He had no authority as master of a vessel whilst there. (See Story *on Agency*, § 116, p. 139, and cases cited; Abbott *on Shipping*, p. 69, c. 3, § 2, and cases.)

It cannot be contended that any one at the isle had any authority, express or implied, from the government of the United States, to do anything in the premises.

No authority by us to relinquish the rights of the United States would have been valid if we had given it, and this for the reasons before stated. (See ante, xvii.)

Lang was no agent of ours—was an interloper—hostile to our interests; had intruded in violation of our just rights, upon the disclosure of Wheeler as to the discovery, and was suffered to remain because we could do no better without violence.

XXIV. THE DIAS CAPITULATION OBTAINED BY THE COMPOUND MEANS OF MISREPRESENTATION AND FRAUD, AND CONSTRAINT, OR FORCE OR "DURESS."

1. *Misrepresentation and fraud.*—Captain Safford's deposition is conclusive on this point; it is annexed, marked A. He says, Dias "*landed an armed force and took possession of the island.*" He says, Dias "*hauled down the American flag, and hoisted the Venezuelan flag in its stead.*" He says also that at the same time Dias *threatened the immediate expulsion of all the Americans on the island.* This was on the 13th of December. He says, "finally, that the said Captain Dias drew up a document in Spanish, which he said was a permit for them to continue to load guano, provided they placed their armament under his control. I was present when the purport of said document was explained to Captain Gibbs, (who did not understand Spanish.) *As explained it was simply* that Gibbs and Lang were to assist the garrison *left* on the island with *provisions and water*, and the most *positive assurances* were given them *that the document contained nothing whereby they assented to the title of the island being in Venezuela.* I am POSITIVE on the point, as Captain Gibbs asked MY opinion in reference to it. And I further certify that said Dias insisted that, unless they signed said document, they must leave the island *forthwith.* Captain Gibbs, under the circumstances, felt compelled to sign the document, hoping, by so doing, they would allow him to load the vessel there, and those expected, saying to me, that if the document contained anything different from what had been explained to him, he did not suppose a paper signed under such circumstances could be considered as of any binding force."

Other depositions have been filed by other parties, but we do not present them or rely on them at present. The "agreement," upon its face, is stamped with the characteristics of fraud.

Its being written in Spanish, no written translation being given by Dias—the certificate or permit given by him to Gibbs and Lang not being signed by any person but himself, though written as if Gibbs's and Lang's signatures were to be affixed—and all the circumstances about it, indicate fraud, if we had not produced this direct and unequivocal proof by a respectable and impartial witness.

The character of the stipulation is, of itself, evidence of fraud or of force being used, or of both combined, to procure the signatures of Gibbs and Lang. Gibbs did not understand Spanish; and if others besides Dias, deceived him as to the contents of the paper, it does not strengthen its validity.

It may be observed that the inconsistency of this document with Captain Gibbs's instructions, and with his bounden duty, and with his fidelity, which is unquestioned, are strong circumstances, if not sufficient of themselves to justify the charge of fraud, to corroborate and confirm the direct testimony on that point.

2. *Constraint and force, or duress.*—The testimony of Captain Safford is equally conclusive on this point. Duress, according to the common law definition—that is, threats of imprisonment or other bodily harm, or putting a party in fear, &c., may not be proved, nor is it necessary that it should be, as we have shown, (see xxi, supra,) but that constraint was induced by Dias being the officer and representative of a government.

XXV. THE ONUS PROBANDI AS TO THE TITLE RESTS ON VENEZUELA.

We were in peaceable possession, and the isle was invaded, and we were ejected by armed force whilst in the enjoyment of that occupation. We had been notoriously in possession for several months, the American flag had been flying there during all that time, American vessels had been continually there, lading guano, and voyaging from thence to the United States and elsewhere.

Right of possession is sacred.—(See Vattel, p. 168, §§ 88, 90; 1 Phill., p. 272, § 253.)

No admissions or acknowledgments of agents without authority to make them, or relinquishments, equally invalid for the same cause, as well as others, should not exonerate Venezuela from the duty of producing, on demand by the United States, the full original proofs of her title, upon which she tortuously assumed such possession, and evicted us. If those admissions are of any validity, the rule is the same; and, indeed, between sovereign States, the honor of the State, outraged by such forcible invasion, demands *that the statu quo ante bellum* (for it was an act of *war*) should be restored, and indemnity made, and apology given, before any discussion of title can be entertained.—(See Vat., lib. 2, c. 18, § 337.)

Possession is *prima facie* evidence of title.

XXVI. VENEZUELA BOUND BY THE CONSEQUENCES OF THE FRAUD AND MALCONDUCT OF HER OFFICERS, AND, HAVING AVOWED THEM, CANNOT HEREAFTER CHANGE THE ISSUE.

Venezuela is estopped by the acts of her officers, having adopted them. She adopted them by producing the agreement or capitulation of Dias.—(See Vattel, p. 160 to 163, lib. 2, c. 4.)

She is responsible for the deceit, misrepresentation, falsehood, and fraud, as well as force and constraint, or duress, by which that paper was obtained; especially as upon its face, upon the first blush, these characteristics are manifest. She must have known of them, for its very form and stipulation are circumstances pregnant with fraud and force.

The fact that she has chosen to rely upon the capitulation and the admissions therein, instead of giving proof of her discovery and actual occupation, is suspicious.

And if anything else was wanting, the official report of Dias, of his exploit at Shelton's Isle, in the *guano war*, of his victories on that bloody field of arms, of his capture of our artillery, of his contributions levied upon us for provisions and water, of his hauling down the Yankee flag (if we could procure a copy) would be conclusive.

We have called the isle a *bloody* field of arms, not because any *American* blood was spilled there, but on account of the *felo de se* of a Venezuelan soldier, in the *feu de joie* by which the hoisting of the Venezuelan flag was saluted.

We trust a copy will be procured by our minister, as we learn that it is an interesting historical document.

XXVII. FORM OF RELINQUISHMENT BY AGENT IMMATERIAL.

It is of no consequence what the form adopted, except in so far as its form and contents indicate its character, and the means adopted to obtain it. A parol relinquishment or verbal admission, if otherwise unexceptionable, would have been as valid as if the form of a public treaty by national representatives had been adopted; or if Gibbs had executed a deed of indenture, or deed poll, or technical release in due form of law, signed, sealed, delivered, and acknowledged before some judicial functionary, it would have been of no more force than mere tradition of the personal property yielded up, or the manual delivery of the vessels and artillery, and verbal acknowledgment of right and title in Venezuela.

All such acts would have been equally void. All such admissions, whether written or verbal, are ineffectual to impair our rights.

A convention or treaty between States may be by parol.—(2 Phill., pp. 63, 64, § 69; Klüber, § 1413.)

All that is necessary is, that the declaration should be positive and clear. The *consensus fictus* of the civil law is unknown to national jurisprudence.

We have before urged that the form that seems to have suited Commander Dias's fancy, that of a military CAPITULATION by an agent and employé without the honors of war, (the United States flag having been forcibly hauled down by Dias on his storming the isle, their artillery and armament demanded, and themselves obliged to engage in aid of the Venezuelans,) is *significant* of the force and coercion employed by Dias, and the *constraint*, "under the circumstances," which induced Gibbs to take the *permit*, (with the misrepresentation and fraud also practiced,) and to yield his signature to that capitulation.

XXVIII. INSULTS TO THE UNITED STATES BY VENEZUELA, AND OUTRAGES UPON OUR PERSONS AND PROPERTY, IN THIS CASE, A JUST CASUS BELLI.

It is forbidden by the laws of nations for one State to attempt to tamper with the citizens or subjects of another, not authorized by their State to do the act sought to be obtained.—(See Vattel, lib. 1, c. 4, § 75, p. 33; Ib. lib., 2, c. 4. § 54, p. 154; Thompson *vs.* Powells, 2 Simon's Rep., p. 294; Taylor *vs.* Barclay, Ib. p. 213; United States *vs.* Palmer, 3 Wheat. Rep., p. 610; "*Santisima Trinidad,*" 7 Wheat., p. 283.)

Especially is it an affront to the United States, and an act forbidden by the *jus gentium*, for a State to arrange with a private subject or citizen in respect of his possession of discovered territory, or his rights thereto, in order to impair or defeat the rights of the United States so acquired and vested. It is seeking to withdraw them from their rightful allegiance and loyal duty. (See Vattel, lib. 2, c. 4, pp. 160–1, §§ 71–2, &c; Ib., lib. 2, c. 4, p. 154, § 54 and supra; Ib., lib. —, c. 18, p. 374, § 332, &c.)

The resort by Venezuela, without notice to the United States, to armed force, to oust us from the peaceful possession of Shelton's Isle, assumed peacefully and enjoyed uninterruptedly by us, after the discovery of guano thereon, and the hauling down the United States flag, without having previously applied to the federal government, was an outrage upon and an insult to the United States, and it should demand prompt reparation and atonement; and this demand should be made, and compliance with it insisted upon, as a preliminary or proemial condition, before considering the question of title. (Vattel, pp. 575–6, before cited.)

This atonement and reparation should be—1. Restoration of isle to *status quo ante* the eviction; 2. Indemnity to us for our damages; and 3. Apology to the United States, and saluting our dishonored flag, as we did the Spanish consul's at New Orleans, and as France insists we shall do to the French consul's at San Francisco. [This is the precise course of the British government in the case of Mears at Nootka Sound, and to which Spain was constrained to accede, to avoid *war.*]

And in Mears's case, too, it is questionable if the ships seized by Spain were not Portuguese, though the British flag was used; and in that case, also, the ships had been given up by the Mexican Viceroy on the Pacific coast before the demand was made. (See Greenhow's Oregon, p. 466 and app.; see British An. Reg., 1790; "Gentleman's Magazine," 1790; "British State Papers.")

Many similar instances can be referred to in the history of nations within the past century.

See the case of the Falkland Islands;* its seizure by England

*Discovered by Davis, Hawkins, *et al.*, about the close of the 16th century. English, French, and Spanish settlements made simultaneously in 1763. Spain then purchased French claim and dispossessed England forcibly from port, and afterwards abandoned the island. English flag rehoisted, but subsequently abandoned. France and Spain acknowledged her right of sovereignty in 1774. In 1825, Buenos Ayres founded a colony under Durbein Vernd, who seized two American schooners sealing. His settlement destroyed by United States ship Lexington. The British government resumed possession in 1833, contending it had only been suspended. In 1845 incorporated by royal charter as British colony.

during last century, and also recently, in violation of national law, and the discussions upon that subject, in illustration of the true principles of international law, violated by the British in both instances.* (See Wheat. *Int. Law*, p. 220.)

Shelton's Isle being a desert and uninhabited isle in the high seas upon its occupation and settlement by us, and our ships being there with the flag of the United States, and that flag being raised on the isle as an emblem of its sovereignty connected with such occupation, the isle became subject to the jurisdiction of the federal government, and subject to its laws, the same as were the vessels of the United States there; and any crime, (murder or robbery and the like) committed upon it—certainly by any American citizen—would be punishable by said laws in the federal courts of the United States.

We conceive, also, the commission of a crime on the isle during that time, if by a foreigner, would likewise be punishable by those laws and by the same courts.

The fact that we were, at the time of the invasion of Dias, in full possession, and in the actual and peaceful occupation of the isle, and had been so for months before the outrage, and that it was notorious, and that no remonstrance was made by the Venezuelan government to our minister to that republic, or through their agent here, or otherwise to the United States, grossly aggravates the insult and outrage perpetrated by her authority—expressly avowed by her by the production of the Dias capitulation. And it is no palliation of this indignity, or excuse for this unjustifiable and hostile act, that it may have been stimulated by a combination of speculators, even though some were citizens of the United States; but, in truth, such circumstances heighten the enormity, and add to the effrontery of her conduct.

The duty of the United States in such case is laid down in the following cases:

Vattel pre. p. lv, note 1; also lib. 1, c. 23, § 283, p. 126; lib. 2 c. 2, § 24, p. 144; §§ 65 to 70, pp. 160–1; lib. 2, c. 18, pp. 275–6, §§ 323–8, pp. 279–80, §§ 332–3–4, p. 281 §§ 339–40.

XXIX. DAMAGES AND INDEMNITY.

With regard to our damages in this case, as heretofore presented, they are in no degree supposititious or hypothetical, or what are generally called incidental, consequential, or indirect damages. They are positive, certain, readily ascertained and liquidated, and immediate and direct:

1. The asportation and the detention of our personal property.
2. The loss by false freight, demurrage, and expenses of our vessels.
3. The obstruction to the labor and employment of our workmen at the isle, taken and sustained there at great expense.
4. Expenses of procuring redress, and interest or augmented damages for delay.
5. And further, we claim the actual value of the guano at the island

*See Dr. Johnson's Works, vol. 12, p. 123; 1 Phill., § 246, p. 262.

at the time of the aggression, deducting only that which may remain there when the possession is restored to us.

We have evidence that since that time numerous vessels have been employed in carrying it off, under the authority of the Venezuelan government, upon payment of what is styled a "royalty," or under some contract with that government.

We are not bound by any improvident contract or arrangement that Venezuela may have made in this regard as the limit of our damages; but, on the other hand, she cannot refuse to yield the full amount she has herself thus estimated the guano to be worth to her at the island, aud in addition, such sum as we may prove that it was worth to us.

She is bound to yield up *at least* the estimated fruits of her contract to the Philadelphia speculators, even though such estimates may not have been realized by their bad faith.

And again, we contend that in addition to these certain damages, we may justly claim of Venezuela, as indemnification for her tortuous outrage and wrong committed upon our rights and property, all the profits we should have probably made by the shipment and sale of the guano, if they had not molested us.

And in addition to this, we claim, also, that evenhanded justice demands that they should indemnify us for the embarrassment in our business and to our credit, and the consequent losses we have incurred, which every merchant can understand and appreciate, and which we are prepared to show are of no trifling amount or moment; not merely has our prosperity been jeoparded, but it is yet uncertain whether it may not result in consequences still more serious; all the result of her unjustifiable *tort*.

Our only hope of redress is in the action of the President and yourself. And we have full confidence in the fulfillment of that pledge he made to the American people on the 4th of March, 1853, that "THE RIGHTS WHICH BELONG TO US AS A NATION ARE NOT ALONE TO BE REGARDED, BUT THOSE WHICH PERTAIN TO EVERY CITIZEN IN HIS INDIVIDUAL CAPACITY, AT HOME AND ABROAD, MUST BE SACREDLY MAINTAINED." * * * "HE MUST REALIZE THAT UPON EVERY SEA AND UPON EVERY SOIL WHERE OUR ENTERPRISE MAY RIGHTFULLY SEEK THE PROTECTION OF OUR FLAG, AMERICAN CITIZENSHIP IS AN INVIOLABLE PANOPLY FOR THE SECURITY OF AMERICAN RIGHTS."

With this we shall be satisfied.

A.

BOSTON, *June* 20, 1855.

I, JOSHUA F. SAFFORD, hereby certify, that on the 13th day of December, 1854, I was master of the bark Carlo Manaran, laying at Aves or Bird Island, in the Caribbean sea, loading guano, shipped by Captain W. N. P. Gibbs, for account of Messrs. Sampson & Tappan and Philo S. Shelton, of Boston. That on the day above named a Venezuelan schooner-of-war, commanded by one Dias, arrived at the island and landed an armed force, and took possession of the island, hauling down the American flag and hoisting the Venezuelan flag in its stead, at same time threatening the immediate expulsion of all the Americans on the island. Finally the said Captain Dias drew up a document in Spanish, which he said was a permit for them to continue to load guano, provided they placed their armament under his control. I was present when the purport of said document was explained to Captain Gibbs, (who did not understand Spanish,) as explained, it was simply that Gibbs and Lang were to assist the garrison left on the island with provisions and water; and the most positive assurance was given them that the document contained nothing whereby they assented to the title of the island being in Venezuela. I am positive on this point, as Captain Gibbs asked my opinion in reference to it. And I further certify that said Dias insisted that unless they signed said document, they must leave the island forthwith. Captain Gibbs, under these circumstances, felt compelled to sign the document, hoping by so doing they would allow him to load the vessels there and those expected, saying to me that if the document contained anything different from what had been explained to him, he did not suppose a paper signed under such circumstances could be considered of any binding force.

J. F. SAFFORD.

COMMONWEALTH OF MASSACHUSETTS, *Suffolk County*, } *ss:*

Then the above named J. F. Safford personally appeared and made oath that the foregoing declaration by him subscribed is his free act and deed. Before me,

CHARLES HOMER,
Justice of the Peace.

BOSTON, *June* 20, 1855.

B.

I, James Wheeler, hereby certify, that I was, in the early part of the year 1854, in the employ of Messrs. Sampson & Tappan and Philo S. Shelton, of this city, collecting guano on an island in the Gulf of Mexico; that some time in the month of March, in said year, Captain Nathan P. Gibbs arrived at the island in the brig "John R. Dow," and informed me that, by direction of our employers, he had visited "Islas Aves," or Bird Island, in the Caribbean sea, latitude 15° 40′ north, longitude 63° 35′ west, and had found quite a large deposit of guano upon the principal island.

I returned to Boston in the month of May of same year. I left the employ of the gentlemen above named, and persuaded Messrs. Lang & Delano to fit me in the brig M. H. Comery for said island for a cargo of guano. I left Boston harbor in said vessel on or about the 22d of June, understanding I was to be immediately followed by Captain N. P. Gibbs, in the brig John R. Dow, sent out by my former employers.

I arrived at the island on or about the 15th day of July, a vessel which I supposed to be the Dow being then in sight, and she also arrived the same evening at the island.

I give this declaration as an act of justice to Messrs. Sampson & Tappan and Mr. Shelton, to whom I was indebted, through Captain Gibbs, for the knowledge that there was guano on said island, of which fact I was previously ignorant, and imparted the information to Messrs. Lang & Delano, to the prejudice of my former employers; and as an act of justice to them I give this declaration.

Given under my hand this 8th day of June, 1855.

JAMES WHEELER.

STATE OF MASSACHUSETTS, } *ss:*
County of Suffolk, }

Then personally appeared the above named James Wheeler, and declared, under oath, the above to be his free act and deed. Before me—

JOHN CLARK,
Justice of the Peace.

BOSTON, *June* 8, 1855.

C.

I, James Wheeler, late master of the brig M. H. Comery, do depose and say: That much of the time when I was on Aves or Bird Island, and afterwards, when I was lying there with my vessel, the American flag of the United States was flying, and that it was a usual practice to keep said flag flying. I further depose, that when visited by the British steamer Devastation, I informed the commander that we held the said Aves or Bird Island for the government of the United States, and expected to be protected by our government, as we were citizens of the United States.

The American flag, which was then flying, was respected, and I was informed by Captain D'Orsey, of said British government steamer Devastation, that we had the right to hold the island in the name of the United States.

JAMES WHEELER.

COMMONWEALTH OF MASSACHUSETTS, } *ss:*
County of Suffolk, }

Then personally appeared the above named James Wheeler, and made oath that the declaration by him subscribed was true. Before me—

GEORGE B. UPTON,
Justice of the Peace.

JUNE 15, 1855.

Extract of letter of instructions to Captain Nathan P. Gibbs, dated June 21, 1854.

"You have an armament sufficient to protect you against all intruders who come for the purpose of taking guano, and we wish you to use it without hesitation against all *individuals* that may *come to molest you;* but we don't wish you to resist *the armed force of any government,* although we feel confident the island does not belong to any nation; yet there may be claims of this kind we do not know of, and we do not wish you to place yourself by any chance in *a false position by resisting any government force that may be sent there.*"

BOSTON, *June* 22, 1854.

DEAR SIR: As you are about to proceed to Islas Aves or Bird Island with a gang of men to gather guano, our instructions are that you take possession of said island and *hold it* against all claimants; to better secure your rights of possession that you put a fence all around it, leaving open your landing only.

Should parties come there to take guano you will order them off and prevent their taking it, *by force,* if necessary, for which you have an armament, *and you must use it,* if threats don't answer. We mean you to keep possession of the island till it is *exhausted;* and if you want more men write home and we will send them out to you; and if the person now sent out as your assistant is not all you want, write and your wishes shall be gratified in this respect. We don't wish to drive hard until the rainy season gets over, in order to have dry guano; but you can, while loading the first two or three vessels, judge how rapidly you can ship it in dry weather. We shall send you as much tonnage as you think you can load, if it is 3,000 or 4,000 tons per month, as we must clear the island this year. The first two or three cargoes you better avoid the top sandy looking guano, and take that which is darker underneath and the crust, which I want you to pound up on a plank platform, so as to have it *fine* mixed in with the guano. The first cargo or two however you need not be so particular. Write home if you want more horses, boats, or scows; all you ask for will be sent you. Write a few lines by every vessel, and let us know if you have any trouble. [If any body claims the island in the name of a government, you must insist that no government can claim it unless it be Spain, who discovered it; no one but yourself has acquired possession, and that you shall hold it till you can hear from your government on the subject. No government have any better claim than we have, and this you can *insist* upon. Don't mind any threats, because there is nothing they can or dare do to injure you. The probability is, if anybody comes under *English, French, Dutch* or *Danish* flags, they will say they are by orders of government; but resist all attention to their orders, and insist they must take you all as prisoners and make *prizes* of your vessels before you will go, and leave it for your government to settle the matter with theirs. I am sure they will not move you, but will frighten you if they can. Against other comers you must take your chance and drive them off.]

Captain N. P. GIBBS.

BOSTON, *June* 22, 1854.

DEAR SIR: As you are about proceeding with a gang of men to collect guano and ship it home, the following is our understanding as to compensation:

You are to receive seventy-five dollars per month and fifteen cents per ton on all the guano shipped from the island, the weight to be ascertained on landing in this country; and it is further guaranteed that your compensation shall in no event be less than one hundred and fifty dollars per month during the time you are so employed. You can draw for seventy-five dollars per month payable here during your absence.

Captain N. P. GIBBS.

DEAR SIR: You will proceed as soon as possible to Sydney, Cape Breton, and take a cargo of coal as per charter party herewith, and proceed to the port of Mole, Island of Guadaloupe, and discharge the same according to bills lading or charter party. You will notice the freight is payable at the rate of $10 per chaldron of name measure or its equivalent. The silver 5 franc piece is a legal tender in this country at 94 cents each. You can take your pay in this coin or in French gold coin at the rate 18¾ to 19 cents per franc, or bills on France of an undoubted character at 18¾ cents our money per franc. I prefer your taking gold or silver for your freight which you can collect yourself, and not pay any commission for collecting the same. You probably will have to pay a commission on your disbursements, which I presume cannot be very large. You will take in sufficient ballast to take your vessel safely down Ilas "Aves" or Bird Island, which you will find down on the chart, latitude 15° 40′ 56″ north, 63° 36′ 54″ west from Greenwich, where you will no doubt find Captain N. P. Gibbs with a gang of men prepared to furnish you with a cargo of guano, which is the object of this voyage; and you will with your boats and crew lend every assistance in so loading your vessel or in any way make yourself useful with your crew in assisting Captain Gibbs. After getting your cargo proceed to *New York* as speedily as possible and report yourself from coast of South America consigned to order. Should you not find Captain Gibbs there, and you cannot with your crew and the means at your disposal load the brig with guano, you will proceed to Turk's Island and get a freight of salt to Boston on the best terms you can with the least possible delay. You will write me from Sydney how much coal you take and when you are to leave, and from Guadaloupe when you expect to get away, and how much money you have over; and if you take bills of exchange for your freights send them to me properly indorsed to my order inclosed to my order. The first and second you can bring with you.

Capt. LUTHER HOWLAND, *of brig Cronstadt.*

D.

AVES ISLAND, *December* 3, 1854.

SIR: I being forced to leave this island, I shall take passage in the Amazon, as she wants 75 tons to make up her load, so I order her to Boston. The Viator will touch at St. Thomas; she has in about 100 tons of guano.

Yours, obedient,

N. P. GIBBS.

PHILO S. SHELTON.

E.

This is to certify that I was visited at Aves Island by a vessel from the government of Venezuela, on the 13th day of December, 1854, and that they claimed the said island, and landed one field piece, ten soldiers, and an officer to guard the island against all other comers, but allowed me to work until they could have further orders from their government. On the 20th of December another vessel came and landed twenty more troops and small arms, but did not attempt to molest us until the 28th, when the same vessel returned and added to their forces, and took possession of the island in the name of their government, and would not allow us to work longer, and ordered us to clear off all our property in twenty-four hours; but by giving them a portion of provisions I was allowed to take the remainder, but we had not time to clear our houses and wharves away, as they had taken forcible possession of them.

NATHAN P. GIBBS.

F.

AVES ISLAND, *December* 25, 1854.

SIR: I send you a line via St. Thomas, by Mr. H. Lang, who leaves here to-day in one of his vessels which he gives up. We are expecting to be stopped every day. Since my last we have had twenty more troops landed, and we are now waiting their pleasure. There is an English brig-of-war now lying here and leaves to-day for Carraccas, to see if this Venezuelan government have a right to take it; if they have not, this government will look into it. He says we have the best right, and he was ordered to come and see if we were still here, if not, to take it himself. I think they may come and help defend it and let us work. He has gone to find out the right of it. The Carlos will sail to-morrow with 800 tons, the Amazon the last of the week. The Viator arrived 23d. We have nothing decisive to depend upon, but I shall stick until the last, but I fear the time will be short. The Carlo will come to Boston.

Yours obedient,

NATHAN P. GIBBS.

PHILO S. SHELTON.

G.

AVES ISLAND, *December* 26, 1864.

SIR: I last wrote you via St. Thomas, informing you of the state of affairs here. We are expecting daily to be stopped, but I shall work as long as I can and get the best. The Amazon will sail Saturday for Falmouth. Her cargo will make a good average. She has in 70 tons, like the Dow's, former cargo, and 300 of No. 4 of my first samples, mixed one third decomposed coral. I shall try to finish her the same as I am going on. The Viator will sail soon. I look daily for the Mary Pearce. I hope I'll not have to wait, as I don't know how long I may be allowed to wait. I am out of coffee and some other trifling things, which I shall not order; if I can get it out of the vessels I will do so. You will probably see Mr. H. Lang, who can inform you the particulars. He sends another vessel away to-day empty.

Your obedient,

NATHAN P. GIBBS.

PHILO S. SHELTON.

H.

UNITED STATES OF AMERICA,
State, City and County of New York, } *ss:*

By this public instrument of declaration and protest, Be it known and made manifest unto all whom it doth, may, or shall concern: That on this twentieth day of February, in the year of our Lord one thousand eight hundred and fifty-five, before me, *John Neilson, a notary public* in and for the county and city of New York, in the State of New York, duly and by lawful authority admitted, commissioned, and sworn, and residing and practicing in the city of New York and State aforesaid, personally came and appeared *George W. Nickels,* master of the ship James N. Cooper, and together with him come and appear *Henry C. Dearborn,* first mate, and *Patrick Scallan,* second mate, all of and belonging to the said ship; all of whom being by me severally, duly, and solemnly sworn on the Holy Evangelists of Almighty God, voluntarily and freely depose and say: That they sailed in and with said ship on the fifteenth day of January, one thousand eight hundred and fifty-five, from the port of New York, bound for Bird Island for a cargo of guano; that said island is situated in latitude 15° 40′ north, and longitude 63° 38′ west, in the Caribbean sea; that they arrived off the said island on the second day of February, one thousand eight hundred and fifty-five, and came to anchor; that at the same time of their coming to anchor the colors of the *Venezuelan government* were flying on the island; that at 5, p. m., the first mate went ashore in one of the boats of said ship for the purpose of making arrangements to load the vessel with guano; that on his landing he was met by an officer of the aforesaid government of Venezuela with *a file of thirty armed men who forbid him in the name of the said government from making any such arrangements and ordered him off the island;* that the said first mate then returned to the ship accompanied by the said Venezuelan officer and three of the soldiers; that on their arrival at the ship the said Venezuelan officer ordered the master of the ship to get underway and leave the island, which he accordingly did, not having the means or power wherewith to resist said order.

GEORGE W. NICKELS, *Master*
HENRY C. DEARBORN, *First Mate.*
PATRICK SCALLAN, *Second Mate.*

Wherefore, the said George W. Nickels, master and commander as aforesaid, hath requested me to *protest,* and I the said *notary,* at such his request, have *protested,* and by these presents *do publicly and solemnly protest* against the governments of *Venezuela* and the *United States of America,* and all foreign princes and powers, and against all and every person or persons whom it doth, shall, or may concern, for all manner of losses, costs, damages, charges, expenses and injuries whatsoever, which the said ship James N. Cooper, her owners, freighters, or charterers, have already sustained, or may hereafter sustain, by reason or means of the foregoing premises.

Thus done and protested, in the city of New York, this twentieth day of February, in the year of our Lord one thousand eight hundred and fifty-five.

[SEAL.] In testimony whereof, I have hereunto set my hand and affixed my official seal the day and year last above written.

JOHN NEILSON,
Notary Public.

UNITED STATES OF AMERICA,
State, City, and County of New York, } *ss:*

I, John Neilson, a notary public in and for said city and county, duly commissioned and sworn, dwelling in said city, do hereby certify that the foregoing is a true and correct copy of an original protest on file in my office.

In testimony whereof, I have hereto set my hand and affixed my [SEAL.] official seal this twentieth day of February, one thousand eight hundred and fifty-five.

JOHN NEILSON,
Notary Public.

I.

Extract from a report or letter from Captain N. P. Gibbs, announcing the discovery of guano deposit on Shelton's Isle, (Aves or Bird Island.)

APRIL 6, 1854.

SIR: I landed on Aves or Bird Island, and it proves to be no harbor, but vessels can anchor on the southwest side of it from one cable's length to a half mile, and not have over eight nor less than five fathoms water clear bottom. There is a heavy swell setting on the beach all around the key. The key is very much like Arenas, it being a coral formation, and very hard to ascertain the quantity of guano there until it is worked. I don't like to make an estimate for fear I might exaggerate, but I think there is more guano there than there ever was at the former key, and the greater part of decomposed coral such as I have the samples of, which I took about two feet under sample No. 2. I tried in several other places, and found the same. Sample No. 1, I think, is nothing but sand. Of such the northwest part of the key is composed of for two feet deep; then comes No. 4, about the same depth. Under this still comes the decomposed coral, the exact depth I cannot tell, but one part of the key it was from three to four feet. From No. 1, I measured 1,000 feet length by 300 feet breadth. Within these bounds I took No. 2, 80 feet long, 80 feet broad, 2 feet deep; also No. 3, 150 feet long, 50 feet broad, 2 feet deep. Under all these samples is decomposed coral, and you will see by the plan that No. 4 is from the edge of the bank. I was near being deceived in the key until I came to this bank where the sea had washed under it and caved it away about 10 feet deep, so I could see what the key was composed of. I then tried in several places back and found it the same. There is no one on board of the brig that knows *what* there is there. It will be hard to keep the mate in the dark, for he knows the keys we stopped at in the passage. I made the key at 9 o'clock, after running through the night by dead reckoning, and made it to a mile, as I expected. I run by English chart and directions, and I am certain the latitude and longitude here is correct. The mate got a good meridian altitude while I was on shore, and made it 15° 50′. I am confident he made a mistake. The key cannot be seen above eight or nine miles.

At 8 o'clock on the 4th instant made the Island of Sombrero, and it proves to be a barren rock, without more than fifty birds, and not one bit of guano on it. There is fifteen fathoms all around it, is perpendicular about thirty feet. It was with a great deal of difficulty I landed; there was but one place where I could get up; there was some grass on the *center* of the key. After looking this thoroughly over, I lost no time in running for Aneyada, which I made at 5, p. m., of that day. The island is full ten miles long, well wooded, and quite a large village upon it. My West Indies directions told me so before, but the coast pilot did not. So, to make sure, and obey your orders strictly, I went, and found it as here described. I did not land, but hauled on the wind and weathered the reef the next morning and proceeded for Aves—not a bird on Aneyada.

On the seventh instant at 1, p. m., was up to Bird Key, laid down on the chart as Frenchman's rock. This key lays about six miles from St. Thomas, and is 200 feet perpendicular, the sea breaking against all sides of it. As it was impossible to land—if I could land I could not get upon the top of it—I lay aback two ships' length from it, and done all I could to obey orders. There was not a bird on it; the top was covered with grass; the sides one solid, and bounded up like a sugar loaf; there is no bottom to be seen close to it. * *

[For plat see original.]

11th. Landed on Nevasa, and there proves to be nothing there.

N. P. GIBBS.

Mr. French to Mr. Marcy.

WASHINGTON, *June* 26, 1855.

DEAR SIR: I have the honor to inclose a letter to you from my brother, Henry F. French, Esq., notifying the department that he is attorney for Messrs. Lang & Delano in their claim against the Venezuelan government for damages in being driven from the Aves Island. He has already notified the department, I believe, that he is attorney for Wheelwright & Cobb, in the same matter.

I now act for my brother; after the 1st July I shall act with him, so that any communication on the subject may be addressed to me here.

I am, with great respect, your obedient servant,

B. B. FRENCH.

Hon. WILLIAM L. MARCY,
Secretary of State.

Mr. French to Mr. Marcy.

WASHINGTON, *June* 30, 1855.

DEAR SIR: I inclose the petition of Lang & Delano, of Boston, Massachusetts, for indemnity in consequence of the outrage committed upon their property and agents at the island of "Aves" by the Venezuelan government.

I accompany it with some views of my brother and myself as attorneys for L. & D., which we beg you to consider, and we hope that you will, in such manner as may seem to you most expedient, cause indemnity to be made by the government of Venezuela to our clients as soon as practicable.

In our view, not only the rights of American citizens, but the dignity of the United States of America, demand both indemnity and concession on the part of Venezuela.

Very respectfully yours,

B. B. FRENCH.

Hon. WILLIAM L. MARCY,
Secretary of State.

To the honorable William L. Marcy, Secretary of State of the United States.

The memorial of John H. B. Lang and William W. Delano, partners under the firm of Lang & Delano, of Boston, Massachusetts:

Your memorialists represent that they are native citizens of the United States; that having learned that a deposit of guano of great value in commerce and agriculture existed on the island in the Caribbean sea known as "Aves," or Bird Island, which lies in latitude 15° 39′ and in longitude 63° 38′ west, they fitted out the brig M. H. Comery to obtain a cargo and secure such rights in the island as might be proper. The Comery sailed from Boston in June, 1854, and arrived at said island and found it uninhabited and unoccupied. She landed her party, who hoisted the American flag, and took formal possession, and proceeded to inclose the island with a fence.

On the day following, the brig Dow, from Boston, owned or chartered by Philo S. Shelton, arrived, and, by consent of Lang & Delano's agent, occupied and inclosed a part of the island, and both vessels loaded with guano.

The Comery having completed her freight first, landed a party of working men to retain possession, build houses, and make other arrangements for procuring further supplies of guano, and left the island and arrived at Baltimore with the first cargo of guano ever brought from the "Aves" to the United States.

It being the hurricane season, but few vessels were sent during the summer, but in the autumn your memorialists chartered many vessels and made extensive arrangements to prosecute the business.

That about the 12th of December a Venezuelan armed schooner came to the island, landed a detachment of armed men, and took possession of the island in the name of that government. There were, at this time, upon the island seventy men, citizens of the United States. Men-of-war of different nations had visited the island, and their commanders had uniformly expressed the opinion that the parties in possession had the right of possession.

There were, at the island, three American vessels taking in cargoes of guano. The Venezuelans hoisted their colors upon the very flagstaff which had been erected by us, and which had borne the American flag. Having no adequate force to repel the means there arrayed against us, the Venezuelans having armed occupation of the island, and asserting an exclusive title thereto, which we were unable to investigate or resist, no resistance was attempted, but we submitted to such conditions as were imposed, trusting to our own government to protect the rights of its citizens, and to procure for us redress, should this assault upon us prove, as we deemed it, illegal.

The commander of the Venezuelan force gave to the agent of each party upon said island a paper in the Spanish language, of which the following is a translation:

"Domingo Dias, captain of the navy, second chief of the Venezuelan squadrons, and commissioned by the supreme government of the republic as supervisor of the Antilles in the Caribbean sea, have come to an agreement, subject to the approval of my government, with Charles H. Lang, agent for Lang & Delano, of Boston, and Nathan P. Gibbs, agent for Sampson & Tappan and P. S. Shelton, also of Boston, whom I have found taking guano at this island.

"1st. They may continue loading with guano the three vessels now taking cargoes.

"2d. They may continue loading until such time as the company arrives with whom the government have made a contract, or until the arrival at the island of the approbation or disapprobation of the government.

"3d. And we, Charles H. Lang and Nathan P. Gibbs, promise to loan to the garrison such auxiliaries as they may require.

"4th. And, in effect, place our artillery and armament at the orders of, and under the flag of Venezuela, to whom the island appertains.

"5th. I, Domingo Dias, second chief of squadron, order the commanders of men-of-war that are cruising in the Antilles, to respect this until the government give contrary orders.

"Island of 'Aves de Barlovento,' 13th December, 1854."

That this paper was forced upon the parties in a strange language, as the only terms to be allowed them, and received by them only because they had been forcibly deprived of possession of the island and were under actual duress; that any admission of title therein contained refers only to the actual possession which had been forcibly taken from the Americans by the Venezuelans, and so was based upon a false, violent, and outrageous assertion of right by a Venezuelan officer, for which his government should be held responsible.

That, under this permission, they continued loading the vessels already at the island; that several other vessels chartered by them arrived, when the Venezuelan armed schooner returned, landed more troops, and placed sentinels over all the houses and on the wharf in the night; that when our men attempted to resume their work in the guano pits, they were threatened by the sentinels with being instantly shot, and were thus compelled to stop; that our citizens were then notified to quit the island, with all their people and vessels, within twenty-four hours, which they were compelled to do, abandoning their houses, wharfs, boats, water, and other property of great value; that the commander of the Venezuelan schooner boarded all the American vessels then at the island, and demanded to examine their papers, and compelled the officers to exhibit them; that many other American vessels chartered by us afterwards touched at the island to procure guano, and were not allowed to do so; that your memorialists are satisfied that the Venezuelan government have no title whatever to the said Island of Aves, although, as appears by the paper aforesaid, that government had contracted, before dispossessing us, with some other party, based upon an assumption of title to the island; that the course of its officers is in violation of the law of nations and an outrage on the rights of American citizens, and of your memorialists in particular; that we have thereby been subjected to great and ruinous losses in our business; that the document aforesaid is dated as at the "Aves de Barlovento," which is the well known name, as laid down on the charts, of an island, or part of a group of islands, more than two hundred miles nearer to Venezuela than this island of Aves, which has never been known by any other name; that whether the conduct of the agents and officers of Venezuela originated in misapprehension or was an intended outrage upon our rights, we are equally entitled to indemnity.

Wherefore your memorialists pray that such course may be adopted by our government that their wrongs may be redressed, and full indemnity awarded them for their losses and injuries by them sustained through the violent and unlawful acts of the said government of Venezuela. And, as in duty bound, will ever pray.

LANG & DELANO,

By their attorneys,

B. B. & H. F. FRENCH.

JUNE 30, 1855.

The evidence on file in the Department of State in support of the claim of Wheelwright & Cobb, for indemnity in the same matter, is referred to, to substantiate the facts above stated.

B. B. & H. F. FRENCH,
Attorneys.

Claim of Lang & Delano vs. *the Government of Venezuela.*

In the matter of the claim of Lang & Delano for indemnity for damages sustained at the Island of "Aves."

It is said that the agents of the Americans, in the arrangement to which they were parties, admitted the title of Venezuela to the island.

To this we answer—

1st. That the Venezuelan government had already taken armed occupation and exclusive possession of the island, and so *de facto* settled, at their peril, the present question of title. From this first decisive and outrageous act, flow, as consequences, all the acts which follow. There is nothing in the arrangement that in the least excuses the original wrong of dispossession, or that can be construed into satisfaction or amends, or into a waiver of claim to indemnity for it.

2d. Had there been, upon the false assertion of title by Venezuela, and express admission by the Americans of such title, it would be but an admission under misapprehension of the fact, which could on no principle bind them. No party can take advantage of his own wrong, or claim a right because his own falsehood has been taken for truth.

An admission, even of title, in another, if not induced by falsehood, is not binding if made under misapprehension, except in some cases where rights of innocent third parties intervene.

3d. The agents of the American owners had no authority to bind their principals in this matter, which could not be within the scope of their authority.

Had the Venezuelan officer claimed one of the American vessels as belonging to his government, and procured, by or without force, an admission from the captain or agent that such claim was just, no one would pretend that the property of the owner could be thus transferred.

4th. But the agents of the Americans were actually under duress, and so, had they made agreements prejudicial to their interests, no one could be bound by them.

B. B. & H. F. FRENCH,
Attorneys for Lang & Delano.

WASHINGTON, *June* 30, 1855.

Mr. French to Mr. Marcy.

WASHINGTON, *December* 17, 1855.

SIR: On the 30th of June last I had the honor to address you as the attorney of Lang & Delano and Wheelwright & Cobb, of Boston, relative to indemnity claimed by them from the Venezuelan government for outrages committed by the agents of that government on their property at the Aves Island, to which I received a reply, dated July 2, 1855, saying "that the department" was then "engaged in the consideration of that subject."

Will you do me the favor to inform me how those cases now stand, and very much oblige your obedient servant,

B. B. FRENCH.

Hon. WM. L. MARCY,
Secretary of State.

Mr. Marcy to Mr. French.

DEPARTMENT OF STATE,
Washington, December 20, 1855.

SIR: In reply to your letter of the 17th instant, in relation to the claim of Lang & Delano and Wheelwright & Cobb, against the Venezuelan government, I have to inform you that as the subject is still under discussion between the two governments, no definite intelligence can be imparted to the claimants at this stage of correspondence.

I may, however, prevent untoward anxiety on the part of the claimants whom you represent, by stating that the contract which the public papers allege to have been made by the United States minister at Caraccas in behalf of a Philadelphia company, expressly reserves, as this department is informed, the anterior claims of the Boston discoverers of the Aves Island guano deposits.

I am, sir, &c.,

W. L. MARCY.

B. B. French, Esq., *Washington.*

Mr. Sanford to the President.

St. Nicholas Hotel,
New York, December 24, 1855.

Sir: In obedience to your verbal direction, when I had the honor of seeing you on Thursday, the 20th instant, at the Presidential mansion, I now address you on the subject of Shelton's Isle and the action of the government thereon, having postponed this communication till my arrival here this morning, in order that I might acquire more certain particulars in Baltimore and Philadelphia and this place concerning the extraordinary circumstances which I intimated to you there was reason to believe had occurred in that business.

The department of State possesses documentary proofs of most of the following facts, and of incidental circumstances strengthening Mr. Shelton's claim to the prompt interposition of the government:

1st. That nearly two years ago, Mr. Shelton's agents, while on a voyage of discovery in the Caribbean sea, expressly for guano, discovered and took possession of that derelict isle, and others, containing valuable deposits of guano, and a short time afterwards he sent thither several vessels and men, and brought several cargoes of guano to the United States.

2d. That after several months' peaceable possession of Shelton's Isle, and after having erected tenements, built wharves, and made other improvements, and hoisted the American flag thereon, Mr. Shelton's agents and men were forcibly ejected by an officer of the Venezuelan navy, in an armed vessel of that navy, and with a military force of that government, and his property on the isle forcibly wrested from his possession by military force, and the American flag struck and the Venezuelan hoisted in its place with a salute, and this outrage was committed by the express order of the Venezuelan government.

3d. That Mr. Shelton sustained damage to an amount at least of three hundred and forty thousand dollars, and he has been utterly ruined thereby.

4th. That the Venezuelan government had no pretense of right nor title to the isle 300 miles or more from its coast, either from discovery, occupation, or transmission of the right thereof from others, and the outrage was totally unjustifiable, and is now so conceded and admitted by all parties.

5th. That there are circumstances connected with the attempt first made to defend this outrage, that superadd fraud to the original violence and insult to the first injury, and that insult extends as well to the federal government of the United States as the outrage does to Mr. Shelton.

6th. That the conduct of the Venezuelan government was prompted by a combination of speculators, partly resident in the United States, including prominent politicians claiming to have influence, and for the purpose of subserving their own selfish interests at Mr. Shelton's expense.

7th. That the combination has been enabled by sinister courses and contrivances to satisfy the Venezuelan officials that the government of the United States was not disposed to interfere for or sustain Mr. Shelton, and that in fact the government of the United States desired the favorable action of the Venezuelan government towards them, the said combination of speculators. It is worthy of note that the present Venezuelan officials denounce the first agreement, to carry out which Mr. Shelton was ejected, made by the influence of predecessors as a fraud obtained by nefarious courses by all parties, and hence the pretended new contract, though really founded on the first so repudiated.

8th. That chiefly through the instrumentality and influence of Mr. Eames, the United States minister at Venezuela, the Venezuelan government has been induced to take such favorable action for such speculators, and give them a new contract for guano in Caribbean Islands, under which, by authority of the Venezuelan government, the guano on Shelton's Isle is rapidly being taken away in fraud of Mr. Shelton's rights, and, as some concerned in the combination boast, it will all be taken before he can get redress.

9th. That while this act of fraud was being perpetrated, the United States minister utterly and inexcusably neglected to enforce the claim of Mr. Shelton, and manifested lukewarmness if not hostility to it.

10th. That a person named Pickerill, dispatched by said combination to Venezuela to perpetrate the arrangements mentioned, was greatly facilitated in so doing by his being, as it were, clothed with an official character as charged with public dispatches, one of which was instructions to Mr. Eames to further Mr. Pickerill's views to a certain extent, but not to allow anything to be done to militate against the claim or rights involved in Shelton's Isle.

11th. That from these various circumstances and others, and the fact that some of those concerned in the combination referred to boast that their political influence in Congress and at Washington and elsewhere, was sufficient to sustain them against Mr. Shelton, and that he could get nothing done for him, have created with Mr. Shelton and his friends a total want of confidence in Mr. Eames, and it may be added, a conviction that he is connected too intimately in feeling, if not otherwise, with those opposed to Mr. Shelton, and who have sought to wrong and injure him.

12th. That the Mr. Pickerill above named has ceased to be the agent of said combination, but has sought to get the control of Mr. Shelton's claim as agent, for a fee of half, which has been denied him, though he was profuse in his assurances of powerful political aid in both countries. The refusal of Mr. Shelton was for the reason that he feared his constitution of such agency would end in the total sacrifice of his claim and rights.

Copies of the papers in relation to the contract made by Mr. Pickerill are unquestionably in the Department of State. I beg of you to examine them. The papers in relation to Mr. Shelton's claim are also on file, and I trust you will examine them personally. I regretted to learn that Mr. Marcy took exception to a long letter addressed by Mr. Shelton to him in a reply to a letter from the Secretary of State, which Mr. Shelton supposed conveyed imputations against his conduct, but it was not imagined the reply was disrespectful, nor was it so intended; and I presume Mr. Marcy is satisfied on that point, as he has been so assured, and also that any portions regarded as exceptionable would be promptly expunged.

My uncle, Mr. Shelton, is advised by counsel that it is proper for him to memorialize Congress to confirm his right of discovery and occupation of Shelton's Isle, if the executive is without full power so to do. This would bring the case up fully before the legislature for its action, and therefore, as it might embarrass the executive diplomatic action, which I am confident you will promptly direct to be further had for the enforcement of his claim against Venezuela for indemnity, &c., I have induced its being withheld until approved whether it meet your approbation or not.

As upwards of a year has elapsed since the outrage, and as the failure of the judicial officers here to arrest the Venezuelan commander who dispossessed Mr. Shelton of his property, Captain Dias, upon a civil process, which failure was occasioned by a sudden departure from this city, every day's delay is adding to the injury he has received.

I will add that frankness induces me to say that circumstances have caused me to have a pecuniary interest in my uncle's claim, and this letter is addressed in my own behalf as well as his. It is proper for me also to state that the State Department was apprised of the purpose of Mr. Shelton to arrest Dias and hold him to bail, above attempted, if no objection existed, and it was intimated that none did exist.

Apprehension that such course might possibly compromise Mr. Shelton's rights as an American citizen, to the interposition of his government for the protection of his rights, and the indemnity for the outrage he has sustained, have deterred him from pursuing the advice of counsel to institute suits of libel or injunction or otherwise against some nine or ten vessels now employed in the asportation of his guano from Shelton's Isle, or by a suit against the combination before mentioned, incorporated by act of the Pennsylvania legislature.

The Venezuelan government has established a military garrison on the Isle, but if authorized by you, Mr. Shelton will promptly rid the isle of it without expense to the government of the United States, though it would perhaps be advisable that Congress should first recognize his right, acquired by discovery and occupation.

May I ask that Mr. Shelton or myself be advised of the action that may be had by the Executive on the subject, and of such course as it may deem it proper and most advisable for him to pursue, as he wishes to conform to its intimations?

Mr. Marcy suggested to me in conversation on Wednesday last that

I should make some proposition as to what Mr. Shelton wanted to be done. Mr. Shelton's letter on file and the printed pamphlet I handed you, also on file in the State Department, contain express propositions of what he wanted, sustained by argument and citations from authorities, and he and his friends feel the present condition of his case to be a great hardship and grievance.

I have confidence that the Administration when fully acquainted with this case will not consent to do anything or to omit doing anything whereby the just claim of an American citizen for indemnity for wrong, outrage, and injury by a foreign government is sacrificed to further the schemes of speculators, who, without merit, seek to avail themselves of the beneficial results of the enterprise. As a question of honor, Mr. Shelton's case is one demanding the attention of the government, and as a question of interest the agricultural community are deeply interested in seeing that his enterprise and industry, pregnant with such advantageous results to them, should be encouraged and protected against the insidious efforts of an unscrupulous and selfish corporate monopoly.

I have the honor to be, sir, with great respect, your obedient servant,

H. S. SANFORD.

The PRESIDENT.

Mr. Sanford to Mr. Marcy.

38 CLINTON PLACE, NEW YORK,
January 3, 1856.

DEAR SIR: The unfortunate condition of the case of Mr. Philo S. Shelton in relation to the outrage committed by the Venezuelan government at Shelton's Isle, and of his claim for indemnity from that government, has constrained the parties interested to decide upon the employment of an agent to go at once to Caraccas to attend to their interests, if such course is not unacceptable to the State Department. Such agent would be more certainly useful if the department would provide him with letters of a similar character to those furnished to Mr. Pickerell, the agent of the Pennsylvania or Philadelphia Guano Company last spring; and suggesting to the minister of the United States at Caraccas to aid him and to confirm such adjustment as the agent might succeed in effecting, not inconsistent with the other official instructions of the department on that subject. Mr. Shelton and associates have not yet fixed upon any agent, and they would take care not to select any person without consulting the department, and not to designate any one unacceptable tô it. I presume I need not say to you that I have not thought of going on this errand, and since I have retired from the diplomatic service of the United States, I have not had the least wish to be invested with any official or quasi official employment. My private and personal affairs have been the object of my undivided attention. The only object of this communication is to endeavor to accelerate the just settlement of my uncle's claim, in which circumstances have constrained me to become deeply interested, and I am controlled only by an anxious desire to conform to the views of the department.

May I beg you to answer this communication to me here, where I shall probably be some weeks.

I have the honor to be, very respectfully, your obedient servant,

H. S. SANFORD.

Hon. WILLIAM L. MARCY,
Secretary of State, &c.

Mr. Marcy to Mr. Shelton.

DEPARTMENT OF STATE,
Washington, January 4, 1856.

SIR: In order that this department may frame further instructions to Mr. Eames in regard to your claim against the government of Venezuela, you are requested to prepare and transmit such a statement of your losses and damages at the Aves Islands as will cover, substantially, all the elements of your claim.

It occurs to me—and the suggestion is offered for the consideration of all the parties interested—that it would be decidedly to the advantage of the several claimants, viz: Messrs. Lang & Delano, Wheelwright & Cobb, and your own house; to confer upon the subject together and agree upon some gross amount which shall embrace all claims, and which shall be distributed by the claimants among themselves in such proportions as may have been previously agreed upon.

A letter of like tenor to this has been addressed to the other claimants mentioned.

I am, sir, &c.,

W. L. MARCY.

PHILO S. SHELTON, Esq., *Boston.*

Same to Wheelwright & Cobb, Boston. Same to Lang & Delano, Boston.

Mr. Sanford to the President.

38 CLINTON PLACE, NEW YORK,
January 5, 1856.

SIR: In connection with my former communication to you, written at your intimation, in relation to the right of Mr. Shelton as discoverer and possessor of Shelton's Isle, and the outrage of Venezuela upon those rights, and his claim for indemnity, &c. I have now deemed it my duty, in behalf of Mr. Shelton, to inclose to you a notice signed by the president of the Philadelphia Guano Company and the Venezuelan consul at Philadelphia, inhibiting all vessels, except authorized by the Philadelphia company, from visiting all guano islands in the Caribbean sea under the jurisdiction of Venezuela. It is taken from the Herald of to-day.

Shelton's Isle is claimed *by them* to be under that jurisdiction, and included in the contract between the company and the Venezuelan officials, and the Venezuelan government have a military force there, as, in my former communication, I stated to you. The instructions from the Department of State in relation to the affairs of that company, and to the good offices of the minister of the United States in its favor, to effect an arrangement with Venezuela, were express to the point that nothing should be done to militate against the right of Mr. Shelton to Shelton's Isle, and his claim for indemnity, based on that right; and, in view of this fact, the inclosed notice is a matter of astonishment.

I have also inclosed a copy to the Secretary of State, whom I addressed yesterday, as well as to-day, in relation to the outrage upon Mr. Shelton.

I have the honor to be, with great respect, sir, your obedient servant,

H. S. SANFORD.

The PRESIDENT.

Notice.

OFFICE OF THE PHILADELPHIA GUANO COMPANY,
December 24, 1855.

The Philadelphia Guano Company having, by virtue of a contract made with the government of the Republic of Venezuela, secured the possession and exclusive right to remove the guano deposits existing on all the islands belonging to and under the jurisdiction of the said republic, hereby give notice that no person or persons other than agents of the said company can lawfully remove guano from any of the said islands, and that all cargoes taken therefrom without a permit from the company, duly signed and sealed with the corporate seal thereof, will be claimed by them on arrival at any of the ports of the United States or Europe, and legal proceedings will be immediately instituted for the recovery of the property so taken, in whose hands soever it may be found.

By order of the board of directors.

D. LUTHER,
President.

Agent in New York, James Lee & Co., 49 Wall street.

CONSULATE OF THE REPUBLIC OF VENEZUELA,
Philadelphia, December 19, 1855.

Captains and shipowners are hereby notified that, there being no ports of entry open to foreign commerce in any of the Caribbean islands under the jurisdiction of the republic of Venezuela, with the single exception of that of the island of Margaritta, all vessels found touching at any of the guano islands, except those having a permit from the Philadelphia Guano Company, duly authenticated, will be seized and held liable for the penalty provided for a violation of the navigation laws of the republic.

JOSÉ A. KEEFE,
Consul.

Mr. Sanford to Mr. Marcy.

38 CLINTON PLACE, NEW YORK,
January 5, 1856.

SIR: Since my letter of yesterday I have been surprised upon reading the subjoined notice, which appears in the Herald of to-day, and which I have cut from the fifth page of that paper, (fourth column.) Although it is signed by the Venezuelan consul at Philadelphia, as well as the president of the Philadelphia Guano Company, I am not prepared to believe that your instructions that nothing be done to militate against Mr. Shelton's right as to discovery and possession of Shelton's Isle, and his claim for indemnity, based upon that right, have been disregarded. I have deemed it my duty, on behalf of Mr. Shelton, to inclose you the within notice.*

A few days since I addressed a communication to the President, at his request, which I presumed would be referred to the department, and therefore thought it unnecessary to duplicate it to you. I have deemed it proper, also, in connection with that communication, to transmit to the President, as well as to yourself, the subjoined notice of the Venezuelan consul and the Philadelphia Guano Company.

I am, with esteem and respect, your obedient servant,

H. S. SANFORD.

Hon. WILLIAM L. MARCY,
Secretary of State, &c.

Mr. Marcy to Mr. Sanford.

DEPARTMENT OF STATE,
Washington, January 7, 1856.

SIR: In reply to your letter of the 3d instant, I have to state that the department perceives no objection to the appointment, by Mr. P. S. Shelton and the other parties interested, of a suitable person to represent them and urge their claim upon the Venezuelan government for the losses sustained by their expulsion from the Aves Islands in the early part of last year.

---

*The notice above referred to accompanies the preceding letter to the President.

The same facilities will cheerfully be extended by the department to such an agent as were offered to Mr. Pickrell, the agent of the Philadelphia Guano Company, on the occasion of his recent visit to Venezuela.

I am, sir, &c.,

W. L. MARCY.

HENRY S. SANFORD, Esq.,
38 *Clinton Place, New York.*

Mr. Marcy to Mr. Sanford.

DEPARTMENT OF STATE,
Washington, January 9, 1856.

SIR: I have received your letter of the 5th instant, with the notice from the New York Herald.

I do not see wherein the notice could excite your surprise, or how it has any relation to Mr. Shelton's claim. The notice relates to islands under the jurisdiction of Venezuela. The ground of Mr. S.'s claim is that Bird Island was not under the jurisdiction of Venezuela when he had possession of it. I see nothing in the notice which can in any way affect that question—nothing which shows [that] the instructions, or rather advice, from this department have been disregarded.

I am, sir, &c.,

W. L. MARCY.

H. S. SANFORD, Esq.

Mr. Sanford to Mr. Marcy.

38 CLINTON PLACE, NEW YORK,
January 12, 1856.

SIR: Your brief note of the 9th, in reply to my communication of the 5th, was received last evening. When I addressed you that communication, it seemed to me that the facts referred to in it, and also in my other recent letters to the President and yourself on the subject of Mr. Shelton's claim, not only justified, but demanded, that the attention of the President and yourself should be called forthwith to the notice I inclosed to you, and in the manner adopted by me, otherwise that notice would probably have escaped your observation. I will recapitulate the facts to which I allude, *seriatim*. You must pardon me for their reiteration. It is done to save you the trouble of an examination of the past correspondence to ascertain them.

1. The Philadelphia Guano Company claim, and the Venezuelan government agrees, that Shelton's Isle (miscalled "Bird Island" in your note) is included, and was expressly intended to be included, in the contract between them definitively arranged under the auspices

and by the assistance of the United States minister at Caraccas, rendered to the contracting parties under the instructions, or (as you suggest) the "advice," of the department.

2. The Venezuelan government has had officers and a military garrison on Shelton's Isle ever since the 13th day of December, 1854, when Commander Dias, of the Venezuelan navy, hauled down the United States flag and hoisted that of Venezuela there, and forcibly ousted Mr. Shelton's agents and workmen, and drove his vessels away from the island, &c., and the Venezuelan government are now exercising jurisdiction over it.

3. The Philadelphia Guano Company has been actively engaged since the ejection of Mr. Shelton's agents, &c., and since the arrangement it made with the Venezuelan government, and are now actively engaged in the asportation of the guano on Shelton's Isle *under that contract*, thus decreasing the quantity of the deposit there and greatly injuring his interests therein, and essentially impairing the value of his rights with respect to the isle and in the guano deposit first discovered by him, (per his agents,) and peaceably and rightfully possessed by him when so forcibly ejected.

4. The Venezuelan government persists in denying Mr. Shelton's rights with respect to the isle, and also have not yielded to him any indemnification whatever for the injuries sustained by him by the aggression of its officers, under its authority, more than a year since, and for the continued usurpation of his rights.

5. The course of the United States minister at Caraccas in reference to Mr. Shelton's claim, has displayed feelings beyond mere indifference to his rights, and Mr. Shelton and his friends had a profound conviction that his course merited reproof beyond that for inexcusable remissness and disregard of the primary instructions of the department in relation to the prosecution of the claims, and that he had lent the influence of his official position in aid of the consummation of measures prejudicial to Mr. Shelton's rights and interests, and that Mr. Eames was in fact interested in feeling, if not otherwise, with the Philadelphia speculators, and in disregard of the instructions or "advice" of the department, in respect to the rendition of his good offices to that company, did aid in effecting an arrangement that materially militates against Mr. Shelton's interests.

It seems to me quite apparent that the facts stated must have inadvertently escaped your particular notice in the haste of dictating your brief and prompt reply.

The official notice I inclosed to you was signed by the Venezuelan consul and the president of the Philadelphia Guano Company. It purported to be the conjoint act of the government of Venezuela and of that company. It was an authoritative, official warning to the government of the United States and its citizens, and to "the rest of mankind." It officially threatened the "*seizure*" of all vessels "*touching at any of the guano islands under the jurisdiction of Venezuela*" in the Caribbean sea, with the sole exception of Margaritta, and excepting those vessels having a permit from the Philadelphia Guano Company! It would seem from your note that you were under the impression that the notice did not relate to Shelton's Isle, and that there is *"nothing in it which can in any way affect"* Mr. Shelton's claims, for as much as the ground of the claim is that the isle *"was not under the jurisdiction of Venezuela* WHEN HE HAD POSSESSION OF IT." This is clearly a misconception of the notice. The jurisdiction referred to in it is that claimed and exercised at the date of the notice, (December 19, 1855,) and not that at the time Mr. Shelton had possession and was ousted by Venezuela, (December 13, 1854.) This notice embraces all guano islands in the Caribbean sea *"under the jurisdiction of Venezuela"* on the 19th December, 1855, excepting only Margaritta; and it makes no distinction between jurisdiction exercised *de jure* as well as *de facto*, and jurisdiction *de facto* only, and where the question of right was in controversy. The only exception the notice does contain, is of one other named island, and it forbids the idea that Shelton's Isle or Bird Island was not intended to be included. But if desired by the department, proof *dehors* the notice, and sustaining the allegation that it was expressly intended by the parties to it to include Shelton's Isle, will be procured. The purposes and objects of the Venezuelan government and of the Philadelphia Guano Company, in this regard, are susceptible of direct and positive proof. If Mr. Shelton were now to send a vessel to Shelton's Isle for guano, and if such vessel should touch at that isle without the permit of the Philadelphia Guano Company, she would be forthwith *"seized,"* according to the notice, on the ground that the isle was *"under the jurisdiction of Venezuela"* when she so touched, and at the date of the notice, December 19, 1855. The misapprehension of the department as to the extent and application of the official notice, and under which it is quite obvious the note to which this is an answer was written, was occasioned by not adverting to the fact that since December 13, 1854, Venezuela has exercised *unmolested jurisdiction over the isle*, and that the notice refers to the Venezuelan jurisdiction in December, 1855, and not that in December, 1854, when, to quote from your note, "the island *was* not under the jurisdiction of Venezuela."

From December 13, 1854, (when Mr. Shelton, after having had several months peaceable occupation of the isle, was forcibly dispossessed by Venezuela,) and up to the date of that notice, and at this time, Venezuela has claimed the isle, has held possession of it by military force, and has exercised such *unmolested* jurisdiction over it. It is true her possession was usurped and her exercise of jurisdiction wrongful, because in violation of Mr. Shelton's rights and in defiance of those of the United States, based upon his discovery and occupation. But the fact that Venezuela has had, since the 13th December, 1854, and still has and exercises, *de facto*, jurisdiction over the isle, cannot be questioned. It is as notorious in Boston, New York, Philadelphia, Baltimore, and every port of the United States into which guano is imported from *"islands under the jurisdiction of Venezuela,"* as the fact that Oregon is at this time under the jurisdiction of the United States. The records of imports of guano in the custom-houses verify this fact, for vessels laden with valuable cargoes of guano from Shelton's Isle, have, since it has so been "under the jurisdiction of Venezuela," entered as from a Venezuelan port. And this jurisdiction, although so acquired, has been so far respected by the United States that the executive has not granted the twice repeated application of Mr. Shelton to be permitted to retake his possessions at his own expense, (which course he could not pursue without such permission, except by violation of the neutrality acts,) and the executive has also refrained from sending a vessel of the navy to the isle.

And now as to the effect of this notice upon Mr. Shelton's rights and interests. A reference to Mr. Shelton's statement, filed in the department several months ago, will show that he claims the restitution of Shelton's Isle to him and to the United States, *status quo ante* the forcible and tortious eviction in December 1854, as just in respect to his rights and due to the honor and dignity of the United States, and he refers to precedents for such course, *vide printed memoranda on file*, pp. 21–22. Such restoration he insists (upon the authority of those precedents) is a just preliminary act to be done by Venezuela; for mark! that government during the six months Mr. Shelton occupied the isle made no complaint thereof to the United States, but proceeded at once to employ military force to effect his ejectment. As the rights of the United States flow exclusively from him and his acts, and are wholly founded upon his discovery and peaceable occupation of this isle, (derelict till he took possession of it,) and as he is a citizen of the United States and most directly interested, it is respectfully submitted that it was not unbecoming for him to urge the adoption of such course. Indemnification for his actual losses and for his damages is also there stated and claimed. He claims compensation for the deterioration in value of the isle between the time of the eviction and such restoration, when made, whether by the abstraction of guano therefrom or otherwise, and damages resulting from the continued occupation and exercise of jurisdiction over the isle by Venezuela, and the exclusion of Mr. Shelton's workmen therefrom and for his being deprived of its use and of the profits of the guano thereon after his having been driven off in December 1854, and also damages for the seizure and detention of his personal property, indemnification for losses by false freights, demurrage of vessels, obstruction to the labor and employment of his workmen at the isle, transported thither from the United States in June, 1854, and sustained there at great expense in erecting houses and landing, &c., for expenses in obtaining redress and interest and augmented damages caused by the long delay. The account of his claim, filed in the department 15th January, 1855, being at that time, in the aggregate $341,000, if scrutinized, will show that the continued occupation and appropriation by Venezuela of Shelton's Isle and her deprivation of Mr. Shelton of the use of it and her exercise of *jurisdiction* over it forms the largest item of his claim.

Every communication addressed to the department urging the enforcement of his claim to the island and the guano on it, and for indemnity, or otherwise connected with it, refers as well to the *continued* exercise of jurisdiction as to the first forcible and tortious assumption of jurisdiction by Venezuela over the island. In fact, part of his claim, as before observed, is founded entirely on such *continued* exercise of jurisdiction.

I assure you it was not apprehended that the official notice of the Venezuelan government and the Philadelphia Guano Company, published in the New York Herald, in December, 1855, could, *ex propria vigore*, demolish the *rights* of the United States to the jurisdiction over and sovereignty of Shelton's Isle, founded upon Mr. Shelton's discovery and possession of 1854, or destroy or even impair Mr. Shelton's *rights*, based on the same discovery and possession of the then derelict isle; and I am gratified at the discovery in your note of an intimation that in this respect your judgment sustains mine. Some solicitude was, however, felt by me when I wrote my letter of the 5th instant that a *tacit acquiesence* by the authorities of the United States (intrusted with the conduct of Mr. Shelton's case) in that notice, and in the claims it puts forth, and the protracted delay, in connection with other peculiar circumstances of this case, might hereafter be invoked by the Venezuelan government and the guano company to assist them in raising obstacles to his indemnification for their violation of his rights, and hence, and in such way, have an injurious effect upon his *interests*. The very material distinction between the *rights* of a citizen, however incontrovertible, and his *interests*, dependent upon the vigilant attention to, and diligent enforcement of those rights by his government, was not lost sight of by me in my letter, and in fact the letter was induced by my exact appreciation of this essential difference.

In this very case his rights may be incontestable, and, if prosecuted with zeal and ability, valuable; and yet, by remissness in the enforcement of them, by delays and by pretermissions of duty by him, or by his agents, or by his government, and other circumstances, his *interests* may become of trifling value and consequence.

I did not conceive it to be necessary, and, indeed, it might have been regarded as indelicate and presumptious in me to suggest to the department the propriety of its prompt notice and rebuke of the admonitory manifesto of the allied powers of Venezuela and the guano company, and therefore I contented myself with the mere transmission to the department of the notice, and the expression of my opinion as to its objects and effect, and of my "surprise" at its appearance; confidently anticipating that so far from being regarded as intrusive or officious, or offensive, my exertions to be of service to it, and to aid it in sustaining the rights and interests of a citizen outraged by a foreign government, would be appreciated and well received.

I beg leave, in order to prevent misapprehension hereafter, to explain more particularly in what "way" (as I believed) I saw that this declaratory notice and its being carried out would certainly affect, and injuriously, Mr. Shelton's interest. The pecuniary responsibility of Venezuela, as is notorious, is of little account. Apprised of this by public rumor, and by a knowledge of the dishonorable failure of that government to fulfill its solemn obligations of several years standing to citizens of the United States at this place, I have looked to its promise of a pecuniary indemnification to Mr. Shelton as of secondary value, and have considered that his chief dependence has been and is the immediate restoration of the island. Unless it is exacted immediately I fear his prospect of obtaining ultimate just redress is remote and dreary. Upon the question of the effect of a tacit acquiescence in the notice, especially in connection with the other circumstances adverted to, as militating against Mr. Shelton's *interest*, I must, of course, defer to your experienced judgment, and I concede also in this case, perhaps, more impartial, for I confess that mine may be influenced by a deep sense of the grievous wrong and injury done to my relative and friend. If, fortunately, the occurrences connected with the Philadelphia Guano Company, and upon which this official notice was predicated, do not militate against Mr. Shelton's rights and interests I shall be gratified, but I have not been able to extinguish entirely my apprehensions on this score for reasons I have suggested.

It only remains for me to explain my statement respecting my "surprise" at reading the notice contained in my letter inclosing it to you. That surprise was excited in part by the effrontery of such publication by the functionaries of a foreign government in a newspaper of this country, and whilst the right to one of the islands to which it was intended to *relate*, and does *relate*, was a subject of diplomatic discussion and contest between the United States and that foreign government. I had, before I wrote, distinctly and certainly ascertained that the notice was intended to include, and it did in terms include, the isle in dispute. And the circumstances before adverted to connected with this notice, and information as to the course of the intelligent minister of the United States at Caraccas in reference to the contract between the Venezuelan government and the Philadelphia Guano Company—claimed by them to embrace Shelton's Isle—and the fact that the contract did include that isle, so far forth, was in derogation of Mr. Shelton's rights and interests, and was calculated to embarrass the measures of his government to obtain reparation and indemnification for him, and did therefore cause surprise that the notice should be thus given in the face of the United States government. Surely the evidence thus boldly put forth that the arrangement was framed so as to include Shelton's Isle, which if made without permission of the government of the United States, and solely by the parties thereto, inasmuch as the title to Shelton's Isle and the guano thereon was at the time a subject of controversy and diplomatic negotiation between the two governments, of which the citizens of the United States concerned in the guano company had notice, was a palpable violation of the act of Congress of June 20, 1799, (1 Stat. at Large, p. 699,) by those citizens, and the bold impudence of the avowal contained in this "notice" was therefore calculated to excite some astonishment to a law-abiding and law-respecting man. And besides, as the consummation of such arrangement so eminently prejudicial to Mr. Shelton's rights and so directly tending to jeopardize his interests, if effected by the good offices and with the concurrence of the United States minister at Caraccas, was, it seemed to me, a disregard of the instructions or "advice" which I had been gratified to understand had been given to him not to countenance anything militating against Mr. Shelton's claims. The evidence this notice gave of a different course having been pursued more particularly created surprise. The contract of the Venezuelan government and Philadelphia Guano Company is, in reference to Mr. Shelton's rights and interests, certainly in disregard of the plainest principles of justice. This must have been manifest to the intelligent minister of the United States at Caraccas, for he could not have been ignorant of Mr. Shelton's case *at the time the contract was consummated*, and information of his course being influenced by prejudices against Mr. Shelton's claim, and of his being interested in feeling, if not otherwise, with the Philadelphia Guano Company, and the conviction that Mr. Shelton's rights and interests had been sacrificed to promote the interests of volunteer speculators, confirmed by the corroborating proof of this "notice," likewise caused surprise. I trust you will with this explanation see that I had grounds for that expression.

Your verbal direction to me when at Washington, a few days since, that if I had anything to say or any propositions to make respecting the case of Mr. Shelton to put it in writing, I presumed would be a sufficient warrant for my addressing you, if I had not had a direct interest in the issue of his claim. Indeed, under such direction, I esteemed it to be an imperative duty on my part to write to you.

I have sent a copy of this to the President in explanation of my former letters to him. I expect, of course, copies of my letters are forwarded to Mr. Eames. Of course Mr. Shelton and myself each have cognizance of our correspondence. You will have received a reply from him to your circular of the 4th, ere the receipt of this. I expect him here to-morrow or next day, when I will again write you.

I am, with great respect, very truly, your obedient servant,

H. S. SANFORD.

Hon. W. L. MARCY,
Secretary of State, &c.

Mr. Sanford to the President.

38 CLINTON PLACE, NEW YORK,
January 13, 1856.

SIR: To prevent further misunderstanding respecting Mr. Shelton's application for the interposition of his government in relation to Shelton's Isle, and for indemnity, and in connection with my former letters to you, I have the honor to inclose you—

1st. A copy of a letter addressed by me to Mr. Marcy in reply to one from him expressing the opinion that he did not see how the notice of the Venezuelan consul could relate to Shelton's Isle.

2d. A copy of a letter from Moses Taylor, Esq., of this city, to the Venezuelan consul at Philadelphia, and the original reply of that functionary under his official seal, (see envelope,) expressly stating that the notice does apply to the island.

Comments upon this manifesto of the Venezuelan government, warning the United States and its citizens in the mode and manner adopted, I am certain, are unnecessary to be made to you.

I expressed my surprise to the Secretary of State at the appearance of this notice in a letter a copy of which I inclosed to you. I am confident you will be satisfied that the expression was not uncalled for.

I have the honor to be, sir, with great respect, your obedient servant,

H. S. SANFORD.

The PRESIDENT.

P. S.—It is wished that the original of the Venezuelan consul's letter to Mr. Taylor be placed on file at the State Department.

H. S. S.

No. 1.

44 South Street, New York,
January 11, 1856.

Sir: A few days since I saw a notice in the Herald, of this city, signed by yourself and the officers of a guano company in Philadelphia about the guano islands of the Caribbean Sea, under the jurisdiction of your government. Propositions having been made to me to send a vessel forthwith to what is called Shelton's Isle, or Aves, or Bird Island, in that sea, for guano, under authority of Mr. P. S. Shelton, of Boston, and fearing that the island he claims may possibly be included in your notice, and desirous to avoid difficulty before dispatching the vessel, I would respectfully request you to inform me if your government and the Philadelphia Guano Company claim said island, or exercise jurisdiction over it or the guano upon it, and whether there is any objection to my going there under Mr. Shelton's authority. I have just been informed that the Venezuelan government had a garrison there, and that the Philadelphia company were engaged in shipping the guano from it; if so, please inform me, and also what price per ton the Philadelphia company or your government charge for guano collected on it or other islands.

Respectfully yours,

MOSES TAYLOR.

José A. Keefe, Esq.
Consul of Venezuela, Philadelphia.

No. 2.

Consulate of the Republic of Venezuela,
Philadelphia, January 12, 1856.

Dear Sir: I have received your favor of the 11th instant, and noted its contents, and in reply beg to inform you that the Island of Aves or Bird Island, of which you write, is in the possession and under the jurisdiction of the Republic of Venezuela, and has a military force upon it sufficiently large to protect it from any depredations. No vessels are permitted to touch at it other than those sent thither by authority of the "Philadelphia Guano Company," who have ratified a contract with my government, granting them the sole right to remove the guano deposits from the said island, and all others in the Caribbean sea belonging to Venezuela.

Under these circumstances, and in view of the official notifications given at the instance of my government, I should deem very injudicious and extremely hazardous on the part of any person to dispatch a vessel to the island referred to, or any of them, without a proper authorization first being obtained, as all vessels found touching at the guano islands, without a duly authenticated permit from the company here, will be seized and held liable for the penalty fixed for a violation of the navigation laws of the republic, there being no ports of entry for foreign commerce at any of the guano islands.

The Philadelphia Guano Company are engaged shipping guano from Bird Island, and haue a large number of laborers upon it. I am not able at this time to inform you as to the price charged by the company for guano, but I presume Messrs. James Lee & Co. of your city can, as they are agents for the company. The government of Venezuela has nothing to do with the sale of the article, nor will it until the term shall have expired for which the contract is to endure.

I am, dear sir, very respectfully,

JOSÉ A. KEEFE.

MOSES TAYLOR, Esq.

Mr. Sanford to Mr. Marcy.

38 CLINTON PLACE, NEW YORK,
January 16, 1856.

SIR: Since my last upon the subject of Mr. Shelton's demand for the protection of his government to his right to Shelton's Isle, and his application for its interposition to procure him proper indemnity from the Venezuelan government, I have been furnished with the inclosed documents.

No. 1 is copy of a letter to the Venezuelan consul at Philadelphia, from Moses Taylor, Esq., of this city.

No. 2 is the reply of that officer to Mr. Taylor. The original has been sent to the President.

You will see by the inclosed, that the notice referred to in my two last letters to the President and yourself, was intended to relate, and does relate, to Shelton's Isle, and was at the "*instance*" of the Venezuelan government, and I am satisfied you will see that my surprise occasioned by its appearance was not entirely uncalled for.

I have the honor to be, with great respect, your most obedient servant,

H. S. SANFORD.

Hon. WM. L. MARCY,
Secretary of State.

Mr. Marcy to Mr. Shelton.

DEPARTMENT OF STATE,
Washington, January 19, 1856.

SIR: Your letter of the 15th instant has been received. Mr. Sanford also has addressed the department in relation to your claim.

Copies of these communications with further instructions will be transmitted to Mr. Eames.

I am, sir, &c.,

W. L. MARCY.

PHILO S. SHELTON, Esq., *Boston.*

Mr. French to Mr. Marcy.

WASHINGTON, *January* 21, 1856.

SIR: I inclose a letter from my brother, Judge French, of New Hampshire, who is attorney, both in law and in fact, of Messrs. Lang & Delano and Wheelwright & Cobb, of Boston, in their claim against the Venezuelan government, which he has forwarded to me, with the account of Lang & Delano stated, *vs.* the Venezuelan government.

I pray you to note particularly the last paragraph but one of my brother's letter, in regard to "the mode of proceeding and *the amount* to be insisted on."

With great respect, your obedient servant,

B. B. FRENCH,
Attorney, with H. F. French,
For Lang & Delano and Wheelwright & Cobb.

Hon. WILLIAM L. MARCY,
Secretary of State.

EXETER, NEW HAMPSHIRE,
January 18, 1856.

SIR: Your letters of the fourth instant to Lang & Delano, and to Wheelwright & Cobb, have been forwarded to me for answer.

I have called on Mr. Shelton, and proposed an arrangement as to the proposition of our several claims, but he for the present declines to enter into any stipulation on the subject. Between Lang & Delano and Wheelwright & Cobb there will be no difficulty in any arrangement, as I have full power to act for both. I forward herewith Lang & Delano's statement of their claim, as they have drawn it up. It is, I have no doubt, correct so far as it purports to give precise statements. Some of the last items are estimates of their own, made by men who embarked their fortunes in this enterprise, and have been ruined by it. They may be exaggerated, and we by no means insist upon being judges in our own case. The statement will give information as to the precise nature of their claim, and we shall be contented to abide the award of any commission that may be appointed to assess the damages upon such principles as the department may deem reasonable.

Mr. Shelton is somewhat impracticable at present, because we will not agree to a mode of prosecuting those claims different from what seems to us legitimate and proper. I do not despair, however, of completing an arrangement such as you suggest with him whenever he perceives that our government is really doing all in its power to procure for all parties suitable redress—a point upon which I and they for whom I act are already satisfied.

Wheelwright & Cobb estimate their losses and damages at $15,000. Their papers already filed disclose the nature of their claim.

Their case contains one element wanting in all the others. You will see by the deposition of Warren Wass, master of the Panola that he actually paid *port charges* to the Venezuelan officer, who agreed to furnish him a cargo, but drove him off, in violation of that agreement.

The department will find me at all times ready to comply with any reasonable suggestion as to an arrangement of these matters, and willing to pay great deference to its views, both with regard to the mode of proceeding and the amount to be insisted on.

My brother, Hon. B. B. French, will act for me at Washington.

With much respect,

HENRY F. FRENCH,
Attorney for Lang & Delano and Wheelwright & Cobb.

Hon. WILLIAM L. MARCY,
Secretary of State.

Statement of claim of Lang & Delano, in the Aves Island matter, against the State of Venezuela.

Lumber, provisions, water, boats, houses, wharfs, &c., at island		$10,000 00
Expenses of passages of laborers out and back		4,000 00
Charter of ship Kentucky, 800 tons, 5 months, at $2,000		10,000 00
Brig Aonian, 275 tons, at $7 50		2,062 50
Bark E. A. Kinsman, 350 tons, at $5		1,750 00
Brig H. H. McGilrery, 250 tons, 4 months, at $1,000		4,000 00
Brig A. Blanchard, 300 tons, at $5		1,500 00
Bark Richmond, 350 tons, at $5		1,750 00
Brig J. Means, 200 tons, at $5		1,000 00
Brig J. H. Kent, 200 tons, at $6 50		1,300 00
Schooner Magdala, 75 tons, 3 months, at $400		1,200 00
Demurrages and expenses		5,000 00
Time of laborers during passage, 25 days, 31 men, at $1 per day	$775	
Foreman, at $3 per day	75	
Agent, at $5 per day	125	
		975 00
Expense and time of J. H. B. Lang to island and home, 3 months		2,500 00
Loss by being compelled to suspend business and damage to credit		50,000 00
Loss on 2,825 tons guano, (above cargoes,) at $15		42,375 00
Interest on outlay and expenses to date of settlement		139,412 50
50,000 tons guano on island, owned by us by right of taking possession, valued at	$30	
Less getting to market	20	
		500,000 00
		639,412 50

Mr. Thomas to Mr. French.

DEPARTMENT OF STATE,
Washington, Jan. 22, 1856.

SIR: I have to acknowledge the receipt of your letter of yesterday, inclosing one from your brother, H. F. French, of the 18th instant, together with a statement of the claim of Lang & Delano against the government of Venezuela.

A copy of these papers will be transmitted to our minister at Caraccas.

I am, sir, &c.,

J. A. THOMAS,
Assistant Secretary.

B. B. FRENCH, Esq.,
Washington.

Mr. Marcy to Mr. Sanford.

DEPARTMENT OF STATE,
Washington, Jan. 25, 1856.

SIR: Your letters of the 12th and 16th instant have been received. A copy of these communications will be forwarded to the minister of the United States at Caraccas.

I am, sir, &c.,

W. L. MARCY.

H. S. SANFORD, Esq.,
38 *Clinton Place, New York.*

Mr. Sanford to Mr. Marcy.

38 CLINTON PLACE, NEW YORK,
February 1, 1856.

SIR: I have received your letter of the 25th ultimo, (post marked 26th,) informing me of the receipt of my letters of the 12th and 16th ultimo, and that copies thereof will be sent to the minister of the United States at Caraccas. I do not perceive that my letters to the President, of which I have advised the department, were intended to be transmitted. If it would save the department any trouble I will myself forward to Mr. Eames, upon its intimation, copies of all the correspondence in relation to the case that may be in my possession.

If not inconsistent with diplomatic propriety, I would request in behalf of Mr. Shelton and those interested with him to be furnished with copies of the correspondence with that minister that has been had in relation to this case, for the copying of which I will cheerfully pay, as in the instance of the brief filed by me in June last.

I have the honor to inclose you a copy of the power of attorney to me from Philo S. Shelton and Sampson & Tappan, with power of substitution, to be filed in the department. I also send the original for comparison by the department and for your satisfaction, but which original, as it is necessary to use it otherwise than before the department, I request may be transmitted to me.

If any additional authentication is necessary it shall be made upon intimation by the department.

I am, sir, with the highest respect, your obedient servant,

H. S. SANFORD.

Hon. WM. L. MARCY,
Secretary of State, &c.

P. S.—Mr. Shelton has sailed for the West Indies from this port, of which I apprise you in order that any letters for him in relation to this case may be addressed to me.

H. S. S.

United States of America.

Know all men by these presents, that we, George R. Sampson and Lewis W. Tappan, merchants, doing business as Sampson & Tappan, at Boston, in the State of Massachusetts, and Philo S. Shelton, merchant, of Boston aforesaid, having, by our agents, in the spring of 1854, discovered a certain vacant, unoccupied, and desolate guano island, or rock, in the Caribbean sea, in north latitude about 15° 40′, and in west longitude from Greenwich about 63° 38′; and whereas the said island was forthwith landed upon and taken possession of by our said agents for us and for the United States of America, of which we are citizens; and whereas, subsequently, and as soon thereafter as was practicable, we dispatched several vessels with materials and many laborers from the United States to said island for the purpose of procuring the guano thereon, to which we had acquired a full right in virtue of said premises; and whereas we, by our agents as aforesaid, having, in June, 1854, taken possession of said island for said object, and called it "Shelton's Isle," (the same having been heretofore denominated "Aves Island," or "Bird Island,) and having employed our said laborers in carrying guano therefrom, and erecting tenements and landings on said island, we remained in peaceful and unmolested occupation and possession thereof and of the guano thereon, and were engaged in procuring said guano, and shipping the same for several months, namely, until in the month of December, 1854, when we were, with our said agents and laborers, forcibly ejected from and dispossessed of said island and guano, and our tenements, materials, implements, and provisions on said island taken from us by the authority of the government of Venezuela under pretense of claim by the said government to said island and guano, which claim we insist is without foundation in right; and whereas our vessels and agents and seamen and workmen aforesaid, were driven away from said island by an armed force of said government, which hath from thence kept us from the use and occupation of said island and guano, and hath kept possession thereof in defiance of right; and whereas we have (in January, 1855,) applied to the Secretary of State of the United States for the interposition of the federal government of said United States, of which we are citizens, for the maintenance and protection of our just rights to said "Shelton's Isle," and to the guano thereon accruing and derived as aforesaid, and also for our redress and indemnity for our losses and for our damages sustained by reason of the outrages and wrongs of the Venezuelan government, as aforesaid: Now, therefore, we do hereby constitute and appoint Henry Shelton Sanford, Esq., as our true and lawful attorney to prosecute and defend for us, and in our behalf, our right and interest to and in said island and said guano, and to represent us to and before the government of the United States, or the government of Venezuela, or elsewhere and otherwise as may be necessary. And to compromise and compound for, demand and receive our claims for redress, indemnification, and damages sustained in the premises, and also for loss of said guano, false freights, demurrages, damages on charters, loss of outfits, fixtures, wharves, boats, cabins or huts, houses and other property in the premises, and all other damages arising in consequence thereof in anywise whatsoever. And we hereby vest in our said attorney full and ample powers in the premises to do and perform all such acts as we might do and perform in relation to the aforesaid premises and to our said claims as if personally present. Giving him power to make arrangements to send an agent to Venezuela, if deemed by him advisable, in order to make a more speedy adjustment of the matter; to substitute the powers herein delegated to him to one or more attorneys under him, giving to him and his substitutes full and adequate power and authority to grant releases in our behalf on receiving satisfaction; to compromise and adjust the same in any way he may deem expedient; and in case any clause of amplification should be deemed necessary in this our power to said Henry Shelton Sanford, Esq., or his substitutes, to give validity to his acts in our behalf, we hereby grant the same and ratify all the acts he may do in our behalf in reference to the said claim and its adjustment.

Given under our hands and seals, this 21st day of January, 1856.

GEO. R. SAMPSON. [SEAL.]
LEWIS W. TAPPAN. [SEAL.]
PHILO S. SHELTON. [SEAL.]

Signed, sealed, and delivered in the presence of—
A. L. FROTHINGHAM,
F. W. REYNOLDS.

Witnesses to P. S. S.—
BENJ. L. MASSITT,
C. A. STETSON.

UNITED STAES OF AMERICA,
State and City of New York, } *ss:*

Be it known to all to whom these presents shall come, that on this 21st day of January, A. D. 1856, before me, John L. Sutherland, a notary public of said city and State, by lawful authority duly commissioned and sworn, and by law authorized to take and receive and certify the acknowledgment of letters of attorney as aforesaid, personally appeared Philo S. Shelton, Esq., merchant of the city of Boston, State of Massachusetts, the constituent in said letter of attorney named, of whose identity I am satisfied, and voluntarily acknowledged that he signed, sealed, and delivered said letter of attorney to said Henry Shelton Sanford, Esq., as his voluntary act and deed, for the uses and purposes therein expressed, and desired me to authenticate and certify the same according to law.

Witness my hand and official seal, as notary public aforesaid, at my office in the city of New York this 21st day of January, A. D. 1856.

[SEAL.]

JOHN LANSING SUTHERLAND,
Notary Public.

STATE OF MASSACHUSETTS,
County of Suffolk, City of Boston, } *ss:*

To all to whom these presents shall come: I, Charles B. F. Adams, a notary public, duly commissioned and sworn in and for the county aforesaid, and practicing therein, do hereby certify that on the day of the date hereof before me personally came George R. Sampson and Lewis W. Tappan, they being to me personally well known, and severally acknowledged the foregoing letter of attorney, by them subscribed in my presence, to be their free act and deed for the uses and purposes therein set forth.

Witness my hand and official seal, this twenty-fourth day of January, eighteen hundred and fifty-six.

[SEAL.]

CHARLES B. F. ADAMS,
Notary Public.

Mr. Sanford to Mr Marcy.

38 CLINTON PLACE, NEW YORK,
February 12, 1856.

DEAR SIR: In acknowledging the receipt of your favor of the 6th instant, it is due to myself to rectify your misapprehension that mine of the 1st—to which yours was a reply—manifested a "desire" that my letter to the Persident should be communicated to Mr. Eames. For several reasons I supposed they would be, but I was entirely indifferent on that point. In that letter I merely noticed the circumstance that your previous communication to me of the 25th ultimo did not refer to those letters, and mentioned only those from me to the department of the 12th and 16th ultimo as intended to be copied and forwarded to him. This circumstance induced the supposition that my letters to the President might have been inadvertently overlooked at the department, or that they might not have been referred to the department or placed on its files. Such supposition was justified by the fact that in no one of the communications from the department had any of my letters to the President or the original documents transmitted with one of them (requested to be filed at the State Department) been in anywise noticed. As I was convinced there could not be any intention to omit noticing them, because of their being addressed and sent to the President instead of the department, I could not account for such omission in any wise than as just intimated, except that possibly they were not to be forwarded to Mr. Eames because of the trouble of having them all copied; and my offer to copy and forward them to our minister was in the first place to attract your attention in a delicate mode to them if they had been so overlooked, or had not been placed on file; and in the second place, if they were omitted on account of the trouble of copying them, as is explicitly expressed in my letter, "to save the department any trouble" on that score. And so also, my letter, as I thought, in distinct terms placed the suggestion that I would willingly forward to Mr. Eames "upon its (the department's) INTIMATION copies of all the correspondence in relation to the case that may be in my possession," entirely upon the ground of saving "trouble to the department," and in compliance with an intimation by it that such aid would be acceptable. I deeply regret to perceive from your letter that I was so unfortunate in my selection of the language employed as to cause the department to misapprehend me, and to judge me as seeking officiously to interfere with its duties. Nothing could have been further from my object; and most surely it was not intended by me in that letter to intimate that it was desired or deemed advisable for the claimants to seek to withdraw their case from the State Department, or pretermit in any degree their solicitations for its advocacy and protection. They were aware and I was aware that such abandonment of the ordinary, proper, and legitimate channel of correspondence, either with the Venezuelan government or with the United States minister at Caraccas, would have amounted to a virtual abandonment of their claim; and as to the questions of national honor and national rights and interests involved, the maintenance and protection of which is the *peculium* of your department, they certainly had not the arrogance or presumption to express any willingness to assume charge of them by "corresponding directly with the legation;" nor was the idea entertained that they or their attorney possessed equal ability to enlighten the minister on this subject of their own rights and interests, or as to the minister's duties as the Secretary of State, who is chosen for his learning, ability, and patriotic impartiality. It is true they and their attorney did imagine that their diligent and vigilant aid, stimulated as they are to such diligence and vigilance by a deep and abiding sense of wrong and injury, and by their important pecuniary interest involved, might be usefully rendered by furnishing copies of papers to the department, and thus saving it trouble and drudgery. More than a year has elapsed since the outrage was perpetrated, and since the interposition of the department was invoked, and it was believed such aid might tend to expedite the settlement of the case and prevent further delay, and the proffer of such assistance was the sole object of my communication of the 1st February. It is lamented that (as would seem from your letter) a somewhat different impression is entertained, but it is hoped that this explanation will be satisfactory.

I transmit to the department by the same mail with this, copies of my letters to the President adverted to, and of sundry other papers on file in the department directed to Mr. Eames with a letter to that functionary, which, I presume, the department will have no objection to forward, with its next dispatches, to him. I hope the department will examine these papers and see if they are correct, for I would not think of communicating with Mr. Eames except with the knowledge and entire approbation of it. In ignorance of what has passed between the department and Mr. Eames respecting this case, except the partial information disclosed to me verbally, it would the extremity of self-reliance for me to venture to make suggestions to him in relation to this claim which might be inconsistent to those made by the department, nor could I answer his objections or those Venezuela. The claimants have concluded that until Mr. Eames is heard from, and the present condition of the case at Caraccas is fully, exactly, and truly known to them, it would be useless expense and trouble and inadvisable for them to send a known agent to Venezuela as formerly intimated, and that the claimants can do little else than rely upon the attention of the State Department to their claims. That attention they would respectfully ask as early as the multifarious duties of the officers of the department may allow.

It is hoped that any omission or deficiency in the proofs filed may be suggested as early as practicable for the reasons heretofore urged, so that the same may be supplied as promptly as possible.

It is anticipated that the claimants may, ere long, be able to furnish the department with some interesting information, in some degree touching this case, derived from confidential sources at Caraccas.

I inclose an advertisement of the time of the next sailing of the steamer "Tennessee" from this city to that port.

I remain, dear sir, with the highest respect, your obedient servant,

H. S. SANFORD.

Hon. W. L. Marcy,
Secretary of State, &c., &c.

Advertisement.

For Laguayra and Porto Cabello, touching at Porto Rico and St. Thomas. The United States mail steamship Tennessee, J. Johnson, commander, will leave for the above ports on Saturday, February 16, at twelve o'clock, from pier No. 2, East River.

Passage to Porto Rico and St. Thomas	$70 00
" to Laguayra and Porto Cabello	85 00
Steerage passage to the latter ports	25 00

This steamer will arrive in time at St. Thomas for passengers to take the British mail steamer to

Guadaloupe,	Trinidad,
Martinique,	St. Bart's,
St. Croix,	Demerara,
Antigua,	Santa Martha,
Granada,	Carthagena,
Barbadoes,	Aspinwall and
St. Martin's,	San Juan, Nicaragua,
St. Kitt's.	

All letters must pass through the post office.
For freight and passage apply to

S. DE AGREDA, JOVE & CO.,
47 South Street.

Mr. Marcy to Mr. Sanford.

DEPARTMENT OF STATE,
Washington, Feb. 6, 1855.

SIR: Your letter of the 1st instant was received this morning. As you manifest therein a desire that your letters to the President, upon the subject of Mr. Shelton's claim, should be communicated to Mr. Eames, expressing at the same time a willingness to prepare and forward yourself copies of those letters, and of any others you may have which will probably enlighten our minister upon the subject. I have to state that there is no objection to your pursuing that course, and corresponding directly with the legation if you deem it advisable.

A compliance with your request to be furnished with a copy of the correspondence of the department with Mr. Eames on this subject would, at least, whilst the affair is pending, be contrary to the usages of the department.

I return the original power of attorney inclosed in your letter. The copy accompanying it has been carefully collated with the original, a few immaterial errors corrected, and it has been filed with your letter.

I am, &c.,

W. L. MARCY.

HENRY S. SANFORD, Esq.,
38 *Clinton Place, New York.*

Mr. Marcy to Mr. Sanford.

DEPARTMENT OF STATE,
Washington, Feb. 20, 1856.

SIR: Your communication of the 12th instant, with inclosures for Mr. Eames, was not received in time to permit the transmission of the latter by the Tennessee, (steamer,) to Venezuela. They will be forwarded, however, by the usual channel of intercommunications between the department and Caraccas, that is, through Messrs. Dallet Brothers, of Philadelphia.

I am, sir, &c.,

W. L. MARCY.

H. S. Sanford, Esq.,
38 *Clinton Place, New York.*

Mr. Sanford to Mr. Marcy.

38 Clinton Place, New York,
March 8, 1856.

Sir: Your letter of the 20th ultimo was duly received. Upon a recent visit to Philadelphia on the 25th ultimo, I made inquiry of Messrs. Dallet & Brothers, mentioned in that communication as having been intrusted with your last dispatches to the United States minister at Carraccas, and also with my letter of the 12th ultimo to Mr. Eames, and its inclosures; and I ascertained that those packets and others, postmarked Washington, in January, then yet remained with them. I trust it will not be deemed officious for me to advise you that the steamer Tennessee sails from this port for La Guayra on the 22d instant, as you will perceive by the annexed advertisement. I have supposed this liberty will be excused in consideration of the importance of the case of Messrs. Shelton and Sampson & Tappan, (represented by me,) and the anxiety they feel as to its early settlement by the Venezuelan government. Every day's delay (for causes heretofore explained,) decreases their prospect of receiving or securing just indemnity.

I learned authentically when in Philadelphia, that the Philadelphia Guano Company have, during the last two months, dispatched more than a score of vessels and a large force of laborers from the United States to the Caribbean sea for guano; part of which are to be employed in "skinning" Shelton's Isle of the guano remaining on it, for shipment to Europe and elsewhere. I was also informed that at least twelve vessels were ice-bound in the Chesapeake with guano from Shelton's Isle. I learned also that all the choice guano remaining on the isle was to be first selected, leaving to the last the middling and ordinary qualities, and other courses were pursued by which to make it seem hereafter that the quantity of guano on the island, and its quality and its value were not so great nor so high as we have represented, and thereby decrease our damages. I learned, also, that between December, 1854, when we were evicted, and the summer of 1855, when the last contract with the Philadelphia Guano Company was perfected, the Venezuelan government authorized large quantities of the best guano on the island to be abstracted therefrom for shipment to Europe and elsewhere, by others than the company, and the shipment was under the supervision of its military officers and officers of the customs, stationed on the isle since the day we were driven off. I have deemed it proper to advise you of these facts in order that the information thereof may be, and remain on the records of the department for future reference and use. It is, as you will at once discover, well nigh impossible for the claimants to adduce legal proof fully as to these circumstances, and especially so as to the cargoes of guano taken away; and therefore I propose to procure testimony, in addition to that already filed, of the quantity and value of the guano on the isle at the time we were dispossessed; deeming it the best proof, *ex necessitate rei*, that we can procure; but I await the advice and suggestion of the department on these points, and as to what it deems requisite and sufficient. The claimants have heretofore, in several different communications, solicited information from the department in this regard, but as yet have not received in reply any signification of what kind of testimony would be expected from them, nor as to what points it would be necessary to file additional proofs, and hence, in some degree, the non-procurement of further proofs. Our witnesses, as heretofore suggested, are all seafaring men, and we can only find them at the times of their return voyages to the United States; and it is therefore hoped that the department will inform us at an early period of what it is wished we should do in this behalf.

I was informed in Philadelphia that the "royalty" paid by the "Philadelphia Guano Company" to Venezuela for the guano, was five dollars per ton, Venezuelan currency; and that the last contract expressly included Shelton's Isle, and contains the extraordinary stipulation that if it should be decided that Venezuela had no right to the island, the company should make no reclamation on account thereof!

I was also informed that some of the Venezuelan officials, and those who uphold them in their course with respect to Shelton's Isle, contend that the United States impliedly recognized the title of Venezuela to Shelton's Isle by having omitted to object to the first contract made by Venezuela with citizens of the United States; and that a still higher recognition of it was given by a less dubious assent (through its functionaries at Caraccas,) to the *last* contract, made months after the eviction of Mr. Shelton, and his claims for indemnity, &c., having been preferred, with a chartered coöperation of one of the States, and against which the British representative at Caraccas did formally object.

I do not for a moment imagine that the facts assumed in such defense would be conceded by the State Department, or that the argument based upon such assumption would be listened to by you as entitled to respectful consideration; and I am satisfied that the President and yourself will both maintain the doctrines so handsomely put forth by Mr. Webster in his dispatch to Mr. Osma, of the 31st August, 1852, respecting the Lobos Islands, in which he says:

"The government of the United States has not, nor never has had, any intention to facilitate the particular purposes of any persons, such as Mr. Osma calls speculators, further than those purposes are conformable to public law, as well as to the laws of the United States. This government knows of no companies, no associations, and no individuals, in whose behalf it undertakes any special protection. The question is a general one, in which all the citizens of the United States engaged in commerce have an interest, and that interest is equally respected by the United States, regardless of individuals."

But you will not, I trust, consider it as improper for me to respectfully request that the department will take measures, as early as convenient, to procure true and authentic copies, *in extenso*, of both the first and second contract of the Venezuelan government with the Philadelphia company, insomuch as it is quite probable we may fail in our efforts to obtain them.

And we deem a copy of Captain Dias's official report to his government of his conquest of Shelton's Isle, and also a copy of the protest of the British representative at Caraccas, important to us in this case. It is presumed the department could readily obtain copies through our minister at Caraccas, and it is believed they will be material to us in establishing our damages and in other respects.

A suggestion has been made, that probably after the island had been "skinned" of the guano, a few weeks hence, the mockery and insult of yielding it up may be proposed by Venezuela, but unaccompanied by any other satisfaction or promise of satisfaction for our injuries. Such offer, without paying, or at least promising to pay, for the guano taken from the island since our eviction, and our damages sustained otherwise, we cannot suppose will be regarded by the department as very complimentary to the United States. If it is distinctly and in good faith proffered as a preliminary to full atonement, as we have heretofore urged should be done, we trust it will be accepted, but in such view only. We will, with the sanction of the department, forthwith resume our possession in such event.

I inclose a declaration of William P. Gibbs, duly certified and marked M, who was at Shelton's Isle in December, 1854, and proves important facts. He is a relation of Captain Nathan P. Gibbs, the agent of Mr. Shelton. I desire it to be filed as testimony in this case. It was inadvertently omitted to be sent to the department whilst I was absent in Europe last autumn. Captain Nathan P. Gibbs is soon expected in the United States from Australia, and his testimony will forthwith be forwarded.

I have the honor to inclose you also a printed pamphlet, published within a few days past by the "Philadelphia Guano Company," marked N, which I regard as important, particularly with respect to four points, viz:

1. It shows that the government of Venezuela and the Philadelphia Guano Company claim Shelton's Isle and the guano on it.

2. It gives testimony of the quantity of the guano, and the importance of the island in their estimation.

3. It establishes the high quality of the guano thereon, of which it gives analyses.

4. It shows the current value and price of this guano is, in the United States, from $25 to $40 per ton.

Neither the Venezuelan government nor the "Philadelphia Guano Company" can ever gainsay the statements in this pamphlet without stultifying and criminating themselves. They are bound by it. I desire it filed as evidence in the case.

You will notice that Mr. Keefe, the consul of the Venezuelan government at Philadelphia, (and the gentleman who had the correspondence with Moses Taylor, Esq., as to Shelton's Isle, heretofore inclosed to you,) is a stockholder and director of this company, and one of those under whose authority the pamphlet is issued. I will send to Philadelphia to have transmitted to you some copies, one of which I request may be forwarded by the department to Mr. Eames.

I deem it proper also to inform you that on Friday last I ascertained that the schooner Indicator, Captain White, burthen about 177 tons, was dispatched by Messrs. J. Lee & Co., the agent of the "Philadelphia Guano Company," from this port on the 1st instant, armed with cannon and manned by a large complement of men for such vessel, and provided with small arms and fixed ammunition, for the purpose of protecting, by force, the claim of Venezuela and the "Philadelphia Guano Company" to all the guano islands in the Caribbean sea, Shelton's Isle included. I inclose you a paper from the custom-house of this city, certifying to the clearance of the vessel, &c., and her papers, &c. I will send some further proofs in reference to her so soon as I can obtain them.

I am advised by legal counsel that a suit in chancery by us against the "Philadelphia Guano Company," and perhaps joining as defendants, Captain Dias, who is now in Philadelphia, and other parties; (and indirectly the Venezuelan government) may be instituted in the federal court at Philadelphia by us, if we are given the express sanction of the department, on the part of the government of the United States therefor, and that the result would probably be advantageous to the claimants, and that at any rate we could, in the progress of such suit, coerce the production of material proofs, and obtain by commission, important testimony that we cannot now procure. The suit would be for the proceeds of the Shelton's Island guano received in the United States, perhaps an action of trover, for the guano, on the ground that it is ours, and a suit in equity to enjoin the payment of the "royalty" yet unpaid by the company to the Venezuelan officials, and to others to whom they have given authority to receive it here. I am referred to the case of McFadden and the Vengeance, in 7 Cranch Reports, as showing that the express authority of the government for such suit is primarily necessary. With such authority, and provided such proceeding would not in anywise interfere with the vigorous prosecution of our claims by the department, it is proposed to institute it immediately. I think it would constrain the Venezuelan officials (who would personally experience some detriment of the "royalty" and the proceeds of the guano) to do us justice; and the course of Venezuela in this business is entirely that dictated by those of her officials who are interested in receiving personally a large share of the profits of this guano. The suit at law against Dias, instituted in this city some months ago, with the assent of the department, for trespass, $350,000, was ineffectual in consequence of his abruptly leaving the day the *capias* against him was attempted to be executed. May I ask the department to sanction the institution by us of the suits in trover and in equity suggested, if, on further counsel, such course is deemed advisable. I most respectfully solicit a reply to this communication as early as convenient.

I have the honor to be, with high respect, your obedient servant,

H. S. SANFORD.

Hon. WILLIAM L. MARCY,
Secretary of State, &c.

I, William P. Gibbs, of East Wareham, State of Massachusetts, by occupation a shipmaster, do hereby certify that on the 13th day of December, 1854, I was at Aves or Bird Island, in the Caribbean sea, in the employ of Messrs. Sampson & Tappan and Philo S. Shelton, of Boston, assisting Captain N. P. Gibbs in shipping guano on board various vessels at that island. That on the day above named a Venezeulan schooner of war, commanded by one Dias, arrived at the island and landed an armed force with a large gun, and claimed possession of the island in the name of the Venezuelan government, at the same time threatening the immediate expulsion of all the Americans on the island. Further, the said Captain Dias drew up a document in Spanish, which he said was a permit for them to continue to load guano, provided they placed their armament under his control. I was present when the purport of said document was explained to Captain N. P. Gibbs, (who did not understand Spanish,) and the most positive assurance was given to him that said document contained nothing whereby he assented to the title of the island being in Venezuela; I am positive on this point; and I further certify that said Dias threatened that unless they signed said document they must leave the island forthwith. Captain Gibbs, under these circumstances, felt compelled to sign the document, hoping by so doing, they would allow him to load the vessels then there, and those expected. Further, on the 30th day of the same month of December, another Venezuelan vessel of war, reported from Laguayra, called at the island, and landed twenty more troops and notified Captain N. P. Gibbs we must cease shipping any more guano, and must quit the island within twenty-four hours; the same night they stationed armed guards, with fixed bayonets, at the doors of our houses, at the guano pits, on our wharves, and on our boats; on the next morning, on attempting to resume our work, as usual, we were forced at the point of the bayonet to desist. Under these circumstances, Captain Gibbs found it necessary to leave the island, leaving in their possession our houses, our wharves, and other implements, together with a portion of our stores, which we were obliged to concede to them in order to get possession of the remainder; sending away the brig Viator with only a few tons of guano, the brig Mary Peirce without any, and leaving ourselves in the bark Amazon, which was also not fully loaded.

WM. P. GIBBS.

BOSTON, *August* 23, 1855.

COMMONWEALTH OF MASSACHUSETTS, } ss:
County of Suffolk. }

Then the above William P. Gibbs, personally appeared and acknowledged the foregoing instrument, by him subscribed, to be his free act and deed. Before me—

CHAS. HOMER,
Justice of the Peace.

BOSTON, *August* 23, 1855.

Extracts from pamphlet, marked N, filed as proof, with Mr. Sanford's letter of March 8, 1856.

* * * * * * * *

We allude to the recent discovery of large amounts of guano, amounting to millions of tons, on the islands of the Caribbean sea under the dominion of the Republic of Venezuela. These islands are but 1,900 miles from our chief Atlantic ports, and their valuable fertilizing deposits can thus be made available at but a comparatively very trifling cost for freight. In 1855, the Pennsylvania Legislature granted a charter to the Philadelphia Guano Company for the purpose of at once commencing an extensive trade in the article in question. By a contract entered into with the government of Venezuela, it possesses the exclusive right, for a series of years, of exporting the guano existing upon all the islands belonging to that republic. The company is now fully organized, and prepared to furnish any quantity desired.

* * * * * * * *

It is thus noticed in an article upon fertilizers, published in the agricultural report of the United States Patent Office for 1854, page 95:

"*Columbian or Bird Island Guano.*—A guano has recently been imported from Bird Island, (which is embraced in the contract of the Philadelphia company,) situate some 400 miles off the coast of Venezuela, 200 miles south of St. Thomas, and 150 miles westward of Guadaloupe. From careful analysis, it has been ascertained that this substance is by far the richest source of phosphoric acid for the farmer yet discovered, as it contains eighty-four per cent. of dry super-phosphate of lime, or about one third more than pure ground bones. It also contains less than one fourth the quantity of water always present in the Peruvian article, and from twenty to thirty per cent. less than any other guano known. One hundred parts of the Bird Island article contains the phosphoric acid necessary to form ninety-five and two fifth parts of bone phosphate of lime. Of dry organic matter and ammonia, it contains six and one fifth per cent."

* * * * * * * *

It will no doubt be gratifying to our agricultural friends to learn that these valuable guano islands have been leased from the Venezuelan government, for a long term of years, by a number of enterprising capitalists of New York, Philadelphia, and Baltimore, who have procured a charter from the State of Pennsylvania with an authorized capital of one million of dollars. The name of the company is "The Philadelphia Guano Company," the office of which is in this city. The whole of the stock has been subscribed; and the company are making extensive preparations for a large importation of the article to meet the demand for the spring crops. We understand that the guano will be sold at a reasonable price, and agencies at all the principal marts.

* * * * * * * *

David Stewart, M. D., chemist of the Maryland State Agricultural Society, in a letter dated Baltimore, September 14, 1855, says:

"Highly as I appreciate the Mexican guano, still I do not hesitate to say that I would rather have four tons of Columbian than ten tons of Mexican, and I would rather have equal portions of Columbian and Peruvian applied to my wheat than Peruvian alone, or any other superphosphate alone. The fact that I have purchased seven tons of the Columbian guano for each of my farms should seem to indicate the confidence which I place in it."

The guano islands of Venezuela are quite numerous, including Bird or Aves Island, Los Hermanos or the Brothers, Los Frayles or the Friars, Los Roques, Sola, Orchilla, Los Mongas or the Monks, Tortugas, Centinellas, and many others. The quality of the guano upon them, to some extent, varies in the amount of ammonia and of the phosphates contained in it. The wholesale price will be from twenty-five to forty dollars per ton, according to quality and amount purchased.

Custom House, Collector's Office,
March 8, 1856.

I certify (at the request of H. S. Sanford, Esq.) that the schooner Indicator, of New York, burthen 177 19-95 tons, registered at New York on the 25th day of February, 1856, (Register No. 108,) built at Marblehead, State of Massachusetts, her owners being Benjamin C. Lee and James Lee, of New York, cleared from this office on the 1st day of this month for the port of Laguayra, in Venezuela, with George V. White as master, and the following named crew: "Daniel S. Downe, John Bell, Thomas Smith, Samuel Pearson, William Keys, James Farland, and Joseph E. Hurlbut," and that the said vessel was in ballast; and it does not appear by any document on file in this office, that said vessel had on board any guns, ammunition, or passengers.

[SEAL.] Given under my hand and seal.

HEMAN J. REDFIELD,
Collector.

Mr. Marcy to Mr. Sanford.

Department of State,
Washington, March 24, 1856.

Sir: Your communication of the 8th instant, with its accompaniments, has been received, and its suggestions have been taken into consideration.

One of these is, that the department should indicate to you what proof it "deems requisite and sufficient" to sustain the claim of Shelton, Tappan, and others against the government of Venezuela for their expulsion from the Aves Islands, and consequent losses and damages.

Upon more mature reflection you will doubtless perceive the impracticability of complying with this request. The claimants themselves, and recently you in their behalf, have presented a case to this department claiming redress from Venezuela upon certain specific and well-defined grounds, and damages have been claimed for losses alleged to have been actually sustained. It is not the province of the department to designate the nature of the evidence by which the claimants should substantiate their claim. It is to be presumed, of course, that the same care will be taken to obtain the most positive proof of which the case is susceptible, as though the claim were to be subjected to the scrutiny of a court of justice.

The department cannot engage in the stipulation which you propose, to the effect that, if the claimants enter the courts of the United States for redress against the Philadelphia Guano Company, the diplomatic negotiations in their behalf shall not be prejudiced or estopped thereby. In regard to a "suit in chancery," or any other judicial proceedings, the claimants must use their own discretion, guided by such legal advice as they may see fit to adopt. In this respect, however, the department does not perceive the analogy between the case under consideration and that of McFadden *vs.* the Vengeance, (*Query Exchange?*) in 7 Cranch Rep., to which you have been referred "as showing that the express authority of the government for such suit is primarily necessary."

I think it fair to acquaint you that on Saturday, 22d, dispatches were received from Mr. Eames, one of which, relating to Mr. Shelton's case, was of the date 12th ultimo. With this Mr. Eames transmitted a copy of the contract made with Mr. Pickrell, a transcript of which, in the original Spanish, I herewith inclose. At the moment of writing Mr. Eames had not received all the instructions and documents which the department has forwarded to him upon that subject,* and he expressly regrets "that, in a case of such magnitude, the claimants have not furnished more ample materials upon which to estimate the amount of the indemnification to which they are entitled. Should such further materials, however, not reach me by the next arrival from the United States, now daily expected, I shall deem it my duty, under your instructions, to urge strongly the claim, as it now stands, upon the attention of this government, without further delay."

That you may understand what documents and data were either in Mr. Eames's hands or on the way to him, I append a schedule of the dates of the different instructions on this subject, and of the documents accompanying each. From this you will observe that a statement of the items of the claim which you represent was first sent out on the 20th ultimo. This schedule will enable you to determine whether any further testimony is desirable in Mr. Eames's future proceedings.

---

*Instruction No. 23 was the last he had received.

The department will delay writing to Mr. Eames until you shall be heard from. Meantime a copy of N. P. Gibbs's affidavit, which accompanied your communication, will be prepared for transmission, with such extracts from your letter as bear upon the merits of the case.

The department is quite ready to comply with your request that Mr. Eames be solicited to procure from the Venezuelan government, if he can do so with propriety, a copy of Captain Dias's report, and of the protest of the British representative to that government.

I am, sir, &c.,

W. L. MARCY.

HENRY S. SANFORD, Esq.,
38 *Clinton Place, New York.*

Mr. Sanford to Mr. Marcy.

DERBY, CONNECTICUT,
April 14, 1856.

SIR: I have the honor to forward to you by this mail the deposition of Captain Nathan P. Gibbs, a witness in the case of the Venezuelan outrage at Shelton's Isle, duly attested, &c., to be filed at the department. May I beg you to acknowledge its receipt?

I send in addition two copies of the same in order, if thought proper to communicate it to our own minister at Caraccas, the department may be saved the trouble of having it copied.

I send also a copy to the President.

My address hereafter is as above.

I have the honor to be, very respectfully, your obedient servant,

H. S. SANFORD.

Hon. WILLIAM L. MARCY,
Secretary of State.

Mr. Marcy to the President.

DERBY, CONNECTICUT,
April 14, 1856.

SIR: I have the honor to inclose herewith a copy of the deposition of Captain Nathan P. Gibbs, a witness in the case of the Venezuela outrage at Shelton's Isle upon citizens of the United States and their property, and of which I have heretofore written to you, the original of which duly authenticated I have this day sent to the State Department.

I have the honor to be, with the highest respect, your obedient servant,

H. S. SANFORD.

The PRESIDENT.

Testimony in the case of the claim of Philo S. Shelton and Sampson & Tappan, against the government of Venezuela.

Interrogatories to be propounded to Captain Nathan P. Gibbs, a witness in the matter of a certain claim against the government of the republic of Venezuela, preferred to the Department of State of the United States of America, by Philo S. Shelton, aud George R. Sampson and Lewis W. Tappan, merchants of Boston, in relation to "Aves," or "Bird Island," now called "Shelton's Isle," in the Caribbean sea, and in respect of the guano thereon, in December, 1854, and of the eviction of said claimants therefrom, by order of said government of Venezuela, in the month and year aforesaid, and of the taking of the property of said claimants thereat by the same government, and of their damages and losses sustained by the same.

I. Are you, or not, a citizen of the United States? Where were you born, and where is your residence and domicil? What has been, and what is your occupation? and what is your age? and in what employment and where have you been employed for a year past? Please state fully.

II. What was your employment in the year 1854, and where were you employed? State fully.

III. Were or were you not employed by said Philo S. Shelton to go on a cruise of discovery in the Caribbean sea for guano islands? If so, state fully; and if you sailed on said cruise, when and where from, and what you discovered, and your conduct and proceedings thereupon; and please state the particulars fully, and especially in relation to Shelton's Isle, if any of them relate thereto; and to your taking possession thereof, if you did so, and describe said isle.

IV. What were your proceedings on your return to the United States; and did you, or did you not, make arrangements for returning to said isle for said claimants, or either of them; and if so, what arrangements were made? State fully.

V. If you did leave the United States for Shelton's Isle, when did you so leave, where, and in what vessels, and for whom, and when did you arrive at the isle; and who, if any one, did you meet there, and in what vessel? and state all the particulars fully, and likewise your proceedings after your arrival at the isle, and the reasons therefor, and how you were employed the first week or ten days thereafter.

VI. State if you did, or did not, continue in the undisturbed occupation and possession of said isle and of the guano thereon, for some time, and whether you were or were not employed in the gathering thereof without molestation for some time, and if so, how long; and how much guano was there shipped, if any, during said time, and by whom; and what vessels, if any, were sent thither by claimants during said time for guano; and all the particulars of your occupation of said isle, that may be material in this matter; and whether you were visited by any foreign vessels of war, and if so, what vessels, and when, and what occurred during their visits; and whether your occupation was ever objected by any, and whether other vessels visited the isle?

VII. When you landed first on Shelton's Isle, had you ever been informed of its being previously inhabited, or possessed, or occupied, or claimed by any person or government, or that any government exercised jurisdiction over it; and particularly, had you, or not, heard of such claim by Venezuela? Please state fully all your knowledge on this subject and any facts connected therewith, of which you have been informed.

VIII. When you visited said isle in April, 1854, did you, or not, examine it with reference to making an estimate of the guano thereon, as to quantity and quality, and if so, what was your estimate? Please state particularly and fully, and also refer to any authenticated facts within your knowledge in confirmation or corroboration of your estimate; and please also state if you have heard any reports in relation to said guano, differing therefrom, and whether or not they have affected your opinion as to your estimate; and state if you had, or had not, experience in respect to gathering guano?

IX. Were you, or were your not, visited on the 13th day of December, 1854, by a schooner of war of the Venezuelan government; and if so, state fully what occurred then and there, and all that passed between you and the officer commanding her? Relate all the particulars as fully as you can recollect the same, and particularly as to a certain paper stated to have been signed by said officer and yourself and Charles H. Lang, and how the same was given, and whether you knew the purport and contents thereof; and say also whether or not you were subsequently visited by an additional military force; and, if so, when, and whether or not you were evicted and dispossessed of said island and guano by said force, and of the property of your employers there; and if you were, state all the circumstances particularly and fully.

X. If you were compelled to abandon the property of your employers at the isle, state the kind of property and value as particularly as you can, and what you think was the cost and value to them of said isle, and answer particularly and fully.

XI. Have you seen a copy of the statement of the claim of the said claimants presented to the State Department, consisting of three items: one of $312,500, one for $20,000, and a third for $8,500; in the aggregate $341,000? If so, please say whether the same is, or is not, in your judgment, exorbitant or extravagant; and state anything in your knowledge having relation thereto, and showing whether the same is just or unjust, reasonable or unreasonable. State fully.

XII. Have you, or have you not, any interest in said claim, direct or indirect, immediate or remote, in any wise? How were you employed by claimants? Have you any feeling in the case? and state fully and particularly; and state also, in answer to this interrogatory, the names of any persons you may recollect that were with you at the isle in 1854.

H. S. SANFORD,
Attorney in fact for Claimants.

NEW YORK, *April* 2, 1856.

The answers of Nathan P. Gibbs to the forgoing interrogatories made before me, Joseph C. Lawrence, a notary public of the State of New York, residing in the city of New York, the said Gibbs being by me first duly sworn to testify the truth, the whole truth, and nothing but the truth, in said answers, and being also duly cautioned according to law. To each of said interrogatories he answers and deposes as follows:

HE ANSWERS TO THE FIRST.

I am a native citizen of the United States of America. I was born at, and my residence and domicil is, Wareham, in the State of Massachusetts. My occupation or employment is that of a mariner, and has been from my youth. I am about twenty-eight years old. I am at present master of the ship Marion, of Boston, now in this port, (New York.) I sailed in command of said ship in the month of April, 1855, from New York, and went to Havana, Matanzas, Marseilles, Genoa, Constantinople, Balaklava, [in the Black sea,] and thence to Palermo, and thence back to this port, where I arrived about the 15th of last month.

TO THE SECOND.

Prior to my taking command of the ship Marion, I had been for a long time in the employ of Philo S. Shelton, Esq., merchant of Boston, in the United States, who was extensively engaged in the guano trade. In the early part of the year 1854, I commanded and sailed the brig John R. Dow, of Boston, owned, I believe, by him; and was also his superintending agent in the procurement of guano in the Caribbean sea, and also to aid him in the Gulf of Mexico, in which business said Shelton had at that time several vessels and many laborers employed at heavy expense.

TO THE THIRD.

Under said Shelton's instructions, and at his expense, and as his agent, and for him, I sailed in said brig John R. Dow on a cruise in the Caribbean sea for the discovery of guano islands, leaving Baltimore in the month of March, 1854, and spent some time in making such discoveries amongst the desert keys or rock isles in said sea, several of which I visited; and whilst so engaged, early in April, 1854, (I believe the 6th day of said month,) I found Aves, or Bird Isle, in said sea, (called since by Mr. Shelton "Shelton's Isle,") being in about 15° 40′ north latitude and 63° 38′ west longitude from Greenwich. I personally landed on said isle, and staid there with my vessel one day, engaged in taking soundings and observations, and I made a sketch of said island and of the approaches thereto. I explored and examined it thoroughly, and ascertained it to be about 1,400 feet in length and from 350 to 400 feet in breadth, and from fourteen to sixteen feet above the ordinary level of the sea, and that it was a desert isle, not having any trees or herbage thereon, and was uninhabited, and that there were not any appearances or indication thereon of its ever having been occupied by men; and I was fully convinced from its appearance, that if it ever had been so inhabited, it had been entirely abandoned for a long time, and was what is usually called a derelict and desert isle, I thereupon, as far as I then could, took possession of said isle and of the guano thereon for and in behalf of Mr. Shelton, my employer, and he being a citizen of the United States, in behalf also of my government and country, as I conceived I had full and lawful right to do; and in so doing I believed I was acting properly, and that thereby the jurisdiction over said isle became vested in the United States of America, and that Mr. Shelton acquired, in virtue of such premises, a right to take and appropriate said guano on said isle, and when in the actual possession thereof, was entitled to hold the same against and over all others who could not show a higher and better title than he had, or until forbidden by some law of the United States, or by the Executive of the United States in the fulfillment of legal duties. After fully examining said isle and the guano thereon, and taking samples of said guano, I sailed from thence on the 7th or 8th of April in said brig, and visited some other keys in said sea, and then proceeded with all dispatch to Arenas and other guano islands in the Gulf of Mexico, where Mr. Shelton's vessels and men engaged in the guano trade were then chiefly employed. Captain James Wheeler was then superintending agent at Arenas for said Shelton, being in charge of said business there, and had the brig Cronstadt, the barque Thorndike, and the ship Lanark, and perhaps other vessels whose names do not occur to me, subject to him. I then informed Captain Wheeler in confidence, as such agent, of my discovery for our employers, and we dispatched all Mr. Shelton's vessels there home as speedily as practicable, and I conveyed the laborers (some fifty odd in number) in the brig John R. Dow to New Orleans and discharged them, and abandoned the Gulf guano trade with the view of enabling Mr. Shelton, as soon as I could return to the eastern States and get our vessels provided with proper materials and laborers, to go again to Shelton's Isle and continue the possession thereof, and after erecting the necessary structures, to gather guano thereon and ship the same to the United States, as I had by letter advised my principal, Mr. Shelton. The said Captain James Wheeler, however, who also went in said brig to New Orleans, immediately left said city in a steamer for a northern port, on his way to Boston, where, failing to induce Mr. Shelton to decide until I should arrive as to sending vessels to the isle and laborers under him as agent, gave private information to Lang & Delano of what I had communicated to him as agent of Mr. Shelton, in confidence, respecting Aves or Bird Isle, and the guano thereon, and persuaded them to fit out a vessel and send him thither for themselves.

TO THE FOURTH.

I arrived at Boston from New Orleans in said brig John R. Dow about the 9th or 10th of June, 1854, and saw Mr. Shelton and Messrs. Sampson & Tappan, of Boston, the last-named gentlemen having been interested with the former—they may have been interested before then, though I have no positive knowledge thereof—and they all constituted me their chief superintending agent, to take control and charge of said isle for them, and to gather and ship the guano on the same, according to their instructions; and said parties and myself made the necessary and proper arrangements to carry out said object. I was accordingly dispatched about the middle, or perhaps the 20th of June, 1854, in the same brig John R. Dow, to Shelton's Isle, there being also shipped by said vessel a large quantity of heavy timbers and other lumber prepared and framed, and fitted in Boston, to be well fastened, in addition to wooden fastenings, with large iron bolts and braces and rods, which, with nails and spikes and tools, were also shipped by said brig, in order to erect a wharf or dock on the shore of said isle, at the place I had ascertained by my soundings and examinations to be most practicable. The said wharf, it was proposed, should extend upwards of eighty feet from the shore into the sea, and was to be constructed by placing or sinking into the sea upwards of twenty piers or horses, made of heavy timbers, framed and fitted, and to be well secured by fastenings and braces of iron as well as wood, and afterwards filling in the same with heavy rocks, to be obtained at the isle, and also by sinking such rocks around them as a support, and to protect them from the surf, and likewise by placing large stringpieces and heavy planks upon them securely bolted and spiked; all of which I had ascertained when at the isle in April was indispensable for a safe landing and for lading the guano on shipboard. There were also extra tackles and falls and cordage, and several extra water casks or tanks, and a large quantity of water, and also of supplies and provisions—meat, fish, bread and breadstuffs—and other articles necessary and proper for a large laboring force at said isle, purchased by said parties and shipped to said isle by said brig and by other vessels subsequently dispatched thither by them up to the time they became apprized of my being dispossessed of said isle on the 26th of December, 1854, as will be stated by me hereafter, (which time, I believe, was about the 15th day of January, 1855.) That materials for the erection of several houses (say seven) were also prepared in Boston, and also materials for sheds and bunks, and upwards of six dozen good wheelbarrows, upwards of ten dozen shovels and several spades and grubs, upwards of six dozen picks, and divers hoes and other implements wherewith to gather the guano, and tackles and falls, spars, ropes, boards, nails, hinges, locks, and the like, more than four dozen baskets, and several large baskets or buckets, expressly made for the lading of guano; and several dozen other buckets and tubs, cooking and other utensils, the necessary articles for the proper accommodation in sleeping of the laborers, and medicine and other stores for the preservation of their health, were also sent at different times by said parties to said island; and likewise several extra boats and appurtenances were furnished by them for the convenient use of the persons in their employ there. My employers also sent two cannon (both six-pounders) and two dozen muskets, and twenty-five large pistols, and several Colt's revolvers, and twenty-five cutlasses, and twenty-five boarding pikes, and a large magazine of fixed ammunition, and also a flagstaff and United States flags for use on the isle. I took in the brig John R. Dow, the trip last mentioned, some twenty-seven or twenty-eight men, being mechanics and laborers, besides her crew, which consisted of fifteen souls; and from time to time afterwards said parties sent others out, so that, upon an average, in addition to the crews of the vessels there, we generally had as many as thirty-five men, and, with the crews, ordinarily, not less than sixty men of the party under my charge, and by me employed on the isle after we got at work, up to the day of our eviction. There were several females who visited the island during the time I occupied it, the wives of persons who came out in the vessels and stewardesses on board the vessels, and one or more families of children, who also came out in the vessels.

TO THE FIFTH.

After leaving Boston in June, 1854, I arrived at Shelton's Isle in the brig John R. Dow, on the first or middle part of the month of July, 1854, I believe on the 15th of that month. On the same day, Captan James Wheeler, before mentioned, also arrived there in the brig Mahala H. Connery, having been dispatched by Messrs. Lang & Delano, merchants of Boston, as I understood from him, upon the information they had derived from him as to the existence of guano thereon, as before stated. Our vessels were in sight of each other when we made the isle, and there was not an hour's difference in the time of our arrival. On the next day we went ashore in company with Captain Wheeler, and although I did not conceive that either he or Lang & Delano had, under the circumstances, any legal, or equitable, or rightful claim to any portion or share of said isle or the guano thereon, and regarded the attempt to appropriate the same to their benefit to be a wrong upon Mr. Shelton, yet to avoid difficulty, and for the sake of peace, and as there was sufficient guano for all, I agreed with him to divide the isle and guano, and accordingly we staked off our respective portions, and came to an unnderstanding not to interfere with each other till I could hear from my employers, but leave the matter to be arranged and settled at home as the parties might deem advisable. Captain Wheeler had also, as I understood, brought out for Lang & Delano sundry materials and articles, though not equal in quantity or number, or in utility or value to those sent by Mr. Shelton and Sampson & Tappan. We immediately erected two liberty poles, or flagstaffs, and hoisted a United States flag on each, which were kept flying constantly by day. Both companies forthwith commenced erecting their respective structures, the two wharves being built near to each other. Several days were employed by all the persons at the isle in building wharves, during which time the vessels remained idle and incurring demurrage or losing time to the owners.

TO THE SIXTH.

I continued in the peaceful and undisturbed occupation and possession of Shelton's Isle, and of the guano thereon, as aforesaid, and was employed gathering and shipping guano therefrom, from the time I got the necessary structures erected, without molestation or objection from any one, until the 13th day of December, 1854. I had erected, besides the wharf, seven houses, and sundry sheds, and covers for my water casks or tanks, and places for my provisions, and places of shelter for my workmen, and up to the time I was dispossessed, as I will state hereafter, I shipped for my employers to the United States, I think about 7,200 tons of guano. The guano so shipped was not selected as being of superior quality, but was gathered as was most convenient for landing, because it was expected to ship the whole; and, in fact, the best guano was left on the island when I was evicted, and what had been shipped facilitated access to it. My employers sent, after I got ready to ship the guano, several vessels to the isle. I remember among them, besides the John R. Dow, the brig Cronstadt, of Boston, Howland, master; the ship Junius, of Hallowel, Erskine, first master, and afterwards Titcomb, master; the ship James N. Cooper, of Boston, Nickels, master; the barque Carlo Mauran, of Providence, Safford, master, (dispatched from Liverpool;) the barque Amazon, of Bangor, Stubbs, master; the brig Viator, of ———, Ellis, master; and the brig Mary Pearce, of Bangor, Pearce, master; the barque Brilliant, of New York, Bailey, master; the barque Mary Smith, of Portland, Fitz, master, and others whose names do not occur to me at this time. Captain Howland, of the Cronstadt, and also his son, died on the passage between the isle and St. Thomas, and several of his crew died also. Some were buried at the isle, and also one of the crew of the ship James N. Cooper. All of said vessels belonged to the United States. I estimate the entire quantity of all the guano shipped by my employers from the isle as about 7,200 tons, and the entire amount shipped by Lang & Delano, including all who shipped under their authority, as not over 2,000 tons. During the time I was in possession of this isle, several foreign vessels visited us. On the same day, or the day after, Captain Wheeler and myself went ashore, a vessel passed near to us, bound to the Island of St. Thomas, and, as I ascertained afterwards, reported there our being in possession of the isle. A few days afterwards, and I believe on the 1st of August, an English man-of-war steamer, called, I think, the Devastation, and commanded by a naval officer, named, I believe, De Horsey, came down to ascertain our objects. The commander was very gentlemanly, and landed and made inquiry, and I concealed nothing from him, and told him of my intention to take the guano. He obtained some samples, and examined the isle. He appeared to be an intelligent man, and I sounded him as to his opinion, whether any government but my own could claim the isle, and he told me frankly that he thought not, and advised me to keep my flag constantly flying, and to keep possession. We were next visited by an armed French steamer, whose commander was also very polite, who also obtained samples of the guano, and who expressed similar opinions to those expressed by the British officer. Afterwards we were visited by a Danish ship-of-war, and her officers told us to hold on to the island, as no government within their time had ever occupied it or claimed it. Several merchant vessels of different nations, and I think another vessel-of-war, touched at the island that autumn and fall, before we were expelled, and no one expressed any doubt of our being in rightful possession. I would observe that no United States government vessel visited us during the several months we were at the isle.

TO THE SEVENTH.

When I landed on Shelton's Isle, I had not been informed that any person had ever inhabited, possessed, or occupied it, or that any government had ever claimed or exercised any jurisdiction or ownership over it in anywise, though I did then, as I do now, regard it as quite as probable that the island had many times been visited, and that the egg gatherers from the islands of St. Thomas, Guadaloupe, St. Kitts, St. Eustatia, and other West India Islands—the nearest inhabited regions to it—had visited it to gather birds' eggs for sale in the said islands, as is their practice in respect to most of the desert rocks or keys in the Caribbean sea, not possessed by any government; and that, in fact, as the said isle was without wood or fresh water, it could not be permanently inhabited by man for any longer period, without supplies of those necessaries from elsewhere. I especially declare that I had never heard at that time, nor, until the 13th of December, 1854, did I once hear it intimated that the republic of Venezuela had any claim whatever to said isle, or that the same was under the jurisdiction of said republic; and if I had so heard, I would have regarded such claim, as I did when I first heard it advanced, as utterly preposterous, insomuch as Shelton's Isle is more than two hundred and fifty miles in the sea distant from the nearest admitted possessions of Venezuela inhabited by her citizens, which is more than twice the distance said isle is from several of the long settled and still inhabited windward West India Islands, possessed by the Danish, Dutch, French, and British governments, all much more ancient than that of Venezuela.

TO THE EIGHTH.

I made as full an examination of said isle when I first landed on it in April, 1854, as I deemed essential to ascertain satisfactorily to myself the quality and quantity of the guano thereon; and in several places on the isle I adopted means to find the thickness of the deposits with which the isle was covered. I had, as before stated, been formerly engaged for several months in the procurement of guano, and had acquired considerable experience therein, and I made up my mind as to the quantity of merchantable guano on said isle, and that there could be obtained therefrom, and laden on board vessels, over one hundred and fifty thousand tons, and that of said quantity at least one half, or seventy-five thousand tons, might be classed as first rate guano; and that said estimate of one hundred and fifty thousand tons was exclusive of a large quantity which, from various causes, should not be classed as good, merchantable guano, although it was mostly of sufficient value to bear freight to the United States, at the prices such guano was selling for in 1854 in the United States. I deem it proper for me, in confirmation of the correctness of my estimate, to state that I have seen an extract from an official letter or report, purporting to have been made by the British naval officer I have before mentioned, dated August 1, 1854, which has been published in England and in the United States, and which purports to have been addressed to the proper functionaries of the British government, and in which it is stated that said isle had then upon it "*two hundred thousand tons of guano, but slightly inferior to the Peruvian.*" I have not seen nor heard anything since I made my first estimate to make me suppose that it was in any degree extravagant, and, on the contrary, my subsequent examinations, and the knowledge acquired during several months' stay on the isle in the summer and fall, and till December 26, 1854, engaged in gathering the guano, satisfied me that my judgment in that estimate was not erroneous. I have knowledge of all the guano taken from the isle after I took possession in July, 1854, until my eviction by the Venezuelan officers, as I shall hereafter state, and I do not think, as I have before stated, it exceeded in the aggregate 9,200 tons; and I would again state, that the cargoes shipped were not selected or picked from the best guano, but were gathered as it was most convenient, as we expected to take all there was on the isle if the demand for it continued; and that, in fact, we took it as it lay, to facilitate access to the shipment of the best guano. I deem it proper to state here that I have heard that reports have been made, stating that the quality and quantity of guano on the isle were much less than my estimate; but that does not affect my conviction of its correctness, for I know that it requires practical experience with respect to gathering the article, to judge of the quantity that can be obtained from a place of deposit, and likewise experience and considerable skill to gather it advantageously; and I place limited dependence on the estimates of those called engineers, however able and scientific, if without such experience acquired by having been engaged in the business. From my knowledge of the business, a very large percentage is likely to be lost, in respect to quantity and quality for market, if gathered by inexperienced persons." After the business of my employers at said isle was broken up, as I will state hereafter, I received applications for my services to gather the guano on said isle and elsewhere, from persons connected with the Philadelphia Guano Company, which I declined, and several of which letters my employers have.

TO THE NINTH.

On the 13th day of December, 1854, a schooner-of-war of the government of Venezuela, commanded by Domingo Dias, an officer of the Venezuelan navy, as he represented, came to the isle, and said Dias landed, and stated that he came by authority of his government to take possession of the isle and guano, as belonging to that republic. He landed one cannon, and ammunition, and ten soldiers, armed with muskets and other arms, in charge of another officer, inferior to him. Dias told me that his government had sold or leased, or was about to sell or lease, the isle to a company in Philadelphia, in which company, he said, were interested gentlemen of great influence and high in office in both countries, who had united to make money out of the guano on the islands in the Caribbean sea, and that their influence was so powerful that it could not be resisted. I told him I had discovered the guano when the isle was derelict, and that I should not leave till

I heard from home, as my employers had encountered very great expenses and much trouble in the business. From his conversations and representations I received the impression that it was probable the government of the United States had made some arrangement, and had perhaps authorized the Venezuelan government and the Philadelphia company he spoke of to take possession of the isle and guano, and that it was likely Mr. Shelton and Sampson & Tappan were concerned in or with such company. I talked freely to Dias, and suggested that even if this were so that that fact furnished good reasons for my holding on to my possession till I heard authoritatively from home; and I finally told him, distinctly and unequivocally, that I would not leave the isle, nor cease gathering the guano till prevented by superior force, and that I would resist, and that he could not affect my expulsion with the force he had there. He then informed me that two other government vessels-of-war of Venezuela—one an armed steamer and the other a sloop-of-war—were coming over to the isle immediately with more troops, and that they had orders, if I had not complied with his directions, to expel me from the isle at once by military force, and to drive away all my vessels, and that he (Dias) was commander of the whole squadron, and that if he did not decide to expel me forthwith, that he should leave the isle in a few hours, (leaving his soldiers there,) and if the other vessels came in his absence, they would resort to military force to expel me, at all hazards; and after some time, he told me that he was willing that I should continue to work till the Philadelphia company sent down, or till he could ascertain if my employers were interested, or procure the final decision of his government; and that it would be best to keep off all other, and if I would assist him in that, he would give me a paper signifying my right to load the vessels there, and which would prevent all difficulty between me and those in command of the other vessels, and prevent them from attempting to interfere with me. I told him several times, distinctly and expressly, that I would not do anything to admit or recognize any right or claim of Venezuela to the isle or guano, or to compromise in any way the title of my employers, and that I had no right or authority from them to do so. I told him we were in possession, and had been so, peaceably, for several months, which title was good till somebody showed a better; and that his government, if it had any right, should bring the case before the federal government of the United States; and that if force was used, I would resist, and appeal to my government for redress if I was overpowered. He assured me that he did not desire me to make any admissions as to the claim of Venezuela, and boasted that her title did not need them; and he assured me also of his kind and friendly feelings, and of his anxiety to avoid difficulty, and handed me a paper that he had drawn up, or had got drawn up, in Spanish, signed by himself alone, which, he said, in case he went away, would prevent the vessels-of-war of Venezuela that might arrive when he was away from molesting me. I did not understand Spanish, and did not know the contents of the paper. I took the paper for what it was worth, and without much inquiry at that time as to its contents, knowing, as it was not signed nor assented to by me, it could not do any harm. He then wanted me to sign a copy, which he had made out in Spanish, and which he had also signed, and said that he desired it to be signed by myself and Mr. Lang, (Lang & Delano's agent,) merely to show to his government in due form what he had done. I unequivocally and emphatically refused to sign anything. I did not, as I have before said, understand Spanish, nor was there any one of my company who did. Dias professed to interpret and translate the paper to me. He said if I signed it he would leave the isle, the ten soldiers and officer already landed to remain there; and that the only thing that he asked of me, and that was in the paper, besides his orders not to molest me, was a statement that I would assist his soldiers with my men and cannon, and other arms, if occasion should arise, to keep off all intruders. He pretended to explain it word for word to me, and declared that there was not in it any acknowledgment of the right of Venezuela, nor anything whatever that could prejudice, or compromise, or affect the rights of my employers. I still refused, when he changed his course, and declared that unless I did sign it he would not leave the isle till he had driven me and my vessels away, and that he would forthwith resort to military force to prevent me from working, and to expel me at all hazards; and that if I resisted, he would resort to extreme measures; and that if the forces he had at the isle were not sufficient, he would soon have such forces when the expected vessels got there; and he even boasted that he might carry all of us and our vessels to Venezuela for trial for having violated her laws and stolen her property, and the like. He then again assured me, on his honor as an officer and a gentleman, that he had interpreted the paper he wished me to sign truly; that it was a mere copy of his "permit," as he called it, that he had signed and given to me, and that it contained nothing conflicting with the views I had expressed to him, and not a word admitting the title of Venezuela in any way. Finally, after consulting with some of my company and the American captains of the vessels there, after several hours delay, by my refusal, I concluded to run the risk of relying on his word, and signed the copy, as did also Mr. C. H. Lang, as agent for Lang & Delano, and Dias kept it. Dias then said he would leave, and I was appealed to to provide his soldiers with some provisions and with water till he came back, or till the other Venezuelan vessels-of-war arrived, as they were short of both; and pretty much as a matter of charity and humanity, I consented to do so, and he left. Some of the persons on the isle aided him with boats and sailors in going to and from his schooner, as he was badly off as to both. I did not anticipate any further trouble, and continued my work. During all this time we kept the United States flag flying by day on the isle on two liberty polls, and also on our vessels. Dias, whilst there, did not attempt to haul it down. I fed the soldiers, and they did not molest us, and I took the officer into my house, and fed him also, and I employed some of the soldiers to collect guano and paid them in clothing and provisions. I feel bound to say that, notwithstanding Dias' menaces and threats, and his apparent demonstrations of an intention to fulfill them, I did not sign the paper from any apprehension of personal consequences to myself, if I persisted in refusing, or because I had any fear that with the force he had then at the isle he could have overcome my party or have driven us away. I had reason to apprehend, however, that he might attempt it, and I was desirous to avoid any extremities in which bloodshed might have ensued. Though I had no doubt that we could have taken him and all his men, and his schooner-of-war, I did desire to avoid such necessity, and, from Dias's representations, I was not satisfied that my government might not have taken such action as to the guano isles in that sea as would have made such resistance improper, and also I did not know how soon the superior naval and military force, represented by Dias as coming there, might arrive; and, as we had no reason to expect a government vessel-of-war of the United States to protect us from their attack, we should have been at their mercy; and, besides all these considerations, if Dias had not dishonestly misrepresented the purport of the paper, it was harmless. I have since seen the translation of the paper Dias signed and gave to me, which I learn Mr. Shelton sent to the State Department of the United States so soon as he received it from me, in February, 1855, and also a copy of the copy signed by myself and Lang, and kept by Dias, and a translation of it procured from the said department by Mr. Shelton; and by said translations it appears said papers are substantially alike, and I unequivocally declare that Dias's representations to me of their contents and purport were false, dishonest, and fraudulent; and if I had known or suspected the import of said copy so signed by me, I would not have signed it, even under his menaces and threats of military force to expel me from the isle, but I would have resisted him at all hazards, and if overcome, appealed to my government for redress. On the 23d of December, 1854, the same schooner (as I believe) came back; as she approached she hoisted the Venezuelan colors, and the soldiers on the isle hoisted the same, and they exchanged salutes, in which one of the soldiers was mortally wounded, and who afterwards died. She landed twenty more soldiers, and sailed immediately for St. Thomas with the wounded soldier, but came back to the isle on the 25th, anchored about 5 o'clock, p. m., and about 10 o'clock, p. m., sent most of her crew ashore fully armed. They charged their muskets, and sentries were then placed around all our houses and stores, and over all our property, and at the guano pits, and on the wharves and over our cannon, and they forbade the hoisting of our colors any more. I was then in bed. When they first landed, I did not anticipate any difficulty, as I supposed Dias's paper would prevent it. The next morning I did personally hoist the colors, in despite of the armed sentry at the flag-staff, and I directed my men to go on with their work. They did attempt it, but were charged upon by the sentries with loaded muskets and fixed bayonets, and desisted only when in peril of their lives; and so also with respect to some guano in barrows, which I directed laborers to wheel to the wharf; they did so till stopped by the sentries, who presented their bayonets and levelled their muskets towards them. Those on board of my vessels, laying off from the wharves a short distance, were expecting me to load as usual, until I signalled them to come ashore immediately, and they put off; but the boats were not allowed to land by the sentries. The United States flag that I had hoisted was hauled down, and it was not hoisted any more. The Venezuelan flag was hoisted in its stead by the soldiers, and continued flying till we left, and a salute with cannon was fired by the Venezuelans on the occasion, from the isle and from the schooner. The officer in charge, whose name I do not recollect, (but it was not Dias, who had not returned,) refused to pay any attention to Dias's paper, and imperiously and imperatively ordered, under menaces and threats, and demonstrations of a violent character of the employment of military force, that all the persons belonging to our parties and their vessels should leave the isle and its vicinity within twenty-four hours, and he refused to allow us a reasonable time to get our implements, water, provisions, and other movable property on board of our vessels, and would not permit such vessels to approach to the wharves; and we were constrained, as he had a superior force, all armed, and acting in the name and under the authority of a government recognized by our own, to yield obedience to his commands, or engage in a combat which would have resulted in bloodshed. There was a British brig-of-war at the isle at the time, the name of which I do not certainly recollect; I believe it was the Mariner, or Marine. The commander left the isle, and said he intended to go to Laguayra, and find out by what right the Venezuelans so acted, and he said I might be certain my government would look into the matter and demand satisfaction.

TO THE TENTH.

In consequence of what I have stated, I was compelled to abandon on the isle a large amount of property, including provisions and water and other stores belonging to my employers, some of which the Venezuelans positively refused to allow me to take away, and then took possession of it themselves for their own use, as they had little else there for their troops, as they admitted, and none of which was I allowed time to bring away, and was, therefore, obliged to abandon, and all of which I have since been informed they appropriated to their own use. It is impossible for me to specify all this property, but I will state some of it. With the wharves and houses and sheds, there were a large number of shovels and spades, and hoes, and hatchets, and axes, picks, and other implements, and wheelbarrows and wheeling plank, baskets, buckets, and tubs, and tools, and water casks and tanks, and hogsheads and barrels, and a large amount of provisions and stores of various kinds, and water in casks or tanks, and two large launches or long-boats and their appurtenances, the aggregate cost of all of which to my employers at said isle (and the aggregate value thereof to them was much greater if they had been unmolested in their business) was, according to the best of my judgment, (and I had a general knowledge of such costs and of their value, derived from my superintendence of said business,) more than ten thousand dollars. I verily believe that by a fair and just valuation it would have amounted to a larger sum, for they kept pretty much all that we had on the isle, and we were abundantly supplied. The residue of the property of my employers, of similar character, on board their vessels sent to said isle for use there, and which was rendered comparatively valueless by reason of said expulsion, was not less than two thousand dollars in value. I further state that, according to the best of my judgment, the cost at said isle of all the materials for the wharf of my employers, and which were left there, and taken possession of by the Venezuelans, and the building of said wharf at said isle, was not less than $4,500. I further state that, according to the best of my judgment, the cost at said isle of all the materials for said seven houses and the sheds built by my employers there, and which we were compelled to abandon, and which the Venezuelans took possession of, and the building said houses and sheds at said isle was not less than $3,500, and the cost of the other property was as much as $3,500 more. I further state, that I do not include in said cost any of the expenses incurred on the cruise for the discovery of said isle, which, including the hire for the brig and crew so employed, were not less than $3,000; nor do I include any of the sacrifices, expenses, or losses incurred or sustained by the breaking up of their guano business at Arenas, in the Gulf of Mexico, in order to go to said isle, which I think must have amounted to several thousand dollars, and not less than $3,500; nor do I include in any of said estimates of any of said property at the isle any amounts except the actual cost of the materials or articles in the United States, and of their transportation to the isle, and the time, labor, trouble, and expense bestowed upon them there; and I consider my estimate greatly below what would have been their value to my employers at the isle if they had not been molested by the Venezuelan government, and if they had been allowed to continue the gathering of said guano.

TO THE ELEVENTH.

I have seen a copy of the statement of the claim presented by P. S. Shelton and Sampson & Tappan to the State Department, of their damages against the Venezuelan government. The first item is "for the guano on said island, estimated as a minimum at 25,000 tons, (probably 50,000 tons,) which, under the management of the subscribers, would have produced a net profit of $12 50 per ton, which on 25,000 tons is $312,500." I regard this item, if they are held to be entitled to the guano and to a fair compensation for it, as much below the amount they might justly claim. As I have stated in my estimate, the quantity stated is less than was on the isle when we were evicted. If Lang & Delano should be considered as entitled to one half, in consequence of the division in July, 1854, made under the circumstances I have stated, the quantity is still, I think, understated, for if nothing had to be paid for port charges or export duties, and if they had been free to load the guano at no expense but the cost of lading it as their own property, with the conveniences and facilities for so doing that they had prepared, then I regard the price or value claimed, viz: $12 50 per ton, as below what might reasonably be claimed for it at the isle, and a fair profit made upon it in the United States. As freights would probably not have exceeded, on an average, $7 per ton to the United States, even if sold at first sale in the United States at $25 per ton, it would have been a profitable trade, and have left also a margin for profit to those who purchased it to sell again. With respect to the second item of $20,000, I know of several vessels of my employers, or of vessels engaged by them, or to whom they had engaged freights of guano from the isle, but as to this item of charge they can, doubtless, furnish more particular statements than I can give. I know they had made extensive arrangements as to the guano trade in reference to this isle, and incurred great expenses thereby, most of which were lost to them. The following named vessels, I remember, were at the isle when we were evicted, on the 26th day of December, 1854: the bark Amazon, the brig Viator, and the brig Mary Pearce. The ship James N. Cooper was expected, and did, I believe, go out in ballast. All these vessels were sent out by my employers, and I understood they had others. The Amazon and Viator were driven off with but little cargo on board, and the Mary Pearce was sent away empty, and the James N. Cooper, I believe, was not allowed to take any guano.

In reference to the third item of $8,500, I have already stated particulars, showing that, in my judgment, it is much less than it might justly have been made. In reference to the entire statement, I feel no hesitation in expressing my deliberate and sincere conviction that if my employers were entitled to hold possession of the isle, and to use the guano as their own property, and if entitled to payment for it from Venezuela, (without reference to the expenses of discovery which I have before alluded to, and without reference to the expenses and losses encountered by the abandonment of the Arenas business, and without reference to the embarrassment and losses consequent to Mr. Shelton from this interruption and interference with his business, by which he was compelled to suspend;) but simply and solely considering the actual and direct losses and damages from the deprivation of their property, the aggregate amount there stated is beneath what might be justly claimed. And even if they are not allowed any compensation whatever for the guano not gathered upon the isle, I verily believe their said actual losses in the premises, including the expenses of discovery, and also the said Arenas sacrifices, and also their direct and actual losses in consequence of their being compelled to abandon their arrangements for receiving, storing, and selling the guano in the United States and elsewhere, could not be reimbursed under forty thousand dollars at least.

TO THE TWELFTH.

I have no personal interest in this claim, direct or indirect, immediate nor remote, in anywise. I was employed as agent, at a salary and for a certain price per ton; I have settled with my employers; but I think in justice I should have more than I received, but I am not promised anything, nor do I expect anything from this claim. I have some feeling in it. I feel humiliated as an American citizen at the insult to my country's flag, and at the outrage upon myself and my countrymen at the isle, yet unatoned for; and I feel, too, sympathy for Mr. Shelton, whose rightful property, as I conceive, was despoiled from him whilst in my care, as his agent, by the fraud and trick and force of the officers of the Venezuelan government, and I have an anxious hope that his wrongs may be redressed by his government. This is the sum of the concern I have in anywise in the claim; but, if I know myself, it has not caused me to swerve from the truth in the foregoing answers, which, after reflection and care, I have caused to be written and printed, and to the correctness of which I now attest. I will name here the following persons who were with me at the isle, and whose names I can now recollect; there were others whose names I cannot remember. The testimony of all will, I am satisfied, sustain the truth of my answers: William P. Gibbs, my brother, who was my assistant, William James Gibbs, Frederick Scott, Kartin Austin, Adolph Ritchart, Charles Sullivan, Richard Thornell, John McCabe, Alfred H. Morgan, Joseph Herbert, John Sweeny, Robert Williamson, George Humphrey, T. H. Whitney, Frederick Kager, William Kalback, Britton J. Hopper, James Smith, Philip Knight, Henry Baker, Charles Knapp, John Carr, Henry Troutman, Gerard Ferrell, George Scotter, William Parker, Charles Johnson, Frederick Taylor, James Johnson, besides the crews of the vessels there. I believe these names are given correctly, but I am not certain.

NATHAN P. GIBBS.

Subscribed and sworn before me, and I certify that the foregoing interrogatories and answers were read to the above named deponent in my presence, this 12th day of April, A. D. 1856.

JOSEPH C. LAWRENCE,
Notary Public, 67 *Wall street*, *New York*.

Mr. Marcy to Mr. Sanford.

DEPARTMENT OF STATE,
Washington, *April* 17, 1856.

SIR: Your letter of the 14th instant, with its inclosures, has been received. One of the printed copies of Captain Gibbs's testimony will be transmitted to Mr. Eames.

On the 24th ultimo the department addressed a letter to you at New York, which contained information supposed to be of interest to the claimants whom you represent. As no acknowledgment of its receipt has reached the department, it is presumed the original failed of its destination. Should this supposition be correct, a duplicate will, at your request, be transmitted to you.

I am, &c.,

W. L. MARCY.

HENRY S. SANFORD, Esq.,
Derby, *Connecticut*.

Mr. Sanford to Mr. Marcy.

DERBY, CONNECTICUT,
April 19, 1856.

SIR: In several former letters addressed to yourself on the subject of Mr. Shelton's claim, and in a letter to the President of the United States, dated December 24, of which I inclosed you a copy, I adverted to the fact that legal counsel advised Mr. Shelton of the expediency of obtaining from Congress a confirmation of his ownership of Shelton's Isle and the guano thereon. I respectfully solicited suggestions from the President or yourself if it was deemed improper. Not having received any intimation of such impropriety, I have supposed you did not disapprove of such course, if deemed advisable.

I frankly state to you that I do not concur in the necessity of such proceeding, and would respectfully solicit your attention to pages 5 and 12, included, of the printed brief I sent to you in June last, of which the original manuscript is on file in the department. Some of the citations are misprinted, but you can readily recur to them by looking at the original brief. The heads of the brief to which I would solicit your attention on this point are—

"X. Faculty of acquisition by the United States of such isle by discovery, &c.

"XI. If faculty not in the United States, it remains in the State of discoverer.

"XII. Executive may enforce and maintain public and private rights resulting from discovery and occupation, without action of Congress.

"XIII. The non-existence of any restraining or directory law leaves plenary power with the President.

"XIV. Discovery by private citizens vests rights in the United States.

"XV. Rights and interests of citizen discoverers.

"XVI. Extent of our rights in the present case.

"XVII. A discoverer has no right or power to alienate rights of his State, or his own, to foreign powers, and admissions by him to such effect are of no force."

I inclose you herewith a copy of a memorial I have this day sent to be presented to both houses of Congress, which you will perceive only claims the interposition of Congress, in case Congress, in its wisdom, should deem such interposition necessary to confirm and maintain our rights. I presume, therefore, it can in no wise embarrass, but, on the contrary, aid the department in its diplomatic negotiations with respect to this claim.

If Congress is disposed, it certainly can nerve and strengthen the executive arm most effectually by making provision for the employment of a naval force to coerce just reparation. I understand that during Mr. Polk's administration, Mr. Buchanan felt the necessity of the executive being invested with power to use the naval force in reference to some of the American republics south of us so strongly, that he urged upon the members of Congress the propriety of a general authority being given in such cases. It certainly seems to me proper.

Venezuela is so utterly indigent and dishonest, (as is proved by the large amount of bonds outstanding and unpaid for years past in the hands of American citizens,) that we have little hope of obtaining pecuniary indemnity from her distinct from the restoration of the isle. We fear that the isle, and indeed we have reason to know such is the fact, has been very considerably decreased in value by the abstraction of the guano therefrom since our eviction. For this they should make compensation, and we trust it is not expecting too much for American citizens to expect that their government will exact, by coercive measures if necessary, such just compensation.

I have deemed it my duty to inclose to you a copy of the memorial, and respectfully request that your efficient aid may be given to accomplish such end in respect to it as you may deem just.

I have the honor to be, with great respect, your most obedient servant,

H. S. SANFORD.

Hon. W. L. MARCY,
Secretary of State.

APRIL 21.

P. S.—Since the above was written, I have had the honor to receive your letter of the 17th instant. That of the 24th ultimo was received on my return to New York.

To the honorable the Senate and House of Representatives of the United States of America in Congress assembled, the memorial of Philo S. Shelton, a citizen of the United States, resident in Boston, in the State of Massachusetts, merchant, in behalf of himself and of other citizens of the United States, his associates, interested with him by transfer from him, respectfully showeth:

1. That in the month of March, 1854, your memorialist fitted out the brig John R. Dow, of Boston, owned by himself, and under the command of Captain Nathan P. Gibbs, also a citizen of the United States, and she sailed from Baltimore on a cruise of discovery in the Caribbean sea for derelict and desert guano keys or isles.

2. That in the month of April, 1854, said Captain Gibbs, in said brig, acting as the agent of your memorialist, discovered and took possession of a desert and derelict rock or isle in said sea, situate in north latitude 15° 40′, and west longitude from Greenwich 63° 38′, then known as "Aves," or "Bird Island," now called "Shelton's Isle."

3. That your memorialist was then engaged in the guano trade from the Gulf of Mexico, but relinquished the same at a great sacrifice for the said isle, which he named "Shelton's Isle," and forthwith, on the return of said Captain Gibbs to Boston, dispatched said brig, under his command, to said isle, provided with extra launches, and laden with materials for a wharf and houses to be erected thereat, and with implements and provisions and water for laborers, and with

many workmen by said vessel, to gather guano at said isle; and that in June, 1854, said brig arrived thereat, and said Captain Gibbs, your memorialist's agent, and the workmen accompanying him, forthwith landed, erected houses and a wharf thereon, and continued in peaceable and undisturbed possession; and that your memorialist continued to dispatch other vessels and workmen, and provisions, &c., until December, 1854, when they were violently dispossessed of and expelled therefrom by an armed military force of the government of the republic of Venezuela, under circumstances of an aggravating character, and combining gross fraud with violence, and being alike an outrage upon your memorialist and the citizens of the United States, whose flag, raised by its citizens there, was struck by the said military force.

4. That your memorialist presented early in January, 1855, to the proper executive department of the United States, his claim for redress against the government of Venezuela, but as yet no satisfaction has been accorded him, and said claim is still pending; that the amount of said claim is $341,000, of which $28,500 is for actual losses sustained in damages occasioned by demurrage, false freights, and forfeited charter-parties of his vessels employed in said business, and for the value of the wharves, houses, boats, implements, provisions, and other property of which he was despoiled by said military force at said isle; and that the residue of said claim is a charge of $312,500 for 25,000 tons of guano, at $12 50 per ton, being, as your memorialist believes, less than one fifth of the quantity and value of the guano on the said isle at the time of his eviction; and he also asked for restoration of said isle.

5. That annexed hereto is a deposition of said Captain Nathan P. Gibbs, (a duplicate of which has been filed in the State Department of the United States,) in said claim, and which sets forth the facts of said case truly and at large. And that there are on the files of the State Department sundry depositions, documents, and papers, exhibiting the justice of your memorialist's claim to said isle and guano, and showing also that his right is incontestable under the laws of nations, and exhibiting also the wrongs and outrages committed upon him, and the damages he has sustained; as to all which as yet no atonement hath been made.

6. That, if not allowed the item for the guano on the said isle as his property, the direct and consequential damages sustained by your memorialist in the premises, in addition to those specified in said two other items of the claim, would, with said items, amount to upwards of $40,000, (those augumenting the aggregate to such amount having been in the stating the claim to the State Department estimated as covered by the item charged for the said guano therein, and therefore omitted to be specifically stated, and also the property of which he is despoiled, being estimated at the cost in the United States, merely, as is shown by the deposition of Captain Gibbs,) and your memorialist also shows that since December, 1854, a large amount in quantity and value of the guano on said isle has been abstracted under the authority of the government of Venezuela, for which, your memorialist respectfully submits, said republic of Venezuela should be compelled to pay to him, upon the restoration of said isle.

7. That the republic of Venezuela has not and never had a shadow

of right or title to the said isle or the guano thereon; and her only pretenses in justification for the forcible expulsion of your memorialist's workmen and agent therefrom, and for despoiling him of his property, are, that your memorialist's agent was not a commissioned officer of the United States, authorized to hoist the flag of the United States thereon and occupy the same; and a fraudulent paper in Spanish, alleged by it to admit the title of Venezuela, procured by misrepresentation, crime, and violence, by the officers of Venezuela from the agent of your memorialist, though said agent was without authority to sign the same. And your memorialist annexes hereto a sketch showing the location of said Shelton's Isle with reference to several of the West India Islands and to the coast of Venezuela, by which it will be seen that said isle is more than three hundred and fifty miles from the latter, whilst it is less than half the distance from several of the former; and, being separated from it by the open sea, Venezuela has no claim upon the ground of contiguity or being appurtenant.

8. That your memorialist claims that, until otherwise declared by a law of the United States, he was and is entitled, as the discoverer of said desert and desolate guano rock called Shelton's Isle, to the exclusive use of the guano thereon and of said isle, in virtue of said discovery and his possession aforesaid, the soveignty and jurisdiction thereof being vested thereby in the United States; but that your memorialist is informed that his claim to said exclusive ownership of said guano and said isle is contested, and alleged to be invalid, unless the federal government of the United States do recognize the same and vest said ownership in him by joint resolution or act of Congress to that effect.

Therefore, your memorialist, humbly but confidently relying upon the just and liberal protection and aid of Congress, prays that such resolution or act may be passed for the benefit of himself and associates, specially referring to said isle, and confirming the right of your memorialist and his associates thereto, provided your honorable bodies may deem such action requisite to confirm said right; or that such other action may be had in the premises to obtain and secure your memorialist justice, as to the wisdom of your honorable bodies may seem meet.

And your memorialist, as in duty bound, will ever pray.

PHILO S. SHELTON, for self and others,
By H. S. SANFORD, *Attorney in fact.*

DERBY, CONNECTICUT, *April* 19, 1856.

Mr. Marcy to Mr. Sanford.

DEPARTMENT OF STATE,
Washington, May 1, 1856.

SIR: I have to acknowledge the receipt of your communication of the 19th ultimo, with the inclosed copy of Mr. Shelton's memorial to Congress.

I am, sir, &c., W. L. MARCY.

HENRY S. SANFORD, Esq.,
Derby, Connecticut.

Mr. Sanford to Mr. Marcy.

DERBY, *May* 9, 1856.

SIR: I have this moment received from the persons I employed to prosecute it, a deposition of Captain James Wheeler, who was employed as agent for Lang & Delano at Shelton's Isle. It is offered in behalf of Mr. Shelton, *et al.*, to show the damages sustained and the quantity and value of the guano. You will notice that Captain Wheeler prefers a claim on his own account, but which does not in any respect conflict with that of Mr. Shelton, or Sampson & Tappan.

I would call your attention to a copy of a letter appended from the Foreign Office, London, to Mr. Dallas, enclosing an extract from the report of Commander De Horsey, of the British Navy, as to the guano on Shelton's Isle. The original papers received from Mr. Dallas, I will forward in a few days.

Very respectfully, your obedient servant,

H. S. SANFORD.

Hon. WILLIAM L. MARCY,
Secretary of State, &c.

Mr. Sanford to Mr. Marcy.

DERBY, *May* 10, 1856.

SIR: I have the honor to inclose, herewith, to be filed in the department as testimony in the case of Philo S. Shelton *et al.*, the deposition of Richard Thornell, one of the employés on Shelton's Isle.

I inclose also a copy of a letter from Mr. Hammond of the Foreign Office, in the absence of Lord Clarendon, to our minister, Mr. Dallas, with extract from a report by Commander De Horsey, of H. B. M.'s ship Devastation, to Commodore Henderson, and which I have lately received from London, to be filed as testimony with Captain Gibbs's deposition in the Shelton's Isle case.

I have the honor to be, very respectfully, your obedient servant,

H. S. SANFORD.

Hon. WILLIAM L. MARCY,
Secretary of State, &c,

FOREIGN OFFICE, *April* 11, 1856.

SIR: I referred to the admiralty your letter of the 4th instant, inclosing a copy of one from Mr. Sanford, requesting your assistance to procure for him certain specified information as to the visit of her Majesty's steamer Devastation to the Aves or Bird Islands, and I have now the honor to transmit to you, herewith, an extract of a letter, dated the 1st of August, 1854, from Commander De Horsey, of her

Majesty's steamer Devastation, to Commodore Henderson, reporting his visit to the above mentioned islands.

I have the honor to be, with the highest consideration, sir, your most obedient humble servant, in the absence of the Earl of Clarendon.

E. HAMMOND.

G. M. DALLAS, Esq., *&c.*,

Extract of a letter from Commander De Horsey to Commodore Henderson, dated August 1, 1854.

"Having obtained information at St. Thomas that two or three vessels had been seen at the small uninhabited islands of Aves, in latitude 15° 40′ and longitude 63° 36′, and the trades hanging well to the northward, enabling me to fetch down, I proceeded there, and, on arriving, found three American vessels—a brig, a brigantine, and a schooner—employed in shipping guano. They had been there about ten days, and were expecting a fourth vessel, a bark, all owned by the captain of the brigantine. The owner of the vessels informed me that the guano was but slightly inferior to the Peruvian, and better adapted for tobacco lands, and that it would be worth $35 per ton in the United States. At a rough estimate, I should say there were about 200,000 tons of guano on the island, which, at £7 per ton, would make the island worth one and a half million sterling.

STATE OF NEW YORK,
County and City of New York, } *ss:*

Before the subscriber, Joseph C. Lawrence, notary public of the said city and State, by lawful authority duly commissioned and sworn, and by law authorized to administer oaths and affirmations, and to certify the same, on this seventh day of May, 1856, personally appeared Richard Thornell, who, being by me duly sworn to testify the truth, the whole truth, and nothing but the truth, in a certain matter of claim against the government of the republic of Venezuela, in favor of Philo S. Shelton and Sampson & Tappan, pending in the United States Department of State, deposes and saith, on his oath, that he is about 22 years old, is a native of Ireland, is by trade a cooper, and at present resides in the city of New York, and is not, as yet, fully naturalized a citizen of the United States; he says he is not interested in said claim in anywise, though he lost a winter's work by the transactions the claimants complain of; he says that he considers that there was 200,000 tons of guano on Aves Island, now called Shelton's Isle, in the Caribbean sea, when he first went there, in July, 1854, with Captain Gibbs; one half of it, he thinks, could be called first class; and the best of it was worth—to any one who had vessels and the privilege of taking it free, and the privilege of the wharves and other conveniences in the establishment that Captain Gibbs had charge of there, and labor sufficient to get it—at least $15 a ton on the island. It costs but $7 or $8 to fetch it to the United States, and the lowest that the best of it ought to bring in the United States was $35 per ton. There was at least 75,000 tons, or more, of the best quality on the island, in his opinion. He says he staid on the island till November 21, 1854, and knows all that occurred previously. What he got off was mostly inferior, as they had to clear away as they went, and take the nearest the wharf, in order to get at the best. He says that he thinks the wharf built by Captain Gibbs was worth there—and he means by worth its cost at the island when finished—at least six thousand dollars, adding in freight and time lost to vessels, and the labor and expenses of all kinds there. We had twenty-eight men besides the sailors on board the John R. Dow, (and the crew were twelve or fifteen more,) and Lang or Captain Wheeler's company and ours helped each other fix the wharves. Ours was prepared in Boston, and ironed, and was of good solid timber, and was built in fourteen feet water at its out end, and extended eighty feet from the land, and was about twelve feet wide, and laid on horses kept firm by being surrounded with heavy rock sunk round each one. Captain Gibbs had seven houses, besides several sheds, which were framed in Boston; and I think the houses cost, to put them up out there, $750 or $800 a piece. They were framed to stand the West India hurricanes. The sheds cost considerable to get them there; I suppose a thousand dollars would pay for them. We generally had at least thirty-five men in our party on the island, and our supplies came out from time to time on different vessels from the United States, and we caught some fish there, though the time lost was as much as they were worth. Captain Gibbs always had a plentiful supply of stores there, such as provisions, and sometimes exchanged with his vessels there. All his water had to be brought there in casks. He kept an ample supply; he had not less than ninety or one hundred large casks generally on hand, and the vessels took away casks nearly every trip, which were returned filled. Captain Gibbs also had plenty of implements—tools of all kinds, barrows, and everything necessary for such an establishment—all of which must, at the island, have stood the owners in at least ten thousand dollars. I do not think his outfit on the island could have cost less there. I do not mean to include in this the wharf, or houses, or sheds, or the extra cables and anchors for moving the vessels which were kept there, or his extra launches or boats, of which there were two launches that must have cost several hundred dollars, used for lading the guano, but I mean only his stores, provisions, medicine, implements, barrows, tools, and the like. He further says he believes the stock was kept up, and was particularly so towards the last of the time, as it was intended to push the business that winter, and he thinks there was more than ten thousand dollars' worth there. He says he never saw a list of them, but has a general recollection of them, and a general knowledge of the cost of such things in the United States, and there was generally supplies for a couple of months ahead for thirty-five or forty men, besides the implements, &c.; and besides that, there was the cannon and sundry small arms, and powder and ball. Any shipmaster or merchant can judge of the freight out. These things were indispensable to the business. I have no doubt if they had not been disturbed that those who were in possession of the guano would have made an immense fortune out of the island. I reckoned Shelton and Sampson & Tappan would make a million of dollars at least, and have no doubt they would if the Venezuelans had not interfered with us. Several of their vessels were disappointed in cargoes, as I heard, by being driven off. I heard that a ship called the J. N. Cooper was driven away in January, 1855. We saw no United States men-of-war out in those parts while we were there, but several of other nations. I think they ought to have been down there. I think Captain Gibbs kept on hand six or seven thousand dollars' worth, at least, of provisions, stores, implements, water casks, barrows, and other property, besides the wharf and houses, and sheds in his charge, and the boats that cost several hundred dollars, while I was there. I think the hiring of the vessels in the trade cost $250 or $310 at least. When I say six or seven thousand dollars above, I mean the cost in the United States. I have before said out there they were worth ten thousand. If they had not been driven off, I should have gone back there. I know Captain Gibbs was there in the M. H. Pomery.

RICHARD THORNELL.

STATE OF NEW YORK,
City and County of New York, } *ss:*

Be it remembered that on the day and year first aforesaid, said Richard Thornell appeared before me in person, and was duly sworn as aforesaid by me, and made answers to questions propounded to him on behalf of said claimants, as above stated, and the same were reduced to writing in my presence, and carefully copied, and read and explained to him, and he deposed that the same so subscribed by him were true, according to the best of his knowledge and belief.

[L. S.] In testimonium veritatis I hereunto set my official seal, at my office, No. 67 Wall street, the day and year first aforesaid.

JOSEPH C. LAWRENCE,
Notary Public.

Mr. Marcy to Mr. Sanford.

DEPARTMENT OF STATE,
Washington, May 16, 1856.

SIR: Your communication of the 9th instant, transmitting the deposition of Captain James Wheeler, in support of Mr. Shelton's claim, and your letter of the 10th instant, covering the deposition of Richard Thornell, and copy of papers from the British Foreign Office, relating to the same subject, have been received.

I am sir, &c.,

W. L. MARCY.

HENRY S. SANFORD, Esq.,
Derby, Connecticut.

Mr. French to Mr. Marcy.

WASHINGTON, *June* 15, 1856.

SIR: The inclosed copy of a certificate, under oath, of Albert Smith, was forwarded to me by Messrs. Lang & Delano, of Boston, to be filed in the department with the papers relating to their claim *vs.* the Venezuelan government.

Respectfully,

B. B. FRENCH,
Attorney.

Hon. WILLIAM L. MARCY,
Secretary of State.

I hereby certify I sailed from Boston, United States of America, in the American brig John R. Dow, Gibbs, master, for the Aves Island, in the Caribbean sea, to procure a cargo of guano, in the month of June, 1854. That I was to take charge of the said vessel on her homeward voyage, provided she procured a cargo of guano, as Captain Gibbs was to remain at the said island. I also certify that I was employed by Philo S. Shelton, merchant of Boston. I further certify that on our arrival at the Ave sIsland, we found there the brig M. H. Comery, and that the island had been already taken possession of for Lang & Delano, merchants of Boston, by their agent, Charles H. Lang, who without pay or remuneration permitted Captain Nathan P. Gibbs, agent for P. S. Shelton and others, of Boston, to inclose a portion of said island for said Shelton and others. And I further certify that we loaded the brig John R. Dow with guano, and that I, as master, brought said brig to Boston, leaving the island in possession of Charles H. Lang, as agent for Lang & Delano, and Nathan P. Gibbs, as agent for P. S. Shelton and others.

ALBERT SMITH.

COMMONWEALTH OF MASSACHUSETTS, } *ss:*
County of Suffolk, }

Personally appeared before me, Daniel Sharp, jr., a notary public by lawful authority commissioned and duly qualified, Albert Smith, and made oath that the within statement by him subscribed is true according to the best of his knowledge and belief.

In testimony whereof I have hereto set my hand and affixed my official seal this day and year above written.

[SEAL.] DANIEL SHARP, JR.
Notary Public.

BOSTON, *May* 22, 1856.

Mr. Sanford to Mr. Marcy.

DERBY, CONNECTICUT,
June 30, 1856.

SIR: I inclose herewith, to be filed in the Shelton's Isle case, a printed deposition of John McCabe, one of the workmen employed on Shelton's Isle, duly authenticated, and which I have this day received from my agent in New York, who took the same. The reason for its being printed is, that the first manuscript contained some informality, and the notary public has explained in his certificate that this is a correct copy of the first, and to save, moreover, trouble in copying.

I inclose also a copy for the use of the department, to be sent to Mr. Eames, if it thinks proper, after appending the notary's certificate.

I have the honor to be, very respectfully, your obedient servant,

H. S. SANFORD.

Hon. WM. L. MARCY,
Secretary of State.

Copy of deposition of John McCabe, original, duly certified, on file at the State Department.

UNITED STATES OF AMERICA.

PHILO S. SHELTON and SAMPSON & TAPPAN, *vs.* THE REPUBLIC OF VENEZUELA.	Claim for indemnity, &c., for dispossession of Shelton's Isle, and taking property, &c., in 1854, and keeping it from their possession.

John McCabe, a witness for claimants, being duly sworn to testify the truth, the whole truth, and nothing but the truth, touching said claim now pending in the State Department of the United States, and being duly cautioned according to law, doth depose: that he is of lawful age, and is a citizen of the United States, and resides in the city of New York; that he is not pecuniarily interested in said claim; that he went to the isle with Captain Gibbs, in the John R. Dow, and arrived there in July, 1854, the same day that Captain Wheeler did, in the brigantine M. H. Comery, and that they both landed next day (sea time;) that he staid there till Christmas, 1854, when the Venezuelans took possession by military force; that he thinks there were 200,000 tons of guano on the island, and that was the general estimate, and one half was first-class if carefully procured. That he won't pretend to give a positive valuation, but he thinks that there were at least 75,000 tons on Captain Gibbs's part of the island, worth $13 or $14 a ton, considering that he had all the means of gathering it and loading it prepared for his use, and hands there also; that he means the value at the isle to the owners, they having these means, (wharves, houses, boats, and the like,) and he thinks the freight ought not to be more than $8 per ton to the United States in the winter time; and if any one bought it at the island for the price he states, at the generally going prices in the United States, they would make good freights, and covering all expenses he supposes would make heavy profits, provided they know how to get it up for market, and how to sell it. The chief part we sent off was the most inferior sort on the island, which Captain Gibbs got out first to reach the best. Captain Gibbs took out twenty-eight men in the Dow, besides the sailors, twelve or fifteen more, and he built a wharf 80 feet out, and in 14 feet water; it was framed, ready to be planted, in Boston, and taking it there, and the labor and time spent there on it, deponent says would make it cost at the island at least $5,500, if not more. Captain Gibbs also carried out and put up seven houses, and deponent thinks that they cost at the isle somewhere about $750 apiece; they were built strong, in order to meet the heavy winds and sometimes hurricanes in that latitude. Besides the houses, there were several sheds, which he supposes cost all together $900 or $1,000. Captain Gibbs took plenty of supplies of all kinds proper for the party, and all sorts of tools and implements, and fire-arms, and two cannon and ammunition, and a supply of boarding-pikes and cutlasses. Deponent says he don't know exactly what to say these things all cost at the island, but there was a full outfit suitable for such an expedition, and keeping up the same, and he thinks taking them, and all expenses attending them, cost for all the time they were there—for supplies and other things kept coming out all the time—must have cost them well nigh to eighteen or twenty thousand dollars in all, leaving out the wharf, houses, sheds, and several extra boats they had, and extra cables and anchors. He thinks they generally had two months' or more supplies of provisions on hand. They had over a hundred water casks. He can't specify all things. He was there when Dias first came, about the 12th or 13th of December, 1854. He had to help boat him and his soldiers ashore, and they were the most miserable, shabby-looking set of vagabonds pretending to be regulars he ever saw. They were badly off in every way, and we had to feed and clothe the poor wretches for humanity's sake. After they eat and drank awhile, some of them would swell and talk large, especially the officers, till they got hungry again. The talk at the island we got from them was, that their government owned all the guano islands in these parts, and that they were part of a squadron going round to take possession and drive away everybody else, and that in a few days a big steamer and other vessels with troops were coming to the island. The Venezuelans said that the "Gobierno Yankos" had given it up to the republic, and that both had formed a company that had several millions capital, and that several of the principal officers and head men of our country and of theirs were joined in it and would make their fortunes by it, and that they expected a good slice themselves. They said our minister or consul in Venezuela knew all about it, and knew that the ships and soldiers were out visiting the guano islands to drive everybody off but the company. They said we should have to go, as the United States had agreed to it. This was their current talk. We all knew that

Dias had given Captain Gibbs and Charles Lang, on the 12th or 13th of December, a paper in Spanish, which we generally understood was a protection against the squadron that he said was coming down, and an order not to disturb us. We heard that afternoon that he wanted Captain Gibbs to sign a paper in Spanish, saying he would allow his soldiers to stay there and keep everybody but our parties off, and feed them, while he was gone down to Laguayra, and see what his government wanted to be done, and what the United States had agreed to about the island. Captain Gibbs refused for several hours; said he did not read Spanish, and he would not sign anything; and that unless the United States had agreed to give up the island, the Venezuelans had no right, and he would not acknowledge any, and he had no right to sign any paper, and it might commit him. Dias said over and over again that it did not acknowledge his claim, and that he did not want any such thing; and after talking smooth awhile, then he would blow and talk big, and then coax again; and he went round among all hands and seemed a good deal troubled, as if he had his hands full. Finally, towards night, Captain Gibbs, through his representations, signed his paper, and Lang also, and he then cleared out, leaving several of his soldiers there and one man who was an officer. We had to give these fellows victuals and clothes and drink and tobacco and cigars, and shelter to sleep on, for about two weeks, but they were all too lazy to work. I never saw such a gang of worthless human beings in the whole course of my life. When the second party came to the island, the fellows ashore undertook to salute them, and one of them got wounded in firing the cannon by his ignorance and awkwardness, and they took him away to St. Thomas for a doctor, and he died. They came back and landed more men late at night, on Christmas or the day after, and stationed their soldiers, with loaded muskets and fixed bayonets, all around, and pretty soon announced that they took possession, and that we should not take any more guano, and must go off the next day. They said we should not hoist our flag any more. Their sentinels were kept stationed around our stores, and at the pits, and on the wharves, and at the flag-staff, all night, and kept there till morning, and till we went away. They helped themselves to all they wanted. In the morning Captain Gibbs did hoist our flag, in spite of the sentinel at the liberty-pole, and hailed the vessels to send their crews ashore. Our party wanted to lick the vagabonds off the island and take the schooner. We could have tied the whole concern in fifteen minutes, and captured their vessels besides; but some of Lang's party were not disposed to go in for the fight, and Captain Gibbs said he did not know what the United States government might have done about the island; and it seemed that our minister must have known the vessels were coming down, and that it would be best, on the whole, not to have any bloodshed, but to make it necessary for the Venezuelans to show force and demonstrations, and then come home and report the facts to the President, and see if he would let our country be run over and cowed down, and such a set rob American property with impunity. We never saw any United States ship-of-war down there, but several of other nations. I think there ought to be some men-of-war cruising about to protect our citizens, and that somebody is to blame that it is not done. Our country is not considered to be of much account in the way of protecting our commerce, as well as I could learn.

The French and English, Dutch and Danish men-of-war people, when they came there, inquired where our men-of-war all were? I felt mighty mean when I saw the stars and stripes hauled down, and the Venezuelan rag hoisted in its place. Captain Gibbs came away in a few hours. He was not allowed, unless he chose to make fight, to take off but very little of the provisions and other things. He left two launches or boats, most all of the implements, and tools, and barrows, and nearly all the provisions, I should say; he left seven or eight thousand dollars' worth, at least, of property, besides the wharves and houses and sheds. What he did bring away was not of much use or value, except the cannon and small-arms, for the Venezuelans kept most of the provisions for themselves to eat. They kept the chief of our water casks. I came off on the Amazon, and went to Holmes' Hole, and got there 28th of January, 1855; and my passage was settled by claimants. The Amazon had about 490 tons of guano on board. The Viator had but part of a cargo, and the Mary Pearce was not allowed to take any. Captain Gibbs got everything he could get away, or was allowed to. He says he feels bound and desirous, as a citizen of the United States, to express his sentiments about these transactions. The island, if well managed, could have been made to yield more than two millions of dollars, and the Venezuelans, in my opinion, had no more right to take it from us than they had to take a ship on the high seas. He says he don't know how this insult may be plastered up; but he considers it a most rascally affair, and if the government don't make the mulatto vagabonds pay for this piratical act, and all damages, and give up the island, they might as well quit trying to be a government. He says he looks at it as worse than the Black Warrior case, or the Greytown case, or any other case that he has heard of, except the late massacres at Panama and Virgin bay; and that he should not wonder if those who perpetrated them, (for they are the same breed of people,) were encouraged to the act by having heard that the United States had not done anything in this case, and that it was safe to impose on a Yankee. He says he has insisted on putting in this expression of his opinions, so that they be wrote down in the records.

JOHN McCABE.

Mr. Sanford to Mr. Marcy.

DERBY, CONNECTICUT, *July* 3, 1856.

SIR: Messrs. Lang & Delano, of Boston, have preferred to the department certain claims for indemnity, &c., &c., on account of the outrage and spoliation in December, 1854, by Venezuela, at Shelton's Isle, and for rights to said isle and the guano thereon. Captain James

Wheeler has also preferred his claims in the deposition I transmitted to the department on the 9th of May last. Wheelwright & Cobb have also preferred claims to the department based on said spoliations. I regard this last as connected with those of Lang & Delano and Wheeler, and in fact derived from and founded thereon, and that they are all one and the same. P. S. Shelton and Sampson & Tappan's claims, represented by me, are not in anywise connected with the others, and my principals do not recognize the others alluded to in the correspondence between the department and myself. Nevertheless, neither my principals nor myself feel it to be a duty to intermeddle in the other claims in any degree, except so far as to see that they do not in anywise compromise or affect injuriously the rights we conceive belong to us. We have reason to believe that the other claims may affect us in that way, unless we take steps in time to prevent such result. In this view of the case it is highly important to Mr. Shelton and Sampson & Tappan, that the letter of Lang & Delano to the Hon. Mr. Cushing, Attorney General of the United States, dated August 29, 1854, and in reply to which your official letter to them ot 12th September, 1854, was written, should be preserved to be used by us as testimony in said case, and especially is it important to Captain James Wheeler that it should be so used. He is referred to in it as "the agent" of Lang & Delano. You will see the importance of this letter by referring to Captain Wheeler's short affidavit, dated June 8, 1855, and that of June 15, 1855, filed in the department in the month of June, 1855. I was not enabled when last in Washington to ascertain whether the original or a copy of the letter of Lang & Delano to Mr. Cushing was on the files of the State Department.

To show further the pertinency of that letter and its impertinence in connection with Captain Wheeler's three affidavits, I have now the honor, at the request of the assignees of Captain Wheeler, who have received from him an irrevocable power of attorney to their use of said contract, and of all his rights under it, and of all the claim he asserts to Shelton's Isle, to inclose a copy of the original contract between Captain Wheeler and Lang & Delano. The assignees will forward the letter of attorney and assignment hereafter. You will perceive that, of course, Captain Wheeler's assignees will be entitled to receive a moiety of whatever Lang & Delano, or those who are connected with them, may receive on account of the guano, or of the island, or of the profits they would have made. It may be observed that the agreement inclosed makes no reference to Aves or Shelton's Isle, which it appears by your letter to Lang & Delano of September 12, 1856, they claim to have discovered by their agent, referred to in their letter to the Attorney General of the 29th August. In Lang & Delano's letter to you, dated January 15, 1855, they state that they had the pleasure to address you in September, and to which they received an answer September 12th. I presume this is an error on their part, and that they mean to refer to their letter to the Attorney General, to which you replied September 12th, as I understand there is no letter of that kind from them to you on file.

May I ask for a copy of the letter of Lang & Delano to the Attorney General, as above specified.

I presume copies of the depositions of Captain James Wheeler, Richard Thornell, and John McCabe, heretofore transmitted to the department, have been sent by it to the United States minister at Caraccas.

I have the honor to be, very respectfully, your obedient servant,

H. S. SANFORD.

Hon. WILLIAM L. MARCY,
Secretary of State, &c.

Agreement made and concluded upon this 20th day of June, A. D. 1854, *by and between James Wheeler, master mariner, of Boston, Massachusetts, of the first part, and John W. B. Lang and William W. Delano, carpenters, under the firm of Lang & Delano, both of Boston, State of Massachusetts, of the second part.*

The above parties agree to fit out vessels as may be required for such time as is hereinafter specified, for the purpose of procuring guano. It is agreed that the party of the first part and the party of second part shall have and divide equally in whatever profit or loss may accrue from chartering and freighting vessels and all expenses connected therewith, and from the sale of guano.

The said party of the first part to have charge of loading all vessels at guano islands, and to aid in procuring vessels when in the United States. The said party of the second part to have the consignment, sale, or disposal of all the guano or other merchandise shipped and receive proceeds of same.

It is understood the party of the second part shall settle, so far as they can with the party of the first part, semi-annually, or at such time after as may be practicable.

It is understood, if the parties of the second part think it for the mutual benefit of all concerned, to purchase any vessel or vessels during the absence of the party of the first part from the United States, they are at liberty to do so, said vessels to be owned in common—by the party of the first part one half, and by the party of the second part one half.

It is also understood and agreed that should the party of the second part be in need of any funds or moneys (during the absence of the party of the first part) for any purpose whatever, they are authorized by this agreement to value on Phineas Coleman, and he is hereby empowered to advance them on account of the party of the first part such sum or sums as they may require, not exceeding ——— thousand dollars.

The agreement to continue in force for the term of — years.

Witness our hands, this 21st day of June, 1856.

LANG & DELANO.
JAMES WHEELER.

[NOTE.—The blanks are unimportant. The context shows the sum was over one thousand dollars and the term over one year.]

Mr. Marcy to Mr. Sanford.

DEPARTMENT OF STATE,
Washington, July 7, 1856.

SIR: I have to acknowledge the recept of your letter of the 30th ultimo, transmitting an authenticated copy of the deposition of John McCabe in relation to the claim of Shelton and others against the government of Venezuela.

I am, &c.,

W. L. MARCY.

HENRY S. SANFORD, Esq.,
Derby, Connecticut.

Mr. Thomas to Mr. Sanford.

DEPARTMENT OF STATE,
Washington, July 8, 1856.

SIR: Your letter of the 3d instant is received, and, in compliance with your request, I inclose herewith a copy of the letter of Lang & Delano to the Attorney General of the 29th August, 1855, and which was referred to this department, and is here filed in original.

In reply to your inquiry whether the depositions of Captain Wheeler, Richard Thornell, and John McCabe have been forwarded to Caraccas, I have to acquaint you that a copy of your letter of the 24th June, 1855, and of the accompaniments, among which were Captain Wheeler's depositions of the 8th and 15th June, 1855, was sent to Mr. Eames on the 20th December, 1855.

It is not convenient to discover with certainty whether, among the many documents forwarded from time to time, the deposition of Thornell has been included; and with reference to that of McCabe, received a day or two ago, I have to state that, inasmuch as the department expects to learn, by the first arrivals from Caraccas, something definite of the views and intentions of the Venezuelan government in the matter under consideration, it is deemed inexpedient to cumulate further testimony until it is known upon what points the government of Venezuela fail to acknowledge the sufficiency of the evidence already presented.

If, however, as the representative of Mr. Shelton, and those more immediately connected with him in his claim, you do not acknowledge the propriety of this reserve, the deposition of McCabe will be forwarded to Venezuela, and, if it be in your power to refer to the letter with which Richard Thornell's statement was inclosed to the department, a copy of that also will be sent to Mr. Eames.

I am, sir, &c.,

J. A. THOMAS,
Assistant Secretary.

HENRY S. SANFORD, Esq.,
Derby, Connecticut.

Mr. Sanford to Mr. Thomas.

DERBY, CONNECTICUT,
July 11, 1856.

SIR: Your letter of the 8th instant has been received, and at same time one from Mr. Marcy of the 7th instant, acknowledging the receipt of what he erroneously calls "an authenticated copy" of the deposition of Mr. John McCabe. It is an original, not a copy, though I inclosed a copy with it, leaving the certificate to be added to it. Another manuscript original was first made and sworn to by Mr. McCabe, but that sent, it will be seen upon an examination of the notary's certificate at the conclusion of the printed one, was again sworn to, and at another date, and again signed by the witness, and is, therefore, equally an original with the first manuscript. I refer to this to prevent mistake hereafter.

You will find, upon an examination of my letter of the 8th instant, that my inquiry there made was not respecting the transmission to our minister at Caraccas of the deposition of Captain Wheeler of the 8th and 15th June, 1855, which, as I was apprized on the 24th of March last, had been sent to Mr. Eames in December, 1855; but my inquiry was whether the third and last full and detailed deposition of Captain Wheeler, transmitted by me to the department on the 9th of May, 1856, and that of Richard Thornell, transmitted by me on the 10th of May, 1856, and the receipt of both which was acknowledged by the department in its letters to me of the 16th of May, 1856, had been sent to Mr. Eames. Both these depositions are in manuscript, and are full, and are deemed important. If mislaid or lost, on advice thereof I will supply the loss by new ones. Unauthenticated copies are filed with the committees of both houses of Congress having charge of Mr. Shelton's memorial there.

As these depositions, and also Mr. McCabe's, are deemed of consequence, I should, as the attorney of Mr. Shelton, and of Sampson & Tappan, certainly prefer that the United States minister at Caraccas should have copies of them sent to him at the earliest possible period. Such great delay has already occurred in the procurement of any satisfaction for this outrage, that the claimants almost despair of getting anything.

In the procurement of proofs in this case, I have been obliged to act on my own judgment as to what might possibly be required. In answer to my inquiry of the 8th of last March as to "what proof the department would deem requisite and sufficient," or rather, as to *what points* the department desired testimony, I was, on the 24th of the same month, told in reply that "it is not the province of the department to designate the nature of the evidence by which the claimants should substantiate their claims. It is to be presumed, of course, that the same care will be taken to obtain the most positive proof of which the case is susceptible, as though the claims were to be subjected to the scrutiny of a court of justice."

I presume from the remark in your letter of the 8th instant, "it is deemed inexpedient to cumulate further testimony," &c., that the department is satisfied that I have already furnished more than sufficient on all the points involved. I feel happy that I am relieved from the task of procuring any additional proofs, though if I err in my construction of your remark and am so advised, and that the department desires further proofs on any point, I will cheerfully furnish it if the suggestion is made before the witnesses are scattered.

I inclose another printed copy of Mr. McCabes deposition, to which the certificate is not appended.

I am much obliged for the copy of the very extraordinary letter of Lang & Delano upon the subject of Lang & Delano's claim, (of the the contents of which I had been previously advised otherwise.) So far as it interferes with that of my clients, I may address the department fully later.

You did not notice the receipt of the copy of Captain Wheeler's contract with Lang & Delano: as it was attached to my letter I presume you did not overlook it.

I have the honor to be, very respectfully, your obedient servant,

H. S. SANFORD.

Hon. J. A. THOMAS,
Assistant Secretary of State.

Mr. Sanford to Mr. Marcy.

DERBY, CONNECTICUT, *July* 15, 1856.

SIR: Information received from my clients in the Shelton's Isle case (P. S. Shelton and Sampson & Tappan, of Boston) induces me to fulfill what I consider to be a bounden duty, viz: to request that their claim should not in any manner or form be connected with that of Lang & Delano, or any other persons who have preferred claims relating to that isle.

In a letter dated 14th January last, you were advised of the wish that these claims should be kept disconnected, and we then refused to have any concern with the others. We trust that the depositions and proofs we have procured and filed will not be allowed to be used by the other parties to supply their own negligence or inability to get proofs; and above all, we trust that our business will in no respect be mingled or mixed up with the others.

These claims are separate and distinct, and in some respects are adverse to each other. At a proper time, when our interests more than now may demand such a course, we may furnish some testimony as to some of the other claims, showing the propriety of our urging the right of having ours kept distinct from all others. We know it is just, honest, and reasonable, and desire it considered by itself, and not contaminated or prejudiced by others.

I may state as one reason for this course, that it is our determination, if Venezuela does not, between this and the next session of Congress, make proper reparation for the outrage committed upon our property in December, 1854, to seek the power of obtaining redress from Congress. Of the particulars of our injuries, the department was furnished a detailed statement January 15, 1856, and which we have understood the department presented to the Venezuelan government, amounting to $341,000. On the first day of next session, if the department does not advise to the contrary, we intend to solicit from Congress to grant us letters of reprisal under the law of nations, to enable us to obtain that justice Venezuela denies us.

If the department desires a reference to the authorities on this subject, it will be cheerfully furnished in full. There can be no doubt of the remedy, and as a "peaceful remedy."

We have not learned that anything having the appearance of an intention to do justice is manifested by Venezuela, and feel that the continued delay is inexcusable. She continues skinning the isle of the guano.

Very respectfully, your obedient servant,

H. S. SANFORD.

Hon. WILLIAM L. MARCY,
Secretary of State, &c.

P. S.—I would respectfully ask that a copy of this letter be transmitted to Mr. Eames, to be shown to the Venezuelan government.

H. S. S.

Mr. Marcy to Mr. Sanford.

DEPARTMENT OF STATE,
Washington, July 21, 1856.

SIR: The urgency of other important business requiring the attention of the department, has prevented an earlier acknowledgment of the receipt of your letter of the 11th instant to the Assistant Secretary, and of the 15th to myself.

In compliance with the request made in the former letter, the depositions of Captain Wheeler, of John McCabe, and of Richard Thornell, will be transmitted to Mr. Eames so soon as it is practicable to make copies of Wheeler's and Thornell's, which, as you are aware, are somewhat voluminous.

In relation to the sufficiency of these proofs, with those formerly transmitted, to sustain Mr. Shelton's claim against the Venezuelan government, I deem it proper to correct the error into which you appear to have fallen in your letter of the 11th, wherein you state that you "presume from the remark in your [the Assistant Secretary's] letter of the 8th instant, 'it is deemed inexpedient to cumulate further testimony,' &c., that the Department is satisfied that I have already furnished more than sufficient on all the points involved;" and you express your happiness that you are relieved from the task of procuring any additional proofs. Were your quotation from that letter precisely correct, your felicitations would not be unfounded. Quoting probably from memory, you have failed to appreciate the spirit of the suggestion offered in the letter of the department of the 11th instant. Therein it was stated that "it is deemed inexpedient to cumulate further testimony until it is known upon what points the government of Venezuela fail to acknowledge the sufficiency of the evidence already presented." This sentence cannot be construed to express either an admission or denial on the part of this office of the sufficiency of your proofs, but had reference solely to the view which might be taken of the case by Venezuela, and as no decisive result had been attained by Mr. Eames in his representations of Mr. Shelton's claim, and especially as the department was in daily expectation of receiving dispatches from him containing the exposition of the views of Venezuela, it was thought that no practical good could be accomplished by forwarding additional evidence until it was seen upon what points it was necessary.

A copy of your letter of the 15th will be transmitted to Mr. Eames with the other papers.

I am, sir, &c.,

W. L. MARCY.

HENRY S. SANFORD, Esq.,
Derby, Connecticut.

Messrs. Sampson & Tappan and Shelton to Mr. Marcy.

BOSTON, *July* 21, 1856.

SIR: We are in a measure unadvised whether the Venezuelan government have indicated any disposition as yet to do us justice for the Shelton's Isle outrage, committed more than a year and a half since.

Our counsel, H. S. Sanford, Esq., has advised us of all that has taken place, except that he has informed us that the department decline, under its rules, to allow copies of the correspondence between the department and the United States minister, and that of the latter with the Dutch government, to be furnished, and that he has little information on the subject.

He informs us, however, that a letter from General Thomas, Assistant Secretary of State, to him, of the 8th instant, informs him you expect dispatches by the next vessel from Laguayra. We trust on the receipt of them you will advise Mr. Sanford forthwith.

Our extreme anxiety on this subject is caused by its importance to us and the long delay that has ensued.

We do hope that if delayed any longer our government will allow a resort to us, under the law of nations, and under the treaty with Venezuela, to letters of reprisals, which eminent counsel say are resorted to by other nations, and which it is said are not war nor any just cause for war. We have written Mr. Sanford to-day to address you on this past point. We supposed that he had made it a point in our memorial to Congress presented by him, but learn from him that he did not. We have advised him of this letter. We have heretofore refrained from saying but very little to the department respecting the claim of Lang & Delano from motives of delicacy, and because it might appear invidious. It is, however, due to ourselves to say that we have never had any concern in it, and have always repudiated it as unjust towards us. They have no claim as discoverers whatever. They pretend that they had a vessel in the Caribbean sea in 1853, the master of which saw the island and landed on it. This is utterly incorrect, and they will not venture to name the vessel or the master, and if the department should require them to do so they will evade it. We trust the department will call for such specification at least, if not for proof. They say, also, that they subsequently sent a vessel to hunt for that island, but got no guano, and the pretended excuse is, that the master they then sent was probably unacquainted with the article. They do not say that he found this island he was sent to find, and though the excuse, as the probable one, (not finding the guano,) would seem to imply that he did find that island. The island that he did find, therefore, if he found any, was not Shelton's Isle, for he could not mistake as to the guano there. They then say that in June, 1854, they sent a vessel first to Aves Isle (though they give the latitude and longitude wrong) with C. Lang, agent, who there found guano. This it seems, is their first pretended discovery distinctly alleged. And they next say their instruction to their agent was, if they found the article of Mexican guano to remain on the island and to take possession, &c. And they say further, they were at considerable expense to find and to get possession of the isle, &c.

Now, sir, we call your attention to the three affidavits of Captain Wheeler, of June 8, 1854, January 15, 1855, and of 6th of May, 1856, on file in your department. Captain Wheeler was Lang & Delano's sole agent. Mr. Sanford has advised us that he has forwarded to you a copy of their correspondence with Wheeler dated June 21, 1854, which the assignees of Wheeler allowed him to do. This fully proves that the alleged agency in June, 1854, of Charles H. Lang, was set up to cut Wheeler, whose name is suppressed throughout by them, of all his claims, if he had any under his agreement; and Captain Wheeler's affidavit of the 15th June, 1855, shows how and by what means Lang & Delano obtained their first knowledge of Shelton's Isle, and confutes all their long rigmarole subsequently made to the State Department completely. These papers show that they first sought a surreptitious advantage of P. S. Shelton and Captain N. P. Gibbs, and next sought to take a like advantage of Captain Wheeler, and actually claimed to be the first discoverers themselves and undermine all the others. Captain Gibb's affidavit, and Captain Wheeler's, show conclusively who were the discoverers of the guano. We do not conceive that their statement of there being only 50,000 tons of guano on the island is at all important. It cannot surely prejudice us or militate against us. It shows they know nothing of the facts, and their claim or statement of damages since filed shows how unguarded they are, for it is impossible to reconcile them. We have been disposed not to interfere with respect to the just demand that Lang & Delano may have for actual false freights, if any, and for pay for their wharf and property on the island taken from them, but this, even, is all founded on the permission of our agent, Captain Gibbs, in July, 1854, as alleged in his and Wheeler's affidavits, and also to Captain Wheeler to occupy part of the island; but we protest that they are not entitled to claim any share of the guano otherwise. We deem it our duty to protest against their claim; and so far as it may in any wise affect ours, and before it is passed upon, we shall claim the privilege of furnishing testimony in this regard.

To satisfy you how little this particular statement of the quantity by them can injure us, we offered, and yet offer, if paid for one half of 50,000 tons—say 25,000 tons at $12 50 per ton, and $28,500 for our property and damages, to waive our right to all the rest of the guano and the isle. But if Lang and Delano's claim is sustained to the guano it decreases our prospect of getting paid by Venezuela, and we conceive it to be our duty to protect ourselves against any unjust pretensions, which may be used to contaminate ours and to give an improper coloring and character to what we know is honest and just. Against this being done we respectfully but earnestly remonstrate. A reply to this addressed to Mr. Sanford, Derby, Connecticut, will reach us, as we have advised him hereof.

We are, sir, very respectfully, your obedient servants,

SAMPSON & TAPPAN.
PHILO S. SHELTON.

Hon. W. L. MARCY,
Secretary of State.

P. S. We are informed that up to this hour Lang & Delano have not filed a single deposition, or affidavit, or other proof of any kind or character in reference to their alleged discovery, or in verification of their statements in reference thereto. We trust they will be admonished to adduce it; our just interests and rights authorize us to make such request.

S. & T.
P. S. S.

Mr. Sanford to Mr. Marcy.

WASHINGTON, *August* 11, 1856.

SIR: I have the honor to inclose herewith the deposition of Joseph Herbert, to be filed in the department in the Shelton's Isle case, and copy of which it is desired may be forwarded to Mr. Eames.

In a few days other depositions will be forwarded. As I presume, from the intimation conveyed in your letter to me of the 17th ultimo that the department is not yet satisfied with the testimony that has been adduced by the claimants, I should be gratified to learn upon what points further the department would desire testimony. I hope I may be advised as to objections made by Venezuela.

Very respectfully, your obedient servant,

H. S. SANFORD.

Hon. WILLIAM L. MARCY,
Secretary of State.

STATE OF NEW YORK,
County and City of New York, } *ss:*

I, Joseph Herbert, being sworn to testify the truth, the whole truth, and nothing but the truth in relation to the claim before the State

Department of the United States, in which Philo S. Shelton and Sampson & Tappan are claimants against the republic of Venezuela, do depose that I reside in Brooklyn, in said State, am of lawful age, and by occupation I am a gunsmith; that I went to Shelton's Isle or Aves Island with Captain N. P. Gibbs, in the brigantine John R. Dow, from Boston, in July, 1854; that I staid at said island till Christmas of the same year, when the Venezuelans forced us away; that I think there was perhaps 200,000 tons of guano there; about one quarter of it could not be called the best quality. Captain Gibbs and Captain Wheeler staked off the island between them, and on Captain Gibbs's part I should say there was 75,000 tons of pretty good guano, worth twelve or fifteen dollars a ton to us, as we had everything ready for loading it to any vessels that might come there. I understood freight was from six to eight dollars a ton to the United States. We gathered from July till we went away, after we got our wharf, houses, and other things prepared. I cannot make an estimate of the cost of the wharf and other structures we built there, but I have read Captain Gibbs's, Captain Wheeler's, Richard Thornell's, and John McCabe's depositions, and don't think any of them state their cost too high; and I agree with them as to their description of the property there, and also as to that left when we were driven off, and that we brought away. I came home in the bark Amazon with the other hands. Captain Gibbs took possession of the isle when we landed in July, as he stated, in the name of the United States, and hoisted the United States flag and fired a salute. He said he claimed to be the discoverer of the guano on it when out on a voyage of discovery the April before, when Captain Wheeler was with him as his mate, both being in the John R. Dow, in the employ of Mr. Shelton. Captain Wheeler went out in July in the M. H. Comeroy for a Mr. Lang, and he and Captain Gibbs disputed about his right to go on the isle and take guano for Mr. Lang, but finally Captain Gibbs, rather than have a row, staked off to Wheeler about half the island. Wheeler built some structures and a wharf, but they were not as good or as costly as those put by Captain Gibbs. Captain Dias, who said he belonged to the Venezuelan navy, came down to the isle in an armed schooner some time near the middle of December, and, with our aid, landed himself and some men. He said he came there to take charge of the isle for his government, and that the United States had consented they should have it. He wanted at first to drive us all off at once, but he found that would not do, and then he got Captain Gibbs and Charles Lang to agree to let some of his soldiers stay there a few days, and to feed them while he went home for further orders, and he promised, if they would do so, he would give a paper ordering any other Venezuelan vessel that might come there while he was away not to disturb us. He did give, I understood, a paper in Spanish; and I heard also that Captain Gibbs and C. Lang gave a receipt for it or something of the kind; and I have also heard that it turned out to be a different paper from what we all understood it was at the time. Captain Gibbs refused to sign anything for a long time, and Dias blustered and coaxed and promised nearly half a day to get it done. He said it was no acknowledgment of the title of anybody, and he didn't want any. He threatened if it was not signed as soon as the steamer of war came down that he expected, that he would send us away by force. After he got the paper signed he went away, and about ten or twelve days afterwards another Venezuelan man-of-war schooner came there, landed more men, and finally forced us off, unless we fought them. Captain Gibbs and his party were disposed to resist, but Lang's folks held back. We could have licked the whole Venezuelan gang and took their vessel very easily, but Captain Gibbs thought we might get into a scrape with our own government, which the Venezuelans said had given up the isle, and he therefore resolved on peace. They put sentries on our wharf, at the pits, and at our houses and stores, armed with muskets and bayonets. They tried to keep Captain Gibbs from hoisting the United States colors next morning, but he run them up in spite of their sentinel at the flagstaff. We kept them flying all the time we were on the isle from the first day we landed. When the Venezuelan schooner first came to the isle on the last visit the soldiers on the isle tried to salute her, and one of them got his arm blown off by his bungling, and she took him to St. Thomas to be doctored, and he died, as I understood. They took possession when the schooner returned from St. Thomas, having landed more men, armed, about 10 o'clock at night. We were visited by several men-of-war of other nations while at the isle, and no one disputed our right, and I have heard the men belonging to them admit it several times, and say we'd got a good prize. I don't think, from the appearance of the island when we first landed, that it had ever been occupied by anything but birds. There was no sign of man ever having lived there. We thought it very strange that no United States men-of-war during the five months and more we were there, and in which time there were so many American vessels there, did not visit us, and were not seen or heard of in those parts. This was one circumstance that made Captain Gibbs and all of us give some credit to what the Venezuelans said about our government having given up the isle. They said that a good many of the principal men of both countries were interested in a guano company that had been raised as a speculation, and that this was the reason the United States would'nt claim the island, and they said the American minister or consul at Caraccas was concerned, and a good many others, and they expected Mr. Shelton was also in the company. I think, after reading the other depositions above mentioned, that none of them estimated the losses and damages of Mr. Shelton and those concerned with him too high, nor do I think they value the guano on the isle too high. I was employed by Mr. Shelton; but I am not interested in any wise in this case or claim, except to see justice done, and to do what I can to aid. I consider the turning oft of Captain Gibbs and his party from the island as an infamous transaction, and that if satisfaction is not obtained from Venezuela for the insult, and she made to pay all damages and give up the isle, and pay for the guano she has stolen since she ejected us, every American citizen should hide his head in shame for the imbecility of his government. Such, I know, is the feelimg of all that were there, and I shall never feel content till I hear that right has been done. I think Mr. Shelton and those concerned with him must have lost more than forty thousand dollars by the dispossession of them from the isle by the Venezuelans, and by the latter taking their property, and this without including Lang's losses, and without including either the guano left on the isle, which was worth several hundred thousand dollars more; I should say, at least a million of dollars, which I believe Mr. Shelton and those connected with him could easily have made out of the guano, net profit, if they had not been molested by Venezuela.

JOSEPH HERBERT.

Subscribed and sworn to by said witness, before me August 6, 1856.

L. PITKIN,
Notary Public.

STATE OF NEW YORK,
City and County of New York, } *ss:*

Be it known that on this sixth day of August, anno Domini one thousand eight hundred and fifty-six, before me, the undersigned, a notary public of said city, county, and State, by lawful authority duly commissioned and sworn, and by law authorized to administer and certify oaths and affirmations, personally appeared Joseph Herbert, the deponent above named, of lawful age, who being by me duly sworn, on the Holy Evangelists of Almighty God, to testify to the truth, the whole truth, and nothing but the truth, as is stated in said deposition, and being by me cautioned as to his said oath, according to law, he informed me that he had had read to him and had also read said deposition, and the same was also again carefully read to him in my presence, whereupon he subscribed the same and deposed that the statements therein made, and all and singular the matters and things therein stated, were truly stated and not otherwise, according to the best of his belief, and he desired me to certify the same.

[SEAL.] Whereof I have hereunto set my hand and affixed my official seal, the day and year last aforesaid.

L. PITKIN,
Notary Public, New York.

No. 22.] *Mr. Eames to Mr. Marcy.*

LEGATION OF THE UNITED STATES,
Caraccas, October 9, 1856.

SIR: I have the honor to acknowledge the receipt of dispatches from the department to No. 36, inclusive.

In compliance with the suggestion made at the request of the Aves Island claimants, and contained in your No. 30, I now transmit, inclosed, a copy of the guano contract concluded between this government and Mr. J. F. D. Wallace, on the 21st of December, 1854. In looking over my dispatch, No. 10, under date of April 26, 1855, in which I gave the department an account of this contract, I perceive that it omits to state expressly the fact, at that time fresh in the recollection of the department, but which now appears proper to be mentioned, that the negotiation of this contract by Mr. Wallace took place during my absence from Caraccas on a short visit to the United States, by the permission of the President. Mr. Wallace arrived here after my departure and had left before my return. I heard nothing of the contract, and knew nothing of any negotiations upon the subject until February, 1855, when the existence of the contract was made known to me, and an abstract of its terms put into my hands by one of the merchants of this city, who, as stated in my No. 10, had previously purchased of this government the drafts drawn in its favor by Mr. Wallace.

I have not yet found an opportunity to make a successful application for the two other papers mentioned in your No. 30—the official report of Dias and and the protest of the British charge d'affaires. The report of Dias may, I think, be difficult to procure. The protest of the British chargé d'affaires may probably be obtained, but I do not think that the Aves claimants are right in supposing that they will derive any help from that document, because my recollection of it after hearing it read, is as stated in my No. 13 to the department, that it proceeded upon the idea that Venezuela being in full jurisdiction over all the guano islands, had opened them all, to all nations, by the resolution of July 26, 1855, (transmitted in my No. 12,) and was, therefore, by her own obligatory act, inhibited from in anywise recognizing or conceding any exclusive right of American citizens in any of the said islands. Certainly it is not easy to perceive how such a protest, based as it is upon an act of Venezuelan jurisdiction over all the islands, including the Aves—asserting as it does the obligation, and, of course, the validity of that act as against any exclusive American right or privilege in the islands—and claiming as it does under that act a common British usufruct in all the guano deposited, can strengthen the case of American citizens claiming indemnification on the ground of their exclusive right, as against Venezuela, to the guano on the Island of Aves. It was in conformity with this view, that while the British legation hereupon, at least, an implied recognition of Venezuelan title, and in avowed maintenance of British interests under Venezuelan jurisdiction over all the islands, was thus by protest opposing my efforts to save the rights of American citizens under the Wallace contract in the other guano islands except the Aves, in pursuance of your instructions, I, in the most express terms, as appears by my Nos. 13 and 20, and their inclosures, refused to sanction or countenance in any manner the insertion of the Aves in the contract with Mr. Pickerill, thus leaving to Venezuela no option but either to forbear from making that insertion, or else, if she persisted in that course, then to do the act of inserting the Aves as she had done the previous act of occupying it, at her proper peril, and in view of the announcement that all the rights and claims of its first American occupants were fully reserved and would be sustained.

To the view of the case in which, under your instructions, this action was taken by me in behalf of the claimants, the British protest appears wholly opposed. Still, as they ask your aid to obtain that paper as part of their case, I will endeavor to procure it if practicable, with the report, but I shall be careful in so doing in no way to accept or admit the idea in which it is written.

In urging the Aves claim to an adjustment by this government, composed as in great part of an estimated value of the guano deposit from which the claimants were ousted, I feel seriously the want of more proof of the value of that deposit. I have nothing of importance on this point but the estimate of Captain N. P. Gibbs, as given in his printed deposition transmitted with your No. 30. On the other hand, it is believed here that the guano taken from the Aves since the Venezuelan occupation amounts to not more than from 800 to 1,200 tons, not all of this quantity being very saleable; and it is known, or at least confidently asserted here, that the Aves have been for some time abandoned as valueless. I am not warranted by any facts in my possession in disputing this last assertion. I infer from the language of one of the inclosures in your No. 30, that the importance in this claim of clear proof as to the value of the Aves guano had not escaped the attention of the department, and had been by you suggested to the claimants. The facts of the case as they are alleged here to have since appeared, show that suggestion of the department to have been alike judicious and important. I hope the claimants will act upon it, and transmit to me, through the department, all the proofs on the point which it may be in their power to obtain.

I have the honor to be, with the highest respect, your obedient servant,

CHARLES EAMES.

CARACCAS, *December* 21, 1854.

Simon Planas, Secretary of State in the Department of the Interior of Justice and of Foreign Affairs, of the government of Venezuela, acting, on the one part, under the express authority of the Executive power and John D. F. Wallace, a resident of Philadelphia, in the State of Pennsylvania, on the other part have entered into the following contract, to wit:

Article first. The right is granted to John D. F. Wallace, to those with whom he now is or may hereafter be associated, and to their lawful successors, collectively and individually, for the period of fifteen years, to extract guano from the desert island called "Las Aves" and from any other islands belonging to the republic in which said article may be found.

Sec. 1. Should Venezuela, by any contingency or cause, happen to lose the right which she now holds over said island, it is understood that the fifteen years settled upon in this article shall be reduced to the time which will have elapsed between the date of this contract and the day when the loss of such right will have occurred; and in such an event, there shall be no ground for an indemnity, and upon a settlement of the account, the balance resulting therefrom shall be paid.

Sec. 2. Said island lies in latitude, north, 15° 45′, and longitude, west, 63° 35′, from the meridian of Greenwich.

Article second. Wallace shall pay to the government the price of four dollars, standard, for each ton which he may extract, all the expenses which may be incurred in the procurement of the guano, or from any other cause, being for his own account.

Article third. On account of what may accrue to the government in virtue of the foregoing article, Wallace shall draw bills of exchange, in its favor, on John Tucker, of Philadelphia, State of Pennsylvania, for the sum of two hundred thousand dollars, payable ninety days after sight.

Article fourth. The right, granted by article first, shall not be exercised so long as said bills will not have been fully satisfied, and should they unfortunately be either protested or unsatisfied, the present contract shall by that fact, and without any declaration to that effect be forfeited, and the government of Venezuela shall be paid for such damages as may have been suffered in consequence thereof.

Article fifth. The extracting of the forementioned guano having duly commenced, in consequence of compliance with the foregoing articles of contract, the government has the right of assigning such agents as it may deem expedient, to supervise operations for the purpose of ascertaining the number of tons, which the contractors may have taken out, in virtue of article first.

Article sixth. The contractors are bound to render a monthly account of the guano taken out to the agent, whom the government may appoint; and, upon calculation of the amount, accruing to the treasury of Venezuela, such amount shall be deducted from the two hundred thousand dollars advanced in virtue of article third, and when said sum will have been entirely redeemed, there shall be a monthly payment into the general treasury of the proceeds of the number of tons which may be taken out during the respective month; said payment to be made in actual money, or by bills of exchange on the United States of the North, at the option of the government.

Sec. 1. Upon failure of payment, for three months of the price of the tons of guano taken out; it is understood that the contract shall be forfeited, and that, in any event, all arrearages shall be satisfied.

Article seventh. For ampler proof of the quantity of the guano taken out, during each and every quarter, the contractors are bound to exhibit to the government the manifests of shipments, which may clearly establish the importations of guano into the ports of the United States or of Europe.

Sec. 1. The government is authorized at all times to adopt all such measures as are calculated to prevent the frauds which may be committed in the excavation of said guano.

Article eighth. In order to guard the islands, with a view of preventing the fraudulent taking out of the guano, the contractors shall be bound to keep up at least three armed vessels, of the larger size, at their own expense and with out any remuneration on the part of Venezuela.

Article nine. In case of a revolution in Venezuela, in which the government may determine to reinforce the national navy, said vessels which shall hoist the flag of Venezuela, shall, with their crews, armaments, and other appliances, be at the disposal of the government, to be employed by it, under the command of Venezuelan officers, for the whole period, during which such revolution may last, and without any indemnification of any kind.

Article ten. The vessels of the contractors in the event of actual injuries or from stress of weather, shall not be held to the payment of any harbor dues as required by law.

Article eleven. The doubts and controversies, which may arise as to the meaning of all or of any of the articles of this contract, shall be settled by arbitrating umpires and amicable adjusters, appointed, one by each of the parties, with a third one in case of a disagreement; the decision to be made in this capital, with an express renunciation, on the part of the contractors of the right of domicil, without any prejudice to any right whatsoever, which may be enforced against the contractors out of the territory.

Article twelve. To the fulfillment of this contract, all the contractors pledge their persons and their property, present and future.

Article thirteen. If, at the expiration of six months, reckoning from the payment of the forementioned bills of exchange, no beginning will have been made in the taking out of the guano; the present contract shall be null.

SIMON PLANAS.
JOHN. D. F. WALLACE.

Mr. Sanford to the President.

BREVOORT HOUSE, NEW YORK,
December 14, 1856.

SIR: You will pardon me for again calling the attention of the Executive to the case of the claim of Philo S. Shelton, and others, of Boston, against the Venezuelan government for an atrocious spoliation committed in December, 1854. It is yet unsettled, and the claimants are almost in despair of justice being obtained for them for a long time to come. The case has been fully made known to the Executive, and the documents and proofs showing its justice, are all on file in the State Department.

On the 18th of August last, the President approved an act entitled "an act to authorize protection to be given to citizens of the United States who may discover deposits of guano." Notice was given by Mr. Shelton long before the passage of the act, of the discovery by his agent for him, early in 1854, of Bird Island, or Shelton's Isle, in the Caribbean sea, and the deposits of guano thereon, verified by affidavit describing said Island, and the latitude and longitude thereof, and that possession was taken in the name of the United States, and that the same was not, at the time of the discovery thereof and of the taking possession and occupation thereof by claimants, in the possession or occupation of any other government, or of the citizens of any other government, according to the requirements of said act. All the papers and proofs have been for many months on file in the department.

The second section of said act requires a certain bond with securities to be given by claimants, and that the President shall designate the amount of the penalty. The claimants are ready to comply with that provision of the act in all things, if the case is one in which they should so proceed, and if such course will in nowise weaken or compromit their claim against Venezuela for the outrages for which they seek redress.

They therefore ask, if the Executive deems the case a proper one for such proceeding under the law cited, that they may be advised of the character, condition, and amount of the bond he will require, and if advised thereof, they will obey such requirement immediately.

I have addressed this letter to you, conceiving that under the law referred to, it is the proper course—the case being intrusted expressly to the discretion of the Executive.

I have the honor to be, with the highest respect, your obedient servant,

H. S. SANFORD,
For the claimants.

The PRESIDENT.

Mr. Sanford to Mr. Marcy.

BREVOORT HOUSE, NEW YORK,
December 16, 1856.

SIR: On the 14th instant I addressed a letter to the President, according to the act of 18th of August last, respecting discoveries of guano deposits, making application under said act in behalf of Philo S. Shelton and his associates, as discoverers of Shelton's Isle, for the benefit of said act, provided it nowise compromits their claim against Venezuela, now being prosecuted by the department.

It has been suggested to me that it is possible the reported claim of the Dutch government made to Venezuela for that island, may create an impediment to such application. Whether the ancient title of the Dutch government was well founded or not, they were not in possession of the island at the time of our discovery and occupation, and it was in fact derelict and abandoned. It is not seen, therefore, how their mere pretense of claim can be interposed to prevent our being entitled to the benefit of the law. You will notice that act expressly applies to discoveries made before the passage, as well as those made subsequent; the phraseology of the bill was so shaped at my express instance to include this very case, and, in truth, the provisions of the bill variant from that originally proposed, were suggested by myself, and were adopted with a view to this case. The debates in the Senate will show the express objects of the bill as I have stated them. The whole matter is, however, in the discretion of the President, to whom, under the law, I have, therefore, directly submitted it.

It is certainly no defense for the spoliation of our personal property by Venezuela that the island belonged to the Dutch, or Danes, or any other nation. It is no defense for the tortious eviction. It would not be in the case of an individual trespass, either by the common law or civil law, to say the property taken from us belonged to a third party. It could not be given in evidence even to decrease damages against a *tort feasor* that the property despoiled from an actual possession belonged to a third person—a stranger—who had not given authority to wrest it from the possessors.

In the action of ejectment—a legal fiction—the existence of a legal outstanding title in a third person may be set up as a defense, but this only is a part of the formula of the action, part of the fiction created for convenience, and is not founded on any principle of law between nations; the admission of the doctrine that any one could become an Anacharsis Cloutz, would lead to infinite disputes and error.

I have the honor to be, very respectfully, your obedient servant,

H. S. SANFORD.

Hon. WILLIAM L. MARCY,
Secretary of State, &c.

Mr. Marcy to Mr. Sanford.

DEPARTMENT OF STATE,
Washington, December 23, 1856.

SIR: On the 28th April last this department, at your solicitation, addressed an intimation to Mr. Eames at Caraccas, requesting him to obtain, if practicable, copies of certain official papers which, it was believed, would be useful in the further prosecution of the Aves Island claim against Venezuela. Herewith you will find a copy of Mr. Eames's dispatch of the 9th October (received on the 28th November) in relation to that subject, and also a translation of the Wallace contract, accompanying that dispatch.

At the date of his last communication to this department, (1st November,) which has been received, Mr. Eames makes no acknowledgment of a dispatch which was addressed to him on the 14th August, in which he was instructed to "express the earnest wish of the government of the United States that the claim may be promptly adjusted," and with which were transmitted copies of your communications of the 9th and 10th May, 15th and 21st July, and of their respective accompaniments.

How far those accompaniments will supply the want which Mr. Eames feels "of more proof of the value of the guano deposit from which the claimants were ousted" it is for them rather than for this department to determine. Captain Wheeler's deposition, transmitted with your letter of the 9th May, estimates the quantity of first class guano on the island when it was taken possession of in 1854 at more than 100,000 tons. Mr. Eames, on the other hand, states that it is believed in Venezuela "that the guano taken from the Aves since the Venezuelan occupation amounts to not more than from 800 to 1,200 tons, not all of this quantity being very saleable." And he further states that it is confidently asserted that the Aves have been for some time abandoned as valueless. This could hardly be the case if Captain Wheeler's estimate were an approximation to the truth. If, as the attorney of the claimants, you are not satisfied that the issue should rest upon Captain Wheeler's deposition as to the quantity of first rate guano, it would be advisable to present such further testimony upon this point as may be accessible to you.

Is is to be regretted that this department is ignorant of the position which the Venezuelan government assumed after Mr. Eames had received my communication of the 14th August, already adverted to, and had presented to that government the views therein expressed. So long ago as the 15th March last our minister in Venezuela expressed the hope of soon being able to submit to this department a proposition for the adjustment of the claim. No such proposition, however, has yet been received from him. It is possible that the accompaniments to my dispatch of the 14th August may have facilitated the adoption of some basis of settlement.

Wishing, as well for the sake of the claimants as for other obvious reasons, to promote the early adjustment of this question, the department would prefer to pursue such a course as would commend itself to the cordial satisfaction of the parties interested. If they are content to await the possible results of the last instructions to Mr. Eames upon the subject, no further measures will be immediately undertaken. If, however, they doubt the sufficiency of the proceedings instituted by the department, and think that their interests would be promoted by the presence at Caraccas of an agent of their own selection, it is not doubted that such a representative might, concurrently with the minister of the United States, do much to effect a more speedy adjustment of their claim.

If this view of the case should be acceptable to them, the department will extend the same facilities to such an agent as were afforded to the private agent of the Philadelphia Guano Company, whose visit to Caraccas under an introduction and with dispatches from this department were not unproductive of its advantages to the party represented by him.

I am, &c.,

W. L. MARCY.

HENRY S. SANFORD, Esq.,
Attorney of Philo S. Shelton, Brevoort House, N. Y.

Mr. Sanford to Mr. Marcy.

BREVOORT HOUSE, NEW YORK,
December 27, 1856.

SIR: I have received but this morning, on my return here from Connecticut, your letter of the 23d instant, with its inclosures, to wit:

a dispatch from Mr. Eames, dated October 9, and a translation of the Wallace contract.

It seems to me strange that neither in that dispatch nor in his last, dated November 1, nor since, has he acknowledged the receipt of the depositions of John McCabe, Richard Thornell, and James Wheeler, nor of the report of Commander de Horsey, transmitted to him by the department some months prior to October, and has made no acknowledgment of the dispatch addressed to him on the 14th August, expressing the earnest wish of the government of the United States that the claim of Mr. Shelton might be promptly adjusted. I trust a satisfactory reason for this can be given.

On the 11th July last, I addressed a letter to the department in relation to those proofs, in answer to a communication from the department of the 8th of that month, saying "it is deemed inexpedient to cumulate further testimony until it is known upon what points the government of Venezuela fail to acknowledge the sufficiency of the evidence already presented;" and the department also, in reply, on the 21st of July, to my letters of the 15th and 11th of the same month, correcting a misapprehension by me of the citation above quoted, says, "it was thought that no practical good could be accomplished by providing additional evidence, until it was seen upon what points it was necessary." In consequence thereof no additional proof has been taken, and we have been anxiously awaiting the expected dispatch from Mr. Eames "containing the exposition of the views of Venezuela," which, I am informed, has not yet been received by the department. I confess I am at a loss what course to pursue. I am not advised authentically, or in any manner, upon what ground Venezuela justifies or excuses her outrage upon and spoilation of our property. I am not told upon what ground she now claims title to the island, or whether she still insists the Dias expulsion of Mr. Shelton's agent and workmen was a lawful act or not. I am not advised of the ground she assumes in relation to the paper called the Dias capitulation; whether she persists in giving it force, or abandons it, nor if any additional proof is required of its being void on account of coercion, fraud, &c., and absence of authority to make it. On all this I am in the dark. Our witnesses are seamen, masters and crews of different vessels, and, it may be presumed, scattered.

All we learn up to the 9th October is, that he is without proof, except Captain Gibbs's deposition, of the value of the guano. If it is possible that the other proofs above mentioned were not received by him from the department, I trust the department will ascertain the fact and remedy the accident.

Reflection upon the whole subject, and especially as the department declines giving any opinion upon the efficiency of the proof as to any point in the case, has satisfied me that the proper course for the claimant will be to procure such additional proofs, if the witnesses can be obtained, and even testimony to rebut the reports and rumors Mr. Eames says are current at Caraccas, and which he says he was not warranted by any facts in his possession from disputing, and the difficulty in regard to which he felt so "seriously." I am more satisfied of the correctness of this course, when I notice that the suggestions of the department to the claimant, made on the 25th April, 1856, in relation to the proofs are approved of by Mr. Eames as "alike judicious and important."

In the meantime, however, I trust that the department will, by such dispatch as it may deem proper, stimulate Mr. Eames to some exertion to procure some answer from Venezuela upon some points, and, by distinct instructions, direct him to present all the proofs in his possession provided by us, and we will not put him to the trouble of argument or comment upon them. All that we wish from him is, to lay before the Venezuelan government the documents sent by the department, and we do not desire his doing any more than this, and insisting upon an answer from the Venezuelan government with reasonable diligence, with such reiterated presentation of our claim, and demand for justice, and protest against any extension of the delay of two years that has already ensued.

With reference to this dispatch, I purpose hereafter to transmit to the department some observations that I think it calls for, for I assure you it has given me pain and mortification. I consider the documents that he has not procured, and upon which he comments at large to show their immateriality instead of getting them, as of importance, and I hope they will be procured. I allude to the British protest, and to the resolutions of Venezuela of May 21, 1855, and July 22, 1855. The Dias report is obviously of the highest consequence, and if a formal "demand of justice" was made under the third section of the thirty-fourth article of our treaty with Venezuela of 1836, (p. 432, 8 vol. Stat. at Large,) being the "statement of the injuries and damages (we sustained) verified by competent proofs," it would place the affair in a tangible shape, and Venezuela would then have to refuse or act justly. She has already "unreasonably delayed," and, I trust, in such demand this unreasonable delay will be adverted to in unequivocal terms.

In regard to your suggestion in respect to the appointment of an agent by Mr. Shelton, I would respectfully enquire whether it is practicable to dispatch such agent in a public vessel to Laguayra, to await some ten days his return, and the character of the instructions he would bear with him; because if not in their nature decisive, it is not anticipated that the expense and trouble incurred would be worth the result effected.

We do not wish that any action by the department should be delayed or pretermitted in anticipation of the appointment of such agent, for, before decision can be made on that point, the claimants have to be consulted with, after hearing from the department in answer to the above inquiry.

I have received nothing in reference to the letter, of which I advised the department on the 8th instant, I had addressed to the President.

I have the honor to be, with great respect, your most obedient servant,

H. S. SANFORD.

Hon. WILLIAM L. MARCY.

Mr. Eames to Mr. Marcy.

No. 30.] LEGATION OF THE UNITED STATES,
Caraccas, January 7, 1857.

SIR: With reference to my No. 22 to the department under date of 9th October last, and to your Nos. 22, 27, and 30, which are the last dispatches received by me from the department, relative to the "Aves" claim, I have the honor to transmit, inclosed, a note addressed by me, under date of 20th ultimo, to the Minister of Foreign Relations of this government, in which I have continued to urge strongly upon his attention the importance of a prompt and satisfactory adjustment of that claim.

There are expressions in some of the papers presenting the case to the department which would seem to indicate that the claimants, or some of them, have not been entirely free from doubt as to the extent in which that part of their claim which demands indemnification for the loss of their profits from the guano remaining on the "Aves" at the time of their eviction, could, as an estimate of future and contingent profits, be properly sustained. But in view of all your instructions, and especially of your Nos. 22 and 27, I have felt myself fully authorized to insist strongly upon this branch of the claim without discussing the question whether it stands in its nature precisely upon the same footing, in all respects, with the demand for indemnification of the immediate and positive losses and expenses brought upon the claimants by their summary expulsion and the sudden breaking up of their business. I have pressed this demand of indemnification for the loss of probable profits with the more confidence and vigor, because, as stated in my No. 10, under date of 25th April, 1855, I have from the first maintained before this government, that the pretense of title in Venezuela to the "Aves," prior to her occupation of it, has not sufficient foundation to justify discussion; and because, moreover, by a whole series of consistent administrative acts, commencing at the time of the Venezuelan occupation of the "Aves," and continued by its qualified insertion in the Pickerell contract, in the face of the denial by the United States of her pretended prior title, and in the face of the express exception and reservation of the "Aves," and all the rights and claims of the present claimants pertaining thereto, and of the further announcement that all those rights and claims could be fully sustained by the United States, Venezuela, on her own sole responsibility, and in full view of it, has persisted in her settled policy of holding the island by force and administering it for her own advantage. The cogency of this view and of the facts of record which sustain it, as heretofore presented by me, and now urged in the inclosed note to Mr. Gutierrez, I do not perceive how this government can confute or escape.

What is now greatly needed by this legation in the prosecution of this claim for indemnification against Venezuela, is, as intimated in my No. 22, exact specification and detail duly vouched and attested—first, of all the actual and immediate losses and damages inflicted upon the claimants by their sudden and forcible eviction from the

"Aves;" and secondly, a statement duly vouched and as exact as possible, of the quantity of guano (with its market value) taken from the Aves since its occupation by Venezuela.

Without positive information on the subject, I presume that the bulk of the guano so taken from the "Aves," and also from the other guano islands under the Pickerell contract, has been carried to the ports and entered or manifested at the custom-houses of the United States. In that event the claimants may probably find greater facility in making up the necessary statement of it than they would have been able to command if Venezuela, instead of inserting the "Aves" in that contract, had seen fit to keep it open to all nations in pursuance of her administrative resolution of the 28th July, 1855.

It is proper to add that since the receipt of your No. 27, inclosing to me information as to the amount of the claim as estimated, I have been constantly awaiting further details of statement and proof upon that point. In my judgment, it is not safe nor expedient for the claimants to rest their case in this respect upon the printed deposition of Captain N. P. Gibbs, transmitted in your No. 30, though that document will of course be useful in the negotiation.

With the highest respect, I have the honor to be, your obedient servant,

CHARLES EAMES.

Hon. W. L. Marcy,
Secretary of State.

Note.—In looking over my dispatches I perceive that in my No. 12, transmitting the resolution of the 28th July, 1855, I give it as dated of "26th July," and the same error occurs again in my No. 22. The true date of the resolution is 28th July, 1855, and I request that the correction may be made.

Legation of the United States,
Caraccas, December 20, 1856.

Sir: Referring to the notes addressed by this legation to the honorable Minister of Foreign Relations of Venezuela, under dates respectively of September 24, 1855, and March 8, 1856, relative to the claim of the American citizens who were expelled from the "guano island of Aves" by the Venezuelan naval forces in December, 1854, and referring also to the several oral discussions of that subject which have taken place since the case was first brought to the notice of the Venezuelan government in April, 1855, the undersigned, minister resident of the United States, has now the honor to urge strongly upon the attention of the honorable Minister of Foreign Relations, the importance of a prompt and satisfactory adjustment of that claim.

The main facts of the case as first presented by the undersigned to the government of Venezuela, and afterwards summed up in his two notes above referred to, do not appear to be disputed.

Nor, in the judgment of the undersigned, is it probable that the Venezuelan government will at this time see fit to insist upon any title in Venezuela to the island in question prior to the occupation of it by her naval forces in December, 1854; and if this be so, it is manifest that, whatever possessory rights in the island Venezuela may have since alleged or exercised, as resulting from her occupation of it, those alleged rights must always be regarded, even by Venezuela herself, and much more by the government of the United States, as arising and existing, if at all, then only as subject to the paramount and previous right of the anterior American occupants of the island, to full reparation and indemnification of all the loss, damage, and injury brought upon them by the government of Venezuela in ejecting them from that occupation, and taking possession herself of the island and proceeding to hold and administer it for her own advantage and profit.

In this attitude stood the question of this claim when first presented, and though its reception then by the government of Venezuela was, in judgment of the undersigned, as he then stated, by no means in conformity with the rights of the claimants, and the just expectations of the government of the United States in their behalf, still the case might probably, at that time, have presented no insuperable obstacles to a prompt adjustment but for the appearance among the documents pertaining to it and in the possession of the Venezuelan government of a paper purporting to be the original of an "agreement" entered into and signed at the "Aves" Island on the 13th December, 1854, by Commander Dias, of the Venezuelan navy, of the first part, and the agents of the American occupants of the island of the second part, by which the possession of the island would seem to be ceded to the Venezuelan authorities by those agents upon certain terms and considerations therein set forth. This paper the undersigned, when properly assured of its authenticity, deemed fit, as new matter in the case, to be referred to his government in order that explanations of it by the claimants might be received and considered. Those explanations, showing that the alleged "agreement" was entered into and signed by the agents of the claimants under *duress* and upon compulsion, were considered by the government of the United States as sufficient wholly to invalidate and void the instrument.

The urgent aspect of the claim resulting from these facts was at once presented to the honorable Minister of Foreign Relations by the undersigned, in personal interviews, and was also shortly after pressed upon his immediate consideration in the note of the 8th of March last already referred to.

The papers which accompany this note, prove also the additional fact that the alleged "agreement" with Commander Dias, being written in a language not understood by the agents of the claimants, and so requiring interpretation, was signed by them under an entire misapprehension of its contents.

The case being thus cleared of the embarrassment occasioned by this alleged "agreement," and the forcible expulsion of the claimants from the island by Venezuelan forces, and its subsequent occupation by Venezuela not being disputed, the undersigned is unable to perceive any ground upon which the right of these claimants to indemnification can be denied or questioned. Any such denial would, in the judgment of the undersigned, impose inevitably upon Venezuela the necessity of maintaining the monstrous proposition that these claimants, having first discovered guano upon that derelict, uninhabited, and uninhabitable island, which had never been embraced within the jurisdiction nor reduced to the possession of any power, had, in that state of the island, no right to land upon it and work upon it; that in fact, from the day when they went there, in June, 1854, up to the day when they were driven away, in December of the same year, they were from the first and all the time, law-breakers and trespassers, engaged in active, open, and persistent violation of the territorial sovereignty of Venezuela. To suppose that the intelligent government of Venezuela could ever undertake to maintain such a proposition, would not, in the judgment of the undersigned, be respectful. But if this proposition be not maintained in its full extent, how can this claim for indemnification be resisted? If the claimants were, as against Venezuela, lawfully in possession of the island when Venezuela found them, then surely they may rightfully claim full reparation for being driven away by her public force.

It would seem, therefore, that in this case little remains to be done but to fix, justly, the amount of indemnification to which the claimants are entitled. This amount should embrace, in the judgment of the undersigned, *first*, a fair and just remuneration for all the actual and immediate injury inflicted upon the claimants in the form of property of various kinds, seized or sacrificed, or expenses or liabilities under contracts, or damages under charter-parties, necessarily resulting from the sudden breaking up of their business, and their precipitate and compulsory departure from the island. These items of the claim are in their nature positive and susceptible of exact statement and proof, and their adjustment will probably not be difficult. *Secondly*, these claimants allege that they are also entitled to a fair and reasonable indemnification for the loss of the profits which would have accrued to them from the prosecution of their business in the guano on the island of "Aves" if they had not been wrongfully disturbed and expelled by the Venezuelan forces. The claimants estimate this item of their claim at a large amount, and they have laid before their government testimony upon which they appear to rely as confirming, not only the fairness, but the moderation of their estimate. Without discussing, at this time, the question whether this second branch of the claim which seeks indemnification for the loss of estimated profits should be adjudged to stand in its nature and in its whole extent precisely upon the same footing in all respects with the first branch of the claim already referred to, the undersigned is yet clearly of opinion that the facts of the case as they appear, unquestioned and of record, strongly and urgently command this branch of the claim to the justice of the Venezuelan government, and require for it a favorable consideration and a fair adjustment.

At the very moment, in December, 1854, when Venezuela was moving forwards to the expulsion of these claimants from the "Aves" island, she was engaged in selling the guano thereon for the benefit of her treasury, and that sale was consummated on the 21st of that month in the contract concluded with Mr. Wallace under that date. All this was done without any knowledge of it, either by the undersigned, then in the United States, or by his government. Subsequently, in May, 1855, the government of Venezuela, upon reasons deemed satisfactory to itself, by executive resolution, declared the contract of Mr. Wallace null and void, but still the armed Venezuelan occupation of the "Aves" continued, in full view of the presentation by the undersigned, in April preceding, of the present claim, with notice that the title of Venezuela to that island at the time of her occupation of it was in no way recognized or admitted by the government of the United States. Soon after, while the case was in this state, and while active negotiations on the subject by the undersigned were suspended solely by the reference of the Dias "agreement" to the government of the United States, the government of Venezuela, on the 28th of July, 1855, by executive resolution reciting the annulment of the Wallace contract, and specifically mentioning the "Aves," declared its purpose to open that island, and all the other guano islands belonging to the republic, to the access, working, and trade of the citizens and subjects of all nations indiscriminately, upon such equal terms and conditions as should be promptly thereafter prescribed by the executive power. This resolution was accompanied by another of nearly even date, July 23, 1855, in which the Venezuelan government declared its purpose to prevent by force the working of any of the above named guano islands by any persons without its permission, and to execute the rigor of its laws upon any trespassers who might be found so offending. About one month afterwards, at the beginning of September, while the Dias "agreement" was yet under consideration at Washington, commenced the effort of the assignees of the Wallace contract, through their agent Mr. Pickrell, to save their rights vested under that instrument; and that effort, with express exception and reservation of the "Aves," and all the claims and rights of the present claimants therein, it became the duty of the undersigned to aid, and such aid was given, subject always to that express exception and reservation, in their full extent, repeatedly and emphatically insisted on from the first, and placed on record before the Venezuelan government, both during the pendency of the Pickrell negotiations and afterwards. At the close of that negotiation, it notwithstanding appeared that Venezuela, persisting in her settled policy of asserting and maintaining jurisdiction over the "Aves," had determined, in full view of all her responsibility in the premises, to specify that island in the contract of the 29th of September with Mr. Pickrell. This policy in regard to the "Aves," first adopted by Venezuela in her negotiation with Mr. Wallace while that island was still in the possession of the present claimants, carried into effect by their forcible expulsion, and subsequently, in the face of their rights and claims, and the interposition of the government of the United States in their behalf, fully adhered to in the continuance of her armed occupation, and solemnly reaffirmed in her administrative resolutions of 23d and 28th July before referred to, appears, in the insertion of the "Aves" in the contract with Mr. Pickrell, to have been only so far modified in view of the decided position adverse to that insertion taken by the undersigned in the name of the government of the United States in maintenance of all the rights and claims of the present claimants, as to withdraw the "Aves" from the primary and principal place which it held in the Wallace contract, and to give to its specification in the Pickrell contract an incidental and qualified form, exempting the Venezuelan government from liability to Mr. Pickrell and those whom he represented, in case of the failure of the Venezuelan possession and alleged title. But this modification could, of course, in no way diminish the profits resulting to Venezuela by the working of the island under her authority.

It thus appears, that in defeat of the claims of the claimants, and in disregard of the prompt and continued interposition of the government of the United States in their behalf, Venezuela, by a whole series of acts, commencing in December, 1854, and constituting since a systematic policy, has forcibly occupied, and in various ways administered, according to her own judgment, upon her own sole responsibility and for her own advantage, the guano island of "Aves;" and the inference, in the judgment of the undersigned, is obvious, that unless it be shown affirmatively and clearly that Venezuela had a title to this guano when she took it into her own hands, in December, 1854, better than the title of these claimants, who had discovered it, taken formal possession of it, and were lawfully and peaceably putting it to use when she found them and expelled them, then, under the law of nations and upon principles of justice, Venezuela is responsible to them, and to their government in their behalf, in a fair and reasonable indemnification for the loss of their profits from the guano, the rightful possession of which she thus wrested from them. The equitable estimate and computation of those probable profits will properly form the subject of future consideration.

Deeply impressed with the importance of a satisfactory adjustment of this claim with the least possible delay, and earnestly urging this view of it upon the government of Venezuela through the honorable Minister of Foreign Relations, the undersigned is desirous to proceed at once in the negotiation, and as a basis of such arrangement he will undertake to entertain and transmit to his government for its consideration a proposition by which the government of Venzuela shall agree:

First. Promptly to indemnify these claimants for all the actual positive losses resulting to them from their expulsion from the Aves in December, 1854, and forming the first branch of their claim as already alluded to.

Secondly. To indemnify these claimants in a reasonable amount as compensation for their loss of probable profits in the guano which may have been taken from the Aves under Venezuelan authority from the day of its occupation by her forces up to the day when the adjustment of this claim may be concluded between the two governments.

Thirdly. To adjust the question of the rightful interest of these claimants in the guano remaining upon the island at the time of such settlement of their claim, either by the relinquishment of such guano to them, or in other manner satisfactory to the two governments.

The undersigned avails himself of this opportunity to renew to the Hon. Señor Gutierrez the assurance of his very distinguished consideration.

CHARLES EAMES.

Hon. JACINTO GUTIERREZ,
Minister of Foreign Relations.

List of papers accompanying this note.

Deposition of Captain Joshua T. Safford as to Dias's agreement, &c., marked A.

Deposition of Captain P. Wheeler, marked B.

Second deposition by the same, marked C.

Deposition of George McGeorge, marked D.

Deposition of Charles H. Lang, marked E.

Certificate of William P. Gibbs, marked F.

Protest of George W. Nichels, master, and Henry C. Dearborn and Patrick Scallam, of ship James N. Cooper, marked G.

Mr. Marcy to Mr. Sanford.

DEPARTMENT OF STATE,
Washington, January 9, 1857.

SIR: I transmit a packet addressed to Mr. Eames, the United States minister at Caraccas. It contains an instruction to him upon the subject of the claim of Mr. Philo S. Shelton against the government of Venezuela, in behalf of which you have addressed this department as agent. As it is understood that you prefer to carry the packet to Caraccas rather than it should be sent by mail, a courier's passport for that city is also herewith inclosed. This department is informed by the Secretary of the Navy that the sloop-of-war Saratoga will probably be at St. Thomas about the first of next month.

I am, sir, &c.,

W. L. MARCY.

HENRY S. SANFORD, Esq., *New York.*

Mr. Sanford to Mr. Marcy.

BREVOORT HOUSE,
New York, January 10, 1857.

SIR: I had the honor this morning to receive per mail the following papers:

1. A sealed dispatch to Mr. Eames, United States minister at Caraccas.

2. A letter of introduction of myself to Mr. Eames, (marked "private,") dated January 6.

3. A courier's passport for myself.

4. A letter from the department to myself inclosing said papers, dated January 9.

5. A letter to me from the honorable the Secretary of the Navy, dated the 9th, advising me simply that Commander Tilton had informed the department that the Saratoga would be at St. Thomas about the 1st of February.

I regret that the last vessel for Laguayra left here on the 8th instant, and none is expected to sail for several days. I have ascertained that sailing from here to Havana or St. Thomas would not expedite me to Laguayra for some days, as the packet from St. Thomas to Laguayra is monthly and leaves St. Thomas on the arrival of the steamer, which leaves Havana on the 9th of every month.

I am not advised by any of said letters when the Saratoga will be in Havana, nor if she will take me from that port, nor if I was at St. Thomas on the 1st of February if she would carry me to Laguayra from that port. Under these circumstances, for the sake of dispatch, and presuming that Mr. Eames would receive the sealed letter addressed to himself at an earlier period if dispatched by the department than if carried by me, I herewith reënclose it, and beg of the department to send it by the earliest opportunity. I presume the Saratoga may afford such means, as the Secretary of the Navy assured me she would touch at Laguayra.

In the meantime, and before I sail, I purpose visiting Washington again in respect to this claim; when, if deemed proper, I may request a duplicate of such dispatch to be sent by me with some additional papers which I may then furnish the department for transmission to Mr. Eames to enable me to aid the department and Mr. Eames effectually in the prosecution of this just claim.

I have the honor to be, with great respect, your obedient servant,

H. S. SANFORD.

Hon. WILLIAM L. MARCY,
Secretary of State.

P. S. I notice in the papers a call by the Hon. Mr. Bell, in the Senate, for the correspondence relating to Aves Island. Lest I might be misunderstood, I desire to state that I have had no participation in this any more than the other call, of which I was ignorant till I saw it in the papers.

H. S. S.

Mr. Sanford to Mr. Marcy.

WASHINGTON, *January* 22, 1857.

SIR: I have the honor to inclose herewith a translation of a report of the Secretary of Finance of Venezuela to the Congress of that State, dated Caraccas, January 20, 1856, which I desire to have filed with the papers relating to the Shelton's Isle case, to which I invite your particular attention, as containing an authentic account of the coöperation of the minister of the United States at Caraccas in obtaining the contract to the Philadelphia Guano Company, by which Shelton's Isle was ceded to it.

I have the honor to be, with great respect, your obedient servant,

H. S. SANFORD.

Hon. WILLIAM L. MARCY,
Secretary of State.

Extract, translated from the report of the Secretary of Finances to the Congress of Venezuela, Caraccas, January 20, 1856.

The bills of exchange, in favor of the general treasury, drawn on John Tucker by Mr. J. D. Wallace, the grantee of a privilege to take guano, for a period of fifteen years, from Aves Island, of the windward, and other islands of the republic, containing guano, having been protested for non-acceptance, the executive power, in furtherance of the opinion of the council, on the 22d of May ultimo, declared the annulment of the contract of December 21, 1854, which, at the preceding sessions, had been transmitted, in its original form, to the honorable the chamber of representatives. Having it in contemplation to bring the management of that article, with a view to the greatest advantage, under the control and the agency of fit officers, until the legislature should decide in the matter, the executive power, among other measures, adopted that of instituting an inquiry abroad, through the diplomatic agents of the nation, and others, specially authorized to that effect, to secure the information necessary to enlighten him fully in the premises, such as the price of our guano and of that of Peru and of Mexico in the United States; the kind most in demand in their markets; the chemical action likely to produce the article; the means to be used to obtain, through a simple scientific process, a knowledge of the best quality of that produce, in consequence of the greater or less quantity of certain substances, resulting from chemical decomposition. The executive power also adopted a measure having, for its object, the keeping up of a naval station of two war steamers cruising about the islands to prevent the fraudulent exportation of the article, in quest of which various vessels swarmed in our seas; the sending of a few cargoes of the article in order to introduce it into the principal markets of Europe and America; the station on Aves and Monges Islands of officers to watch over the guano and see to its exportation, to which end minute instructions were issued to them; the denouncing of seizure and other legal penalties for all vessels apprehended for fraudulent taking of the guano, or which may be at the islands taking such article without the due authority; the ascertainment in which of said islands the guano is found, and what the quantity and quality are. In consequence of the last requirement, guano was discovered in Monges Island, on the islet of Pié, belonging to the cluster of Los Hermanos. Some specimens received from the localities have been submitted to analysis in this capital. It is also known that there are deposits of the substance in the north and leeward islands of Aves, in Orchila, in the Tortugas, and the Frailes. This knowledge is derived from the statements made by the various agents of the national navy commissioned minutely to explore the archipelago, and to return surveys with all necessary details relative to all that may have come directly under their personal observation, or which may have been obtained through information supplied by the navigators who visit the archipelago. As to the character of the article, the comments of the press in different portions of the United States, as our consular agents inform us, and the various tests to which it has been subjected by chemists, show that the Venezuelan guano is of variant qualities, though the superior kind is found in a favorable classification.

A circumstance, however, which need not excite surprise, intervened to counteract the intentions of the government, even to the extent of making them illusory, just at the time when the data which the former administration could not have had on hand were duly coming in, and when there was an expectation that the information would be supplied in so full a measure as to justify a complete organization and development of the undertaking. So far, indeed, had the matter proceeded, that wonder was expressed that the contractor himself should have afforded the republic the opportunity for a reversion to it of the free and immediate management of that product, and for a supply, at the same time, for the somewhat reduced condition of the treasury.

The agent of an association entitled "The Philadelphia Guano Company," which had assumed the rights acquired by Wallace in virtue of the contract made with the preceding administration, reached Caraccas, and, maintaining the existence of the contract on the ground that the present administration had not the authority to issue the declaration of the 22d of May, filed in the department under my charge a protest for damages, which were set at $500,000, besides the further sum of $50,000, which were claimed for expenses already incurred by the company. The position in which this claim placed the government was, beyond doubt, painful and embarrassing, for at the very time that it was preferred, two mercantile firms of this city were urgently pressing their claim for $200,000, with 15 per cent., for cost of protests and damages on the bills drawn by Wallace, the contractor, on the 21st of December, 1854, which they had taken from the government for value received, but which were dishonored for want of payment. It is proper here to remark, that in view of such a contingency, and for securing the amount outlaid by them, the purchasers, among other privileges, had the right of being absolutely substituted for Wallace, in the execution of the contract, by articles drawn up by them and the preceding administration, on the 17th of January of last year.

Still, however complicated the guano question and its concomitants turned out to be; however trying it might have been for the government, in view of the straitened condition of its treasury, immediately to devise the means, in money, to honor its indorsement on the protested bills, and even, should it so be urged, to indemnify Wallace's successors; nothing of this could have ultimately induced the government, after nearly a whole month expended in daily conferences, to relax from its firm purpose of maintaining the rescision of the contract, had it not been for the ardent and hourly official advocacy of the United States minister resident in Caraccas. By him the attorney in fact of the company was presented to the government, and with him he was present at the daily conferences; and as the result of those conferences, after so long and uninterrupted a discussion, was adverse to him, he asked and obtained at the hands of the head of the nation a special audience in reference to the matter, a record of which is now to be found on the files of the department of foreign affairs.

The question then assumed a broad and serious aspect, through which was descried a disagreeable contest, as well as a painful issue, between the government of Venezuela and that of the United States, where public opinion and the daily press, by their energetic demonstrations, gave additional impulse to the claim, as we learned from the official information, from time to time, received from the diplomatic agent of Venezuela near the government of Washington.

Under such circumstances, aware that the object which the company had in view, was the recovery of the rights which it had acquired under the contract, the nullity of which had been declared by the executive power—that power appreciating the importance pressing on Venezuela, not to disturb her relations with a friendly nation, and looking to the difficulties of every kind to make available the guano industry, by a system of administration carried on over so many and isolated localities, almost all of them deserted and unsupplied with potable water; many of them wanting even a landing place, and forbidding, unless at great risk, the residence of the officers ashore, which circumstance necessitated the employment of a fleet to watch the coasts, at the time when there was not even one vessel for that service about Aves Island, and in consequence of which fact, authority had to be obtained for the purchase of such vessel; viewing all these things, said executive power authorized the secretaries of the departments of finance, of the interior, of justice, and of foreign relations to agree upon a previous recognition of the declaration of the 22d of May, with the representative of said company, which, on the preceding 30th of April, had obtained an act of incorporation from the legislature of Pennsylvania, in conformity with the law of that State, to grant the privilege of said island for a period of fifteen years; and it was accordingly granted by contract, signed on the 29th of September ultimo, for the excavation, sale, and exportation of guano, on condition of payment into the treasury of five dollars (single) for each and every ton, instead of four dollars, the consideration under the former contract; all expense incident thereto to be at the cost and on account of the contractors. It was also conditioned that they should sell the guano on the islands at an uniform and like price, to all individuals or nations whatsoever; that said islands should be guarded by officers of the republic, and by such naval or land force as it may deem expedient to provide; that said agents or officers should see to the due compliance with our civil and political laws; that they should intervene in the excavation and the importation, the latter to be verified and vouched for by the bills of lading; that the contractors should pay a fine of ten dollars for each ton taken out without due formality, without prejudice to the compliance with the laws, and with governmental regulations, enacted in relation to abuses against the national property and revenues; that all doubts and differences as to the construction of the contract should be decided by the supreme court of justice of Venezuela; and lastly, that the government should work out and explore, on account of the nation, a quantity of guano sufficient to load a certain number of vessels, which was subsequently, by agreement, fixed at twelve in the month of October last.

Such are the stipulations of the agreement of the 29th of September last, and though the executive power is conscious that they are much more advantageous than were those previously contracted for, still I cannot refrain from submitting to Congress that, had it not been for the mass of reasons and special circumstances which operated in favor of the agent of the company, even the recourse of diplomatic means in his purpose of asserting the validity of the agreement which had been rescinded, or failing in this, of claiming enormous indemnities, his excellency the President of the republic would have dwelt longer on the consideration and settlement of the question.

Mr. Sanford to Mr. Marcy.

BREVOORT HOUSE, NEW YORK,
January 26, 1857.

SIR: The vessel in which I sail for St. Thomas has been delayed by the ice, and will not leave till to-morrow. Reflection upon the position of Mr. Shelton's case, as it is disclosed to me by the official correspondence published by the Senate and by the other information I received whilst at Washington last week, has induced me to prepare and submit an additional statement or memorandum of the damages claimed by Messrs. Shelton and Sampson & Tappan, and which is now inclosed to be filed in the department. You will notice, first, that the damages now claimed are augmented since the statement filed January 29, 1855; and second, that we have now presented a statement of what we claim based upon the contingency that Venezuela may offer to restore the isle, and that the United States may possibly deem it advisable to accept such restoration.

I deem it proper that an explanation should be made in this communication on both these points: first, as to the augmentation of the claim; and secondly, as to the claim now made, if the isle be restored.

1. In reference to the additional quantity of 12,500 tons of guano at $12 50 per ton, now claimed, we have to say that when we made our former statement we anticipated the speedy settlement of our just claim by Venezuela, and were not disposed to be exacting or exorbitant. We

supposed that the conduct of Dias might possibly have been through his error or mistake. We then supposed that the guano, then charged, was not more than one fourth of what was on that part of the isle staked out between Captain Gibbs and Wheeler in July, 1854, to our party on the isle, and less than half of the first class guano on that part, not including the "good merchantable guano" and that of inferior quality, but which would bear freight to the United States. The fact of the guano, on our part, exceeding 100,000 tons is proved by five witnesses and by Commander De Horsey, R. N., in his report to his government.

We made it as we did because, although we believed our right to the whole was just and valid, we were desirous to avoid all appearance of being hard or unreasonable, and to prevent any imputation being made of exaggeration. We had not been at the isle ourselves, and did not know what we could certainly prove on that point by reputable witnesses.

We deemed it advisable also, in order to procure speedy payment of any indemnity from Venezuela, believing that satisfaction might be obtained more readily for such part of our rightful dues than for the whole; and besides, it was of pressing importance then to have the matter settled forthwith to avert other embarrassments and injuries, the results of said outrage, which, if the claims had been settled in the winter of 1854–55, or spring of 1855, we should not have been compelled to suffer. We claimed then, and claim now, only in reference to the moiety of the isle our Captain Gibbs took exclusive occupation of, on his division with Captain Wheeler, in July, 1854. We forbore to claim for the other part, because it was claimed by Lang & Delano under that division, and although we did not, and do not now, admit their claim is well founded, as against us, our position in January, 1855, induced us to forego at that time opposition to it, though, at the proper time, we purpose to have our respective rights as to said isle and guano decided upon by a competent tribunal. We do not imagine that there will be any question about our rights to add to our claim in respect of this additional charge for guano. Our former statement is no legal "*estoppel.*" Its not being made in January, 1855, may be regarded as evidence against the propriety of such additional claim. Be it so. In the face of the incontestable proof of the justice of the addition, and that it is still less than one half of the guano we might charge for, such argument may pass for what it is worth in such regard. Besides, the terms of our past statement show that we then supposed the quantity of guano on our part of the isle was 50,000, worth $12 50 per ton, and in presenting our charge for 25,000 only, we stated it as the "minimum" quantity; which word you will find in the statement.

In reference to our former statement of January 29, 1855, you will find, upon recurring to the deposition of Captain Gibbs, that he first arrived in the United States, after the eviction, at Holmes' Hole on that very day.

We saw him a few moments only, and made and forwarded that hasty and loose general estimate on the spur of the occasion. We repeat that we were then willing to take the amount there stated, if the case had been settled promptly. But we submit, that in a court of strict law even, a party would not be limited to a general hasty estimate (the brief statements of which show it was made without specific data) thus prepared, and which is clearly shown by incontestable proof subsequently obtained, was below what it ought to have been. It would be amended by leave of a court, if it had been filed as a bill of particulars, upon suggestion of the facts, on the ground of mistake and error, and the having subsequently obtained correct information, especially if the party was in a position (as Mr. Shelton was in this case) in which he might be supposed to be ignorant of the facts at the time. As to this additional charge, it is shown by the testimony, that added to the 25,000 tons before charged, and both together make out little more than one half only of the quantity then actually on that part of the isle we occupied of "first class" guano; (worth more than our claim per ton;) and such addition of this additional charge claimed by us, making the 37,500 tons in all, gives but a little more than a third of all the guano on such part. When Venezuela offers to pay the first charge of $312,500, she may properly discuss the additional charge now made.

And so as to the "false freights and damages, &c.," which we now charge at $36,320, instead of $20,000 formerly charged. We stated the charge generally in the statement of January 29, 1855; we had not sufficient data to do otherwise. Any one having any knowledge of such business can see our statement was mere guess-work. Now, we give the items. They are proved to be correct and just. The law does not require impossibilities of a party. In January, 1855, we did not give specifications; in fact, some of these damages had not then fully eventuated, though they did occur, and as the result of the expulsion. The items show this. Our first estimate we are willing, under these circumstances, should pass for what it is worth in weakening our claim to the said damages now set forth and proved. We are content on such score. When the $20,000 first stated is paid, it will be time enough to object to the overplus. That sum would have been worth more to us in January, 1855, than the $36,320 can be. If the $20,000 had then been paid (and the other accompanying charges equally as just) it would have released us from embarrassment, saved the necessity of grievous sacrifices, and protected the commercial credit and prevented the insolvency and pecuniary ruin of Mr. Shelton.

And as to the augmentation of the charge of $8,500 to $14,600, or what is the same thing, the additional charge of $6,100 for losses on wharves, houses, &c., it is clearly sustained by proof of items, by bills, accounts, &c., verified by witnesses, in addition to the indisputable testimony in the depositions filed. If this was a case between individuals, every honest man, after he had examined the papers, would be ashamed to dispute it. The particulars need not have been adduced. Proof of what such wharves, &c., would cost there, how much it would cost to keep thirty-five or forty men there seven months, and how much the implements ought to have cost, ought to be all-sufficient. In a court of law it would be. We have furnished such proof in the depositions, and then in addition, and to corroborate them, we furnish proof of items of actual expenditure. They amount to $6,100 more than we charged in January, 1855. If Venezuela insists that we are estopped by our first statement, she is at full liberty to do so; and if it should ever be decided that under all the circumstances we have adverted to we are precluded from claiming this $6,100, we shall acquiesce; but still we desire the present statement presented with the proof of its justice, as in such case we presume Venezuela would not demur to paying the $8,500 and interest immediately.

All the other damages charged in the inclosed statement it will be seen upon examinatian of them are direct effects and consequences of the trespass by Venezuela, and of her most unreasonable and unjust delay in respect to the fair and moderate claim preferred in January, 1855, amounting to a little more than half of what we now prove we could properly have claimed, and therefore now demand. If she had settled this case within a reasonable time after it was first presented to her, nearly two years since, or even given any answer that would have afforded us some reasonable prospect or hope of its early adjustment, none of the items composing the $97,490 now charged would probably have been preferred, and most of them would then not have had foundation. That they have arisen since January, 1855, justifies their being added to the former statement.

We do not suppose that you will have any objection to this memorandum or statement being presented, especially under the circumstances mentioned, and to its being transmitted to Mr. Eames, to be submitted to the Venezuelan government as our present claim. If you have any doubt as to the propriety of the augmentation of the amount formerly stated, or if you should deem it inexpedient to forward the inclosed to Mr. Eames as the basis of his action, we presume all difficulty on your mind will be removed by the unequivocal declaration we now make, and give full authority for him to repeat, in the most binding form, that if Venezuela will yet forthwith adjust and give reasonable assurances of payment in the aggregate of the claim *first* presented, $341,000, with her own legal rate of interest thereon, we will still give her a full discharge for it, and we will personally abandon all claim to the isle; but this statement of our just dues ought to be presented to preclude the most hypercritical from objecting to the other. The present statement is founded on the proofs adduced, and if it serves no other purpose it will show that Venezuela should not whisper a word in derogation of the first.

2. As to the restoration of the isle to us. We make the separate and distinct statement of our claim in such case, because we notice in your dispatches, published in Sen. Doc. No. 25, 3d Sess. 34th Cong., (present session,) you refer to such atonement; and also that Mr. Eames in his dispatch No. 22, of October 10, 1856, (not published,) but of which you furnished me a copy, alludes to the reported "abandonment" of the isle by "the Philadelphia Guano Company" as "valueless," &c. We cannot believe that you will agree that such restoration, in part satisfaction to us, is at the option of Venezuela. We were willing to take it back in January, 1855, in part satisfaction, and even for some months afterwards, before our property there had been eloigned, wasted, delapidated, and become worthless, and before any guano had been abstracted therefrom, and especially before

Aves Island guano had, by the bad management and ill judgment of Venezuela and her transferrees, depreciated in reputation, demand, and price, and the market ruined by them, and which has rendered the isle now of comparatively little value to them or to others. We hold that we have the option or choice to accept a restoration of the isle or not, in part satisfaction. At any rate, our government has such option. Between individuals it would be preposterous that a trespasser when arraigned for his tortious acts, after he had kept the property two years, and used it, taken away part of its only valuable product, and rendered it well nigh worthless, (and even if it had become valueless, without his expressly causing it,) should be allowed to say "here it is, take it back and be satisfied." We are not now in the guano trade, and are not disposed to go in it again. Besides, what are we to do with the Philadelphia company? Two years since we asked to be restored; eighteen months—nay, a year ago we were willing to take back the isle in part satisfaction. In May and June, 1855, we begged of the government to send a naval force to give us possession, or to allow us to do the business ourselves. We could have used it then profitably. *Now* to ask us to take it back as part satisfaction to any considerable amount, would be a bitter mockery. And, besides, the President hath not granted our application under the act of last session, respecting the isle, and though our claim for damages against Venezula may be good, we may have trouble hereafter, which we should not have had in 1854 as to the isle. I trust that you will suggest to Mr. Eames that the restoration of the isle in part satisfaction of our damages, on terms essentially different from what we now state, will not be just, and that the Venezuelan government be so informed.

May I ask that the inclosed be filed, and a copy I have made and sent in another envelope, (with also a copy of this,) be sent to Mr. Eames, and a second copy certified to be a true copy, and sent to me. I would ask that the latter be sent to the Brevoort House, New York, addressed to me, where I have left instructions how to forward it by the first conveyance some five or six days hence to Laguayra. Any other communication to me respecting this case can be addressed in the same way during my absence.

I have the honor to be, sir, yours, very respectfully,

H. S. SANFORD,
Attorney for claimants.

Hon. Wm. L. Marcy,
Secretary of State.

P. S.—Mr. Philo S. Shelton expects in a few days to sail for the West Indies; he will address the department before he sails, and after his departure Edward N. Shelton, Esq., will communicate to the department in answer to any letters to me addressed as above.

Memorandum of claim vs. Venezuela, if isle is retained.—Philo S. Shelton, and Sampson & Tappan claimants.

GUANO.

I. One half of 50,000 tons—say 25,000 tons, $12 50 per ton only was charged as per statement January 29, 1855			$312,500
It appears the quantity was estimated too low, and we charge, therefore, for 12,500 tons additional at same price		$156,250	
II. We charged per statement of January 29, 1855, for false freight, damages, &c			20,000
We have since ascertained the following false freights, damages, losses, &c.:			
1. Brig John R. Dow, false freight, &c	$2,500		
2. Loss on sale and sacrifice of said brig since said statement	3,000		
3. Ship Junius, false freight	850		
4. Ship James N. Cooper, false freight	5,950		
5. Bark Carlo Mauran, false freight	2,500		
6. Bark Amazon, false freight	2,210		
7. Brig Viator, false freight	1,450		
8. Brig Mary Pearce, false freight	1,820		
9. Bark Mary Smith, false freight	500		
10. Lining and fitting for guano trade, &c., Junius, J. N. Cooper, Carlo Mauran, and Amazon, at $250 each	1,000		
11. Additional loss of profit of $2 per ton on freight, at $7 per ton, the same being worth $9 per ton in winter and spring of 1854-5	3,040		
12. Losses on engagements, &c., for other vessels besides the above, (bark Brilliant and others,) estimated at $5,000	5,000		
13. Expenses of discovery of isle in J. R. Dow, in 1854	3,000		
14. Loss on abandonment of Arenas	3,500		
Amount	36,320		
The actual losses are therefore $16,320 more than stated January 29, 1855, for false freights, damages, and losses, &c., and since *ascertained* as the result of the expulsion		16,320	
III. Loss on wharves, houses, sheds, and property at the isle, as per statement January 29, 1855			8,500
It is ascertained that the cost *at the isle* of the wharves, houses, sheds, and property, putting them up, and of implements, tools, &c., and of provisions, water, &c., sent to isle up to December 26, 1854, and freight thereon, &c., was at least	21,500		
Deduct value of provisions consumed up to said day, and value of the provisions and property allowed to be brought away	6,900		
Value taken by Venezuelans	14,600		
The same amounting to $6,100 more than the amount ($8,500) charged January 29, 1855, is accordingly charged as now ascertained		6,100	
IV. We claim additional cumulated and augmented losses, partly from the delay of reparation for two years, viz:			
1. Injury and damage to credit and business from embarrassments consequent on losses from eviction		50,000	

STATEMENT—Continued.

2. Attorney's expenses, &c., on visit to Caraccas......	$5,000		
3. Agents, clerk hire, printing, witnesses, official fees, and other expenses..............................	5,700		
4. Commission for collection, (a portion,) say 10 per cent. commission charged to Venezuela, which, on $341,000, is..	30,690		
		$41,390	
5. Interest on $341,000 only, from December 26, 1854, to February 26, 1857, two years and two months, at 6 per cent. (But one half legal interest of Venezuela)......................................	....	44,330	
[If further accumulation of interest the same to be charged.]			
Amount of augmented damages since January 29, 1855..	....	314,390	$341,000
			314,390
Aggregate now claimed if isle be not restored..........	....	....	655,390

If isle is offered to be restored, and if accepted by claimants, we should be paid as follows:

I. 1. For all the guano taken from the isle since December 26, 1854, at $12 50 per ton, correct quantity to be properly ascertained.....	....	....	$
2. For depreciation in value and price of the residue of said 25,000 tons and said 12,500 tons, in all 37,500 tons, at $7 50 per ton, since December 26, 1854, at $5 per ton, being the present maximum value owing to mismanagement of it since then..	....	....	
II. 1. All the foregoing items from No. 1 to 14 (II) should be paid as..	$36,320		
III. 1. We should be paid the above item of $14,600, less 10 per cent. on cost, being present estimated value of what of it, it is presumed, is yet there if restored—say deduct $1,460	13,140		
IV. 1. Damages to credit and business as above............	50,000		
2. Attorney's expenses to Caraccas, &c., as above. } 3. Agents, clerks, &c., $5,700........................... }	10,700		
		....	110,160
4. Commissioners, at 10 per cent. on amount paid....	....	....	
5. Interest on amount paid as above........................	....	....	
Amount	....	....	

H. S. SANDFORD,
Attorney for Claimants.

NEW YORK, *January* 26, 1857.

Mr. Shelton to Mr. Marcy.

BOSTON, *January* 31, 1857.

SIR: I am informed that by a vessel which arrived at New York the day after Mr. H. S. Sanford sailed for St. Thomas, (the 28th,) that an agent (a Mr. Leon de la Cova) of the Philadelphia Guano Company arrived from Caraccas *via* Porto Cabello, with a new contract made about the 15th of December last, between the present Venezuelan government and that company, for all the guano islands in the Caribbean sea, the company agreeing to yield six dollars per ton "royalty" hereafter for all the guano gathered, and to pay all the damages and protest fees on its dishonored bills of exchange under the old contracts, and being thereupon released from all liability on account of said bills.

I am informed also that the contract in the possession of said agent, and shown by him, was duly authenticated and certified by the United States minister at Caraccas, under his official seal, and presume therefore that he has transmitted a copy or fully advised the department thereof.

With reference to the fact of the increase of the royalty, the contract may be an important piece of evidence for us, as showing what the parties value the average of Venezuelan guano at, at the islands where they are at no expenses for lading it, and also in other respects; and this whether or not (in express and specific terms) it includes Aves or Shelton's Isle. As I cannot divine any good reason why it would be improper for us to be supplied with it, if it is in the department, I beg to ask you that I may be furnished such copy if it is received, or if received hereafter, so soon as it is received, and if it is not transmitted, that I may be furnished with any information respecting it the department may have.

I should not trouble the department if I was not satisfied that my information was correct.

I would also respectfully solicit to be advised if anything has been received from Mr. Eames since the dispatch of the 10th of October, a copy of which was furnished to Mr. Sanford; and if so, please address me, directed to H. S. Sanford, Brevoort House, New York, with which direction I shall soonest see it, and it be sooner sent to Mr. Sanford. I can send it to him from thence in a few days.

I am, very respectfully, your obedient servant,

PHILO S. SHELTON,
For self and others.

Hon. WM. L. MARCY,
Secretary of State.

Mr. Marcy to Mr. Sanford.

DEPARTMENT OF STATE,
Washington, February 3, 1857.

SIR: I have to acknowledge the receipt on the 31st ultimo of your communication dated the 22d ultimo, with its accompanying memorandum, both of which papers are in triplicate.

One of these has been placed on file, another authenticated under the seal of the department is herewith returned to you, and the third copy similarly attested, has been transmitted to Mr. Eames with a corresponding instruction.

I am, &c.,

W. L. MARCY.

HENRY S. SANFORD, Esq.,

Mr. Marcy to Mr. Shelton.

DEPARTMENT OF STATE,
Washington, February 3, 1857.

SIR: In reply to your letter of the 31st ultimo, I have to acquaint you that Mr. Eames has not communicated to this department a copy of the contract which you have been informed was executed in December last, between the Philadelphia Guano Company and the government of Venezuela, and duly authenticated under the seal of the legation, nor has Mr. Eames mentioned the existence of any such contract.

Our dates from Caraccas, however, only reach the 6th of December. Should the department receive any such document as that referred to, and there should appear to be no reason for withholding it, a copy will be forwarded to you as you request.

I am, sir, &c.,

W. L. MARCY.

PHILO S. SHELTON, Esq., *Boston.*

No. 46.] *Mr. Marcy to Mr. Eames.*

DEPARTMENT OF STATE,
Washington, February 3, 1857.

SIR: Mr. Henry S. Sanford, the attorney of Shelton and other claimants, against Venezuela, who is now on his way to Caraccas with important dispatches to you in relation to the Aves Island question, has addressed to this department a memorial respecting the claim which he represents, accompanied by a new and corrected memorandum of the items forming that claim. A certified copy of these papers is, at Mr. Sanford's request, herewith forwarded to you.

Without entering upon a detailed examination of the items composing the claim as now presented, it may be remarked, that the grounds upon which it is offered are sufficient to warrant the department in transmitting it to you as the basis of your demand upon the government of Venezuela. The claimants, by their attorney, allege that their former statement of losses, &c., was hastily made up from crude and unreliable data, and that the substituted amounts are susceptible of proof from authentic sources.

Mr. Sanford has also made up a statement of the claim, based upon the supposed proffer by Venezuela to restore the Aves Isle in question, as either a partial or complete atonement to the claimants for their lossess. The remarks which, in his memorial, he makes upon such a contingency, are approved by the department, and it is not deemed necessary to do more than commend that part of his argument to your particular attention.

I am, sir, your obedient servant,

W. L. MARCY.

CHARLES EAMES, Esq.

To the Department of State of the United States:

Detailed statement of the injuries and damages sustained by Philo S. Shelton and George R. Sampson and Lewis M. Tappan, in consequence of their being tortiously evicted, in violation of the law of nations, and of justice and right, by the naval and military forces of the Republic of Venezuela, acting under authority of the government thereof, in the month of December, 1854, of the isle in the Caribbean sea, situate about north latitude 15° 40′, and west longitude from Greenwich about 63° 38′, formerly called "Aves" or "Bird Island," and now called "Shelton's Isle;" and by reason of their being dispossessed in like manner, by said forces, of the guano on said isle, and of the houses, sheds, wharves or piers, timber, planks, and other fixtures and utensils, boats or launches, barrows, implements, tools of various kinds, buckets, tubs and baskets, water-casks, water and provisions, and other articles, their property, then being on said isle, taken by said forces; and likewise of their injuries and damages otherwise sustained by reason of their expulsion as aforesaid, and the expulsion of their said agents and workmen, and of their vessels therefrom; and the prohibition and exclusion by said government from visiting said island and taking the guano therefrom, and by the breaking up of their employment and business in the guano trade at the said island; and by keeping the said isle and guano and their said other property from them. The said outrage having been perpetrated without any application, or notice thereof, to the government of the United States.

I. These claimants claim for 37,500 tons of guano on that part of said isle occupied by them December 26, 1854, of the value of $12 50 per ton, being..$468,750

(See memorandum of claim transmitted to department January 27, 1857, and letter from H. S. Sanford, Esq., to department, of same date, inclosing the same for explananation of the above charge.)

Proofs as to quantity, quality, and value of guano on the isle at the time of the eviction, December 26, 1854:

1. These claimants, May 9, 1856, filed in the department a copy of a letter from the Hon. E. Hammond ("in the absence of the Earl of Clarendon") of the British "Foreign Office," dated April 11, 1856, to George M. Dallas, the minister plenipotentiary and envoy extraordinary of the

United States of America at London, in answer to a request by Mr. Dallas at their instance, inclosing an extract from an official letter or report of Commander DeHorsey, of the British navy, who visited said isle in July, 1854, which report is dated August 1, 1854, and wherein Commander DeHorsey, after stating his visit and information given to him as to the price of the guano in the United States, being $35 per ton, says: "At a rough estimate I should say there were about 200,000 tons of guano on the island, which, at £7 per ton, would make the island worth one and a half million sterling." In corroboration of this estimate, claimants state that they have been informed that a larger one was published, soon after they occupied the island, in the summer of 1854, in a French West India paper, called "L'Outre Mer," which stated the quantity at 250,000 tons. They annex a copy of a notice of said publication in an American newspaper, given to them by Mr. F. Colby; and also an extract from a publication in the New York Tribune, written by Mr. Colby in July, 1855, noticing Commander DeHorsey's report; and also a notice in the "American Agriculturist," of November 8, 1854, of said report, which are part of the publications referred to in Captain Gibbs' deposition.

2. The printed deposition of Captain Nathan P. Gibbs, dated April 12, 1855, transmitted by claimants to the United States State Department, April 14, 1856. (See Ex. Doc. No. 25, 3 Sess. 34th Cong., pp. 61 to 75.)

He states, in answer to eighth interrogatory, (p. 67,) that from his first examination of the isle and guano, when he landed on it in April, 1854, his estimate of the guano was "over 150,000 tons," of which 75,000 tons was "first rate," and the rest "good merchantable guano;" and that this estimate of 150,000 tons did not include a large quantity of inferior guano that would, however, then (in 1854) "bear freight to the United States." In same answer he states that from the knowledge he subsequently acquired, by being nearly six months on the island getting guano, he does not regard Commander DeHorsey's estimate as "extravagant" or "erroneous." In his answer to the eleventh interrogatory, he quotes the item stated for the guano, in the claim filed in January, 1855, "minimum 25,000 tons, probably 50,000 tons," at $12 50 per ton, $312,500, and says it "is much below the amount" these claimants "might justly claim." He states the aggregate quantity shipped from the isle, whilst occupied by claimants, was, by claimants, about 7,200 tons, and by Lang & Delano, 2,000 tons: in all 9,200 tons, and that it was not the best on the isle. (See answer to sixth int. p. 65, and to eighth, p. 68.)

3. Mr. John McCabe, in his printed deposition, made June 28, 1856, sent by claimants to the State Department

June 30, 1856, (see Ex. Doc. above cited, p. 81,) says: "That he went to the isle with Captain Gibbs in the John R. Dow, and arrived there in July, 1854, the same day that Captain Wheeler did in the brigantine M. H. Comery, and that they both landed next day, (sea time;) that he staid there till Christmas, 1854, when the Venezuelans took possession by military force; that he thinks there were 200,000 tons of guano on the island, and that was the general estimate, and one half was first class, if carefully procured; that he won't pretend to give a positive valuation, but he thinks that there were at least 75,000 tons on Captain Gibbs' part of the island worth $13 or $14 a ton, considering that he had all the means of gathering it and loading it, prepared for his use, and hands there also; that he means the value of the isle to the owners, they having there means, wharves, houses, boats, and the like, and he thinks the freight ought not to be more than $8 per ton to the United States in the winter time, and if any one bought it at the island for the price he states, at the generally going prices in the United States, they would make good freights, and, covering all expenses, he supposes would make heavy profits, provided they know how to get it up for market, and how to sell it. The chief part we sent off was the most inferior sort on the island, which Captain Gibbs got out first to reach the best."

4. Captain James Wheeler, in his written deposition, made May 7, 1856, transmitted to the U. S. State Department, May 9, 1856, (see Ex. Doc., above cited p. 90,) says:

"I think there was 50,000 tons and more of first class guano on Gibbs's part of the island, staked off by me, and as much also on my part, and this was not half on either lot, but I estimate that the rest was not all good merchantable guano; say 50,000 tons and more on each. I consider the 50,000 tons which I call first class guano, on each of the two lots, as worth at the isle, with the privilege of preparations for getting it and loading it there, use of wharves, &c., there, fully $15 per ton, and much more, there, and the residue was not worth so much, but it would bear good freight. There is great skill and experience in gathering and shipping guano, and sending it to market. The practical experience I refer to is, in my opinion, worth a great deal more than the quackery of men who call themselves chemists about this article. I have always, since June, 1854, regarded the island and guano as worth about two millions of dollars, if properly managed."

And again, (p. 91, ibid.,) "I am informed that little or no profit was made on the guano brought from the island whilst we had it, because we gathered mostly the outside and indifferent guano nearest the wharves, before we could get at the best, and because also the difficulties caused by the eviction, forced them to sacrifice it. I have heard, however, it brought between $23 and $30, (the account of sales will show,) but the expenses were great, as we were just starting the establishment, and the profits afterwards would if we had been allowed to go on, have been pretty much clear gain."

5. Mr. Richard Thornell, in his written deposition, made May 7, 1856, (Ex. Doc., above cited, p. 78,) transmitted to the U. S. State Department May 10, 1856, concurs fully in respect to the quantity, quality, and value of the guano on the isle, with the other above-named witnesses, showing that claimants' charge is much less than what they might rightfully have charged.

6. Mr. Joseph Herbert, who was also several months at the isle, in his deposition made in August, 1856, transmitted to the United States State Department by claimants, in August, 1856, corroborates the statements of the other witnesses, proving that claimants' charge for the guano is just and reasonable and below the true quantity and fair value at the isle.

Every one of these witnesses was on the isle several months and engaged in gathering guano. None of them are interested in the claims of Mr. Shelton and Sampson & Tappan. No proofs have been adduced, so far as we have been informed, to impeach their testimony, or in contradiction of the verity of their statements or correctness of their estimates. Evidence is on file in the State Department of their respectability and credibility, and also on the files of the United States Senate. (See Ex. Doc. above cited, pp. 76–78 for some of said evidence.)

7. The printed pamphlet, published in 1856 by the Philadelphia Guano Company, whose agents occupied the isle under authority of Venezuela after our eviction. The names of the directors of the company are appended to it, one of whom is Don José J. Keefe, the consul of Venezuela, at Philadelphia. For value and quality of guano at the isle, see page 9, (an extract from page 95 of Agricultural Report of United States Patent Office of 1854, and other publications there quoted and adopted;) and see also page 15, where the wholesale price of this guano in the United States, is stated to be from $25 to $40 per ton. See also *ibid. ut passim* for the quantity and value, generally, of the guano on the isles in the Caribbean Sea. The Venezuelan government cannot gainsay these statements of their substitute, without self-stultification or self-crimination. Several copies of this pamphlet were sent to the United States State Department in the spring of 1856, to be used as evidence in this case.

8. An official letter of Don José J. Keefe, consul of the Republic of Venezuela, addressed to Moses Taylor, Esq., of New York, dated January 12, 1856, in which he states

that the Philadelphia Guano Company were at that time "engaged in shipping guano from said island, and had a large number of laborers on it;" and likewise the "Notices" referred to therein, and the letter of Mr. Taylor to him.

9. Accounts of certain sales of guano imported by claimants in the winter of 1854-55, and spring of 1855, showing its value at that time in the United States.

10. The "Wallace contract," dated December 21, 1854, by which Venezuela exacted from Wallace, for all the guano he or his assigns might gather in fifteen years, from all the isles claimed by Venezuela in the Caribbean sea, (and expressly designating, first, this isle,) $5 per ton; and the contractors to bear all expenses, and pay in advance $200,000 by ninety day bills on Philadelphia; and to exhibit manifests of all shipments to the officers of the Venezuelan government, who were authorized to supervise them; and besides, Wallace was, without remuneration, to keep up three armed vessels of the larger size, at his own expense, for said government, which, in case of revolution, should reinforce the Venezuelan navy, and be under the command of its officers whilst the revolution lasted; and the guano vessels to be liable to harbor dues, except in case of stress of weather or actual injuries; and Venezuela not to be liable for indemnity or damages if dispossessed of the isle. These conditions were equal to at least $12 50 per ton, and Venezuela cannot gainsay her own valuation of the average of all the Caribbean guano (good, indifferent, and bad) thus made; though, if less than real value, we are not bound by it.

11. The "Pickerell contracts," dated September 29, 1855, (see Ex. Doc. above, pp. 22 to 26,) granting a monopoly of the guano to the Philadelphia Guano Company, as successors of Wallace, for the same price of $5 per ton, the same term of fifteen years, and similar conditions, except with regard to the armed vessels.

12. Claimants have been informed that a contract has been entered into, within a few weeks past, between said company and Venezuela, renewing the Pickerell contract, but exacting $6 per ton for such guano, besides sundry damages; which, if made when obtained by claimants, will be offered as evidence of the like effect as the other contract above cited.

13. Official statistical accounts of the imports of guano into the United States from July 1, 1854, to January 1, 1857, showing that the average valuation of Caribbean guano exceeds that made by claimants of $12 50 per ton; and also of the exports from United States same time to like effect.

It will be seen that claimants ask, above, compensation for less than one fourth of the guano on the island. They have not estimated for the "good merchantable guano," and the "inferior guano," not certainly worth the $12 50 charged, but shown to be on the isle in addition to that charge, and to be of value. The lowest estimate, by any of the witnesses, of the "first class guano," exceeds the quantity claimed more than thirty per cent., and some of them exceed it sixty per cent. and even more.

II. The brig John R. Dow was owned by Philo S. Shelton, and was registered as of the burden of 197 85-95 tons; but she could carry from said isle to the United States at least 280 tons of guano. She was on a return voyage from Shelton's Isle to Boston, with a cargo of guano, at the time of this eviction. Her cargo was landed, and preparations made for sending her back for another cargo, and to send provisions, stores, water, and other articles, by her to the isle for our use there, when, January 15, 1855, being then first advised of any difficulty at the isle, she was detained for the receipt of more definite information; and on the receipt, January 29, 1855, of the tidings of the eviction, her outward voyage was consequently necessarily abandoned. The expenses and losses encountered, being reasonable demurrage or hire for her for the time she was so detained, and the outlay for the voyage sacrificed by such abandonment; the losses on the purchases for shipment by her on her outward voyage, and the valuelessness of many of them, and the uselessness of equipments for said vessel in said trade, and the frustration of the arrangements in regard to the employment of said vessel, caused by being forced to abandon said voyage and business, and the loss resulting from her remaining idle and out of employment at Boston till sold in the latter part of February, 1855, are estimated to be not less than.. $2,500

(See depositions before referred to, and other proofs, with our attorney in Venezuela. See Captain Gibbs, ans. to int. six, p. 66, and eleven, p. 74.)

III. In addition to the foregoing charge respecting the brig John R. Dow, the claimants state, by reason of the embarrassments caused by the breaking up of their said business, and commercial disappointments and difficulties, the direct consequences thereof, said P. S. Shelton was constrained to sell said vessel at a sacrifice, being unable at that season to obtain for her, at Boston, but $3,800, when he had been offered in June previously, and had refused, $7,000 for her; the loss on said sale of said brig being, estimating the ordinary wear and tear and increase of age, at least $3,000, and which amount it is considered is justly chargeable as damage resulting from said eviction.......... 3,000

(See depositions before referred to, and other proofs, with our attorney in Venezuela. See Captain Gibbs, ans. to int. ten, p. 72; eleven, p. 73; and twelve, p. 74.)

IV. The ship Junius, registered at 561 71-95 tons, but she could and did carry from the isle to the United States

850 tons of guano. She was on her return voyage from the isle to the United States when the eviction took place, and arrived with a cargo of 850 tons in New York, December, 1854; value stated, in manifest, at $15 per ton; for which freight was paid $5,100. She was chartered at $6 per ton for guano, delivered in New York, which was a very advantageous charter for these claimants, but the charter was abandoned in consequence of the difficulties at the isle. On account of this vessel, it is conceived they are entitled to reasonable damages for being compelled to abandon the charter, each trip not less than $1 per ton, and at least one trip.. $850

(See depositions before referred to, and other proofs, with our attorney in Venezuela.)

V. The ship James N. Cooper, was, at the time of the eviction, on her way from New York to the isle. She sailed from New York, January 15, 1855, before advices could be sent to Boston for her detention. Her registered tonnage was 549 30-95 tons, but she could carry from the isle to the United States 850 tons of guano. On her arrival, about the 2d of February, 1855, at the isle, she found it in possession of the military forces of Venezuela, which prohibited the vessel from taking guano or any thing else from there, and peremptorily ordered her off, and she came home in ballast. She could and would, if she had not been prevented by the Venezuelan forces, have laden and brought to the United States at least 850 tons of guano, which, at $7 per ton freight, would have amounted to $5,950, and therefore these claimants regard the said sum as justly chargeable by them as "false freight" to the government of Venezuela, and it should be paid by said government... 5,950

(See depositions before referred to, and other proofs, with our attorney in Venezuela.)

VI. The bark Carlo Mauran was at the isle at the time of the eviction. Her registered tonnage was about 566 tons, but she could carry from the isle to the United States 900 tons of guano. She was chartered at $1,100 per month for the vessel, the claimants to pay the wages of the officers and crew, and the expenses of victualling, fitting out, &c., each trip, (not including lining and port charges;) the whole amount being about $2,250 per month. She was ordered away from the isle on the 25th day of December, 1854, and brought but 800 tons to the United States. The false freights on the deficiency in her cargo, say 100 tons, at $7 per ton, amount to $700. In consequence of the breaking up of the business at the isle, we were compelled to relinquish her charter, which was an advantageous one, and also lost the expenses of fitting her out, (not including lining,) and of sundry provisions, &c. We estimate the whole at $2,500, and consider it chargeable to the Republic of Venezuela.. 2,500

(See depositions before referred to, and other proofs, with our attorney in Venezuela.)

VII. The bark Amazon was at the isle when the eviction was made, and was but partly laden when she was ordered off. Her registered tonnage was 385 tons, but she could carry from the isle to the United States 600 tons of guano. On her return to the United States, she brought but 490 tons. We charge for false freight, in the deficiency of her cargo, 110 tons, at $7 per ton, making $770. We paid for the passages of part of our employés at the island to Boston, in her, and for the provisions used by them on the passage. She arrived at Holmes' Hole about January 29, 1855, and in Boston a few days later, up to which time the wages of said employés were paid. The passages, expenses, and the wages of said employés, and provisions, amounted to at least $1,440, which, added to said $770, false freights, makes $2,210, that we consider justly chargeable to the said Republic of Venezuela........................ $2,210

(See depositions before referred to, and other proofs, with our attorney in Venezuela.)

VIII. The brig Viator arrived at the isle whilst the Venezuelans were there, before the final eviction, and had laden but about 80 tons aboard, when it was made. Her registered tonnage was about 208 tons, but she could carry 280 tons of guano from the isle to the United States. After being driven away from Shelton's Isle, she went to St. Thomas to procure a freight, and prevent loss, but failed. We were enabled to compromise for the false freights of this vessel by paying $1,005 92, but we conceive we have a just right to charge for all that she would have brought to the United States, and was prevented from bringing, viz: 280 tons, (deducting the 80 tons she did bring,) being at least 200 tons at $7 per ton, being $1,400, and also her expenses and port charges going to St. Thomas for freight to save loss, $50.. 1,450

(See depositions before referred to, and other proofs, with our attorney in Venezuela.)

IX. The brig Mary Pearce, was at the isle when the eviction took place, and was ordered off without being allowed to take any cargo. She returned to the United States in ballast. Her registered tonnage was 192 tons, but she could have carried from the isle to the United States 260 tons of guano. We were enabled to compound and compromise for her false freights for about $1,470, but we conceive that we have a just right to charge for all that she could and would have brought to the United States for us, if she had not been prevented from so doing by the military force of Venezuela. This at $7 per ton is.. 1,820

(See depositions before referred to, and other proofs, with our attorney in Venezuela.)

X. The bark Mary Smith was in Boston at the time of

the eviction. Her registered tonnage was about 333 tons, but she had landed in Boston, from the isle, 440 tons, and could have brought 500 tons. In consequence of the information of the eviction, these claimants were constrained to effect a cancelation of her charter, which, if they had not been expelled from the isle, was highly advantageous to them. The loss thereby was at least $500.................... $500

(See deposition before referred to, and other proofs, with our attorney in Venezuela.)

XI. In reference to the ship Junius, the ship James N. Cooper, the bark Carlo Mauran, and the bark Amazon, these claimants expended considerable sums on each, in lining their holds throughout, and otherwise rendering them suitable to carry guano, as is necessary with respect to large vessels in this trade, to prevent injury to the ship from the cargo; and the expenses thereof, for each vessel, averaged more than $250, or, in all, the sum of one $1000, all of which expenses were lost to claimants as the result of said eviction, and of their being compelled to abandon the employment of said vessels in said trade, and relinquish their charters, say $1,000.. 1,000

(See depositions before referred to, and other proofs, with our attorney in Venezuela.)

XII. And these claimants state, in reference to the preceding charges for false freights, that whilst it is true that they were evicted at a season of the year, (December, 1854,) when freights are generally lower from the northern Atlantic ports of the United States to the Caribbean sea than at other seasons, and when, also, labor for that southern climate can be more readily procured, yet such facts afford no ground for Venezuela being exonerated from the payment of fair and usual freights, though beyond the amount claimants actually paid for such false freights. If claimants were fortunate in obtaining freights or charters for themselves Venezuela has not acquired, by her wrongful and tortious act, any just claim to them. Besides, whilst freights are low, the markets of the United States for guano, both as to demand and prices, are always better in the late winter and in the spring months than in the summer and fall; and, as in this case, the cargoes belonged to claimants, the less the freights they had to pay the greater their profits on the cargoes; and their charters, in nearly every instance, extended, at same prices, into the season when freights became higher. Some of them were for $6 per ton only; others by the month or by the trip. All conversant with such affairs know that there are numerous charges outside the mere freight or charter of various kinds—port charges, custom-house dues, quarantine fees, pilotage, advertising, brokerage, small casualties, and the like—and that there is no little labor and trouble necessarily encountered by those who employ vessels, and which swell to a considerable amount in short voyages. These claimants have charged at the rate only of $7 per ton for false freights, for some 1,520 tons, amounting to about $10,640, without including the charges for the brig John R. Dow, the ship Junius, and the bark Mary Smith, for damages, &c., at the same rate of $7 per ton. They however insist that the facts above stated should not only be considered in deciding as to this charge, but they further insist that, insomuch as such price is actually from $1 to $2 lower than the usual freights for articles carried less than is paid for guano, with a prospect of cargo, in and out, between the West India Islands contiguous to Shelton's Isle, and either Boston or New York, as there was no outward freight to Shelton's Isle, except their own shipments of supplies, &c., they may, under the circumstances of this case, justly increase their charge to $9 per ton for all said false freights, and which amounts to $13,680, being a difference of $2 per ton, or $3,040...... $3,040

(See depositions before referred to, and other proofs, with our attorney in Venezuela.)

XIII. These claimants had, in 1854, and in January, 1855, before they heard of the eviction, made arrangements for the employment of sundry other vessels besides those above named, for continued employment in said trade to said isle, on favorable terms, and incurred considerable trouble and expense in making such arrangements, and they were compelled by said eviction to abandon and renounce all said arrangements, and to give up the said vessels, insomuch as, by reason thereof, their business at said isle was destroyed, and said vessels rendered utterly useless to them. The damages resulting from being so obliged to adopt such course must necessarily be a matter of general estimate. The claimants allege that they sustained thereby at least $5,000 damage, without reference to the effect otherwise on their other business. This was not specifically set forth in their statement of January 29, 1855, for reasons given, and likewise, in part, because claimants had then but imperfect means of estimating them, and were not certain that the same might not be avoided in some way, and perhaps by the continuance of their guano trade, if not to said isle to some other place, making the additional amount of 5,000

(See depositions before referred to, and other proofs, with our attorney in Venezuela. See Captain Gibbs's Ans. to int. 6, p. 66, as to bark Brilliant and others.)

In addition to the foregoing, the claimants insist that they are justly entitled to the following charges, as actual losses and "damages" connected with the establishment at Shelton's Isle, and of which they were prevented, by said eviction, from obtaining the reimbursement, the same not being specifically stated in said estimate of January 29, 1855, viz:

XIV. These claimants conceive they have a just claim to reimbursement of the expenses of the cruise of discovery, in which said isle and guano were discovered, as a derelict and desert isle, in April, 1854, by the agent of said Philo S. Shelton, in the brig John R. Dow, owned by him, burden 197$\frac{85}{95}$ tons, being the value of the hire of said brig and the wages of an extra crew, consisting of eleven or twelve men, and provisioning said crew and insurance of said brig so employed, say nearly three months.............. $3,000

(See depositions before referred to, and other proofs, with our attorney in Venezuela. See Captain Gibbs's Ans. to int. 3, p. 62, and to 10, p. 73, as to expenses, and Captain Wheeler's affidavit, p. 90.)

XV. These claimants conceive also they have a just claim to reimbursement of the expenses, losses, and damages occasioned by the relinquishment, by Philo S. Shelton, of his guano trade at Arenas, in the Gulf of Mexico, and the abandonment of his wharf and houses there, and by the sacrifices and losses by reason of his being obliged to transport his workmen thence to New Orleans, and to sell his implements at New Orleans at a sacrifice, and the expenses of said transportation, in order to take possession of said isle; all of which are properly chargeable to the expenses of making the settlement and establishment in said isle, and which were lost to claimants by said eviction, and which amounted to upwards of...................... 3,500

(See depositions before referred to, and other proofs, with our attorney in Venezuela. See same as referred in XIV.)

XVI. These claimants also claim for the value at said isle of the timber, lumber, planks, iron bolts, rods, bars, joists, pine boards, nails for houses, canvas, ropes, tackles and pulleys, and other like materials for coverings and awnings; table, stools, benches, chairs, posts, poles, materials for bunks, used for the comfort of the workmen at night, or when prevented from work in the day, and for conveniences for sleeping, water-casks, water, provisions and stores of various kinds, and spirituous liquors, and oil and lamps, pots, kettles, pans, knives and forks, cups, plates, and other dishes and utensils for cooking and for the table, and medical and surgical instruments, etc.; also, two six-pounders. and two dozen muskets and twenty-five large pistols, and ten Colt's revolvers and twenty-five cutlasses, and twenty-five boarding-pikes, and a magazine of fixed ammunition, and powder and ball for cannon and small arms, and an extra flag and flag-staff, a liberty pole, &c.; in fact, everything that was appropriate and necessary for a company of forty men employed at a place where nothing could be obtained except from such supplies. Wheelbarrows, wheeling-plank, buckets, tubs, baskets, shovels, spades, picks, hoes, rakes, drags, extra anchors and cables wherewith to moor vessels at the isle when they could not lie at the wharves or piers, and extra boats and launches to load the guano on board such vessels, and some of the other articles and property were also purchased and shipped to the island for use thereat in said business; and likewise for the freight and other expenses incident to their transportation to said isle of said articles, and the time, labor and trouble and expense of landing and taking care of said articles at said isle; and for the time employed and labor and trouble and expense of getting rock at said isle, and for the time, labor, trouble, and expense of constructing said wharves and pier, houses, sheds, &c., at said isle, and the wages of the guano laborers during the time they were delayed from work till said wharves and houses were constructed, (demurrage of vessels not included herein.) $21,500

From this amount their may be made the following deduction, viz: estimated value of the supplies, provision, &c., at the isle, consumed by the persons in our employment in the guano business at said isle from the day of the embarkation in June, 1854, of the first company of laborers, and from other different days subsequently, when others were sent out to the isle, up to the day of the return of the last company to the United States, January 29, 1855; and to other days previously when others came back, including some supplies furnished to our vessels and those supplied to the other party on the isle; and also those given, from motives of humanity, to the starving and distressed Venezuelans, before the eviction, (which claimants scorn to charge for, even after the wrong they have suffered,) and those dispensed in hospitality to visitors to the isle in vessels that touched there, (none being sold,) estimated at an average of thirty-five men for the term of seven months, and at $20 per month each, $4,900, and also the value and avails of that portion of said property and supplies of every kind that claimants' agent had any opportunity or was allowed to bring away when expelled, and received and disposed of in the United States, and the value of that undisposed of, mostly useless and unsaleable, estimated at the outside at $2,000, in all 6,900

Amount due claimants as above............. 14,600 $14,600

Said sum of $14,600, these claimants insist should be allowed to them as the value of the property of which they were despoiled by the Venezuelans at the isle, and that of which they were not allowed opportunity or time to bring away, and which the Venezuelans used, and their losses on the residue as above stated.

(See depositions before referred to, and other proofs, with our attorney in Venezuela.)

These claimants, in addition to all said above-stated items of losses and damages, claim the following as further accumulated or augmented damages, which have occurred since their statement of January 29, 1855:

XVII. By reason of said disturbance by Venezuela of their possession of said isle and guano, and their expulsion therefrom, and the spoliation of their said property by Venezuela, and the breaking up their business at said isle, and the great injuries, losses, and damages they sustained thereby, as aforesaid, their other affairs and business as merchants engaged in general commerce and navigation became and were embarrassed, and suffered great prejudice and detriment; and although said Sampson & Tappan have not been so deeply injured by such effects, and have sustained all said losses without suspension of payment, yet the said Philo S. Shelton, by reason of his more restricted means, has, in consequence of the embarrassments caused thereby, been obliged to suspend his said business as a merchant, stop payment, and wind up his affairs, and yield up all his property in liquidation to his creditors, and was greatly injured as to his commercial credit and means; all of which injuries, damages, and losses of the claimants were the direct consequences and effects of said wrongful acts of Venezuela, and which it is estimated may be reasonably set down at $50,000, and which claimants therefore charge; and they insist that the same ought to be allowed and paid to them by Venezuela in addition to said other charges............... $50,000

(See depositions before referred to, and other proofs, with our attorney in Venezuela.)

XVIII. By reason of the wrongful refusal of Venezuela to adjust and settle the just demands of the claimants presented to the United States State Department January 29, 1855, and reclamation for which was forthwith made by the United States from the government of Venezuela, which opposed and resisted said claim, and by said act made it necessary that the claimants should procure full proofs of the justice of the same; and by reason, also, of the unreasonably protracted delay that has taken place by the conduct of said government in the settlement of said just demands, these claimants have been constrained to employ, at heavy expense, legal counsel and attorneys, agents and clerks, to give necessary aid in the prosecution thereof by the procurement and collection of the testimony and proofs therein. And that said expenses, to wit: in the ascertainment of witnesses and their residences, and when and where their depositions could be obtained, writing depositions and copies, searches for procuring documentary proofs and copies, official fees for depositions and attestations and official copies, conduct of correspondence and copies, legal opinions and arguments in support of claim and in refutation of the objections made by Venezuela, printing depositions, arguments, and other papers; necessary journeys of P. S. Shelton from Boston, and of his attorney from Derby, Connecticut, and from New York to Washington, to attend to such claim; and other actual expenses in the prosecution thereof, amount up to this date to upwards of $5,700; and they have also been obliged to employ their said attorney to go on a voyage from New York to Caraccas, to attend to said case, the expense whereof, and his compensation therefor—if he should not be detained there but a few days—is estimated at $5,000 in all.. $10,700

(See depositions before referred to, and other proofs, with our attorney in Venezuela.)

XIX. Moreover, these claimants will necessarily have to pay commissions upon the collection of said claim when realized; what that percentage may be is not very material, except to the parties interested. They conceive that Venezuela should pay to them a reasonable portion of those commissions, and ten per centum on the amount Venezuela may admit to be due and ultimately pay as such reasonable portion, beyond which these claimants forbear to charge. Said portion of said commissions on the amount of $341,000 only, at ten per cent., is $34,100, which, deducted from said amount, leaves $306,900. Ten per cent. thereon is... 30,690

(See depositions before referred to, and other proofs, with our attorney in Venezuela.)

XX. And these claimants further insist that, in consequence of the unreasonable and inexcusable delay of Venezuela to adjust and pay the said claim, they ought to be allowed and paid, by Venezuela, interest on the amount due to them, and from the 26th day of December, 1854, when the wrong was committed, until the same be fully paid. They learn the legal rate of interest in Venezuela is twelve per cent. per annum. They conceive they are entitled to claim it if such be the fact. But at present they charge but six per cent. per annum, the legal rate in the United States, and in the State of their residence, Massachusetts. And they deem it entirely proper to declare that it is their purpose, under favor of Divine Providence, and with the aid of the federal government of the United States, to persist in the prosecution of their just claim for the atonement, reparation, and indemnification by Venezuela, for her grievous outrage upon and wrong of them, and to exhaust all the legal and honest means and remedies to which resort can be had, till the same is fully satisfied and paid; and that, although further procrastination may be used, and still further delay may be had, for all such procrastination and delay they shall insist that additional interest and augmented damages must be yielded to them. At six per cent., on $341,000, said interest amounts, if calculated from December 26, 1854, up to 26th of February, 1857, (before which time it is supposed

our attorney may not reach Caraccas and procure the settlement of said claim, being two years and two months, to the sum of	$44,330
(See depositions before referred to, and other proofs, with our attorney in Venezuela.)	
Total claim of P. S. Shelton and Sampson & Tappan, now presented	655,390

Mr. Eames to Mr. Marcy.

No. 35.] LEGATION OF THE UNITED STATES,
Caraccas, February 28, 1857.

SIR: I have the honor to acknowledge the receipt of your dispatch No. 42, under date of 3d ultimo, which was put into my hands by Mr. Sanford on the 21st instant, and which then gave me the first information I have ever had of the existence of your dispatch No. 37, of 14th of August last, relative to the "Aves" claim, which, with important accompanying papers, now appears to have been prepaid and forwarded from the department at the very time when I, having nothing from you respecting that claim later than your No. 30, of 25th April last, was in great need and in confident expectation of a further communication from the department on that subject. I waited impatiently till the 9th of October last, and then I wrote and sent my No. 22, stating my need and my expectation of further papers from the department relating to the "Aves" claim and the grounds of that expectation.

Meantime, the department doubtless has already received my No. 26, of 5th December last, acknowledging your Nos. 39 and 40, and stating that "your Nos. 37 and 38 are wanting, No. 36, under date of 9th August last, being the last dispatch previously received by me." This No. 36 is the dispatch in which you inform me that the general treaty negotiated by me last spring and summer, and transmitted to the department in July last, has been sent in to the Senate for ratification. Before this date, also, the department will doubtless have received my No. 30, of 7th January last, inclosing copy of my note of 20th of December last to Mr. Gutierrez, continuing to urge strongly the "Aves" claim, and indicating a basis of settlement. By my No. 30, the department will see that I wrote that note to Mr. Gutierrez solely on the basis of Nos. 22, 27, and 30 from the department, and in some perplexity at not receiving from you any thing later on the subject. I hope confidently that the department will consider, as I do, that in my note to Mr. Gutierrez of 20th December last, while laboring under the disadvantage of failing to receive your important No. 37, of 14th August last, with its inclosures, I have yet, to a considerable extent, if not entirely, anticipated the views of the department as therein set forth. If so, it is fortunate; for Mr. Sanford has brought with him and shown to me the proof sheets of the Senate document, containing both your missing dispatch No. 37, of 14th August last, and also your No. 42, of 3d January last, as communicated to the Senate and printed, and I cannot doubt that the whole document, as soon as published, will be forwarded at once to this government by some of its agents. Seeing your No. 37 in this form for the first time, I shall regard it of course as authentic, though, in view of my previous advices, I have no doubt that a duplicate has already been sent to me. I trust so, because as printed, it gives no list of its accompanying papers, and for these, so far as they may be contained in the printed document, I am obliged to rely wholly on Mr. Sanford's recollection. He tells me that he feels quite sure that Wheeler's second long deposition and McCabe's deposition were accompaniments of your No. 37, though they appear to have been printed as accompaniments of his printed memorial. Be this as it may be, I shall regard and use them as fairly in the case.

During the past week, since the arrival of your No. 42, I have been pressing the business with all possible activity in the sense of your instruction No. 42, and expect to receive, without delay, the reply of this government to my note of 20th December last, which I hope reached Washington with my No. 30 to you of 7th January last, in time to go into the Senate with the other papers, if the department shall have deemed that course expedient.

I write this dispatch in great haste to go forward by a vessel which sails to-day, and shall have the honor to write you further upon the subject by the first opportunity, which will, I anticipate, occur in a few days.

With the highest respect, I have the honor to be, your obedient servant,

CHARLES EAMES.

Hon. W. L. MARCY, *Secretary of State.*

[Extract.]

Mr. Cass to Mr. Eames.

No. 49.] DEPARTMENT OF STATE,
Washington, April 1, 1857.

SIR: * * * * * * *

Your dispatches to No. 35, inclusive, have been received. The last, announcing Mr. Sanford's arrival with instruction numbered 42, reached this department on the 20th ultimo. The loss of Mr. Marcy's No. 37 to you accounts for the delay which has been experienced in the prosecution of the Shelton claim. It is hoped, however, that the duplicates which were at once forwarded to you, (February 3,) together with the very minute statement of the items making up that claim, transmitted with another dispatch (No. 46) to you of the same date, will have enabled you before this to make a final and satisfactory adjustment of this claim.

I am, sir, your obedient servant, LEWIS CASS.

CHARLES EAMES, Esq., *&c.*

Mr. Eames to Mr. Cass.

No. 36.] LEGATION OF THE UNITED STATES,
Caraccas, April 1, 1857.

SIR: In my No. 35 I had the honor to inform the department of the receipt, on the 21st of February last, of its No. 42 in relation to the Aves claim, giving me, then, my first information of the existence of its No. 37 of the 14th August last, which, however, was next day shown to me by Mr. Sanford in the proof sheets of the Senate document in relation to the Aves, which he had brought with him. In my No. 22 of 9th October last, which, I perceive, was not sent to the Senate, the department was informed of receipt by me of its dispatches "to No. 36 inclusive," and my No. 26, of 5th December last, acknowledging Nos. 39 and 40 from the department, stated "that Nos. 37 and 38 are wanting."

I have now the honor to acknowledge the receipt on the 17th ultimo from the department of No. 43, of 6th January, and Nos. 47 and 48, both of 24th February. But none of these three numbers relate to the Aves question, and the three intermediate Nos. 44, 45, and 46, have not been received, and are probably lost, because since the receipt of Nos. 43, 47, and 48, other vessels have arrived here, both from Philadelphia and New York, bringing me other correspondence, but nothing from the department. I presume that these lost Nos. 44, 45, and 46, contain important matter relating to the Aves claim, as I am advised by Mr. Sanford that he has reason to believe that such papers have been forwarded to me from the department since the date of its No. 42, which is the latest I have on the subject.

The department will thus perceive that of its *twelve* dispatches forwarded to me since the 9th of August last, the date of its No. 36, I have failed to receive *five*, namely: Nos. 37, 38, 44, 45, and 46; all of which are still wanting, and of which others, as well as No. 37, doubtless relate to the Aves. Considering the urgent attitude of this question, and that the published correspondence in regard to it may have already reached this government, the department will, I am sure, fully appreciate the extraordinary and, perhaps, unprecedented difficulty and embarrassment to which this series of unfortunate casualties has subjected this legation in that business.

I deem it proper to add that I am entirely confident that these lost dispatches never reached Laguayra, because by reference to the "memorandum" accompanying my contingent account, and transmitted with my No. 25, the department will perceive the effectual precautions which, in order to avoid the risk and delay of the mail service here, I took more than two years ago, and have ever since maintained, to have all my dispatches, with a list of them, transmitted to me immediately upon their arrival at Laguayra through our consulate there, and by a special messenger. This duty has been performed by our consul with exact attention. As the dispatches for this legation have ever since its establishment been transmited through the commercial house of Messrs. Dallett Brothers, of Philadelphia, and as its records show that no dispatch has been lost prior to No. 37 to me from the department, my conjecture is that by some untoward accident these lost dispatches have failed to reach the counting-house of those gentlemen. I mention these details in view of the probability that the department may deem it desirable to make investigation as to the cause of the loss of nearly half its dispatches forwarded to this legation in a somewhat critical period of its business, during the last eight months, no such loss in any case here having occurred before.

With these preliminary observations, deemed proper under the circumstances, and referring to my No. 30 under date of 7th January last, which transmitted to the department my note of 20th December last to the Minister of Foreign Relations of this Government, continuing to urge the Aves claim, and indicating a basis of settlement, I have the honor now to transmit, in copy and translation, (1 and 2,) his reply, dated 28th February and received on the 3d of March, to my note of 20th December. I transmit, also, my answer to that reply, (3,) under date of 31st ultimo, which in view of the instruction, (No. 42,) from the department, I have prepared and intended as closing on the part of the government of the United States the discussion of the general question of the obligaticn of the government of Venezuela to make due reparation to those claimants.

By reference to the note of Mr. Gutierrez the department will perceive that, as anticipated in my note of 20th December, this government does not undertake to dispute the main facts of the case; but that it adheres substantially to the positions announced in my dispatch (No. 10) to the department under date of 26th April, 1855, as constituting the reply of this government to the reclamation as first presented by me in execution of the instruction (No. 12) from the department, then recently received.

The first of these, as stated in the note of Mr. Gutierrez, is that the right of Venezuela to the Aves was recognized and admitted by the agents of the claimants in their so-called "agreement" with Dias, of the 13th of December, 1854, which was referred by me to the department, "as new matter in the case," in my No. 10 of 26th April, 1855. In that, (No. 10,) I stated to the department that, in my judgment, that paper was regarded by this government as its main defense in the case. The observations on that subject in my answer to Mr. Gutierrez, I regard, however, as disposing effectually of that defense.

The extraordinary and inadmissible pretension indicated, though not fully alleged by this government in the note of Mr. Gutierrez of a right to molest citizens of the United States in actual occupancy in their private capacity of a derelict island, has been repelled by me in my reply in terms intended to be decorous, but, I trust, sufficiently decided to meet the approval of the department.

The allegation of Mr. Gutierrez in bar of this claim of the negotiation to protect the rights of the assignees of the Wallace contract in the other guano islands, except the Aves, accompanied as that allegation necessarily was by a total suppression of the fact of the complete and effectual official reservation and exception by me in that negotiation of the Aves, including all the rights and claims of the present claimants therein, has received in my note refutation and exposure, which, I hope, the department will consider both conclusive and exemplary.

The department will perceive that Mr. Gutierrez in his note has ventured to allege title to the Aves prior to 1854, in Venezuela, as the successor of Spain. The pretension is utterly futile; and, as I have from the first expressed myself emphatically in that sense, both to the department and to this government, I have deemed it proper in my reply to go thoroughly into that question, and put it at once beyond the necessity of any further discussion. The department will perceive that the maps and geographical work of Codazzi, the Venezuelan commissioner, as presented by me, are wholly conclusive against this government on the point; and it is in this view that I have demonstrated so much in detail their entirely official and authoritative character. I shall, if possible by the next opportunity, send to the department a copy of these maps, with the explanatory volume, especially as they are nearly out of print and hereafter may not be easily procured.

With the highest respect and consideration, I have the honor to be your obedient servant,

CHARLES EAMES.

Hon. LEWIS CASS,
Secretary of State.

REPUBLIC OF VENEZUELA,
Caraccas, February 27, 1857.

The undersigned, Secretary of State in the Department of Foreign Relations, has had the honor to submit to the executive power the note directed to him by the honorable minister resident of the United States, under date of 20th December last, and in conformity with the orders of his excellency the President, he proceeds to express the opinion which the government has formed on the subject of that dispatch, in which three forms of indemnification are demanded in favor of the Americans who are said to have occupied the guano Island of Aves, and to have been expelled from it by the Venezuelan forces.

On the occasions in which Mr. Eames has conferred upon this subject with the predecessor of the undersigned, and with himself, they have both expressed to him the views of the government in regard to that reclamation, to which no answer has been given before now in writing, both because up to the present time it has only been presented, and because when reference to it has been made by the legation in its dispatches, it has been only in an incidental manner in connection with the petition of Mr. Pickrill and the question of Venezuela with Holland. Mr. Eames repeats in his note aforesaid, in which he for the first time formalizes the demand that he deemed it necessary to consult his government as to the convention entered into with Commander Dias, the force of which induced him to delay the presentment of the subject.

Mr. Eames supposes that the question becomes free of this difficulty by reason of the explanations given by the claimants as to the validity of that document; but the government cannot share in an opinion founded simply on the assertion of persons interested in causing their assertion to be believed. Neither by the elements in their power, nor by their number compared with that of the Venezuelans, nor by the acts performed after their departure, nor by any of the other circumstances of the occurrence can any one assert that the Americans were compelled to sign a document which they did not understand. Had they opposed any resistance, had they protested on the spot or afterwards against the violence which they allege was done them, or made reclamation immediately against its effects, then their assertion would deserve some credit; but it seems extraordinary and not justified by any precedent that an attempt should be made to invalidate an act by the very party that granted it, upon his mere allegation that it was the result of violence and not voluntary. If such pretension were admissible, it would authorize every one who should repent of a solemn engagement contracted to free himself from it without other difficulty than by simply affirming that he acted under duress and not of free will. That the legation is certainly aware that the laws of every country consider valid a contract which, on its face, appears to have been concluded voluntarily, and the very grave proofs required to annul it for want of consent, both in respect to the facts of violence and the sort of fear that they may impress upon the mind. Nevertheless the tardy depositions which the legation has transmitted to this department, in mere copies, are all the proof with which it seeks to destroy the validity of a document which must be presumed legitimate and obligatory, as long as violence is not proved in the most incontrovertible manner. The circumstance is remarkable that, of the two persons who are said to have signed it, and to whom the other witnesses attribute ignorance of the Spanish language, one has not deposed, and the other who has deposed does not allege that objection, nor does he allege that the convention contained nothing in which the title of Venezuela is recognized; neither does he assert that he was impelled to act by any other cause than the desire of avoiding outrage. The government submits to the consideration of Mr. Eames the appreciation of this fact, which presents the doer of an act less informed of its motives than others who took no part in it.

But supposing that the Americans had been compelled to acknowledge the right of Venezuela, which is persistently denied, still they could never complain of their expulsion except after demonstrating that it was lawful for them to land upon the island and take away therefrom the guano it contained. The island belonged before 1854 to the republic, as the successor of Spain, its discoverer, and to whom various authorities attribute it, the circumstance of its not having been inhabited being of no consequence, since Mr. Eames himself asserts that it cannot be so; and moreover, nearly all the other islands pertaining to the republic are in the same state. The Americans went to the Aves, as they had gone to the Monks and other national islands, from which they have clandestinely shipped cargoes of guano, for the value of which the government of the United States ought to indemnify Venezuela, without being authorized by the Cabinet of Washington to proceed in that manner, and without taking care to investigate in the Department of State, as has been done in other similar cases, whether they had a right to the usufruct of those places.

The Island of Aves is not derelict, nor is it conceived how Mr. Eames can assert it to be so, when he lays it down in the same paragraph that it has never been reduced to possession nor has been under the jurisdiction of any power. If no one has ever occupied it at any time, who abandoned it, leaving it voluntarily as lost? But how can a thing be reputed as abandoned, concerning which two nations have been for a long time in controversy? The assertion that characterizes the citizens of the United States as discoverers of the Aves is entirely unfounded; and the guano thereon being the accession of the soil, it pertains to the owner of the land, not to those that discovered that substance. The United States did not commission the Americans in question to occupy the Island of Aves, and to take possession of it in their name. Thence it is clear that they could not hoist thereupon the flag of their country, nor assume the authority to say that they acted in its name, as Wheeler asserts that he informed the captain of the English ship Devastation. Reduced, therefore, to the class of mere private persons, they did not possess the faculty of acquiring as inherent in nations; they did not possess the right to compete with any nation, nor consider as occupied an island, the posseession of which they would in vain struggle to maintain by defending it against the States that would desire to appropriate it.

If the island of Aves was a thing common to all, of which, therefore, all could avail themselves, it is not to be inferred from this fact that any obstacle can be alleged to its occupation by Venezuela or any other nation; and this act once executed, it would from that time have entered into the special dominion of the occupant, ceasing thereby to be common property. Every one would then be compelled to respect a right that each one might have appropriated, and of which no one before sought to avail himself exclusively. Will the United States maintain that an object so capable of an appropriation as an island, could ever be reduced to private dominion on the ground that private individuals of different nations had enjoyed the use of it from time to time? Undoubtedly not. Then they have no doubt in regard to the eminent domain of Venezuela in the Aves, as Mr. Eames has often said to the undersigned, and they only dispute the private property of the guano found on that spot. So certain is this, that the federal government being perhaps ignorant in December, 1854, as probably might have been the case with Mr. Eames, even if he had been at that time in Caraccas, that there existed any guano at all on the Aves, and still more that countrymen of his were in the enjoyment of it, not only did not dispute the validity of the Wallace contract, but even made efforts to renew it when annulled by the executive power, and has since protected with great zeal the contractors of guano existing on the Aves and other islands pertaining to Venezuela. To suppose that Venezuela had the domain and the dominion over the Aves, necessary to enable it to dispose freely and for its own benefit, as Mr. Eames says, of the only substance that makes the island valuable, and to assert at the same time that the Americans preserve their right to that substance, implies a contradiction difficult to understand. If they are still the proprietors of the guano already taken away and of the that remaining on the island; if they are to be indemnified for the loss, caused by their expulsion, of the profits which they would have gained from the guano business since December, 1854, up to the settlement of their reclamation; if they have a right to demand that the remainder of that substance be delivered to them, or that they be satisfactorily compensated for their right to it, the result then evidently would be, that Venezuela had no authority to maintain the assignees of the Wallace contract in the enjoyment of the rights that it conferred upon them, nor to conclude a new one with them, nor to administer the island, nor to sell its products, since all these acts are the legitimate and exclusive effects of dominion which Venezuela could have refused, as was recognized in the act of soliciting her to perform them. After having thus clearly agreed on the point of the sovereignty of Venezuela over the Aves, the United States demand, without right, that she should disavow the legality of her proceedings, and that she should destroy her own title! Upon such a supposition, what would the republic have gained? To make herself the officious and gratuitous protector of the Americans; to defend the place for them from the pretensions of other nations; to keep for them, and, at great expense, their property; to employ in their behalf the citizens, arms, and national ships; to save them from the contingencies and risks of their possession, and ultimately to return it to them, or what is just the same, to pay them the reclamations made through their legation under three heads, in order that they should have all the advantages resulting from the dominion of the island, while all the charges of the same devolving upon the republic. These are consequences which ought to have great weight with the justice of the Cabinet of Washington, and make it abstain from protecting the cause which lead to them, especially in view of the consideration that the profits of the labor of the guano business on the Aves have already been obtained by other Americans whom their government so earnestly protected in obtaining for them the continuance of that same contract to which, as is now indicated, it would have been opposed either by that government or its legation, if it had been known when granted, and which could not have appeared to them so objectionable. To what is then reduced the indisputable title of Venezuela on an uninhabited and barren place, without property, in fact without any other value except that derived from the guano, if this substance belongs to those who now claim it? Thus the consequence of its occupation would not have been limited to the portion of that product which they really took off and shipped, being all to which, in the most favorable case, they could pretend; but it would extend to all which they had no capacity to occupy or defend, notwithstanding their having ceased to take care of and preserve it, without which acts property in things cannot be maintained.

But, moreover, the United States maintain that the island was common, so that the use made of it by some parties did not exclude the right of others, and this is proved by the fact of the existence among the documents of a declaration relative not to those entitled the first occupants of the island, but to others who, at the end of January, 1855, sailed from New York, bound to that island in quest of guano, and did not obtain it by reason of its not having been consented to by the Venezuelan forces there, in consequence of which they protested on their return to that port. Then, if such are the views of that government, how does it pretend that not the private citizens of Venezuela, but the State itself, had no right to compete with its citizens for a share of what was common to all, or that it had no right to take possession of it for its own private benefit, when it was not subject to the incapacity of those few private persons whose occupancy was not accompanied by all the circumstances necessary to constitute a source of property?

The government confidently hopes that the preceding observations may be considered as justifying its grave objections to the admission of a reclamation, the formal discussion of which commences now when the legation has received the documents and other proofs that it expected, in order to present it, and cannot, therefore, have acquired such a degree of urgency as a subject would have when examined in all lights in which no difficulties and no necessity of considering them had been presented, and in which, from the first, all identity of opinion in both the parties to it had not failed to appear.

The undersigned renews to the Hon. Mr. Eames the assurance of his high consideration.

JACINTO GUTIERREZ.

Hon. Charles Eames,
Minister Resident of the United States.

Legation of the United States,
Caraccas, March 31, 1857.

Sir: The undersigned minister resident of the United States has the honor to acknowledge the note of the honorable Minister of Foreign Relations of Venezuela, under date of 27th ultimo, in reply to that of the 20th December last, in which the undersigned continued to press upon the attention of the government of Venezuela the urgent importance of an immediate adjustment of the very grave question which has been pending between the two governments for nearly two years in relation to the expulsion of certain citizens of the United States from the guano island of Aves, in December, 1854, by the armed public force of the Venezuelan government.

The government of the United States has from the first presented this question through the undersigned to the government of Venezuela in the form of a demand for full indemnification to these its citizens for all the loss, damage, and injury resulting to them from the grave and wholly unjustifiable outrage which it considers to have been perpetrated upon them in the act of their expulsion, in the spoliation of their property which then took place, and in their continued exclusion, to their great loss and injury, by Venezuela from the peaceable possession and usufruct of the guano on that island; and it was the principal object of the undersigned, in his note of the 20th of December last, having in view the maintenance of friendly relations between the two governments, first, to impress upon the government of Venezuela his clear conviction that little then remained to be done in the case but to fix justly the terms of that indemnification, and, secondly, to indicate and explain a basis of arrangement upon which, in his judgment, the satisfaction so imperatively demanded by all the character and circumstances of the case, and by the attitude of the two governments in respect to it, might be properly and promptly made.

Mature consideration of the note of the honorable Minister of Foreign Relations, with careful reference both to what it alleges and to what it omits to allege, has fully confirmed the undersigned in the views which he then had the honor to urge, and he does not doubt that such will also be its effect upon his government. From the whole tenor of that note it sufficiently appears that the government of Venezuela does not dispute that these claimants, by their agents, were the first discoverers of the guano on the Island of Aves, nor that, at large expense, they soon after, in the summer of 1854, took and maintained for several months peaceable and undisturbed possession of such guano; nor that they fully intended and were fully prepared to retain such peaceable possession till the whole valuable supply of that article there should be by them exhausted; nor that they were forcibly expelled and ousted from such possession in December of that year by the Venezuelan government, acting through its public armed force; nor that Venezuela has since continued to occupy and hold the island and the guano on it for its own profit, against these claimants, by such armed force; nor that great losses and damages, both immediate and consequential, have resulted to them from that expulsion and adverse possession. Of all these facts (and they are the main facts upon which the government of the United States has heretofore demanded and now demands full indemnification to these claimants) the very elaborate note of the Hon. Mr. Gutierrez, as it alleges no denial, must evidently be taken as confession.

It is, moreover, observable that the Hon. Mr. Gutierrez nowhere in his note alleges, in clear and express terms, that the expulsion of these claimants, as it took place, was a lawful and justifiable act, nor does he anywhere expressly and absolutely deny the obligation of the Venezuelan government to make reparation to them for that act.

The undersigned, in his note of 20th of December, distinctly alleged that "if these claimants were, as against Venezuela, lawfully in possession of the island where Venezuela found them, then surely they may rightfully claim full reparation for being driven away by her public force."

This proposition, unless it be confuted, carries along with it, inevitably and manifestly, the justice and validity of this claim for indemnification; yet the Hon. Mr. Gutierrez has nowhere expressly denied either the fact or the inference which it contains. He has nowhere asserted that these claimants were in fact, as against Venezuela, unlawfully upon the island when Venezuela found them. He has neither cited nor alluded to any law, ordinance, decree, or regulation of the Venezuelan government, which they infringed by going there and working there and remaining in possession there. He has wholly failed even to aver distinctly that they committed by those proceedings any violation of the established territorial sovereignty of Venezuela.

The absence of these averments, in a note purporting to reply to the precise and stringent proposition of the undersigned above cited, is of course confession. It is confession that these claimants, from June to December, were not as against Venezuela law-breakers nor trespassers, but were lawfully engaged in lawful occupation. Indeed, such confession by the government of Venezuela could with no show of reason have been withheld, because the fact is of universal notoriety that these claimants in landing upon the "Aves" in June, 1854, and proceeding to make the best use they could of that desert island, did no more than all men had been free to do and had done, whenever they saw fit, from a period long antecedent to the existence of the republic of Venezuela, and through the whole period of that existence, without any sort of hinderance, molestation, prohibition, or remonstrance by any government, and least of all, by the government of Venezuela.

But the Hon. Mr. Gutierrez, apparently convinced of the impossibility of denying the liability of his government to make full reparation to these claimants upon the assumption that they were lawfully upon the "Aves," when Venezuela found them and expelled them, proceeds in this connection to state that these claimants "can never complain of their expulsion unless they demonstrate that it was lawful for them to land upon the island and take away the guano found on it." This observation of the Hon. Mr. Gutierrez has been read by the undersigned, and will be read by his government with regret and astonishment. In the prosecution, as they consider, and as their government maintains, of a legitimate commercial industry these claimants took peaceable possession of an article of value which they had first discovered on a desert and derelict island, near, indeed, to the possessions of several great powers, but understood to be not then claimed by any of them, and separated by several hundred miles of open sea from the uttermost known limits of Venezuelan jurisdiction, as then existing or pretended in that direction, and upon which, up to that time, no citizen of Venezuela in any capacity, public or private, is proved or even asserted to have ever set his foot.

Remaining in this peaceable occupation for several months, these claimants were visited by ships-of-war of at least four of the great powers having possessions in the immediate vicinity, no one of which manifested the least right or disposition to disturb them, and some of which expressly confirmed their right to remain undisturbed. In this state of facts the government of Venezuela, without any previous public allegation of title to this island, without the slighest complaint or remonstrance against its occupation by these claimants, and without any notice to them or to their government of its hostile purpose, organized and sent forth an armed expedition to pass far beyond the uttermost limits of Venezuelan jurisdiction, to traverse four degrees of latitude on the open sea, to seek and find them at their peaceful work, to menance them, and finally to eject them from the island at the point of the bayonet; and then, with depredation upon their property, to drive away there ships from before the mouths of her cannon. All this was perpetrated; and now, when the government of the United States demands from the government of Venezuela full indemnification to their claimants for her act in thus treating them as law-breakers, trespassers, and criminals, the unexampled and inexplicable answer of the honorable Minister of Foreign Relations, as understood by the undersigned, appears in substance to be: "Let them first prove that they are not law-breakers, trespassers, and criminals; till they do this, they have no right even to complain for being treated as such." Solicitous to receive with all proper consideration every observation offered by the honorable Minister of Foreign Relations in behalf of his government, and therefore avoiding upon this point all unfit warmth of expression, the undersigned contents himself with declaring that such answer to this reclamation is, in his judgment, totally inadmissible; and that he is by no means prepared to assure the government of Venezuela that the government of the United States, in justice to itself and to its citizens, must not regard such answer, if insisted on, as constituting aggravation of the original injury.

By every principle of justice, and by the law of every civilized nation, the burden of proof and justification is upon the aggressor, and not upon the victim of his aggression. It is for the assailant to justify his assault. It is for the ejector to justify, in law, his violent act of ejectment. Not by the undersigned, not even by his government alone, but by the voice of the venerable code of public law, by the collective conscience of civilization as embodied in legal institutions everywhere, is it proclaimed to Venezuela that, by reason of the perpetration of this deed of violence by her public force upon peaceable and law-abiding men, she must stand in the attitude of a wrong-doer until she either makes due atonement for the act or presents and proves for it affirmatively a clear and complete justification.

But, if all this were otherwise, and if the burden of proof were in this case not upon the aggressor, but upon the sufferers of the aggression, still it is wholly manifest that Venezuela, by her own act, has precluded herself from alleging that these claimants were, as against her, unlawfully upon the island. Venezuela has produced, and the Hon. Mr. Gutierrez in his note seems to rely upon the so-called "agreement" between Commander Dias and these men, as her justification for driving them away. That "agreement," in the judgment of the United States, is wholly invalid and void, if not for other reasons, then, at least, for duly proved force and fraud. Venezuela denies that the force and fraud are duly proved, insists upon its validity, and terms it a "convention." But, if these claimants were not, as against Venezuela, lawfully at work on the island, then they were trespassers and law-breakers, engaged in depredation upon Venezuelan property, and in criminal violation of Venezuelan law and territorial sovereignty. Now, assuredly the enlightened government of Venezuela will never acknowledge that, acting through high official functionaries in command of her public force, she makes "conventions" with characters of this description found by her in *flagrante delicto*. Yet this is just what she must not only acknowledge, but maintain, unless she now admits that these men, when she found and ejected them, were not, as against her, law-breakers, trespassers, and depredators, but were, on the contrary, lawfully engaged in lawful occupation.

Proceeding, then, upon the conclusion that Venezuela in presenting the alleged "agreement" or "convention," as entered into by her with these claimants and attempting to sustain its validity, has precluded herself from maintaining that they were, as against her, lawbreakers, whom she might lawfully expel by force. The undersigned will now, in reply to the observations of the Hon. Mr. Gutierrez on this point, establish beyond all doubt the total invalidity of that alleged "agreement" as against these claimants. That the positive and direct proof of force and fraud in extorting the signatures to that paper, deemed upon very mature and careful consideration by the government of the United States fully sufficient to invalidate and avoid it, should, when presented to the government of Venezuela, be pronounced insufficient is matter of regret and surprise.

The purpose of the honorable minister's observation, that the depositions duly specified and transmitted by the undersigned in his note of the 20th of December last were "mere copies," is not distinctly perceived. It is impossible for the undersigned to doubt that copies of depositions transmitted in due course of business from the Department of State at Washington to this legation, and then by this legation duly transmitted in copy to the government of Venezuela, will have with that government precisely the force, neither more nor less, of the originals, of which they purport to be copies. The phrase "mere copies," applied to such papers, is inappropriate. They are more than "mere copies," they are authenticated copies.

The Hon. Mr. Gutierrez alleges that the deponents are interested in this claim, and intimates that they are therefore incompetent witnesses. This is not an exact statement nor a correct inference. The deponents are the salaried agents of these claimants, having no proved interest whatever in the claim, and as such they form a class of witnesses recognized as fully competent by the tribunals of all countries.

The Hon. Mr. Gutierrez observes that if the agents of these claimants had resisted or protested at the time or made immediate reclamation of their property, then their assertion that they signed the alleged "agreement" upon compulsion would be credible. They did all this; they did reluct and resist, and signed at last not only under a mistake, but avowedly and only to avoid violence and bloodshed at the hands of the public force of a government. They complained at the moment of the whole proceeding, including the seizure and sacrifice of their property, and made reclamation for full reparation without delay before their government, and that reclamation was at once presented clearly and strongly by the undersigned, in pursuance of his instructions, to the government of Venezuela. So prompt, indeed, was all this action of reclamation, that it outran all knowledge by the undersigned and by his government of the alleged "agreement," and caused that paper, when authentically made known by the Venezuelan government, to appear then before the undersigned as new matter in the case, and as such, and only as such, fit, on its face, to be referred to his government for explanation and consideration.

But on this point of force and fraud in that alleged "agreement" the Hon. Mr. Gutierrez principally complains of the absence of the testimony of one of its signers. This cause of complaint the undersigned is now fortunately enabled in the most effectual manner to remove. He presents with this note a long extract from the deposition of Captain N. P. Gibbs, one of the signers of the alleged "agreement," and invokes to it the especial attention of the government of Venezuela. Its minuteness of detail, its frank admissions, and its temperate yet firm tone, all stamp it as a trustworthy paper, while its clearness of statement shows it plainly to be the testimony of an intelligent witness. The Hon. Mr. Gutierrez will observe that the witness swears distinctly that the so-called "agreement" was fraudulently interpreted to him; that he would not have signed "anything" except to avoid violence and bloodshed; that he yielded only to the command and force of a government recognized by his own; and that had the contents of the paper been truly interpreted to him he would have refused his signature to at it all hazards.

Now, the Hon. Mr. Gutierrez will also observe that in the testimony of these witnesses there is no possible chance of mistake. Two of them, chief actors in the transaction, swear positively to their own motives in signing the paper; the others swear to what they personally knew of those motives as eye and ear witnesses of the transaction, and as participants in it by consultation. There being no possibility of mistake on their part, the government of Venezuela must either receive their testimony on this point as true, or it must take the position that they all willfully commit wholesale perjury. This last position the government of Venezuela assuredly will never assume; for the professed purpose of the Venezuelan expedition was to occupy the island and eject these men from its possession. That possession they had lawfully, in their judgment, and in the judgment of their government, established at great expense and were sedulously and profitably maintaining. It is against all reason—it is against every principle of human nature, to suppose that they could possibly be so ejected from such a possession without the employment of force or fraud, or both. The Venezuelan expedition was provided with guns and bayonets, and powder and ball, and does not appear to have been provided with any other arguments to accomplish its purpose. Here were the means of force. The commander of the expedition understood the Spanish language, which one of the two chief agents did not understand at all, and the other, if at all, very imperfectly. Here was a ready method of fraud. The paper was drawn and signed only in Spanish, and not, as would have been natural, both in English and Spanish. Here was a badge of fraud. The paper now urged by Venezuela as an "agreement" or "convention" was presented to these agents as a "permit." Here was an overt act of fraud. The purpose of the expedition plainly requiring for its accomplishment the use of the means of force or fraud, which were at hand, was accomplished. These witnesses swear that force and fraud were used for its accomplishment. Their collective solemn oaths, therefore, only confirm and establish the strongest possible antecedent probability. Such testimony to such fact must command irresistible credence.

It is obvious to say that these facts were not known when this paper was first presented to the undersigned; that if they had been known it would never have been even referred by him to his government, and that if, in that case it had been so referred, the rejection of it as wholly void against these claimants must have been alike summary and conclusive.

As against these claimants, therefore, this alleged "agreement" is null and of no effect; but the force and fraud which as against them invalidate and avoid it were not theirs, and therefore they and their government have a right to claim that the "agreement" being now insisted on by Venezuela shall as against the Venezuelan government remain in the case to establish—

First. That through its authorities that government even in the act of expelling them from the island acknowledged them to be not lawbreakers, but, on the contrary, of a character and in a position fit to be negotiated with; and, *secondly*, to establish as against these authorities that in the negotiation forming a part of the *res gesta* of their expulsion, not force only, but fraud also was employed against them, and to their injury.

Another consideration in this connection claims from the government of Venezuela thoughtful attention. The signature of this paper by the agents of these claimants, thus extorted, alone appears to have prevented conflict, bloodshed, and, in the heated passion and stern retribution of the hour, but too probable slaughter. That a paper preventing such dire and bloody work and its ulterior consequences, and sworn to have been signed by these men only in that purpose, should be insisted on in bar of this claim for just indemnification is, in the judgment of the undersigned, most extraordinary and unjustifiable.

The Hon. Mr. Gutierrez, making a distinction between things "common" and things "derelict," observes that "the Island of Aves is not a derelict thing, nor can it be conceived how Mr. Eames asserts it to be so, when, in the same paragraph, he states that it has never been reduced to possession, nor under the jurisdiction of any power." The undersigned would regret that the government of Venezuela should continue under the totally erroneous impression that the government of the United States has presented or urged this claim in any other than precise and appropriate terms. The Hon. Mr. Gutierrez is, therefore, in reply informed that, in the judgment of the United States, this Island of Aves having long been known but not reduced to possession nor embraced within any jurisdiction, was in the strict legal and lexicographical sense of that term derelict in the month of June, 1854, when the guano upon it was lawfully taken into actual possession by these claimants who had discovered it, and whose right to retain such possession undisturbed was good against the whole world, when they were, to their great injury, wrongfully and unlawfully driven away by Venezuela.

But in this connection the note of the Hon. Mr. Gutierrez presents other observations of far more extended reach, and which require direct response. It alleges that as the government of the United States gave no commission to these claimants to occupy the island "in its name," they, as "mere private persons," "had not the capacity of acquisition which nations have, and could not compete with any nation, nor consider as occupied an island whose possession they had not force to maintain by defending it against the government which might desire to appropriate it to themselves." This observation and some of those apparently in a somewhat similar sense which follow it, in the note of the Hon. Mr. Gutierrez, seem to be rather vaguely expressed, and the undersigned is not sure that they are exactly understood. But in his opinion they may be considered as implying, or at least intimating, though they do not in terms assert, the doctrine that, when citizens of the United States, in their personal capacity, as first discoverers of the guano thereon, are in the actual occupancy and use of an island previously known to exist, but at the time of its occupation by such citizens derelict and not embraced within the sovereignty or jurisdiction of Venezuela, then the government of Venezuela has the right, and may, in its discretion, lawfully and justifiably exercise the right to overpower and expel such occupants by its public force, and appropriate to itself the island and the guano existing thereon. Such a doctrine, opposed alike to private right and public law, and carrying on its face its own condemnation, cannot be made by the undersigned in this case a subject of discussion. Should such doctrine be formally advanced by the government of Venezuela in bar of this claim, the duty of the undersigned will be limited to the announcement of that fact to his government. In view of the settled policy of the government of the United States as established in ancient usage, recognized by other powers, and reaffirmed by recent legislation, the maintenance of such doctrine by any power, and its persistent application against citizens of the United States, are not perceived to be compatible with the preservation of peaceful relations. The undersigned trusts, therefore, that the observations referred to have not, in fact, the full scope and intention which some of the terms in which they are expressed may be considered to contemplate. Yet if these observations do not imply and embrace substantially the doctrine referred to, then their bearing against this claim is not to be perceived because they certainly proceed upon the assumption that this island was not Venezuelan at the time when Venezuela by force expelled these claimants from it and reduced it to her own armed occupation.

The Hon. Mr. Gutierrez observes that: "They (the United States,) have no doubt as to the eminent dominion of Venezuela in the 'Aves,' as Mr. Eames has repeatedly stated to the undersigned, and only dispute the private property in the guano found thereon." This statement, in order to be exact, requires material modification. If it be intended to assert that the undersigned has repeatedly stated that Venezuela, since her unlawful expulsion of these claimants, has maintained an armed occupation of the Aves adverse to the rights, and so excluded them from the use of their right of property in the guano thereon, then the statement is accurate; and the fact stated constitutes an important element in this their claim for redress. But if it be intended to assert that either the government of the United States or the undersigned has ever admitted that Venezuela has now, or ever did have, the rightful eminent domain of the Aves, then the statement is wholly inaccurate. No such admission has ever been made, and there is, in the judgment of the undersigned, no probability that it ever wil be made. It may be that the forcible expulsion of these claimants, and the subsequent armed occupation of the island are regarded by the Venezuelan government as constituting in Venezuela, during the continuance of such occupation, an eminent domain there *de facto*. Such an assumption on her part would appear to be indicated by her course in administering the island on her own responsibility, and for her own advantage. But respecting the correctness of this assumption, neither the undersigned nor his government has seen occasion to express to Venezuela any opinion, for the plain reason that such eminent domain *de facto*, if it exist at all, can obviously exist only as subject to all the responsibilities attaching to the mode of its acquisition and maintenance, and as subject especially to the previous and paramount right of these claimants to full indemnification for the outrage perpetrated on them in their expulsion and exclusion. This consideration effectually disposes of the several observations in which the honorable minister of foreign relations has set forth the inconvenience which must result to Venezuela, upon the supposition that those claimants are entitled to the full indemnification now demanded. Inconveniences, more or less grave, always flow from the perpetration of wrongful acts. The expulsion of these claimants and their subsequent exclusion by Venezuela from the enjoyment of their rights on the Aves were, in the judgment of the United States, unquestionably wrongful acts. It would be a strange doctrine indeed which would withhold from peaceable and law-abiding men, thus gravely inferred, a just indemnification on the ground of inconveniences thereby resulting to the perpetrator of the injury.

The Hon. Mr. Gutierrez has in his note referred to the contract concluded in December, 1854, by the Venezuelan government with Mr. Wallace, to the alleged course of the government of the United States in sustaining the validity of that contract, and to the negotiation which, after the annulment of that contract by Venezuela, took place with the aid of the undersigned under his instructions, in order to protect the rights and interests vested by that contract in the several guano islands regarded as rightfully belonging to Venezuela, and of course other than the Aves which was not so regarded. In this series of occurrences, as referred to in his note, the honorable minister of foreign relations appears to allege or intimate the existence of an obstacle to the admission of this claim for indemnification. But in order to prevent any such obstacle, the honorable minister of foreign relations has manifestly felt himself inevitably compelled to omit or suppress in his note all mention of the most capital and conspicuous facts of record in those occurrences.

Neither the government of the United States nor the undersigned, at that time in the United States, knew anything of the Wallace contract, nor of any purpose in any quarter to conclude any such contract until months after its conclusion.

This fact is wholly omitted in the note of the Hon. Mr. Gutierrez.

Both the government of the United States and the undersigned distinctly and affirmatively refused all manner of sanction to that contract, in so far as it related to the island of Aves in question, and this refusal of all such sanction was officially made known to the government of Venezuela by the undersigned in his immediate notification to the government of Venezuela in the month of March, 1855, of the claim of these claimants for full indemnification for their unlawful expulsion, in consequence of that contract, from the island of Aves.

All mention of this fact is omitted in the note of the Hon. Mr. Gutierrez.

In the negotiation which took place in September, 1855, to protect the just rights of the assignees of the Wallace contract after its annulment by Venezuela, not only was all manner of sanction or countenance of that contract, in so far as it related to the Aves, withheld and refused by the government of the United States and by the undersigned, but, on the contrary, the undersigned, under express instructions then referred to, made known officially and in the most formal and effectual manner to the government of Venezuela, that the Aves, and all the rights and claims of the present claimants therein, were, in their whole extent, reserved and saved from being in any manner or in the slightest degree affected or impaired by that negotiation or by any aid which the undersigned might render it.

This most conclusive fact, announced by the undersigned to the government of Venezuela at the commencement of that negotiation, insisted on during its continuance, and five days before it closed, placed on record officially before the government of Venezuela, and afterwards, in subsequent record, insisted on, is, in the note of the Hon. Mr. Gutierrez, in the face of all that record, totally and incomprehensibly suppressed.

It is thus made the duty of the undersigned now to reproduce that record.

The negotiation in question closed in a contract concluded and signed between the government of Venezuela and the agent of the assignees of the Wallace contract on the 29th of September, 1855. On the 24th of that month, the undersigned delivered to the government of Venezuela an official note of that date, being a memorandum of an audience granted to the undersigned three days before by his excellency the President of the republic, in the presence of his excellency's minister, the Hon. Mr. Aranda (then minister of foreign relations) and the Hon. Mr. Gutierrez, (then minister of finance.)

From that note of the undersigned of the 24th of September, 1855, the following are extracts defining the position then taken upon this subject by the undersigned, in pursuance of express orders from his government:

"After this preliminary reference, and having previously presented to his excellency the agent of the company, the undersigned proceeded officially to make known to his excellency what he had previously declared to the ministers of his excellency's government, that in rendering his good offices in aid of the purposes of the agent of the company to save their rights as the assignees of the Wallace contract, the undersigned was emphatically instructed to forbear from saying or doing anything which could in the slightest degree affect or impair the claim against the Venezuelan government for full reparation on the part of those American citizens whom Venezuela had found in possession of the Aves Island in December last. The undersigned explained, therefore, fully and clearly to his excellency, that all which he might say or do in aid of the agent of the company, must be understood with this express reservation, that the Aves claim was a wholly separate matter, in no way to be compromised or affected by any arrangement which might be made in respect to the rights under the Wallace contract, or by any aid which the undersigned might render in bringing about such an arrangement."

Certainly this language of reservation and exception of the present claim in its full extent from being in any way affected, or impaired, or compromised by that negotiation, or by any action of the undersigned in relation thereto is, and was intended to be, just as clear, explicit, and comprehensive as language can be. But the undersigned, as appears by the same record, did not stop with this. The same note proceeds to state that:

"In reply to a remark from his excellency expressing his preference that the claim in regard to the previous occupation of the Aves Island, should, if possible, be disposed of in any arrangement which might be made with the agent of the company, the undersigned answered to his excellency as he had previously answered to his excellency's ministers upon the same point, that any such disposition of the Aves claim was wholly impossible, not only by reason of the entirely distinct character of the two subjects and of the duty of the undersigned to treat them separately, but also by reason of the fact that the undersigned was not yet fully in possession of all the information requisite for the due adjustment of the Aves claim. He felt himself authorized, however, in view of recent instructions, to repeat the expression of his confident conviction that the government of the United States would deem it its duty to maintain the right of those claimants to full indemnification."

Surely this was a language which did not admit and could not admit any possible misapprehension; but out of abundant caution, and to define repeatedly, and, if possible, with still more exactness, the position of the government of the United States and its legation upon this point, the undersigned again referred to the topic, and representing to his excellency the very grave and serious aspect presented by this Aves claim, even when viewed exclusively upon its own character and circumstances, and urging his excellency to consider the great additional complication and aggravation which must be brought upon it by the Venezuelan government if it should persist in a course of policy inflicting serious loss and injury upon other citizens of the United States having other rights and interests vested under the Wallace contract in the several guano islands considered to belong to the republic, the undersigned proceeded to state that the effect of concluding a satisfactory arrangement with the agent of the company would only be to leave this Aves claim to be afterwards adjusted upon due consideration of its own rights and merits, without such additional and extrinsic embarrassment and aggravation.

The undersigned will quote again from the same note of the 24th of September, 1855, his exact language on this point, which is as follows:

"The undersigned then, proceeding more immediately to the objects and purposes of Mr. Pickrell, the agent of the company interested in the Wallace contract, desired his excellency to consider the extremely unfortunate aspect in which this whole guano question, between Venezuela and the citizens of the United States interested in it, now presented itself to the government of the United States. A whole series of events of a grave and highly unsatisfactory character, each of them a separate occurrence, but all having a common reference to the rights of American citizens in the guano islands, had followed each other in rapid succession. The forcible dispossession of the American citizens on the Aves, the contemporaneous conclusion of the Wallace contract, its annulment by Venezuela in defeat of the rightful expectations and to the great damage of those interested in it, were facts each of which tended to aggravate the other, and to complicate the negotiation looking to a satisfactory adjustment of any or all of them. The undersigned earnestly desired his excellency to consider the grave additional complication and difficulty which must ensue if the agent of the company now present, through the refusal of Venezuela, should find himself unable, after all his efforts, even when aided by the good offices of the legation of the United States, to make any satisfactory arrangement to protect the rights and interests which he represented. It was the duty of the undersigned most respectfully to urge upon his excellency's consideration that in the judgment of the government of the United States this guano question was a matter of great and public concernment, that it involved not only important rights and large interests, but also a grave question of good faith, the determination of which, under the circumstances in which it had arisen, could not but have its effect upon the relations of the two countries; and that the undersigned, while carefully avoiding an expression which could be possibly construed in any unfriendly or minatory sense, or in any sense not perfectly compatible with the most perfect consideration for the dignity of the Venezuelan government, yet felt bound in frankness to make known to his excellency that both the people and the government of the United States felt a deep interest in this subject, and would see with extreme regret and sensibility any course now taken by Venezuela which should result in a loss and injury to those of our citizens interested in the contract above referred to. On the other hand, the undersigned did not hesitate to say that, in his judgment, an opposite policy on the part of Venezuela, recognizing and restoring, in a satisfactory manner, the rights of those citizens, would produce an excellent effect upon the relations of the two governments, not only as in itself an act of good faith, but also as leaving the very serious question which had previously arisen between the two governments in regard to the forcible occupation of the Aves Island by Venezuela to be considered and adjusted upon its own character and circumstances, without the additional aggravation which must be brought upon it by the persistence of Venezuela in a course of policy productive of great loss and injury to other citizens of the United States interested in the Wallace contract."

Thus formally and fully was the government of Venezuela, from the very commencement of this negotiation, officially assured that the claim of these claimants could in no manner nor in the slightest degree be affected by it; that the Aves Island and all their rights and claims therein were fully reserved and saved; that those rights and claims were a wholly separate matter, and would as such be effectually and fully sustained by the United States, and, finally, that the conclusion of a satisfactory arrangement with the agent of the assignees of the Wallace contract would, by freeing these anterior claims from formidable additional aggravation and difficulty, leave them, as a very grave and serious question, to be afterwards adjusted upon due consideration of their own separate character and merits.

And, after full consideration of the whole matter, the government of Venezuela, with this recorded position of the government of the United States upon that subject in its hands, did, in full view of this record, five days afterwards, conclude the arrangement with the agent of the assignees of the Wallace contract. That the government of Venezuela should take notice of this record in framing that arrangement was a matter of course, and that such notice was taken may be inferred from the fact that the new arrangement, departing from the form of the Wallace contract, omitted all mention of the Aves in the article granting the usufruct of the guano islands of the republic to the assignees of that contract, and afterwards, in another article, specified the Aves with the apparent object of relieving Venezuela from liability to those assignees in the event that her possession and use of it for her own profit should, in view of this claim or from any other reason, terminate. Such was the view taken by the undersigned when, in reference to the subject of the cession to the government of Holland of the then armed possession of the Aves by Venezuela, he, in his note of the 8th of March, 1856, after formally and urgently protesting against such cession upon the main and principal ground of the rights and claims of these claimants to that island, and of the international reclamation by the government of the United States in their behalf then pending in its full extent, considered it proper also to address the government of Venezuela, in that note, the following additional language, fully recognizing and restating the recorded position taken by him in regard to the Aves in the whole course of the negotiation in question:

"The undersigned in this connection deems it his duty further to state that he has in his possession a copy of a contract entered into on the 29th of September last between the government of Venezuela and John F. Pickrell, a citizen of the United States, conveying to the said contractor and his associates certain exclusive privileges in the guano islands of Venezuela, in which contract the undersigned perceives that the island of Aves in question is specified under certain conditions and stipulations therein set forth. Though it is undoubtedly true that the inclusion of that island in the said contract, in any form and to any extent, took place without any manner of countenance or sanction on the part of the government of the United States or of the undersigned, by whom, on the contrary, all the rights and claims of its prior American occupants were fully and expressly reserved from being in any way affected or impaired by that negotiation; and though the undersigned, in view of that reservation, now abstains from giving any manner of sanction to the insertion of the Aves Island in that contract to operate thereby any defeat of those reserved rights and claims in their full extent, yet he deems it his duty to state in reference to the cession of the island now under consideration, that it appears to him that Venezuela, on her own sole responsibility, did by that contract voluntarily transfer, for good consideration, to a citizen of the United States, in their full usufruct, as against any foreign power whatsoever possessory claims in that island she may have set up, be the same in her own judgment greater or less, and that therefore upon any view of her case, the proposed cession of the island to Holland, is objectionable, and the undersigned again hereby makes known that such cession, if it be made, must take place, subject to all and singular the rights and claims in the premises of the government of the United States, and of any and all of its citizens against whomsoever the same may concern.''

These two notes of the 24th of September, 1855, and of the 8th of March, 1856, were repeatedly referred to by the undersigned in his note of the 20th of December last, and such having been from the first and up to the present time the recorded and steadily-maintained position of the undersigned and of the government of the United States as to the rights and claims of the present claimants in their relations to the two contracts now alleged by the Hon. Mr. Gutierrez in bar of their claim, the undersigned is entirely unable to comprehend the motive and policy of the honorable minister of foreign relations in making that allegation, accompanied, as it is, by a total suppression of this most complete and effectual reservation made by their government and by the undersigned in their behalf. The undersigned cannot indulge any disrespectful doubt that the Hon. Mr. Gutierrez clearly perceived that this reservation wholly annihilates the force of his allegation of these contracts, and utterly precludes it from having any force against this claim. As introduced and insisted upon by the Hon. Mr. Gutierrez, it can tend only to convince the government of the United States even more fully and completely that Venezuela has against this claim no valid defense. Had any such valid defense existed in the case, then surely the ability of the Hon. Mr. Gutierrez would never have felt itself constrained to allege a defense so wholly invalid and unfounded as this, the very presentation of which has required the total suppression of the most important and conspicuous fact appearing in the whole negotiation, and which suppression was sure to encounter at the hands of the undersigned this swift and signal and conclusive exposure.

The Hon. Mr. Gutierrez, without one word of proof or argument to sustain his statement, has alleged "that the island of Aves belonged to the republic before 1854, as the successor of Spain who discovered it." This allegation at this time was not expected by the undersigned, who has from the first maintained before the government of Venezuela that any pretension of Venezuelan title to the Aves prior to 1854, has no sufficient foundation to justify discussion. Continued research upon this point has fully confirmed the undersigned in this emphatic view, and he desires that the observations now submitted by him on the subject may be considered exclusively in that sense.

Before entering upon an examination of the proposition of Mr. Gutierrez, above cited, it is proper to notice the undisputed facts which, appearing as antecedent to any such discussion, seem to the undersigned to preclude its necessity.

It is not pretended that Venezuela can claim any title to the Aves Island in question by reason of a contiguity. No single authority of any character whatever is alleged to have ever recognized in any manner that island as a Venezuelan possession prior to 1854. On the contrary, all the geographical authorities who have described the islands in that vicinity, and among these Balbi Alcedo and the official Derrotero de las Antillas, in speaking of these islands, have entirely failed to mention any such pretension of title to the Aves Island in question. It is not asserted that in any constitution, law, ordinance, decree, or other State paper whatsoever, emanating from the authority either of the captain-generalship of Venezuela, the republic of Colombia, or the republic of Venezuela, has this island of Aves ever been named, prior to 1854, as a possession, or claimed possession of either of those governments. No proofs have been offered and no assertion has been made that any pretension of title in Venezuela to the Aves prior to 1854, has been even mentioned and much less countenanced by any writer whatever. The undersigned maintains the firm conviction, that up to the year 1854 no printed mention of such title or pretension of title can anywhere be found. The undersigned has no reason to believe that any *unpublished* document written before 1854, and existing in the archives of any government, can be produced, in which such Venezuelan pretension of title is even alluded to. It is not pretended that Venezuela ever established any such jurisdiction upon the Aves, or ever made any such manifestation of title there prior to 1854, as other governments are bound to respect; and, as already stated, it has not been proved or, to the knowledge of the undersigned, anywhere asserted that prior to 1854 any citizen of the republic of Venezuela, in any capacity, either private or public, ever visited that island.

In view of such undisputed facts existing antecedent to any discussion of the title now alleged by Venezuela prior to 1854, it would certainly seem that no discussion on that point is now necessary.

But there is another line of facts which have not, so far as the undersigned is informed, been heretofore alluded to in this connection, though undoubtedly of the most conclusive character. To these facts the undersigned has now the honor to invoke especial attention of the honorable Minister of Foreign Relations.

The undersigned confidently alleges that the government of Venezuela itself, acting through its duly authorized commissioners, has at a yet recent date announced to the world its official repudiation of all title or pretension of title to the Island of Aves in question; and that in June, 1854, when these claimants took possession of that island, that official repudiation of all Venezuelan title or claim to it stood unmodified and in full force.

As the exact demonstration of this proposition, while exploding all pretension of title in Venezuela to the Aves, must present, in the strongest light, the extraordinary character of the outrage complained of by these claimants, and the consequent signal obligation of Venezuela to make to them full reparation, the undersigned deems it proper to present that demonstration with exactness of detail.

Soon after the establishment of the republic of Venezuela its constituent congress, in a decree under date of 13th of October, 1830, reciting the importance to Venezuela of a statistical delineation of the territory of the nation, and of its limits in "all its provinces," directed "the executive power to authorize a skilled official functionary to accomplish that work." Under this law Colonel Codazzi, a scientific engineer, who had been previously extensively engaged in such service under the authority of the republic of Colombia, was duly appointed and commissioned to perform within the period of three years, by authority of the government of Venezuela, the work proposed. By another law of congress under date of 3d May, 1833, the prescribed period for the work was extended, in compliance with an official report of the Department of War, two years longer. By another law of congress of 22d April, 1835, also in pursuance of the official report of the Department of War, the period was again extended to the 31st of December, 1837. Another law of congress of 17th of April, 1837, reciting that "the previous extension is not long enough to enable the commission to complete the delineation of the province Guayana," again extends the period to the 31st of December, 1838, and further enacts "that the commission, as soon as it has completed the delineation of that province, shall make the general delineation of the republic." By yet another law of congress, 18th of April, 1839, it is enacted that the commission shall continue till the 31st of December, 1839, and that its duty shall be "to form the general delineation of the republic, to form a descriptive chart presenting its physical aspect, and to note and explain the leading facts in the political history of Venezuela in their relation to its geography, and that the government shall place at the disposition of the commission all the delineations, itineraries, statistical information, and other documents existing in its archives, and which may be deemed by the commission proper to be consulted in the discharge of these its duties; that the works may be engraved and printed by the commission for its account, but one hundred copies shall be the property of the government for purposes of instruction and for the public officers; that if the time given by this law for the completion of the work be not sufficient, then the executive power, by consent of the council of government, may extend the same six months more." By yet another law of congress of the 16th of March, 1840, reciting "that although by the law of 18th of April of the year last past permission was given to that commissioner (Colonel Codazzi) to print and engrave his said work for his own account, as a reward for his absolute devotion to the duty with which he was charged, the economy of the public treasury being at the same time thereby considered, it has not on that account ceased to be a national work, the prompt completion of which is of the utmost importance," it is enacted that "the executive power shall cause to be placed at the disposition of Colonel Agustin Codazzi ten thousand dollars out of the public treasury, as a loan, for the printing and engraving of the work with which he was charged by the executive power under the law of 14th of October, 1830." By another law of congress of 23d of February, 1841, making the same recital, and again referring to the high national importance and utility of the work and of its prompt conclusion, it is enacted that the executive power shall place five thousand dollars more at the disposition of Colonel Codazzi for the same purpose.

On the 4th of September, 1840, M. Berthelot, general secretary of the central committee of the Geographical Society of Paris, read to that society in its session of that day a "report upon the geographical and statistical labors executed in all the extension of the territory of Venezuela by Colonel Codazzi." From this report the following remarks are extracted:

"M. Codazzi, colonel of engineers, recently arrived in Paris, is charged by his government to cause to be engraved in France the great chart of the republic of Venezuela and the atlas of its provinces composed of twenty sheets. A special work dedicated to public instruction will accompany these productions, and will form two handsome volumes embracing the whole political history of Venezuela, the description, geography, and the statistics of that region." * * * *

"I shall be able to give you only a succinct idea of the work which the congress has thus ordered to be printed under the direction of Colonel Codazzi, to whom has been granted the obsolute ownership of the same as a national recompense." * * * * *

"The great map of Venezuela, the reductions and separated portions of which form an atlas arranged by provinces, is the result of ten years of incessant labors. This general map or chart presented to the institute by M. Arago has attracted the fixed attention of our *savants*."

* * * * * * * *

"It remains for me, in concluding this report, to express a desire which you will doubtless grant, that this excellent work of Colonel Codazzi be admitted to compete for the annual premium which you adjudge to those voyagers who have best served the cause of science."

On the 15th of March, 1841, a committee of the institute of France composed of Messrs. Arago, Savary, and Elie de Beaumont, presented, through their reporter, Mr. Bossingault, a "report upon the geographical and statistical works executed in the republic of Venezuela in pursuance of the orders of its congress."

From this report the following extracts are cited:

"By a decree of the 14th of October, 1830, the congress of Venezuela authorized the executive power to cause to be formed a general chart of the republic, and to cause to be collected in a single work the documents relating to the history and statistics of the country." * *

"Colonel Codazzi was charged with the direction of this important work by the President of the republic. Mr. Codazzi has traversed during the period of ten years and in all directions the vast territory of Venezuela. * * * The government having afforded to this engineer the means of proceeding to Europe to publish the result of his labors, he has selected France for that purpose, where his first step has been to submit to the judgment of the Academy of Sciences the fruit of his long and laborious researches." * * * * * *

"The examination of your committee has, with propriety, especially been devoted to the value of the elements employed by Mr. Codazzi in the construction of the atlas, and to the degree of confidence which the statistical documents forming the basis its text should inspire. These documents are numerous and authentic, and emanate directly from the general administration, because the government in creating the topographical commission placed its archives entirely at the disposition of the skillful officer who was at its head." * * * *

"The number of observations of latitudes and of chronometrical longitudes made by Mr. Codazzi is considerable. This indefatigable observer has established 1,002 notable points, it being observable that among these there are 58 which have sustained a comparison with the observations published by M. de Humboldt and with those unpublished of one of your committee."

"Venezuela is situated at the northern extremity of South America. Its political limits give it a very irregular figure, the circumference of which is 566 miriametros, comprising upon the Sea of the Antillas an extent of coasts of 144 miriametros. The superfice of the territory is 11,094.5 square miriametros, distributed in the following manner:

Tops of high mountains	47.2
Elevated mountains	2,756.9
Table lands	471.9
Plains	6,795.2
Lakes	222.8
Lagoons and ponds	68.2
Lands liable to inundation	716.7
Islands	15.6

* * * "The labors of Colonel Codazzi having required on his part so much perseverance appear to us as a whole and in all respects worthy of the most effectual encouragement. Your committee would not hesitate to solicit for them the highest proof of your estimation in causing their insertion in the *memoirés* of foreign *savants*, if such a request could be granted in the case of materials so voluminous, and which, besides, are on the eve of publication. Solely by reason of this impossibility your committee restrict themselves to the proposition that you offer your thanks to Mr. Codazzi for his important communication. They think, also, that by reason of the enlightened protection which the government of Venezuela has always granted to the labors of this skillful official, it would be just and useful that a copy of this report should be transmitted to the congress of that republic through the Minister of Foreign Affairs."

The conclusions of the report were adopted.

Thus formally was the geographical and topographical delineation of the republic of Venezuela in the whole extent of its jurisdiction, both continental and insular, as existing or pretended, laid before the world by the government of Venezuela itself.

Thus formally was it in that character received, analyzed, and reported upon by the learned societies standing in direct official relation with the government of France, and thus their reports reciting the exact number and measurement of all the islands claimed by Venezuela as Venezuelan, was officially transmitted to the government of Venezuela by the Department of Foreign Affairs of the French government.

And then all this official and scientific appreciation of the work of the Venezuelan commission was formally recognized and accepted by the Venezuelan government, for which, in consequence of these proceedings, Colonel Codazzi received from the French government the decoration of the legion of honor. The Venezuelan government by a special law of Congress of 22d ——, 1844, enabled him to accept that distinction, and afterwards by other law of Congress of 17th of May, 1845, reciting "that the services of Colonel Codazzi in the formation of the map of Venezuela, and in its publication with the geography and history of the country, are of great importance," it is enacted "that in payment of $15,000 granted to him by the laws of 16th of March, 1840, and 23d of February, 1841, for the purpose of engraving the map of the republic and printing its geography and history, the one 1,322 existing copies of the said work shall be received and sold for account of the nation."

Such being the legislative and administrative and diplomatic history of this official geographical delineation of the whole of Venezuela by the Venezuelan government, it is most manifest and indisputable that the islands claimed by this work as Venezuelan, are so claimed by that government; and to the islands which this work does not claim as Venezuelan, all claim is by that government repudiated, and that repudiation is published to the world.

Seventy-one islands of all classes, the greater part of them small and uninhabited, are so claimed as Venezuelan. They are all delineated on the great chart of Venezuela. They are all—every one of them—mentioned in the accompanying volume, numbered, named, and distributed among those sea-board provinces of the republic to which they are considered as respectively belonging. They all reappear, each in its place, on the separate maps of these provinces which are found in the atlas. They reappear, the whole seventy-one, in the map which in the atlas delineates the republic of Colombia. They reappear, every one of them, in the two maps which in the atlas delineate the republic of Venezuela as it was in 1810, and as it was in 1840.

But neither on the great chart, nor on any one of these maps of Colombia, of Venezuela, or its provinces, does the island of Aves in question appear, nor is it anywhere mentioned in the geographical volume. To perceive the whole conclusive force of this fact, it must be borne in mind that the great chart of Venezuela covers twenty-four square feet, bears date of Caraccas, 1840, is dedicated to the constituent Congress of 1830, and contains an inscription setting forth "the ten years' labor" dedicated to the perfecting of its "most minute details," and referring to acts of the government, above cited, which give it its undisputed official character.

But if this omission of the Aves in question on the maps of Venezuela and Colombia were all, there might perhaps seem to be a possibility of some pretext, or shadow of pretext, for the allegation that its omission was accidental, or the result of oversight, and so should not be held as affirmatively excluding all pretension of title to it by the government of Venezuela. But even for such a pretext, no opportunity is left. The island of Aves in question was not forgotten. It was put where it belonged, in the map of another region, and far outside of any pretended Venezuelan jurisdiction.

Besides the maps of Venezuela in its various forms, the atlas intended for public instruction contains a map of the World, a map of North and South America, and a map entitled "a map of the coasts of Terra Firma, from the Orinoco to Yucatan; of the Antilles; and of the greater part of the Lucayan Islands, with routes of navigation and discovery by Columbus and other navigators." And upon this map, in its proper place up among the "Little Antilles," known as the "Windward Islands," in the immediate vicinity of Saba, Monserrat, and Guadaloupe, and three degrees of latitude away from that portion of the sea shaded as containing the group of Venezuelan islands, we find the Aves in question plainly delineated and named.

Here, then, is seen the positive and purposed exclusion, by the government of Venezuela, of the "Aves" from any claim of Venezuelan jurisdiction in its furthest reach. Turning now to the geographical volume made up from the Venezuelan archives, we find under the chapter of "Islands," the Venezuelan government, through its commission, rendering its reasons, and very sound reasons, for this exclusion, in stating that the "northernmost" of the seventy-one Venezuelan islands are those of the chain "extending along the coast of the Province of Caraccas," and nearly "in the same parallel of latitude with the Dutch islands of Curaçao, Bonaire, and Oruba." For this reason, doubtless, the chart of Venezuela, and all the maps of Colombia, and of Venezuela and its provinces, while excluding the Aves in question, are extended so as to include this northernmost chain of islands claimed as Venezuelan.

Thus is fully demonstrated the proposition above stated, that the government of Venezuela, as late as 1845, formally and officially repudiated, and announced to the world her repudiation, of all pretension of title to this Island of Aves. There is no pretense any where that this repudiation was in any way revoked, or did not stand in its full force in June, 1854.

The cogent effect of this fact in manifesting the enormity of the outrage perpetrated on these claimants, for which redress is demanded, cannot escape the attention either of the United States or of Venezuela.

Resting upon these grounds, his position that the Venezuelan pretension of title to the Aves in 1854 has not sufficient foundation to require discussion, the undersigned will now, out of respect to the Venezuelan government, proceed to examine the proposition above cited, that "the island belonged to Venezuela prior to 1854 as the successor of Spain, who discovered it." A brief analysis will suffice to explode this proposition and scatter it to the winds.

In the first place, it is manifest that this proposition, in order to present any precise legal or political meaning, must be modified in its terms. The phrase "successor to Spain," without qualifying words, means "general successor to Spain." Venezuela is no such "general successor." Her succession is special, and limited by the important possessions which Spain has retained; by the possessions of other powers on this continent and in its seas, which have succeeded to certain former possessions of Spain; and finally, by the words of the Venezuelan constitution, limiting the jurisdiction of Venezuela "the territory denominated the captain generalship of Venezuela."

Therefore, in order to be precise and clearly intelligible in its bearings on the question in hand, the proposion should read, "the island belonged to Venezuela prior to 1854, as the successor to that part of of the dominion of Spain known as the captain generalship of Venezuela."

Not the slightest doubt or difficulty can arise from the fact which has been stated to the undersigned, that the captain generalship of Venezuela, being formed in 1751, was the last of the continental governments constituted by Spain, and included that part of the *continent* of South America which had not been embraced in the several continental governments previously formed; because all the territory of these continental governments formed originally part of the jurisdiction of the government of Santo Domingo, and were successively excinded out of it. But besides this vast continental territory, the government of Santo Domingo, as appears in the "Leyes de las Yudias," published at Madrid in 1786, liber II., pit. XV., comprehended also "all the Windward Islands," among which, as we have seen, the Aves in question is found; and this group of islands was never taken out of that jurisdiction by Spain, or assigned to the jurisdiction of any of the continental governments, and least of all to that of Venezuela, which was at first a dependency of the vice royalty of New Granada, and so continued till 1751. The *cedula real*, or royal ordinance establishing the captain generalship of Venezuela, does not appear to exist in print, and has not, after diligent search, been found in manuscript; but this is immaterial, because the historical portion of the work of the Venezuelan official commission, drawn from the Venezuelan archives, thus gives the limits of the captain generalship which it established:

"It had for limits on the north the Atlantic ocean and the Caribbean sea."

It is of course hardly needful to say that, independently of all these ancient Spanish territorial regulations, the United States maintain that this Island of Aves either was never reduced to possession by Spain, or if so reduced to possession, was soon abandoned and left derelict.

In view of these observations, the undersigned perceives to be involved in the proposition of Hon. Mr. Gutierrez, above cited, the truth of the following nine subordinate propositions embraced in it:

1st. The Aves was discovered by Spain.

2d. That by such discovery, or in other manner, Spain established her title to the Aves.

3d. That Spain maintained such title to the Aves till the date of the establishment of the captain generalship of Venezuela.

4th. That Spain then included the Aves in that captain generalship.

5th. That the Aves remained under the jurisdiction and in the possession of that captain generalship up to the date of its independence under the name of Venezuela.

6th. That at the establishment of the republic of Colombia, the

Aves, as a part of Venezuela, came into the possession and under the territorial sovereignty of that republic.

7th. That the republic of Colombia maintained such title and possession of the Aves until it was dissolved, in 1830.

8th. That upon the dissolution of the republic of Colombia, the title to and possession of the Aves reverted to Venezuela.

9th. That since the date of her existence as an independent republic, Venezuela has, previous to 1854, in no way lost or relinquished the possession and sovereignty of the Aves, but has, up to that year, constantly maintained the same by such manifestations of title and possession as other governments and their citizens and subjects are bound to respect.

Now, it is wholly manifest that the truth of every one of these nine propositions is indispensably necessary to establish the title of Venezuela to the Aves, as it is alleged to have existed at the beginning of the year 1854 in her, as the successor of Spain, and if any single one of these nine propositions be not true, then such alleged title of Venezuela at that date falls to the ground. In fact, every one of these nine propositions is true in relation to Margarita, and to all the islands belonging to Venezuela.

But not one of these nine propositions, with the possible exception of the first, has been or can be proved to be true in relation to this Island of Aves.

In the confident judgment of the undersigned, every one of these nine propositions in relation to the Aves, except the first, is untrue; and the last three, being the most important, have been, as we have seen, officially announced to be untrue by Venezuela herself.

Of such a pretension of title to an island known and used as derelict for two hundred years; a pretension never heard of till the end of 1854; a pretension alleged to rest only on a chain of succession of which all the important links are wanting; a pretension, in fine, which the government now setting it up did formally and officially and publicly repudiate in 1840. Of such a pretension of Venezuela to title in the Aves prior to 1854, nothing more remains, in the judgment of the undersigned, to be said, save this: that such a pretension, not having sufficient foundation, nor color of foundation, to form a profitable subject of speculative historical disquisition, has no appropriate place in a discussion between governments, and when alleged in justification or excuse of a serious outrage upon citizens of the United States cannot justly claim further consideration.

The undersigned has now disposed of all the observations in the note of the Hon. Mr. Gutierrez which appear intended to bear in any way against the obligation of the government of Venezuela to make full and prompt reparation to these claimants.

If this reply of the undersigned, intended to close, on his part, the discussion of the general question of the liability of Venezuela to make redress in this case, shall appear to the government of Venezuela as complete and conclusive as it is full and minute, this fact should be attributed to the impregnable and irresistible force and justice of this reclamation. The careful examination which the undersigned has now bestowed upon the subject, will, he trusts, also indicate to the honorable Minister of Foreign Relations his desire to give just and respectful consideration to every observation, however destitute of foundation it may appear, which has been, in the present attitude of the case, presented in behalf of the Venezuelan government.

For now it is the duty of the undersigned to announce to the government of Venezuela that further procrastination in the adjustment of this claim cannot be regarded with indifference by the government of the United States. The case is one of grave and rash outrage upon citizens of the United States and their property, inflicting upon them great loss and injury. To their government, it appears abundantly sustained by evidence and fortified in principle as regards the right of the claimants to expect redress from Venezuela.

The undersigned is therefore instructed by his government to press in its name, the demand for such redress in a formal and decisive manner, and to request the determination in the case of the government of Venezuela. If liability be admitted, a basis of adjustment may be fixed without delay. If reparation be refused, reasons for that course, satisfactory to the government of the United States, and not yet assigned, will be expected, especially in view of the stipulations contained in the third section of the thirty-fourth article of the treaty of 1836, which contemplates special modes of redress in a case where either party "considering itself offended, shall first have presented to the other a statement of such injuries or damages, verified by competent proofs, and demanded justice, and the same shall have been either refused or unreasonably delayed."

The undersigned avails himself of this occasion to renew to the Hon. Señor Gutierrez the assurance of his distinguished consideration.

CHARLES EAMES.

Hon. Jacinto Gutierrez,
Minister of Foreign Relations.

Accompanying this note is a printed paper, entitled "testimony in case of Philo S. Shelton and Sampson & Tappan against the government of Venezuela," and containing extracts from the interrogatories propounded to, and the answers given under oath by, Captain N. P. Gibbs. This paper, transmitted to this legation from the Department of State, is presented in its printed form, with the seal of this legation upon it, instead of a manuscript copy thereof, solely with a view to the convenience of business and facility of reference. A duplicate of the same, printed in the same form, and duly certified by the Department of State to be a true copy of the original on file there, remains in the archives of the legation.

Mr. Cass to Mr. Eames.

No. 50.]

Department of State,
Washington, April 3, 1857.

Sir: At the request of the claimant, P. S. Shelton, Esq., I transmit, herewith, a certified copy of the statement of his claim against Venezuela; presented in detail. The items composing this statement correspond with those set forth in the memorandum furnished by Mr. Sanford, and transmitted with the instruction of my predecessor to you of the 3d February last. I need do no more than reiterate the views therein expressed.

I am, sir, your obedient servant,

LEWIS CASS.

CHARLES EAMES, Esq., *&c.*

Mr. Cass to Mr. Eames.

No. 52.] DEPARTMENT OF STATE,
Washington, May 25, 1857.

SIR: Not a little surprise was occasioned by the receipt on the 8th instant, of your dispatch No. 36, of the 1st ultimo, acquainting the department of the non-arrival of the instructions to you numbered 44, 45, and 46, although those numbered 47 and 48 had not failed to reach you. Before undertaking to prepare duplicates of the missing dispatches, which would have been in some respects impracticable, an effort was made to discover whether your failure to receive them was the result of neglect, fraud, or accident. A letter received this morning from D. B. Taylor, dispatch agent at New York, discloses the fact that it was owing to the gross and culpable neglect of Mr. J. A. Hill, late dispatch agent in the same city. Mr. Taylor states, in his letter, that he found the packet of dispatches among the books handed over to him by his predecessor, and he has returned it to the department. No time is lost in transmitting it once more en route to its destination.

A more unfortunate and ill-timed mishap than the detention of this packet of dispatches could scarcely have occurred; referring principally to the claim of Mr. Philo S. Shelton, to promote and expedite the adjustment of which, Mr. H. S. Sanford, as Mr. Shelton's agent and attorney, visited Venezuela, and covering very important evidence and statements in support of that claim, upon which Mr. Sanford placed much reliance as aiding you in its complete development and entire verification, as well as inclosing a duplicate of the missing numbers 37 and 38, of August last, the former of which conveyed to you the emphatic views of this government in regard to the same claim; the absence of these instructions must to a great extent have embarrassed your official movements, as well as have, probably, counterbalanced the benefits proposed by Mr. Sanford in repairing to Caraccas.

One of the dispatches contained the leave of absence granted by the late executive, with an accompanying private letter from my predecessor to you. From the post-mark on the original envelope, you will observe that it was mailed in this city on the 7th February last.

I have to express to you the high appreciation entertained by the department of the ability, earnestness, and research displayed in your note of the 31st March to the Venezuelan minister for foreign relations upon the subject of the Shelton claim; and its approval of the manner in which you have in that note presented it for adjustment. It is only to be regretted that from any untoward circumstances so long a time has elapsed before you were enabled, in your judgment satisfactorily, to demand that consideration of the subject to which its importance and the extent of interests involved entitled it.

Your No. 37 was received on the 14th instant. The department hopes to receive the reply of Venezuela to your note of the 31st March, by the next mail from Caraccas.

I am, sir, your obedient servant,

LEWIS CASS.

CHARLES EAMES, Esq., *&c.*

Inclosures.

Duplicate of instruction No. 37, with its inclosure.
" " " " 38, " " inclosure.
Original, No. 44.
" 45.
" 46, with its inclosure.

Mr. Eames to Mr. Cass.

No. 38.] LEGATION OF THE UNITED STATES,
Caracas, June 13, 1857.

SIR: I have the honor to acknowledge the receipt, on the 23d ultimo, of your Nos. 49 and 50, under dates respectively of 1st and 3d of April last, being the latest dispatches received from the department. But Nos. 37, 38, 44, 45, and 46, are still wanting. All the duplicates of them referred to in your No. 49, as having been forwarded early in February last, having failed to reach this legation: thus making a loss in all, duplicates and originals, of not less than ten dispatches from the department since August last, most of them appearing to relate to the Aves claim. For the reasons stated in my No. 36, under date of 1st April last, I am convinced that those duplicates, like their originals, never reached Laguayra.

With reference to my No. 36, and its inclosures, relating to the Aves claim, I have now the honor to transmit, inclosed, copies of further correspondence with this government on that subject, being three notes addressed to me by Mr. Gutierrez, under dates, respectively, of 28th ultimo, and 2d and 12th instant, with two notes addressed by me to him, under dates of 29th ultimo and 11th instant.

Your No. 49, of 1st April last, expressed the hope that the Aves claim had already been finally and satisfactorily adjusted by this government, and referred to the probability that I might, at that time, be on my way to the United States, under the leave of absence asked by me to take effect in February last, and then granted. Such would have been the case, had I not for four months past, and until now, forborne to avail myself of that leave in order to urge the Aves claim.

But, by the correspondence now inclosed, the department will perceive that the government of Venezuela, up to this time, has not only failed to conclude or to recognize its obligation to conclude any such adjustment of that claim; but that, on the contrary, in the face of the formal and decisive demand of the United States, it still persists in withholding its determination even as to the preliminary question of its liability in the case.

By my note to Mr. Gutierrez of the 29th ultimo, the department will perceive that the decisive requirement by the government of the United States of that determination without delay, was formally announced by me to the Venezuelan government as early as the 23d of February last in the strong terms of the instruction No. 42 from the department; that it was reiterated and pressed in the same sense, and in connection with the demand for reparation, in my note to Mr. Gutierrez of the 31st of March last, intended in pursuance of that instruction to close, on the part of the United States, the general discussion; and that I have continued to insist upon the same requirement in the most urgent manner ever since its announcement.

The course of the Venezuelan government in failing to indicate a purpose to afford redress in the case, and in withholding for such a length of time its determination, when thus demanded, appears to me not only wholly unjust to the claimants, but also to be not in conformity with a due respect to the position assumed upon the subject by the government of the United States.

I, therefore, under my instructions, deemed it most conducive to the attainment of justice in the case, and most compatible with the dignity of my government, not to sanction, nor seem to sanction, this unexpected and unjustifiable procrastination by continuing to await, for a time indefinitely longer, the required answer of Venezuela as to her liability in the case. With this view, in my note of the 29th of May, I announced to the Venezuelan government my determination not to wait for such answer beyond a fixed period, and failing then to receive it to proceed to Washington, and submit in person the whole state of the case to my government for its consideration.

My conviction of the expediency of this announcement has been confirmed by the reply of Mr. Gutierrez. That reply, under date of the 2d instant, is, in my judgment, nothing more than a series of pretexts for further and indefinite delay; and it is observable that only a single one of these — the further inquiry as to the alleged Dias "agreement"—has even in appearance the slightest pertinency to the merits of the reclamation or the duty of Venezuela in respect to it. Nor can even such inquiry in respect to that paper be regarded as really material, unless Venezuela intends to maintain that she did not forcibly expel the claimants from the Aves, which, in view of all the proofs, I suppose to be impossible. The other points of the reply are obviously an attempt to substitute new and irrelevant issues in the case in place of that presented in my notes of the 31st of March and 29th of May. Such an attempt to complicate and prolong the controversy should not be in any way countenanced by me, and therefore I distinctly declined to discuss these extraneous allegations.

Though all official announcement of the determination of the Venezuelan government in the case has been withheld, I deem it proper to state that from the best means of information within my reach, I have become convinced that up to the date of my note of 11th instant, the purpose of Venezuela ultimately to refuse all reparation, was but too probable. Some of the expressions in the answer of Mr. Gutierrez, under date of 12th instant, to that note, may perhaps bear a construction somewhat less unfavorable to the claim. This change of tone, in so far as it may exist, I attribute to an apprehension, probably strengthened by my note of the 11th instant, that the government of the United States may now see fit to press the claim in a manner so stringent as to be effectual.

With the highest respect and consideration, I have the honor to be, your obedient servant,

CHARLES EAMES.

Hon. Lewis Cass,
Secretary of State.

Republic of Venezuela,
Caracas, May 28, 1857.

Reverting to what he has verbally stated to the minister resident of the United States in various conferences, the undersigned, secretary of foreign relations of Venezuela, now has the honor again to state that the lengthy note of the American legation in reference to the guano of Aves Island, a note extending over thirty-two sheets, which it was necessary to have previously translated, together with a long printed document annexed, setting forth the declaration of N. P. Gibbs, is now under consideration by the government, which has submitted the question to the deliberations of its council. As it is the desire of the executive power to proceed with accuracy in the matter, and to invest its decisions with the stamp of mature reflection and justice, time for deliberation is necessarily required. And the undersigned again and by its order here declares that the discussion of the claim did not formally commence before the 20th of December last, when it was first presented to this department in a direct way, and accompanied by vouchers; whence, therefore, the government resists every charge of dilatoriness which may be attempted to be preferred against it.

On the other hand, the government has thought proper that its answer should be preceded by certain acts relative to putting in a clear light the imputations of violence and fraud alleged by Mr. Eames in support of his claim; preliminary proceedings which have been delayed by various circumstances, among which is the absence from this place of those whose declarations are to be taken in the premises. To-morrow, at twelve o'clock, the interrogatory of Lieutenant Colonel Domingo Dias and Lieutenant Nicolas Pereiro will be proceeded with before the commandant-at-arms of this province, notice of which is hereby transmitted to you, in the event that you may wish to be present at it in person or by representative. The executive power has endeavored to expedite this matter in view of the information communicated by Mr. Eames that, in consequence of the permission obtained from his government, he intended to return to the United States, and had settled on the 9th of June next as the period of his departure.

The undersigned tenders to Mr. Eames renewed assurances of his distinguished consideration.

JACINTO GUTIERREZ.

Hon. CHARLES EAMES,
Minister Resident of the United States.

LEGATION OF THE UNITED STATES,
Caracas, May 29, 1857.

SIR: The undersigned, minister resident of the United States, has the honor to acknowledge the note, under date of yesterday, of the honorable minister of foreign relations, by which he is informed that the testimony of two Venezuelan naval officers will be taken to-morrow, before the proper military authority, in relation to certain points involved in the Aves question, and this information is given in view of the possibility that the undersigned may desire to witness the proceedings.

The courtesy of the Hon. Mr. Gutierrez in making this communication is properly appreciated; but, as the proceedings seem to be, in form at least, a mere military inquiry touching the conduct of the officers in question, the undersigned does not perceive any special inducement to be present on the occasion. In fact, both the undersigned and his government regard the facts of the case as having been already fully developed and abundantly proved.

The honorable minister of foreign relations in the same note reiterates the expression of the opinion that the discussion of the Aves claim did not commence "formally" till the 20th of December last. The point as stated, turning as it does upon a mere verbal distinction, is not, in the judgment of the undersigned, of the slightest importance in its bearing upon the present critical aspect of the case; but the statement, when presented by the Hon. Mr. Gutierrez, as exonerating the Venezuelan government from the responsibility of undue and perilous delay in this matter, can by no means be accepted by the undersigned as an accurate or just appreciation of the facts. These are of record and speak for themselves.

Two entire months have now elapsed since the undersigned, by express order of his government, upon rendered reasons and in the most decisive manner, in its name, made known to the government of Venezuela that this case of the Aves was, in the deliberate judgment of the government of the United States, a clearly proved, grave, and wholly unjustifiable outrage upon its citizens, inflicting on them great loss and injury; that further procrastination in the due adjustment of their claim for reparation could not be regarded with indifference; and that, therefore, the determination of the government of Venezuela in the matter, was required, in view of those modes of redress recognized in treaty stipulations between the two governments as proper and applicable in cases of proved injury, and of the refusal or unreasonable delay of just redress.

Nor did the note of the 31st of March, in which the undersigned made these solemn announcements, take the government of Venezuela by surprise. Five weeks before, on the 23d of February last, the undersigned in a formal interview, sought for that sole purpose, fully explained, with careful exactness, to the honorable minister of foreign relations the position thus deliberately and definitely assumed by the government of the United States. In addition to all this, the undersigned, in view of the urgency and grave responsibility of the case, has not ceased to press in every possible manner upon the attention of the government of Venezuela the importance of prompt and satisfactory action in the premises. He has solicited and obtained a special audience of his excellency the president upon the subject, and has availed himself to the utmost of that opportunity to enforce its urgency. No week has passed since the announcement in question in which he has failed to press the case with the minister of foreign relations.

It is with regret and astonishment that the undersigned now finds himself compelled to inform his government that the only answer yet received in this case from the government of Venezuela is, that the matter is under consideration.

This is manifestly a state of things full of peril to the friendly relations between the two governments; and the undersigned deems it proper to state that he is confirmed in this conviction by instructions very recently received. Just respect to the attitude of the government of the United States in this case demands that the definitive answer of the government of Venezuela, as required in the note of the undersigned of the 31st of March, should no longer be withheld. Should such answer reach this legation on or before the 6th proximo, and that such is the purpose of the Venezuelan government may, perhaps, be inferred from the note of the Hon. Mr. Gutierrez, then it will be fairly and maturely considered with a view to the prompt adjustment of this question upon principles of equity and justice. Should that day pass without such answer from the government of Venezuela, the undersigned, under his instructions, will deem it his duty to proceed at once to the United States and report in person to his government the unreasonable delay of the government of Venezuela, and the total failure of his best efforts to obtain such answer, as constituting in his judgment substantially a defeat of justice in the case.

The undersigned avails himself of this opportunity to renew to the Hon. Señor Gutierrez the assurance of his distinguished consideration.

CHARLES EAMES.

Hon. JACINTO GUTIERREZ,
Minister of Foreign Relations.

REPUBLIC OF VENEZUELA,
Caracas, *June* 2, 1857.

The undersigned has communicated to his government the note of the legation of the United States of the 29th ultimo, and the executive power has directed the following in answer.

Mr. Eames has presented a claim against Venezuela, the admission of which, in the view of the republic, is attended with serious difficulties. An attempt has been made to set aside one of the most considerable of these difficulties by saying, on the faith of the declarations of certain individuals, that a document signed by two individuals was not the spontaneous act of their will, but the result of compulsion and fraud on the part of the officer to whom they delivered it. Since the argument used against such statements in the first note of the undersigned, Mr. Eames has persisted in advancing them as an evidence of the nullity of an act which, even had it been compulsorily consented to, could not be invalidated, unless the means of violence resorted to against the declarants should be made out with precision and by proof. It was natural, therefore, that measures should have been taken to ascertain what took place between Colonel Domingo Dias, the other Venezuelan officers at Aves, and the Americans found in the island.

If the United States extend confidence to the allegations of their citizens; Venezuela, which must not discredit the reports of her citizens, much less the reports of those who, by the position which they occupy and the functions which they exercise, are worthy of every consideration and respect; Venezuela, which cannot but defend their rights, has believed that it was its right also to be informed, on its part, of the real state of the occurrences, and to seek the information at the hands of those who ought to possess the necessary knowledge. The government had supposed that it was contemplated to discuss a question between two equal States; that it had the power to set forth its objections to rebut the proofs of the claimants, and to take all necessary time to deliberate; and for this reason, unwilling to build up its defence without the intervention of the adverse party, it invited Mr. Eames' presence at the taking of two declarations. Yet he has declined thus to intervene, upon the averment that in his judgment and in that of his government the facts are amply elucidated and abundantly proved. Granted that this is the judgment of the one and the other, but such it is not of the government of Venezuela and of the minister who pens this answer. Mr. Eames will not pretend that Venezuela is held to subscribe to foreign judgments, for the mere reason that they are such. In that case all that would be necessary were to impose them upon the government without the necessity of discussion, and with no other limitation than that of the will of the claimants.

But it is further required that the decisions of the executive po[illegible]er in the matter—and this is not the only one commended to its care—should be made in a short and peremptory period of time, suited to special circumstances, prepared and arranged beforehand, without the slightest reference to the condition of the affairs of the two republics, in which the American legation finds itself, as has been learned from the conversations of Mr. Eames with the undersigned. Such a proceeding is incompatible with the relations of friendship under which both countries live. Of that friendship Venezuela has recently given a valid proof by her signature to a treaty of commerce, amity, navigation, and extradition, proposed to her by the United States, and now awaiting ratification. Great and repeated were the efforts made by the executive power, under the daily and pressing instances of Mr. Eames, to obtain the assent of congress to this convention. When in the act of doing this, it was far from foreseeing that it would ever be pressed upon, and in terms such as are contained in Mr. Eames' note, for a matter which had been allowed quietly to slumber for two years. Besides this, it took Mr. Eames more than a month and twenty-two sheets of paper to answer the first note of the department, which covered five sheets only; yet it seems extraordinary to him that, surrounded by numerous matters of various kinds, the executive power should take a little more time to answer his latitudinous dissertation. The undersigned has already stated that the executive power is expediting the termination of this matter, because he is privy to the intention of Mr. Eames for some time entertained, of returning to his country in virtue of permission asked and obtained from his government. Yet, although he should depart, means of continued communication would not be wanting between the two governments, since Venezuela maintains a legation in Washington.

The undersigned renews to Hon. Charles Eames assurances of his distinguished consideration.

JACINTO GUTIERREZ.

LEGATION OF THE UNITED STATES,
Caracas, June 11, 1857.

SIR: The undersigned, minister resident of the United States, has the honor to acknowledge the note of the honorable Minister of Foreign Relations of Venezuela, under date of 2d instant, in relation to the case of the Aves. Many of the views presented in that note wholly fail to command the assent of the undersigned, but in the present state of this negotiation, further discussion of them by the undersigned at this time does not appear to be necessary nor useful.

The expectations and demands of the government of the United States not having been complied with by the government of Venezuela, nothing for the present remains for the undersigned but to submit the state of this case to the consideration of his government in the sense and manner indicated in his note of the 29th ultimo.

Intending, therefore, to proceed to the United States without further delay, the undersigned has the honor to request that the usual passport may now be forwarded to him for that purpose.

The undersigned avails himself of this opportunity to assure the Hon. Mr. Gutierrez of his very distinguished consideration.

CHARLES EAMES.

Hon. JACINTO GUTIERREZ,
Minister of Foreign Relations.

REPUBLIC OF VENEZUELA,
Caracas, June 12, 1857.

The undersigned, Secretary of State in the department of foreign relations, has the honor of sending to the honorable minister resident of the United States the passport to those States asked for in his note of yesterday, which was not received until this day.

The government regrets that it should have been impossible for it to communicate, as it desired to do, to Mr. Eames the pending answer in relation to the Aves question previous to the period of his return to his country, for the reason that the compendium of the case, a form which the executive power has deemed proper to give to the claim, could not be completed in time. But, although this difficulty compels it to defer this communication, it hopes that it will not be for any long period, and then, should there be no legation of the United States in Caracas, both cabinets will confer through the medium of the chargé d'affaires of Venezuela, in Washington.

His excellency the President of the republic has specially ordered the undersigned to reiterate to Mr. Eames the assurance of his desire to maintain the most amicable relations with the United States, one of which he has at all times given proofs, and of which he never will lose sight.

Having thus complied with the directions of his excellency, the undersigned tenders to Mr. Eames renewed assurances of his distinguished consideration.

JACINTO GUTIERREZ.

Hon. CHARLES EAMES,
Minister Resident of the United States.

Mr. Sanford to Mr. Cass.

WILLARD'S HOTEL,
Washington, August 10, 1857.

SIR: The present position of the claim of Philo S. Shelton and Sampson & Tappan against the Venezuelan government for the outrage and spoliation committed in December, 1854, at Shelton's Isle, seems to require this communication.

The demand for redress, I would remind you, was made by the claimants on the 15th January, 1855. It has been incessantly followed up by them since. No neglect, no delay, can be imputed to them. On the contrary, their importunity and the pertinacity with which they urged their claim received from the late administration more than one significant intimation that it was not altogether necessary, as the claim was being enforced by the government. The accumulation of depositions by these claimants was as early as July 8, 1856, hinted, as quite superfluous, until the Venezuelan government should make some response.

The claimants, dissatisfied with the unaccountable delays at Caracas, with the assent, nay, at the instance of this government, dispatched an agent to Caracas early last winter, who remained there nearly four months, urging the justice of the claim upon the Venezuelan government.

Whilst there that government was informed that if justice was conceded to these claimants, every disposition existed to agree to reasonable terms with respect to the amount of indemnity and mode of payment.

Notwithstanding the decisive terms of the instructions sent by the late administration to our minister at Caracas, and of which the Venezuelan government were apprized, notwithstanding the urgent applications of the claimants for just redress, and though the minister of the United States presented in December, 1856, the case, under the instructions of the department, in a manner that rendered further procrastination on the part of the Venezuelan government inexcusable, up to the time of the departure of the undersigned from Caraccas, on the 10th of June, that government withheld not only payment or assurance of payment of any indemnity, but disputed their right to claim remuneration upon a most frivolous and unfounded pretext. It did not deign to yield to our minister even a respectful response to his communication.

In the last communication received from Senor Gutierrez in reply to the intimation by Mr. Eames that, should the 6th of June pass without a definitive answer from the government of Venezuela, he would, "under his instructions, deem it his duty to proceed at once to the United States, and report in person to his government the unreasonable delay of the government of Venezuela, and the total failure of his best efforts to obtain such answer, as constituting, in his judgment, substantially a defeat of justice in the case;" the department will notice the insulting sneer, "that even should he (Mr. Eames) leave, means of communication between the two cabinets will not be wanting, since Venezuela has a legation at Washington."

Two months have elapsed since the date of that communication of Senor Gutierrez. Mr. Eames was detained at Caracas till the 13th June last, and has since arrived in the United States. Up to this day, though several vessels have arrived in the United States from Venezuela since his departure, no communication has been received by the government from Venezuela or its minister here in relation to this case.

These claimants respectfully insist that, as appears by the dispatches of the Department of State under the late administration, (see dispatch of 14th August, 1856, and 2d January, 1857,) and which the same department under the present administration have reiterated, but one question remains open, and that is, the amount of damages to be paid them; and upon this point they contend that their demands should be considered distinctly and separately from Lang & Delano, and others who have presented their claims to the department.

From the outset P. S. Shelton and Sampson & Tappan have declined to have their just claim connected or intermingled with the others alluded to. They have protested against allowing the other claimants to invoke the testimony they procured at enormous expense, in which Lang & Delano have not participated, and because also objections existed against such claim, which can be made manifest by an examination of the evidence in the case, and others which these claimants may feel themselves constrained to produce.

It is a mistake if it is supposed that all the claims stand on the same footing, or are equally meritorious and just.

With reference to the amount of damages claimed by Philo S. Shelton and Sampson & Tappan, the department has on file the several statements thereof made by them. The department has also the proofs (depositions of witnesses and documentary) sustaining generally the aggregate amounts claimed to be just. If further testimony, if further proofs, setting forth particulars of details, should be considered requisite, is respectfully suggested to the department as was suggested by the claimants in 1855, that the matter be referred to the Chamber of Commerce of New York or Boston, or to any respectable merchants of those cities, to examine the same, take any additional testimony produced, and make report to the department of the amount justly due, by which the claimants will abide. It is well nigh impossible to furnish evidence to the department in an authentic form except by some such proceeding.

With respect to the course to be pursued by the department in the interim, if such measure is adopted, the claimants would respectfully suggest that if the United States government would again dispatch a public vessel to Venezuela, with an open letter to that government by the hand of an agent, who should have the full power of the claimants for an arrangement of the claim; and if in such letter it should be distinctly stated that all questions are foreclosed except the amount to be paid, and referring the Venezuelan government to such agent as authorized to arrange such amount, and that it was expected a just settlement should be had immediately; and that if, on the return of such vessel, such settlement should not have taken place, the United States would feel itself bound not to allow its minister to return to Venezuela, and to tender the Venezuelan minister here his passports, and that it should also feel bound to resort to the remedy provided by the third clause of the thirty-fourth article of our treaty with that country, I do not doubt would insure a prompt adjustment of the claim.

The misfortune in this case has been that in the incipient stages of it, and until December, 1856, our minister at Caracas did not seem fully to understand or appreciate its merits; and hence it was not so strenuously and positively urged upon the Venezuelan government as the flagrancy of the outrage and its large amount demanded.

The pertinacity with which the Venezuelan government insist upon the capitulation by Gibbs to Dias, as precluding these claimants, it is respectfully submitted, should receive emphatic rebuke from the government of the United States. The proof of fraud and duress in relation to that document cannot be disputed by the assertions of the instruments of the Venezuelan government, who perpetrated that fraud and committed the violence.

But concede, *arguendo*, that this instrument was not tainted by fraud, nor stained by duress, who ever heard that agreement made by an agent in fraud of his principal, without authority from or consent of that principal, destroying his very agency, yielding up the property intrusted to him, &c., was valid and binding upon his principal? By the common law and by the civil law and by every dictate of common sense and common justice such rule with regard to agents and their acts must be recognized.

It betrays a lamentable ignorance of the elementary principles of justice, upon which those rules are all based, to question their existence. Not a law book on the subject of agency can be found that does not reiterate them as well settled, and it applies to all acts, whether the acts of individuals or of governments.

Even if a minister of the United States should, whether in lamentable ignorance of the law or not, fully cognizant of the facts, or disposed to pretermit the just rights of his government or its citizens, make concessions or admissions, either of law or of fact, in derogation of these rights, without instructions from his government, who can pretend that the government should be bound by them?

With respect to the ulterior action of the government, in case Venezuela should persist in withholding justice, the claimants, P. S. Shelton and Sampson & Tappan, would suggest:

First. They have heretofore *ex abundante cautela*, presented to the President of the United States in December last a formal application to be placed in possession of Aves Island under the act of 18th August, 1856, a law framed expressly to meet this very case, and to which the executive decision still remains suspended awaiting the action of Venezuela.

The formal petition to the President, and a copy of which is on file in the department, is referred to, and a copy of the act herewith inclosed, and the fifth section is respectfully referred to, which authorizes the President, "at his discretion, to employ the land and naval forces of the United States to protect the rights of the said discoverer or discoverers, or their assigns, as aforesaid."

Second. These claimants insist, also, most respectfully that it is their right to demand of their government, if payment of their just and manifest indemnity is denied them, special letters of reprisal against the Venezuelan government under the law of nations; and they insist, also, that it is the constitutional duty of the Executive Department of the government of the United States to see these laws faithfully executed by the granting of such letters.

Whilst they concede that the power to issue general letters of marque and reprisal (*quasi* acts of war) is not vested by the Constitution upon the Executive without previous authority of Congress, they contend that such restriction does not apply to a special letter of reprisal, which is in no sense an act of war, or even a *casus belli*, but that it is an executive function, to be exercised and performed by the Executive at his own sound discretion, and upon his sole official responsibility.

If, however, any doubt existed on this point under the act of August 18, 1856, above cited, so far forth as it respects Shelton's Isle, legislative authority unquestionably exists.

Upon the subject of reprisals, whether the exercise is stipulated in the treaty or not, and as to the distinction between general and special reprisals, and as to special reprisals being the proper remedy in this case, these claimants will, if desired by the department, submit a full brief.

The long endurance of our government and these claimants of nearly three years under an unparalelled outrage upon its flag and upon them, the absolute and positive necessity of exemplary measures to put a stop to such acts by some of those irresponsible institutions called governments south of us, demands a resort to most cogent means. Their administrations continually changing by successive domestic revolutions, shirking responsibility for the acts of their predecessors, well nigh takes from them all claim to the benefit of the beneficent principles of the laws of nations that may be extended by a superior power to a feeble nation. Certain it is, that with respect to most of the Hispano-American governments, the records of the department will show that amicable remonstrance, diplomatic correspondence, and negotiation are totally unavailable to procure justice for outrages upon American citizens, unless accompanied by use of means of coersion.

It is no consolation to these claimants that they are one of several hundred in like condition.

I have the honor to be, very respectfully, your obedient servant,

H. S. SANFORD.

Hon. LEWIS CASS,
Secretary of State.

AN ACT to authorize protection to be given to citizens of the United States who may discover deposits of guano.

Be it enacted by the Senate and House of Representatives of the United States in Congress assembled, That when any citizen or citizens of the United States may have discovered, or shall hereafter discover, a deposit of guano on any island, rock, or key, not within the lawful jurisdiction of any other government, and not occupied by the citizens of any other government, and shall take peaceable possession thereof, and occupy the same, said island, rock, or key, may, at the discretion of the President of the United States, be considered as appertaining to the United States: *Provided, however,* That notice be given by such discoverer or discoverers, as soon as practicable to the State Department of the United States, of such discovery, occupation, and possession, verified by affidavit describing said island, rock, or key, and the latitude and longitude thereof, as near as may be, and showing that such possession was taken in the name of the United States, and that satisfactory evidence be furnished to the State Department that such island, rock, or key, was not, at the time of discovery thereof, or of the taking possession and occupation thereof by the claimants, in the possession or occupation of any other government, or of the citizens of any other government.

SEC. 2. *And be it further enacted,* That the said discoverer or discoverers, or his or their assigns, being citizens of the United States, may be allowed, at the pleasure of Congress, the exclusive right of occupying said islands, rocks, or keys, for the purpose of obtaining said guano, and of selling and delivering the same to citizens of the United States for the purpose of being used therein, and may be allowed to charge and receive for every ton thereof delivered alongside a vessel in proper tubs within reach of ship's tackle, a sum not exceeding eight dollars per ton for the best quality, or four dollars per ton in its native place of deposit: *Provided, however,* That no guano shall be taken from said island, rock, or key, except for the use of the citizens of the United States, or of persons resident therein, as aforesaid: *And provided also,* That said discoverer or discoverers, or his or their assigns, shall first enter into bonds, with such penalties or securities as may be required by the President, to deliver the said guano to citizens of the United States, for the purpose of being used therein, and to none others, and at the price aforesaid, and to provide all necessary facilities for that purpose within a time to be fixed in said bond. And any breach of the provisions thereof shall be taken and deemed a forfeiture of all rights accruing under and by virtue of this act.

SEC. 3. *And be it further enacted,* That the introduction of guano from such islands, rocks, or keys, shall be regulated as in the coasting trade between different parts of the United States, and the same laws shall govern the vessels concerned therein.

SEC. 4. *And be it further enacted,* That nothing in this act contained shall be construed obligatory on the United States to retain possession of the islands, rocks, or keys, as aforesaid, after the guano shall have been removed from the same.

SEC. 5. *And be it further enacted,* That the President of the United States is hereby authorized, at his discretion, to employ the land and naval forces of the United States to protect the rights of the said discoverer or discoverers or their assigns, as aforesaid.

SEC. 6. *And be it further enacted,* That until otherwise provided by law, all acts done, and offenses or crimes committed, on every such island, rock, or key, by persons who may land thereon, or in the waters adjacent thereto, shall be held and deemed to have been done or committed on the high seas, on board a merchant ship or vessel belonging to the United States, and be punished according to the laws of the United States relating to such ships or vessels and offenses on the high seas; which laws, for the purposes aforesaid, are hereby extended to and over such islands, rocks, or keys.

Approved August 18, 1856.

POINTS ON SPECIAL REPRISALS.

1. Special letters of reprisal are, in time of peace, means of redress allowed by the law of nations to a State for injustice by another State.

2. A resort to such remedy by the injured State is, in a rightful case, entirely consistent with a state of peace, and does not justly constitute a *casus belli.*

3. Such resort may be had, as well to obtain just redress for a citizen or a subject who has been wronged, as to obtain reparation for injuries directly to the State.

4. Such reprisals may be made, as well for the unlawful acts of individuals of the State complained of, as for the acts of such State itself by its authorities.

5. Such a remedy may be rightly adopted by a State in behalf of its citizens or subjects, whether the injury complained of be the withholding of a just debt to its citizens or subjects, or the denial or unreasonable delay of justice to such citizens or subjects of the State against which it is used, to the persons or the property of the citizens or subjects of the State adopting such remedy.

6. Such remedy should not be used in a questionable case; a claim should not only be manifestly just, *in res minime dubia*, but there must be a clear and open delay of justice or denial of right.

7. The claim should be fully presented to the State complained of by the State alleging the wrong, and a request made that justice be done, and a reasonable time allowed, according to the circumstances, for the reparation of the alleged wrong, or for the answer of such State to the demand made.

8. If the complaint be the unreasonable delay or denial of justice in relation to a debt, all the legal remedies allowed to the claimant must be sought by such claimant before the application to his government for reprisal; and it must be shown that such debt is certainly and manifestly due.

9. If the demand be for damages sustained by violence done to the persons or property of a citizen or subject of the complaining State by the authorities or citizens or subjects of another State, the claimant must produce full proof to his own State of all the circumstances of the case, and of the wrongs and injuries sustained and damages incurred, which ought to be forthwith submitted to the State complained of, in order that it may adduce rebutting or explanatory evidence; and that if the authorities of the complaining State, after a careful and impartial consideration of all said testimony, still regard the case as one to be prosecuted by special letters of reprisal, they should, by such process as may be devised to attain an enlightened, impartial, and just decision, (of a judicial character, if practicable,) ascertain and adjudge the amount justly due, and the character and extent of the satisfaction to be required, and forthwith notify the State complained of thereof; and that if, within a designated reasonable time, it still refuses or fails to do justice, the complaining State, on such continued refusal or failure, after such time, may issue special letters of reprisal against the property of such delinquent State, and against the property of the citizens or subjects, in order to obtain satisfaction for such injuries.

10. Special letters of reprisal are in the nature of a national *distress-warrant*, and authorize the seizure and detention of the property of the citizens or subjects of the delinquent State, as well of the property of such State itself, to be brought in and detained as a pledge, and disposed of under judicial sanction, and the proceeds to be first applied to the payment of the reasonable expenses incurred thereby, and next to the satisfaction of the claim, and the surplus to be returned to the State complained of.

11. The State granting such special letters of reprisal may issue them to those of its citizens or subjects who claim redress, upon such conditions and restrictions as it may deem proper to prevent the unlawful use thereof; and it should in all cases exact a caution and

surety from the party demanding such letters to respond in damages to any person illegally damnified by the abuse thereof, and also to all persons injured thereby in any manner whatsoever; or, if it should be subsequently made to appear that said party has fraudulently made a false or exaggerated statement of his claim, and misled the authorities of the State into the granting of such letters. And the State granting such special letters of reprisal may, at its option, direct that they be executed by the citizens who are the claimants, and by officers, also citizens, appointed by the claimants, and by the private armed vessels of such citizens; or it may direct that the same be executed under the supervision of officers of its regular navy, or such letters may be issued immediately to such officers, and the execution thereof may be directed to be made by them, and in a public ship-of-war.

12. Special letters of reprisal can only be granted by order of the sovereign of the State, or that branch of the public authority to which the power of directing the intercourse of such State with other States is entrusted.

13. Until diplomatic action has been had, and has failed to cause justice to be done, such letters ought not to be granted, except in extraordinary cases, marked by circumstances of great atrocity.

14. The right to make private property the subject of special reprisals is founded upon the principle that each member of a State is bound for the liabilities of his State, and that it is not unjust to collect such liability from him, insomuch as, in such case, he has full resort to his State for indemnity, and to his fellow-citizens or subjects to make contribution.

15. To deny justice is injustice, and unnecessary delay is equivalent to a denial. Justice is every man's right by the *jus gentium*, which is therein agreeable to the natural law, as well as to the civil law and the common law; and such unreasonable delay of justice by a State to a citizen or subject of another State will, after diplomatic request and expostulation, if the case be manifest and undoubted, justify the issuance of special letters of reprisal, equally in the case of debt as if the wrong complained of was a *tort*.

16. It is the duty of the authorities of a State, when one of its citizens or subjects is wronged by another State, to espouse his cause and, if need be, to constrain the aggressor to make a just reparation; for otherwise individual security, the great object of every political association, would not be obtained.

Mr. Sanford to Mr. Cass.

DERBY, CONNECTICUT,
August 16, 1857.

SIR: The inclosed brief on special reprisals as a rightful and peaceful remedy in the case of Philo S. Shelton and Sampson & Tappan for the outrage perpetrated by Venezuela at Shelton's Isle in 1854, is submitted for the consideration of the department.

I trust the department will recollect that in this case, at this time, for the issuance of letters of reprisal on the demand heretofore made of the Venezuelan government by the United States under the treaty, we only ask that a letter of request, of the character heretofore indicated in my letter of the 10th instant, may be sent open to that government, with copies of all the proofs duly authenticated by such person or in such mode as the department may deem proper, which letter of request, (*lettre de requête*) according to the formula of established precedents, should designate a reasonable time (and the claimants think thirty days amply sufficient) within which Venezuela should make satisfaction of the claim to the claimants, or conceding the liability, leave the question of amount to be ascertained and determined by the United States, according to the law of nations.

If this be done, and it should be deemed necessary that any general or special legislation regulating the mode of procedure in cases of special reprisal is indispensable to enable the executive to act, this case may then be back in time to be submitted to Congress at next session, in order to procure such law. If the time for answer is not limited, and further delay is allowed, the case cannot be so returned in season for congressional action.

I have the honor to be, with great respect, your most obedient servant,

H. S. SANFORD.

Hon. LEWIS CASS,
Secretary of State.

P. S. Full extracts from the authorities referred to in this brief, and most of them translated, (for another object,) can be forwarded to the department for its temporary use in reference, (to be returned when requested, and to be kept exclusively in charge of the department till returned,) if it is desired, as facilitating its investigations.

H. S. S.

P. S. SHELTON AND SAMPSON & TAPPAN,
vs.
THE REPUBLIC OF VENEZUELA.
} *Claim for indemnity.*

Brief, by claimants, on application for "lettre de requête," and special reprisals for spoliation at Shelton's Isle in December, 1854.

In the "Points" submitted with the letter of the 10th instant, no reference is intended to be made to what are designated "general commissions of reprisals," or "letters of marque," sometimes called "extraordinary letters of reprisal," as contradistinguished from "special or ordinary letters of reprisal in time of peace." The difference between the two remedies, and the distinctions between the cases in which they are respectively appropriate, are all settled by the approved authorities upon international law. Sciolistic essayists, and those authors whose want of legal acumen and discrimination and limited research have restrained them from referring in any but general terms to reprisals, have often confounded these different and distinct; whereas, in their character, objects, mode of procedure, results, and effects, they are as different as is the "right of visit" from the pretended "right of search."

I. In the exposition of the *jus gentium*, it is a great misfortune that so much difficulty is encountered in meeting in many works, loose, general theories, advanced by authors who seem wanting in the faculty of analysis and power of discrimination, and devoid of that experience necessary to perceive the true results and effects of their visionary Utopian theories. For instance, certain modern writers (rather controversal essayists than jurisconsults) and some military or naval officers, who deem themselves competent to expound the principles of international law—but who seem to have a superficial idea of the law of reprisals, "ordinary" or "extraordinary," "special" or "general," and confounding them as before observed—have denounced them both as *quasi* acts of war, or as tending to war, and as remedies of an "obsolete" character, and more in harmony with the *jus gentium* as it prevailed in ancient times, than as ameliorated and improved by modern progress. As it relates to extraordinary or general reprisals, we concede that they are often acts that tend to war, and are "a kind of imperfect war," but with reference to special or ordinary letters of reprisal, in their character, objects, and effects, they are emphatically preventives of war; and because they are such preventives is it that the right to issue them should be maintained, and in proper cases enforced. Witheut them, if diplomatic negotiation fails to effect reparation for wrong, war is the only alternative.

Special, or ordinary letters of reprisal, are the appropriate remedy for a wrong to the individual subjects of a State to effect redress.

General or extraordinary commissions, or letters of marque and reprisal, are the appropriate remedies for an assault or wrong to a State, other than those committed against a State through its citizens.

Several theoretic writers upon the continent of Europe refer to the law of reprisals, special and general, as existing anterior to the era of Roman power; but the distinction between such special and general reprisals was not, in ancient times, so clearly defined as in later days, and for the reason that, in those times, the power of governments and the rights of feudal leaders were not so definitely limited and established, and often the latter exercised the attributes of sovereignty since acknowledged to belong only to established governments.

It is, however, a gratification to advert, on this subject, to the writings of the ancient sages of the common law of England. So early as the eleventh century, the principles upon which the law of special, as well as of general reprisals, are founded, and the formula for the execution of that law, are all distinctly and forcibly set forth in the records ef English jurisprudence which have come down to us; nay, in the great charter these principles are announced as among those, adherence to which was assured by the King in that compact, (*vide* C. 29, 2 and C. 30, 2,) and the reference to the "ancient" and established customs and laws of the realm therein made, including the custom and law of special reprisals.

The remedy of special reprisals in behalf of a subject who has sustained wrong from a foreign State is in the nature of an attachment or distress warrant, or capias *ad Withernam* against the property of an offending delinquent State, and hath been held to be a writ of *common* right, not to be "denied," or "withheld," or "delayed" to any "freeman."

Several ancient English statutes prescribe and regulate the mode of procedure by a subject to obtain such suit.

"Commissions or letters of *general* reprisal or letters of marque" rest more completely in the discretion of the executive power, and in which those considerations of prudence and expediency often controlling the intercourse between nations (waiving strict rights) have governed "*ordinary* or *special* letters of reprisal," being, as before observed, in the nature of a judicial process, to which the subject is entitled of right, such considerations should not, except in extraordinary cases, be allowed controlling influence.

And to the honor and glory of England it may be said, that from the time of Magna Charta no instance is known to have occurred in which her monarchs have hesitated to exert the royal authority in behalf of a subject seeking just redress from a foreign State by the use of a "special letter of reprisal."

A memorable case, a worthy example to all governments, occurred during the time of the Lord Protector CROMWELL, and is related by British historians with pride, though a celebrated French writer styled it "insolent justice."

An English Quaker having had some property seized by the French in the time of Cardinal MAZARIN, and meeting with no success in his efforts to procure reparation from that government, called personally on CROMWELL and made his complaint, who, after hearing him, gave him a letter to MAZARIN, and told him to deliver it in person, and to wait three days for an answer and then return. Receiving no answer on his return, Cromwell issued a "special letter of reprisal" and seized a sufficiency of French property to indemnify the English Quaker. The French acquiesced in the peaceful remedy.

It is true that, in 1752, when the law of special reprisals was applied to Great Britain by the King of Prussia in the celebrated Silesian loan case, the British court illustrated the moral of that famous fable of Æsop in relation to the bull goring the ox, in a way not uncommon with that power, by objecting to this application to *her*, and since that case it may be noted that some British publicists seem disposed to adopt the doctrines of Sir Dudley Ryder, Lord Mansfield, and the Duke of Newcastle in their correspondence with the Prussian minister, repudiating principles before then maintained by every British writer of established reputation. It may be said, however, that the sequestration by the King of Prussia of the money due to British merchants on the Silesian loan for the capture of Prussian vessels by the British, for an alleged violation of neutrality, was a case of some doubt, especially insomuch as the parties injured had full redress in the prize or admiralty courts of Great Britain, into which the captured property had to be taken, and which had full judicial power to award damages for an illegal capture. Nevertheless, though the fact (as it is conceived from false notions of what was the true glory and honor of that country) is concealed by every British author who has adverted to the case, the British government ultimately yielded to Prussia, and adjusted the damages due to the Prussian subjects on account of the capture referred to, and the King of Prussia released the reprisals. Annexed hereto is a copy of a dispatch from Lord Holderness to Mr. Mitchell, dated May 11, 1756, showing such to be the fact, and which the counsel for claimants in investigations on the subject of the law of reprisals procured from the British foreign office by permission of Lord Clarendon.

A memorandum of British authorities is annexed. If reference be made to those authorities, what is above stated in respect to ordinary and special, or extraordinary and general reprisals, will be found fully sustained by them.

Viner, 5, 18; quoting Molloy, ch. 2, § 57, and "2d General Treatise of Trade, 211." 1 F. N. Br., p. 114. 2 Co. Inst., 56, 204, 205. 4 Co. Inst., 124, 125, 137. 1 Hale's Hist. Pl. of Crown, p. 162. 1 Ward's Law of Nations, c. 9, p. 294. 3 Hallam's Middle Ages, c. 10, pt. 2, p. 332. Stephens' Comm., vol. 2, book 4, pt. 1, § 4, p. 515. 1 Blackstone's Comm., c. 7, p. 259, E. ed. 2 Brown's Civil and Adm. Law, c. 7, p. 334. Wildman's Institutes, p. 186, *et seq.* Polson's Law of Nations, p. 37. Chitty's Law of Nations, p. 73, *et seq.* 3 Phillimore, c. 2, p. ii, &c.

In France the same principles have been sedulously maintained since the tenth century, and the forms and mode of procedure of French subjects asking the interposition of their government by special letters of reprisal, have been regulated by the royal ordinances of marine. See the French authorities cited in the list annexed, (*ut passim.*) See also the American authorities, and see several treaties between the United States and other nations recognizing special reprisals. (8 U. S. Statutes at Large, *et seq.*, published laws, &c.) See also European authorities cited in list, and many treaties, ancient and modern, between European States recognizing such right therein referred to.

Not a publicist of repute, prior to the middle of the eighteenth century, questioned the right to issue special letters of reprisal under the law of nations, and that it was a peaceful remedy and preventive, instead of a cause, of war. In numerous treaties between continental States the right was recognized and regulated; and England has also sanctioned it in the same way. It is true that some few modern theoretic assayists of the character described in the commencement of this brief, confounding special with general reprisals, have referred to both as an "obsolete" remedy, an "ancient practice not recently followed," and one of whom quite sagaciously insists that to justify its use, there ought to be "in every case a recent treaty" between the complaining and delinquent States recognizing it. Some of these writers seem as much at fault in their opinions as to what is the law of nations, as with respect to their opinions, as to what ought to be that law. One of them just referred to (Sir James Reddie) has written three volumes about international law, (and writers upon it,) the principal object of which books seems to have been to maintain the British doctrine, hostile to neutral rights, of "the flag not covering the cargo," and to berate all who maintain the principle of "free ships, free goods." His inconsistency is manifest in condemning reprisals as "ancient" and "obsolete," and his contending that the doctrine of "the flag not covering the cargo" is the true doctrine, because it was the doctrine of the "time-honored" *Consulato del Mare* of the eleventh century. As England in 1856, by the convention of Paris, agreed that if such principle of "the flag not covering the cargo" had been the law it ought not to be any longer, it is presumed he would not now insist that those opinions ought to be completely yielded to by others.

But upon this subject, and as a conclusive answer to all the objections about this remedy being "obsolete" and having "fallen into disuse among civilized nations," &c., the treaty of 1836 between Venezuela and the United States is decisive. It recognizes and sanctions the resort to the precise remedy of special reprisals; it provides for resort to that remedy, in proper cases, instead of other remedies given by the law of nations, to either State injured in the persons or property of its citizens. In providing for the resort to such remedy, it is important to observe that the provisions of that treaty not merely regulate, but are, all of them, in restraint of its exercise, whilst it clearly and unequivocally recognizes its legitimacy. (See Art. 34 of Treaty, 3d clause, 8 Stat. at Large, p. 482.)

Yet we do not rest the right to special reprisals upon this treaty. We place it upon the universal law of nations.

Suggesting the idea that a State may not pursue the remedy of special letters of reprisal unless a "recent treaty" with the State against which such letters are issued, we conceive to be an arrant blunder. The right of a State to adopt such remedy to obtain satisfaction for injuries by another State, and in order to avoid a resort to declared and general war, rests upon the well established principles of the law of nations, and not upon treaties allowing it. Treaties between States may regulate the exercise of such right by these States as to each other; may restrain or agree to abandon or prohibit the resort to such remedy by either against the other; but the absence of a convention on the subject in no wise impairs the right to have recourse to a remedy so founded upon the ancient and approved customs and rules of international law. Empirics as to international law and international morality have always endeavored to cut off what they thought excresences, and to patch up what they considered rents in the science of international law in various ways, some by treaty, and some by denying ancient principles and rules; but the same class of persons, whensoever any of their favorite notions are assailed by the provisions of a treaty, are loud in their denunciation of the impolicy of the removal of the ancient landmarks of the *jus gentium*.

All publicists allow that treaties altering or restraining ancient laws or customs are not to be regarded with favor, and are to be strictly construed. 1 Reddie, p. 173. 2 Wynn's Jenkins, p. 759. 1 Molloy, book 1, chap. 5, note to § 12. 2 Burke's Works, p. 521.

No difficulty can arise from the non-existence of a treaty prescribing the formula of procedure, or the cases in which the remedy may be adopted. The cases in which it is proper to resort to such remedy, and the general modes of procedure, may be readily ascertained by an examination of the authorities above referred to, and no difficulty can ensue as to the application of the principles on which this remedy is based, if the State preparing to adopt it, whilst it refuses to submit to wrong, asks for nothing that is not right.

Those writers who advance the opinion that the resort to special reprisals is "obsolete," must have omitted to advert to the constant exercise of the right to resort to such remedy by European nations up to this day, shown by the numerous cases which have occurred even within the last decade, and some of which are referred to in the works most recently published on the laws of nations. 1 Cussy, *Phases et Causes Célèbres*, p. 126; 2 ib., p. 56, 486. 3 Phill. Comm., p. 11, &c; ch. II., §§ 22, 23, &c. Hazlett & Roche's Manual, pp. 89 to 96.

The right is founded upon the immutable principle of the law of nations, that every sovereign State possesses the right to redress its wrongs by just means, and this particular remedy has been adopted to avoid the necessity of a resort to war. A sound and just principle cannot die. It might as well be contended that because a State has long maintained peace, she lost the right to resort to war; that such just right and remedy had become "obsolete." It might as well be said that because a State has failed in the fulfillment of the duty of protecting its citizens or subjects, (reciprocal upon their allegiance,) therefore her right to do so when she becomes awakened to a just sense of that duty, could not be exercised, because the practice had with her "fallen into disuetude," and thence "become obsolete." Special reprisals are not "obsolete." The law of nations allows and sanctions them. They are recognized by numerous treaties, ancient and modern, and constant practice to this day maintains them. And with reference to the government of the United States this remedy is peculiarly appropriate. It is a remedy for the protection of the citizen. As to those governments administered more for the benefit of the rulers than for that of the people, there may be reasons for its abandonment, by those rulers, that do not exist with the functionaries of the federal government of the United States. There are a class of naval and military persons who look to open war as the proper remedy in all cases of wrongs by a State, and these may deride this conservative remedy; And some diplomatists may think there is greater superiority and efficacy in protracted negotiation and reiterated remonstrance, voluminous correspondence and interminable discussion, than in "special reprisals;" and some may regard arbitration (even against all experience) as the most certainly just remedy, and as the most easy and effectual. But it is enough to answer all these suggestions by urging the right of the injured citizen to insist that recourse shall be had in his behalf to the admitted law of nations, and the established practice under it, and to cite the course of one of the most illustrious chief magistrates of this confederacy (General Jackson, in 1834) against one of the most formidable powers in the world, maintaining all we contend for.

II. That special reprisals are appropriate and consistent with a state of peace, and, if justly resorted to, do not constitute a *casus belli*, or tend to war, is fully proved by the authorities, British and European, and also American.

All the confusion existing on this point is attributable to the confounding ordinary and special reprisals, in time of peace, with extraordinary and general reprisals, or letters of marque, in time of war, or immediately preceding it, which latter are in themselves a kind of informal war. 1 Molloy, (c. 2, § 8,) says: "The granting of letters of reprisal does not, in the ordinary way, for particular satisfaction, amount to the breach of the peace." (3 Phill., c. 2, p. 11. 1 Kent's, p. 61. 1 Le Page's Elements, p. 326. Valin, Comm. on Art. 1 of Ord. of 1681, p. 414, &c. 2 Azune, p. 2, c. 5, § 9. 1 Elliot's Deb., p. 110; 4 Ib., 458.)

III. Special reprisals have been usually allowed to obtain redress for a citizen or subject who hath been wronged, and general or extraordinary reprisals, as before observed, are more appropriate for injuries directly to a State; but it cannot be doubted that a State may direct special reprisals for pecuniary injuries to itself in the same manner as for injuries done to one of its citizens or subjects.

The authorities, also, sustain this position. 1 Massie, p. 138, § 131, and authorities cited there, and those contained in list annexed *ut passim*.

IV. The unjust, illegal, and injurious acts of individuals of a State, equally as the acts of such State by its authorities, if no redress is given against such offending individuals, constitute a proper cause for special reprisals. (See same authorities.)

A State is liable for the acts of its citizens, if means of just redress are withheld or not afforded against them to the injured party.

The citizens or subjects of a State are each and all liable *per my et per tout* for the liabilities of a State; and, on the other hand, the State is responsible for the acts of its individual members in so far as it does yield just remedies for redress against them to an injured party. (Vattel 6, 2, § 81, 82, 342, 344. Grot. 6, 3, c. 2, p. 538. Wildman, c. 5, p. 187. Felice, v. 12, p. 178. 5 St. Edme, p. 270. 1 Massie, p. 134, § 137. De Garden 64, § 3, p. 229, &c. 2 Azuni, c. 5, a. 2, 5, 7. Ruth. Inst., 516, 517, v. c. ix, § 13.)

V. The withholding payment of a just debt from a State or citizen, or subject of a State, or the denial or unreasonable delay of justice in regard thereof, it is conceded, though it constitutes a case for special reprisals, is not so strong a case as that where redress is sought for illegal violence by the authorities or citizens or subjects of the State against the persons or property of citizens or subjects of a State resorting to such remedy. The English denied, in the Silesian loan case, that reprisals extended by the law of nations to cases of debt, except in cases of justice absolutely denied, first by tribunals, and afterwards by the prince, and such denial must be in *re minime dubia*. (1 Reddie R., 269. Contra W. Inst. c. v. p., as to limiting remedy to case, violence, &c.) Precedents can be found, both of debt and of violence. In case of debt, however, the creditor is bound to submit to the *lex loci contractus*, and to the *lex fori* as administered by the State complained of to and between its own subjects or citizens; and, if equal rights are conceded, and the same remedies yielded, no just cause of complaint exists. This principle cannot, however, apply in terms to cases of debt due by a sovereign State, as in most countries such sovereignty cannot be made a defendant in its own courts. In such case the complaining State may resort, *in limine*, to special letters of reprisal to coerce the fulfillment of an admitted obligation, for the enforcement of which no other remedy exists except war.

Cases of *tort* by a State are governed by the same rule, and so, also, cases of *tort* by the individual subjects or citizens of a State without its sanction or authority. Special reprisals should not be resorted to till judicial remedies have been sought in vain, for it is only when such remedies are withheld or denied that such State is responsible for the acts of its individual members, though this rule does not apply in cases of *tort*, even if criminal acts, when they are avowed by the State as committed under its authority. (See authorities in the celebrated McLeod case in New York.)

VI. The doctrine that the claim for which "special reprisals" are sought must be manifestly just and without doubt, is unquestionably reasonable; but this rule doth not apply, and cannot, in the nature of things, be made to apply, in cases of *tort*, to the precise amount claimed by the party injured, or to anything beyond the right to damages to some extent. Such damages are more or less uncertain in all such cases, until final investigation and adjudication, and in such cases where special reprisals are granted, as hereinafter is fully shown, the delinquent State is fully protected in the judicial proceedings for the trial and condemnation of the property seized under the letters, and the ascertainment of the amount of damages justly due by judicial authority, and the resort to the caution with security exacted from the claimants to respond in damages for any injury sustained in consequence of an extravagant and unreasonable demand, or for any abuse of the letters of reprisal. The ordinary rule in England is, to receive "the oath of the party injured, or other sufficient proof touching the pretended injury, and of the certain loss and damage thereby sustained." (See 1 Molloy, c. 2, § 6; Viner's Abr., 17, &c.) If the circumstances be of a corroborating character, the oath of the party is deemed *prima facie* true, and it is held will justify the granting of the letters of request, and even the issuance of the letters of reprisal, which rests in the discretion of the king.

(See, also, Valin Comm on Art. 1 and 5 of Tit. X. of Ord. of 1731, (before cited,) as to preliminary proof of wrong, &c., page 414, &c.)

It seems by the precedent in Molloy of the letters of special reprisal granted to Turner *et al.*, that without any express statute directing or authorizing it, a preliminary reference was had to the admiralty court to assess the damages.

In this case, we have furnished the testimony of several competent disinterested witnesses, and also documentary proofs of the act of violence, and of the damages also.

VII. The *lettre de requête* is the incipient step to letters of special reprisal. Forms are to be found in the ancient English registers, in F. N. B., in Rymer, and other books of historical and legal documents, and are referred to by modern English legal authors. Ordinarily they state merely the circumstances of the case and request that justice be done, and designate a reasonable time, according to circumstances, for reparation to be made, or for the answer of the State complained of to be given, and formerly the proofs were not usually communicated with such letter. Indeed no recorded case can be referred to in which such proofs were transmitted. By the treaty between the United States and Venezuela, however, it is required, (see Cl. 3, of Art. 34, of treaty of 1836, 8 Statutes at Large, p. 842,) as in many other of our treaties with the Hispano-American Republics, "that neither of the contracting parties will authorize or order any act of reprisal, nor declare war against the other, on complaints of injuries or damages, until the said party considering itself offended shall first have presented to the other a statement of such injuries or damages, verified by competent proofs, and demanded justice, and the same shall have been refused or unreasonably delayed."

In this case, the proofs in the schedule below have been communicated to the State Department of the United States by the claimants for transmission to the government of Venezuela, at the dates therein designated. If heretofore communicated to it, (and there is no reason whatever for any portion of them being withheld,) the treaty has been complied with; but if they have not been fully communicated to the Venezuelan government, and if any part of them has been suppressed, the omission, it is submitted, must be supplied by annexing the same to the letter of request, in order that the terms of the treaty may be complied with by the United States.

Such proceeding is proper, in order that the State complained of may be apprised precisely of the alleged wrong, and have an opportunity to adduce contrary or explanatory proofs.

In this case, two years and a half have been spent fruitlessly in applications for redress, in remonstrance, in correspondence, and other efforts, to procure the adjustment of the case without resorting to any harsh course. Venezuela is fully apprised of all the circumstances of the case, both as to facts and law. They have all been made public by the Senate of the United States. (Sen. Ex. Doc., No. 25, 3d Sess. 34th Cong.) The letter of request, in this case, ought to exact an adjustment within a brief period. (See, as to time, Wildman, Inst. of Int. Law, c. 5, p. 190, and cases there cited designated by treaty, &c., &c.)

Schedule of proofs referred to.

No.	Schedule.	Dated.	Transmitted to State Department.
1	(A.) Deposition of Captain Safford as to fraud of Dias with respect to "agreement," and hauling down United States flag by Dias	June 20, 1855	1855
2	(B.) Deposition of Captain James Wheeler, discovery of guano on Shelton's Isle	June 8, 1855	1855
3	(C.) Deposition of Captain James Wheeler as to United States flag being hoisted and kept flying on Shelton's Isle, and as to declaration of commander of H. B. M.'s steamer Devastation	June 15, 1855	1855
4	(D.) N. P. Gibbs to P. S. Shelton, received about January 20, 1855	Dec. 30, 1854	1855
5	(E.) Certificate of Captain N. P. Gibbs, in his handwriting, made in January, 1855		1855
6	(F.) Captain Gibbs to P. S. Shelton, received *via* St. Thomas, January 15, 1855; landing second company of Venezuelans	Dec. 25, 1854	1855
7	(G.) Captain Gibbs to P. S. Shelton, received in January, 1855	Dec. 26, 1854	1855
8	(H.) Memorandum of protest of G. W. Nickels, master, and two mates of ship Jas. N. Cooper	Feb. 20, 1855	1855
9	(I.) Extract of report, or letter, from Captain Gibbs, announcing discovery of guano deposit on Aves or Bird Island	April 6, 1854	1855
10	(I[2].) Map of Shelton's Isle		
11	(J.) Copy of instructions to Captain Gibbs, Boston	June 22, 1854	June 20, 1855
12	(K.) Sampson & Tappan and Philo S. Shelton to Captain Gibbs	June 22, 1854	June 20, 1855
13	(L.) Extract of a letter of instructions to Captain Gibbs	June 21, 1854	June 20, 1855
14	(M.) Declaration of William P. Gibbs	Aug. 23, 1855	March 8, 1856
15	(N.) Printed pamphlet of Philadelphia Guano Company, (published)	Feb. —, 1856	March 8, 1856
16	Official notice of Venezuelan consul and Philadelphia Guano Company, published in New York Herald	Jan. 5, 1856	Jan. 5, 1856
17	Copy of the capitulation to Commander Dias	Dec. 13, 1854	Feb. 26, 1856
18	Extracts from the Wallace and Pickrell contracts, showing that Shelton's Isle was included, with express refusal by Venezuela to guarantee title		
19	Copy of report of Commander De Horsey, obtained from foreign office, of quantity and quality of guano on the isle	Apr. 11, 1854	May 9, 1856
20	Extract from "*L'Outre Mer*," (French W. I. paper,) in 1854, of the quantity of guano on the isle		May 9, 1856
21	Printed deposition of Captain N. P. Gibbs, (Ex. Doc. No. 25, 3d sess. 34th Cong., pp. 61 to 75)	Apr. 12, 1856	April 14, 1856
22	Deposition of John McCabe, (Ex. Doc. above, p. 81)	June 28, 1856	June 30, 1856
23	Deposition of Richard Thornell, (Ex. Doc. above, p. 78)	May 7, 1856	May 10, 1856

SCHEDULE—Continued.

No.	Schedule.	Dated.	Transmitted to State Department.
24	Deposition of Joseph Herbert	Aug. 6, 1856	Aug. —, 1856
25	Deposition of Captain James Wheeler, (Ex. Doc. above, p. 90)	May 7, 1856	May 9, 1856
26	Moses Taylor, Esq., to Don José J. Keefe, Venezuela consul, as to notice No. 16	Jan. 10, 1856	Jan. 15, 1856
27	Don José J. Keefe, Venezuela consul, to Moses Taylor, Esq	Jan. 12, 1856	Jan. 15, 1856

It is deemed important that all the papers above mentioned, of which full and exact copies have not been duly presented to the government of Venezuela, should accompany the letter of request; and those which have been presented to Venezuela should be noticed, with the date of presentation in said letter:

Firstly. Because the treaty imperatively demands such course; and

Secondly. Because it may be deemed requisite to entitle claimants to offer said documents in evidence on the trial before the *admiralty* court.

VIII. As a State is in nowise liable for the debts of its individual citizens, except in so far as it denies a creditor justice against such debtors, it follows that a resort must first have been had by a creditor to all such remedies as are allowed him by the State complained of before applying to his own government for special reprisals, and the amount of debt claimed must be shown to be clearly due *in re minime dubia*. (See authorities above referred to.)

IX. It will be noticed that in the points preceding this argument it is conceded that if satisfaction is not accorded agreeably to the requirements of the *lettre de requête*, in a case of damages for a *tort*, the complaining State, before it issues letters of special reprisal, ought, for the prevention of injustice *ex abundante cautela*, for its own satisfaction, direct an inquisition of a judicial character, if practicable, for the ascertainment of the true damages. There is a similar requirement in the ancient ordinances of marine in France, and most other States pursue an analogous practice in relation to special reprisals. (See article 1, Ordinances, page 1681, referring such preliminary investigation to the courts of admiralty on petition. See Sea Laws.) No one can question the power of any government to direct such inquisition for its own satisfaction before it will act by granting the letters demanded. Nor can the competency of the executive of a government be questioned to indicate a form of such procedure assimilating (*cy pres*) to the proceedings of a judicial tribunal. Similar directions are constantly made by this government in various cases, as necessary to effect the purposes of justice, and to prevent those who administer the government from being misled.

It is not contended that such inquest of damages is conclusive; it is a precautionary measure to prevent injustice, and for the satisfaction of the government itself, and neither the claimant nor the government complained of can except to it, for it is a measure of prudence with reference to one and of security with regard to both.

The true amount of damages is subsequently, upon the execution of the letters of reprisal, judicially determined, and adjudged upon judicial proofs and investigations, and before this appointed tribunal all parties can be heard. The question of the right to issue reprisals, of the proper and legitimate exercise of the executive function, in resorting to that remedy on behalf of claimants, is the only question which is not permitted to be contested in such court. The question of damages, and all questions as to any alleged abuse of the letters, are rightful subjects for its investigation and decision; and, under the law of nations and under the practice of nations, the admiralty or prize courts of the State giving such letters of special reprisal, are the proper tribunals to make such decision. When property is seized by virtue of the letters of reprisal, it must be brought *infra præsidia* so soon as possible, according to the rules observed with respect to captures in time of war by public ships or by private armed ships with commissions of general reprisal or letters of marque. (See 1 Kent, p. 62; Wheaton's Hist., § 12, p. 108; Valin's Comm. on Arts, 1 and 5, Tit. X, of Ord. of 1681. See, also, Molloy, before cited, *Form of Letters of Reprisal*, &c., p. 53, also § 21.)

All the proceedings subsequently are judicial by libel or information, according to the practice of these courts.

And it may be observed that, whilst the English statutes and the French ordinances and Spanish regulations and those of other countries all prescribe similar rules conformable to the law of nations, yet they are all merely directory, and if they did not exist the general laws and practice of nations, and rules of judicial proceeding adapted to such remedy, would be all-sufficient. They are merely self-imposed restraints by a government upon itself and upon the acts of its own officers, rather than being *per se* rules of the *jus gentium*, though in conformity with the latter.

The English common law writers, as well as the international publicists of that nation, all contend that the early English statutes regulating the issuance of special reprisals, did not either strengthen or impair the royal (executive) authority, under the law of nations, to issue such writs, and that these statutes are merely directory regulations in regard to the exercise of such authority by the administrative officers.

In Viner's abr. before cited, [II,] it is said, (referring to the ancient British statutes as to proceedings to obtain special reprisals,) "letters of reprisal were granted long before the statutes by the kings of England, by virtue of their prerogatives, nor was the king's prerogative in the least diminished by them, but remained at common law, (general treaties of trade, &c., 212,) and this statute does in no respect restrain the king's prerogative and authority which he had at the common law in judging the conveniency and time when to be executed." Viner cites Molloy, 30, cap. 2, § 9. Molloy, b. 1, c. 2, §§ 7 and 8, referring to the statutes of King John, of Edward III., and Henry V., and Henry VI., says (§ 7,) that letters of reprisal "may issue not only by the *jus gentium* and *civile*, but by the ancient municipal laws of the kingdom;" and (§ 8,) that the statutes are made "for the subject and letters of reprisal, they being granted long before the statutes, and the king's prerogative not the least diminished, but remaining at the common law to judge when expedient."

Stephens, in his Comm., before cited, p. 264, pt. 1, § 4, p. 515, says: "As the delay of making war may sometimes be detrimental to individuals who have suffered depredations from foreign potentates, our (the English) laws have in some respect armed the subject with powers to impel the prerogative by directing the ministers of the crown to issue letters of marque and reprisal upon due demand," &c.

Valin, in his Comm. on the French Ord. of 1681, as to special reprisals, p. 444, before cited, says "it is conformable to the law of nations received among all nations; but further, it has perfected that law by the wise precautions it has taken in addition to those that the author of the Guidon, c. 10, had already demanded, to abate the excesses and temper the rigor thereof."

Mr. Reddie, 1 Maritime Int. Law, 157, says: "It is but justice to observe that the ordinance (1681) and the administration under it are, in the great majority of rules and cases, in conformity with the natural and common consuetudinary law of nations, and declaratory of the principles previously recognized by the European nations," and excepting the provisions in relation to neutral rights, that it is "an able declaratory exposition of the common maritime international law of Europe."

And it has even been contended that letters of special reprisals issued to an individual subject, for injuries committed by a foreign State, were not revocable by a domestic act, and even if a war intervened before final execution, that they were not revoked by a subsequent treaty of peace between the two countries till satisfaction was had upon them, and the power of the king to revoke such letters before such satisfaction was had, was even questioned by some eminent English common law jurists. (See 1 Molloy, c. 2, § 8, as to revocations. King *vs.* Caren, 3 Swan, 669. 1 Vern., 54, 55, parch., 1682.)

In the reign of Edward II., according to Lord Campbell in his "Lives of the Lord Chancellors of England," vol. 1, p. 205, the power of issuing letters of marque and reprisal against a foreign State that denied a delayed justice to Englishmen, resided in the high court of chancery, and those letters were in the nature of a judicial process, and the property captured was detained as a pledge or security till justice was rendered by the offending State.

The reasonable term in which an answer is to be required, of course depends on the character and circumstances of the case, the contiguity of the respective governments, &c. In Europe, as to ordinary cases of spoliation, four or six months from the allowance of the application from the injured party to his government is the longest term designated in which such answer should be made. (See Wildman Inst., c. 5, p. 190, &c.)

In the present case the spoliation was committed in 1854, nearly three years ago. Our claim for damages was presented to the Department of State of the United States, January 15, 1855, so soon as we became apprised of the outrage. We have diligently followed up that demand for justice by reiterated applications to the same department since that day, and by furnishing to it from time to time proofs by depositions of numerous witnesses, and by documents of different kinds, some obtained from Europe, all of which, careless of any advantage the same might afford to Venezuela, we asked should be forthwith furnished to that government. So unremitted have been our efforts, that we have on more than one occasion received from the department something like a rebuke for our importunity and for cumulating such proofs unnecessarily, and in certain public prints we have been reproached with "pestering" and "bothering" the department improperly with respect to our indemnity; and, besides all this, we have, with the assent of the department, and, in fact, at its suggestion, at an additional expense of several thousand dollars, dispatched an agent to Caraccas to obtain, if practicable, a compromise of our just claim and its settlement upon something approaching reasonable terms, and yet it has not resulted in effecting any promise by Venezuela to indemnify us in any degree or any concession of their liability; and, on the contrary, the government of the United States and ourselves have as yet only received in answer the repudiation of our claim upon the most frivolous pretexts, coupled with indignity and insult to the representative of the United States in relation to it.

Under these circumstances, fully cognizant as Venezuela is of all he facts of the case, and has been since the wrong was committed, nearly three years since, apprised as she has been from time to time of the proofs we have adduced, according to the terms of the treaty of 1836, it is submitted that any further forbearance to her to enable her to indulge her disposition to shuffle and equivocate, should be limited to the time necessary to understand the character of the demand made by the United States. And Venezuela should not only be peremptorily required to admit liability to make indemnity, and to give assurance of just satisfaction to the claimants, but with respect to the amount of damages, she should be held to show to the satisfaction of this government that the amount claimed by us is exorbitant, and wherein the same is exaggerated, and her willingness to pay what is not so controverted by proofs to be promptly adduced by her. And upon this point we contend that without indubitable proof so adduced, the amount claimed by us, especially if previously determined by process of ascertainment above indicated, must be regarded as the just amount due.

Especially should this rule obtain, as such amount is not conclusive; but, if it is proper, it may be reduced by deductions on the trial before the judicial tribunals when the letters of reprisal have been issued and executed by the seizure of property brought before such tribunal for condemnation and sale.

The idea of referring, *lite pendente*, the amount of damages to the arbitrament of a third power, is not only derogatory to the dignity of the complaining State, but it is vexatious and unjust to the individual claimants, and is also inconsistent with all proceedings looking to the issuance of special letters of reprisal as the ultimate remedy. It breeds procrastination and delay, and causes great and unnecessary expenses to the claimants. It is the abnegation, by the complaining State, of the rightful jurisdiction of its own judicial tribunals over the ultimate decision of the question of damages with which such tribunals are invested by the law of nations, and to the benefit of which its citizens are entitled. They should not be deprived of that benefit (or advantage if it be such) in such cases, and shuffled off by a reference to a third power or party not administering justice under judicial sanction, and often subject to influences to which a court of justice is impregnable, and affected by considerations other than the strict maintenance of the principles of international law. It is an interference with the regular course of proceeding, and a departure from the rules sanctioned by the practice of ages as best promotive to the ends of justice. As well might a State abnegate the exclusive jurisdiction of its own prize courts in time of war, under the laws of nations, and agree to refer the decisions of questions of prize or no prize, or of any incidental question arising in the progress of a prize cause, to a third power or person, as to refer this incidental question of the amount of dam ages to such arbitrament. Such course, in the argument of Ryder and Mansfield, on the Silesia loan case, it is declared would be "manifestly unjust, absurd, and impracticable." (1 Reddie Int. Mar. Law, p. 269. 1 Magens, *on Insurance*, p. 491.) Such procedure must be founded upon the theories of the speculative philosophers of the era of the French revolution, who vainly insisted that it was only necessary to establish one supreme court of justice for the whole world to effect the coming of the millenium and secure universal peace forthwith, but who were never able exactly to agree upon the formula for the execution of the decrees of such august tribunal to effect their object, nor neither have any peace societies since.

And here it may be observed (as is conceived not inappropriately to this case) that this entire class of pseudo-philanthropic philosophers, whether anti-war, anti-privateering or general reprisals, anti-capture of merchant vessels in war, anti-retaliation or retorsion, or "anti-special reprisals in time of peace," all begin at the wrong end to effect the consummation of their sublime wishes. To crown their hopes with favorable success peace societies should alter their names, and style themselves anti-quarrel, anti-spoliation, and anti-wrong and injustice leagues, and adopt measures to effect the objects indicated by such change. Prevention of wrong, and not the abolition or lessening of the penalty for the commission of such wrong or weakening the means of redress and of establishing right and justice, is the true course. National injustice is the cause of all wars. War is, in fact, but an effect of and result from such injustice. Prevent the cause and there is no such effect. And this can only be done by enforcing the principles of right, and a respect for and adherence to them upon the individuals who compose a nation or rule a State. War is a punishment for national crimes. In every war one or the other State acts wrongfully, and often both. There is no case of a war just on the part of both. As in civil society, so it is with respect to States, that the least salutary of all modes of preventing crime is to abolish or weaken and render ineffective the punishments therefor. It gives impunity to crime. Would it tend to prevent murder to provide that the murderer should not be hanged or imprisoned, but merely censured or reprimanded by the judge? If a State persists in injustice, what other effective punishment than war, *in ultimâ ratione*, is there? How is she to be constrained to do justice or make reparation? Will the rebuke or reprimand of other nations suffice? Just in so far as the punishments now allowed by the law of nations, and, it is believed, by the divine law, are abated, and in so far as the means of redress now given are weakened, will the apprehension of them be less likely to deter nations from the perpetration of wrong. Who does not know that the fear by merchants of the capture of their ships and goods by privateers, and by public ships in war, and their consequent opposition to war, is a powerful restraint to every commercial nation from engaging in war? Abolish privateering and the capture of merchant ships in war, and this commercial influence, now pledged by its interests to peace, will not be, as heretofore, exerted to preserve it.

The penalty for the commission of national crimes, it is admitted, will be rendered less severe, but the effect of such exemption will also be to make such punishment unequal with regard to the different classes in a State, and likewise to make the means of reparation less coercive against the delinquent nation, and therefore less effective in maintaining justice and preserving peace.

If a new remedy is proposed in lieu of general war between people of different nations, perhaps the most effective would be that suggested by the Emperor Paul of Russia, in his famous letter written about two thirds of a century since, viz: That in all cases of dispute between nations the ministers of State of both, when they failed to adjust the difficulty amicably, should be compelled to settle it by duel to the death between themselves, and the people generally, often not interested, should take no part, but remain at peace.

If special reprisals were abolished, or regarded as obsolete, spoliations and injustice would be more frequent, for the efficacy of the means of redresss would be weakened, and a cogent preventive abandoned. Destroy this remedy, and if a nation persists in injustice and wrong, general war is the only resort. But why should the government constrain claimants to abandon a plain *judicial* remedy and adopt any other uncertain recourse?

Experience hath proved that the hope of effecting arbitraments is, in most cases, illusory. Certainly the experience of the government of the United States will not warrant the expectation of a speedy and equitable and legal decision. Excepting the reference to the Emperor of Russia, under the treaty of Ghent between the United States and Great Britain, not a solitary case of arbitration by this government has ever resulted in a decision that has been satisfactory as just and rightful to its citizens. The memorable award of the King of the Netherlands with respect to the northeastern boundary, discarded by both parties as absurd, is one instance in point of the practical inefficacy of such mode of adjustment.

The General Armstong case, as to which the United States Court of Claims has, since the decision of the then President of the French Republic, decided that the United States were responsible to the claimants for having failed to enforce just reparation from Portugal, notwithstanding the decision of the arbitrator that Portugal was not amenable, is another illustration of the little value of such arbitration. There are many other cases in the history of our government of like character.

Cases of joint commissioners to ascertain damages, where there were many and divers claimants, under treaty stipulations, have occurred, and even these have failed in effecting justice, as is proved in the case of the Mexican commission, under the treaty of 1839, (in which ultimate reference, in case of a difference in the joint commission, was had to an umpire, a distinguished minister of a foreign power,) is an additional illustration of the worthlessness of such means of adjustment. In this last case, the failure of the joint commission to do justice, and even in some cases when aided by the distinguished umpire, is shown by the fact that by the decision of the board of commissioners established under the treaty of Guadaloupe Hidalgo, and in which proceedings the United States and its citizens were the sole parties, thousands of dollars were awarded to claimants under the treaty of 1839, to whom partial justice only had been meted out by the joint commission!

In truth, the resort to arbitration, though a favorite means with certain theoretic essayists and statesmen who indulge the fanciful idea that they can better the rules and usages of the law of nations, sanctioned by the wisdom of ages, may, perhaps, be well adopted in a bad cause, but should never be consented to in a good one.

These claimants deem it due to themselves, and not disrespectful to the government, to say that in view of the further procrastination and delay consequent on the adoption of such mode of ascertainment of the precise amount justly due to them, and in view of the great additional trouble that would be caused to them, and in view, also, of the increased expense to be incurred, they trust no such reference or arbitrament will be consented to by the United States.

The claimants suggest, as they conceive it is proper for them to do, that the question of damage in this case should be investigated, as before indicated, in some manner decided by the federal authorities and for their satisfaction, after the formal letter of request is transmitted, and prior to the issuance of letters of reprisal, and that the ultimate investigation and decision most appropriately and exclusively belongs to the judicial prize tribunals upon the execution of such letters and trial of the property seized thereon; and they deprecate an abandonment of the established rules and formula practiced under the law of nations, as being unwise, useless, and uncertain, and creating great delay and expense to them.

X. As before observed, special letters of reprisal are in the nature of a national distress warrant, or a *capias ad withernam*, or writ of foreign attachment, authorizing the seizure and detention of property as a pledge to answer the just claims of the parties who obtain the writ, to be proved by such parties before the court into whose jurisdiction the property is brought. It is an error to suppose the seizure or capture of such property by virtue of the letters of reprisal is absolute. It is no more absolute than the taking of property under the common-law *writ of replevin;* and, in truth, the proceedings in an action of and under a writ of replevin at common law bear a close resemblance to the proceedings under the *jus gentium* upon special letters of reprisal. (See 1 Black. Comm., p. 259, and notes to Am. ed., and 3 ib., p. 146, &c.; 3 ib., p. 6, &c., 129, 146, 413, 280, 231. 1 Lord Campbell's Lives of Lord Chancellors, p. 205, before cited.)

The preliminary caution, with surety demanded of the party seeking a letter of special reprisal, is analogous to the bond or stipulation required of the plaintiff in replevin. And so, too, where the property is replevied from seizure under a distress for rent due.

The question to be decided by the court is not ordinarily the legality or illegality of the distress, except as dependent upon the fact whether any rent was actually due as claimed, or whether the amount claimed was due, or the distress was unreasonable. And so the court, in case of a seizure by letters of reprisal, determines only the amount of damages due the claimants, and whether there hath been an abuse of the writ in that regard.

The property seized is disposed of by the direction of such tribunal, and the proceeds first applied to the payment of the reasonable expenses incurred in the case, next to the satisfaction of the claim, and the surplus is to be returned to the State complained of.

After seizure, it remains *in the custody of the law* till adjudicated upon and disposed of by admiralty court. The seizure is a mere *stop-*

page or *detainer*, and does not, of itself, till adjudicated by the court of admiralty, change the property. This is the well-settled rule, according to all the authorities.

XI. It is conceded that a State granting special letters of reprisal, may require such reasonable conditions and restrictions necessary to prevent the improper use thereof, not in derogation of the rights of its citizens to such full remedy according to the *jus gentium*, and not of a character rendering it ineffectual. The consuetudinary law of nations, and the practice under it, requires that in all cases a caution and surety should be exacted from the party demanding such letters, to respond in damages to any person illegally damnified by the abuse of such letters, and also to all persons injured thereby in any manner whatever, if it should be subsequently made to appear that the claimants fraudulently made a false and exaggerated statement of their claim, and misled the authorities of their State into granting such letters.

This stipulation is an ample guarantee to the whole world against illegal damnification by the issuance of such letters, or the proceedings under them. It deprives the State, whose property, or the property of whose subjects or citizens, is seized under such letters, of all pretext for resisting their execution. It takes away from the letters everything like a belligerent character, and makes them mere judicial process for the enforcement of just indemnity for a wrong, or collection of a just debt.

The authorities show that all States, within the last six centuries at least, have exacted such caution.

Among the restrictions and conditions that a State issuing such letters may rightfully exact of its citizens demanding them, is the preliminary investigation before alluded to, to ascertain, for its own satisfaction, the amount of damages or debt justly due from the delinquent State; though, as we have before stated, such preliminary investigation was not required either by England or any of the continental States, except France, by Art. 1, of Tit., 10, of Ord. of Marine, 1681, and prior ordinances, in cases of letters of special reprisal. (See Cleirac, Valin, and Pardessus before cited *ut passim* in notice on said article.) Such course is now suggested as a wise and precautionary measure to avoid subsequent contest on that point, to prevent an abuse of the letters, and injustice and injury to the State complained of, and all other parties.

Anciently, special letters of reprisal were issued to the individuals complaining, and who also executed them by vessels armed by themselves. It is not questioned that a State may, for its own security, and to prevent an abuse of its writ and injustice being done, direct, at its option, that the letters be executed by the individual claimants, as according to past practice, or that they be executed under the supervision of its naval or other officers, or such letters may be issued immediately to such officers, and the execution thereof directed to be made by them, and in a public ship-of-war.

Doubless no departure from the rules and usages of the *jus gentium*, having in view the security of the alleged delinquent State, and third parties, would be justified on the part of the State issuing such letters, but the prescribing of regulations and restraints by such State upon its own citizens, tending to *enhance* such security, cannot be complained of. The only question in relation to such regulations and restrictions *is between such State and its citizens*, and as to their not being in derogation of the rights of the latter, or impairing those rights under the law of nations.

The abolition of privateering by the convention of Paris of 1856, so far forth as respects the seven States, parties to that convention, is at least suggestive of the self-imposed prohibition, by all of those States, against the granting thereafter of commissions to private armed vessels, in principle extending to both kinds of letters of reprisal. Whilst we do not accede to the policy of the abolition of general reprisals or privateering, insomuch as the employment of public vessels is less expensive to the claimants than their own private vessels; insomuch as abuses are less likely to occur in the execution of the writ of special reprisals; insomuch as resistance would be less likely to be made to public officers in public ships; insomuch as public officers intrusted with the execution of such letters would be more fully under the control of the State issuing them, and would be disinterested and impartial, it is submitted that the employment of such officers and such vessels to execute this particular duty, is consistent with sound policy and reason as well as with the law of nations.

XII. All the authorities require that special letters of reprisal should be granted by order of the sovereign of the State, or that branch of the public authority to which the power of directing the intercourse of such State with other States is intrusted by its constitution.

We concede that the power to issue or authorize the issue of general or extraordinary commissions of reprisal or letters of marque is, by the first article, eighth section of the Constitution, vested in Congress; but the authority to issue special reprisals, under the law of nations, is, we contend, appropriately *an executive function*, not included in that delegation, but left to be exercised by the executive branch of the government, as one of the necessarily inherent and implied powers, founded on the constitutional duty to "take care that the laws be faithfully executed;" (see art. 2, § 3;) the *jus gentium* being included in that requisition.

The Articles of Confederation between the United States of America, adopted during the war of the Revolution, contain two clauses pertinent to this subject. (See 1 U. S. Stat. at Large, p. 4.)

Article 6, section 5, among other prohibitions upon the respective States, contains the following: "Nor shall any State grant permission to any ships or vessels of war, *nor letters of marque or reprisal*, except it be *after a declaration of war* by the United States in Congress assembled, and then only against the kingdoms and State, and the subjects thereof, against which war has so been declared, and under such regulations as shall be established by the United States in Congress assembled," &c. (1 U. S. Stat. at Large, pp. 5, 7.)

Article 9, section 1, provides that "the United States in Congress assembled, shall have the sole exclusive right and power of establishing rules for deciding, in all cases, what captures on land and water shall be legal, and in what manner prizes taken by land or naval forces in the service of the United States shall be divided or appropriated; of granting letters of marque and reprisal *in time of peace*, appointing courts for the trial of piracies and other felonies committed on the high seas, and establishing courts for receiving and determining finally appeals in all cases of capture, provided no member of Congress shall be appointed judge of any of said courts." (Ib. p. 6.)

It will be noticed that the delegation of power by the federal Constitution to Congress "to declare war and grant letters of marque and reprisal," is not accompanied by a similar provision to that in the first section, ninth article of the Articles of Confederation above quoted, referring to such letters "in time of peace," and therefore the delegation in the federal Constitution must be construed as referring only to such general or extraordinary commissions or letters to be issued in time of war. And this construction is strengthened by that delegation being coupled with the power of declaring war, and connected in the same clause and section. And such contraction leaves the power of issuing *special* letters of reprisal "*in time of peace*," to be exercised as an inherent power or function of the executive branch of the federal government *under the law of nations*, unfettered by any constitutional restriction or inhibition, as was contained in article six, and also in article nine, of the Articles of Confederation above quoted.

This is no novel construction; for it has, with great force, been contended by distinguished statesmen in Congress that the power to grant special reprisals in time of peace, to their citizens, by each of the States, for injuries sustained, either against a co-State or foreign government, hath not been relinquished by the federal compact, and that the eighth section, first article, refers only to general or extraordinary reprisals *in time of war*, and has left the right of special reprisals unaffected by the Constitution; and as it exists by the law of nations alone, and that it may be so exercised by the federal or State governments in all proper cases. [Vide speech of Senator J. M. Mason, in Senate of the United States, on the fugitive slave bill in 1850.]

We do not think it necessary to discuss the question of the existence of this power in the several States, or its exercise against each other or against foreign governments. It is sufficient for us that there is not any express delegation by the Constitution to Congress of the exclusive power to grant special reprisals. It is sufficient for us that by the common law of England, and by the civil law, as well as by the universal law of nations, such letters of special reprisal, in time of peace, are in the nature of *a judicial writ*, and are demandable *of right* by the subject or citizen of a State from its government when he hath been aggrieved and injured by a foreign State, its subjects, or citizens.

It is sufficient for us that the *jus gentium*, and the usages and practices of all nations under it, have provided rules and formula of procedure *that save the necessity of congressional legislation* to enable such rights to be maintained by the Executive.

It is not a sound argument to urge that the Executive may endanger the peace of the country by authorizing the issuance of such letters without the authority of Congress. Such argument is founded upon the presumption that the Executive is incompetent or incapable of exercising the functions of government justly and properly, and that

Congress is the only immaculate and safe depository of public power. If carried to its full extent, it annihilates all executive power whatever, and places every thing under the control of Congress; whereas, according to the true principles of the federal compact, the separate powers of the executive branch of the government are as independent of those of the legislative branch, and are as well defined and maintained, as the latter. We are not informed of any case of special reprisals that has occurred in this government since the adoption of the federal Constitution.

Cases of general and extraordinary reprisals have repeatedly occurred, and in which the legislative as well as the executive power has been exercised under the Constitution to authorize the issuance of such letters, which were recognized as a kind of imperfect war.

The act of Congress of July 9, 1798, (1 Stat. at Large, pp. 574, 579,) authorizing general reprisals against the French government, are of this character. So, too, the act of February 6, 1802, (2 ib. 130;) and also the acts of June 18, and June 26, 1812, (ib., pp. 755, 759,) declaring and during the war with Great Britain. So, too, the act of March 3, 1815, (3 ib., p. 230,) as to the letters against Algiers; and so also the message of General Jackson to Congress, (December 1, 1834,) with reference to the authorization of general reprisals against the French government for the public debt due to the United States by treaty stipulations, is of the same character; and the distinction obviously exists between all these cases and the case of special reprisals to enforce rights of individual citizens in time of peace, must be apparent to the most ordinary intellect.

No one contends that there is any special statute investing the executive branch of this government with power to grant special letters of reprisal in time of peace, or with power to lay a blockade or embargo in time of peace, in a case where by the law of nations such blockade or embargo would be justified; or to take possession, by armed force, of territory in dispute between the United States and a foreign State; or of resenting by violence an insult to and outrage upon a public diplomatic representative of the United States in a foreign country; or of committing acts of hostility against another people for insults and outrages upon the American flag and American citizens. Yet it hath been found that such measures must be adopted, and such legitimate executive functions fulfilled; and though several such cases have occurred, no Executive hath been arraigned and censured for violating the Constitution in so doing, but in every instance he hath been applauded and sustained.

We prefer to be strict constructionists of the Constitution, but not so much with reference to the necessary powers of the federal government for the protection of its citizens against the aggressions of foreign States, as in regard to encroachments upon the rights of the individual States of the Confederacy, or the rights of the individual citizen by the federal government. By such liberal construction from the former, no danger is to be apprehended: on the contrary, the greatest danger is, that timid statesmen, holding the reins of federal authority in future times, (when the doctrines of Exeter Hall shall more exclusively prevail,) may be deterred from acts of necessary justice by the facility to find excuses for their neglect or timidity in alleged doubts as to their constitutional power. Over fastidiousness in this regard by Mr. Jefferson, would have prevented the taking possession of the Spanish ports on the Southern Mississippi border under the treaty of 1795, or the subsequent occupation of Mobile and the country west of the Perdido fifty years since, as included in the Louisiana cession. No act of Congress existed authorizing Commodore Rogers to fire into the Little Belt just before the war with Great Britain. If Mr. Polk and his cabinet had been squeamish in 1845–6, about the occupation by the Army of the United States of the country between the Nueces and Rio Grande del Norte without congressional authority, the history of this country would have been very different. General Jackson would not have invaded the Floridas in 1814 or 1818 if he had believed an act of Congress was necessary. If Captain Percival, some thirty years since, had awaited the instructions of the President, and the President had awaited the authority of Congress, before that gallant officer permitted himself to fire upon the savages at Quallabbattoo ; if Commodore Armstrong or Captain Towle, more recently, had refrained from punishing the Chinese for their outrages, till Congress had passed a law to allow it; or if President Pierce had asked authority from Congress to allow him to bombard Greytown, and chastise the negro and mulatto vagabonds there congregated, for their outrage upon the American minister; if Captain Ingraham had deemed an act of Congress necessary for him to act in the Kozta case, the chronicles of our country would have been greatly variant from those now written. The idea of an Executive of this great Confederacy possessing no attributes unless Congress had sanctioned them, of being helpless as an infant (unless the previous authority of Congress be given to him) to uphold and execute the law of nations, to protect and enforce the rights of American citizens, and to maintain the honor of the American flag, is degrading to the exalted position of the Chief Magistrate of the United States. The concession that the citizens of this government cannot receive the same redress yielded to the subjects of European monarchies, until the Executive asks leave of Congress to fulfill such duty under the law of nations, and the soliciting congressional direction as to the mode of such fulfillment, is derogatory to the character of our free institutions.

The argument that would inhibit the Executive from exercising the power of issuing special letters of reprisal without the previous legislative permission of Congress, it is presumed, is founded chiefly upon the idea that the issuance of such letters is a belligerent act, or an act tending to war. The authorities heretofore cited show that it is not; but, on the contrary, is a pacific, conservative remedy. Doubtless congressional legislation, analogous to that of the British Parliament as early as the time of Edward III and Henry V, and analogous, also, to the French ordinances of marine as early as the thirteenth century, embodied in the tenth article of the famous ordnance of 1681, and to similar *leyes* of Spain and *placarts* of Holland on the subject of special reprisals, with such improvements as the progress of mankind render proper, would be beneficial. But such legislation is no more wanting to warrant the Executive in the fulfillment of his duty on the case of special letters of reprisal under the law of nations, and according to its usages and practices, than it would be for the prompt defense of our country by the Executive in case of hostile invasion by a foreign power without declaration of war. The idea of the necessity of such previous congressional legislation is as ridiculous as the fastidiousness of the Englishman who declined exerting himself to save a drowning man, for the reason that he had never been regularly introduced to him, and could not venture for that reason to speak to him, much less take hold of him. The belief by foreign governments that the Executive of the United States was impotent to redress wrongs upon our citizens by special letters of reprisal before he had sought and obtained the authority of Congress, would tempt them to the commission of acts of violence and outrage, whilst, on the contrary, the knowledge that the Executive of the United States possesses such power, and will exercise it without the delay of recourse to Congress, would deter those disposed to act unjustly. It would secure the prompt payment of many just claims of our citizens against foreign governments; it would tend to prevent difficulties; to prevent the creation of hostile feelings and the commission of hostile acts, and would prevent wars. This power, properly exercised by the Executive, might have prevented the war with Mexico, for the long delay in the adjustment of the just claims of our citizens for the spoliations of that republic tempted it to further aggression after the treaty of 1839. And we believe if special reprisals had been promptly resorted to, both against the British and French governments for their spoliations under the orders in council, and the Berlin and Milan and Rambouillet decrees, the war of 1812, between this country and Great Britain, would never have occurred. Had the remedy of special reprisals been adopted by those who administered the executive powers of the government of the United States in the cases of the atrocious outrages perpetrated by the Spanish officials in Cuba some years ago upon the persons and property of citizens of the United States, and for the outrages upon our flag, instead of the idler measures of diplomatic remonstrances, those wrongs would not have been repeated. Inertness in exacting just redress and atonement created the belief of impunity, and tempted such repetition.

Loccenius, in his work, (cited in the list annexed,) refers to the practice of certain princes refusing letters of special reprisal for fear of provoking war, as to which practice Valin remarks, it is "no proof of moderation of the governments that have adopted it, nor of their love ot peace, but rather of their feebleness or pusillanimity; and that any sovereign who should refuse them on such a pretext would be regardless of his own honor and of the justice which he owes to his subjects." (Valin Comm. on Ord. of 1681, b. III, Tit. X, art. 1. Wildman's Int., c. V., p. 190.)

But though there may not be any special statutes of the United States referring in express terms to special reprisals, as before observed, yet it is submitted that such reprisals, and a resort to them by the President, "at his discretion," in the mode we have indicated, is clearly embraced in the purview, and is within the spirit, meaning, and object of the fifth section of the act of 18th August, 1856, passed, in part, on the application of these claimants, and with this very Shelton Isle case in view. (See memorial, &c., on file in Senate, and a copy whereof was sent to the State Department at the time it was presented.)

The act is entitled "an act to authorize protection to be given to citizens of the United States who may discover deposits of guano," but includes, in terms, those who "may have discovered" at the time of the passage of the act. And the fifth section expressly authorizes the President, "at his discretion, to employ the land and naval forces of the United States to protect the rights of such discoverers," &c. The employment of these forces to enforce special reprisals, surely is within (because a less hostile course) their employment in using warlike force against another nation, and in acts of unequivocal hostility.

XIII. In the present case diplomatic action has been had. Nearly three years have elapsed, and no result has been obtained, except a display of shuffling and equivocation and evasion by the Venezuelan officials, and an insult and indignity to our minister, and this, too, it must be borne in mind, in a case of gross outrage upon the American flag, and despoiling the property of American citizens, perpetrated under circumstances stamping the outrage as an atrocity. Further diplomatic action by the United States government, it is submitted, would be a compromise of the national honor and character.

The example of the British government in the Nootka Sound case is worthy of imitation in this, and they are similar in character. (See Brief, page 46, Ex. Doc. Misc. 25, 3d sess. Thirty-fourth Congress, for this case.)

XIV. No one can contest the justice of the rule recognizing the right to make private property subject of special reprisals for the liability of the State under the law of nations. Each member of a State is bound for the liabilities of a State, and it is not unjust to collect such liabilities from him, insomuch as in such case he hath full and plain resort to his State for indemnity, and to his fellow members thereof for contribution.

This is analogous to the principles of the common law in relation to the debts or liabilities of a municipal corporation, (cities, towns, &c.,) and of the individual corporators or members thereof. (See Common Law and authorities on this subject.)

He who cannot see that the true principles of justice and right and morality and sound policy are maintained by these rules must take a superficial view of the subject, and be perversely blind to their operation and effect. They afford the sole means of enforcing justice against such corporations. The effects of the original wrong are thereby brought home to the community, and it is constrained by its own members to do them the justice it has denied to strangers.

XV. It is not supposed that any one will deny the propositions stated in the "points" filed under this number.

XVI. The citation of authority to support the doctrine asserted in the points filed is deemed useless to statesmen, who, we have every confidence, fully appreciate the duty there noted.

But it may be remarked that the non-fulfillment of such duty by any government would justify the reproach Sir Henry Bulwer cast upon that of the United States in 1850, in his famous "Chatfield letter" of being "a weak government," wanting decision, firmness, promptness, and energy; and it may be also said that the continuance of such neglect will, in many cases, excite the injured citizen to attempt the redress of his wrongs by his own strong arm, and with such means as the SUPERIOR of all governments may extend to him, without relying on his country for aid. If procrastinated palavers and protocols, the scribling of endless diplomatic dispatches, and everlasting discussion and negotiation be all the results he can attain; if delay, evasion, shuffling, and trifling by the State which has wrong him be unrebuked and overlooked by his government, except by the stereotyped phrase "they do not look on it with indifference," can it be wondered at if, maddened by his wrongs, he becames a *filibuster* and engage in schemes hostile to the nation which has wronged him, and, perhaps, ruined him, in order to avenge those wrongs, and, perchance, obtain some indemnity for them by plundering it in retaliation?

By rigidly and promptly enforcing the law of special reprisals in every case, we shall not so often witness such acts by American citizens, now the subject of such sharp reproach against us by the people of other States.

The claimants in this case forbear to ask for special letters of reprisal in their case until a technical formal *lettre de requête* hath been sent to Venezuela with full and authentic copies of all the proofs and depositions filed by these claimants in said department. These claimants are apprehensive that in this regard the treaty stipulations with Venezuela have not been fully complied with on the part of the United States by such full rendition of the proofs adduced in regard to the spoliation and the damages sustained therefrom, and they would submit that such *full* proofs be forthwith communicated to that government according to treaty, and accompanied by a technical *lettre de requête* for reparation, with a view to the ultimate granting of letters of special reprisal; and, in the meantime, they would respectfully solicit the adoption of measures by the government of the United States to ascertain for its own satisfaction the amount of damages justly due, and the payment of which should be enforced by such letters of reprisal, if necessity exists for their issuance after the time specified in the *lettre de requête* has expired.

These claimants decline in this brief to comment upon the testimony sustaining their claim for damages to the amount of $655,590 filed in the State Department and printed for its use, and a copy whereof hath been or should have been communicated to the government of Venezuela, as was anticipated when said document was filed. Those depositions and proofs sustain in general terms every item of said claim as just and reasonable; but in the investigation solicited the claimants will be able to adduce evidence verifying particulars and details, so as to leave no question of fact in respect to said damages in doubt. The questions of law in relation to the damages which we claim can then be more readily decided in a manner satisfactory, because just to all parties; but in such case the decision, as to damages, of the Executive preliminarily to the issuance of letters of reprisal, will be subject to the review and supervision of the judicial tribunal before which the property seized under the letters may be brought for adjudication.

These claimants, Philo S. Shelton and Sampson & Tappan, do not regard their case as blended in any degree with that of Lang & Delano and others. The latter have adduced no proofs, and have not adopted any measures or made any application for a technical letter of request nor for letters of reprisal. We protest against their being allowed to use our proofs, which we have procured at great trouble and expense to us, to which they have in nowise contributed. We consider them to be interlopers, not having any rights in this case nor entitled to any aid or redress, and at the proper time we will show it. We desire our claim and case to be kept separate and disconnected. They have no right to be joined with us.

BRITISH AUTHORITIES.

17 Viner's Abr. Tit. *Prerogative,* Na., p. 2, 3. Viner is copied from Rolles' Abr., 1668, published by Lord C. J. Hale. See 2 Rolles' Abr., N. 175. *Vis.*

1 Runn. *Stat. at Large,* p. 273, (127. *V.*) Stat. 27, ed. III, c. 17, A. D. 1353; ibid p. 507, (456.) Stat. 4, Hen. 5, c. 7; A. D. 1416.

1 Fitz-Herb. N. Brev., 9th London ed., 1794, vol. 1, p. 114.

2 Ibid (2 F. N. B.) lit. *Libra Requesta.* The last of these citations contain precedents of "letters of request."

1 Molloy's *de Jure Maritimo,* 9th ed., 1769, ch. 2, p. 33, *et seq.*, § 1 to 28, regarded as the best authority on the subject of reprisals, and it contains a form of special letters of reprisal, which see. The letters cited were issued 17 Car. 11, May 19, (in 1646,) to James Caren *et al.*

1 Waret's *Hist. of Laws of Nations in Europe,* ch. 9, p. 294.

3 Hallam's *Hist. of Middle Ages,* ch. 9, p. 2 and 332. Am. Ed. of 1853.

2 Stephens' *New Comm. on Laws of England and of States,* Pt. 1, § 4, p. 515. London ed. of 1842.

1 Black. *Comm.*, ch. 7, et notes, tit. *Prerogative,* § 4, p. 259. Am. ed. 1841.

2 Brown's *Cir. and Ad. Law,* c. 7, p. 334. 2d London ed.

Rutherford's *Inst. of Nat. Law,* c. 17, p. 200, &c. 2d Am. ed.

Wildman's *Inst. of Nat. Law,* (v. Am. Law Lib., vol. 52,) Eng. Ed., p. 186, Am. ed., p. 117.

Pritchard's *Admiralty Dig.*, London ed. 1847, p. 193.

Polson's *Principles of the Law of Nations,* (vol. 78, Am. Law Lib.,) Eng. ed., p. 36, Am. ed., p. 39, &c.

Chitty's *Law of Nations,* Eng. ed. of 1812, ch. —, p. 73, &c.

Manning's *Comm. on the Law of Nations.*

3 Phillimore's *Comm. on Int. Law,* ch. 2, p. 11, &c. 1 Ib., §§ 48 and 344.

Hosack *on the Rights of Neutrals,* § 6 and 7, citing Stat. of 29 Geo. II, ch. 34, and 19 Geo. III, ch. 67, vesting the admiralty with the power of issuing letters of reprisal exercised by Lord Chancellor under prior statutes above cited.

McCulloch's (J. R.) *Com. Dict.*, p. 1105, edition of 1850.

1. Magens, *on Insurance,* App. p. 491.

Correspondence on Silesian loan case. Dispatch of Lord Holderness to Mr. Mitchell, dated May 11, 1756, respecting the adjustment of said case.

1 & 2 Reddie's *Maritime Int. Law.*

Reddie's *Researches on International Law.*

Hazlitt & Roche's *Manual*, p. 84 to 96.

EUROPEAN CONTINENTAL AUTHORITIES.

Loccenius, *De Jure Maritimo et Nevale*, lib. 3, c. 5, p. 257, &c.

Vattel, *Droit des Gens*, b. 2, c. 28, p. 283, &c. Am. ed. of 1854.

Grotius, *De Jure Belli et Pace*, b. 3, c. 2, p. 663. Lat. ed., with Grusnovio's notes. Ibid, p. 215. French edition, with notes by Barberac added. Ibid, p. 538. English ditto.

Bynkershoek, *Ques. Jur. Pub.*, b. 1, ch. 24, p. 184. Duponceau's Am. translation.

DeWicquefort, *on Embassadors*, &c., ch. 22, § 4.

Puffendorff, *Law of Nature*, &c., b. 8, ch. 6, §§ 12 and 13, et Notes Eng. ed. of 1760.

2 Klüber, *Droit des Gens mod. de l'Europe*, p. 1, §§ 12, 1, 231, &c.

Wesenbee's *Comm.*, lib. 3, cod. tit. 13, p. 493.

Struve, *Juris. Civ. Syntagma*, exer. 8., lib. 5, tit. 1, p. 309.

Besoldus, *Thes. Prac.*, R. 52; tit. *Reprisals*, p. 789.

Leyser, *Med. ad Pandectas*, p. 30, book 2, tit. 2, p. 306, § 4.

Voet, *Comm. on Pandects*, lib. v, tit. 1, § 30, p. 248.

Putter, *Inst. Jus Pub. Ger.*, p. 415, § 383.

Roccus, *de Navibus, &c.*, and notes, § 22, p. 168, and notes; and see Am. translation by J. R. Ingersoll.

Wolfe's *Jus Natura*, p. 196, 197, and notes to § 572.

Targa, *Reflections on Com. Marine*, c. 67, p. 158.

1 Milnitz, *Manuel de Consuls*, p. 474 and inde.

1 DeRayneval, *Inst. of Int. Law*, b. 2 ch. 12, p. 205, Spanish edition.

Ibid., French edition.

Magerus *De Advocatia Amata, &c.*, c. 14, p. 738.

AMERICAN AUTHORITIES.

Danes' Abr., ch. 227, p. 676, § 66.

1 Kent's *Comm.*, 6th edition of 1848, part 1, lecture 3, p. 60, &c.

Wheaton's *El. of Int. Law*, 6th edition of 1855, part 4, c. 1, §§ 12 and 13, p. 361, *et seq.*

Wheaton's *History of Laws of Nations.*

2 *Peter's Decisions*, Pref. to App., vol. 2, p. 1; Obs. on Ord. of 1681, &c.

1 *Elliot's Debates*, p. 110; Mr. Sitgreves's speech, p. 453.

General Jackson's Message, December 1, 1834.

Hon. J. M. Mason, speech in Senate of United States on Fugitive Slave Bill, asserting right of States to issue reprisals for non-delivery of Slaves in 1850.

FRENCH AUTHORITIES.

1 Corbin's *Code de Louis XIII*, b. 3, art. 52, p. 89, tit. 34.

Ceirac's *Guidon de la Mer*, part 2, p. 300, &c.

Ibid., notes on same, ib., p. 301, &c.

2 Pardessus *Lois Maritimes*, tit. X, p. 410, &c.

Ordinance of 1681 *as to Reprisals*, by Louis XIV, and Valin's Comm.; *vide* 2 Valin's Comm., p. 414, tit. X, b. 3.

Same ordinance, as translated in "British Collection of Sea Laws."

2 Valin's Comm., p. 414.

Valin's *Tracte de Prises*, c. 201, p. 320, *on Reprisals*.

6 Pardessus, *Cours de droit Commercial*, p. 380.

Boucher, *Nouveau Valin*, art. 161, (350,) p. 472.

Ordinances by Kings of France of the Third Race, &c., by *De Lauriere*, vol. 1, p. 516, &c.

Felice's *Code of Humanity*, &c., vol. 12, p. 177, *et seq*.

Un. Dict. of Sciences, by Robinet, vol. 17, p. 551, tit. *Reprisals*.

DeGarden's *Treatise on Exterior Rel. of Nations*, vol. 2, b. 6, § 3, p. 220.

Encyclopedia of French Academy, tit. *Reprisals*, vol. —, p. —.

Chameane's Dict. of Legislation, part 2, p. 631.

1 LePage, *Elemens de la science du droit, &c.*, ch. 4, art. 3, § 33, p. 326.

5 Saint Edme., *Dict. of Penalties throughout the World*, &c., p. 270.

G. Von Marten's *Law of Nations*, trans. by Cobbett, b. 4, p. 269, ch. 1, &c.

2 Marten's *Précis du droit des gens M. de l'Europe*, Paris, 1831, b. 8, p. 145, art. 160.

1 Marten's *Précis du droit des gens*, with Ferreira's notes, ch. 3, § 96, p. 224.

DeMarten's *Essay on Privateers*, translated into English by T. H. Horne, cited as *Horne on Captures*, ch. 1, § 4, p. 9, &c.

Emerigon on *Insurance*, § 4, p. 59, § 5, p. 63, ch. 12, § 36, p. —, American edition.

Bouley Paty, *Notes on Emerigon*, vol. 1, ch. 12, § 36.

1 Azuni's *Maritime Law*, American edition of 1806, translated by Mr. Johnson, p. 1, c. 4, art. 14, § 2, p. 194, &c., and art. 2, § 1.

Schmalz, *Le droit des gens (l'Europe,)* b. 6, c. 1, p. 213.

1 Massé, *Comm. Law*, b. 2, ch. 2, sect. 1, § 1, p. 130.

2 Mauzet, *Treatise on Ins.*, p. 37, § 273.

18 DeLocri, *Civil Leg. of France*, p. 411; *Comm. on art.* 350 of *Code of Commerce*, &c.

1 T. Ortolan, *Int. Laws of the Sea*, b. 2, c. 14, § 549, p. 386, French edition.

1 DePistoye & Duverdy, tit. 1, ch. 3, p. 85, § 3, &c., p. 135, tit. *Embargo*.

1 DeCussy, *Phases et Causes Célèbres du droit Maritime des Nations*, pp. 124, 118, 120, 390.

2 Ibid., pp. 8, 56, 533, 557, 558, 486.

Mr. Cass to Mr. Eames.

No. 53.]

DEPARTMENT OF STATE,
Washington, August 31, 1857.

SIR: Your dispatch No. 38, of the 13th of June last, has been received. From this and from your personal report on the subject, it appears that the wrong done to Messrs. Shelton & Co. by the violent eviction of their agents from the Island of Aves, still remains unacknowledged by the Venezuelan authorities. Considering the aggravated character of this wrong, the very serious damages which it occasioned to innocent parties, the period of time which has elapsed since it took place, the promptness with which it was brought to the attention of the government at Caraccas, and the urgent manner in which, under the instructions of the President, you have demanded reparation for it, the continued indifference of Venezuela, is so extraordinary in its character as to become itself an occasion of serious complaint. The injury which claims redress occurred so long ago as December, 1854. In the month of March following, it was brought to the attention of the Venezuelan government. In repeated instances during the same year it was prominently referred to by you, both in personal interviews with the President of the republic, and in communications to the minister of foreign affairs, and always mentioned as a subject of grave importance, which would unquestionably be pursued by the United States to a just conclusion. In the proceedings which attended and led to the Pickrill contract, this Aves claim was scrupulously reserved for separate adjustment on its own merits, and at an audience of the President, about the middle of September, 1855, you expressed to his excellency your "confident conviction that it would be effectually sustained." On the 8th of March, 1856, you renewed the reclamation which you had made twelve months previous, and informed the minister of foreign relations that you had "recently received emphatic instructions to continue to urge the same upon the government of Venezuela." In August, following, and again in January, 1857, the department expressed great surprise at the protracted delay which this claim had encountered, and demanded in the gravest manner that it should be brought to a speedy conclusion. "There remains no course, then," you were informed, "but to press the demand for redress upon Venezuela in a formal and decisive manner, and request, in behalf of your government, her determination in reference to this case. If she admits her liability for the spoliations committed, the basis of adjustment may be fixed without difficulty or delay. If she refuse redress, she will be expected to offer such reasons for that course as will be satisfactory to this government, especially in view of the stipulations contained in the 3d section of the 34th article of the treaty of 1836, which contemplates certain modes of redress in a case where either 'party, considering itself offended, shall first have presented to the other a statement of such injuries or damages, verified by competent proofs, and demanded justice, and the same shall have been either refused or unreasonably delayed.' Before the reception of this dispatch, you had, on the 20th of December, in some degree anticipated its directions, and had submitted a formal and urgent request that the action of Venezuela with reference to it might no longer be delayed. But on the 31st of March, you renewed the demand for redress in the very language of the department, replying, conclusively, at the same time, to the only communication on the subject in which Venezuela had ever noticed the reclamation since it was first brought to her attention in March, 1855. To this demand no reply has been received, except an acknowledgment of its receipt on the 28th of May, and a statement that it required time for consideration; while the long forbearance of the United States to make it in a formal and peremptory manner, is most unreasonably urged as a justification for further delay. It is true that you were also informed in this reply that an examination of the two officers who were chiefly concerned in the Aves expedition, was to be had on the subject the next day, and that you were at liberty to attend. But since these officers had been the mere agents of the Venezuelan government in the transaction complained of, had been constantly within its reach for consultation, and had officially reported their proceedings on their return, without any appearance of disapproval by their government, it is difficult to see why any delay of the case was necessary in order to receive their formal testimony.

Nor is it readily perceived, in view of those facts concerning it which are not controverted, how the justice of the Aves claim can be shaken by any testimony whatever. It is not denied that the island in question was on the 13th of December, 1854, in the peaceable and open possession of American citizens, and had been so for at least six months. It is not denied that they had first discovered that it contained a valuable deposit of guano; that they had erected buildings upon it; that they had hoisted the flag of their country as evidence of their citizenship; and that they were engaged with all the necessary materials and arrangements which they had procured and established at great cost in shipping the guano which they had discovered to the United States. It is not denied, but appears clear, on the contrary, from the evidence and the correspondence, that these facts were all brought to the knowledge of Venezuela. It is beyond controversy, that with this knowledge in its possession, and without any previous notice whatever to the United States or its minister at Caraccas, the Venezuelan government sent out an armed force to take possession of the island and drive out the American citizens who were its rightful occupants. It is undisputed, of course, that this force accomplished precisely what it was sent to do, and evicted the occupants of the island under circumstances of indignity to the flag of their country, which no American could witness without emotion, and with a degree of violence which they were unable to resist. It is certain that, in consequence of these proceedings, Mr. Shelton and his associates, without having committed any fault or violated any law, sustained loss and damage to a very large amount, while he himself was reduced from affluence to a condition of comparative want. It may be added, moreover, that the armed expedition of Venezuela seems to have been undertaken with a view to divide with others the very profits of an enterprise which rightfully belonged to Mr. Shelton and his associates, and that a large part of these profits has actually been paid into the Venezuelan treasury. Taken in connection with the acknowledged want by Venezuela of any title to the island, (for its suggestion of a title growing out of successorship to Spain can hardly be seriously insisted on,) if these admitted facts do not constitute a clear case of aggravated wrong, and do not urgently require the most prompt disclaimer and redress on the part of the Venezuelan authorities, it is impossible to conceive how such a case can ever be presented. In the view here taken of the transaction, the conduct of Commander Dias, who led the first Venezuelan expedition to the island, becomes quite unimportant. Whatever may be the character of the paper to which he procured the signatures of Messrs. Gibbs and Lang, and under whatever misrepresentation or misapprehension they may have signed it, it is quite certain, not only that they did not leave the island in consequence of it, but that they never expected to do so. Their eviction was only accomplished by the arrival and violent measures of a superior force, and not in pursuance, but in direct contravention of the arrangement which is said to have been made by Dias. If this were otherwise, the introduction of the Dias transaction far from palliating the wrong complained of, could only render it more aggravated, by showing that the occupants of the island were the victims alike of fraud and violence.

Entertaining these views of the Aves claim, the President cannot consent that its just acknowledgment shall continue to be delayed under any circumstances whatever. While he has the strongest disposition to maintain the most friendly relations with Venezuela, he is bound by still higher obligations to maintain the honor of his country, and to protect every citizen of the United States in the possession and exercise of his just rights. If these rights can be violated and outraged, as they unquestionably were in the case of Mr. Shelton and his associates, without acknowledgment and without redress, no matter by what government the injury is done, the character of an American citizen must cease to command respect, and it will be little else than a mockery to invoke the protection of the American flag. You will, therefore, lose no time upon your return to Caraccas in bringing this whole subject to the renewed attention of the Venezuelan government. You may read this dispatch to the Minister of Foreign Affairs, or to the President, and, if they desire it, you may give them a copy of it. At the same time you will assure them that a settlement of the Aves claim cannot be further procrastinated without serious injury to the friendly relations of the two countries. The adjustment of damages ought not to occasion any considerable difficulty or dispute, but these may possibly require some further examination. On the question of liability, however, you will regard the discussion as closed. If this is not admitted within a reasonable time, the question will be withdrawn from the ordinary channels of negotiation, and the President will be obliged to consult with Congress in reference to its further prosecution. You will remain in Caraccas for thirty days, in order to receive the answer of the government there to this dispatch. Before the end of that time, it is confidently hoped that the just claim of our citizens in the case presented will be acknowledged by the Venezuelan authorities; but should this expectation prove unfounded, and you should have no assurance that such an acknowledgment will speedily be made, you will close the legation, request your passport, and return home.

I am, sir, your obedient servant,

LEWIS CASS.

CHARLES EAMES, Esq., *&c.*

Mr. Sanford to Mr. Cass.

DERBY, CONNECTICUT,
August 31, 1857.

SIR: In the month of April last, there appeared in the "Diario de Avisos," a newspaper published in Caraccas, a communication, dated Philadelphia, 20th March, from a Mr. Leon de Cova, now or formerly an agent of the Philadelphia Guano Company, making some assertions intended to prejudice the Aves Island claim, and among others, that Mr. Guthrie, while Secretary of the Treasury, speaking of this case, had said to him, that "neither said Shelton nor his attorney, Sanford, had a right to a dollar from our (the Venezuelan) government," &c., &c.

This statement, our minister at Caraccas, Mr. Eames, seemed to think the Venezuelan government attached much importance to, and, accordingly, on my return to this country, I wrote to Mr. Guthrie, inclosing the article, and asking him to inform me if the assertions of the article with respect to himself were correct.

The inclosed is his reply, stating that the account of what he is ascribed therein as saying, is "either a mistake, a misapprehension, or a fabrication."

I inclose his letter to be filed in the department, and in order that our minister at Caraccas, now in Washington, may have cognizance of it, and be relieved of any apprehensions which these false assertions may have caused him to entertain.

I have the honor to be, with great respect, your obedient servant,

H. S. SANFORD.

Hon. LEWIS CASS,
Secretary of State.

LOUISVILLE, *August* 20, 1857.

DEAR SIR: On my return to Kentucky after an absence of six weeks, yours of the 9th of July was received.

The extract from the Venezuelan paper of what I should have said in Washington whilst Secretary of the Treasury, about the claim of Mr. Shelton against the Venezuelan government, for which you were agent, is a mistake, misapprehension, or fabrication. I have no recollection of such a conversation, nor of having expressed any opinion upon the subject, and am confident that I had no distinct opinion upon the subject, not having examined it, but was then, and am now, under the impression that the island did not belong to that government, and the use of force was a great wrong and unwarranted; and if it proved the island did not belong to Venezuela, that Mr. Shelton was entitled to all damages sustained, and full compensation for the willful wrong.

Respectfully, JAMES GUTHRIE.

Mr. Appleton to Mr. Sanford.

DEPARTMENT OF STATE,
Washington, September 4, 1857.

SIR: I have to acknowledge the receipt of your communication of the 31st ultimo, with the inclosed original letter to you from the Hon. James Guthrie, of the —— ultimo, in which he emphatically denies having expressed himself unfavorably respecting Mr. Shelton's claim upon Venezuela, as is ascribed to him in a letter purporting to be addressed to the "Diario de los Avisos," of Caraccas, and published in that paper of the month of April last.

As you think that the impression which would naturally be created by such a statement from such a source should not remain uncorrected, a copy of your letter, and of its inclosure, will be forwarded to Mr. Eames.

I am, &c., JOHN APPLETON,
Assistant Secretary.

HENRY S. SANFORD, Esq.,
Brevoort House, New York.

Mr. Cass to Mr. Eames.

No. 54.] DEPARTMENT OF STATE,
Washington, September 4, 1857.

SIR: I inclose a copy of a communication, of the 31st ultimo, from H. S. Sanford, Esq., and of the inclosure therein referred to, in which the Hon. James Guthrie denies having given utterance to certain expressions, imputed to him, unfavorable to Mr. Shelton's claim upon Venezuela, and which were published in the "Diario de Avisos," of Caraccas, in April last, under the signature of Mr. De la Cova.

If you think, as Mr. Sanford believes you do, that Venezuela places any reliance upon these supposed views of Mr. Guthrie, as sustaining her resistance to the claim of Mr. Shelton and his associates, or if you find upon returning to Caraccas that such a disposition is manifested, the letter of Mr. Guthrie will enable you to remove any missapprehension of that character.

I am, sir, your obedient servant,

LEWIS CASS.

CHARLES EAMES, Esq., *&c.*

Mr. Ribas to Mr. Cass.

[Translation.]

LEGATIO OF VENEZUELA IN THE UNITED STATES,
Washington, September 4, 1857.

MOST EXCELLENT SIR: The undersigned, Chargé d'Affaires of the Republic of Venezuela, has the honor to make known to the most excellent Secretary of State of the United States that he has received a communication from his government, bearing date of 22d of June, of the present year, in which it is stated that Mr. Eames, Chargé d'Affaires of the United States in Venezuela, has sent a note to the Minister of Foreign Relations of Venezuela demanding that within a very brief period the pending question about the Island of Aves should be settled, and threatening, if this were not done, that he would withdraw from Caraccas for the purpose of reporting to his government. He was told, as regarded this, that it was considered necessary that the claim should be further substantiated, since, if in his view it was sufficiently proved, the same opinion had not been formed of it either by the President or the Secretary of Foreign Relations, who could not determine the matter in the brief and peremptory time which he had assigned. He was reminded of the proof of friendship which Venezuela had just given to the United States by concluding with them a treaty of friendship, commerce, navigation, and extradition, which they had proposed, and the Congress had sanctioned only by the strong and well known exertions of the executive authority. His attention was called to the difference of circumstances between a department loaded with business and a legation which had very little; and, finally, he was told that the conclusion of the claim was hastened by the knowledge of his intention to leave; and that, even if this should take place, there would not be wanting means of communication between the two cabinets, as that of Venezuela had a legation at Washington. The day fixed arrived without Mr. Eames receiving the reply. On absenting himself, he told very respectable persons that he left with the determination of employing the press, of which he was a member, as a means of waging war on Venezuela, so as to force Messrs. Buchanan and Cass to follow the popular movement, and that he calculated on returning very soon accompanied by a fleet.

Complying with the orders which the undersigned has received from his government, he communicates to the most excellent Secretary of State of the United States what has been related, in order that he may see that it has not been in the power of the government of Venezuela to satisfy the demands of Mr. Eames; and that, if he (Mr. E.) has been willing to absent himself from Caraccas without giving that government time to satisfy his demands, for this there is not the slightest responsibility resting on that government.

The undersigned avails himself of this opportunity to renew to the most excellent Secretary of State the protestations of his highest consideration and respect.

His obedient servant,

FLORENCIO RIBAS.

Most Excellent Mr. LEWIS CASS,
Secretary of State, &c.

Mr. Cass to Mr. Ribas.

DEPARTMENT OF STATE,
Washington, September 11, 1857.

SIR: I have had the honor to receive your communication of the 4th instant, in which you inform the department of the circumstances under which Mr. Eames, the American minister, left Caraccas on the 13th of June, and of the intention which your government then had of transmitting through you its decision in reference to the claim of Messrs. Shelton *et als.*, who were evicted from "Aves" island in 1854 by the Venezuelan authorities. It is deeply to be regretted that this decision has not yet arrived, because the case is one of peculiar aggravation, and has now been pending for more than two years and a half. What you say of the comparative business of a Department of State and a legation, is undoubtedly true; but it is difficult to see how much time could be required in the "Aves" case in order to determine the preliminary question of liability, whatever investigation might be necessary to adjust the amount of damages. About the prominent facts upon which the claim is based, there is no controversy. The discovery by the claimants of guano on the island, their preparations for working it, their peaceable possession of the locality, the dispatch of an armed force by Venezuela in order to evict them, without notice to the United States, and the accomplishment of this design by the force employed, are facts too clearly proved to be susceptible of doubt. The report of the officers who had charge of the expedition sent out must have been made to the Venezuelan authorities soon after its return, and all the facts in the case must, therefore, have been long known at Caraccas.

Yet, so far has Venezuela been from acknowledging the wrong done to our citizens and expressing its willingness to make just compensation for it, that it has indicated a disposition, on the contrary, to justify the expedition by intimating a claim of title and a right of possession to the island. It is not believed, however, that this claim can be deliberately insisted on, because it is impossible to discover any good reason to sustain it. It does not appear that the island was ever occupied by Venezuela or by the citizens of that republic. It was never inhabited, and was not capable of supporting a permanent population. There was nothing about it whatever which could lead Messrs. Shelton & Co. to believe that Venezuela had a claim to it. It was not contiguous to the Venezuelan coast, but was more than three hundred miles distant from it, and much nearer to the possessions of other countries than to Venezuela. Under such circumstances, knowing, as the government of Venezuela did, that it was occupied by a party of American citizens, who had established works on it, and were exporting its guano under the protection of the flag of their country, for that government to send out an armed force to pull down the American flag and substitute that of Venezuela, to drive away the occupants of the island and destroy their business, and to establish in their place a new company, from which Venezuela expected to derive large profit, and to do this without notice to the American government or the American minister at Caraccas, was a wrong to the United States and their citizens who occupied the island, which appears so entirely manifest, that it is difficult to understand how a friendly government, like Venezuela, could have authorized it in the beginning, or can hesitate now to acknowledge it. Certainly, it cannot remain much longer unadjusted without imminent danger to the amicable relations between the two countries which now so happily subsist, and which, it is earnestly hoped, may never be interrupted. On this point you are already in possession of the views of this government, as they have been given to you in a personal interview, and as you will doubtless communicate them to Venezuela. It is believed that the wrong committed against Mr. Shelton and his associates is too clear to justify any further discussion of it, and it is hoped, therefore, that your government, regarding this point as settled, will proceed at once to investigate the damages which the wrong is alleged to have occasioned. These may require to be carefully examined, but the United States feel it to be due to their self-respect that the forcible injury done to their flag and to their citizens should no longer remain unacknowledged.

I avail myself of this occasion to renew to you, sir, the assurances of my high consideration,

LEWIS CASS.

Senor FLORENCIO RIBAS,
&c., &c., &c.

Mr. Ribas to Mr. Cass.

[Translation.]

LEGATION OF VENEZUELA IN THE UNITED STATES,
New York, September 18, 1857.

EXCELLENT SIR: I have had the honor of receiving your note of the 11th instant, through which you have been pleased to answer mine of the 4th instant, in relation to the departure of Mr. Eames from Caraccas.

As I have received no instructions from my government for any other purpose than that of submitting to the government of the United States the slight cause which Mr. Eames had for requesting his passport, whilst the minister of foreign relations was preparing satisfaction for the claims preferred by said Mr. Eames, I am not now in a condition to state to you anything in reference to your note of the 11th instant. Complying, however, with the wishes of your government, I shall immediately report to mine all that you have been pleased to communicate to me touching the question, and I trust that I shall soon have the gratification of notifying you of the determination which may be reached in the premises.

The undersigned avails himself of the present occasion to reiterate the assurances of his most distinguished consideration and respect.

Your obedient servant,

FLORENCIO RIBAS.

His Excellency LEWIS CASS,
Secretary of State.

Mr. Gutierrez to Mr. Cass.

[Translation.]

REPUBLIC OF VENEZUELA, SECRETARYSHIP OF FOREIGN RELATIONS,
Caraccas, September 21, 1857.

The undersigned, Secretary of Foreign Relations of Venezuela, has received orders from the executive power to announce to the Secretary of State of the United States of America, that the answer to the reply of Mr. Eames, in relation to the question of Aves Island, being now completed, it will, as well as this note, be transmitted to Washington, through the channel of the legation of the republic at that place.

In giving out this announcement, which will be speedily followed by its accomplishment, the government of the undersigned has for its object, besides coming to an understanding with that of the United States, the submitting for its consideration some of the very controlling circumstances which prevented, as was required, the immediate answer insisted upon by the American legation in a demand recently put up in this secretaryship.

Although the correspondence shows, and it is necessary here to repeat the fact, that what though, in the course of various conferences with the predecessor of the undersigned, in an audience sought with his his excellency the President to enforce the claim of Pickrell, and in a note addressed to the undersigned, relative to a certain question between Venezuela and Holland, Mr. Eames had incidentally touched on the demand now under consideration, he never proceeded to present it formally and accompanied by proofs, until the 20th of December, 1856. When the President himself, on that occasion, urged Mr. Eames to discuss it, before Mr. Pickrell's application, Mr. Eames stated that he labored under the impossibility of doing so for want of the necessary documents; and, under other circumstances, assuring Mr. Aranda that the main object of his government looked to the renewal of the Wallace contract, he decidedly gave it the preference, and so extraordinary a one, that he threatened a rupture if the claim were not allowed. All at once, and when the period was drawing near for his availing himself of the leave of visit to his country, which he had obtained from Mr. Marcy, and this a few days before Mr. Sanford's arrival in Caraccas, he devoted himself exclusively to the agitation of the question, and wrote his first note asking for an indemnity, and stating that he had not applied for it before, in view of the necessity under which he was placed of consulting his cabinet on the point of the document signed by Lang and Gibbs, which, in his opinion, required certain explanations. He spoke also of certain instructions of his government, which, sent to him since the month of August, 1856, did not reach him, through the fact of loss or miscarriage, and of the purport of which he did not become possessed until a copy of them was shown to him by Mr. Sanford, who had brought it over. To his aforesaid claim of the 20th of December, he annexed certain declarations, which could not have been all that he had in his possession, since there was missing the declaration of Gibbs, one of the signers of the permit, and if he sent it with his second communication, when the circumstance was adverted to in the first answer of the undersigned, it was in the shape of a printed and mutilated paper, the meaning of which is, up to this moment, ignored.

When the executive power perceived this insistance on a claim, which, judging from the conduct of the United States legation for two years, could not be held in very high regard; and one, too, which merely rested on the testimony of some of the interested parties themselves, he deemed it his duty, on his part, to adopt measures of investigation, necessary not only in his view of the matter, but in the opinion also of the government council, to which the question had been referred. Those investigations were not closed by the time of Mr. Eames's departure, nor are they all so even at the present day, whence the depending facts that neither has the record of proceedings been returned by the council, nor has it yet been made known whether the arguments of the legation have changed the government's view of the case.

His Excellency also desires to convince the government of your country that Venezuela, in acting as she has done, was far from any intent, in the least degree, of offending the Americans found in Aves Island, as it stands to reason that he who uses his own right inflicts no injury on another, and that he holds full mastery over a thing to exclude others from its enjoyment. And even were this not the case, the Americans themselves, by recognizing, in the manner in which they did recognize, the dominion of Venezuela and the unlawfulness of its possession by them, would have justified the proceedings of the national force. Besides, in no form or shape was violence resorted to in their regard, to secure their dispossession, nor could it have been so done. A verbal warning was given to them, and without threats; nothing more. The number of their vessels, of their laborers, of their arms, cannons, guns, muskets, boarding pikes, cutlasses, and pistols; their large supply of powder—all this, in comparison with twenty-five soldiers under Colonel Dias's command on board of the Venezuelan schooner, with ten individuals constituting the whole number of the garrison left on the island, even with the additional force of fifteen by which said garrison was increased when another schooner of Venezuela reached the port, could have enabled them, in any one of those three occasions, and especially on the second, to resist and victoriously repel those whom they considered as disturbers of their lawful possessions. Notwithstanding this, they complied with the summons; and this proves that the consciousness of their duty was more powerful than the conviction of their indisputable superiority. Their departure was voluntary, rather than enforced. Mr. Eames has no doubt viewed it in this light, since, up to this moment, he has confined his reclamation to the payment of an indemnity, and not to the requirements of an evacuation and surrender of the island, which he would have demanded in the case of a violent and illegal spoilation.

On the other hand, we must take in consideration the fact, that contemporaneously with the deliberation on the note of the 31st of March, one of the most laborious of Congresses was in session, and one so because its duties turned upon no less an object than the reformation of the institutions and of the general laws, which were to be shaped in harmony with the alterations made in the organic law. All of these demanded the unceasing and undivided attention of the Executive power. One of the points on which his action was most applied and concentrated, was the treaty concluded in the course of the preceding year between the two countries, which but for such action, would have evidently been disapproved from the very incipiency of the debates, so great were the objections by which it was combatted, so great the opposition raised against it, so deep and various the parliamentary stratagems devised by its antagonists for the purpose of preventing its acceptance. And it is to be observed that whilst its success was wrapped in uncertainty, namely, until the day of the adjournment of Congress, on the 20th of May, when with the resolution of adjournment the decree of approval was passed, Mr. Eames, though without any exception as to day or time, however inopportune, he had frequent access to the Department of Foreign Relations never denied to his expressed wishes, urged no action on the Aves question, a decision on which he afterwards insisted on in a summary and peremptory manner.

The undersigned avails himself of this occasion to tender to his excellency the Secretary of State of the United States, the assurances of his distinguished consideration.

JACINTO GUTIERREZ.

The SECRETARY OF STATE OF THE UNITED STATES.

Mr. Sanford to Mr. Cass.

LA UNION, SAN SALVADOR,
September 29, 1857.

SIR: I desire to send to Boston immediately a copy of the power of attorney in my favor of P. S. Shelton and Sampson & Tappan in the Aves Island case, a copy which duly collated is on the files of the department, the original of which is not at this moment in my possession.

May I beg you to have the goodness to direct that a copy be made and sent to P. S. Shelton, Boston, for which I shall be grateful?

I have the honor to be, with great respect, your obedient servant,

H. S. SANFORD.

Hon. LEWIS CASS,
Secretary of State.

Mr. Cass to Mr. Eames.

DEPARTMENT OF STATE,
Washington, October 6, 1857.

SIR: The department received with surprise your communication of the 3d instant from Philadelphia, announcing your immediate departure for Venezuela. It was expected and understood that you were again to visit this city prior to your return to Caraccas.

The object of this dispatch is to acquaint you that Mr. Ribas, chargé d'affaires of Venezuela, has personally visited this city, and has had my dispatch No. 53 read to him. The substance of that dispatch has been also communicated to Mr. Ribas in a note from this department of the 11th ultimo, a copy of which and of his reply are herewith transmitted. He has in his personal interviews expressed the hope that you would be permitted to delay the presentation of the subject discussed in my note No. 53 to the government of Venezuela until he had himself written to his government in relation to the matter, which he engaged immediately to do. In compliance with this request, it has been thought desirable to instruct you to await for a brief period after your arrival in Caraccas the result of Mr. Ribas's communications to his government. You will doubtless be apprised of their decision in due time. Should it not be made known to you, it will be proper for you to intimate that you have been instructed to receive that decision in behalf of your government before presenting in formal terms its demands for the adjustment of the Aves Island claim. In the event of unnecessary delay in rendering a reply, you will then be governed by the instructions contained in my No. 53.

I am, sir, your obedient servant,

LEWIS CASS.

CHARLES EAMES, Esq., *&c.*

Mr. Eames to Mr. Cass.

No. 40.]

LEGATION OF THE UNITED STATES,
Caraccas, October 31, 1857.

SIR: I have the honor to inform you that having embarked at Philadelphia on the 3d instant, by the first practicable opportunity after leaving Washington, I arrived at Laguayra by a direct passage of twenty days on the afternoon of the 23d instant, and the next day I reached this city.

Bearing with me from Washington your instruction No. 53, under date of 31st August last, I received at Philadelphia just before embarking your Nos. 54 and 55, both under dates of 9th September last, and on arriving at Laguayra I found in the hands of Mr. Consul Golding your No. 52 of 25th May last, with its large packet of specified duplicate and original inclosures. I have thus received at last, either in duplicate or original, the long missing numbers from the department 37, 38, 44, 45, and 46, the detention of which is explained in your No. 52, and I can now congratulate myself upon having the complete series of numbers from the department up to your No. 55 of 9th September last, inclusive, which is the latest communication received from you.

I beg leave to express by this first opportunity after the receipt of your No. 52 my high and grateful appreciation of the commendatory terms in which it refers to the manner in which, in my note of the 31st of March last to Mr. Gutierrez, I urged and sustained before this government the "Aves" reclamation.

Mindful of the instruction contained in your No. 53 "to lose no time" after my return to Caraccas in bringing that question to "the renewed atttention" of this government, and fully conscious of the new power with which the reasoning and the conclusions of that important paper clothed the reclamation, I on the second day after my arrival here, addressed to Mr. Gutierrez my note of the 26th instant—a copy of which I transmit inclosed—asking at his earliest convenience an official conference with him on that subject. His reply under date of the next day, 27th instant, a copy and translation of which I also inclose, appointed the conference of the 29th instant, and informed me that this government had, during my absence, through its diplomatic agent at Washington, "commenced an understanding" on the subject with the government of the United States. The conference took place at the hour appointed.

I opened the subject by refering to the terms of my note, and expressing the hope that he was now prepared to make to me on behalf of his government an acknowledgment of the claim. He replied by reference to the terms of his note, and added that a definitive or at least full reply in the case was now nearly completed, and at the moment under consideration by the council of government; that it would be sent to Washington very soon, he trusted by the first opportunity. I informed him that he could send direct to the United States on Tuesday next, (3d proximo,) and he said that he believed it would then be ready, and would use every effort to do so.

I then said that I trusted he was prepared now to assure me that the reply would admit the preliminary point of the liability of Venezuela in the case.

He replied that it was out of his power to give me now any assurance as to that or any other point of the reply, which was still under consideration.

I told him that it was then my duty, under my instructions, to assure him—*first*, that in the judgment of the United States the liability of Venezuela in the case was too clear for further discussion, and that my government had for some time past considered discussion on that point as closed; *secondly*, that the President of the United States could not consent that the adjustment of the claim should be procrastinated, and that longer delay in its acknowledgment must result in serious injury to the friendly relations of the two countries. I added that other points were embraced im my instructions which were of a definitive character, but that in view of his statement that his reply was to be given at once, and as I did not doubt to be promptly made known to me, I would take the responsibility of limiting myself for that interview to the two declarations above made, which were manifestly important to be known and kept in view by the Venezuelan government in framing its reply in the case. I said further that I might also conclude to wait two or three days longer before asking a special audience of his excellency, the President, with a view to the full execution of my instructions; that I would consider the propriety of this course, and advise him of my conclusions.

He replied, that as to the discussion being closed, Venezuela had a right also to her own views on that point; but that the matter being under consideration at Washington, he did not see how it could be further discussed here.

I said, in reply to this, that I was not here to reopen discussion, but primarily to make known to him, in the words of my government, and upon its rendered reasons, its position as to the point of liability, and to receive his answer as to that point, which I hoped might be speedily given in a satisfactory sense.

As I rose to take my leave, he said that he trusted that the United States would only ask for justice in the case.

I told him nothing more was demanded, but that I trusted that justice in the case would be speedily done by Venezuela, and thus the conference closed.

My course, in deferring for that day the reading to Mr. Gutierrez of your No. 53, may not be, perhaps, in the strictest compliance with the letter of that instruction, but I trust the department will consider the discretion exercised by me as warranted by the statements made to me by the minister and the state of the case.

To-day, after careful consideration of the whole subject, I have deemed it proper, in view of my instructions, to request, in conformity with my intimation to Mr. Gutierrez, a special audience of the President. I have endeavored to draw up this request (copy of which I inclose) in such a manner as to induce, if possible, this government to frame their pending reply in the case in a satisfactory sense, and give me promptly the proper assurance in regard to it. It is my purpose to be governed in some degree by what his excellency may say at the audience, in then determining whether to read my instructions to him at once, or to wait some short time longer. I suppose the audience will take place on Monday or Tuesday next, being the 2d and 3d proximo.

I hope to send you an account of any further proceedings which may take place in the case on or before the 3d instant, by the same vessel which carries this dispatch.

With the highest respect and consideration, I have the honor to be your obedient servant,

CHARLES EAMES.

Hon. LEWIS CASS,
Secretary of State.

LEGATION OF THE UNITED STATES,
Caraccas, October 26, 1857.

SIR: The undersigned, minister resident of the United States, having returned to Caraccas to resume his official duties near the government of Venezuela, under special instructions to lose no time in bringing in a prescribed form to the renewed attention of the Venezuelan government the whole subject of the international reclamation now pending between the two governments, in relation to the expulsion and exclusion by the Venezuelan public force, of certain citizens of the United States, from the guano island of Aves, in December, 1854, has now the honor, in pursuance of those instructions, to request an official interview with the honorable Minister of Foreign Relations, and that he will appoint such early time for that purpose as may be compatible with his convenience.

The undersigned with pleasure avails himself of this first occasion since his return to Venezuela, to offer to Hon. Señor Gutierrez the assurance of his distinguished consideration.

CHARLES EAMES.

Hon. JACINTO GUTIERREZ,
Minister of Foreign Relations.

[Translation.]

REPUBLIC OF VENEZUELA, DEPARTMENT OF FOREIGN RELATIONS,
Caraccas, October 27, 1857.

The minister of foreign relations of Venezuela has the honor to acquaint the honorable minister resident of the United States that his note of yesterday to the undersigned has been received, giving information of his return to Caraccas to continue his official functions near the government, and that in virtue of instructions respecting the subject of the Island of Aves, he desires an interview with the undersigned.

The executive power is advised of Mr. Eames's return, and has directed the undersigned to observe to him that, during his absence from the country, the government, having in Washington a minister of the republic, has commenced an understanding in relation to the question of the Aves through that agent with the government of the United States. As to the conference solicited, the undersigned will receive Mr. Eames next Thursday, at one o'clock, p. m., to-morrow, being a fast day.

The undersigned hastens to reciprocate to Mr. Eames his assurance of distinguished consideration.

JACINTO GUTIERREZ.

Hon. CHARLES EAMES,
Minister Resident of the United States.

LEGATION OF THE UNITED STATES,
Caraccas, October 31, 1857.

SIR: The undersigned, minister resident of the United States, with reference to his note of the 26th instant, to the reply of the honorable minister of foreign relations thereto under date of 27th instant, and to the official conference in pursuance thereof, held on the 29th instant, has now the honor to make known in writing to the government of Venezuela what he has already mentioned to the honorable minister of foreign relations in the conference referred to, that he is charged with a communication of an important and definitive character, to be made by the undersigned in person, without delay, and in a prescribed form, by the authority and in the name of his excellency the President of the United States, to his excellency the President of this republic, in relation to the Aves reclamation, now pending between the two governments.

The undersigned, therefore, in pursuance of his instructions, and for their due execution, has the honor to request a special official audience of his excellency the President of the republic.

Considerations of the greatest weight, arising out of the origin, nature, and history of this reclamation, and the attitude of the two governments in respect to it, combine with the grave tenor of the instructions under which the undersigned is acting, to make it his imperative duty to request, as he now requests, that the audience solicited may take place at the earliest time compatible with a proper and perfect consideration of his excellency's convenience.

The undersigned renews to the Hon. Señor Gutierrez the assurance of his distinguished consideration.

CHARLES EAMES.

Hon. JACINTO GUTIERREZ,
Minister of Foreign Relations.

Mr. Gutierrez to Mr. Cass.

[Translation.]

REPUBLIC OF VENEZUELA, SECRETARYSHIP OF FOREIGN RELATIONS,
Caraccas, October 31, 1857.

Aves Island constitutes one of the Windward Islands, which are situated in the Caribbean sea. The government of Venezuela sent a garrison thither, in the month of November, 1854, upon learning that in this, and in other national islands, strangers had clandestinely entered and were removing the guano from its deposits. Some Americans were found in the act of loading three vessels with guano. They made no opposition to Colonel Domingo Dias's landing, who had been commissioned to visit the islands and to prevent persons, having no right to them, from making use of them. Neither did they offer any resistance to the two officers who had accompanied the colonel, nor to the ten soldiers who went ashore after those officials, there to remain as a garrison—nor yet did they prevent the taking in of water, provisions, &c., &c.; but, on the contrary, assisted the operation by their own launches. The vessel was nothing more than a small schooner, which carried not more than twenty-five or twenty-seven men, with as many muskets, one four-pounder, a few provisions, and some packages of powder. As soon as communication was established, Colonel Dias put the first questions to them, for the purpose of learning the cause and object of their presence on the spot. They did not answer that they were engaged in a lawful occupation, making use of a certain article which was theirs, the United States', or the whole of mankind's; but they acknowledged that they had gone to other islands of the republic, and thence taken some of the same produce, and afterwards came to Aves Island to do the same thing, as they considered the spot as one where it would be more difficult for the national authorities to discover them. Thereupon, as Colonel Dias declared to them the nature and object of his commission, notifying them that it was imperative that they should leave the island; they spoke to him of the expenses and losses which their undertaking had caused them, appealing to his humanity to allow them, in order to recuperation, to continue digging out the guano. The Colonel moved to compassion, deferred to their request, although unauthorized to do so, under the condition that the government should approve his conduct; moreover, and upon their solicitations, and for their greater security, he agreed to give them the permit prayed for in writing; this so much gratified them that they beset that officer with attentions; offered to supply him with provisions, of which he stood in need; put the arms belonging to them under his protection, and finally deported themselves like men who had just been the recipients of a priceless favor. In the permit, signed by the two individuals who, in the name of two American companies whose agents they purported to be, directed the excavations, the title of Venezuela to the island was recognized, by an act of spontaneous will on their part, and without the least shadow of violence.

Colonel Dias retired, leaving in the island a single officer, with ten men as a garrison, to which were added fifteen more men when, on the 21st of said December, another war schooner landed there, which, having put them ashore, made sail for St. Thomas. Upon his return to Aves, the commander was informed by the officer to whom supervision over the island had been intrusted, that the permit granted by Colonel Dias was abused, which permit was restricted to the complement of the cargo of three vessels, and was subject to the approbation of the government, which declined to ratify the permit; besides this, that the laborers had failed to comply with his orders; in the meantime, three brigs and two ships had anchored and were receiving cargoes. This led to a new notification to the Americans that they should leave the island. They did so, without requiring the use of force to compel them to it; nor did they protest in the act itself, or afterwards, against their ejection.

Upon Colonel Dias's arrival, there were two American vessels, with two six-pounders, eighty laborers, something over two hundred weight of powder, besides arms, such as rifles, muskets, guns, pistols, revolvers, pikes, carbines, cutlasses, in addition to the laboring implements, which might be used as arms. Yet, though all these means of defense gave them a decided superiority over the few Venezuelans mentioned, they did not resist them; a conduct which will admit no other possible explanation than that of a conviction, on their part, of all absence of right to make use of an article which they knew to belong to Venezuela.

About the end of December of the same year of 1854, an agreement was made in Caraccas with Mr. J. D. Wallace, an American citizen, which permitted him and those whom he might associate with himself under certain conditions, to take guano from Aves Island and the other islands of the republic in which the article might be found. The contractors, among other obligations, bound themselves to pay a certain sum, for the amount of which Wallace drew on the United States, in favor of this government; and as the stipulations were not complied with, and as this failure caused the protest of the drafts and the consequential damages resulting from it, the executive power was reduced to the necessity of declaring an annulment of the contract. This resulted in an application made to the government of Venezuela by the other Americans, to whom Wallace had ceded his rights, asking a redintegration of the annulled contract, or the arrangement of a new one with them, and, with slight differences, like to the former agreement.

Trusting that its decision would be respected, which was one in consonance with justice, and provoked by the conduct of the contractors, the government had proposed to manage the guano islands in a suitable manner, and so as to derive the highest advantage from them. It made an announcement to that effect, and promised to frame the necessary regulations, communicating its intentions to the diplomatic agents of the nations represented in Caraccas, and therefore to the minister resident of the United States.

On some occasions Mr. Eames had spoken of the affair of the Americans who had been on the island. He had given to understand that they might prefer some claim. But the licentiate Francisco Armada, the Secretary of Foreign Relations, ever denied their right to do so; and when, as a conclusive argument, he used that which was supplied by the paper which they had signed and which was delivered to Colonel Dias, it was fairly perceived that it struck the minister resident with force; and this is borne out by his note of the 20th of December, 1856, which gives the assurance that the case had been submitted to his government as a preliminary step to their procuring and considering the explanations of the parties interested. Out of this grew the declarations which accompanied the demand of last December.

In the course of September, 1855, Mr. Pickrell came to Caraccas as the representative of the Philadelphia Guano Company, and from the fact of the annulment of the contract with Wallace, which had been transferred to them. From that time that matter claimed Mr. Eames's attention, in preference to all else. Presented to Mr. Pickrell, he became his inseparable companion; the advocate of his cause; intervening in the discussion of all the points debated with him; coming daily to the government-house urging its settlement; purporting to take the Secretary of Foreign Relations and of the Treasury to his residence, in order not to lose a single moment, even on a holiday; offering to smooth all difficulties in the way of the new arrangement; and wielding, as a powerful instrument, the certainty of trouble with the United States. Every one of these is a clear indication that he had taken this business at heart, and that his ministry was not confined to merely good offices. Mr. Eames intervened in the matter more largely than Mr. Pickrell. In this connection it now occurs, and the fact is recorded in a memorandum, that in the first interview of the Secretaries of State and of the Treasury with Mr. Pickrell, at which, as at all other subsequent ones, Mr. Eames was present, doubts were expressed on the part of the organs of the government as to the validity of the powers of this private agent, because they contained no clause which, as in all like cases, should make his acts binding upon the company. This observation, not addressed to Mr. Eames, and by him not allowed to be translated for Mr. Pickrell, and not understood by him, because it had been made in the Spanish language, Mr. Eames answered with the statement that the instrument was in due form, and that, from his knowledge of the laws of the United States, he could assure the ministers that the company was bound by whatever act which Pickrell, as their attorney, might perform, although it was not actually so mentioned in the instrument.

At the same interview Mr. Eames stated that he had been instructed to make a reservation, and that was, that the good offices which he was directed to interpose in behalf of Mr. Pickrell were not to be understood as affecting a claim made and likely to be presented by Americans, who were in possession of Aves Islands before its occupation by the government of Venezuela. At the same time Mr. Aranda, the Secretary of Foreign Relations, pointed out the impropriety of blending two distinct and, to a certain extent, incongruous questions. For in the very act, on one side, of supposing the right of Venezuela to the Aves Island to be perfect, its ownership was, on the other, controverted; whence he concluded that, in his opinion, if both phases had to be held up, it were better to take up that to which allusion had been made in the former instance.

Mr. Pickrell's business proceeded in its course, under the patronage of Mr. Eames, the minister resident. As, however, it did not do so with all the desired speed, and as the propositions of the government, initiated for the purpose of bettering the improper and vicious contract of 1854, did not suit the present negotiators, Mr. Eames carried his good offices to the point of considering it most urgent and absolutely indispensable, in order to remove the dangers which impended over the peace of both republics, directly to inform his excellency the President of the gravity of the case, for which purpose he begged that an interview should be granted to him. Through the merest condescension, the President granted the interview; and what then took place, according to the very language of the legation, tends to set forth, in unobstructed light, the course pursued by Mr. Eames under the circumstances, and how he applied all the efforts of his energy to procure the preponderance of Pickrell's claim, subordinating Shelton's to its success.

It will immediately strike any one that the motive and the object of such an audience were merely to create a deep impression on the mind of the government touching the consequences which might result from its refusal to go into the new contract, for which Pickrell had applied, and that all else that was said in the course of that audience was mere tinsel, with which it was attempted to conceal the threat. After recapitulating the facts, according to his mode of viewing them, up to the time of Mr. Pickrell's arrival in Caraccas with dispatches, which went to say that, in view of the public and, indeed, national importance of the business, he should, by his good offices and by the personal and official influence of the legation, sustain Mr. Pickrell in the defense and in the recognition of the rights conferred on citizens of the United States by the contract of 1854. Mr. Eames then touched upon the case of those Americans by a repetition of what he had already stated before. His excellency having, thereupon, remarked that it was preferable, in the first instance, to adjust this claim, or that the company should assume its adjustment upon themselves, he declared that such a thing was entirely out of the range of possibility, not only from the essentially distinct character of both questions, and on account of his duty separately to treat them, but because, also, he was not yet fully in possession of all the information required for a proper preparation of the claim for Aves Island. He added that he considered himself authorized, in view of recent instructions, to state again a conviction that the government of the United States would deem it its duty to sustain the right of the claimants to a full indemnification.

"The undersigned," he continues in the statement of that conference, "then passing to the more immediate objects and aims of Mr. Pickrell, the agent of the company interested in Wallace's contract, begged his excellency to consider the extremely unfortunate aspect under which all this guano question, between Venezuela and the citizens of the United States, presented itself to that government. That a whole series of grave and highly disagreeable circumstances, each of them a separate occurrence, although all bore a common relation with rights of American citizens in the guano islands, had followed each other in rapid succession. The violent dispossession of American citizens who were on Aves Island, the making, at the same time, of a contract with Wallace, its annulment by Venezuela, baffling the lawful hopes of the interested parties, and inflicting great injury upon them, were facts, each of which tended to aggravate the other, and to complicate any negotiation which might seek a satisfactory settlement of all or of any of them. The undersigned earnestly begged his excellency to consider the serious and new complication and difficulty which would follow, if the agent of the company, who was then present, should, through a refusal of Venezuela, find himself in the impossibility, after so many efforts made by him, even with the help of the good offices of the legation of the United States, to come to some friendly arrangement with the view of protecting the rights and interests which he was representing. That it was the duty of the undersigned to submit, with deepest respect, to his excellency that, in the judgment of the government of the United States, this guano question is one of great and public interest, involving not only important rights and considerable interests, but also a great question of good faith, the settlement of which, according to the circumstances under which it had arisen, could not but have its effect on the relations of both countries; and that the undersigned, whilst carefully avoiding any expression which might, perhaps, be construed into an unfriendly or threatening sense, or one not thoroughly compatible with the most perfect consideration for the dignity of the government of Venezuela, deemed himself, notwithstanding, obliged frankly to inform his excellency that the people and the government of the United States, alike, took a deep interest in this matter, and that they would, with extreme pain and regret, witness any proceeding, now had by Venezuela, which might result in loss or injustice to those of our citizens interested in the said contract. On the other hand, the undersigned did not hesitate to say that, in his judgment, an opposite course, in accordance with which Venezuela should recognize and restore in a satisfactory manner the rights of those citizens, would produce an excellent effect on the relations of both governments, not only as an act of good faith in itself, but also because it would leave, on its own character and circumstances, the consideration and settlement of the very serious question, which had previously arisen between the two governments, as to the violent occupation of Aves Island by Venezuela, without the new aggravation and complication which must result from the persistence of Venezuela in a policy productive of great loss and injury to other citizens of the United States interested in Wallace's contract. The undersigned, in continuation, submitted to his excellency some observations going to show that the undersigned concurred in the justice and the reasonableness of the conditions under which the agent of the company was disposed to enter into a new contract, in lieu of that which had been made with Wallace; and with these words the statement of the undersigned closed. The undersigned experienced great satisfaction at hearing his excellency the President state, in answer, that, moved by the desire of manifesting his deep interest in the full maintenance of the good faith of the Venezuelan government, and especially his ardent wish of cultivating the most friendly relations with the government and the people of the United States, he had resolved that a satisfactory arrangement should be made; and that the government would immediately turn its attention to it through the action of its ministers."

Although this memorandum, extended by Mr. Eames himself, has softened the harsher expressions which he used in that conference, and which rung from the President this exclamation: "What! threats, Mr. Eames!" still it may be clearly enough perceived that he exerted himself in exaggerating the proportions of things. At one time he aggravates the conduct of Venezuela to the highest pitch; at another he lingers on the extent which the difficulties might reach if the application for a renewal of the contract were set aside; now he invests the question with an importance not its own; then he suggests that the relations of both countries depend upon its settlement. In the sequel he represents the people and the government of the United States advocating, with unparalleled zeal, the cause of Wallace's transferees, and here he favors us with a glimpse at a recourse to force should Pickrell's application not be granted. Essaying then to enforce the expediency of yielding to it, he adds that it would produce an excellent effect on the relations of both governments, and would signally conduce to the settlement of the other claim. Lastly, on that occasion, speaking with his excellency, he goes even into the details of the contract which Pickrell intended to make, as if an agreement had already gone that far, and as it were to leave no doubt as to the character of his intervention.

It is proper to observe that the note referred to, signed by Mr. Eames, in which it was his object to record the passages of that conference, is the only paper that issued from the legation touching Pickrell's affair, and that there is absolutely nothing said in it about not including Aves Island in the contract which might be made with him. The contrary is shown by the tenor of his observations. If, besides this, it be borne in mind that he alternatively demanded the restoration of Wallace's contract, which included Aves Island, or the conclusion of another similar one, it will easily be ascertained that he did not combat the insertion of Aves in the Pickrell arrangement, as he now pretends to have done.

So far as concerns the note of the 8th of March, 1856, here follows the showing made by the records in relation to it, Holland having contested the right of Venezuela to Aves Island, the consul general of the former presented to the government of the latter an ultimatum, by which it demanded a recognition of its rights to and a withdrawal of the Venezuelan troops from the Aves Island. This having been bruited about, Mr. Eames applied to the department of foreign relations in writing, for the purpose of inquiring whether the statement were correct. He was answered that, in fact, the recognition and evacuation of Aves Island within three days had been required, and that the government were considering the claim. Thus officially informed of transpiring events, he wrote the communication mentioned above, which, in substance, amounted to his interjecting opposition to a cession of Aves Island to Holland, on one part, for the claim which was said to be pending in relation to it between the United States and Venezuela, and in favor of certain Americans, who had discovered the guano and occupied the island, and on the other part, for the rights to the island conferred upon Pickrell. It is true that he there alluded to a pending claim, which existed nowhere, although it had afforded matter for Mr. Eames's conversations with the secretary of foreign relations, but circumstances prevented this assertion from being noticed and triumphantly refuted. Even he himself did not consider that to be the proper manner of setting up the claim; and that he never again recollected such a note is a self-convincing proof of the fact. The mention, therefore, which he then made of the matter was an indirect or incidental one; one which would not have occurred had it not been preceded and caused by the question with Holland. So that, had not the latter supervened, the note had never been penned. Add to this that Mr. Eames grounded the delay of discussion on the want of documents, and as those must have been the declarations which he subsequently transmitted, and as the last bears date April 12, 1856, it is but right to infer that they could not be in Caraccas before May or June following, and that hence it was not in his power to submit the claim through his note of the 8th of March. Finally, on the 20th of December, 1856, he formally presented the claim in writing, accompanying it, as vouchers, with simple of copies of various declarations taken by justices of the peace and notaries in the United States, without any intervention of the party against which they were intended to work, and urgently requiring at once—"First. An indemnification for all the actual losses resulting to American citizens from their expulsion from Los Aves. Secondly. Indemnification for the loss of the probable gain which they would have derived from the guano taken thence, with the authority of Venezuela, from the day of their occupation to that of the settlement of the claim. Thirdly. The settlement of the question of legitimate interest which they have in the guano that may still remain in Los Aves at this time, either by abandoning it to them or by any other mode that may be satisfactory to both governments."

The government of Venezuela allowed no delay in framing and expressing its opinion adverse to the application, and this in keeping with repeated declarations made to Mr. Eames every time that he touched this question in the various conferences. The answer was directed to show, first, the absence of all urgency in a matter which had been allowed to slumber for two years, or merely mentioned by accident during that time, and that solely to announce its existence; secondly, the force of the document, in which the right of the republic was admitted; thirdly, the title of the republic to the ownership of the island; fourthly, the incapacity of individuals to acquire international dominion in competition with a State; fifthly, the consequences of the present expensive possession of this country; sixthly, the impossibility under which the United States had laid themselves of maintaining that the island did not belong to Venezuela, when the reverse was shown by the protection which had surrounded Wallace's successors with so lively an interest; seventhly, the nullities of the delarations brought forward in support of the demand.

To these Mr. Eames answered *in extenso*, concluding that, for his part, the discussion was closed. The executive power, by the suggestion of the council, to which the records had been transferred for consultation, then deemed it his duty to take some measures to embody the real state of things, and, among others, to procure from Colonel Dias, and the other officers who accompanied him in his mission, a declaration of all that had occurred in its course. By courtesy, and for fear that their testimony should suffer from the *lâches* adverted to in the proof brought forward by the claimants, the secretary of foreign relations gave notice, in writing, to Mr. Eames of the day, the place, and the hour when their declarations were to be taken, in order that should he desire to be present in the act, he might do so, as he had expressed orally a desire to that effect, when it was first proposed to receive the depositions. But although Mr. Sanford, who was interested in the question, since he came exclusively to hasten its dispatch, was present when the declarations were taken, the American minister, altering his mind, abstained from an appearance, alleging, as an excuse, that, in his judgment, as well as the judgment of his government, the facts were fully evolved and abundantly proved. He then gave notice that if a final answer were not sent to him by the 6th of June, he would be under the necessity of proceeding to the United States, in compliance with instructions, to account in person for the delay, and state the uselessness of his efforts. Under these circumstances, it became necessary to intimate to the minister that the admission of his reclamation had presented serious difficulties, the most stubborn of which looked to the document signed by the two agents of the companies which were taking out the guano, and attempted to be set aside by a mere statement of the interested parties themselves, to the effect that the document was a consequence of the compulsion and fraud exercised by the officer to whom they delivered it. It therefore became necessary that what had really occurred should be ascertained; because, if the statements of American citizens were entitled to the credence of their legation, Venezuela, on her part, could not disregard the reports of her citizens, much less so of those who, from the position which they occupied and the duties which they performed, were entitled to every respect and consideration. She could not but defend her rights, whilst there was no way of ascertaining what had occurred but that of interrogating those who must be acquainted with the occurrences. It was supposed that the object was to discuss a question between equal States, and that Venezuela had the right to set forth her objections, rebut proofs adduced by the claimants, and take time to deliberate; it was for this reason, and because, also, that the government would not have its defense made in the absence of, and without notice to, its opponent, that the minister was invited to be present at the investigation. Now, if, in the judgment of Mr. Eames, the facts were fully evolved and abundantly proved, such was not the opinion of the government and of its secretary of foreign relations. It could not be pretended that Venezuela was bound to subscribe to extrinsic judgments merely because they were such; for, in that case, discussion were nugatory, and nothing more were required than to amerce the government at the discretion of the claimants. But besides this, it was required that the decisions of the executive power should be given within a short and peremptory period, made coördinate with special and previously arranged circumstances, in which the American legation found itself without the slightest relation to the state of affairs between the two republics. Several times did Mr. Eames state in conversation that he had asked and obtained from Mr. Marcy, the Secretary of State, leave to visit his country; he even exhibited an official note in which this was mentioned, one, particularly, from General Cass in reference to the treaty pending between the two countries, who had thought him *en route,* by virtue of the leave given to him. It is to be supposed that Mr. Eames might have desired to be in Washington by the time of the inauguration of the new President; still he would delay his departure, in order to take along with himself the approval of a treaty, and the recognition of the pretended duties of certain Americans. Thus it was that whilst the treaty was imperilled in the Congress, he abstained from pressing the other matter. So soon, however, as the crisis had been gone through, he returned to the charge with increased vigor, as if, on one side, he was impatiently fretting for his absence from the United States, and on the other, for the lack of a speedy and favorable settlement of the Aves claim, which held him here as though in a state of imprisonment. In this stress, he considered that by throwing out a threat in the shape of a peremptory demand, and an application for his passport, he would advance the attainment of his wishes; thus leaving room for a belief that the relations of both countries were in danger, and a dissemination of the alarm which this rumor was calculated to produce, especially in the midst of the peculiar condition in which the republic stood under the reform of its organic laws.

From himself, perchance, proceeded the news, published also in an American newspaper, to the effect that his excellency, the President, had refused to ratify the treaty concluded in the course of last year. There is the truth of the case. That convention was approved by the congress of Venezuela just as it had been negotiated by the plenipotentiaries, but a like result was not obtained in Washington, for the American Senate agreed on all its articles, with the exception of some words in the twenty-eighth article, which were stricken out. Speaking of this result, Mr. Eames said that it ought not to prevent the ratification, as the legislature of this country had had the Spanish text only under their eyes, and the Senate of the United States the single English text; the change made in the letter was in no way essential, much less so as the omission went to lay down, with greater accuracy, the limits of one of the grounds of extradition, leaving the English clause mutilated, with the same sense, however, as the Spanish gives in its integrity. The secretary of foreign relations answered him, that he did not judge that the executive power had the right to alter the text of a law, such as the treaty had already become, even though it should be in the copy of the English, which was presented to the congress as a faithful version of the Spanish text; that an omission from one part of the treaty required a like omission from the other part; and lastly, that due attention would be given to the matter before definitely passing upon its merits. Besides, Mr. Eames had not by him the instrument of ratification, nor was it possible that it should have been sent to him pending this difficulty. Hence it is absolutely inaccurate to say that the executive power declined, in that instance, complying with an obligation contracted towards the United States. The difficulty—and the thing is self-evident—has grown out of their own action. But it may be said that through a wish of charging our adversary we impute assumed facts to him.

Now, such a degree of exasperation was exhibited by Mr. Eames that, as though some serious offense had been committed against him, he was beyond measure irritated because his wishes were not realized; and about the time of his departure he gave out, both personally and through persons of a high character and of social standing, and of others, his echoes immediately about him, that he had taken the resolution of using the engine of the press, whose nursling he was, to wage war against Venezuela until he should compel Messieurs Buchanan and Cass to follow the popular movement, intending speedily to return accompanied by public vessels.

After demonstrating by the foregoing *historique* the groundlessness of the charge of dilatoriness brought against Venezuela, and also how inaccurate it is to assert that the question has been for more than two years pending between the two governments, the undersigned proceeds to consider the arguments on which Mr. Eames rested for insisting on his demand with a confidence so overweening as to deem it unnecessary to continue the discussion.

It is supposed by him that because Venezuela did not deny the main facts upon which the reclamation is grounded, such a denial must be taken as an admission of the facts themselves. In this category it is laid down in the first instance, "that the claimants through their agents were the first discoverers of the guano on the Aves Island." No attention was paid to this point, because it was considered to be of no importance to the question. Passing by this—that the matter is not proved, and that it might even be impossible to prove the negative, which it involves, and let it be granted that it is invested with all the truth which is claimed for it, and then what would be the inference drawn from this? Does any one acquire a right to another man's land because he had seen it before the lawful owner had done so? Then, indeed, would the effects of property be extremely precarious; all things connected materially with property would have to be concealed from the sight of those who have no right to it, for from the moment that they should be discovered by them they would be lost to the rightful owner. The fruits which the tree may have produced in the absence of its owner, the buried mines of the earth, the existence of which were unknown; the rain-water which from time to time may come down from the clouds; all other matters embodied in the earth and not previously noticed, might be contended for by him whom chance or an unlawful act had put in the way of happening upon them before the owner of the property. The American legation maintains that Aves Island, though discovered by Spain, does not belong to her; so that it considers that the discovery by itself confers no title even when the question turns upon the property "*nullius;*" and, withall, it considers such as a source of property with respect to what is incorporated with the possessions of "somebody." The first and essential requisite of occupation is that the thing to which a claim is preferred shall be the property of no one. "*Quod autem nullius est, naturali ratione occupanti conceditur.*" Then it is that ownership can result from possession, which constitutes the second requisite. Now, the claimants having failed to prove that Aves Island was "*res nullius*" when their agent went thither, no force attaches to their allegation as to their landing and taking possession of it, &c. If the island was another's, these acts, far from conferring the least title upon them, made them liable to its owner, in the first place, for a tort committed by the invasion of his territory, and, in the second place, for the value of all the produce thence derived, and for the damages accruing from the act of spoliation. Yet so great is the impossibility of giving credit to circumstances of such enormity, that Mr. Eames studied particularly to escape from the stress in which he was placed; and if he is told that "it was incumbent on the Americans to show that it was lawful for them to go to Aves Island and dig out the guano which it might contain," he answers that the burden of proof does not lie with them, but that it does on Venezuela. They could not ignore the fact that a spot situated so short a distance from other places amply known—a spot which must have been frequently observed by navigators; which bears, in its very name, the mark that was stamped upon it by Spain, its discoverer and sometime owner; which is assigned to that power by various works on geography, and sometimes to Holland also by some writers—which is mentioned and described in various books—which is laid down on almost every chart published—which figures in certain maps as connected with Saba through a sandbank; that such a spot must necessarily belong to some one, and hence that it was not allowable to suppose it thitherto undiscovered, and open to occupancy and possession. This consequence acquires additional force when certain indubitable antecedents are recalled to mind. Enough, therefore, to adduce the recent and notorious fact that Americans in the course of 1853 pretended to take possession not only of Lobos Islands, in Peru, to which they dispatched vessels to take out guano, but of various islands also of Venezuela, upon which they went, settled down, and clandestinely continued, availing themselves of the circumstance that they were uninhabited and that their owner put them to no use. Such was the case with Monjes Islands, upon which, as on Aves Island, were found houses, tools, and other necessary appliances to carry out the pursuit in which the usurpers were engaged, and where the American bark Tom Corwin, Captain Hiram Bart, was detected, on her trip from Boston to said islands, whither she had sailed to take in the guano, which was, as stated, to be delivered by the people whom they had working there. Such was the case with the Heronanos Islets, where the armed schooner General Monagas found a merchant schooner of the United States, which, making off suddenly, left ashore eighty sacks of guano for want of time to take them in. Such the case with Pié Island, which, being examined by said Venezuelan vessel, gave evidences of bags of guano, ropes, pickaxes, &c., and where afterwards, on the 3d of October, 1855, the same schooner, General Monagas, discovered the American schooner White Swan, of Baltimore, Captain J. Henry, who acknowledged that he had proceeded from Laguayra; that he was taking in guano, of which he already had ten tons aboard and sixty-five bags ashore, and then, by flight, escaped a trial and its consequent penalty. Facts of this nature warrant a conviction on the part of Venezuela that the conduct of the Americans in Aves Island was not more lawful than it was in the other mentioned islands.

If, as they assume, they were the first discoverers of the guano of Aves Island, and that they could therefore make that discovery the basis of their appropriation of it, with like reason might they claim the guano of other Venezuelan islands, since it cannot be seen why they should not thus apply the new and unauthorized principle which assumes that the discoverer of a thing which is an adjunct to another thing, though it should belong to another person, acquires rights to that thing without taking in consideration those of the owner of the principal.

But, it is added, neither does Venezuela deny "that the claimants, a short time after the discovery of the guano in Aves Island, in the summer of 1854, took possession of it, at no slight cost, and peaceably and uninterruptedly kept that possession for several months; nor that they intended to keep such peaceful possession until they had exhausted the valuable substance of that article."

The silence of the government on that point does not imply an acknowledgment of what is here asserted, and it proceeded from the same cause mentioned above. It has been said and it is proper here to repeat it, in order that it may remain deeply impressed upon the minds of the American Cabinet, that the principal question under view is not the discovery of this valuable, nor the expenditures which the appropriation of it entailed, nor yet the period of time for which they intended to continue possessing the island; for if there was no good faith on the part of the occupants, all these considerations must be of no avail. To substantiate that good faith, they would have to bring forward the facts, which would go to establish this other fact, that Spain, which is admitted to have been the discoverer of the island, had determined to abandon it, because she wanted it no longer. Then, indeed, would it appear to have passed from a condition of private property of a nation to that of a derelict, and to come within the possibility of being acquired by any one. But presumptions are not sufficient; let the doctrine of Klüber speak: "From the moment that a State leaves or abandons the ownership of an *island,* for instance, it ceases to constitute a portion of its territory, and thenceforward belongs to no one, (*res nullius.*) From that moment it is lawful for any other State to appropriate it to itself and reduce it to its dominion. Still an unmistakable declaration, either expressed or tacit, is required to put an end to the previous right; but as no mere conjecture or supposition can be equal to such a declaration, much less can it work the forfeiture of the property by prescription." (Klüber, *Droit des gens, &c.*)

But on the other hand, in the proof, if it be proper so to call it, adduced by Mr. Eames in support of his action, there is nothing to sustain the assertion that the claimants went into heavy expenses in the undertaking. To judge by the declarations of the functionaries of Venezuela who were on the island, and whom the distortion of truth could in no way benefit, there was not there more than a dozen of huts, frame built, a sort of a wharf, some sixty or eighty wheelbarrows, the necessary spades, some timbers from the wreck of a vessel, and other articles procured from the same. So that, if to what is herein described be added the freight of the vessels engaged, and if we lay aside all interested exaggerations, we will have a correct idea of the extent of the speculation. What the value of the huts was, all of them built of old stuff, may be inferred from the fact that the best of them was sold by Lang, its owner, to Lieutenant Nicholas Pereira for the price of one pound sterling. The others, with the exception of one, which was ceded for the use of the troops, and which belonged to Gibbs, were unroofed and ruined by the Americans themselves, previously to their departure from the island.

Neither is it probable they could retain a peaceful and undisturbed possession of the guano, as it is well known that the Dutch held the island to be theirs, and other nations preferred claims to it, and as, according to their affirmation, they were visited by an English vessel, the captain of which told them that his nation had purchased the island from Spain, as appears from the deposition of the above mentioned Lieutenant Pereira. If they were not driven more early away from their lawless occupation, the fact is to be ascribed, so to say, to the seclusion of the spot, or, in other words, to its latent position, a circumstance which induced the Americans to select it for their operations; for, having first gone to other islands of Venezuela, as they were easily seen in the act, they withdrew from them under no other impulse than that of fear. It is a point not to be overlooked in this question, that the very individuals found on Aves Island were the identical ones who had already gone to other national islands.

It is readily conceived that they should have desired to carry away all the guano which they found; but, unfortunately, will is not the best rule of right, nor yet a thing which can justify the self appropriation of another's property. Let it be noted that hitherto no answer has been attempted to be made on the subject of guano exported from Venezuelan territory, in every place where it has been explored and robbed by the Americans, who have, at the least, made themselves liable for the value of the substance which they have taken, and for damages consequent on their act, not to speak here of the wrong committed against national sovereignty. If the government of the United States claims the guano of Aves Island on the ground that the claimants have acquired a right to it, and because the island was not within the jurisdiction of Venezuela, it is but reasonable that, even setting aside Aves Island, they should take upon themselves to answer for the guano which has been taken from places to which the dominion of Venezuela has never been questioned, and from which fact, therefore, they never could have claimed the guano as their own. Will it be maintained that Los Hermanos, Los Festigos, and Los Monges islands constitute no portion of her property? Mr. Eames, in his reply, has ignored this important chapter, although the note of this government laid down, in explicit terms, the responsibility of the American government to the government of Venezuela for said appropriations of guano. Now, therefore, we must insist on this reclamation, which is grounded upon manifestly proved usurpations. That cabinet which is so observant of justice, cannot fail admitting that on both points, we have it on our side.

In Mr. Eames' opinion, the abstaining also of putting in a denial goes for an acknowledgment that the Americans "were violently expelled and driven from such possession in December, of that year, by the government of Venezuela, acting through the means of a public armed force."

This cannot be allowed to pass by without suitable explanations. These rest on the declarations, made under oath, of Colonel Domingo Dias, First Lieutenant Nicholas Pereira, and First Commandant Manuel Cotarro, persons who intervened in the matter, as officers of the Venezuelan navy, during the occurrences at Aves Island. Their depositions are in no way to be confounded with those presented by Mr. Eames. In this lies she difference; the latter came from unknown individuals; the former from public functionaries; the latter were taken without the knowledge of Venezuela; the former might have been witnessed by Mr. Eames, who was invited to hear them, and failed to be present, as was done by Mr. Sanford; in the latter, the very persons interested are witnesses and parties both; in the former no such disability is found; in the latter, interest, stimulated by avarice, figures as the prime mover; in the former, the love of truth alone controls; the latter do not fitly accord with the circumstances of the event; the former are most easily explained by them; the latter cannot cease to be mere copies, although they come through a very respectable channel; the former are transmitted through an equally worthy channel, and are, moreover, accompanied by certificates in all due form; in the latter, perchance, it might be impossible to find the witnesses and subject them to the test of cross-examination; in the former, the declarants may be brought forward whenever desired, and be submitted to the searchings of counter-proofs, or any other scrutiny of truth.

Now what did occur, according to the unvarying statements of those persons of character, is as follows: On the 12th of December, at 7, p. m., Colonel Dias arrived at Aves Island, where he found three vessels at anchor. In the morning of the following day he went ashore to ascertain what they [?] were doing there, and found that they had come to take in guano; were on shore with eighty men digging it out and putting it on board; having in their possession, among other articles, two pieces of artillery, six-pounders, with the necessary ammunition, some fifty muskets, thirty rifles, thirty cutlasses, twenty-five pikes, fifty pairs of pistols, and balls, eleven to the pound, revolvers, and two hundred weight of powder. Whilst, in the Venezuelan war-schooner, there were not more than from twenty-five to twenty-seven soldiers, with that number of guns, and a four-pounder. When the Americans were asked what they were doing there, they said that they were working out guano, as they had done in other islands of Venezuela; for instance in Hermanos Island, whence they took a schooner load; that they had settled upon Aves Island, because their discovery there, by the republic, could not prove so easy. They alleged no right to the island, but, on the contrary, they admitted that it did not belong to them or to the United States. When, in pursuance of his order to prevent the clandestine exportation of guano from the republic, Colonel Dias directed them to stop digging, they then stated to him the losses which they had suffered, and the expenses incurred, begging him, in view of these considerations, to allow them, for humanity's sake, to continue loading the three vessels there anchored, which had not guano enough on board to serve as ballast.

Having obtained leave to do so, yet still doubtful whether it would not be withdrawn, the Americans asked that it might be laid down in writing, in the event of their falling in with some Venezuelan vessels, to which they would have to account for the guano on board. It was accordingly given to them in that form, and the document, which they signed, was written in one of their huts, and on paper and with pen and ink which they themselves supplied, Mr. Lang acting as interpreter, and with such familiarity with the Spanish language that he corrected a few trifling mistakes which appeared in the instrument. In the act of their subscribing it, there was not a single government soldier on shore; and besides this, they asked that the officer who was to remain on the island in command of the garrison, should not prevent said vessels to continue taking in their cargo.

So voluntary on their part was the act of signing that they mentioned the names of the houses to which they belonged, which it would not otherwise have been possible to express in the document. They not only returned thanks to Colonel Dias, but they also forced upon him various presents, some of which he carried to Laguayra. Besides this, they afforded assistance to the garrison, and put their artillery and armament at the disposal of the officers and under the flag of Venezuela. Colonel Dias shortly after went away from the island, leaving upon it ten men only, under the orders of First Lieutenant Nicholas Pereira, with no more arms than a musket apiece for the soldiers, a few bundles of cartridges, and the small cannon, with twenty-five charges, for the landing of which, and of the water and provisions, the Americans sent out their launches, instead of opposing such landing, when they might have done so in view of their superior force.

Another Venezuelan armed schooner arrived at Aves Island on the 21st of December. It there found three brigs and two square-rigged vessels taking in guano, although the permit given by Colonel Dias did not go beyond allowing them to take in the complement of the cargoes of the three vessels which he had met on the 13th of December, and this under condition that the permission should be approved by the government of Venezuela. He landed fifteen men, whom he had under his orders, and proceeded to Santomas to put in fresh water. On the 24th of December, 1855, an armed British brig bore up for Aves Island, and stood off whilst the captain went ashore, and expressed his astonishment at meeting with Venezuelan troops there, because the island had been purchased from the Spaniards by his government. This was his language, and not that ascribed to him by J. James Wheeler, to the effect that the Americans had a right to hold the island in the name of the United States. The Venezuelan war schooner returned from Santomas on the 29th of December; and, as it became known that the Americans were misapplying the permission granted to them by Colonel Dias, and which was confined to completing the loading of certain vessels, subject to the approbation of the government, which was withheld, they were notified on the 30th to quit the island. The Americans did leave it without any demurrer, departing with their vessels in the evening of the 30th, and leaving no guano collected, for they had stowed it aboard in proportion as it was dug out.

The result of this is: 1st. That the Americans acknowledged that they had no right to be on the island. 2d. That they recognized the right of Venezuela to said island. 3d. That they could, with the greatest ease and best success, have resisted the landing of the inconsiderable Venezuelan force, or expelled it after it got on shore. 4th. That they had abused the conditional permission which had been granted to them after the intimation to depart had been given to them. 5th. That a mere order, without resort to violence, was sufficient to enforce such departure. 6th. That they themselves would have rendered a resort to force lawful in the event that it should have proved necessary to use force. 7th. That they had vessels in which they could embark, not some merely, but the whole of them, and go to the nearest place and extend protest; and that, instead of such a course, they continued availing themselves of the permit, which they now allege was interfered with in violence, error, and fraud. 8th. That they were well informed of the tenor of the document, and signed it with perfect understanding of its contents.

Mr. Eames proceeds and says: "That it is not denied that, since such expulsion, Venezuela has continued occupying and possessing the island and its guano, for her own benefit and against those claimants, through the appliance of such armed force; nor is it denied that great losses and damages, both immediate and consequential, have resulted to their detriment from said expulsion and adverse possession."

The advantage which Venezuela may have derived from Aves Island is but trifling; for, from her having sold the guano for an insignificant price to other individuals belonging to the United States, the profits of the transfer must have inured to them, and this, too, from the pressure exerted on this government in the name of that of the United States, as it has already been amply stated. When the executive power annulled Wallace's contract for, among numerous reasons, a failure to comply with its conditions, it had intended to manage the administration of the guano interest in such a way as to be beneficial to the nation, and to derive from it all the advantages which it held out; but Mr. Eames became so urgent for a reinstatement of the former contract, or the execution of a new one, little differing from the annulled instrument, that trifling were the advantages secured for the State; whilst the main of those advantages were, in the transaction, reserved for the citizens of the United States who were so zealously sustained by their legation in Caraccas. Had it not taken up Pickrell's contract with all its might, nothing is more certain than that it would not have been made, and in that case the guano might have been disposed of in a desirable and proper manner. It should, therefore, not be forgotten that the profits spoken of have accrued to the Americans, and that nothing but the turn which the question took, and the extent to which it went, added to a wish to preserve friendship and peace between the two nations, prevented Venezuela from deriving the best returns from the guano, both in Aves Island and in the other dependencies of the republic. A statement to that effect was made by the Secretary of the Treasury and by the Secretary of Foreign Relations in the reports of their respective departments, transmitted to Congress in 1856, of which Mr. Eames must have been informed, as both were sent to him. Besides this, he had taken cognizance of the report of the former minister whilst it was still passing through the press, and, without demurrer to the truth of its contents in relation to this question, he merely begged the minister, who acceded to his request, to soften somewhat the warmth of tone in which he had, naturally enough, written one of its paragraphs.

Had Mr. Eames pursued another line of conduct; had he abstained to intervene in the manner in which he did in the Pickrell question; had he seasonably presented Shelton's claim—matters would not have come to the state in which they are now found. But he postponed it because he could not, at the time, bring it forward for want of the documents in the case; and this delay of his, or of the parties in interest, which must necessarily have resulted in this, namely, that the scanty price which some Americans paid for the guano would not be sufficient to satisfy the claims of other Americans, is now imputed to the government, although it had urged the examination of this question in preference to every other. It is easy to conceive how the prosecution of pretensions so diverse, and even mutually conflicting, may have contributed to bring about existing differences. Pickrell's defense necessarily supposes and implies a most unequivocal recognition of the property of Venezuela in, and her sovereignty over, Aves Island; whilst that of the claimants stands out against such a right, and leads to the conclusion that the pretended employment of force against them is a sufficient title to acquire sovereignty, but not private property, although both of these things are one and inseparable. Either the title of the country is good—and in that case it must cover the eminent and private domain of the island—or it is vicious, and cannot justify any form of acquisition. To make a show of disclaiming dominion over a thing in the very act which recognizes it—an act voluntary, and more than voluntary, since it was Mr. Eames himself who was urging on a contract with Pickrell for the working of the guano—is a matter which cannot be easily understood.

The losses and damages that may have resulted to the Americans occupying Aves Island—losses and damages which, as it has been seen, must be very limited—are to be referred to those who, knowing that they had no right to it, proposed at all hazards to occupy and use that island, without reflecting that from the moment that their proceeding could become known, they would have to depart thence and suffer all the consequences of their unlawful act.

On the other hand, the government holds it to be a fair cause for surprise, that up to this hour it should not have been clearly informed as to who are those who claim indemnity at its hands for the occurrences at Aves Island. If, as it appears, the claimants are all the individuals to whom the declarations produced have a reference, then there is just ground to affirm that the island continued to be in common, its occupation by some only notwithstanding, and that, by the fact itself, the republic was not excluded from participating in the island. Indeed, the depositions speak of Shelton & Co., of Lang & Delano, and lastly of George W. Nickels; but the American legation, in order to be self-consistent, and under the supposition that the question turned upon *res derelicta*, were bound to maintain that those only of the claimants who first really took possession had acquired the *derelict*. If the claimants, protected by the American Cabinet, are reduced to the partners of the first two companies, we cannot see the object of adding to the other declarations the deposition of Nickels who, in the month of January, 1855, went with a vessel to take out guano at Aves Island, and who, upon being prevented doing so by the garrison, extended his protest on his return to the city of New York. This point has already given rise to certain observations laid down in the first answer of the government; but Mr. Eames has absolutely neglected to notice them in his answer. Admitted, as they are, their consequences ought to be accepted, instead of being resisted, as is the case.

Mr. Eames further remarks, that "it is not in clear and express terms that the expulsion of those claimants, in the manner in which it was made, was a lawful and justifiable act; nor is it anywhere denied, expressly and absolutely, that the government of Venezuela lies under the obligation of repairing the wrong which it inflicted upon them by its act."

In the very words used by Mr. Eames it was not necessary to declare the judgment of the government in relation to the act which gave rise to the claim; it was enough that the latter should have been, as it was, met by a denial, to understand that it did not admit the principle of responsibility which was attempted to be fastened upon the nation. All the arguments adduced in the first answer made to the American legation converge to a defense of the republic from the charges brought against it, and a repelling of the indemnifications demanded at its hands. That answer made out the absence of right on the part of the Americans to appropriate the guano of Aves Island to themselves; their assent to the right of this country to the island; the origin of its acquisition; the fact that the government of the United States had recognized it through the protection which it gave to Pickrell's claim; the inability of individuals to acquire in competition with a State; the contradiction of Mr. Eames in asserting that the island was *derelict,* and never had been subject to the jurisdiction of any power, and that, as a thing common, Americans might enjoy it, but other individuals or nations might not. It concluded with a hope, that in view of the reasons adduced, the equitable Cabinet of Washington would desist from a claim which there were powerful grounds not to admit. It was impossible more formally to deny the application. Its rejection necessarily involved a denial of the assertions upon which it rests.

But the expulsion so repeatedly mentioned did not take place. Neither the Executive power, nor the force acting in its name, had the most remote intention of offending the Americans, although they lacked no right to proceed against them. Convinced that Aves Island was the property of the State, they exercised one of the rights derived from property, namely, that of preventing its enjoyment by other persons, a course which can in no way inflict injury on any one. But even should not dominion over the island reside in Venezuela, the conduct of the opponents has taken away from them all right to complain of violence. First, when Colonel Dias arrived at the island, he there found three vessels at anchor, the smallest of which was 500 tons and another one 800 tons. Engaged in loading them with guano, were eighty individuals, who had in their possession two pieces of cannon, with their supply of balls, forty or fifty rifles, fifty pairs of pistols, guns, revolvers, muskets, pikes, axes, two six or eight pounders, and two hundred weight of powder. They were holding the island, on which they had built some frame cabins. The Venezuelan schooner, from her small size, the small number of her soldiers, not exceeding twenty-seven men, from its armament, composed of so many muskets and a four-pounder, would have in vain attempted to force the Americans in any way. As it has already been seen, in spite of the difference existing between the two parties, no opposition was made to the approach of Colonel Dias, nor to his landing, and that of the troops, which afterwards took place; but on the contrary, they assisted in such landing by sending their launches out.

The Colonel reaches the shores, and asks them the cause of their presence on the island. Perhaps they may have answered that they had no account to give to any one of their rights? Without alleging that the United States had any right to the island, nor they as to a property in common, they answered that they had been upon other islands of Venezuela, in many of which they had found and taken guano; for instance, in the Hermanos, where they had loaded a schooner; that they had selected Aves Island because it was not so easy for them to be discovered by Venezuela. They made no difficulty in acknowledging to that officer that Aves Island belonged neither to the Union nor to themselves. He, therefore, bearing in mind that he had orders from the government to prevent the continued stealthy exportation of guano from the national islands, notified them to put a stop to their work. But they represented to him the losses which they had sustained from one vessel's going upon the bar, and another one's being stove, the outlays for the cabins and wharf, begging him, in consideration of this, and for humanity's sake, to allow them to continue loading those vessels which had not yet a sufficient quantity of guano. Then took place all the circumstances already adduced as to the permission of Colonel Dias, their expressions of gratitude, &c.

In the instrument of grant, or permit alluded to, they, with all desirable clearness, averred that the Aves Island belonged to Venezuela; and if, in their act of invoking the protection of their government, any thing can be deduced from their silence in relation to said permit, it must be that they considered their application destructive of their pretensions. Indeed, Mr. Eames, in his note of the 20th of December, 1856, states the following:

"In this attitude stood the question of this claim when first presented, and though its reception then by the government of Venezuela was, in the judgment of the undersigned, as he then stated, by no means in conformity with the rights of the claimants, and the just expectations of the government of the United States in their behalf, still the case might probably at that time presented no insuperable obstacle to a prompt adjustment, but for the appearance among the documents pertaining to it, and in possession of the Venezuelan government, of a paper purporting to be the original of an 'agreement' entered into and signed at the 'Aves' Island, on the 13th of December, 1854, by Commander Dias, of the Venezuelan navy, of the first part, and the agents of the American occupants of the island of the second part, by which the possession of the island would seem to be ceded to the Venezuelan authorities by those agents upon certain terms and considerations therein set forth. This paper, the undersigned, when properly assured of its authenticity, deemed fit, as new matter in the case, to be referred to his government, in order that explanations of it by the claimants might be received and considered. These explanations, showing that the alleged 'agreement' was entered into and signed by the agents of the claimants under duress, [fraud, in the Spanish translation,] and upon compulsion, were considered by the government as sufficient wholly to invalidate and avoid the instrument."

This passage puts it beyond all doubt that the claimants, at the time of soliciting the interposition of their government, took particular care in concealing from it the existence of such a document; and, in fact, it is seen that Mr. Eames says not a word about it before he learned here that it was in possession of the government of Venezuela, and among the documents bearing upon the question. He therefore turns his attention to scrutinizing its authenticity, and satisfied of it, he deems it proper to refer it to the Department of State, as it appeared to be "new matter in the case," which required explanations which it was necessary to consider. He accordingly holds up the claim and asks for further instructions. When he is told that the explanations have been received, and that they are sufficient for the invalidation of the instrument, he then prosecutes the matter anew, and lays it down in written form.

Who communicated a knowledge of the existence of this document, it is immaterial here to state. Certain it is that the information did not come from the Secretary of Foreign Relations, who, from the very fact that the question was not yet opened, although conversations in relation to it had taken place, did not deem it expedient then to make use of said proof. But afterwards, however, Mr. Eames exhibited to him a copy of the permit, with which he had been furnished, and most urgently begged to be allowed to see the original, for the purpose of comparison. His wishes were complied with. We are, for this reason, compelled to believe that the document in the power of the government is not the only one that had been drawn up, since Mr. Eames procured a copy of it from some other source. Besides this, there is no doubt that the claimants, from the very first, had a knowledge of the permit, from the copies taken by the agents. This is corroborated by the language of Shelton's application to Mr. Marcy, the Secretary of State, under date of May 14, 1855, in which he speaks as follows:

"Said Dias, on the 13th of December, had drawn up and signed a paper in the Spanish language, (which is on file in your department,) which Captain Gibbs, our agent, was, under the circumstances, constrained to sign, and which Dias called his "permit." It has been asserted that we admit the right of Venezuela to Shelton's Island, and that of Captain Dias to eject us. In other words, that we were violators of the territory, and this, too, in the paper which Dias gave to Captain Gibbs."

The following passage from Charles H. Lang's declaration, speaking of the document which he signed with Gibbs, "that said Domingo Dias finally drew up a document in Spanish, copy whereof is annexed, ordering the rest to sign it or immediately to leave the island." And especially this from the declaration of N. C. Gibbs, in which he speaks of the document, and affirms the following: "I have since seen here the translation of the paper which Dias signed, a paper which I know was sent to the Department of State of the United States by Mr. Shelton, as soon as he received it from me in February, 1855, and also a copy of the copy signed by Lang and myself, and retained by Dias, and a translation of it procured by Mr. Shelton from said department, and from said translations it appears that such papers are substantially the same."

The Americans having assented to the right of Venezuela to the island, and being left at liberty to continue, conditionally, working out the guano, Colonel Dias departed, leaving on the island no more than one officer, attended by ten soldiers numbering as many muskets, together with a four-pounder piece. What has already been related then took place.

Now, then, let us revert to three periods of time: the arrival of the former Venezuelan schooner, the occurrences after its departure and until the appearance of the second one, and the facts attending the arrival of the latter, and inquire whether it be possible that violence should have been offered to the Americans? It is a morally and physically impossible fact, standing in contradiction of what the world knows of the courage, of the daring, of the love of property, and of the other qualities which mark the American character, that, with the elements of power which the Americans had at command, twenty-five soldiers, with Colonel Dias's single small vessel, should have reduced to fear eighty men, armed with every form of weapon, masters of an island, for the defense of which they relied on three vessels supplied with artillery, threatened, in the possession of their own, with having their property wrested from them, and with interruption in the peaceable exercise of an industry from which they expected great profits and fabulous wealth. The violence which annuls contracts is that which neither can be avoided nor causes empty fear. Who, then, shall say that eighty men, under most favorable circumstances, were not in a condition to defy twenty-five men at every disadvantage, or, at least to relieve themselves from their fears by a withdrawal from the island? But, it may be asked, they made some show at least of resistance, to evince their sense of the unlawful order which commanded them to depart? Nothing of the kind. They appeal to Colonel Dias's benevolence. They beg of him permission to continue taking in guano. They thank him for it in courteous words; compel him to eat with them, and add a few presents bespeaking their gratification. Was this the natural conduct of men who had yielded to compulsion; of men who must have been excited and enraged by the act of those who had just wrung from them so important an acknowledgment; men who could have room for no other thought than that of wreaking signal revenge; men who, in the act itself, would have proceeded to protest and demand reparation, supposing that they had not made the protest before Colonel Dias himself? But they went further in their exhibition of compliance and good will. As Colonel Dias, from the small number of his force, entertained great fears for its safety, he requested the Americans to put their arms under his charge, and they acceded to the request. To crown the whole of the transaction, they pledged themselves to give the garrison all the assistance which it might require.

In the second period, between the 13th and the 21st of December, ten men only were detailed to keep watch over the island. The facility of baffling their charge, and even driving them from the post, became still greater; because, in proportion as the force of Venezuela decreased, just so was that of the Americans increased by the arrival of additional vessels. The three which were at the island on the 13th, stood five by the 31st of December.

By the reinforcement supplied by the second schooner, the garrison then amounted to twenty-five men, a number equal to that which had been originally detailed. The American force had also increased, and from what cause has already been stated.

But it is not necessary to go out of the question for arguments to prove that they had everything in their favor, and that they did not seek to offer any resistance. Let the statement made to the Department of State by Shelton himself on the 14th of May, 1855, speak for itself:

"It has been asserted that we admitted the right of Venezuela to Aves Island, and that of Colonel Dias to drive us away from it! In other words, that we were violators of the territory, and this, too, in the paper which Dias gave to Captain Gibbs. Entirely frivolous, and more than frivolous, is such a pretense. We could have resisted Dias, at the cost of a few lives on both sides. Perhaps we should have done so; we believe that we could have easily captured the whole of his force, soldiers and vessels included, had we had recourse to arms and the spilling of blood. But we preferred to rely on the protection of our country. We yielded to Dias's orders because he was an officer of a sister republic of America, with which our country was at peace, acting under her authority and with a public force. We suggest to you, and to the President, that our moderation was commendable; the orders and conduct of Captain Dias were unnecessarily harsh; his soldiers took possession of some of our tools, utensils, materials, and provisions, driving away the laborers from the cabins. The losses which we have suffered in consequence of this, amount to many thousands of dollars. We were prevented from taking in the guano which was ready to be stowed aboard of our vessels, and constrained by the military force to abandon the island, utterly failing to load some of our vessels, whilst others had to take in but a part of their cargo. The extensive contracts, therefore, which we have made to furnish guano cannot be executed, and hence we have suffered heavy injury. The salaries of our laborers, who could do nothing on account of this unlawful and unjust interruption, amount together to a heavy sum. The whole of the expenses which we have incurred in the business is a dead loss. We have had to pay forfeit for charters and expenses of demurrage and damages; besides all this, the consequences which have directly resulted to us from the outrage, are such that they may be easily foreseen by any merchant. They are embarrassing, and may well lead to our ruin were not a speedy satisfaction granted to us. We beg of you to consider the whole matter, and we trust that it will induce you to take immediate steps for our protection."

Here it is laid down by the Americans themselves, and with boundless arrogance, that they might, and even should, have resisted Colonel Dias, and that they deemed it an easy thing to capture both him and all his force, including his vessels. Thus speaks Shelton, although the Venezuelan officer had but a single vessel under his command. According to his showing, his enormous expenses, his numerous laborers, the ruinous consequences of his submission, the frivolous pretense of Colonel Dias, the consciousness of his rights and of his physical force, the certainty of his victory, confidence in the protection of the powerful United States, the important interests of every kind involved in his business, and the lawfulness of his occupation; each and all of these impelled him to prevent the interruption to his undertaking. But, as they did not act in this way, and as he, who has it in his power, and holding it to be his duty, to do one thing, yet performs the reverse of it, may well charge himself with the consequences, it will not appear strange that Venezuela should maintain that they, if perchance they had any right, which is denied, stripped themselves of that right by their own will, and are bound to put up with the consequences of their own acts. No one will believe that they obeyed, in consideration of the fact that Colonel Dias was an officer of a sister republic of America, at peace with their country, and was acting under the authority and through the public force of that republic. Persons, convinced of the rectitude of their conduct, and of an intended unjust violence against them, would not have abstained from the use of their force against any one thus attempting to offend them, and especially against the agents of a small and weak Spanish-American republic, as they are all small and weak, which from those very circumstances could not impress them with much respect. We find the proof of this in the fact that they have explored other national guano islands and taken that article from them, without any regard for the rights of their lawful owner. What, they, who in the pursuit of gain, did not hesitate to commit a *tort*, for they had been clandestinely exporting guano from other islands of Venezuela, would have abstained from justly repelling a causeless injury inflicted by functionaries of that State, in the transactions of Aves Island! But let us suppose them controlled by a feeling of humanity. What stood in the way of their leaving the island and entering protest, reserving to themselves the rights which they now claim to have, instead of using the permit as they did, and thence disqualifying themselves at all points, for denying Venezuela a right, which they recognized, while on the island?

The result of all that has been said is that the departure of the Americans was not the upshot of a lawless and unjustifiable act, but, on the contrary, the consequence of one assented to and authorized by themselves. They did not then, nor afterwards, make opposition or enter protest, either against the document or the order to leave. And if they did, where is it? Why has it not been presented? For what time and for what use is it held back?

Mr. Eames attributes great importance to the argument that, "if the claimants were, as against Venezuela, lawfully in possession of the island when Venezuela found them, then surely they may rightfully claim full reparation for being driven away by her public force," because neither the fact or its inference has been either rebutted or denied, nor yet has there been adduced any law, ordinance, or decree of the republic, with the violation of which they are charged, and that, therefore, the absence of such affirmations must be taken as an acknowledgment.

Even though there were no express law forbidding the entrance, appropriation, and advantages referred to, still no one could suppose them to be lawful, for the following reason:

"Every State, therefore, has not only the right of sovereignty, (*imperium et potestas publica,*) that is, the conjunction of all the sovereign rights and powers necessary to the ends of the State, but it is capable also of acquiring and holding property. The right of State property (*jus in patrimonium reipublicæ,*) consists in the power of excluding all other States, or foreign individuals, from the use and appropriation of the territory and of all things lying therein. The objects of this right are not only, first, the common property of the society of which the State is composed, the public domain or the public property, properly so called (*patrimonium reip. publicum*) things, the property of which so belongs to the State, that the use of them, like that of private property, is exclusively and immediately destined for the ends of the State; but also, second, the estates or the property of individuals, (private property, *patrimonium privatum,*) put under the protection of the State, as things that may and should equally subserve, in case of need, the attainment of a general end; and lastly, property without an owner, (*adespota,*) constituting a part of the territory of the State, which is to be considered as unoccupied or abandoned, in reference to that State only and to its subjects, but not in reference to foreign States or individuals." (Klüber, vol. 1, p. 108.)

"The State property is coextensive with the whole territory of the State, namely, with that portion of the earth, with its appurtenances, over which the State independently and exclusively exercises the right of sovereignty."

"Not only the public property and that of individuals, but the property also which has no owner (*adespota*) and which is found in the territory are at the disposal and in the sovereign power of the State. Now, all things included within the territory being referable to one of these three classes, the general rule obtains that everything which exists in the territory of a State is adjudged to be subject to the sovereignty of said State until proof to the contrary. For this reason, not only the inhabited soil, but uncultivated districts also, and the seas, contained within the boundaries of States, constitute a part of its territory, and all the products, natural or created by human industry, which the territory embraces, belong to the State."

"By virtue of the right of property the government may, to the exclusion of all strangers, not only possess and use the territory of the State, but also dispose of it at will, and increase it by the right of accession."

"The right of State property being independent of all foreign influence, the result is, 3dly, that the State may exclude every stranger, not only from the occupation of things which have no owner, (*adespota,*) and from the use of its territory in cases of necessity, but also from any other use that might be made of them, without the other party imflicting any injury, in any manner, upon him; such, for instance, as in cases of transit or residence, of commerce, settlement, or acquisition. The State is free not to allow such uses save under certain conditions and restrictions, such, for instance, as that of allegiance, of the payment of certain imposts, of subjection during sojourn in the territory to the laws of the land, particularly to the right of escheat, (*droit d'aubaine,*) to treatment as a temporary subject, &c. If, in some States, policy, self-interest, or the humanity of the government have induced it not rigorously to exercise those rights; foreigners cannot, therefore, require such deference as a matter of right, unless by virtue of a convention, which cannot be supplied even by relations of good neighborhood. To arrogate such a use to one's self would be to violate territory and incur a treatment appropriate to an offender."

[These passages are extracted from Klüber, Modern Law of Nations of Europe, tit. 2, section 1, chap. 1, property of the State.]

"Every nation has a right, peculiar to itself, as well as exclusive, to the dominion of the whole of the territory which it occupies. This right embraces two things: 1st. The domain, by virtue of which the nation may use, for itself alone, the territory for its own wants, dispose of it, and draw from it all the advantages of which it is capable. 2dly. The empire, or the right of sovereign command, by which it ordains and controls, at will, everything that transpires in the land.

"The right of absolute domain is necessarily a peculiar and exclusive one; because, if one have a full right to dispose, as he pleases, of a thing, it follows that others have obsolutely no right to that thing; for, if the latter had any, the former could not freely dispose thereof. The private domain of individuals may in various ways be limited and restricted by the laws of the State—and it is invariably so by the eminent domain of the sovereign—but the general domain of the nation is full and absolute, seeing that there exists no authority on earth from which it can receive any limitation. As a consequence, therefore, it excludes all right on the part of foreigners; and, as the rights of one nation demand respect at the hands of other nations, so no nation can claim any right to the country of another nation, nor dispose of it or of anything which it contains, without the consent of the latter nation. The national domain, by a lawful title, extends over whatsoever the nation may possess. It embraces its former and original possessions and all the acquisitions which it may have secured by titles just in themselves or admitted as such among the nations, as by cessions, purchases, conquests in lawful war, &c. And by possessions of a nation, we mean not the lands alone, but also all the rights which that nation enjoys." (Vattel, Law of Nations, lib. 2, cap. 7.)

"When a nation has duly occupied a territory the right of property which, *ipso facto,* it acquires to all it parts, authorizes their use to the exclusion of all strangers, and the disposal thereof in any manner, provided it shall not injure the rights of third parties." (Marten's Law of Nations, tome 1.)

"The country inhabited by a nation constituted into a political society belongs to that nation by virtue of its right to exclude all the other nations. Two essential elements are included in this right—the domain, by which alone the nation can use the country for its wants and dispose of it for every necessary object, and the empire, or right of sovereignty and command, by which it ordains and controls at will all the transactions of the land." (Olmeda y Lem, Elements of Public Law of Peace and War, vol. 1.)

"A State, independently of the exercise of sovereignty over its territory, has the right of acquiring and possessing property."

"The right of property includes the right of excluding all foreign States or individuals from the use and disposal of the territory, and of all things therein lying, or of prescribing laws and conditions for those to whom the State may grant such uses." (Diplomatic Treatise by a Former Minister, vol. 2)

"The effects of domain consist in vesting a nation with the exclusive right of enjoying its forests, mines, fisheries, and of generally appropriating to itself all the products of its lands and waters, whether ordinary, extraordinary, or accidental; the right of permitting passage or navigation through them, or allow it under determined conditions, saving always the rights of necessity and of innocent use as well as those defined by treaties or usage; the right of imposing taxes on travelers or navigators for the use of roads, bridges, causeways, canals, ports, wharves, &c.; the right of exercising jurisdiction over all sorts of persons within its territory; and the right of requiring entering or passing vessels to pay the accustomed honors in recognition of its sovereignty." (Bello, Principles of International Law.)

"The exclusive right of every independent State to its territory and other property rests in the original title acquired by occupation, conquest, or cession, and subsequently confirmed by the presumption resulting from the lapse of time, or by treaties or other compacts with foreign States."

"This exclusive right includes the public property or the domain of the State, and things belonging to individuals or corporations within its territorial limits."

"The right of the State to its public property or domain is absolute, and it excludes that of its own subjects as well as that of other nations. The right of national property with respect to things belonging to private individuals or to corporations within its territorial limits is absolute, inasmuch as it excludes that of other nations, but with respect to the members of the State it is merely superior, and constitutes what is defined as the eminent domain." (Wheaton's Elements.)

"When a nation takes possession of a territory which belongs to no one it is deemed to occupy empire, sovereignty, and mastery over that territory at one and the same time, because, admitting that it is free and independent, it cannot be its intention at the time of establishing itself in that territory to leave to the other nations the right to command, or any of the prerogatives whatsoever which constitute sovereignty. The whole of the circuit to which a nation extends its dominion constitutes the limits of its jurisdiction, and is called its territory." (Lectures on Natural and International Law, de Felice.)

The laws hereinafter laid down, and ruling both in Spain and Venezuela, were also violated by those who made entry in Aves Island and other national islands, besides the principles of the law of nations already quoted, which are so many laws to the observance of which the nations are reciprocally bound.

"Waif property, (*bienes mostrencos*,) the movable or self-moving property that is found to have been lost or abandoned, and the owner of which cannot be ascertained, is called *mostrencos* in Spanish, because it is to be pointed out, exhibited, and published, in order that the owner may be informed of its discovery and claim his right."

"Waif property is not to be confounded with vacant or with *ab intestate* property. Vacant property is that, which being immovable, has no ascertained owner; *ab intestate* property is that which remains without an owner through the demise of one who has left no will, and who has neither descendants, ascendants, nor collaterals to succeed to his rights. This three-fold class of property is alike in this—that all of them lack owners, ascertained owners at least, whilst there is this distinction—that waifs are movable, landed estates immovable, and that *ab intestate* property may be both movable and immovable. Besides this, property may be in the condition of a waif through loss or estray; it may be vacant for causes sometimes unascertained; and again, it may be *ab intestate* from the death of the owner. Notwithstanding this, all these properties are commonly known under the general name of '*mostrencos*' property, to be pointed out, made patent, and reclaimed."

"By the law of nations the '*mostrenco*,' vacant, and *ab intestate* property ought to belong to the first occupant, because it is really *res nullius*, no man's property; but by the positive law, princes reserving to themselves the right of occupation, have appropriated it as their own; and that which belonged to no one they have, not without reason, applied for the common benefit. Our legislation has moved in this course, and it gives to such property the forms which we are about to exhibit." (Escriche's Law Dictionary.)

If the authority of Venezuelan law be called for, although all the quotations herein made work as law, we refer to the prohibitions involved in the following paragraphs of the law on seizures of the 10th of May, 1839, and in force in the year 1854:

"ART. 2. The penalty of seizure shall extend to everything that may have been landed, or may be found landing without a lawful permit or landing, or intended to be landed without a manifest and a written permit of the proper custom-house or competent authorities in ports not declared open, on coasts, in bays, creeks, or rivers, in canoes, boats, or other crafts, of what tonnage soever; and the vessel itself shall incur the same penalty, with all its tackle and apparel."

"ART. 8. To all the effects of the foreigner which may have been landed, and which may be found concealed, collected, stored, or deposited, or in any other manner whatsoever in the houses, bays, stations, or other points of the coast or uninhabited points removed from the inspections of the custom-houses and of the ports of entry, which places lie under suspicion of fraud from their locality and their proximity to bays, creeks, rivers, or ports not open to entry."

"ART. 9. To every foreign vessel, with its tackle and apparel and cargo, which may be detected anchored in any of the ports not open to entry in any roadstead, bay, creek, or river, without permit from some custom-house, for the purpose of receiving cargo of the produce of the country in conformity with the exportation law.

"ART. 10. To every national or foreign vesssel which may prove to have made a voyage from the ports or coasts of the republic to any foreign point without a lawful clearance, and to every vessel, national or foreign, that may prove to have sailed directly from foreign ports to a point or to a port on the coast not open to entry for importation."

Article first of the law of the 28th of April, 1854: "Immediately as a vessel will have moored in any of the ports open to foreign trade, it shall be visited by the collector, or by such deputy appointed to that end, and by the chief of inspectors, where such shall be employed, accompanied by a chief and one, or more than one, inspector. If the vessel should have come from a foreign port and with a cargo, the captain shall be held to exhibit his letter of clearance and the manifest of the cargo, on which must be stated the name of the vessel, the nation to which it belongs, the captain's name, that of the port or point from which it comes, the number of packages which make up the cargo, specifying whether they are boxes, barrels, trunks, hogsheads, &c.; stating, also, the numbers and marks, and the port for which the articles are intended, the number of the consignees, in accordance with the bills of landing that may have been signed. There shall, besides, be appended to the manifest a list of the ship's provisions and the other stores on board, for sails, rigging, and other uses of the same. After the visit, one or more than one inspector will remain on board. If the vessel shall have come on ballast, the captain will merely be required to exhibit his clearance and a detailed list of the provisions and stores for ship use, and a formal and rigorous examination shall be had to ascertain whether she really sails a ballast."

We further invoke the authority of all the other articles of this law, a compliance with which can only be enforced in ports open for foreign trade. Equally applicable are those which have force in relation to all the requirements which it prescribes as to the manner of carrying on exportation, and especially that article of the law of May 6, 1833, as follows:

"ART. 1. No growth or production of any kind, intended for foreign countries or ports, shall be exported except from ports open to foreign commerce."

The law of the 11th of May, 1854, upon maritime inspection, amending the law of 1843, which contains a like provision, makes it the duty of the revenue cutters to observe the following requirement of the sixth article:

"It shall be the duty of the captains of the revenue cutters to take to the nearest port of entry—

"1st. All foreign vessels, which they may find in any ports not opened to foreign commerce, having on board goods, growths, and products of any kind."

"4th. All national or foreign vessels, navigating from our coasts to any foreign port, with or without cargo; provided that they shall exhibit no documents showing that they have cleared from some custom-house."

According to the law of the 15th of April, 1854, the ports open for importation and exportation were those of Ciudad Bolivar, Laguayra, Puerto Cabello, La Vela, Maricaibo, and Barcelona, for importation for consumption only; and for exportation, the ports of Cumaná, Carupano, Cariaquito, Caño Colerado, Barrancas, Pampatur, Juan Griego, Soledad y Cumarebo; and, temporarily, the ports of Guiria and Maturin, until the establishment of custom-houses at Cariaquito and Caño Colerado.

With the exception of Margarita, there is no island of Venezuela in which ports have been designated and opened for foreign commerce, nor for any other object of any nature whatsoever; it is, therefore, evident that the Americans could not lawfully, and without violation of all the principles and laws which have been adduced, either anchor at Aves Island, land thereon, or introduce houses and implements, &c., certainly much less apply to their own benefit and export a product of the territory, or one inherent to it, such as is guano.

Mr. Eames thinks that Venezuela cannot, with any show of reason, deny the acknowledgment, to which we have already referred, "because it is a fact of universal notoriety that these claimants in landing on Aves Island in June, 1854, and proceeding to make the best use that they could of that desert island, did nothing more than what all men had been at liberty to do, and which they would have done whenever they might have deemed it expedient, at any period anterior to the existence of the republic of Venezuela, and during that of its existence, without any kind of impediment, prohibition, or reclamation of any government, and less from all, from the government of Venezuela."

Mr. Eames has been contented to assert these facts without adding any proof of their consistency, even of the slightest kind. But in view of the multitude of Spanish laws which forbid access to the possessions of his Catholic Majesty in America, and which are still in vigor in all cases in which they have not been supplanted by other enactments of Colombia and Venezuela, in which States, though the rigorous policy of the ancient metropolis may have been relaxed, this prohibition has been kept up in the manner already explained, it is no easy task to secure belief for such assertions as these. It may be that, in some cases, foreign vessels, driven by stress of weather and by storms, or availing of the circumstances of locality and of the seclusion of the island, may have approached it, and that masters and passengers both may have visited it, as was done, it is said, by the Dutch for the purpose of fishing and gathering birds' eggs. These facts, however, admitting their veracity, which we do not admit, would not make in the least against the dominion of Spain or of Venezuela, because as transient and clandestine visits only are here spoken of, without the slightest idea of appropriating the island and putting themselves in lieu of its owner, without his privity, they could in no degree influence the integrity of his rights. If evidence were adduced that the fact of such visits came to the knowledge of one or the other of the States, and that they, in spite of the knowledge that every one made such use of the island as was exclusively reserved for the Spaniards or the Venezuelans, tolerated such use, then, indeed, might it be argued that they had made abandonment of it, since it seems to imply a tacit renunciation of the advantages of ownership. But Mr. Eames never can succeed in vindicating such a position, nor yet that of the Americans and other foreigners in arrogating to themselves the rights of dominion over the island; and, certainly, strange would it be that being derelict, as is supposed, and being convertible to gainful uses, it never occurred to any nation, not even to the United States, to which its acquisition would have been so advantageous, according to Shelton, to take possession of it and reduce it to its jurisdiction. It is well known that prescription rests on good faith, lawful titles, continuous possession for length of time; and that, as there is no one qualified to determine its duration among States, unless it be by mutual consent, many public writers do not admit it to be an instrument for either the acquisition or the loss of rights, holding that universal law does not sanction it, nor positive law introduce it; that, indeed, the powers frequently invoke it, and provide against its effects by protests to secure their rights, which presupposes in them the obligation of breaking their silence when that which they have no intention of abandoning is usurped by any one; that their language, on this head, has been various and contradictory, and that as no treaty or no usage has determined the time required by prescription, nothing could be gained by admitting it in mere theory.

"Still, we must confess, that it is often difficult to apply usucaption and prescription among nations when these rights rest upon a presumption derived from a diuturnity of silence. Every one knows that it is generally very dangerous for a weak State to put forth the merest glimmer of pretension to the possessions of a powerful monarch. It is, therefore, no easy thing to base a lawful presumption of abandonment on the circumstance of a long silence. Add to this that the head of a society generally not having it in his power to alienate what belongs to the State, his silence cannot work detriment to the nation or to his successors, even though it were held sufficient to warrant a presumption of abandonment on his part. For, in such case, the question would be whether the nation have forgotten to supply the silence of its chief, or whether it has participated in it by its tacit approbation." (Vattel, Law of Nations.)

Both regret and astonishment has Mr. Eames experienced that the Secretary of Foreign Relations should have said "the Americans could never complain of their expulsion, unless they could show that it was lawful for them to enter on the island and export from it the guano which it contains."

What! Does Mr. Eames forget that no one can justly deem himself the owner of a thing of which he has possessed himself by virtue of a title which, by its nature, cannot convey the right of property, nor yet of a thing which he has wrested into his power without any title at all? The observation was most natural when speaking of a claim which is especially based on the circumstances of the Americans having landed on the island, of their occupation of it, and their working upon it—a thing that, it is assumed, any one had the right to do, and which for many years had been done upon convenient occasions before and since the existence of Venezuela, without the infringement of any law and the violation of any jurisdiction—a legitimate pursuit, the continuance of which it is supposed was disturbed and broken up by the forces of Venezuela! It is necessary, therefore, to ascertain the reasons which they had to imagine that Aves Island had been abandoned by its owners, and that, being *res nullius*, it was open to first occupation. This inquiry ought to have suggested itself to them before their visit and settlement on the island, because by such only could they have gathered the conviction that they were about to enter upon a lawful pursuit. This, notwithstanding it does not appear from the documents produced by the legation that they proceeded with that usual prudence which would have controlled any in the like circumstances. What does appear from their concerted declarations is that various American vessels went sailing over the waters of the Gulf of Mexico, and to other parts, in search of guano islands; that one of them found Aves Island; and that subsequently, without further concern, they proceeded to work it for their own benefit. Their occupation of it was not a peaceful one; they went to tempt fortune, with the hope, no doubt, that their occupation being clandestine, would not be discovered, led on, as they were, by the desire of easy and inexpensive gain. But unfortunately for them the event was contrary to their anticipations. The government was informed of their acts there, and in other parts, and it took measures to put a stop to the injury. Neither the possession nor the property of a certain thing can be found, in its entireness, in several individuals; so that, in case that Aves Island belonged to any one, the Americans, who laid hands upon it, could not have acquired a right to it; and then, even if they were operating in good faith, which is denied, no injury was inflicted upon them in the act of excluding them from the enjoyment of such property. *Non facit injuriam qui jure suo utitur.* It was the right of the owner not to allow others to make use of productions inherent to his property. "It is certain that, according to admitted principles, possession is exclusive. In the same manner that I cannot occupy the spot on which you are, and that you may not sit down on the chair which I fill; even so two persons cannot entirely possess any object at the same time. One possession necessarily excludes another possession bearing the same nature and resting on the same pretensions. If you take possession of my stead, I cease to possess it; if I continue possessing it, you cannot possess. But what is impossible is, that two coequal possessions, both of the same nature, should concur in one and the same act; the one necessarily rejects the other." (Troplong, De la Prescription.)

"As it is impossible that when two individuals contend for the property of one and the same thing, each one of them can have an exclusive right to that property; so neither can it happen that if two individuals who contend for the possession of one and the same thing, each one of them, singly, should have a right to that possession. Hence there being but one only that can be the true owner, there is only one real possessor; whence it follows that if he who possesses it is discriminate from the owner, his possession cannot be anything but an usurpation." (Merlin, Rèpertoire de Droit.)

Although Mr. Eames does not admit that the burden of proof lies upon him, he has withal always alleged, probably to justify the conduct of the Americans, that Aves Island, though it may have been discovered in remote times, was never taken into the possession nor brought under the jurisdiction of any power; that it was a thing derelict, and that, therefore, the discoverers of the guano on that island had a right to appropriate it to themselves, without detriment to any one. But one of two things, either this proposition ought not to have been laid down, or, laid down, it ought to have been backed by the necessary proof; because the *onus probandi* was either incumbent upon Venezuela, as has been pretended, and, in that case, the Americans were not bound to open their lips even in their own behalf, or the burden lay on the Americans, and, in this view, little would it have availed them to allege the exception. It is an axiom of jurisprudence that he who avails himself of an exception passes from the attitude of a defendant to that of a plaintiff, and assumes all the obligations of the latter. Certainly it would be very just to invade the property of another man, and then say to the owner, "this is mine, if you do not prove to me that it is yours!"

Mr. Eames insists that Venezuela is the aggressor, and that the claimants are the victims. This no doubt grows out of the fact, that he takes for granted the very question in debate. The question whether the island is, or is not, a portion of the public domain; whether it belongs to the country or to the Americans, and, in either case, he avers the contrary. (?) He argues *con.*, and the republic maintains the *pro.* She maintains that the real aggressors were the explorers, the invaders, and usurpers of another one's property. She argues that they were the violators of the principles of the law of nations, and of the laws above adduced; that they were those who, in an armed attitude, without authority from any sovereign, in the prosecution of a voyage of discovery to guano islands, introduced themselves in Aves, Hermanos, Testigos, Munjes, and other groups of Venezuelan islands; that they were those who held no consideration in respect; those who failed to take the most obvious precautions in the act of proceeding in a hazardous undertaking; those who cloaked their operations in darkness; those who skulked from the most visible parts to go to others that were less so; those who had not the hardihood to defend themselves, even by the allegation of the merest right; those who confessed their wrong; those who resorted to beseechings, so that they might be allowed to take in more guano; those who left their own to enter the country of another people; those who were found armed at all points; those who had gathered together a large number of laborers; those who, in the act of entering a foreign territory, committed an act of violence; those who, in vindication of their conduct, have not alleged a single, well established reason; those who readily yielded to the merest intimation to them to depart; those who spontaneously admitted the absence of all title on their part, and the existence of Venezuela's dominion; those who forewent the sacred right of lawful defense to resist the supposed interruption of their pursuit; those who committed other depredations, if possible; those, finally, who, as the sum of these observations will show, have stood forth in the light, and with all the characteristics, of piracy.

It is not conceivable that the republic should be styled the aggressor in this case, even had she, in order to drive them away, really applied force, a course which, on one side, the proceedings of those men would have amply warranted, whilst it would, on the other, have been justified by the rights, and even the duty, of the republic. To pretend that individuals armed for war, could claim the right to approach places not open to commerce, to land there with their armaments, to import therein various articles, to settle on them to make use of a substance which is an accretion of the territory, to carry off, in reality, several cargoes of that substance, and that Venezuela, the owner of those places, should have been called upon for a public fore-announcement of her title and right, before she could complain and claim back; to pretend, lastly, that she was called on to give notice thereof to them, and her representative to their government, informing them that she was about to organize and dispatch an armed force there, is to attempt to establish, between the Americans and the republic, a difference to which no State, jealous of its own dignity, can never consent; for all men are reciprocally held to the observance of consideration, respect, and duty among themselves, and he who is the first to fail in such observance, concludes himself from all right of complaint if they are not maintained in his regard.

In a passage of the note, to which this is in answer, it is said that Venezuela sent out an expedition to look out for the Americans, find them, drive them from the island, and discharge their vessels, at the cannon's mouth, and despoil them of their houses, "with depredation on their property." Mr. Eames has not been satisfied with visiting military agents of the country with most serious imputations of violence and fraud, but he proceeds, in a note to the government of Venezuela, to say to it that it has ordered "robbery." The action of the United States which, in the 1849, resulted in the expulsion of Minister Pengrin, for indulgence in language no way respectful to American functionaries, though not within the excess to which Mr. Eames has allowed himself to go, holds out a salutary example, and one worthy of imitation as the best corrective for outrages which a diplomatic agent may take the liberty to commit, keeping sacred the bounds of moderation and respect, and defining in the most efficacious way the path which he ought to pursue in the prosecution of his charge. It is to be hoped that the Cabinet of Washington will turn its attention to the manner in which Mr. Eames treats the government of the republic to which he is accredited, and will compel him to make reparation by a recall of the offensive language, considering that Venezuela, astonished, and patient beyond the requirements of her own self-respect, refrained from acting for herself, as was done in Washington in the case adduced, merely to avoid complicating the question in debate with a novel incident—a sacrifice offered to her desire for the unalterable maintenance of the friendly relations between both countries; otherwise there could be no other answer to such a charge.

Passing by this insult, the State is not accountable to any one for its acts, provided they do not affect the rights of others. Hence it is not called on to go into an investigation of the orders and instructions of Colonel Dias, and the reasons which may have justified his dispatch to Aves Island. If the execution of his duties have resulted in unjustifiable damages to any one, let them be asserted; but beyond this, let no one claim liberty.

On the other hand, it can be no cause for astonishment that the Americans should be asked for proofs of the lawfulness of their conduct. They are the plaintiffs; they accuse Venezuela of having disturbed their enjoyment of a right; they say that they were unlawfully expelled; they look for a reparation for their pretended grievances; they maintain that Aves Island belonged to no one; they allege that things derelict belong to the first occupant; they assert that the island was never claimed by any power; they affirm that it had never been reduced into the possession, nor submitted to the jurisdiction, of any one. They speak, besides, of the large outlays which they made, and of the great losses incurred; of the consequences, immediate and remote, of their ejectment; and, in virtue of all these, they claim, from the republic, an indemnification not yet definitely set forth. Is it too much, therefore, to ask them to make good all they advance? We confess ignorance of any principle of law which puts upon the defendant the burden of proof. On this head, see what Merlin says of the word "proof:"

"In this matter, jurisprudence admits three great principles. The first is, that he who lays down a fact is held to the proof, because facts are not to be presumed, and consequently the denial of the adverse party is sufficient in itself to warrant the idea of their non-existence; whence it follows that the denial requires no proof. The second is, that the plaintiff must prove the fact on which he grounds his complaint, and that, in like manner, the defendant is held to prove the fact on which he rests his defense. The third principle is, that he who lawfully possesses a thing is not bound to prove that it belongs to him, but that he who disputes the right to the property is held to make proof of the fact, or of the titles on which he grounds his claim."

By all three of these principles, the claimants are compelled to meet the obligation incumbent upon them, and, in consonance with universal jurisprudence, to prove the facts which they advance, to prove the facts on which they rest their demand, to prove the facts on which they stand to contest Venezuela's right to the proprietorship, or to the usufruct of the island.

Mr. Eames appears to think that Venezuela cannot allege the agreement or document signed by Lang and Gibbs "because its enlightened government will assuredly never recognize that, acting through the agency of high functionaries, the commanders of its public forces, it entered into agreements with usurpers and with violators of law, engaged in depredations upon the property of Venezuela, and caught *flagrante delicto*, in the violation of its law and its territorial sovereignty."

On this point Mr. Eames mistakes. The convention, or "agreement," since Mr. Eames has chosen to give it that name in his note of the 20th of December, is an act which cannot be imputed to the government, because Colonel Dias's commission had a special character, and his orders prevented him from granting such a permit. Thus he acted without any authority of any kind, and therefore he could not bind the government by his act. [!] Besides this, from the moment that the government became informed of what had been done, it unconditionally disapproved it, and stood free from all co-responsibility with its delegate, that had arrogated to himself functions which did not belong to him. Still, this notwithstanding, his error grew out of an excess of forbearance, and even of kindness, for the Americans, not to mention the stress in which he found himself from shortness of provisions for his garrison, with which the Americans offered to supply him. Guilty though they were, and deserving of an entirely different proceeding, seeing that it was not adopted, they ought to have been, as indeed they were, grateful at the time, to him who treated them with such consideration. In spite of the evident nullity of the permit to which allusion has been made, there can be no obstacle thrown up against the incontestable validity of the voluntary acknowledgment of Lang and Gibbs, made on the spot, that the island belonged, not to them, but to Venezuela. This voluntary acknowledgment they carried out by confirming in writing what they had stated in words, and made it every way ample to give a correct insight into their notion as to the proprietorship of the island. Let the paper permit be called "agreement," or whatsoever you please, it will still bear upon its face the clear and unequivocal proposition that Aves Island belongs to Venezuela.

They were, certainly, characterized as mere copies, those rejected depositions which Mr. Eames produced with his note of the 20th of December, 1856, and this because it is the proper name for transcripts of documents the authenticity of which is vouched for by no signature at the bottom, whether in the Department of State or in the American legation in Caraccas. Nothing of the kind is given to understand in even the official note which describes them.

When the question of proofs, as admitted in Venezuela, is spoken of, and when she is called on for no less a task than that of assuming a great burden upon herself, it is thought proper that they should at least accord with the provisions of her laws. According to those laws, "documents are public and private: public documents are instruments acknowledged before a register, or any other competent public officer, the acts of courts, duly authenticated, and all acts of public functionaries, and transcripts, copies, or certificates of said instruments of writing and said acts, legalized in the form prescribed by law.

"Extrajudicial statements of witnesses, or anticipatory certificates or vouchers shall not be admitted, unless those who have signed or certified them shall make appearance and publicly and judicially confirm the truth of their contents, in which case it shall be the right of the parties to cross-question those who have signed the documents. From this are excepted those declarations and proofs made by virtue of citation on the adverse party, on account of the impending departure of a witness, or of such persons as are called on to depose, or on account of malicious delay on the part of the plaintiff to come to trial, to be proved in the manner provided for by this code." (Code of Practice, 4th law, tit. 1, art. 13 and 16.)

It will be seen from the above, that the remark that the declarations had not been brought forward with those requirements, could have no other object than that of breaking the concluding force, which is attributed to them.

Mr. Eames denies the objection, namely, that the deponents have an interest in the claim, and that they are, *ipso facto*, incompetent; whilst he avers that, as salaried agents of the claimants, the courts of all countries hold them to be proper witnesses.

The objection still stands, even were the quotation above perfectly certain. Let it be borne in mind that the declarations were brought forward to invalidate the document signed for Colonel Dias, because, as it is said, it was procured by fraud and violence. If fraud and violence there were, they could have been exercised upon those persons only found on the island, namely, Lang, Gibbs, and the laborers. In fact, Lang and Gibbs were the individuals who signed the permit; and yet the attempt is made, through their verbal statements and those of other individuals, to defeat what they declared in writing. In the hypothesis that the violence and fraud were committed in respect to Lang, Gibbs, and their companions, and not to their principals, it is clear that the latter, who were in the United States, had nothing to do with it, and that the former are solely and exclusively the parties interested, even if it be only through their responsibility to their constituents. If a fact were spoken of, in which the claimants might have intervened, in the presence of their salaried agents, their testimony might be admitted in behalf of the constituents, although even then not without some difficulty; because the relations which grow out of subordination and dependence are too closely binding entirely to exclude the presumption of partiality from such a declaration. But this is not the case. Lang and Gibbs have deposed to acts in which they themselves were the actors, and to pretend to turn off the force of those depositions, because the selfsame persons afterwards contradicted them, is to put them in the attitude of parties and witnesses in the case.

The other witnesses are entirely blemished by this fact, namely, that being ignorant of the Spanish, a language in which Colonel Dias was compelled to speak and write, as he was equally ignorant of the English language, it was not in their power to understand a single word, except through the medium of an interpreter; a task which Lang performed, and consequently their declarations as to force, threats, &c., come into the category of recollections of Lang's conversations, or, what amounts to the same thing, they are nothing but the multiplied testimonies of Lang himself.

Before dismissing this point, it may not be out of place to mention a very significant circumstance. Mr. Eames, for reasons not known, suppressed Gibbs's deposition, as he did not transmit it with the other declarations in December last. The attention of the secretary of relations having been drawn to this, he observed, that of the two who signed the document, one had not deposed, and that the other assigned, as a motive for his conduct, things different from those stated by the other witnesses. At the time of his reply, Mr. Eames transmitted the declaration which had been left out without explaining the reason why it had been previously withheld; and then it was sent, not in manuscript, but printed on a paper, pieces of which had been cut out. The meaning of this it has been impossible to ascertain; and as the paper, in view of the caption at the top, was to contain nothing but some questions put to Gibbs, and his answers to them, and in view of the silence maintained on this point, it is lawful to infer that, in the mutilated portions, there was something that damaged the claim, whilst the object was to conceal it from the government.

Mr. Eames, in consequence of another observation of the Venezuelan note, in the relation to the absence of resistance and of protest by the parties, as also the failure immediately to claim against the effects of the pretended violence, not a claim for their property, as he understood it, proceeds to affirm that the parties did all of this.

The contrary fully appears from the frequently quoted as well as respectable testimony of the three officers of the Venezuelan navy, Colonel Dias, Lieutenant Pereira, and Commander Cotarro. Conviction may be enforced by the following reflection. Had the Americans believed themselves secure in their rights, they would not have failed to go to work and resist the landing of the Venezuelan force, excluding it from the occupation of their property, repelling it by the force of arms, or, at least, making some show of the reluctance with which they yielded to violence; stating to Colonel Dias himself the necessity, in which they were placed, of submitting to him, and then, stopping their work, depart from the island. What they did, instead of this, we have already shown, and repetition is unnecessary.

But as they did not put up a protest on the act itself, which would have been the proper time, they might have done so when they returned to their own country. In so doing they could have had no other object in view than the preparation of their claim, or that of their principals, against Venezuela; if it be true that they were conscious that their act had been one of a lawful character, not one of mere usurpation, and the removing of all doubt from their intention not to submit to the consequences of their spoliation, making use of such document when the occasion should offer for the discussion of this claim. If they did not do so then, for what time did they reserve it? And if they did so, why has it not been produced?

Mr. Eames took care to notice the protest of the individuals who went over to Aves Island in January, 1855, to take in cargoes of guano, which they were not allowed to do, as they found the island guarded by a Venezuelan force. Now, from the circumstance that other papers of this nature were not sent, we may well infer that that is the only one in existence. It also labors, in every respect, under the defects which have been pointed out because either its transmission is useless or it drives Mr. Eames into a circle of contradictions. It is for this reason that he has been asked clearly to State in whose behalf the claim of indemnification has been preferred, an information which cannot with justice be denied to the State which it is attempted to burden with the consequences of an unjustifiable responsibility.

All the witnesses are discredited, particularly Lang and Gibbs, for the good and incontestable ground specified by Mr. Eames himself when, in order to enforce the value of their testimony, he says "that they were the leading actors in the occurrences that took place." As such, and the act by which they signed the document which speaks against them, bearing all the characteristics of a voluntary one, that they should now allege that it is of no value, because it was the result of force and fraud, with the hope that it will be believed on the strength of their words, is a pretension which cannot be admitted, unless we would, at the same time, authorize man to sport with the most sacred acts and laugh at his fellow beings. In no case can a document be invalidated, under a plea of fraud and violence, by the mere say of him who signed it, and who, in spite of that say, is met by the best grounded presumptions.

The reasons assigned by those individuals for their conduct are not the same, neither do they accord with those which are assigned for it by what is termed the eye-and-ear-witnesses of the act, who were participants in it by the fact of consulting together in that act. Let us, however, cursorily examine their declarations, and ascertain whether it be or not possible to find in them some likelihood of error:

"Joshua F. Spofford, master of the bark Carlo Mauran, loading with guano on Aves Island, for account of Tappan and Philo S. Shelton, of Boston, says that a Venezuelan armed schooner arrived on the 13th of December, 1854, landed an armed force, and took possession of the island, lowering the American flag and hoisting in its place the banner of Venezuela, threatening, at the same time, every American there with expulsion from the island. Finally Colonel Dias drew up a document in Spanish, which he said was a permit for them to go on loading the guano provided they put their armament under his authority; that he was present when the tenor of the document was explained to Captain Gibbs, said Gibbs not understanding the Spanish language; that, according to the way in which it was explained to him, it was merely that Gibbs and Lang had to assist the garrison left on the island with supplies of water and provisions, and he was assured, in the most positive manner, that the document contained nothing that went to establish the existence of a title to the island in behalf of Venezuela; that he positively knows this fact, because Captain Gibbs asked him his opinion about it. Besides this, he certified that Dias insisted, if they did not sign the document, that they should have to leave the island forthwith; that Captain Gibbs, under these circumstances, was compelled to sign the document, with the hope that by doing so they would be allowed to load the vessels that were there, as well as those which they were expecting; that Gibbs then told the witness that if the document contained anything different from what had been explained to him, he did not suppose that a paper signed under such circumstances could be considered to be one of binding force." This declaration is dated "Boston, June 20, 1855," and acknowledged before Justice of the Peace Charles Horner.

This witness makes no mention of the employment of force, but he does of threat; nor does he speak of any reluctance on the part of the signers, or of any indications of resistance or opposition. He positively knew that the paper contained no admission of the title of Venezuela, because he was present when it was explained to Gibbs, and because he consulted him as to what he should do. He does not refer to Lang, and he was the only one who was consulted.

James Wheeler, in his first declaration made in Boston on the 8th of June, 1855, acknowledged by him before John Clark, justice of the peace, does not speak of Colonel Dias, nor of the document, nor of the departure from the island. He merely relates the breach of trust which he committed against Sampson, Tappan, and Philo S. Shelton, when employed by them in taking guano from a certain island in the Gulf of Mexico, he was informed that Captain Gibbs, by order of his constituents, had visited Aves Island and discovered a large deposit of guano; he returned to Boston, gave up the service of that company, and, revealing the secret of the discovery to Lang & Delano, prevailed upon them to send him with the brig Comery to procure guano there, and did procure it, arriving at the island before Gibbs's vessel.

In his second declaration of the 15th of June, 1855, acknowledged before Geo. B. Upton, J. P., he states that while he was on Aves Island the American flag was kept continually flying, and that the man-of-war Devastation having visited the island, he informed Captain D'Orsey that they held the island for the government of the United States, and that they hoped that he would protect them as citizens of that republic. He adds that the American flag was respected, and that D'Orsey informed him that they had the right to keep the island in the name of the United States.

The word of a witness who, from his own confession, stands forth as a betrayer, deserves to be held for little or naught.

The third deponent is George M. George, first mate of the brig M. H. Comery, and afterwards foreman for Lang & Delano, who acknowledged his declaration on the 1st of June, 1855, before Daniel Sharp, Jr., a notary public of the city of Boston. After many irrelevant details, he gives an account of Dias's arrival and landing; his taking possession of the island, and the drawing up of the document. He goes on setting forth that the other foremen were required to sign it under threat of expulsion, and that Lang and Gibbs signed it, the former in the name of Lang & Delano, and the latter in the name of P. S. Shelton, in bodily fear, and to prevent outrage and bloodshed! That the document having been signed, the Venezuela armed schooner left the island, having detailed a certain number of soldiers for shore service. That the same vessel returned about three weeks afterwards, and that the commander ordered all his people to leave the island within twenty-four hours, but that the next day being Sabbath day, they knocked off work. That on Monday they were surprised to find a guard with crossed bayonets at their cabin doors, in the guano pits, and on the wharf. That orders were given to the laborers to proceed to the pits at the usual hour, and to pass on to load the boats; but that the guard then ordered them to desist from all work, and that, as one of the laborers insisted on working, a Venezuelan struck him with a bayonet. That orders were then given to the foremen to immediately leave the island, with all the laborers under their charge, within a period of twenty-four hours, which was done by him, as he then was head foreman in the absence of said Lang, leaving ashore a large quantity of water, provisions, houses, the wharf, [the gangways?] and the boats, because time was not allowed them to carry them off.

This witness states that the document—the contents of which he does not describe—was signed through bodily fear, and to prevent outrage and bloodshed, without adducing any reason that could produce such fear, nor why, by signing it, they were preventing outrage and bloodshed. Although the foreman of the works, he was not even consulted by Lang and Gibbs, he being, like the former of these, an agent of Lang & Delano. Then he had no reason to inquire into what was occurring. His statement is inaccurate when he swears that the vessel in which Colonel Dias sailed to Aves Island returned thither three weeks afterwards, because Colonel Dias had come on board of the General Falcon, but the latter was the schooner Trece de Diciembre.

The next declaration is that of Charles H. Lang, foreman to Lang & Delano, and one of those who subscribed the document. The declaration is acknowledged in Boston, June 21, 1855, before Samuel Brackett, J. P. He, too, understood Spanish, having sailed for a number of years in the Pacific ocean, along the coasts of Peru; so that, according to the statement of the officers of Venezuela, they would readily have taken him to be a Spaniard, had he not declared that he was an American. So well did he understand the Spanish language, that he went on correcting a few slight mistakes that had crept into the document. Besides, neither has he denied this, nor have the witnesses referred to any one but Gibbs, when they speak of not understanding the Spanish language and the explanations which were made of the contents of the paper at the time when it was signed. This is so much the more evident from the fact, that in order to understand Colonel Dias, some interpreter was required, as he did not know the English, or they the Spanish, language.

"He deposes to the arrival of Dias, who hoisted the Venezuelan flag, in which particular he is in contradiction with Gibbs; and that Dias immediately insisted that they should depart from the island, and, seeing that they were not disposed to go off with such readiness, he made some show of his forces, such as putting his soldiers through the exercise, firing their guns, &c. That, finally, said Domingo Dias drew up a document in Spanish, copy of which was annexed, ordering the foremen to sign it or immediately to leave the island. That finding themselves unable to leave then, because they had no vessel that could carry him and some thirty laborers, citizens of the United States, he saw himself compelled to sign the document, not thinking that, the circumstances considered, it could be of any value except so far as it put them beyond the reach of outrage for the time. That a few days after he found an opportunity to proceed to the United States, and he did so to give an account of the occurrences to those who had employed him, Messrs. Lang & Delano, of the city of Boston."

He is the only deponent who expresses anything like unwillingness at the time to depart from the island, or who asserts that Dias made ostentation of his force, as, for instance, putting his soldiers through their maneuvers, &c., a false assertion, because, as has already been stated, the soldiers had not yet left the vessel for shore. He does not even hint that he was deceived as to the contents of the document, or that he was utterly unacquainted with the Spanish language; much less does he hint that violence was offered to him, or that he was put in bodily fear. The reason for his conduct was the want of vessels to take him and his laborers away, and for this reason he felt compelled to sign the paper, not considering it to be of any value save that, for the time, it protected them from outrage. The reason is a false one, because there were at the time three large vessels at anchor, one of which of eight hundred tons' burden, the other of five hundred tons, the former being amply sufficient to carry all the laborers, their apparatus and armament included. Besides this, the want of vessels could have had no other effect than that of delaying their departure, not of forcing them to the signature of the document.

"William P. Gibbs, master of a vessel, on the 23d of August, 1855, in the city of Boston, before Charles Herner, J. P., declares to the same effect as J. F. Safford, and almost in his very words. What is added by him to the declaration had, with some slight variations, already been stated in George McGeorge's deposition."

George W. Nickell's declaration refers neither to Colonel Dias's permit nor to the departure of the agents and laborers of the Boston companies. It merely sets forth the circumstance of his having sailed from New York on the 15th of January, 1855, for Aves Island, with the object of loading with a cargo of guano, which he was prevented from taking in, because he was forbidden doing so by the Venezuelan garrison of the island, from which he was ordered by the public force to depart.

This very singular protest does not mention the ground on which the protestant stands to urge the responsibility of Venezuela for the damages which he suffered on that occasion. Whose was Aves Island? Was it Lang & Delano's, whose agents arrived there first? Was it Shelton & Co.'s, whose representatives reached there at a later period? Was it George W. Nickell's, who went to the island in January, 1855? In order to maintain an attitude of consistency the legation has been compelled to sustain the rights of Lang & Delano alone, without attending to the fact, on the score of acquisition, that others, the agents of Shelton & Co., had seen it before, but had not taken possession of it. If in January, 1855, the island continued to be *res nullius*, the whole structure of Mr. Eames' claim falls to the ground, resting, as it does, on the principle that "the discoverers of guano in a derelict, uninhabited, and uninhabitable island, which was not included in the jurisdiction nor reduced into the possession of any power, had a right to land thereon and make use of it." This Mr. Nickell did not discover the guano; he neither took nor kept possession of it; he had no intention of retaining the island until he had exhausted that substance; he was not ordered to quit the island; he incurred no expenses in the undertaking; he did not present himself, for the first time, to the island until it was actually occupied by the public force of Venezuela. Lastly, he does not come within any of the cases applicable to the other claimants. The observations suggested by the discovery of this document among the others transmitted by Mr. Eames seem not to have deserved an answer, a silence which argues that he discovered no way of issue out of the difficulty.

The tardy and mutilated deposition of N. C. Gibbs was made on the 12th of April, 1856, before a notary of the city of New York, sixteen months after the occurrence of the facts which it relates. Although it ought not to engage the attention of the government, so long as no explanation is given of the reason why it was not added to the others, and how it happens to be mutilated by the clippings made in the paper, still it contains several important points, which strengthen the defense of Venezuela. For instance: "Dias landed one gun with its ammunition, and ten soldiers, armed with muskets and other weapons." "I told him (Dias), in precise and unequivocal language, that I would not leave the island, nor cease to gather guano, until I should be prevented from doing so by a superior force; that I would resist, and that he could not effect my expulsion with the force that he had there." "I told Dias that we were in possession, and had been so peaceably for several months, on a title which was good until some one showed a better one." "Dias stated that he interpreted and translated the paper to me, word for word." "Dias boasted that he would take us, vessels and all, to Venezuela to be judged for our violation of her laws and robbery of her property." "I fed the soldiers, and they did not molest us; I took the officer to my house and found him also, and I employed some of the soldiers in gathering guano, paying them in clothing and provisions." "I am bound to say that, in spite of Dias's threats, and the evident demonstration of his intention to carry them out, I did not sign the paper from any fear of personal consequences if I persisted to decline, or from any apprehension that, with the force which he then had on the island, he could either subdue or expel our people. Still I had reason to fear that he might make the attempt, and I wished to avoid extremities, which might have resulted in effusion of blood. Although I had no doubt that we could have taken him, his soldiers, and his armed schooner, I wished to avoid such a necessity."

"My employers also sent two cannons, (both six-pounders,) two dozen muskets, twenty-five pistols of the larger size, several revolvers, and twenty-five cutlasses, twenty-five boarding pikes, and a full supply of ammunition; also, a flagstaff, and a stand of American colors, to be exhibited on the island. I took in the brig John R. Dow in the late mentioned voyage some twenty-seven or twenty-eight men, mechanics and laborers, besides the crew, which consisted of fifteen hands. Afterwards, from time to time, said employers sent other hands, so that, on an average, besides the crews of the vessels, we generally had there no less than thirty-five men, and, with the crews, they numbered sixty men in the party which was under my charge, and which I employed on the island from the day that we undertook the work until the day when we were dispossessed of it."

"In pursuance of instructions of Shelton and at his cost, as his agent and for his behalf, I sailed in said brig John R. Dow to cruise along the Caribbean sea to discover guano islands. Leaving Baltimore in the month of March, 1854, I spent some time in such discovery among the desert reefs or rocky islands of said sea, several of which I visited; and whilst I was thus engaged, about the beginning of April, 1854, (the 6th of the month, I believe,) I found, in said sea, Aves Island, afterwards named by Shelton 'Shelton's Island,' which lies something like 15° 40′ latitude north and 63° 38′ longitude west of Greenwich." "After due exploration of the island and of its guano, specimens of which I gathered, I sailed thence on the 7th or 8th of Apri in said vessel and I visited other groups of said sea, (the Caribbean,) and then proceeded as fast as I could to Arenas and other guano islands in the Gulf of Mexico, where Mr. Shelton's vessels and men were then principally engaged in the guano business." "After sailing from Boston in the year 1854, in the month of June, I arrived at Shelton's Island in the brig John R. Dow about the beginning or middle of July, 1854, (the 15th of the month, I believe.) On the same day arrived the aforementioned Captain James Wheeler in the brig Mahala H. Comery, dispatched by Messrs. Lang & Delano, merchants, of Boston, as he stated to me, in consequence of information which had been communicated to them of the existence of guano there, as I have already mentioned. Our vessels were in sight of each other when we discovered the island, and there was not one hour's difference in the time of our arival. The next day I went ashore in company with Captain Wheeler; and although I did not conceive that, under the circumstances, either he or Lang & Delano had any lawful right, or, indeed, an equitable one to any portion of the island or to its guano, and I thought that their claim to appropriate it to themselves was a wrong done to Shelton; still, with a view of avoiding difficulties and for the sake of peace, and because there was enough of guano for all, I agreed with him to divide the island and the guano, and we accordingly marked out our respective portions and concluded not to interfere with each other until I had communicated with my principals, leaving it to the parties interested to settle the question in the United States as they should think best.

Let it not be forgotten that Gibbs's is the declaration which the legation has put forth with most confidence and commendation. The legation says, "that the minuteness of his details, his frank admissions, and his moderate tone, though firm, everything stamps it with the seal of a faithworthy document; whilst the clearness of his narrative distinctly proves that it is the testimony of an intelligent witness." This being laid down, such a testimony gives most force to the argument adduced against the resort to force and the commission of fraud. Gibbs declares that "he told Dias, in plain and unequivocal language, that he would neither leave the island nor stop taking in guano, unless prevented by a superior force; that he would resist, and that the Colonel could not effect his expulsion with the force which he then had on the island; that he had no doubt that they could have captured Dias, his soldiers, and his schooner, and, to make good his declaration, he enumerates the supply and quality of the arms with which his own single party was provided, &c., &c.; that he did not sign the paper through any fear of personal consequences had he persisted in a refusal to do so, or that he apprehended that, with the force under Dias's orders on the island, his people could be subdued or expelled." There was, therefore, no reason for Gibbs entertaining any fear, present or remote; but he was, on the contrary, satisfied that Dias's force was powerless, as opposed to his, and hence the boastful language of his explanation. After these asseverations, he goes on to show that he acted entirely in opposition to what would have been expected at his hands, considering the posture of things; and this, too, according to the statement of the self-same Gibbs. He goes on to say that he had reason to believe that Dias would attempt to eject him, and that he wished to avoid the effusion of blood. The decision and the desire are so incompatible, that it is not perceived how they could have emanated from one and the same individual at the same time. If they were so resolved on resistance, and so sure of the issue of the conflict, how comes it that he refrained in order to avoid coming to extremities? Did he not care about them when he came to the conclusion not to yield? Will the man who had no intention of yielding, except to superior force, explain how violence could have been inflicted upon him by a force which he despised, because he deemed it insufficient to compel his departure, and because he entertained no doubt that he could capture the Colonel, his men, and his schooner? Neither could the second schooner have been adequate to subdue and eject his people, because the detachment of fifteen men which she had brought put things in the same condition in which they stood during Colonel Dias's visit, whilst, with the arrival of other vessels, the Americans had bettered their condition.

Mr. Eames insists that the two Americans who signed the document acted under the influence of violence and fraud, being completely in error as to its contents, from the fact of their not understanding the Spanish language in which it was couched.

It will not be irrelevant here to transcribe the permit, which plays such a part in this matter. Copied literally, it states as follows:

"I, Domingo Dias, a captain of vessel, second chief of the Venezuelan squadron, and commissioner of the supreme government of the republic, to watch over the uninhabited islands belonging to it in the Caribbean sea, have agreed, provided that my government shall approve it, that Messrs. Charles H. Lang, agent of the firm of 'Lang & Delano,' of Boston, and Nathan P. Gibbs, agent of the company of Sampson & Tappan and P. S. Shelton, also of Boston, whom I have found taking guano out of this island, shall—

"First: Continue to take in cargo in those vessels which are now loading.

"Secondly: That they shall continue to take in guano until the arrival of the company, with which the government has made a contract, or until the approbation or disapprobation of the supreme government shall reach the island.

"Thirdly: And we, Charles H. Lang and Nathan P. Gibbs, bind ourselves to afford all the assistance that may be required by the garrison of this island.

"Fourthly: That, to this effect, we put our pieces of artillery and our armament at the disposition and under the flag of Venezuela, to which the island belongs; and

"Fifthly: I, Domingo Dias, second chief of the squadron, order the commanders of the war vessels cruising in the Antilles, to respect this grant, until the government will have otherwise disposed.

"Aves Island of the Windward, December 13, 1854.

"Signed,

"NATHAN P. GIBBS.
"CHARLES H. LANG,
"*Agent for Lang & Delano, of Boston.*
"DOMINGO DIAS."

This document, in the first place, shows a preamble, by which Colonel Dias, relying on the commission received from the government to watch the uninhabited islands in the Caribbean sea, states that, on condition that his government shall approve it, he grants to Lang and Gibbs:

First: The privilege of continuing to take in guano on board of the vessels which they had then loading.

Secondly: That they should do so until the arrival of a company, with which the government had contracted, or until the decision of said government should be received.

On their part, Lang & Gibbs bound themselves—

First: To extend all the assistance which the garrison of the island might require.

Secondly: To put their artillery and armament at the orders and under the flag of Venezuela, to which they acknowledged that the island belonged.

Finally Colonel Dias directs all commanders of vessels of war cruising along the Antilles, to respect his grant until the government should otherwise ordain. And all three of them sign the document in Aves Island of the Windward, on the 13th of December, 1854, Lang appending to his name, and in the English language, the words "agent for Lang & Delano, of Boston."

Now, the signers of the document understood perfectly well, as appears from the declarations, that it was a document allowing Lang and Gibbs to continue taking in guano, provided they were to put their armament under the authority of Colonel Dias, and imposing upon them the obligation of assisting the garrison left on the island with water and provisions. They add that they were most positively assured that the document contained nothing by which they assented to the existence of any title to the island in Venezuela. Thus Safford asseverates; thus P. Gibbs, and especially thus, the shrewd N. C. Gibbs; so that the violence and fraud consisted, according to the declarants, in the words of the document, which embraces the acknowledgment that the island belongs to the Venezuelan flag, and in all the rest they agreed, knowingly of what they were doing, and with their free consent. So certain is this, that N. C. Gibbs states that had he truly known the contents of the paper, he would, at all hazards, have refused to sign it; that is, that had he known that "it contained any word admitting the title of Venezuela." He, without any doubt, was ignorant that "it was a mere copy of his permit, which contained orders that they should not be molested; and that they should assist the soldiers, with their men, guns, and other arms, to keep off intruders; and that he consented to supply said soldiers with provisions and water;" and he thought that "if the paper was such, it could not damage him, and its effect would be to prevent all new difficulties."

Even setting aside what has been stated in the commencement of the document and the close of the fourth article, and reducing it to the mere fact of the permit, it stands against the claimants in full force as an acknowledgment of the dominion and sovereignty of Venezuela. They, in the sense of their legation, were exercising a lawful pursuit, using an article, their own property, and availing themselves of the advantages inherent to an acquisition, which the whole world could not dispute. What! could they consent that what belonged to them, as masters, to do by right, should be granted to them as a favor by a few intruders? that they should have a short period of time allowed them for their pursuits, when they had the power to carry it on indefinitely? that they should be reduced under the authority of the government of Venezuela, when they were independent of all? that they should submit to conditions, although they were so resolute? When, in the range of the history of mankind, was any master of a thing ever seen thus to abdicate his rights? But if they did all this; if, more than this, they carried out, by act of compliance, the obligations which they had contracted in exchange and return for the permit which they had freely accepted, acknowledged, and made use of, how dare they maintain that they considered themselves as exclusive masters of the island and of its guano? Of the guano, the price of which they had in part to make good by the provisions, which they actually supplied? Did they not know that the bare fact of admitting on the island a garrison, allowed to remain stationed there, occupying, guarding, and governing it in the name of Venezucla, was on their part an explicit acknowledgment both of their own lawless possession and of the title of the republic to that island? What can be the meaning of this obligation to feed the garrison, and feeding it in reality? And this, at what time? Why, when Colonel Dias, being absent, and having left behind him ten men "who troubled no one," "whom Gibbs employed as laborers," and an officer whom "he entertained in his own cabin," and all of them living in good understanding with the eighty American laborers. All pretext, even the slightest, had ceased to justify the idea of ascribing their conduct to the effect of fear. To allow Colonel Dias and his men to come ashore; to consent that they should occupy, garrison, and control the island; to receive and obey his orders; to accept and sign his permit; to comply with the condition of delivering up their armament and supplying provisions, under which conditions the permit was granted; to remain there in harmony and concord with those appointed as their guard; to feed, and even, indeed, to employ the soldiers at work, after the pretended threats had passed away, and they had men, vessels, and arms; all these constitute a series of facts that speak loudly against the claimants, and the power of which it were vain to attempt to destroy. This is sufficient to decide the question, since the foregoing reflections are suggested by the testimony itself of the claimants, examined in the light of their own statements.

It has already been stated that the object of Venezuela was to prevent the exportation of her property, which was carried on in her islands; and it is evident that in order to attain it, she required the application of force, since its absence had encouraged foreigners in disregarding her rights. Still it was applied neither to procure Lang's or Gibbs's signature to the permit, nor to enforce their departure from the island of Birds; so much so, that in the act of speaking of a permit, and of signing the document, Colonel Dias, Commander Cotarro, and Lieutenant Pereira were the only persons ashore. Indeed, it is no matter for wonderment that force should not have been required to obtain that some men, who had possessed themselves of an island to which they knew they had no right, should depart from it as soon as its lawful owner presented himself there. If the expedition of Venezuela came with cannons, bayonets, and powder, the Americans had more cannons, more arms of every kind, more powder, and more men for the defense of what they call their property. According to Mr. Eames's note of the 20th of December, 1856, the agents of the company did not understand Spanish. One of them, according to Mr. Eames's note of the 31st of March, 1857, did understand it, although very imperfectly. The observation as to the paper having been couched and signed in the Spanish language only, and not, as would have been natural, both in English and in Spanish, is so much the more strange in view of what Wheaton says: "The original equality of nations authorizes each of them to make use of its own language in its intercourse with the others; and, to a certain degree, this right is still maintained in the practice of some States." Greater and more evident does that right become when we speak, not of diplomatic correspondence between nations, but of merely domestic acts. We know no State that has so abdicated its independence as to issue its orders, or to reduce its acts to writing in the language of all those who are required to respect them. The argument involves the idea that the Americans constituted a power capable of entering into relations with Venezuela.

Mr. Eames says that it is a declared act of fraud that the paper should now be presented as an agreement, when it had been given to the agents in the character of a permit. But he forgets that it was he himself who thus characterized that document. In his note of the 20th of December, 1856, and no less than six times, he used the word *agreement* to designate it; and because, in imitation of his language, the government in its answer has so called it, it is therefore brought under an imputation of fraud. There is no language to qualify such a mode of proceeding. In the event of force being necessary to secure the end of the expedition, the amount required would have been dispatched. Fraud was neither required nor was it necessary that it should coexist with force. That which is required having been obtained by means of one of these two things, the use of the other is superseded, because either is sufficient for the object in view. The witnesses, it is true, have declared under oath that there were violence and fraud; but it is equally true that the officers of Venezuela have deposed also under oath to quite the reverse, and, in this matter of evidence, declaration stands opposed to declaration.

We cannot get at the motive which led the claimants to conceal the existence of the document from their government; nor why they did not at once furnish those explanations which, to Mr. Eames, appear so satisfactory to invalidate it and strip it of all effect.

Sum up all that has been alleged in relation to the document, and it will be seen that there was no possibility for the employment of either fraud or force. Not of the former, first, because there were among the Americans some who understood the Spanish, and especially C. H. Lang, one of the agents, who was well versed in the language. Secondly, because not only Commodore Cotárro, but Lang, interpreted the permit, word for word. Thirdly, because in case that they were not satisfied as to what they were doing, they ought not to have signed it. Fourthly, because if, as supposed, resort was had to force, and the end attained, fraud could have been of no use, and thus *vice versa.* Fifthly, because the title of Venezuela existed independently of any other consideration. Not of the latter, because, first, only three officers were ashore before the signing of the document and in the act of concluding it. Secondly, because the evident superiority of the Americaus refute the possibility of fear which they allege. Thirdly, because the agents stated the names of the constituent companies, and provided the paper, ink, pen, and other appliances of writing. Fourthly, because far from departing, they remained on the island and availed themselves of the permit. Fifthly, because their whole conduct is inconsistent with that of men who yield to violence. Sixthly, because neither before signing, in the act of signing, or after signing, did they offer the slightest resistance or protest. Seventhly, because they did not protest in the United States. Eighthly, because no act of violence is adduced, nor blows, nor wounds, nor death. Ninthly, because the supposed threat of expelling them from the island was in fact impracticable. Tenthly, because the officers of Venezuela declare that no such thing occurred. Eleventhly, because there is no proof of violence. Twelfthly, because the witnesses brought forward to establish the fact of violence are the very individuals who pretend that they were the objects of that violence. Thirteenthly, because a document cannot be annulled by the verbal declaration of the very individual who signed it. Fourteenthly, because the declarations were taken without notice to, and without the intervention of Venezuela. Fifteenthly, because they are copies certified by no one. Sixteenthly, because Gibbs's declaration has been mutilated—for what cause is not known. Seventeenthly, because it was not exhibited, except upon the advertence of this government. Eighteenthly, because the declarations of the Venezuelan officers contradict them at all points. Nineteenthly, because, if force was used, fraud was useless and *vice versa.* Twentiethly, because three of the declarations do not mention force. Twenty-first, because in the unadmitted supposition that threats had been uttered against them, having passed off unexecuted, the Americans complied with the conditions of the permit, thus confirming their own consent. Twenty-second, because all the presumptions make against them. Twenty-third, because they could defend, and ought to have defended, a possession which they said was a lawful one; and yet they did not do so. Twenty-fourth, because, admitting that they had rights, they renounced those rights by their own act. Twenty-fifth, because the reasons on which they ground their submission are wholly frivolous and incredible. Twenty-sixth, because the declarants, with one exception, not understanding, as they affirm, the Spanish language, their declarations fall back on Lang's, their interpreter, himself one of the signers. Twenty-seventh, because they alleged no right to the island, but, on the contrary, stated that they were there, as they had been in other islands of Venezuela, for the purpose of filching guano. Another fact which makes conclusively against the claimants, is the secret and unlawful manner in which they acted in the dispatch of the vessels sent to Aves Island, even to the infringement of the laws of their own country. From information sent by the legation of Venezuela in Washington, it appears that in the custom-house at Baltimore there is no entry made of the arrival of the brig M. H. Comery, which left Boston, on ballast, for Mogador, on the 22d of June, 1854, and proceeded to Aves Island; nor that the same custom-house shows any registry of the clearance of the ship Kentucky, which sailed for Aves Island in the month of September, 1854.

That the bark Carlo Mauran, the master of which, says Gibbs, was Safford, and which was dispatched from Liverpool, at what date is not stated, did not sail directly for Aves Island in December, 1854. Neither the custom-house of New York, Philadelphia, nor Baltimore, shows a registry of her clearance.

That the brig John R. Dow went from Boston to St. Thomas in March, 1854, for account of Shelton and others. N. P. Gibbs deposes that he sailed from Baltimore in this brig in the month of March, 1854, at Shelton's cost, upon an excursion to the Caribbean sea in search of guano islands, and that having found the Aves, and gone to Boston, he sailed thence about the middle, or the 20th, perhaps, of the month of June, 1854, for Aves Island, with lumber, &c. The vessel goes out with a destination to St. Thomas, and Gibbs says for an excursion to the Caribbean sea. He conceals his true destination, and deceives the American authorities themselves. In the month of March he undertakes a voyage from Boston, and in his declaration he substitutes for that port the port of Baltimore. Are such falsehoods the concomitants of an honest and lawful occupation?

There is another point which deserves notice. This Gibbs was acting in common with Lang. Both, in the beginning, were in Shelton's service. They agreed to divide the island and the guano between themselves, leaving the question of ownership to their principals. They moved in accord on every point. It even appears that Lang's opinion was the preponderant one; Gibbs, at least, to justify his conduct in signing the document, invokes the example of Lang. Besides this, the latter understood Spanish, and was, with Gibbs, the organ of communication. In spite of all this, it is noticed that the legation is inclined to separate the case of the one from that of the other, leaning to Gibbs's side.

Lastly, all the declarations appear to have been taken in June, 1855, either by anticipation or after Mr. Eames had suggested that the document altered the character of the question, and that the Americans should be applied to for explanations in relation to it. It is easily to be conceived that in such a juncture nothing was to be expected but that by every means at hand they should bend themselves to the securement of the triumph of their interests at the expense of truth, and of everything else that stood as an obstacle in their way. Thus it was, and in no other way, that those declarations were framed.

Mr. Eames considers it to be a most extraordinary and unjustifiable thing that, in order to shut the door against this claim for indemnification, we should insist on a paper which was signed solely to prevent, and which did prevent a conflict, and perhaps a very probable destruction of life.

This is mere declamation, as we shall proceed to prove. The threat which led them to sign the paper was that of compelling the Americans immediately to quit the island, if we are to attach any credit to the declarations. Going off, therefore, they would have avoided the consummation of the mischief, satisfying at the same time every wish of Colonel Dias, and, indeed, their own wishes, which certainly did not turn to a fight. This is evidently proved from the fact that when on the 31st of December they were notified to leave, although they were placed in more favorable circumstances than those in which they stood at Colonel Dias's arrival on the island, there was no conflict, no bloodshed, no killing, but there was a quiet departure from it. Besides all this, had they voided the island from the beginning, they would have stood on more favorable ground to advance their claim.

Mr. Eames maintains that the term *derelict* applied to an island which was known long time before but not reduced to any possession or included in any jurisdiction—an island which he sometimes calls *res nullius*—comes within the strictly legal and lexicographical meaning of the word; one which perfectly applied to Aves Island in June, 1854, (perhaps July, see the declarations,) when the claimants commenced taking out guano, and that there is no inconsistency in calling derelict a thing that no one, that is, no power, either possessed or controlled.

The inconsistency does exist, as will be seen. Things derelict are things abandoned by the owner with the intention not to hold them any further as his own, and which may thus be acquired by the first occupant. The digest of the Roman law, from which the expression has been borrowed, thus lays it down: "*Quâ ratione verius esse videtur, si rem pro derelicto á Domino habitam quis occupaverit, statim eum Dominum effici. Pro derelicto autem habetur quod Dominus eâmente abjecerit ut id in numero rerum suarum esse nolit, idelque statim Dominus ejus esse desinit.*" (Instit., lib. 2, tit. 1, § 47.)

"The Digest, in a series of separate articles, lays down the principal circumstances which verge into a lawful ground of possession: such are those in which a man possesses * * * *pro derelicto*, when one possesses himself of a thing that has been abandoned. In all these examples, if he who sold, donated, settled in dower, gave in payment, or abandoned, was not the owner, then property is not entirely acquired, but there is a ground for prescription." (Ortolan, Historical Explanation of the Institutes.) "Things that really belong to nobody, *res nullius*, are as follows: first, those of which man has not yet possessed himself, or which he has entirely abandoned; in the second place, things segregated from human commerce, and which are termed things of divine right, *res divini juris*. As to the first, they are the objects which the owner casts off, because he no longer requires them," &c., &c. (Ortolan, ibidem.) "The abandonment of a thing made by any one with the will that it shall no longer be his, becomes, for him who may possess himself of such thing, a just title, a conveying title, to the property; he who abandons, tacitly consents that the dominion of the thing which he foregoes shall pass over to him who took possession of it." (Pothier on Prescription.) "If the owner abandons anything movable or immovable, with the intent no longer to include it in the tale of his possessions, whether because it be useless or onerous to him, or indeed through a mere whim of his mind, he loses his dominion over such thing, and the first occupant thereof converts it into his own." (Laws 49, 250, tit. 28, part 3.) "*Si res pro derelicta habita sit, statim nostra esse desinit, et occupantis fit.*" (Escriche, Dictionary of Legislation—*ad verbum*, abandoned.)

But beyond this, the Latin verb *derelinquere*, from which *derelict* is derived, signifies the same thing as *abandonar* in Spanish, which means a man's voluntary disseizing, and forever, of his own property. Webster's American Dictionary of the English Language, after adducing the etymology above referred to, defines the word derelict to mean left, abandoned, as an adjective; and as a substantive, in law, to mean "an article of goods, or any commodity thrown away, relinquished by the owner."

But why quote other authorities, when Mr. Eames himself, driven by the force of things, has uttered the following words: "Not the slightest doubt or difficulty can grow out of the fact, to which the undersigned has been referred, namely, that the captaincy general of Venezuela having been established in 1751, was the last of the continental governments constituted by Spain and embraced that part of the continent of America which had not been comprehended in the several continental governments previously formed. Because all the territory of those continental governments originally formed a part of the jurisdiction of the government of St. Domingo, and they were successively cut off from that jurisdiction. But besides this vast continental territory, the government of Santo Domingo, as appears from the laws of the Indies, published in Madrid, 1786, book 2, tit. 15, included also all the Windward Islands, among which, as we have seen, is found the Aves in question; and this group of islands never was separated from that jurisdiction by Spain, nor assigned to the jurisdiction of any of the continental governments, much less to that of Venezuela, which, in the beginning, was a dependency of New Granada, and thus continued until the year 1751."

If the government of Santo Domingo comprehended all the islands of the windward among which Aves Island, now in question, is found; and if this group of islands never was, by Spain, separated from that jurisdiction, nor assigned to the jurisdiction of any one of the continental governments, it is evident that it was reduced to the possession and embraced within the jurisdiction of Spain, to which Santo Domingo belonged. Let this acknowledgment be viewed in conjunction with the one subsequently made by Mr. Eames, namely, that it was Spain that discovered the Aves.

The Aves, therefore, being derelict, as it is called by Mr. Eames, must have had an owner, because, on the contrary, no one abandoned his property in the island with the intent never to claim it again as his own; and it could bear no other appellation than that of a thing common to all, both before and after its discovery, under the supposition that every one who chose might visit it, and make use of it, going off immediately and leaving to others the privilege of doing the same thing.

It being thus established that, even in Mr. Eames's view, the Aves belonged to some power, and was by it abandoned, and it returned to the condition of a thing liable to be acquired by occupation, it now devolves upon him to point out the acts of the owner, significant of this abandonment. "As everything embraced in a country belongs to the nation; and as none but the nation, or the person intrusted with its powers, is authorized to dispose of any such thing, if it have left waste and uncultivated places in the country, no one has the right to take possession of them without its consent. Although they may not actually be put to uses, still those places belong to it; it has an interest in preserving them for future use, and it is answerable to no one for the manner in which it makes use of its property." (Vattel, Law of Nations.)

In view of this principle and of the law maxim that the mere intention of possessing is enough to preserve possession for us, although we may not be in the actual enjoyment of the thing; *licèt possessio nudo animo acquiri non possit, tamen solo animo retireri potest;* and a consequence of the above mentioned point being that the ceasing of enjoying a thing is not sufficient to warrant the loss of it, but that there must also be an intention of abandoning its possession; it follows, beyond doubt, that proof of the abandonment is necessarily required, and so much the more required that if such proof be not made, presumptions of bad faith must stand against the claimants, because they do not ground their claim of possession on any title, in consonance with the generally admitted doctrines.

Although many examples might be quoted to show how nations accept and apply the rule of Vattel, it will be enough to mention one, which is adduced by Raynal in his philosophical history of the Indies, in relation to the Lucayas Islands: "There are something like two hundred of them," he says, "all lying north of Cuba. The majority of them are bare rocks on the surface of the waters. Columbus, who discovered them upon his arrival in the New World, and gave the name of San Salvador to the island where he landed, left no settlement there, nor did the Spaniards thereafter make any establishments. But in 1507, all their population was removed, and it soon perished in the labor of the mines or in the prosecution of pearl fishery. This small archipelago was left entirely deserted, when, in 1672, it occurred to some Englishmen to go and take possession of Providence Island. Having been expelled, seven or eight years afterwards, by orders from the court of Spain; they returned in 1690, to be again expelled in 1703, by the united forces of Spain and France."

Here we have islands the bare and naked discovery of which Spain could claim, islands in which she made no settlement, islands over which she exercised dominion, and from which she repeatedly drove away the English, who had occupied them, although they were uninhabited at the time.

To the observations of the note of Venezuela as to the inability of private individuals acquiring property in competition with a sovereign State, Mr. Eames returns no answer, save one of threat; and the question being thus forced from its appropriate ground, there is nothing left of it but the extent of power of the contending parties. But the government of the United States, which is aware that the rights of nations are independent of their greater or less degree of strength, will not choose, like its minister in Caraccas, to discuss with this species of argument which would necessarily defeat every attempt to go into a question of principle. In this behalf we will add that such observations were intended to make manifest that, even though Venezuela should not have acquired a title to Aves previous to the year 1854, the occupation of that island by her must have countervailed the occupation by the Americans and produced effects which theirs could not operate. But in order to show that the argument, which commended itself to a threat in lieu of an answer, is not so very brainless, a few quotations will be allowed from various expositors of the law of nations, by way of sustaining authority:

"An independent individual, whether he have been expelled from his country or have lawfully abandoned it, may settle down in a country which he finds without a master and there occupy independent dominion. Any one afterwards attempting to possess himself of the whole of the country will not be at liberty to do so with justice unless he shall respect the rights and the independence of this individual. If the same individual find a sufficient number of men who may choose to live under his laws, he can found a new State in the country which he has discovered and occupy its empire and dominion. But should that individual merely pretend to arrogate to himself an exclusive right over that country to constitute himself a monarch over it without subjects, his foolish pretensions may well be laughed at, because a rash and ridiculous occupation can produce no effect in law."

"There are also other means through which an individual may found a new State. Thus, in the eleventh century, a few Norman knights founded a new empire in Sicily, after having rescued it from the common enemy of christendom, because the usages of their country allowed men to leave their native land in quest of fortune on other shores." (Vattel, Law of Nations.) "This right includes two things: 1st. Dominion, by virtue of which the nation can use the country for its needs, dispose of it, and derive from it all the uses that are requisite. 2dly. Government, or the right of sovereign command, though it controls and disposes, at will, everything that transpires in the country." "When a nation takes possession of a country that does not already belong to some one it is considered to occupy in that country empire or sovereignty at the same time that it exercises dominion; because, its freedom and independence being granted, its intention in the act of establishing itself in a region, cannot be to abandon to others the right of commanding within it, nor to any of those who continue under its sovereignty." The same author says: "The general dominion of a nation over the lands which it occupies is naturally united to empire, because, in the act of establishing itself in a vacant country, the nation cannot intend to depend, in that country, on any other power. And how can it be possible that an independent nation should not command within itself? For this reason we have remarked that when a nation occupies a country it is presumed at the same time to occupy the empire inherent to it, but now we proceed further, and we show the connection which naturally exists between those two in relation to an independent nation. How could it govern a country which it inhabits, and after its own notion, if it could not fully and absolutely dispose of the country? And how could it have full and absolute dominion of a spot which it could not command? The control of another, and the rights inherent to it, would deprive the nation of the free disposal of the place. If to this be added the eminent domain which is an integrant of sovereignty, the intimate connection between the dominion of a nation and its control will be better understood. Thus, that which is called the "eminent domain" being nothing but the dominion of the body of the nation, or of the sovereign who represents the nation, is ever considered to be inseparable from the domain of the sovereignty. The "useful domain," or that which is reduced to the rights which may belong to an individual in the State, may be separated from the empire, and there is no obstacle to its belonging to a nation in those places which are not under its obedience. Thus, we find many sovereigns holding fiefs in the land of other princes, and in that case they possess them as private individuals." The same author:

"From the moment that a State foregoes or abandons a portion of its property, an island, for instance, it ceases to be part of its territory, and hence it belongs to no one—(*res nullius.*) From that moment it is allowable for any other State to appropriate it to itself, and to bring it under its dominion." (Klüber, Law of Nations.)

"States acquire all that they can acquire, and they acquire it by those means that are appropriate, and peculiar to those moral beings or entities, and in proportion to their conditions of existence considered, whether in relation to other States with which they form a secondary society of a different order, or in relation to the individuals who make up the whole body of each of them. The characteristics of property and its different divisions impart a varied character to acquisition, whilst, according to the nature of the latter, the conditions required for this act of appropriation will be distinct, as will also the consequences be. States acquire *pari passu*, or in competition with other States. States acquire within their own territory in the cases which are determined by the laws." "The former of these two classes of acquisitions, namely: when a State acquires without its boundaries, presents no important division. Either the acquisition is made of *res nullius*, of a thing belonging to no one, because it is not possessed by any of the other States, or it is made of property that was occupied by some one, whichsoever, of said States." (Spanish Law Encyclopedia.)

"A company purchased the rights of the original grantee, and other companies succeeded the purchaser of the rights. The king abandoned to them not only the useful domain, but also the empire, the jurisdiction, and the military power. He merely reserved to himself the direct domain and the right of appointing a governor, whose power was merely nominal. Even, then, it was the company that had the preferment of the governor whom the king was to appoint, and it had the privilege of removing him."

"All these possessions were ultimately brought under the domain, and they finally came to be national property in the year 1674."

"But in all these transfers of ownership, it is invariably supposed, the right of first occupancy had not vested proprietorship in the islands; that the king's grant was the only title to property. This principle deserves elaboration; but, in this instance, I am a mere historian. (Merlin's Repertory of Jurisprudence—*ad verbum*, occupation.)

Mr. Eames denies having said that "the United States in no way doubt as to the eminent domain of Venezuela over the 'Aves,' and that they merely contest the peculiar right to the guano found in that place," or, at least, he so modifies those words that they do not say what they really import. Unfortunately there exists no written record of what occurred when Mr. Eames gave assurance of this thing, and that more than once, without any reservations of any kind, unless, indeed, mental ones; but this, notwithstanding the assertion of the undersigned, will not be called into doubt by any one who will reflect that it tallies with and it is confirmed by the nature of the demand set up against the republic. The United States do not claim the island at her hands as their property; they do not ask for its evacuation and surrender; they do not ask what the claimants desired; but they do ask, solely and exclusively, for pecuniary indemnifications. The parties interested in applying to their government baptized the "Aves" under the name of "Shelton's Island," and proposed to cede it to their government, an offer which does not appear to have met with an acceptance. It is also known that the question has been debated in the United States as to whether the right of acquisition lay with the Congress of the Republic or with the executive power; and that an act has been deemed necessary declaring that the islands that might hereafter be discovered, as "Aves" is pretended to have been, shall belong to the United States.

Mr. Eames endeavors to overthrow the reasons deduced from the assistance which he lent to Mr. Pickrell, supposing that nothing can be inferred from it against the present claim.

Although this has already been amply spoken of in the beginning, it may not be irrelevant to take the American note in consideration. It begins, on this point, by saying that Mr. Eames' intervention was directed to protect the rights and interests which the Wallace contract secured as to the guano islands considered as justly belonging to Venezuela, and, of course, in contradistinction with the "Aves," which was not so considered. If such were Mr. Eames' instructions, he certainly had no heed of them when he was protecting Pickrell. A copy has already been given of what he stated to his excellency the President when he came to urge him to reinstate the Wallace contract; and in that there is certainly not one word which goes to except Aves Island. At no time, more opportune, could it have been proper to state such a reservation. Especially ought he to have proceeded with due frankness and sincerity, when his excellency remarked to Mr. Eames that it might be more apposite to settle the matter of the claimants before Mr. Pickrell's, pointing out to him at the same time that there was no connection between the two things, because the "Aves" were excepted in the contract. But to induce the government, even by resort to threats, to agree with Pickrell on conditions almost identical with those agreed to with Wallace, to begin to insinuate, after the execution of the new contract, and that in a manner indirect and circumlocutory, that the insertion of Aves Island in it was made without any kind of sanction or of support on the part of the government of the United

States, or of Mr. Eames; and now to assert that he excepted the "Aves," when he was lending his assistance to Pickrell, is a conduct which cannot be properly characterized. Never did the President of the Republic, or the Secretary of Foreign Relations, or that officer for the Interior and Justice, or any other person connected with the government, hear Mr. Eames say that he made such an exception, and the testimony of all those persons is now invoked in opposition to Mr. Eames's. No such exception was made. Nor is it certain that the note of the Secretary of Foreign Relations omits all mention of the principal and conspicuous facts which are revealed in the protection extended to Pickrell. The secretary spoke, as he ought to speak, in this manner: "On such occasions as Mr. Eames had conferences on this subject with the undersigned, and with his predecessor, both of them stated to him the views of the government as to that claim, in relation to which no written answer was hitherto given, both, because at the time a mere announcement of it was made, and when it was mentioned in an official note of the legation, it was so in an incidental manner on the occasion of Mr. Pickrell's application, and of the question between Venezuela and the Netherlands. Mr. Eames himself repeats, in the note alluded to and in which he puts in a formal demand, that he deems it necessary to consult his government on the agreement made with Colonel Dias, in view of which he is induced to delay the presentation of the subject." "The government hopes that the foregoing observations will be considered as justifying the serious objections which it entertains in regard of a claim, the formal discussion of which is just *in limine,* now that the legation has received the documents and other vouchers which it was expecting to accompany the presentation of said claim, which, therefore, cannot be invested with the pressing character that would naturally attach to a matter fully examined in every light; a matter not unattended by serious objections, requiring much reflection in the very act of its presentment; a matter which from the start had labored under a variance of opinion on both parts."

From the explanations which appear in the beginning of this note, it will have been seen that this was all that the secretary of relations could say, or ought to say, because, in truth, nothing else had taken place, as may be easily inferred from the contents themselves of the communication of the 20th of December, 1856; and hence the tumbling down, as a baseless fabric, of all that Mr. Eames recalls and lays down for the purpose of establishing the fact that there was an omission, with the view of giving force to certain arguments, of circumstances which, in his judgment, it was absolutely necessary not to allow to pass in silence. The government of Venezuela was not called on to inquire whether Mr. Eames was or was not in Caraccas in the month of December, 1854. Neither is it accurate to say that Mr. Eames clearly and peremptorily refused to sanction the contract, inasmuch as it referred to the Aves, although, in the year 1855, in a conversation with Mr. Aranda, the minister of foreign affairs, he touched upon a claim which certain individuals, which found the island, intended to bring forward.

Equally inaccurate is it to say that during the negotiation touching

Pickrell's agreement, that there was any reservation as to the "Aves" and all the rights and claims of the present plaintiffs, whilst the proper allusion as to what did occur on this head is made in the already quoted passage, which appears in the opening of the Venezuelan note of the 27th of February last. The words quoted further back from the note in which Mr. Eames summed up the observations made to his excellency, with the view of securing the new contract—words which are a pure fountain of truth against him in this matter—do not involve the sense which it is now attempted to give to them; but they thoroughly do the reverse. Will any one ever imagine that an island, in which the existence of guano was positively ascertained—ridiculously exaggerated into myriads of tons—could have been excluded from the Pickrell matter on a claim of the legation which sustained him?

This note attempts to give some coloring of truth to such an exception, by insinuating that it was in consequence of it that there was "omitted all mention of the 'Aves' in the article, by which the transferees of Wallace, with a difference in his contract, are granted the usufruct of the guano islands of the republic; and afterwards another article specified the 'Aves,' evidently with the object of releasing Venezuela from all responsibility to said transferees, in the event that, on account of this claim, or for any other reason, she should cease to possess or use it for her own benefit." Admitting that in article fifth of the contract with Pickrell it was expressed that, if from any contingency, or from any cause, Venezuela should lose or renounce her dominion over the island of Aves, lying in 15° 45′ latitude, and longitude 64° 45′, the term of fifteen years, in reference to said island, should be understood to have elapsed, without any obligation on the part of the government to make any indemnification for the unexpired time, it is, in spite of such admission, roundly denied that the claim, not yet presented at that time, was the cause, immediate or remote, of such a stipulation. The truth is, that ever since 1854 "Aves" Island had been an object of contention between Venezuela and the Netherlands, and that her claims specially engaged the attention of the government at the time when the arrangement with Pickrell was being made. It was solely and exclusively in view of this controversy of an international character, that the secretaries of the treasury and of foreign relations conceived the idea of such an article, which anticipated and excepted the case laid down; and this, not through any doubt as to the rights of the nation to the island, but because it might suit it to cede that island, or in any other manner to dispose of it.

But there is one reason, above all others, of a conclusive character. Mr. Eames's efforts to obtain the reinstatement of Wallace's contract either did, or they did not, include "Aves" Island. If they did not, there was no room for the involvement of such a question with that of the other Americans, nor for the reservations made in their behalf; nor was there any for the salutary influence which the satisfaction given to one application would exert on the other, nor for any of the views which Mr. Eames advanced upon that occasion. If, on the contrary, as it indubitably was so, he wanted the "Aves" to continue to be the subject-matter of the contract, then the following doctrine must be applied to him:

"The second point which we have noted down, is not susceptible of much controversy, and all the doctors agree in proclaiming the following maxim: *Protestatio contra factum nil relevat.* In fact, what should a protest avail when the act, against which the protest is made, cannot be maintained on any other ground than on that of renunciation?"

For instance, if I pay an amount which I owe, protesting in the act that I do not renounce the right of prescription, there is, in that case, in my conduct a flagrant contradiction, which destroys entirely the value of my protest, and warrants its being considered as unwritten; because, if my indebtedness be barred by limitation, there is nothing to compel me to pay it, and if I pay it, it is because I renounce the right of prescription. The act is bound to carry more effect than can empty words; a real, effective, and voluntary payment is more telling, more worthy of consideration than lip reservations and words, often scarcely weighed. (Troplong's Treatise on Prescriptions.)

Mr. Eames does this, and nothing else. He sustains a claim which necessarily implicates the sovereignty and dominion of Venezuela over the Aves Island; but, at the same time, he protests against the effects that must result from his intervention in the matter, by closing the door against another matter. In other words, the island belongs to the republic, when she is wanted to grant its usufruct to Wallace's transferees; but it no longer belongs to the republic when she wishes to discredit the pretentions of the claimants. If the guano be not given to Pickrell she is threatened with a rupture of the friendly relations existing between the two countries; if the value of the pretensions of the present claimants be not acknowledged, the same good understanding is brought into jeopardy. In requirements thus conflicting it is no easy matter to alight on the means of pleasing and of securing the peace and friendship of the two States. There is no assurance that what is requested and preferred as necessary and most pressing may not, in other circumstances, be converted into a wrong which would also suggest a necessary and most urgent reparation.

Be this as it may, there is, from what has been shown, abundant reason for denying any value or consequence to the reservation made by Mr. Eames in behalf of the claimants; at the very time, too, when he was working, sustaining as he did, even to the extent of threats, the reinstatement of the rights conferred on Wallace, or, what amounts to the same thing, the inclusion of Aves Island in the Pickrell contract. Venezuela, therefore, is bound to insist on all the arguments which she has alleged on this head.

Mr. Eames has not confined himself to pretending that the Americans are not held to prove the legality of their conduct, but he actually shifts the burden over to Venezuela, which he calls the aggressor. He has gone further, and declared that whatever pretension to title is preferred by Venezuela in Aves Island does not present sufficient grounds to justify a discussion; and he said this after having stated that he had not expected to be told that Aves Island belonged to the republic previous to 1854, as the successor to the rights of Spain that discovered that island. So that, whilst he wishes to put the burden of proof on

Venezuela, he considers as useless whatever evidence she may bring forward to make good her dominion over the island; or, in other words, that his demand should be acceded to without any discussion, merely because, in his judgment, there is nothing to justify it—a judgment which he rests on this: that it is not pretended that Venezuela can allege any title to Aves Island here spoken of on account of contiguity; that nowhere is there mention made, in print, of any title or of pretense of a title to the island on the part of Venezuela; that there is no reason to believe that there can be produced any unpublished document written previous to the year 1854, and existing in the archives of any government, in which the pretension even of such a title is alleged on the part of Venezuela; that it is not pretended that she ever asserted jurisdiction over the "Aves," nor that she ever made, prior to 1854, any exhibition of title to it such as another government should respect; that neither has it been proved, nor yet ascertained that prior to 1854 any citizen of the republic of Venezuela had ever visited that island either in a private or in an official capacity; that the government of Venezuela, acting through its commissioners thereto duly authorized, announced to the world her official renunciation to all title or pretension to Aves Island, by not mentioning it as a part of the territory of the republic in her large map, nor in Mr. Codazzi's geography, an agent intrusted with the management of that extensive work, in reference to which he goes into an extensive dissertation, for the purpose of establishing the perfection of his labors, both from the assistance and remuneration which were given to the author, and from the estimation in which it was held in foreign countries, not to speak of that of the government of Venezuela.

The right of Venezuela to Aves Island cannot be rejected on the score of contiguity, because, according to the law of nations, islands adjacent to a continent are reputed to be natural dependencies of the territory of the nation which possesses it, unless there be proof to the contrary; because to such a nation, infinitely more than to any other nation, is the dominion of such islands important for its security both by land and by sea; and because Aves Island has no continent more immediate than that of Venezuela, since, although it be nearer to the possessions of other nations, those possessions are mere colonies or isles themselves, which up to a certain time also belonged to Spain.

Without admitting the necessity of a previous declaration of right to a territory, in order to secure its effective possession, we hold it to be certain that what is found in print is not a mere mention, but contains express declarations that the Aves Island under discussion belonged to Colombia, and belongs to Venezuela. Such are the declarations contained in article sixth of the fundamental law of union of the people of Colombia, and of the constitution of that republic, which in the former says: "The territory of the republic of Colombia shall be that which is comprehended within the limits of the ancient captaincy of Venezuela and the vice-royalty and the captaincy general of the new kingdom of Granada; but the designation of its more precise boundaries is reserved for a more opportune period." Whilst the second says: "The territory of Colombia is the same that was comprehended in the ancient vice-royalty of New Granada and the captaincy general of Venezuela." And article fifth of the constitution, which obtained in Venezuela in the year 1854, which says: "The territory of this republic includes all that, previous to the political transformation of 1810, was denominated captaincy general of Venezuela," in which captaincy was comprehended Aves Island, according to the royal letters patent which created the audience of Caraccas, as will hereafter be explained, subjecting said island to its jurisdiction. The jurisdiction of Venezuela was, therefore, established over the island under the Spanish domination by virtue of a document which is, perhaps, unpublished. Now, admitting the case that this island should never have been visited by any Venezuelan, it certainly is no proof that it had no owner, since, as has already been stated, a country may remain uninhabited and still have an owner; whilst to be susceptible of occupation it must be uninhabited and without an owner. That Mr. Codazzi should have been commissioned for the construction of plans of the provinces of Venezuela—that he should have collected geographical, physical, and statistical information—that the time for the presentation of the results of his commission should have been extended, because much of his time had been otherwise devoted to a different service—that orders were given to assist him with funds and all such data as he might deem necessary for consultation—that his work was appreciated in France—that the Venezuelan congress considered Mr. Codazzi's services to be highly important in the construction of the map of Venezuela and in the publication of the geography and history of the country, and for these reasons allowed him a number of copies of his work in payment of the $15,000 which had been furnished him for the engraving of the map of the republic and the printing of his geography and history. Nothing of all these proves that his work was an official one in the true sense of the word, and much less that it has been approved for perfection or accuracy in all its parts. Let it be remarked that his publication was not made at the nation's expense, nor that it was declared official by any public act. A work may be worthy of appreciation, yet not, therefore, be free from errors; much more so if it be an intricate work and require a long examination of the matters treated of. Mr. Eames goes on with the analysis of the proposition that the island belonged to Venezuela prior to 1854, as the successor of Spain who discovered it, for the purpose, as he says, of pulling it to the ground and scattering it to the winds; but instead of weakening he has strengthened it still more, as will be seen.

The United States, says Mr. Eames, maintain that the "Aves" was never reduced to the possession of Spain, or that, if it was so, it was soon abandoned and derelict, and that if the title of Venezuela to claim a right to that island is derived from that which Spain had, it would then become necessary to prove the truth of nine propositions which he lays down, the first of which only he admits, namely: "The 'Aves' was discovered by Spain."

Spain discovered the new continent, and by her exertion conquered a large portion of it, introducing there her population, her civilization, and her industry. Equity demanded that she should be considered by the European powers as the original mistress of those lands, and she effectually was so considered. The right of first occupancy, and the act of taking possession in the name of the sovereign of him who made the discovery, was the controlling law of those days—a law which was recognized and sanctioned by the bull of Alexander VI, issued on the 4th of May, 1493, and which was received and observed as a lawful exponent of the public law of those days. Hence it was that the emperor Charles V, and his son Philip II, declared in the law 1st Tit., 1st Book, 3d Digest of the laws of the Indies, that by act of donation of the Holy See, and by other just and lawful titles, they were lords of the Western Indies, islands, and mainland of the Ocean sea, discovered and to be discovered. If other European powers came to occupy some lands on the continent or in the islands within the limits assigned to Spain, it was only by direct concession or by act of war. Hence the fact, that the island possessions of powers other than Spain, rest on the treaties of peace by which she has ceded such dominions, and has recognized them in other conventions. But the lands that are possessed by sale, cession, or treaty of peace, are necessarily limited by the contract; and there is no act by which Spain cedes the island spoken of to any other power. It must, therefore, be considered as the original property of Spain, excluding the presumption of an abandonment of it on her part, in view of Law, Title, and Book of the Digest of the Indies, already quoted, as also 2d book, title 15, of the Laws of the Indies, published in Madrid, in 1786, quoted by Mr. Eames himself to prove that the Windward Islands, and among them Aves Island, formed part of the jurisdiction of the government of Santo Domingo, adding that this group of islands never was separated by Spain from that jurisdiction, nor assigned to the jurisdiction of any other of the continental governments, and much less to that of Venezuela, which, in the beginning, was a dependency of the vice-royalty of New Granada, and thus continued to be until 1751.

Mr. Eames, doubtless, is ignorant of the fact that his Catholic Majesty, by royal order of the 13th of June, 1786, decreed that Maracaibo should continue united, as it was, to the captaincy general and the intendency of Caraccas; and to avoid the grievances suffered by the inhabitants of said captaincy, in being compelled to go on appeals in their suits to the pretorial court of Santo Domingo, he established another one in Caraccas, composed of a controlling dean, three auditors, and a crown attorney, allowing the same number of officers to the court of Santo Domingo, and restricting its district to the Spanish portion of that island, to Cuba, and to Puerto Rico. The jurisdiction of the court of Santo Domingo was therefore limited by the territory of the islands mentioned; whilst to the jurisdiction of Caraccas, then recently created, was subjected the rest of the territory, which previously was placed under the jurisdiction of the former court. If, as Mr. Eames says, all the territory of those continental governments originally formed a part of the jurisdiction of the government of Santo Domingo, and were successively cut off from it; if, according to the laws of the Indies, the Windward Islands were part of the territory subject to the jurisdiction of Santo Domingo; and if, by virtue of the royal letters already quoted, said islands were not comprehended in the territory to which the jurisdiction of the court of Santo Domingo was confined, Mr. Eames will be compelled to acknowledge that said royal letters cut off the Windward Islands from the jurisdiction of Santo Domingo, and, among them, Aves Island, and brought them under the jurisdiction of Caraccas, if they had not been placed within it long before and from the very creation of the captaincy of Caraccas.

Spanish America becoming independent, and different governments having been organized in the different sections, each one of them resumed, within the territory of each section, the rights of the original government, because each one of them, in that respect, stood in the stead of Spain, the original conqueror.

The dominion of a nation in a certain territory is attended by its jurisdiction over it; in other terms, by a mixed empire; and *vice versa*, jurisdiction over a territory involves dominion in that territory, unless there be proof to the contrary. Colombia having asserted her independence, resumed her dominion in all the territory which had previously been subject to the jurisdiction of the sections of which it was composed, and the latter being cut off from the former, they fully passed into the mixed empire over that part of the territory which Spain had originally intrusted to their jurisdiction. This explain- the expression "successor of Spain," which was used in regard of Venezuela in a previous note, without intending to ascribe a general character to that succession, as Mr. Eames seems to have understood.

Admitting, as Mr. Eames has done, the first of his propositions, the government of Venezuela will only have to advert to the deductions from that admission, and to the analysis of the following propositions. In the controversy which arose between the United States and Great Britain, they maintaining their right to the territory situated between the Rocky Mountains and the Pacific ocean, and between 42° and 54° 40′ of north latitude, rested their claim on the following grounds:

First. A prior discovery of the mouth of the Columbia river, made by Captain Gray, of Boston, in the year 1792. Secondly, in the first discovery of the headwaters of that river, and a survey of its course down to the sea, made by Captains Lewis and Clark in 1805 and 1806, and on the establishment of the first posts and settlements made by citizens of the United States in the disputed territory. Thirdly, on the acquisition, by the United States, of all the titles of Spain which were derived from the discovery by Spanish subjects to the coasts of the region in question, before they had been seen by people of any other civilized nation. Fourthly, on the ground of contiguity, which ought to give the United States a right to those territories stronger than any that could be adduced by any other power. "If," says Mr. Gallatin, "Great Britain have considered that a few factories on the shores of Hudson's Bay give her an exclusive right of occupation as far as the Rocky Mountains; if the new establishments on the more southern coasts of the Atlantic justify a claim to the southern seas, which in fact was asserted as far as the Mississippi—the right of millions of American citizens, who are already within reach of those seas, cannot be repelled without inconsistency. It will not be denied that the extent of a contiguous country to which an actual settlement gives a prior right, must, in a considerable degree, depend on the magnitude and the population of the establishment and on the facility with which adjacent and vacant lands may, in a short time, be occupied, settled, and cultivated by such population, connected with the probability that their occupancy and settlement may come from other parts. This doctrine was admitted, in all its latitude, by Great Britain, as appeared from all the privileges which, extending from the Atlantic to the Pacific, she granted to colonies then established on the rivers only of the Atlantic. Much more natural and much stronger is the claim when it is made by a nation whose population extends to the central parts of the continent, and whose dominion is acknowledged by all who reach the Rocky Mountains." (Wheaton's Elements.)

Here we see that the United States themselves have alleged discoveries, and especially Spanish discoveries, as a source of right to the Oregon territory. It is evident, therefore, that they cannot object to those principles which they themselves have invoked and maintained in questions of proprietorship of territory, when Venezuela, in her turn, applies those principles to her use, as the successor of Spain.

It follows, in like manner, from the fourth of those grounds, that Venezuela, being a portion of the continent nearest to Aves Island, and of a greater extent, and having a greater population than any of the islands neighboring on the Aves, no one can call in doubt the superiority of the title which Venezuela holds to claim Aves Island as adjacent land.

Mr. Eames's second proposition is, "that Spain grounded her title to Aves Island on the right of discovery, or on any other ground. No one has hitherto denied to Spain the right of first occupancy and discovery of the new world. All nations have either tacitly or expressly recognized that right. She did not discover Aves Island only to which she gave the name. She discovered continents and islands. She peopled the former and the majority of the latter. Many of these were adjacent to Aves, which remained, as it were, clasped within her immense American dominions. She therefore required no actual and continuous occupation of Aves Island, whether "because all that is found within the precinct of the territory of which a nation has possessed itself, and which has not been divided among the individual members thereof, or the particular communities of which it is composed, continues to be common to the whole nation, and constitutes what is called public property," (Merlin's Repertory,) or because the island was naturally to be considered as an appendage or dependency, physically and politically of the continent, which belonged also to said Spain.

On the other hand, an island which the claimants call a barren and uninhabited rock, offering no inducements, was not susceptible of a permanent occupation, equal to that held by the Spaniards in other localities, calculated to sustain life, to warrant cultivation, hunting, and fisheries, &c., but of an occupation *in habitu*, such as Venezuela has held and she still holds of that island, and of almost all the other islands of her right. But why longer discuss this point, if Mr. Eames here recognizes, against his will, perhaps, the just title of Spain to "Aves" Island, and the fact that she exercised jurisdiction over it, when he quotes book second, title fifteenth, of the Digest of the Indies, to prove that the government of Santo Domingo comprehended the

Windward Islands also, and among them Aves Island, adding that this group of islands never was separated from that jurisdiction by Spain, and thus recognizing that the eminent domain was in said island. To the book and title already quoted, may be added book ninth, title forty-second, Digest of the Indies, by which, through various letters royal, from 1591 up to 1634, the navigation and commerce of the Windward Islands were regulated and controlled; title second, book fourth, also of said Digest, which regulates discoveries by sea, providing, by the first law, that no one should proceed to the Indies, to make new discoveries, without royal permission. Do not all these provisions reveal the exercise of jurisdiction on the part of the government of Spain in the Western Indies, islands, and mainlands of the ocean sea, of which the King has been declared lord and master by the first law, title first, third book of the Digest of the Indies, whilst they indicate his decided intention to retain the dominion of all that vast territory? Is it not a principle recognized in law, that the mere intention is enough to retain possession? Merlin, in his Repertory of Jurisprudence, *ad verbum* "possession," says: "In order to lose possession of a thing, it is not enough that we should cease to have the enjoyment thereof. It is required that we should have had the intention of abandoning that possession."

The foregoing expositions demonstrate the truth of the third proposition: that Spain maintained her title to Spain, not only up to the date of the foundation of the captaincy general of Venezuela, exclusively deemed satisfactory by Mr. Eames, but that she also maintained it subsequently to that time.

The fourth proposition is, that Spain included, at the time, Aves Island in the captaincy general of Venezuela. In the absence of the original document by which this captaincy was erected, we have the royal order already quoted, bearing date June 13, 1786, instituting the court in Caraccas, and circumscribing the district of Santo Domingo, to Spanish portion of that island, to Cuba, and to Puerto Rico, thus bringing under the jurisdiction of Caraccas, the territory dismembered from that of Santo Domingo, a part of which the Windward Islands, the "Aves" included, had been. The Windward islands, therefore, remained under the jurisdiction of the captaincy of Caraccas, where the new court had been instituted to obviate all prejudices to its inhabitants.

The fifth proposition is, that the "Aves" continued under the jurisdiction and in possession of that captaincy general until the date of its independence, under the name of Venezuela. The truth of this proposition lies in the fact that Spain made no change in the jurisdiction allowed to the captaincy general and to the court of Caraccas, and neither adjudicated nor ceded the "Aves" to any foreign power.

The sixth proposition is, that when the republic of Colombia came to be organized, the "Aves," as a part and parcel of Venezuela, fell into the power and came under the territorial sovereignty of that republic. Than this, nothing more natural. The jurisdiction, delegated by the government of Spain, and which was exercised by the captaincy and court of Caraccas, inured to the independence of Venezuela, and she resumed her dominion in the territory, over which her ancient authorities had exercised jurisdiction in the name of the sovereign, whose allegiance was abjured; and when the republic of Colombia was founded, the dominion and soverignty which Venezuela held over her territory passed over to Colombia, which dominion and sovereignty she maintained until Venezuela, in separating from her, reassumed them; and she has maintained them, because there is no evidence that either the one or the other has made any cession of territory, or an express declaration of abandonment of any portion thereof, so as to justify the judgment that it is derelict. On the contrary, if Venezuela have made any manifestion, it has been in the inverse sense, so that her rights should never be deemed to have been abandoned. Thus it may be seen that the law of May 3, 1838, declares the existence in full vigor of the pragmatic (ordinances) *cedules*, orders, decrees, and resolutions of the Spanish government, sanctioned up to the 10th of March, 1808, which had been held in observance under said Spanish government within the territory which now forms the republic, and also of the laws of the Digest of the Indies, and of other enactments. Thus it is seen, in the treaty of peace and recognition between Venezuela and his Catholic Majesty, that the latter, after renouncing by article first all sovereignty, rights, and actions over the American territory known under the ancient name of captaincy-general of Venezuela, recognizes her, in article second, to be a free, sovereign, and independent nation, consisting of the provinces and territories mentioned in her constitution and other laws, and of other, whatsoever, territories or islands which may belong to her.

This much, said in relation to the sixth proposition, proves the truth of the three following ones enunciated by Mr. Eames: that Colombia preserved the title and possession of the "Aves," both of which passed over to Venezuela when she separated from the former, and which she has preserved up to this hour, without being disturbed therein by any one, since no one had there exercised any act that ever tended to question her possession until a few Americans, disregarding the rights of property, commenced to take out guano from said island, and that after having done the same thing in other islands belonging to Venezuela. From the moment that she was informed of this, what was her duty to prevent the prevalence of the idea that the law renounced her rights? Her forbearance might afterwards have been invoked to justify against her the presumption of a *juris et de jure* abandonment; and, in order not to leave room for such an allegation, the President ordered that the island should be garrisoned by a force of the government, and the Americans on the island be notified of the fact that said island belongs to Venezuela, so that they should not plead ignorance; and, if he instituted no proceedings against them in pursuance of the laws of the country, it was to avoid, by all means, whatever might effect in any way the friendly relations of the United States; and it is to him a source of regret, of deep regret, that what was an impulse of generosity on the part of the government, should be adduced by Mr. Eames as a proof that the proceeding of the Americans were lawful. By this act the government furnished sufficient evidence that it had no intention of abandoning its rights, and barred prescription, "for which there is no determinate period of years, because it depends on the nature of circumstances and things." (Vattel, vol. 2, § 142.)

After the nine propositions, which Mr. Eames thinks are not proved, or not susceptible of proof, the first excepted, and yet which have already been proved, he goes on to say that the "Aves" was known and used as derelict for a period of two hundred years, just as he had already stated in the same note, namely: "That, in the judgment of the United States, this 'Aves' Island, having been known for a long period of time, but not having been reduced to possession, nor included in any jurisdiction, was derelict, according to the strictest legal and lexicographic sense of the word, in the month of June, 1854." And how can Mr. Eames maintain that "Aves" Island was not reduced into possession, nor included in any jurisdiction, when he himself has maintained in the same note that, according to the laws of the Indies, the Windward Islands, the "Aves" included, were part of the territory subject to the jurisdiction of Santo Domingo? And how can Mr. Eames maintain that "Aves" Island "was known and used as derelict for two hundred years?" when the very laws of the Indies were on the 18th of May, 1680, ordered to be respected and observed, as may be seen by the law at the head of the Digest, which defines the authority of the laws of said Digest, among which are found those which exclude the idea of the abandonment of "Aves" Island, so that two hundred years have not elapsed, not even since that date, and much less since any other posterior date, from which the abandonment of the island could have commenced. This never took place; but Mr. Eames, wishing to make it appear so, has been, in spite of himself, forced into such contradictions. Mr. Eames involves himself in difficulties. He maintains that Aves Island is derelict, which presupposes that it had a former owner, who abandoned it; and at the same time he maintains that it never was reduced into possession, nor included in any jurisdiction, which is tantamount to saying that it never had an owner; and, again, and at the same time, he maintains that it was submitted to the jurisdiction of the government of Santo Domingo, a dependency of Spain, which means that Spain was the owner of the island. The document upon which he grounds all this does not date two hundred years back for its sanction, and yet he says that Aves Island was known and used, as a derelict, for two hundred years.

One by one have all the arguments of Mr. Eames's note of 31st of March last, been met and answered. And this has been done as promptly as was consistent with the necessity of taking some measures to sift out the truth and, among these, of procuring certain information from the United States themselves, and abiding the consultation of the government council, to which it was the duty of his excellency, in his judgment, to submit the question, and upon whose opinion, which it was necessary to await, the present note has been prepared. New reasons have been advanced; the title of Venezuela to the Aves has been produced; adverse principles have been impugned; how much the other party ignored has been brought forth into knowledge; what it considered to be impossible is demonstrated; the conduct of Venezuela is completely justified. She still more fully unravels the causes which have forbidden her accepting a responsibility for damages.

The duty of watching over the national interest, joined to an assurance that she had committed no wrong against the claimants, made it imperative upon her to maintain herself as she has done. The President of the republic cannot bring himself to believe that the President of the United States, in the opinion of whose minister, according to his declaration on the 31st of March last, the discussion, so far as he was concerned, stood closed, can think in a manner very different from Venezuela's in view of the foregoing defense and of the substantial grounds upon which it rests. To entertain any other expectation would be to warrant the idea that an extraordinary change has taken place in the sentiments of the United States in respect to Venezuela, and that every notion of good will and even of mere consideration has disappeared from the relations of both countries. The republic could not have had the intention of giving offense either to citizens or to the government of the United States, and it deems that this declaration, as spontaneous as it is sincere, will dispel even the shadow of a doubt on this head. Every claimant, it cannot be denied, calls into action all the influential means which he may command to reach the ends of personal advantage, without much sparing of imputations, serious and absurd as they may be, against the State from which he makes a demand. But the government of the United States is far too enlightened not to appreciate the peculiar circumstances of each individual, or to adopt the swervings of personal interest. Could the government have satisfied itself that it has committed an act of injustice, it would not have delayed to make a due reparation. That the government has acted under the control of mature deliberations and deep convictions, and not in mere caprice, will be evident to any one who will peruse the present document with calm reason. It can have no interest in justifying wrong, much less in doing so, to the detriment of the United States, whose esteem it labors to deserve by every possible means. If it refuses to acknowledge the responsibility in question, it completely vindicates its course of proceeding. If it repels the charge of dilatoriness, it shows on how slight a foundation it rests. If it questions the proofs brought forth by the claimants, it opposes to those better proofs and unanswerable objections. It relies as much on its just rights as it does on the high equity and rectitude of the government of the United States, without which all attempts to establish conviction were worse than vain. This is one of the principal reasons which have moved the government directly to appeal to that of the United States, which will immediately, and for itself, inquire into things with an unprejudiced mind. Venezuela has given proofs not to be disregarded, some of them quite recently, of the high esteem in which she holds her friendly relations with the United States. She has, upon all occasions, deferred to their wishes, accepted the compacts which were proposed to her, has done justice to their reclamations, has strived to remove all the obstacles that might trammel her purpose of drawing the two countries into closer bonds. Such are her sentiments now and such will they continue to be, notwithstanding a regretful difference of opinion about a pecuniary claim, which ought in no event to assume such an aspect as to jeopard the peace of two republics admonished by their mutual interests of the necessity of living in cordial harmony.

His excellency the President of Venezuela hopes that his excellency the President of the United States will stand in this expected position, under an abiding trust that he will not overlook these considerations when he will have come to weigh in the scales of his eminent and impartial judgment, all and each one of the reasons scattered through this note.

The documents used herein are marked by the letters A, B, C, D, E. The first embraces the measures taken previous to the declarations of Colonel Domingo Dias, First Lieutenant Pereira, and First Commander Manuel Cotarro, together with the declarations themselves. The four following letters refer to official communications of the minister of war and of the navy, and of Messrs. T. Leon Coronado and P. S. Laroche, commanders of the national armed vessels to which they refer. Finally, the letter F looks to the royal order of his Catholic Majesty, given at Aranjuez, on the 13th of June, 1786, which constitutes Venezuela's title to Aves Island.

The undersigned, Secretary of Foreign Relations of Venezuela, avails himself of the present occasions to tender renewed assurances to the Secretary of State of the United States of his most distinguished consideration.

JACINTO GUTIERREZ.

His Excellency THE SECRETARY OF STATE
of the United States.

A.

[Translation.]

SECRETARYSHIP OF STATE IN THE OFFICE OF WAR AND MARINE, DIVISION OF MARINE.

Caraccas, May 15, 1857.

To the Commanding General of the Province:

Under date of the 13th instant the Secretary of Foreign Relations says to me what follows:

"The executive authority, having agreed to the recommendation of the council of government on the subject of the reclamation made by the legation of the United States in behalf of the Americans who were taking guano from the Island of Aves, has determined that Colonel Domingo Dias and the subordinate officers who accompanied him thither, or who remained there until the 31st of December, 1854, shall depose before the competent authority, and with due solemnity, in reference to the points contained in said report, which says:

"'The council of government has made itself acquainted with the statement of reclamation made by the minister resident of the United States in behalf of the Americans who set about taking guano at the Island of Aves; and one of the principal points of that statement being the imputation of fraud and force which is made against Colonel Domingo Dias in order to invalidate a document signed by the two overseers of the laborers on the island, acknowledging Venezuela's title therein; it is deemed proper, before this body gives an opinion, to place in a clear light what really occurred on the occasion as well as other points, which it thinks will be successfully done by the following interrogatories to Colonel Dias and other officers of the marine of Venezuela who accompanied him, or who remained on the island until the 31st of December, on which day in the afternoon the Americans who were there retired.

"'1st. How was the island of Aves at the time of your arrival; who were on it; what were they doing; what had they there; and in what manner did they justify their presence there? Did they oppose the landing of the Venezuelan force, and allege any right to the island, either by considering it as belonging to the United States, or as a thing common or peculiar to them?

"'2d. What took place between the Americans and you, and led to the drawing up of the document which you and two of them signed?

"'3d. Who acted as interpreter to explain to Lang and Gibbs the tenor of said document, or of the permission you gave them to continue taking guano?

"'4th. Whether said gentlemen or others of those who accompanied them were acquainted with the Spanish language? and state, in that case, who they were.

"'5th. Whether the Americans who signed the document were well acquainted with the value and force of each and all of its articles?

"'6th. Whether the act of signing it was entirely voluntary on their part, or was it the effect of compulsion in any respect?

"'7th. How many individuals composed the Venezuelan guard, and what munitions of war had they, and how many Americans were there, and what were their means of resistance?

"'8th. What provisions, implements, machines, timber, rope, houses, furniture, or other effects, had the Americans on the island; and of these things, what remained there, and for what reason, when they retired from the island on the 31st of December, 1854?

"'9th. What preparatory labors had been performed for removing the guano; what labors are requisite for the digging out of this substance; whether they had already any guano piled up ready to be shipped; whether they shipped it in virtue of the permission which you gave them to continue doing so, or it remained on the island?

"'10th. What is the size of the island of Aves, and what are its productions and its capacity for habitation; and is it easy to approach it and to land? And

"'11th. Whether on the arrival of Colonel Dias at the island of Aves, and before signing the document to which the second interrogatory relates, there were anchored at the island any American vessels, of those which were loading with guano, on board of which might have embarked not only Charles H. Lang and thirty laborers, which he says he had, but also all the other Americans who were on the island?'

"You will be pleased to indicate to me the day on which this act takes place, in order that Mr. Eames may be invited to witness it, if he thinks proper?"

And the executive authority having directed me to send you a transcript thereof, and to authorize you to be pleased to cause Colonel Domingo Dias, the captains of frigate Manuel and Luis Cotarro, who commanded the schooner-of-war Falcon, which performed the commission to the island of Aves; the second lieutenants, Avelino Rodriguez and Pablo Garcia, subordinate officers on the same; the first lieutenant, Nicolas Pereira, adjutant to the first named officer; and the second lieutenant, Jesus Maria Arrillaga, now second in command of the schooner-of-war Monagas, to appear before your command, in order that they may give their depositions in regard to the points mentioned, it being incumbent on you to notify in advance the minister resident of the United States of the predetermined day, in order that he may be present at the proceeding, if he thinks proper.

I am your obedient servant,

CARLOS L. CASTELLI.

A copy.
GUTIERREZ.

COMMANDING GENERAL'S OFFICE,
Caraccas, May 18, 1857.

Let the determination of his excellency the executive authority be complied with. For this purpose the 30th instant, at twelve o'clock in the day, is fixed—being appointed as secretary, Lieutenant Olegario José Meneses, who swears duly to discharge the duties intrusted to him. Let the suitable summonses and notifications be made.

MANUEL CALA,
General.

T. F. DE LA GUERRA.
Adjutant of the post.
O. JOSÉ MENESES.

On the same date the necessary notifications were made.

On the 30th of the same month appeared before this command Colonel Domingo Dias, thirty-three years of age, commander of the post of Laguayra, who, having first been sworn according to law, said:

Question. How was the island of Aves at the time of your arrival? He replied, that when he reached it, on the twelfth of December, at seven o'clock at night, three vessels were anchored there. In the morning of the following day he went ashore, in order to ascertain what they were doing there, and it turned out that they were anchored for the purpose of loading with guano; and, moreover, that some eighty individuals were on shore, engaged in digging it out and putting it on board.

Question. Who were on the island? He replied, some Americans, who were directed by two individuals that represented two firms in the United States.

Question. What were they doing? He replied that he had already stated.

Question. What had they there, and in what manner did they justify their presence there? Did they oppose the lauding of the Venezuelan force, and allege any right to the island, either by considering it as belonging to the United States, or as a thing common or peculiar to them? He replied, that they had there some twelve houses and a kind of wharf to facilitate the shipping of the guano; that on examining them in regard to the matter of their presence there, Mr. Lang, one of the agents of the two firms referred to, replied that they had been on a number of the islands belonging to Venezuela; that on many of them they had found guano; that from some they had dug this substançe, as from the Brothers; that they had taken a schooner load, and that they had fixed themselves on the island of Aves because there it was not so easy for Venezuela to discover them. This is the way in which they justified their presence there. In regard to the landing, there was no resistance, and they not only alleged no right to the island, but agreed with the deponent that it belonged neither to the Union nor to themselves.

Question. What took place between the Americans and you, and led to the drawing up of the document which you and two of them signed? He replied that on their answering in the manner they did, and in pursuance of the orders of the government to prevent them from continuing to take off guano clandestinely from our islands, he summoned them to stop their labors. Thereupon they made known the losses they had sustained, one of their vessels having stranded, and another having been stoven in, and the sums which they had expended on the houses and wharf, in order that in view thereof, they might be permitted, on the score of humanity, to continue loading their vessels, which had not yet sufficient guano on board to serve for ballast. This is what took place between us, and occasioned the document to which the interrogatory refers.

Question. Who acted as interpreter to explain to Lang and Gibbs the tenor of said document, or of the permission you gave them to continue taking guano? He replied, Mr. Lang, who spoke Spanish perfectly well, for he said he had navigated for a long time in the Pacific on the coast of Peru, and who, if he had not said he was an American, would have been taken for a Spaniard; that he, Dias, did not know at that time a single word of English, as the little knowledge of it he now has was acquired in the United States, where he lived for one year, from 1855 to 1856. It ought also to be observed that Captain Manuel Cotarro, who commanded the schooner-of-war which conveyed him, knew a little English, and assisted Lang, though imperfectly, in the translation.

Question. Whether said gentlemen, or others of those who accompanied them, were acquainted with the Spanish language, and state, in that case, who they were? He replied, that of those who accompanied them, two of the laborers, one a Peruvian and the other a Chilian, spoke Spanish, but he does not know their names; that the rest he has stated.

Question. Whether the Americans who signed the document were well acquainted with the value and force of each and all of its articles? He replied, yes, they were well acquainted with their value and force, for Mr. Lang and Captain Cotarro translated the document a second time for Gibbs, who was the one who did not understand Spanish.

Question. Whether the act of signing it was entirely voluntary on their part, or was the effect of compulsion in any respect? He replied that it was entirely voluntary; that they not only thanked him verbally, but with demonstrations of gratitude for the benefit he had conferred on them, compelling him not only to dine with them that afternoon, but loaded him with presents, which he took with him to Laguayra. On the other hand, he could not have had printed in said document the names of the houses to which they belonged.

Question. How many individuals composed the Venezuelan guard; and what munitions of war had they; and what were their means of resistance? He replied, that the garrison that he left on the island consisted of ten men under command of First Lieutenant Nicolas Pereira; that they were taken from the twenty-five to twenty-seven which formed the schooner's whole complement; that they were armed each with his musket and he does not remember how many cartridges, (*paquetes*,) and a four-pounder with twenty-five loads; that he has already stated that there were some eighty Americans; that they had about fifty pairs of pistols, carrying an ounce ball, forty or more guns, some boarding pikes and axes, two small cannon, six pounders to eight pounders, with corresponding balls and a certain amount of powder, which was not less than two quintals.

Question. What provisions, implements, machines, timber, rope, houses, furniture, or other effects had the Americans on the island; and of these things what remained there, and for what reason, when they retired from the island, on the 31st of December, 1854? He replied, that he does not know what provisions; that in regard to implements, they had some seventy to eighty wheelbarrows, and the shovels requisite for that number of individuals to work, of whom some were filling and others were loading; that in regard to machines, he did not see any; that the only timber was that of the vessel which had been lost; that he did not see any rope; and that he has already mentioned the houses; that the furniture which he saw was that belonging to the cabin of the brig which had been lost, and consisted of a table, a looking-glass, some ship's chairs, and a chronometer; that he cannot say which of these things remained there, nor for what reason, if any remained, as he was only on the island on the 13th of December; that concerning this last matter, information can be furnished by Captain Joaquin Vale, and the first lieutenant, Nicolas Pereira.

Question. What preparatory labors had been performed for removing the guano; what labors are requisite for the digging out of this substance; whether they had already any guano piled up ready to be shipped; and whether they shipped it in virtue of the permission which you gave them to continue doing so, or it remained on the island? He replied: A wharf had been constructed for shipping it; that for digging it no labor was requisite but removing a foot of earth from the top, it being already in a condition to be taken up with a shovel; that they had no guano piled up, because such an operation was not necessary; but that, according to the accounts of Lieutenant Pereira, they continued loading the vessels which were there and those which arrived afterwards.

Question. What is the size of the island of Aves, and what are its productions and capacity for habitation; and is it easy to approach it and to land? He replied, that it was about 700 *varas* [Spanish yards] long, and 125 broad, and some twelve to fifteen feet high, [Spanish feet;] that its sole production is guano; that it is not adapted for habitation, because in violent storms it is covered by the sea, and it is impossible to obtain fresh water on it; that it is easy to land on it, but not so easy to approach it, as it is remarkably flat.

Question. Whether, on your arrival at the island of Aves, and before signing the document which was agreed to, there were anchored at the island any American vessels of those which were loading with guano, on board of which might have embarked not only Charles H. Lang and thirty laborers, which he says he had, but also all the other Americans who were on the island? He replied, that he had before stated there were three vessels, and that they would very well hold all the individuals who were laboring on the island, with all their effects, as one of them measured eight hundred tons, and was of itself alone capable of holding them.

At this stage, the witness made known that, as the interrogatories were terminated, he had something to add on his own part, which being allowed by the court, he stated as follows: That Lang had made known to him that the island was divided into two portions, and thereupon showed him the boundaries; that one portion, to wit, the larger, was that on which he was digging, and that the other, on which Gibbs was digging, had not enough guano to load the two vessels which were at anchor.

And the witness having signified that he had concluded, and this deposition having been read to him, together with his additional statement, he said he had nothing more to add, and that what he has stated is the truth, and he formally ratifies and signs it.

MANUEL CALA, *General.*
DOMINGO DIAS, *Deponent.*
O. JOSÉ MENESES.

On the 1st of June, of the same year, appeared the first lieutenant, Nicolas Pereira, thirty-one years of age, who, having been sworn according to law, on being interrogated, said:

Question. How was the island of Aves at the time of your arrival; who were on it; what were they doing; what had they there, and in what manner did they justify their presence there; did they oppose the landing of the Venezuelan force, and allege any right to the island, either by considering it as belonging to the United States or as a thing common or peculiar to them? He replied that there were three vessels of the American flag anchored at the island; that there were on it some eighty Americans, all men, and no women or children, and were under the direction of Mr. Lang and of Mr. Gibbs; that these Americans were taking guano from the island; that they had two pieces of artillery of six-pound caliber, with the appropriate ammunition, some fifty muskets, some thirty rifles, thirty cutlasses, some twenty-five boarding-pikes, and some fifty pairs of pistols carrying an ounce ball; and that, as regards their justification for being on the island, they represented that they were there taking guano, and that they did not take it from islands nearer the mainland, although they had found guano on them, because they might be discovered, and that from one of them only they had taken a schooner load; that he does not state the name of the island from which they took a schooner-load because he does not remember it; that they did not oppose the landing of the Venezuelan force, nor allege any kind of right to the island; and that they asked Colonel Dias to allow them to load the three large vessels which they had there, and others which, dispatched by their firms, might subsequently arrive, and this in consideration of the losses they had suffered and the expenses they had incurred, to which request Colonel Dias yielded, but only till the government should otherwise dispose, his act being wholly one of humanity, since he had not the power to concede so much, as the colonel himself told them.

Question. What took place between the Americans and Colonel Dias, and led to the drawing up of the document which he and two of them signed? He replied, that Colonel Dias granted them a favor in permitting them to continue taking guano, and they asked that he would grant it in writing; at the same time, they offered to render the guard every assistance which it might need, for the colonel had made known to them that he left but little provisions and water, and it was under these circumstances that the writing was drawn up which has been spoken of; and observing that they had a large number of fire-arms and side-arms in proportion to the small guard which remained, he said to them that those arms were to be guaranteed by the military, to which they agreed. That the arms referred to have already been mentioned.

Question. Who acted as interpreter to explain to Lang and Gibbs the tenor of said document, or of the permission which he (Dias) gave them to continue taking guano? He replied that Mr. Lang acted as interpreter to Mr. Gibbs; that Mr. Lang spoke Spanish with such entire perfection that he needed no interpreter, but, on the contrary, corrected some small mistakes which were made in the writing; that the document was written by the deponent in his own handwriting, in their house, on their paper, and with their pen and ink, which they voluntarily presented to him for that purpose.

Question. Whether said gentlemen, or others of those who accompanied them, were acquainted with the Spanish language, and state, in that case, who they were? He replied that besides Mr. Lang, who, as he has said, spoke Spanish, there was a Peruvian Indian, called Santiago, and a young Chilian, called Francisco, whose surnames he does not know, who acted continuously as interpreters after Mr. Lang had done so.

Question. Whether the Americans who signed the document were well acquainted with the value and force of each and all of its articles? He replied that with respect to Mr. Lang, he could answer that he was well acquainted with their value and force; that, with respect to Mr. Gibbs, he believed that he perfectly understood them, for when the deponent wanted bread, he had nothing else to do than to point to the number of the article in the manuscript, which has been mentioned, in which it was stated that whenever the deponent should need any provisions they would furnish them, until some government vessel should arrive.

Question. Whether the act of signing the document was entirely voluntary on their part, or was the effect of compulsion in any respect? He replied that it was voluntary; that he did not see among them the slightest appearance of doubt, apprehension, or mistrust; and that there was no kind of threats or coersion in that act.

Question. How many individuals composed the Venezuelan guard, and what munitions of war had they; and how many Americans were there, and what were their means of resistance? He replied that during the act of signing the writing that was made, there was not a single soldier on shore; that afterwards ten men were landed to form the guard; that they had ten guns, ten cartridges, and a four-pounder cannon, with its ammunition; that with respect to the number of Americans, he has stated it; and that their means of resistance was the arms which have been mentioned, and the powder to be used with the fire-arms.

Question. What provisions, implements, machines, timber, rope, houses, furniture, or other effects, had the Americans on the island; and of these things, what remained there, and for what reason, when they retired from the island on the 31st of December, 1854? He replied that with regard to provisions he was entirely ignorant of what they had; that they had hand-barrows and some shovels and picks; that they had no machine; that they had some pieces of board on which they ran the wheelbarrows; that they had no rope; that they had from eleven to thirteen wooden shanties, the best one of which was sold to the deponent for a pound, and belonged to Lang; that another, in which Gibbs lived, was granted to deponent for the guard, at the time of deponent's going ashore; that the rest, almost entirely, were unroofed and completely demolished by them; that these houses were so fragile, that those to the eastward were heavily stowed with coral stone to protect them from the force of the wind; that, moreover, they had some launches by which they conveyed the guano on board, one of which they sold to the captain of frigate Joaquin Vale, at from a doubloon to twenty-one dollars; they left two worthless ones ashore, because they could make no use of them: another worthless one they set on fire, and the rest they took with them; that there remained, therefore, on the island, the leavings of the demolished houses, the house which they sold to the deponent, the one which they gave for the guard, and in the water some floating timbers of a wharf, which they destroyed contrary to their will, and which was composed of some pine logs, some useless pine flooring, and pieces of board already worn out by the frequent use which had been made of it; that after they had made known that they had finished loading, and that there was nothing more which they wished to carry away, they sold him twenty-five barrels of water that were on shore for twenty-five dollars in coin.

Question. What preparatory labors had been performed for removing the guano; what labors are requisite for the digging out of this substance; whether they had already any guano piled up ready to be shipped; whether they shipped it in virtue of the permission which was given them to continue doing so, or it remained on the island? He replied that, for the removal of the guano on the Island of Aves, no preparation was necessary, except to take a little sand from the top, to place the guano in the carts, and to ship it, an operation which is performed with the shovels, and consequently there were no preparatory labors; that there was no guano piled up, because it was not necessary, as may be understood from what he has already stated; that, accordingly, they went on taking guano, and went on shipping it in virtue of the permission which had been given to them.

Question. What is the size of the Island of Aves, and what are its productions and its capacity for habitation; and is it easy to approach it and to land? He replied that he did not know its exact size, but that it is some five hundred varas from the northeast to the southwest, which is its greatest length, and some hundred and fifty varas wide at the center, which is its greatest breadth; and that it is from about eleven to thirteen feet high; its latitude 15° 40′ 20″ north, and its longitude is found in the meridian of Isla Blanca; its only production is guano; it has no capacity for habitation, because it lacks water and is washed by the sea in storms, a thing which happens every year at the equinox; it has a cove to the west southwest, which is very dangerous when the winds are from the north, and everywhere else it is surrounded with reefs which render a landing impossible.

Question. Whether on the arrival of Colonel Dias at the Island of Aves, and before signing the document to which the second interrogatory relates, there were anchored at the island any American vessels, of those which were loading with guano, on board of which might have embarked not only Charles H. Lang and thirty laborers, which he says he had, but also all the other Americans who were on the island? He replied, that there were three vessels there of heavy tonnage, as he has before said, and that one of them alone was sufficient to carry eighty men, according to Spanish regulations, for the vessel measured eight hundred tons, as he was informed by her own captain and Mr. Lang; that there was another measuring five hundred tons, which was the bark Corcor, belonging to the firm of Lang & Delano; that, as to the third, he does not know how many tons she measured, but she was also a vessel of large size; that the first-mentioned vessel was called the Amazon, and her captain spoke Spanish; that this statement in regard to the captain refers to article four, or the fourth interrogatory of those which he has already replied to, and that, in consequence of what he has already stated in regard to the capacity of the vessels, he thinks that all of them could have embarked, with all their goods and chattels, if they had so desired.

On this, his deposition being read to him, he said that what he has stated is the truth, that he has nothing to add or take away from it, and that he ratifies and signs it.

MANUEL CALA, *General.*
NICHOLAS PEREIRA, *Deponent.*
O. JOSÉ MENESES, *Secretary.*

On the fifth of June, of the same year, appeared before this command Captain Manuel Cotarro, forty years of age, an officer, with an invalid's certificate; and he having been sworn in legal form to state the truth in answer to what he should be asked, the commanding genal proceeded to address to him the eleven interrogatories mentioned in the letter of the Secretary of State in the offices of war and marine, dated the 15th of May last, which begins the papers in this record.

To the first interrogatory he said, that on the 12th day of December, 1854, he arrived at the Island of Aves, and landed on it on the 13th, at six o'clock in the morning, by direction of Colonel Dias; that he found on the island some eighty Americans, who had three vessels at anchor; that these individuals were employed in taking guano and in shipping it; that they had there a kind of wharf, which consisted of some wooden beams of a wrecked vessel, fragments of which still remained on the shore; that they had also about a dozen small houses or shanties, which were constructed of old timber, perhaps of wrecked vessels; that the Americans stated to them that they were on the island in search of guano, as they had been on other islands of Venezuela with the same object; that they did not oppose the landing of the Venezuelan force, but on the contrary, sent them launches in order to land the soldiers, the water, provisions, and a four-pounder cannon, with its corresponding ammunition, as a defense for the guard; that they did not allege any right to the island, but, on the contrary, after making known the reason of their being there, which was to seek for guano, they said they might be permitted to finish loading their vessels, as they wanted to compensate themselves for the damages they had sustained by the loss of some of their vessels, expenses of the enterprise in which they were engaged, and labor on the small houses and a kind of wharf which has been mentioned; that these representations were made in such a supplicating manner that nothing less could be done than to yield to their request; that the Americans referred to were all men, no women or children being seen among them, were clad in the dress of sailors, and belonged to two companies, at the head of which appeared two gentlemen named Lang and Gibbs.

The second interrogatory being addressed to him he said: That on granting them the favor to finish loading the vessels, as already mentioned, the Americans demanded that the permission should be given to them in writing, in consideration that they might meet Venezuelan vessels and have to prove their right to the cargo they were carrying; that on this account the document mentioned was granted to them, in which was specified the concession made to them, and the reason for it; and the national vessels-of-war were prohibited from preventing said persons from finishing their loading; that, besides said document, the Americans asked for an order to the officer who remained on the island in charge of the guard, to the end that the vessels mentioned should not be prevented from continuing to load.

The third interrogatory being addressed to him he said: That the deponent acted as interpreter to explain the document in conjunction with Lang, an individual who understood Spanish.

The fourth interrogatory being addressed to him he said: That, besides Mr. Lang, he remembers that there were two persons from the

East Indies who were also acquainted with Spanish, whose names he does not recollect.

The fifth interrogatory being addressed to him he said: That the Americans were as well acquainted with the force and value of each and all of the articles of the document as the deponent; it was read and translated to them more than ten times, and explained article by article.

The sixth interrogatory being addressed to him he said: That it was voluntary, as well as solicited by themselves for a security, as has been stated; and, consequently, that there was no appearance of compulsion in any respect.

The seventh interrogatory being addressed to him he said: That the Venezuelan guard was composed of twenty-five men, of whom ten remained on shore; that they had ten muskets, ten cartridges (*paquetes*), and a four-pounder cannon, with its ammunition; that the number of the Americans he has already stated; that the Americans had two four-pounder cannon, with their corresponding balls and powder, a number of rifles, say forty or fifty, and a like number of pairs of pistols, a few more or less.

The eighth interrogatory being addressed to him he said: That they had some casks, some containing water and others empty, two barrels of meat, half a one of pork, a barrel of flour commenced on, and a hog; this in regard to provisions; that of implements, he saw shovels, crow-bars, and wheelbarrows, but all in very small number; that they had no machines; that they had no timber; that the houses he has already mentioned, twelve small shanties; that of furniture, he saw some, such as a table, a sofa, a looking glass, and a chronometer, articles belonging to a wrecked vessel, as he noticed by the make of them, and as Mr. Lang himself said they were; that, besides what he has stated, there were no other articles of any kind on the island; that he cannot say whether those articles remained on the island or not, the whole or a part of them, as the deponent left on the said thirteenth day.

The ninth interrogatory being addressed to him he said: That there were no preparatory labors for removing the guano; that to dig out this substance it was only requisite to take off a layer of sand and take it out with shovels; that there was no guano piled up, because as fast as they dug it out they shipped it; that during the thirteenth day the deponent saw the Americans continuing to load with guano in virtue of the permission which Dias gave to them.

The tenth interrogatory being addressed to him he said: That the Island of Aves is about 700 varas long by about one hundred and twenty-five wide, and some twelve to fifteen feet high; that it produces nothing but guano, as there is not even a single bush on it; that it is not adapted for habitation in consequence of being frequently inundated during heavy storms, and because it is impossible to obtain fresh water on it; that it is not easy to approach it and to land, because there is a heavy sea, and the anchoring ground is distant.

The eleventh interrogatory being addressed to him he said: That before the signing of the document or permission, to which the second interrogatory relates, the same three vessels which have been previously mentioned were there, for he found them on his arrival and left them at his departure from the island; that these vessels were sufficient for Mr. Lang and his laborers to embark on, as the smallest one would hold five hundred tons, and one of them measured eight hundred tons; that, as he only staid at the island one day, he does not remember the names of these vessels.

On his deposition being read to him, he said that he had nothing to add or take away, and that all that he has stated is the truth, which he ratifies in form and signs.

MANUEL CALA, *General.*
MANUEL DEL COTARRO, *Deponent.*
O. JOSE MENESES, *Secretary.*

COMMANDING GENERAL'S OFFICE,
Caraccas, June 10, 1857.

Let these proceedings be returned to the Secretary of State in the offices of War and Marine, inasmuch as the other officers mentioned are not now at this post.

MANUEL CALA, *General.*

A copy. GUTIERREZ.

B.

[Translation.]

Republic of Venezuela.

SECRETARYSHIP OF STATE IN THE OFFICES OF WAR AND MARINE, DIVISION OF MARINE.

CARACCAS, *October* 25, 1855,
26*th year of the law and* 45*th of Independence.*

Mr. Secretary of State in the Office of Treasury:

In the log-book of the war-schooner Monagas, which has arrived at Laguayra from the Island of Aves, is a paragraph of the following tenor:

"*Tuesday*, 2d, *to Wednesday*, 3d *of October.*—At 4 p. m. of this day came in sight of The Brothers. On passing through the channel between Orquilla and El Pié, we found anchored at the latter an American schooner. We lay to and hoisted our flag; she did not display hers. The boat was launched, and the second officer went on board. On the boats drawing near, it was noticed that many persons came hurriedly down to the beach of the island. The boat waiting for them on the shore, they got in, and went on board and hoisted the American flag. The second officer asked the captain for his papers, and he gave him a passport and a contract; he did not want to give him the vessel's register. He was then summoned, on the part of the commanding officer, to come on board of our schooner, which he was unwilling to do. The second officer came and returned in company with the commanding officer. The captain then said that he was there loading with guano; that he had ten tons on board and sixty-five bags ashore; that he had gone there from Laguayra; and he showed his register. The schooner was called the White Swan, of Baltimore, Captain J. Henry. The commanding officer informed him that he must remain at anchor until daybreak, when he would communicate his orders. The captain agreed to this. The boat came alongside and we then commenced beating between Orquilla and El Pié, not being able to anchor because we were unacquainted with the anchoring ground. In one of the tacks, a little longer than the rest, the schooner made sail. (It was then 1 o'clock of the morning.) On noticing it we pursued her. Finally we descried her, and continued in her wake until four o'clock, a. m. On getting within average cannon shot distance from her we fired several loads of ball and grape at her. She again left us. We made all sail, although our sails were reefed, and we kept up the pursuit until 11, p. m., when we could no longer overtake her. Then we tacked ship, and again returned to The Brothers."

Which I have the honor to inclose to you for your knowledge and further purposes.

I am your obedient servant,

FRANCISCO ORIACH.

A copy.

[SEAL.] GUTIERREZ.

C.

[Translation.]

Republic of Venezuela.

SCHOONER-OF-WAR MONAGAS, AT ANCHOR IN THE CRUCITA,
October 16, 1855.

Mr. Minister of State in the Office of Treasury:

In the long and painful voyage I have had to make since I left Laguayra on the 19th of August last, I went finally to the Island of Aves and anchored there on the 28th of September, and, after having put ashore Senor Rafael Miranda, superintendent of the guano in that island, I was informed by Lieutenant Francisco Atiles, the commander of that garrison, that the official communication which was transmitted to him by Colonel Jelambi, his immediate superior, did not impose on him the duty of allowing any vessel to load, though it were dispatched by Senor Gusman, until the supreme government should prescribe its regulations through the regular channel, empowering Senor Miranda to dispatch vessels with guano from that island.

I deem it proper to inform you that I leave this port for La Orchila and Los Rogues in the fulfillment of my duty, and, although I expect to arrive in a few days at Laguayra, I make known to you that at the small islands The Brothers, to the north of Macanao, I found an American schooner loading with guano stealthily, and, although I pursued her with the vessel under my command, I could not overtake her, but I captured eighty bags of the substance, which she was unable to ship, and I retain it on board.

I am your obedient servant,

J. LEON CORONADO.

A copy.

[SEAL.] GUTIERREZ.

D.

[Translation.]

Republic of Venezuela.

SCHOONER-OF-WAR MONAGAS,
At anchor at Laguayra, October 23, 1855.

Mr. Secretary of State in the Office of Treasury:

I have now, at 4, p. m., just cast anchor in this roadstead, on my way from Barcelonce, Tortuga Island, and Higuerote.

* * * * * * * *

On the 29th, I set sail; I arrived at Juan Griego, but did not enter harbor. I went to the Brothers and to the small island known by the name of El Pié. On coming out I found an American schooner stealing guano. I immediately lay to, and the second officer proceeded to visit her. I afterwards went myself. I learned from the captain that he was there loading with guano. He brought to me at the side her papers, which did not seem to me to be legal, and I imposed on him the duty of remaining at anchor until the following day—it was then six in the evening—when I would communicate to him my orders, and I continued tacking between El Pié and La Orquilla, the other island. The wind was blowing strong; we had the least possible sail set. I was aft and the second officer forward all night, detained giving orders, and ourselves working side by side with the sailors. From time to time I heard the voice of the second officer telling me that the bonnet of the jib was torn to pieces, and that another was being set, &c., and I replied to him—keep courage. In one of the tacks, a little longer than the rest, the schooner escaped from us. Immediately we crowded sail and pursued her. At daybreak we were within average cannon-shot distance, and fired several times at her with ball. Immediately she again went ahead of us. I followed her until the following day at noon, when, perceiving that I was unable to continue the pursuit, I returned to El Pié. We searched the whole island, and found there some bags filled with guano, some with stone, and others empty, implements, rope, picks, &c., left there by the Americans. In the fissures of the stone guano of various kinds was found, samples of which I have on board, and also have the articles left by the persons belonging to the schooner. I then returned to Juan Griego, communicated what had taken place to the governor, and thereupon went to Barcelona. I was there two days. From thence I came to La Tortuga, and afterwards to Higuerote, to gather information about the state of Laguayra and Caraccas, and moreover, to take in a fresh supply of water. There I got sick, and could not leave until the 22d, and to-day I have arrived in this port.

I remain your obedient servant,

J. LEON CORONADO.

[SEAL.] A copy.
GUTIERREZ.

[Translation.]

E.

Command of the war schooner, "13th of December, 1848.

VELA DE CORO, *September* 17, 1855.

Mr. Secretary of State in the Office of Treasury:

In fulfillment of the commission and orders which his excellency the executive authority has thought fit to intrust to me in regard to my keeping strict watch over the islands of Los Monges and coast of Paraguana, I have to communicate to you the following:

On the 13th of the last month, I came to anchor in this port, for the purpose of landing General Falcon, agreeably to your official order; and on the 14th, at daybreak, I set sail for the islands of Los Monges. On the same day I arrived at those islands, and on the following day I examined them, one by one, carefully; finding on the first isle, which lies to the southward, two small shanties made of boards and temporarily constructed; and on the latter, lying further north, another shanty made of boards, and smaller than the shanties on the former island, but of the same construction. In these shanties were living the North Americans, who were removing guano. I ought to state to you that the kind of guano which is on these islands must be of superior quality to that heretofore discovered on the other islands, on account of its being without any mixture of sand, and on account of its stronger smell, for it is composed of the stones, themselves petrified with earth, or limestone dissolved from those stones. This is a sufficient reason for believing that it is better; but there is also much difficulty in removing it, and consequently a vessel of regular size, coming to these islands to load with guano, may calculate on a period of a month when laboring with a sufficient number of men, unless it does not receive much stone, for on these islands there is really no convenient position for getting it at once on board. After the greatest labor in getting it out and separating it from the stones, it has to be placed in large launches at the openings of the island, in order to convey it to the vessels. These launches are liable to be frequently broken to pieces, owing to the desolate character of that island. On the 23d of August last, availing myself of a period of fair weather, I came to the determination of mooring the vessel with a chain to the shore, in a cove or small harbor formed by the southern isle. This cove is somewhat sheltered by the island, and I remained there through the whole night, with uneasiness, for the want of cables. On the following day an American bark made her appearance near me, and was moored in the same fashion. Her captain afterwards came on board, and on my inquiring into the object of his coming to the island, he replied that he came freighted from Boston to load with guano; that the bark was called the Tom Corwin, Captain Hiram Burt, and that they had been assured that they would find persons on the island who would deliver to them the cargo. After this statement, he told me that they took the loose stones to which the guano adhered, ground them, and mixed them with Peruvian guano. This intimation of the captain was caused by some bags filled with stone which I had found on the island.

After being there for two hours, he set sail for Caraçao. From that date I have nothing more to add, continuing always on my cruise between those islands and the coast of Paraguana, meeting on the latter many Dutch and Venezuelan vessels which were going to load with salt at the saline of Guaranao.

On the 26th of the same month, on our water giving out, I went to obtain some at the point of La Macolla; I there found a sunken launch full of water. I then went ashore, when some individuals informed me that they lived on the grazing farm of Señor Luis Hermoso; that that launch had brought from the island of Oruba twenty-four persons, a body of laborers, which the Americans had for working at the guano, and that the captain of the bark which had loaded with guano on those islands was about to convey them to Oruba; but being prevented by the strong currents and the scarcity of provisions, and not being able to go to that island, the captain determined to give the launch of the vessel to these individuals, in order that they might transport themselves to that island; but this being also prevented by the currents, they left the launch at anchor, and afterwards embarked in a small sloop. The launch is in my possession.

Yesterday I anchored in this port, where I had been on the 13th of the last month, and left on obtaining provisions, and to-morrow I shall set sail for the Monges, where I shall continue, in order to fulfill my instructions.

All of which I have to communicate to you, in order that you may deign to lay it before the supreme government.

I am, with every attention and respect, your obedient servant,

P. S. LAROCHE.

[SEAL.] A copy.

GUTIERREZ.

[Translation.]

F.

The king having made himself well acquainted with the petition of the municipal corporation, court of justice, and regiment of the city of Maracaibo, in regard to his majesty's deigning to reintegrate their province to the dominion, rule, and government, political and military, with all their incidents, of the vice-royalty of Santa Fé, from which it was segregated by royal decree of the 6th of September, 1777, and likewise with what the late viceroy of the kingdom, Don Manuel Antonio Flores, and the attorney of his royal treasury, as well as your lordship and the governor of that province, have reported on the matter, his majesty has determined, in view of the whole, that the province of Maracaibo shall continue united, as at present, to the captain generalship and superintendency of Caraccas, attention being paid to what is prescribed by royal decree, of the 15th of February of this year, in regard to uniting the city of Truxillo, and its jurisdiction, to the government of Maracaibo, and in regard to the erection of the province of Varinas into a separate command of its present rank. And in order to prevent injuries from arising to the inhabitants of said province of Maracaibo, and to those of the province of Cumana, Guayana, Margarita, and Trinidad, comprised in the same captain generalship, in resorting by appeal in their affairs to the superior court of Santo Domingo, the king has determined to create another superior court, to be composed now of one chief justice, three associate justices, and an attorney, leaving a like number of judges in that of Santo Domingo, and circumscribing its district to the Spanish part of that island, the island of Cuba, and the island of Porto Rico, for which purpose his majesty appoints, at the present time, the three judges which are to serve in each of them.

I make this known to your lordship by royal order, for your knowledge and government.

God preserve your lordship many years.

Aranjuez, June 13, 1786.

SONOXA

To the INTENDENT OF CARACCAS.

CARACCAS, *November* 27, 1786.

Let this royal order be communicated by circular, and recorded in the court of exchequer and general auditorship of army and royal treasury.

SAAVEDRA.

This royal order has been recorded at Caraccas, on the 5th of December, 1786.

[SEAL.] A copy.
GUTIERREZ.

Mr. Eames to Mr. Cass.

No. 41.] LEGATION OF THE UNITED STATES,
Caraccas, November 3, 1857.

SIR: With reference to my No. 40, of 31st ultimo, it is now with great satisfaction that I have the honor to acknowledge the receipt, at ten o'clock of the evening of that day, (a few hours after sealing my No. 40,) of your No. 56, of 6th ultimo, with its inclosures. It has of course removed from my mind all doubt of the propriety of the course I adopted in suspending the reading of your No. 53 in my first interview with Mr. Gutierrez; and it gives me what I deem just the necessary discretion as to my future course in the Aves case.

Of course I have lost no time in taking my position in conformity with the state of the case disclosed in the dispatch and its inclosures; and in taking that position, I have fortunately found myself aided rather than embarrassed by the action I had already taken under your No. 53.

I inclose copy and translation of the note of Mr. Gutierrez, of yesterday's date, in reply to my request for a special audience, and copy of my note of the same date waiving for a brief period that request. Of my personal interview with the president, referred to in my note of yesterday to Mr. Gutierrez, I have only to inform the department that it was entirely courteous, and I think even cordial on the part of his excellency; and it is proper to add, that at the interview with Mr. Gutierrez of yesterday morning, the form of his reply to my note requesting the audience was arranged, and also the general character of my answer to it. This answer itself being somewhat full and explicit, supercedes the necessity of any further account to the department in this dispatch of the action I have taken since the receipt of its No. 56.

It is gratifying to me that without the aid of that dispatch, I made in my first interview with Mr. Gutierrez, in view of the information which he then gave, the very points as to the position of my government in the "Aves" case, which I perceive to have been made to Mr. Ribas in your note to him of 11th of September last, doubtless upon similar information.

With reference to the first paragraph of your No. 56, in which I am informed that it was expected and understood that I should again visit Washington before embarking for Caraccas, I have to express my great regret that I was not aware of such expectation or understanding; because, in that case, I should at once and very gladly have acted upon it by reason of my high sense of the importance to a diplomatic agent, especially when charged with a question of any difficulty, of personal communication with the Department of State. In fact, when I left Washington, I was under the contrary impression that the department desired me to reach Caraccas as soon as practicable, and I regulated my movements accordingly, at some sacrifice of personal convenience.

In great haste, I have the honor to be, with the highest respect and consideration, your obedient servant,

CHARLES EAMES.

Hon. LEWIS CASS, *Secretary of State.*

[Translation.]

Republic of Venezuela.

DEPARTMENT OF FOREIGN RELATIONS,
Caraccas, November 2, 1857.

The minister of foreign relations of Venezuela has the honor to make known to the honorable minister resident of the United States, that on the day before yesterday, at three o'clock, p. m., being Saturday, and thus the day of the session of the council of government, he received the note of that date in which Mr. Eames requests an audience of his excellency the president of the republic, in order to make to him a communication with which he is charged by his excellency the President of the United States.

The undersigned will give account of the said note in his first audience with his excellency, and will at once communicate to Mr. Eames the answer.

The undersigned renews to the Hon. Mr. Eames the assurances of his distinguished consideration.

JACINTO GUTIERREZ.

Hon. CHARLES EAMES,
Minister Resident of the United States.

LEGATION OF THE UNITED STATES,
Caraccas, November 2, 1857.

SIR: The undersigned, minister resident of the United States, has the honor to acknowledge the note of this day's date of the Hon. Mr. Gutierrez, in reply to that addressed to him by the undersigned on the 31st ultimo, in reference to a special audience of his excellency the president of the Republic.

The undersigned now hastens to inform the honorable minister of foreign relations, that at a late hour on the evening of the 31st ultimo, and several hours after his note of that date had been received by Mr. Gutierrez, the undersigned had the satisfaction to receive dispatches from his government inclosing copies of the official correspondence on the "Aves" question, had (since the undersigned received his instructions and left Washington *en route* for Venezuela) between the honorable Secretary of State of the United States and Hon. Mr. Ribas, the Venezuelan *charge d' affaires* at Washington, and by which the undersigned is also informed that the important paper which he was instructed to communicate to his excellency the President was read, as the undersigned desired and expected that it might be, to Mr. Ribas; that Mr. Ribas requested that the undersigned might be authorized by his government to delay the communication of the paper in question to the Venezuelan government until Mr. Ribas could himself communicate with his government, which he undertook forthwith to do; and that accordingly such authority to suspend or delay that communication for a suitable time has been given to the undersigned.

The undersigned promptly avails himself of this authorization to announce that the immediate necessity for a special audience of his excellency the president of the republic for the purpose of making that communicatión which, under the instructions of the undersigned, existed when his note of the 31st ultimo, to Mr. Gutierrez, was written, has now been, for a short time at least, removed, and that the request for such audience as contained in that note, is for the present waived.

It will be highly agreeable to the undersigned, and he permits himself now to hope, that by a prompt and satisfactory disposition of the "Aves" question, duly made known to him by the Venezuelan government, all necessity for a formal presentation of that communication may be finally removed, in a manner conformed to the justice of the case and the dignity and friendly relations of the two governments.

The note of the 11th September last, addressed by the honorable Secretary of State of the United States to Mr. Ribas, defines the unchanged position of the government of the United States in respect to the "Aves" reclamation in terms exactly coincident with the expressions used by the undersigned upon the same subject to Mr. Gutierrez, in the conference of the 29th ultimo; and the fact that that note has doubtless been for some days known to the Venezuelan government, when taken in connection with the statement made at that conference by Mr. Gutierrez, that the answer of his government in the case would be immediately forwarded to Washington, seems to the undersigned to justify the hope that this long pending question now approaches that satisfactory solution which its gravity and urgency clearly demand.

Though the undersigned had the honor yesterday to mention briefly to his excellency the President the substance of most of the above observations in a personal and informal interview, and though they were this morning, at the first practicable opportunity, also briefly stated in conversation to the honorable minister of foreign relations, the undersigned yet deems it proper to request that this note may be also laid before his Excellency, with the note of the 31st ultimo, to which it refers.

The undersigned renews to the Hon. Señor Gutierrez the assurance of his distinguished consideration.

CHARLES EAMES.

Hon. JACINTO GUTIERREZ,
Minister of Foreign Relations.

Mr. Cass to Mr. Gutierrez.

DEPARTMENT OF STATE,
Washington, November 12, 1857.

SIR: I have the honor to acknowledge the receipt, on the 4th instant, of your excellency's note of the 21st September, ultimo.

The communication on the subject of the Aves Island claim, to which it refers as having been completed, has not yet reached the Department, but whenever it arrives, it shall receive all that respectful consideration to which the views of your excellency must always be entitled.

In the mean time, I forbear to add any thing to what has recently been urged on the part of this government with respect to the claim in question, except to express the earnest hope that the anticipated communication of your excellency may be of such a character as to lead to its prompt and amicable adjustment.

I avail myself of the opportunity to offer, &c.,

LEWIS CASS.

His Excellency Señor JACINTO GUTIERREZ,
Secretary for Foreign Affairs of the Republic of Venezuela, &c.

Mr. Eames to Mr. Cass.

No. 42.]

LEGATION OF THE UNITED STATES,
Caraccas, December 3, 1857.

SIR: With reference to my No. 41 and its inclosures relating to the Aves Island claim, I have the honor now to transmit inclosed to the department further correspondence with this government on that subject, being copies and translations of two notes of Mr. Gutierrez to me under dates respectively of 3d and 23d ultimo, with copies of two notes addressed by me to him under dates respectively of 21st and 30th ultimo.

The department will perceive by this correspondence that in reply to my request under date of 21st ultimo to be apprised of the determination of Venezuela in the Aves Island case, and of any action taken for its prompt adjustment, I am informed by Mr. Gutierrez under date of 23d ultimo that the answer of this government to that reclamation, prepared before my return here, has been forwarded to Washington through the Venezuelan legation there, and that in addition to that legation a special mission of the grade of envoy extraordinary and minister plenipotentiary has now been established, and is about to proceed to the United States charged with the same subject. The special minister appointed is Señor Mariano Briceno. He informs me that he shall proceed to the United States by way of St. Thomas and Havana by the packet of the 8th instant, and that he expects to be in Washington on or before the 1st of January next. Mr. Briceno is the editor of the only daily newspaper published in this city, and is reputed to be a man of ability and accomplishment, but he has not heretofore taken a prominent part in politics here, his journal being considered as neutral.

I have considered that a special mission instituted by any government to settle a reclamation pending against it is a proceeding of such a character that the resident diplomatic agent of the government making the reclamation can rarely, if ever, with propriety interpose objection to it, except in obedience to specific instructions so to interpose. I have also considered that the institution of such a mission to settle a claim is always a virtual acknowledgment that there is a valid claim requiring settlement; and such acknowledgment is still more clearly implied when, as in this case, the special mission is instituted by Venezuela in full view of the previous announcement by the United States that the liability of Venezuela is too manifest to justify or admit further discussion.

It has not appeared to me probable that the department will now consent to reopen the discussion on the point of liability, or will allow the negotiation in the hands of the special mission to assume any shape not compatible with the position taken upon the undisputed facts of the case by the government of the United States in your note of 11th of September to the Venezuelan chargé d'affaires. Should the department in this view see fit to make the formal and explicit admission of liability by this government a condition precedent to the reception of the special mission, I have no sufficient ground to conclude that such admission will be withheld. My note of the 30th ultimo to Mr. Gutierrez is conceived in this sense.

Your No. 56 acknowledged in my No. 41 is the latest dispatch received from the department.

With the highest respect, I have the honor to be, your obedient servant,

CHARLES EAMES.

Hon. Lewis Cass,
Secretary of State.

(Translation.]

Republic of Venezuela.

Department of Foreign Relations,
Caraccas, November 3, 1857.

The Minister of Foreign Relations of Venezuela has the honor to acquaint the honorable minister resident of the receipt of his note of yesterday, concerning the subject of the Island of Aves, and that his excellency the President being, as is known to Mr. Eames at this time indisposed, the undersigned will not be able to take his orders for a reply until he shall have recovered from his illness.

The undersigned renews to Hon. Mr. Eames the assurances of his distinguished consideration.

JACINTO GUTIERREZ.

Hon. Charles Eames,
Minister Resident of the United States.

Legation of the United States,
Caraccas, November 21, 1857.

Sir: The undersigned, minister resident of the United States, has the honor to bring to the renewed attention of the honorable Minister of Foreign Relations of Venezuela the note of the 2d instant in relation to the Aves reclamation, in which the undersigned, in view of the state of that reclamation at that time, expressed the hope that a satisfactory disposition of it, promptly made known to him by the Venezuelan government, might preclude the necessity of further action on his part under his instructions to obtain the determination of Venezuela in the case.

That note was acknowledged by the Hon. Mr. Gutierrez under date of 3d instant, and the acknowledgment was accompanied by an intimation that as soon as the health of his excellency the President would permit, his excellency's orders would be taken for the preparation of a further reply; but up to the present time no such reply, nor any official communication from the government of Venezuela in reference to the Aves question, subsequent to the note of the 3d instant referred to, has reached this legation.

It is, therefore, the duty of the undersigned, under his instructions, to request, and he now requests, to be informed what determination has been arrived at in regard to the "Aves" reclamation, and what action, for the purpose of effecting a speedy and satisfactory adjustment of it, has been taken by the government of Venezuela since the official conference of the 29th ultimo between the undersigned and the honorable Minister of Foreign Relations on that subject.

The undersigned renews to the Hon. Mr. Gutierrez the assurance of his distinguished consideration.

CHARLES EAMES.

Hon. Jacinto Gutierrez,
Minister of Foreign Relations.

[Translation.]

Republic of Venezuela.

Department of Foreign Relations,
Caraccas, November 23, 1857.

His excellency the President of the republic has been informed of the communication of the 21st instant, addressed to this department by the honorable minister resident of the United States, referring to his previous one of the 2d instant, which, as well as the other making mention of it, the executive power has ordered to be answered in the manner in which the undersigned now proceeds to answer it.

Before the departure of Mr. Eames from Venezuela for the United States, five months' ago, the question respecting the guano of the Island of Aves not being as yet concluded, the undersigned announced to him that there being a legation of Venezuela in Washington the government, in the absence of the American legation from Caraccas, would enter into an understanding with the government of the United States through its agent there. This agent was instructed to communicate this determination, and he made it known to General Cass. Afterwards, and before the return of Mr. Eames to Venezuela, the undersigned, on the 21st of September last, commenced an understanding with the said Secretary of State of the Union, completing afterwards the answer in the month of October last past. That answer was given as soon as the decision of the council of government, which had been asked and which had to be waited for, was received. In addition to this, a special minister has been appointed, with the character of envoy extraordinary and minister plenipotentiary, in the person of

Dr. Mariano Briceno, to proceed to the United States, notwithstanding the presence there of another diplomatic agent of the republic. All this will convince Mr. Eames of the interest with which the republic views a subject which now occupies it in so many ways, and with such provisions, through the desire to live in the most perfect understanding with the United States, which is a constant aspiration of his excellency the President, as his conduct towards them has always manifested, even in the midst of this regretable difference occasioned by the Aves reclamation.

The undersigned renews to the Hon. Mr. Eames the assurances of his distinguished consideration.

JACINTO GUTIERREZ.

Hon. Charles Eames,
Minister Resident of the United States.

Legation of the United States,
Caraccas, November 30, 1857.

Sir: The undersigned, minister resident of the United States, has the honor to acknowledge the note of the Hon. Mr. Gutierrez under date of 23d instant, in which the undersigned, in reply to his notes of 2d and 21st instant, is informed that a reply by the Venezuelan government to the "Aves" reclamation having been, in the absence of the undersigned from Venezuela, commenced on the 21st of September last and concluded in October last, has been forwarded to the government of the United States through the Venezuelan legation in Washington, and that an additional special mission upon the same subject has now been, also, instituted by the government of Venezuela by the appointment of Hon. Senor Mariano Briceno to proceed to Washington with the character of envoy extraordinary and minister plenipotentiary of the republic, and this information is communicated to the undersigned as satisfactory proof of the deep interest in the state of that reclamation, by which the Venezuelan government is now induced to adopt such various and special measures for its adjustment.

It is not the purpose of the undersigned in this note to anticipate the judgment which the government of the United States may form as to the sufficiency and propriety, in the present state of the "Aves" reclamation, of this course of action by the Venezuelan government to accomplish the object proposed. But the undersigned is certainly by no means prepared to dispute that the establishment by any government of a special mission of high grade for the settlement of a reclamation pending against it, is at all times a very formal proceeding, of grave significance as to the recognized validity and urgency of such reclamation. Nor does the undersigned fail to perceive that the antecedent facts existing in the present case, and in view of which this special mission has been established, greatly augmenting its significance. Prior to the adoption of this measure the Venezuelan government received, both from the undersigned and through its own diplomatic agent in Washington, full assurance from the government of the

United States that the liability of Venezuela in the case is too manifest to justify further discussion; that discussion on that point is, therefore, considered by the United States as closed; and that the acknowledgment and adjustment of the claim cannot be longer delayed without serious injury to the friendly relations of the two governments. These assurances, moreover, were repeated and emphasized in the note addressed, under date of 11th September last, by the honorable Secretary of State of the United States to the Venezuelan chargé d'affaires in Washington, which, after expressing the expectation that the Venezuelan government, regarding its liability as settled, will at once proceed to investigate the damage done and the amount of indemnification proper in the case, concludes with the declaration that "the United States feel it to be due to their self-respect that the forcible injury done to their flag and to their citizens should no longer remain unacknowledged."

In such a state of facts all previously made known to the Venezuelan government and placed in record before it, the only appropriate basis and purpose of the special mission upon the subject which it has now announced cannot be considered as doubtful.

In regard to the reply of the Venezuelan government in the Aves case which appears to have been sent to Washington, but which has not yet been communicated to this legation, the undersigned now deems it proper to repeat what he had the honor to state to the Hon. Mr. Gutierrez in the official conference of the 29th ultimo on the subject, that the undersigned arrived in Caraccas specially charged and instructed by his government to receive in its behalf that reply, particularly in respect to the point of liability of Venezuela. The subsequent and recent instruction which in view of the representations and requests made by the Venezuelan charge d'affaires at Washington, authorized the undersigned to delay for a brief period the presentation of the subject in the definitive form presented by his government, also announced its assured expectation that the decision of Venezuela in the case would be duly communicated to this legation, and further directed the undersigned, in case it should not be so communicated to him, to inform the government of Venezuela that he has been instructed to receive "that decision in behalf of his government before presenting in formal terms its demands for the adjustment of the claims."

Referring to the express mention in his note of the 2d instant, of such prompt communication of that decision to the undersigned, as constituting a part of the "satisfactory disposition" of the case then contemplated, and referring also to the specific request in his note of the 21st instant, to be so informed of that decision, the undersigned now presents this state of facts upon that point to the attention of the government of Venezuela in order that it may take such course in the premises as may appear regular and proper and most conducive to the good understanding of the two governments upon the subject.

The undersigned renews to the Hon. Mr. Gutierrez the assurance of his distinguished consideration.

CHARLES EAMES.

Hon. JACINTO GUITERREZ,
Minister of Foreign Relations.

Mr. Cass to Mr. Eames.

DEPARTMENT OF STATE,
Washiugton, December 15, 1857.

SIR: Your dispatches numbered 40 and 41 were received on the 24th ultimo. From their tenor the department is not without hope that prior to the receipt of this communication, the government of Venezuela will have evinced such a disposition in respect to the adjustment of the Aves Island claim as to enable you to proceed in the examination of the subject of damages. On this point it is unnecessary at present to go into detail. My predecessor's dispatch of 3d February last, No. 46, transmitted to you a printed statement of the claim, together with a reference to the proofs by which it is supported; and although some of the items embraced in this statement may be rejected or reduced in amount, it can be safely employed nevertheless as a convenient basis of adjustment. Mr. Sanford, the attorney and representative of Messrs. Shelton, Sampson & Tappan, the principal claimants, will carry these instructions to you, and will doubtless coöperate with you in your efforts to bring the claim to a satisfactory result. You will find it desirable to confer with him, and, for a thorough understanding of a matter so important to him, you may afford him access to such papers and correspondence as relate to the subject. Having full powers from the principal claimants, he will be prepared to decide on the spot in reference to any settlement which may be proposed of their claim. The department will not object to one which may be satisfactory to you and to him. But it may be not inopportune to suggest, whether in your conferences with Mr. Sanford, prior to the presentation of his statement of damages, a favorable issue would not be promoted by your reduction, jointly, of his claim to such an amount as would fall within the scope of the moderate resources of Venezuela. A different policy may defeat its own object.

It must be borne in mind, whilst urging this claim to a settlement, that there are other citizens of the United States who claim indemnification upon the same grounds as Messrs. Shelton & Co. You have in your possession the papers which they have furnished on this subject, and in making an agreement with reference to the Shelton claim, you will be careful to guard against any sacrifice of their rights. They will be entitled, of course, to whatever damages they may be found to have sustained by their wrongful eviction from Aves Island.

You will receive with this dispatch copies of Mr. Gutierrez's note of the 21st of September, and of my reply thereto of the 12th of November. It is proper to remark, that it is not the intention of this government to remove the discussion of the Aves case from Caraccas to Washington. It is believed that it may more promptly be adjusted in Venezuela. The note of Mr. Gutierrez, of September 21, had reference only to the preliminary question of Venezuela's liability. His promised communication on the subject which, in the same note, he announced as being completed and ready for speedy transmission, has not yet reached the department. Had it been received, and had it contained an admission of the liability referred to, the department would be still disposed to refer the question of damages to our legation in Caraccas, where it seems most appropriately to belong. An attempt at this time to transfer the subject to Washington, would obviously tend to occasion further delay in a case which has already been protracted to an unreasonable extent.

In committing this subject in this shape to you, it is earnestly hoped that you will be enabled, without further delay, to bring it to a satisfactory termination.

I am, sir, your obedient servant,

LEWIS CASS.

CHARLES EAMES, Esq., *&c.*

Mr. Shelton to Mr. Cass.

BOSTON, *December* 17, 1857.

SIR: A report has reached us, and we have reason to suppose it is true, that F. Copeland, of this city, has presented a claim for spoliation or ejectment at Aves Island, in behalf of himself and others. We wish to state distinctly to you, that neither Mr. Copeland nor any one connected with him, had any men employed on Aves Island during its occupation by us, nor any vessel or vessels ejected from thence by any officials of Venezuela; of this fact we shall be able to give the most ample proofs should your department deem it necessary.

The claim, if such has been made, is entirely without foundation in fact, nor can we comprehend the object of said claimants, unless it be to injure or embarrass us in obtaining our rights.

We are, with much respect, your obedient servants,

PHILO S. SHELTON.
SAMPSON & TAPPAN.

Gen. LEWIS CASS,
Secretary of State, Washington, D. C.

Mr. Cass to Mr. Briceno.

DEPARTMENT OF STATE,
Washington, February 24, 1858.

SIR: The necessary delay in translating the extended communication from the Minister of Foreign Affairs of Venezuela, which reached this department a few days before your arrival here, and which referred to the Aves Island claim, now pending between this government and that of Venezuela, has prevented an earlier attention to what was understood to be the prominent subject of your mission.

This claim was presented by the minister of the United States at Caraccas in the month of March, 1855, and after full discussion there, which was duly reported to this department, the deliberate views of this government concerning it were communicated to him in a dispatch dated August 31, 1857, of which I have the honor to inclose a copy herewith.

It will be seen from this dispatch that the government of the United States regarded the discussion as closed on its part, so far as the question of the liability of Venezuela was concerned, to make a reasonable indemnity to the claimants, leaving the amount thereof quite open for further consideration, and to be determined hereafter.

The President had great satisfaction, therefore, upon receiving a special minister from Venezuela on this subject, believing that this view of the claim had been conceded, and that it was the purpose of your mission to arrange for an equitable adjustment of damages with the parties concerned, either here or at Caraccas.

Upon reading, however, the communication from Mr. Gutierrez, already referred to, he regrets to observe that it embraces only an elaborate argument in favor of the alleged title of Venezuela to Aves Island, and against the right of the claimants, Messrs. Shelton & Co., to any indemnity whatever. This communication, addressed directly to this department, and not transmitted through the minister of either country, has, nevertheless, received that respectful consideration to which it was entitled in consequence of its distinguished source, but it has wholly failed to change the views of the President in respect to the liability of Venezuela in the case referred to, or to render it desirable, in his judgment, that after a delay of three years, since the claim was presented, the discussion on that point should be renewed.

Before replying, however, to the communication of Mr. Gutierrez, I shall be glad to see you at the department on Thursday, the 25th instant, at one o'clock, and to converse with you upon the subject to which it refers. Allow me to express the hope that the whole subject may have been intrusted to your care, and that you may find yourself authorized to make arrangements for its adjustment upon the basis of an admitted claim.

I avail myself, &c.

LEWIS CASS.

Señor M. de Briceno, *&c.*

Mr. Eames to Mr. Cass.

No. 43.] Legation of the United States,
Caraccas, February 24, 1858.

Sir: I have the honor to transmit herewith to the department, in copy and translation, a note addressed to me by the minister of foreign relations of this government, under date of 18th instant, in reply to mine to him under date of 30th November last, a copy of which accompanied my dispatch No. 42.

My main purpose in that note was to take the ground before this government, that the special mission which it had then established and announced as about to proceed to Washington with a view to the adjustment of the Aves claim, must be regarded as implying an admission of the responsibility of Venezuela in the case. The reply of the minister, though purporting to be now given upon mature consideration of the whole subject, neither expresses nor intimates any dissent from that conclusion.

The reasons now assigned by the minister for declining to communicate to this legation a copy of the answer of this government in the case, which was prepared in my absence, and which, as he states, was forwarded and reached the department in advance of the special mission, may be considered as not wholly destitute of plausibility. A more cogent inducement to this course, however, may have probably existed in the desire that the paper should be considered by the department unaccompanied by any counter observations on my part.

However this may be, the fact cannot have escaped the attention of this government, although any recognition of it appears to have been studiously avoided, that in my note of November 30, the communication to this legation of that answer was requested directly by the department in advance in its own words, and the refusal to comply with such a request would seem to be predicated upon the admitted purpose of a prompt and satisfactory settlement in Washington, inasmuch as upon any other view, it may be considered as constituting aggravation of the previous unsatisfactory course of Venezuela in the case.

With the highest respect and consideration, I have the honor to be, your obedient servant,

CHARLES EAMES.

Hon. Lewis Cass,
Secretary of State.

[Translation.]

Republic of Venezuela.

Department of Foreign Relations,
Caraccas, February 18, 1858.

Sir: The undersigned has had the honor to present to the executive power the note addressed to him on the 30th of November last by the honorable minister resident respecting the subject of the Aves Island; and, after full consideration of the case, the secretary of foreign relations has been directed to make the following reply:

The answer which Mr. Eames requests has been given to his government, to which he doubtless would have had to transmit it; so that what is now sought to be done in an indirect manner, has been already directly accomplished, and is besides useless, because on the 17th of December last, the answer referred to was delivered to the Hon. General Cass. Moreover, Mr. Eames has been informed that the republic, notwithstanding it has a legation in Washington, has accredited another extraordinary and especially charged with the Aves Island reclamation. This has already entered upon the discharge of its duties, and in view of all, his excellency believes that the negotiation should continue there, its prosecution simultaneously in two places being impossible.

I reiterate to Mr. Eames the assurances of my distinguished consideration.

JACINTO GUTIERREZ.

Hon. CHARLES EAMES,
Minister Resident of the United States.

Mr. Briceno to Mr. Cass.

[Translation.]

LEGATION EXTRAORDINARY OF VENEZUELA TO THE UNITED STATES,
Washington, February 24, 1858.

EXCELLENT SIR: I have just received, this day, your excellency's note of the 22d instant, in which you set forth the precedents connected with the question of Aves Island, in the sense of the note of the 31st of August, 1857, (copy of which was annexed,) transmitted by your excellency to the United States legation in Caraccas. Your note states that Mr. Gutierrez's of the 31st of October last, has in no way succeeded in altering the opinion which the President of the United States has formed as to the responsibility of Venezuela in the claim referred to, and concludes with a proposition to the effect that, before an answer be given to Mr. Gutierrez's said note, an interview should take place at the Department of State, to-morrow, at one, p. m.

I duly appreciate the position in which the government of the United States places itself in the transfer of the question to this capital. Although I see with regret that Mr. Gutierrez's last note, accompanied by convincing proof, has failed to justify, in the judgment of the Chief Magistrate of the State, the conduct of Venezuela in the premises, still I rejoice at the disposition which he evinces of hearing the envoy extraordinary in this negotiation, before he shall definitively judge of the value of the defense, and of the incidental charge of willful procrastination, which it is my duty, in the name of my government, to repel with an irresistable power, derived from the official correspondence itself, between Mr. Marcy and Mr. Eames, on this question, the merits of which the cabinet at Caraccas could not put forth, because it was not in possession of the whole of it.

With the assurance that I shall be punctual at the appointment to-morrow, I remain, with sentiments of most distinguished consideration, your excellency's very respectful servant,

M. DE BRICENO.

His Excellency General LEWIS CASS,
Secretary of State.

Mr. Cass to Mr. Briceno.

DEPARTMENT OF STATE,
Washington, February 26, 1858.

SIR: I have had the honor to receive your note of the 24th instant, and regret that I was unavoidably absent from the department at the time of our proposed interview. If it will be convenient for you to meet me on Monday at one o'clock I shall be glad to see you at that hour.

In the meantime, I desire to correct some erroneous impressions which you seem to have derived from my note of the 22d on the subject of the Aves Island claim.

In transmitting to you a copy of my dispatch to Mr. Eames of the 31st October last, and at the same time informing you that there was nothing in the recent communication of Mr. Gutierrez which rendered it desirable, in the opinion of the President, to reopen the discussion of the question of the liability of Venezuela in the case referred to, I supposed that on that point there was no danger that the position of this government could be misunderstood; yet you seem to have reached the conclusion that I desired still further to discuss that branch of the subject in our contemplated interview before coming to a definite judgment concerning it. It is right to inform you that this conclusion is directly the reverse of that which I intended to convey, and that the only question connected with the Aves case which this government regards as now open for consideration is one of detail with respect to the character and amount of the indemnity which the claimants in the Aves case ought to receive from Venezuela.

In expressing the hope, as I did in my note of the 22d instant, that your powers would be found sufficient to enable you to arrange for an adjustment of these details either at Washington or Caraccas, it was far from my intention to intimate any desire on my part to "transfer the question" from Caraccas to Washington. On the contrary, if you found yourself authorized to proceed to this adjustment, I hoped to be able to satisfy you that it might be most conveniently accomplished at Caraccas, where the evidence in the case has been already presented, and where an agent representing the claimants has recently gone with the purpose of rendering any aid in his power towards accomplishing such an adjustment.

I avail myself, &c.,

LEWIS CASS.

Señor M. DE BRICENO, *&c.*

Mr. Briceno to Mr. Cass.

[Translation.]

SPECIAL LEGATION OF VENEZUELA IN THE UNITED STATES,
Washington, February 27, 1858.

MOST EXCELLENT SIR: It is important to the government of Venezuela that its accredited envoy extraordinary and minister plenipotentiary at this capital should answer promptly the estimable note of your excellency of yesterday's date, received to-day, in which, after offering the undersigned an interview on Monday, if he should deem it convenient, he is informed that the only question relative to the case of the Island of Aves which the government of the United States considers open is one of detail in regard to the character and amount of the indemnity that the claimants are to receive; that this conclusion is exactly the reverse of the erroneous one which the undersigned inferred from your excellency's note of the 24th, supposing a disposition in the chief of the State to hear the envoy extraordinary of the negotiation before finally determining on the value of the defense; and that, in your excellency's expressing, in your note of the 22d, a hope that the powers of the minister of Venezuela would authorize him to arrange those details, it was not your intention to intimate any wish that the question should be transferred from Caraccas to Washington, but that, on the contrary, you expected, in that case, to convince him of the propriety of having the settlement effected at Caraccas, where the proof has been offered, and where an agent of the reclamation now is for the purpose of lending any assistance which may conduce to such an end.

In the name of his government, the undersigned replies as follows:

He is obliged to accept the explanations which represent as erroneous the conclusion which has been spoken of, but, in making this acknowledgment, the undersigned may be permitted to set forth the facts and circumstances which relieve him from the obligation of atonement for having adopted a forced or arbitrary inference.

He knew that Mr. Eames, who initiated the discussion on the 20th of December, 1856, closed it three months afterwards by fulminating against the government of Venezuela the serious and in every respect unfounded charge of protracting it since March, 1855. He knew that your excellency's government entertained the same mistaken opinion, from your note of the 11th of September last, in which it assumed the right of refusing to Venezuela the right which every sovereign State possesses of opposing reasons with reasons, proofs with proofs, and, in fine, of presenting her title to the sovereignty of the Island of Aves. He has read, finally, in your excellency's note of the 22d, that the note of Senor Gutierrez of the 31st, of last year, a long justification of Venezuela in the matter, had not succeeded in changing the opinion of the President in regard to the point of responsibility, or as respects the propriety of renewing the discussion; but in the same document he has read the words: "Nevertheless, before replying to the communication of Senor Gutierrez, it will be very satisfactory to me to see you," &c.

Even supposing that the cabinet at Washington adhered strongly to its system of laying down as unquestionable the cardinal point of the controversy, without waiting for the reasons from the opposite side, as, it would seem, ought to be expected from equity and from treaty, still it was natural to believe, in view of the words quoted *verbatim*, that the President of the United States, after Venezuela's special mission, would be found disposed to hear the undersigned before definitively determining on the value of the defense. The following circumstances necessarily concurred in the support of so rational an interpretation:

1st. The minister of Venezuela, in his speech of audience, announced the determination of his government to conduct the negotiation in this capital, and signified his hope that its solution would be in conformity to the principles of justice. 2d. The President replied substantially that the envoy would find the best disposition, if, as was to be believed, he came here animated with the spirit of justice for the necessary settlement. 3d. The Secretary of State, on the 11th of January, acknowledges the reception from the undersigned of the last note of Senor Gutierrez, and offers to consider it as soon as it should be translated. 4th. The consideration that, as it only needed, according to your excellency's system of government, to fix the amount of the indemnity, the special mission of Venezuela was entirely without immediate object, and no investigation having been made, either as to the amount of the alleged injuries and damages embraced in the reclamation, there was lacking a basis of negotiation in regard to this point, and such a consideration is so much the more huge as the government of Venezuela does not know this day whether, in case it declares itself responsible for the compensation abstractedly demanded, the agent, who, according to your excellency, is in Caraccas, unites all the representations of the damage, or whether there are others, as he is induced to believe is the case from the additional motion of Mr. Wilson, made in the Senate on the 18th of the expiring month.

As will be perceived, the interpretation to which allusion has been made was not a forced but a very logical one. Moreover, it was altogether compatible with the most exaggerated claims of the interested parties protected by your excellency's government, since nothing would be lost even in time, if, as is to be expected, they should present a basis for the settlement of the damages, in their own fashion, within the short period that the audience of the envoy extraordinary might take. The practical utility of a contrary course is not comprehended, nor that of attaching importance to the false imputations which the secret agents of the reclamation are propagating through the American press, attributing sinister intentions to the executive authority of Venezuela in appointing a special plenipotentiary for the affair — imputations which, by the way, it is to be hoped, are not made by your excellency's circumspect government, although it overlooks the honorable precedents of the statesmen who are attacked.

So powerful are the reasons that sustain the interpretation which has been referred to, that now the undersigned, satisfied as he is that the government of the United States has not, and cannot have, any wish or interest to refuse to Venezuela even the means of declaring herself honorably responsible for the damages claimed, if justice demands it, expects, from the impartiality and rectitude of the cabinet in Washington, a change of procedure in deference to the very claimants who are protected. The minister of Venezuela calls the respectable attention of your excellency to this matter, which is, in truth, serious.

The employment of force, which can only be supposed in the affair through the unavoidable necessity of considering it under all its aspects, would assuredly secure no more favorable nor more prompt results than the conciliatory means by which nations are in the habit of terminating their disagreements.

For your own interest, therefore, even if other high reasons of policy, which cannot be hidden from the wisdom of your excellency's government, were worth nothing, it would seem to be not improper to expect from it the road of negotiation in this capital.

The Republic of Venezuela, for its part, is not disposed to accept from any nation, however powerful it may be, the humiliating law of silence, especially when it concerns a right so sacred and illimitable as is that of defense.

Neither can the government of Venezuela, even if it should prove to be responsible, come to an understanding with the present minister resident of the United States at Caraccas, absolutely incapacitated from continuing the discussion of the question, whether from the hostile attitude which he suddenly assumed on his demand not being satisfied within the term, which he permitted himself to fix, of three months from the beginning of the discussion; whether from the moral certainty as to the extremes to which he wished to go last year; or whether, in fine, from having then exceeded all the limits of moderation and of respect, causing grave imputations to rest on the military officers of the country, and what is more, saying, in one of his notes, that the government of Venezuela had ordered a robbery.

All the reasons set forth make it plain that it is in the well understood interests of both nations to start, continue, and conclude the negotiation entirely in Washington, maintaining intact the unity of action on the reclamation, and if it is desirable to divide, doing so in due time, without impairing the rights which Venezuela enjoys as an equal with the United States in general society.

To oppose so rational and expeditious a course, the government of your excellency would only plant itself upon an assertion which Venezuela denies.

Your excellency lays it down as certain that the reclamation was presented in March, 1855; and the government of Venezuela asserts, on its part, that such presentation did not take place until the 20th of December, 1856. It is a question of fact.

Although yesterday's note, which is replied to, is absolutely silent as to this incident, of much importance in the present controversy, the undersigned will not therefore venture to infer that the government of the United States is not willing to hear the subscribing minister in regard to this subject. It has been said to be of much moment, because, if it is true that the act of presenting the reclamation took place at the date fixed by Venezuela, the determination which closed the discussion at three months from its commencement would be without foundation, and there would then be no plausible reason to refuse the full discussion of the affair at this capital.

The orders which the undersigned envoy extraordinary and minister plenipotentiary has received from his government, are so positive and so formal, that they place him under the necessity of soliciting from your excellency the favor of an answer to these two questions:

First. Is the negotiation of the island of Aves fixed (taken up) or not at this capital?

Second. If it is so fixed, (taken up,) will your excellency's government refuse to hear the envoy of Venezuela on the charge of procrastination, which has been made against the cabinet of Caraccas?

As on Wednesday there will be an opportunity for Laguayra, at Philadelphia, and as your excellency has been pleased to submit the interview to the convenience of the undersigned, he may be permitted to request it at one, of the afternoon of Tuesday next, in order that your excellency, on your part, may have time to consider calmly the interrogatories, and the undersigned, on his part, to communicate the result to his government.

With sentiments of respect and of high consideration for your excellency, he subscribes himself,

M. DE BRICENO.

His Excellency the SECRETARY OF STATE OF THE UNITED STATES.

Mr. Cass to Mr. Briceno.

DEPARTMENT OF STATE,
Washington, March 4, 1858.

SIR: Your note of the 27th only reached me, in a translation, on Monday, the 1st instant.

I regret that you were unable to meet me on Monday, and that thus your interview has been necessarily delayed beyond the day of sailing of the packet which was about to leave Philadelphia for Laguayra. If you can conveniently call at the department on Saturday, at 2 o'clock, I shall be glad to converse with you at that time on the present position of the "Aves" case, and to learn how far you are authorized and may feel yourself at liberty to make arrangements for its complete adjustment.

The intimation contained in your note that "the government of Venezuela, even if it should prove to be responsible, cannot come to an understanding with the present minister resident of the United States at Caraccas," has been received with much surprise, because no complaint of his conduct had been communicated to the department by your government prior to your arrival here, and no request had been made for his recall. If he is thought to occupy "a hostile attitude" towards Venezuela, only because he has expressed in decided terms the view entertained by this government of the transactions upon which the claimants in the "Aves" case found their demand for indemnity, such a belief is as manifestly unjust as it would be for this government to impute a "hostile attitude" to the minister of Venezuela in consequence of the very strong and decided terms in which he has felt it his duty to protest against the policy adopted by the United States on this same subject. If, however, in his intercourse with your government, Mr. Eames has exceeded "the limits of moderation and respect," either with reference to the "Aves" case or any other, which has been a subject of discussion at Caraccas, he has certainly failed, in so doing, to represent the disposition of the President, and his conduct, in this respect, would be deeply regretted by his government. It is my duty to add, in justice to Mr. Eames, that from his correspondence in the "Aves" case, which has been transmitted to this department, I have not observed any such evidences of a "hostile attitude," as from the intimation contained in your note you evidently suppose to exist; and I trust, therefore, that a full inquiry on the subject may satisfy both Venezuela and this government that his motives and conduct in the discussion of the "Aves" case have been wholly misapprehended. With reference, however, to the question whether the final adjustment of the case shall be arranged at Caraccas or Washington, I shall be glad to converse with you on Saturday.

On the point of liability, or the right of the claimants to a just indemnity, this government has no disposition to enter into a new discussion. Whatever may have been the precise period when, in the judgment of Venezuela, the subject was first brought to its attention, and whether the proofs and arguments of the Venezuelan government had or had not been fully presented at the time when Mr. Eames left Caraccas in June last, it surely cannot be doubted that they have been so presented now. The late communication of Mr. Gutierrez, dated 31st October last, contains a most elaborate review of the whole case, and it would be unjust to that distinguished gentleman not to admit that it is alike full, ingenious, and able. Yet upon the few points which must control the subject, it has not changed the views of this government, as they had been previously expressed to Venezuela.

The question of how much or how little delay has been had in the negotiation, is obviously a question of only secondary consequence. It is not to be taken for granted that in every instance of a claim for just indemnity a certain amount of time must necessarily be occupied before its acknowledgment or adjustment. There are plain cases where little delay is needed, and flagrant ones which require prompt reparation. The present case appears to the President to belong to the latter class, because, since this government cannot admit any title in Venezuela to the island in question, it is obliged to regard the summary eviction from it of the American citizens who were pursuing there a lawful occupation as a grave violation of their rights, and a wrong done to the country under whose flag they thought themselves protected.

When you inquire, therefore, whether the negotiation on this subject is fixed at Washington, I have to inform you that, with respect to that part of it which is now open, I shall be happy to discuss with you the question whether it shall be closed at Caraccas or here.

On the subject of the delay of the question in Venezuela, I am, also, quite ready to hear any observations which you may think proper to make; but I must repeat, that after the case has been fully presented by that republic, the fact that it was not presented at an earlier period ought not to prevent in any way its prompt adjustment now.

I avail myself, &c.,

LEWIS CASS.

Señor Doctor M. De Briceño, *&c.*

Mr. Briceno to Mr. Cass.

[Translation.]

SPECIAL LEGATION OF VENEZUELA IN THE UNITED STATES,
Washington, March 4, 1858.

The undersigned, envoy extraordinary and minister plenipotentiary of Venezuela, in acknowledging to his excellency General Cass the reception of his estimable note of to-day, has the honor to make known to him at the same time that he reserves to himself to consider its contents along with the result of the conference, which is appointed for Saturday, the 6th instant.

The undersigned reiterates to his excellency General Cass the assurances of his distinguished consideration.

M. DE BRICENO.

His Excellency the SECRETARY OF STATE OF THE UNITED STATES.

Mr. Briceno to Mr. Cass.

[Translation.]

SPECIAL LEGATION OF VENEZUELA IN THE UNITED STATES,
Washington, March 8, 1858.

The undersigned, envoy extraordinary and minister plenipotentiary of Venezuela, has the honor to present in writing to his excellency the Secretary of State of the United States, the substance of all the observations which he submitted to his upright judgment at the special audience that he granted him on the 6th instant. He will add on the occasion some others which are suggested by his excellency's note of the 4th instant, to which the undersigned in acknowledging its reception reserved his reply until after the proposed interview. Both are summed up in the following memorandum:

Your excellency avers that your government has received with much surprise the announcement of the inconveniences now felt in order to exclude Mr. Eames from the negotiation in Caraccas, inasmuch as it heard nothing in regard to this matter previous to the arrival of the undersigned in this city. In turn, the undersigned is surprised at your excellency's assertion; for Senor Ribas, chargé d'affaires of Venezuela, had a conference with your excellency in regard to this affair, complying with the orders which were communicated to him by Senor Gutierrez in a note of the 28th of August last, and the note of October 31 of last year set forth minutely the complaints against the minister resident.

Your excellency signifies a belief that a hostile attitude is attributed to Mr. Eames solely because he expressed himself in decisive terms in support of the views of his government. The undersigned permits himself to remember the enumeration of insults which has been made in official documents, the most recent of which is the note of this legation, in which it is stated that Mr. Eames, in one of his communications, has charged (*imputado*) Venezuela with having ordered a robbery. This does not now admit of the investigation which your excellency has been pleased to suggest in your note of the 4th instant. Venezuela considers herself a judge of her own dignity, and does not doubt that she would have the right to proceed against Mr. Eames as the government of the United States did against Mr. Roussin in a less serious case, if she did not deem it prudent to await the same result from the upright, benevolent, and conciliatory policy of your excellency's government.

The government of the United States, in the note and at the audience which have been mentioned, has defended its present position imperiously; that is, by laying down as unquestionable truths exactly all that is controverted—the principal point of responsibility and that of delay in the discussion. In its opinion, it is evident that the Island of Aves has not been legally occupied by Venezuela; and this premise being established, it easily deduces everything which is adapted to support its reclamation. In its opinion, the discussion between the two nations has lasted three years, owing to the fault of Venezuela; and this premise being established, it easily deduces everything which is calculated to sustain the party which has set about closing the discussion, in order to investigate solely what is due the claimants. In its opinion, the case has been from the beginning clear and indisputable; and this premise being established, a prompt, summary, and violent proceeding against the nation which seems to be the aggressor is justifiable; and consequently it exempts itself from the obligation to admit middle terms, to which it would be subject by the law of nations under any other presupposition.

At the audience mentioned the undersigned was able also to defend imperiously the position of Venezuela, by laying down that it was a question of nothing less than property the most inviolable, its own territory, which had been occupied clandestinely and against the will of its owner by the citizens who are the claimants, and by laying down that not only is Venezuela assisted by clear and indisputable right in rejecting the pretentions which they maintain, but in looking upon their acts on the Island of Aves as a serious insult, which might be promptly avenged and all compromise refused, in order that toleration should not bring on many other such acts. Yet the government of Venezuela, which is very far from wishing to compromit the great interests of the State in a rash contest, and which anxiously desires to earn the sympathies of the powerful republic called to protect its weaker sisters, and to exercise over them the rational and pacific influence that is derived from the homogeneousness of their institutions, the republic of Venezuela has, for these reasons, reached the extreme of shutting its eyes to the offense, in order to devote itself to examining, in an honorable and candid discussion, the demands of the questioned reclamation.

On this account the undersigned, at the audience mentioned, defended the position of Venezuela, stating that, in the main, her version was opposite to that of the United States, and that that version being established as true and unquestionable by the same right which assisted her opponent, consequences also indestructible flowed therefrom; that it was to be observed that the proceeding of the United States, relative to the incident of closing the discussion before time, produced two effects of much importance—one, that of exempting their Secretary of State from the duty of setting forth the reasons for not attaching any value to the note of October 31 and its documents; and the other, that of impeding the entrance of the satisfactions which the undersigned had to bring forward in view of official documents which the government of Venezuela had hitherto been ignorant of; that the United States lost nothing by opening the discussion on the principal point, for the reasons adduced in the note of the undersigned, dated the 27th ultimo; but that Venezuela did, not only because the proceeding of the United States in the principal question would authorize a similar proceeding in the arrangement of damages, if she should admit her responsibility while cut off from her defense, but because it was a grave question of honor for her government to be precluded from a hearing, even supposing that in a final analysis it should be without justification for denying, as it did deny, that responsibility; that when forms involved questions of honor, they are then much more important than questions of cash; and that the weaker nations were, the more jealous they ought to be in preserving intact their own dignity. Finally, the undersigned rejected the harsh position in which the government of the United States attempted to place him—a position in which he would only have to consider the formula of *how much;* and he concluded by asseverating that he harbored no secret intention in asking that the principal question should continue to be discussed at this capital; but that, far from this, he had well-founded hopes of arriving by this means to a settlement satisfactory to both parties much sooner than it could be done by any other course of procedure.

It is important not to omit, that in the course of the interview of which he speaks, the undersigned observed to his excellency, General Cass, that his government at the same time it seemed to make concession, hypothetically assumed—doubtless without wishing to do so—an inadmissible superiority, very incompatible, certainly, with the rights of equality belonging to Venezuela. If Venezuela alleges that she has not been able to defend herself because the discussion was closed to her before time, the reply is, that after the note of the 31st of October it cannot be doubted that she has alleged all that she had to allege; so that his excellency's government does not admit the defense, but only under-values it *prima facie,* without considering it, and without believing itself obliged to say why the royal order is worth nothing which incorporated the island of Aves in the captain-generalship of Venezuela. So that, if it permits the undersigned to speak, and even consents to hear him on the incidental point of delay, which might, as previously, lead to a fair discussion of the responsibility, it makes known beforehand that it is only through pure form, and virtually places the minister of Venezuela in the inadmissible condition of talking, only for talk's sake.

The government of the undersigned, and the whole nation of Venezuela, can only perceive with great displeasure such extremities. The Cabinet at Washington has certainly the right to judge and decide in its own way as to the means to be employed in the settlement of its reclamations; but from its very high position, its discretion, its prudence, is to be expected a conscientious regard for that opinion which, in the last instance, will have cognizance of its acts.

The undersigned avails himself of this occasion to renew to his excellency, the Secretary of State of the United States, the assurances of the distinguished consideration of his obedient servant,

M. DE BRICENO.

His Excellency the SECRETARY OF STATE OF THE UNITED STATES.

Mr. Eames to Mr. Cass.

No. 48.] LEGATION OF THE UNITED STATES, *Caraccas, March* 25, 1858.

SIR: With reference to my No. 47, under date of 23d instant, informing the department of the definitive establishment of the new government in this republic, I have now the honor to transmit inclosed, in copy and translation, a note of Mr. Urrutia, minister of foreign relations, addressed to this legation, under date of yesterday, but received this afternoon, by which I am informed that this government has withdrawn both of its legations now in Washington, being the special mission of Señor M. Briceno, minister plenipotentiary of the republic, charged with the Aves Island negotiation, and the chargéship d'affaires of the republic intrusted to Señor Florencio Ribas.

The information of the determination so promptly formed by this government within the first four days after its establishment, to recall the special mission of Mr. Briceno, was, when it reached me two days ago, quite unexpected, and still less could I have anticipated that such determination would have been so quickly carried into effect. Two sealed packages, however, addressed respectively to Mr. Briceno, in Washington, and to Mr. Ribas, in New York, and stated to contain the letters of recall of those gentlemen, were delivered to me yesterday with the inclosed note of Mr. Urrutia, and with a request that I would do this government the favor to let them go forward by the first opportunity. They will go by the same vessel with this dispatch, which is announced to sail to-morrow.

The note of Mr. Guiterrez, addressed to me under date of 18th ultimo, and forwarded in copy to the department with my No. 43, under date of 24th ultimo, gave me the latest information I have as to the state of the Aves Island negotiation, and led me to infer, as I then intimated to the department, that it might be at that time proceeding to a satisfactory conclusion in Washington. It is stated, however, that dispatches of a late date arrived four or five days ago from Mr. Briceno. The contents of these may possibly have had some effect in inducing the course now taken by this government. However this may be, it is clear from the tenor of Mr. Urrutia's note, that this government is now not only disposed to continue and conclude the negotiation in Caraccas, thus concurring with the view taken on that point by the department in your No. 58 of 15th December, but that having ascertained that there are sufficient powers in this legation to settle the business, it expresses the anticipation that the republic, having now entered upon an era of reformation in its public policy, may with greater facility accomplish results favorable to the friendly relations of the two countries. I perform no more than my duty in stating to the department that my intercourse with this government up to the present time induces me to concur distinctly in that opinion.

Your No. 59, of 22d December last, is the latest dispatch received from the department, the series to that number being complete.

With the highest respect and consideration, I have the honor to be your obedient servant,

CHARLES EAMES.

Hon. LEWIS CASS,
Secretary of State

P. S. I inclose also copy of the inclosure in Mr. Urrutia's note of 24th instant, giving an account of the progress and policy of the revolution. I regret that the great haste in which I am obliged to prepare and transmit this dispatch leaves me no time to send also a translation of it.

C. E.

[Translation.]

Republic of Venezuela.

DEPARTMENT OF FOREIGN RELATIONS,
Caraccas, March 24, 1858.

SIR: The minister of foreign relations of Venezuela has the honor to communicate to the honorable minister resident of the United States that his excellency the general-in-chief of the liberating army, charged with the provisional organization of the republic, has been pleased to withdraw the legations which the republic had in Washington, because the urgent economy demanded by the present regenerative condition of the country required that course, and because he believes that, as the honorable minister of the United States is sufficiently authorized, there will be no difficulty in continuing in this city the discussion of the same business which is now being considered by the Cabinet at Washington in relation to Venezuela.

These have been the only motives of the determination referred to, which has been in no way the result of a desire to impair the relations of both countries, which, on the contrary, Venezuela wishes always to unite more fully, flattering herself that she may now be able to secure that result with greater facility, inasmuch as she has entered upon an era of order and morality, in virtue of the glorious transformation just completed, in a few days; the origin, course, and fortunate development of which are described in the circular, a copy of which is now inclosed to your honor. His excellency hopes that Hon. Mr. Eames will continue his manifestations of sympathy in favor of the present order of things, and will endeavor that his government shall regard it with the benevolence which it deserves.

The undersigned renews to the Hon. Mr. Eames the assurances of his distinguished consideration.

W. URRUTIA.

Hon. CHARLES EAMES,
Minister Resident of the United States.

Mr. Briceno to Mr. Cass.

[Translation.]

LEGATION EXTRAORDINARY OF THE UNITED STATES,
Washington, April 7, 1858.

EXCELLENT SIR: The government of the United States having abruptly closed the discussion on the Aves Island claim, now maintains that the responsibility of Venezuela in the premises is unquestionable, and that all that remains to be done is to ascertain the merit of the indemnifications demanded.

Such conclusions being denied by the government of Venezuela, it maintains, on its side, that the discussion of the responsibility is still pending, and that its right of defense, if it is to be real and effective, necessarily presupposes in your excellency's government a moral obligation both of listening to those exceptions, which have not yet been alleged, and of setting forth the grounds on which it disregards the reasons adduced in Mr. Gutierrez's note of the 31st of October ultimo.

By the exhibit of the annexed printed memorandum my government intends to demonstrate in every light, that it is not for the purpose of abusing the sacred and imprescriptible right of defense that Venezuela thus maintains.

Her government, which thus furnishes a singular proof of rectitude and good faith, hopes that the government of the United States, in that view, far from persisting in its purpose, will thoroughly examine the matter in a manner entirely in unison with the close relations of friendship existing between both countries.

Meanwhile, I tender to your excellency renewed assurances of my esteem and of my very distinguished consideration.

M. DE BRICENO.

His Excellency General CASS,
Secretary of State.

[With Mr. Briceno's note of April.]

Memoir justificatory of the conduct of the government of Venezuela on the Isla de Aves question, presented to his excellency the Secretary of State of the United States, by the envoy extraordinary and minister plenipotentiary of Venezuela, Doctor Mariano De Briceno.

STATEMENTS.

1854, *June.*—About the middle of the year, 1854, two mercantile firms of Boston, Lang & Delano, and Sampson, Tappan & Shelton, dispatched vessels for the purpose of discovering guano on desert islands lying in the Caribbean sea, and taking possession thereof. The vessels, which sailed clandestinely from Boston on the expedition, were the John R. Dow and M. H. Comery, the former belonging to Shelton & Co., and the latter to Lang & Delano. The fact of their clandestine departure from Boston is clearly proven by the books of the custom-house at that port. Other vessels sailed afterwards during the same year from various ports of the United States for Isla de Aves.

1854, *July.*—James Wheeler, agent of Lang & Delano, invaded Isla de Aves. A few hours afterwards, William P. Gibbs, as the agent of Shelton & Co., also arrived there. The island is situated in 15° 45′ north latitude, and 63° 35′ west longitude from Greenwich, W. $\frac{1}{4}$ SE. from the French island of Guadaloupe. Its dimensions are about 700 yards in length by 125 in breadth and 12 in height. It is liable to be overflown by the sea during storms—waterless, and uninhabited. The filibusters immediately employed themselves in the extraction of the guano they found there, within the limits they prescribed for their respective operations.

1854, *December* 12.—The government of Venezuela, on being informed of the invasion of the island, dispatched thither a national armed schooner, under the command of Colonel Dias, which arrived at its destination on the evening of the above date. He met there three vessels at anchor, ready to take cargoes of guano on board, one of 800 tons, and another of 600 tons. The crew of the Venezuelan armed schooner consisted of 27 men; her armament of 27 muskets, one four-pounder, with a suitable quantity of munitions of war. The filibusters at Isla de Aves were 80 in number, armed with 50 pair of pistols carrying ounce balls, about 40 muskets, boarding pikes and hatchets, two six and eight pounders with a proportionate quantity of balls, and about two quintals of powder.

1854, *December* 13.—Colonel Dias being in the peaceful occupation of the islands, ascertained from the said filibusters that they were engaged in clandestinely exporting the guano from Isla de Aves, and other uninhabited islands belonging to Venezuela.

1854, *December* 13.—At the request of the filibusters, Colonel Dias, as commissioner of Venezuela, gives permission at the island for three American vessels to complete their cargoes without molestation from any of the West India cruisers. By this permit, which was signed by Colonel Dias and the two agents, Nathan P. Gibbs for Shelton &

Co., and Charles H. Lang, for Lang & Delano, the filibusters were allowed not only to complete the loading of the three vessels with the guano, but to continue the further exportation thereof until the arrival of the legitimate contractors of the Venezuelan government, on the following conditions, viz: first, that the latter should approve thereof; second, that the two Boston agents should furnish certain supplies required by the Venezuelan garrison; and third, that they should place the whole of their armaments under the orders of the authority of Venezula, and under its flag; all which was accordingly done to the satisfaction of all the parties, except the government at Caraccas, which disavowed the transaction.

1854, *December* 21.—The government of Venezuela at Caraccas, makes a concession for fifteen years to Mr. Wallace, a citizen of the United States, of all the guano on Isla de Aves, and of the other islands of the republic, in consideration of certain cash payments which the contractor obligated himself to make by means of drafts which he drew in favor of the government.

1854, *December* 30.—By order of the agent of the Venezuelan government the filibusters peaceably left Isla de Aves, laden with all the guano they had shipped, without avowing the least intention of making the international claim which they afterwards interposed.

1855, *January* 15.—Shelton and associates make application to the government of the United States, soliciting its intervention to be indemnified by Venezuela not only for the losses they alleged to have suffered by reason of their expulsion, but likewise for the ulterior profits they expected to realize from the further exportation of the guano.

1855, *March*.—Mr. Eames, minister resident of the United States in Caraccas, obtains privately the copy of a document filed in the office of the secretary of state of Venezuela, in which the agents of Shelton and his associates acknowledged, when on the island, the sovereignty of Venezuela over the same. Mr. Eames, who was not aware of the existence of such a document, brings it to the knowledge of his government, and thereby retards the formal presentation of the claim until the time hereinafter mentioned.

1855, *April* 30.—Mr. Wallace assigns his contract to a mercantile firm composed of American citizens, under the title of the "Guano Company of Philadelphia," which obtained an act of incorporation from the legislature of Pennsylvania of the above date.

1855, *May* 22.—The drafts having been protested for non-acceptance, the Wallace contract was annulled by the government of Venezuela.

1855, *June and August*.—In these months Shelton & Co. take the declarations of their agents, and other persons, with the object of sustaining their projected reclamation on account of their having been expelled from Isla de Aves.

1855, *July* 28.—Decree of the president of Venezuela opening to foreign commerce the exportation of guano from Isla de Aves, and the other islands of the republic.

1855, *August*.—In this month the American filibusters returned to export guano clandestinely from the desert islands on the coast of

Venezuela. During this and the following months were detected at Los Monjes, the American bark Corwin; at the island of Pié, the American schooner White Swan, and at Los Hermanos, another American schooner that left eighty bags of guano in its flight.

1855, *September* 2.—The American Guano Company, of Philadelphia, on being apprised of the canceling of the Wallace contract, solicits the protection of the government of the United States, and obtains it, to compel Venezuela to sustain them as the assignees of the Wallace contract; John Pickrell was, in consequence, dispatched as its agent, in the American schooner White Swan, which arrived at Isla de Aves on the above mentioned date. As was naturally to be expected, she was prohibited from loading with guano; he then entered a protest, making the actual costs amount to $50,000, and the contingent damages to $500,000.

1855, *September*.—Arrival of Pickrell at Caraccas. Sustained by the legation of the United States, he demands the restoration of the Wallace contract, the principal object of which was the working of the guano on the Isla de Aves.

1855, *September* 24.—Date of the memorandum of the conference with the president of Venezuela, signed by Mr. Eames, minister resident of the United States in Caraccas, which shows, 1st, the importance attached by the American legation to the Pickrell claim; 2d, the first written mention of the other claim of Shelton, which he contemplated establishing by reason of the dispossession of American citizens at Isla de Aves; and 3d, of Mr. Eames declining the discussion of the two conflicting claims at the same time.

1855, *September* 29.—The government of Venezuela, out of its regard for the public peace, renews in favor of the Philadelphia company the Wallace contract, with certain modifications in regard to the price of the guano to be exported.

1856, *March*.—Netherland vessels of war arrive at Laguayra with an ultimatum, demanding the recognition of the Dutch right to the Isla de Aves, and the withdrawal of troops stationed there. Mr. Eames, on being made officially informed, at his own request, of the matter, addressed a note, on the 8th of March, to the secretary of foreign relations of Venezuela, opposing the Dutch demand for the surrender of the island, partly on account of the claim which it was his intention to make in regard to that island in favor of the Americans who had first discovered guano thereon, and also in behalf of the rights conferred on Pickrell in respect thereto.

1856, *April and May*.—During these months, Shelton & Co., take the last extrajudicial declarations, before a notary in New York, to invalidate the permit of December 13.

1856, *December* 20.—The minister of the United States addresses the government of Venezuela, his first official note, holding it responsible for the occupation of Isla de Aves, and demanding indemnity in favor of citizens of the United States expelled therefrom, without stating who they were.

1857, *February* 27.—The government of Venezuela repels the claim in a judicious note.

1857, *March* 31.—Mr. Eames insists, in an official communication notable for its length.

1857, *April*.—The President of Venezuela submits the matter to the consideration of the government council.

1857, *May*.—The government council orders that proof be taken to refute the assertion of Shelton that his agent had signed the permit of December 13, by means of fraud and violence.

1857, *May* 29.—The legation of the United States addresses a note to the government of Venezuela, charging it with undue delay in acknowledging the justice of the indemnity demanded, and alleging that such delay was calculated to place in imminent peril the friendly relations between the two countries!

1857, *June*.—The proof ordered by the government council was completed. Mr. Eames was invited to be present at the taking of the testimony, but declined attending.

1857, *June* 11.—Mr. Eames, having the permission of his government to return to the United States, makes a formal demand for his passports as the result of the pending question.

1857, *June* 12.—The government of Venezuela sends Mr. Eames his passports, informing him that the substantiation of the pending claim was not yet concluded. It added, that both cabinets would come to a direct understanding on the subject in the event of there being no minister of the United States in Caraccas.

1857, *August* 5.—Convention between Venezuela and Holland, submitting the question of Isla de Aves to arbitration.

1857, *October*.—Mr. Eames returns to Caraccas. The government of Venezuela victoriously refutes the claim in a note of the 31st of the same month, remits the negotiation to Washington, and sends a special minister plenipotentiary to this capital.

Argument.

Such are the facts connected with the Isla de Aves question, all of which are most clearly proved by official acts.

Among these facts there stands one which constitutes the actual state of the controversy now pending between Venezuela and the United States; namely:

The prohibition to export guano from Isla de Aves, imposed by Venezuela on American citizens, who occupied it in December, 1854.

The two contending parties agree upon this point, but differ in its qualification. The government of the United States look upon it as an act of violent encroachment upon rightful property. Venezuela denies this qualification. It is, therefore, a case in which rhetoric and law have jointly, and from the most remote antiquity, consecrated the principle that:

"It lies upon the accuser to approve what the other denies. In this case, the state of the cause is taken from the indictment."

Otherwise the advantages of the aggressor would become far greater. Filibusters, for instance, could take possession of any uninhabited island, any desert territory never trodden by human foot, of which there is so much in Spanish America. This island or territory has an owner; but filibusters consider it as a derelict domain. They invade and establish dominion over it. The rightful possessor thereof repels the aggressor, who, in his turn, assumes the character of the party aggrieved, and with that arrogance which always accompanies bold injustice, exclaims: "This island, this territory, is not yours; whatever you may aver to the contrary, I disregard; you must produce the proofs, for the simple reason that I choose to constitute myself both judge and party in this matter." Common sense suffices to show how untenable such a supposition would be.

If the claimants, the Secretary of State, Mr. Marcy, and the minister resident at Caraccas, Mr. Eames, have alleged that the proof on the question appertains to Venezuela, it is because they have supposed as unquestionable the identical matter in controversy; that is to say, "that Isla de Aves, up to July, 1854, had no owner; for, being uninhabitable, it was never taken possession of by any government." So true it is that such a proposition has only proceeded from mere supposition, that Mr. Marcy, without sufficient knowledge of the case, and on the claim being presented to his department, decides upon the question, in January 24, 1855, in these terms:

"Aves Islands have been known probably more than three hundred years, but have ever been regarded uninhabitable and valueless. No nation has deemed them of sufficient importance to be reduced to possession. As we understand the case, Aves Islands were not embraced within the sovereignty of any power, but were derelict." (Official note from Mr. Marcy to Mr. Eames. Documents respecting Aves Islands referred to the Committee of Foreign Relations of the Senate, January 20, 1857.)

It would have been natural to expect that Mr. Marcy, in view alone of the unquestionable fact of the discovery of Isla de Aves three centuries ago, had deduced and recognized its occupation by some government, and abstained from officially countenancing the claim introduced by Shelton and his associates. He would thus have respected the principle in virtue of which Spain, about the year 1679, expelled from the desert islands of Providence those Englishmen who had unlawfully occupied it; the same principle which the United States invoked in favor of the Oregon question with Great Britain, and the very identical principle which Mr. Dobbin, a colleague of Mr. Marcy during Mr. Pierce's administration, left untouched in his instructions of October 20, 1855, which, in relation to an uninhabited island in the Pacific ocean said to have been discovered by an American citizen, he (Mr. Dobbin) gave to Commodore Mervine, directing him to abstain from occupying it, and to confine himself to acquiring information, should he find that island had been discovered by other people.

Notwithstanding such valuable precedents, Mr. Marcy overlooked the fact of previous discovery when the subject of Isla de Aves was brought up; and not only did he overlook that fact, but even allowed himself to suppose that it remained abandoned and without an owner, at the time of transmitting the claim of Shelton and his associates to the United States legation at Caraccas.

Mr. Eames replies, however, "that the island had always been considered by all governments as derelict, is, perhaps, not quite so certain," and he proved it by the pretensions which Holland was about interposing thereto. (Note from Mr. Eames to Mr. Marcy, Caraccas, April 26, 1855—document aforesaid.)

But afterwards this doubt was removed from the mind of Mr. Eames, establishing, as unquestionable, a controvertible spoliation in order to deduce therefrom the liability of Venezuela, notwithstanding the additional strong reasons he had for such doubt, arising out of the formal claim presented by Holland.

From the above premises, it clearly results that Venezuela is not bound to furnish the proofs. Nevertheless she has already adduced them, because she has justice on her side, and loses nothing thereby.

The complete justification of Venezuela results from the following propositions, all of which are set forth in the note of the Hon. Jacinto Gutierrez, Secretary of Foreign Affairs, dated October 31, 1857, to which reference is made in this memoir, the object of which is to furnish a condensed statement of the arguments in said document, and to present some additional ones of importance:

1st. Isla de Aves was discovered and taken possession of by Spain.

2d. Isla de Aves was incorporated under the captain generalship of Venezuela at the time of her emancipation from Spain, and is, therefore, at the present day an integral portion of the republic of Venezuela.

3d. Even if Isla de Aves did not belong to the republic of Venezuela, it could not be regarded as derelict in July, 1854, since Holland still persists in asserting her claim, however unjustly, to the ownership thereof.

4th. Supposing that Isla de Aves was derelict in July, 1854, which is the ground taken by the claimants, Venezuela as a nation should, in competition with private citizens, be considered the rightful occupant according to international law.

5th. The government of the United States itself recognized the sovereignty of Venezuela over Isla de Aves when, in September, 1855, it interposed an energetic demand in favor of the Pickrell claim.

6th. Venezuela has in no manner whatsoever incurred any responsibility towards the United States by her prohibition to export guano from Isla de Aves, imposed on American citizens who, in 1854, had occupied it.

PROPOSITION FIRST.

Isla de Aves was the property of Spain.—The history of discoveries shows that Spanish navigators visited all that group called the Windward Islands, extending from St. Domingo in a semi-circular direction to the coast of Guayana, in Venezuela, as well as all others of the littoral of that republic. The very name of Isla de Aves plainly shows the nation which discovered it in the ocean.

The Compilation of Indies contains a law prescribing the formalities by which Spanish discoverers were to be governed in taking possession of territories in America. It runs thus: "We command chiefs, captains, and any other persons who may discover any island or main land, on landing thereon, to take possession thereof in our name, performing such acts as may be deemed expedient, and authenticating the same in a public form and manner to serve as testimony. (Law 11, tit. 2d, book 4th of Compilation of Indies.)

In 1526 all the Windward Islands, among which Isla de Aves is included, and those on the coast of Terra Firma, were comprised, together with the dependency of Venezuela, in the jurisdiction of the Audiencia of St. Domingo. (See Law 2d, tit. 15th, book 11th of Compilation of Indies.)

In said compilation we read the regulations of subsequent date which the Spanish government dictated for the navigation and commerce of the Windward Islands. They are acts of jurisdiction, showing indubitably that Spain did possess Isla de Aves until the early part of this century, when it became the property of Venezuela, as will be seen in the sequel.

It is, therefore, evident, in respect to an uninhabitable island, that the possession in dispute could not have been material, but, as it is termed in law, civil, *in habitu*, which consists in holding the thing habitually or mentally, just such a possession as the various nations of Europe and America, and even Venezuela, still maintain of other uninhabitable islands in the Caribbean sea, Los Monjes, Los Hermanos, &c., figuring among them.

By no possible logical argumentation can it be asserted that Spain, as it pleased Mr. Marcy to suppose, ever renounced the right of possession during the period of her sway, on the plea of Isla de Aves being uninhabitable or worthless at that time. If these conditions were necessary for the retaining of possession, no nation could rest secure in relation to such islands as are unsusceptible of material occupation. This is the reason why the law of nations has consecrated the doctrine "that, when there are in any State desert and uncultivated places, no one is authorized to take possession thereof without the consent of the sovereign. Although not in actual use of such places, he is, notwithstanding, the possessor; it is his interest to preserve them, and he is not accountable to any person for the manner in which he makes use of the property."

Moreover, the same Compilation of Indies precludes all doubt upon this point, granting there was any. The Emperor Charles V. and his successor, by various express royal acts, on declaring themselves lords of the West Indian Islands and continents already discovered, and in the way of discovery, dictated the following: "And considering the faithfulness of our subjects, and the hardships endured by the discoverers and settlers in the discovering and settling thereof, we do, in order to their greater certainty of and confidence in those lands always remaining united to our royal crown, promise and pledge our faith and royal word, for us and the kings, our successors, never to alienate nor separate them, neither their cities nor towns, for any cause or reason, or in favor of any person; and, if we or our successors should make any donation or transfer in defiance of the above, the same to stand null, and so we declare it." (Law 1st, tit. 1st, book 3d of Compilation of Indies, still in force.)

If such strong foundations were lost sight of by a distinguished statesman, which is excusable in the hasty proceedings for the substantiation of a claim, it is to be hoped they will bring irresistible conviction to the just administration now ruling in the United States, where the question must be finally decided.

It then appears as absolutely untenable that Spain has ever spontaneously and tacitly renounced the possession of, or has she alienated Isla de Aves, without those previous express acts in virtue of which she has from imperious political circumstances, given up some of her American colonies.

It has already been proved that Spain did possess Isla de Aves up to the time when it became the property of the Venezuelan nation, for the reasons manifested in the following—

PROPOSITION SECOND.

Isla de Aves the property of Venezuela as succeeding to the rights of Spain.—With pain indeed does Venezuela disinter from dusty archives her title of property over Isla de Aves, in order to free herself from the indemnity demanded by fillibusterism repelled from a territory where the rightful owner has but exercised acts of sovereignty, for which no accountability is incurred if better title is not produced.

The representative of the United States at Caraccas, Mr. Eames, in an official note of 31st March, 1856, has acknowledged the following:

"All of the territory of these continental governments formed originally part of the jurisdiction of the government of St. Domingo, and were successively excinded out of it. But besides that vast continental territory, the government of St. Domingo, as appears in the 'Leyes de Indias,' published at Madrid in 1786, lib. 11, tit. 15, comprehended also all the Windward Islands, as we have seen the Aves in question is found, and this group of islands was never taken out of the jurisdiction by Spain, or assigned to the jurisdiction of any of her continental governments, and least of all to Venezuela, which was at first a dependency of the vice royalty of New Granada, and so continued till 1751."

It is therefore acknowledged that Isla de Aves was never taken out of the jurisdiction of Spain. Although the adverb never is a surplus word, for the reason further on to be explained, it is important however to remark that Mr. Eames agrees to Isla de Aves having never been abandoned, and consequently he has thus left the claim without even the ground upon which he thought to be able to establish it. Nor is this the only contradiction incurred by Mr. Eames; but they cannot be pointed out, as it is not the purpose of this memoir to enter into any other expositions than such as directly and substantially relate to the question.

Mr. Eames, we have seen, agrees that Isla de Aves was owned by Spain, but does not admit her having been assigned to the captain-generalship of Venezuela. The contrary is proved in this manner.

In 1526 all the Windward Islands (Aves included) and those of

Costa Firme, were assigned to the district of the Audiencia de Santo Domingo. (L. 2 tit. 15 lib. 11, Comp. Ind., already mentioned.)

In 1751 the captain-generalship of Caraccas, or Venezuela, was established, and here is the authentic document showing how the Windward Islands (Aves included) were assigned to the Audiencia of Caraccas. Mr. Eames has overlooked or been ignorant of such an official act.

The royal decree, dated June 13, 1786, creating the Audiencia of Caraccas, runs as follows:

" * * * In order to avoid the prejudices which are originated to the inhabitants of the province of Maracaibo, also to that of Cumana, Guayana, Margarita, and Trinidad, (a Windward Island,) comprised in the captain-generalship of Caraccas, from having to recur for appeal in their affairs to the Pretorial Audiencia of St. Domingo, the king hath resolved to create another one in Caraccas, composed, for the present, of one senior judge, three auditors, and one fiscal, leaving an equal number of judges in that of St. Domingo, and limiting their district to that of the Spanish portion of that island, Cuba, and Puerto Rico, to which end his majesty doth from henceforth appoint such judges as will serve in both islands."

If, therefore, it is unquestionable that in 1786 the Windward Islands—Aves included—were attached to the Audiencia of St. Domingo, it should also be clear of all doubt, that since the 13th of June of the same year, they were excluded from said Audiencia, to be assigned to that of Caraccas.

The royal decree of 1786—the right of Venezuela to Isla de Aves—stands of irresistible conviction, from the peculiar circumstance that this islet is found among a group of important islands, named altogether the Windward Islands. Without this circumstance, it had been impossible to fix the series of their jurisdictional allottings.

If an analogous question should in future arise in relation to the desert islands in the littoral of Venezuela, the inquiry would prove more difficult, because not being embraced within a common important denomination, their trifling value has been the cause that no mention of them has been made in any law of territorial decision, either in Colombia or Venezuela; so that, officially, it is not known to which province of the republic they belong. However, no one doubts by what nation they are possessed.

But it will be said that those islands are contiguous to the littoral of Venezuela, and that the one in question is so far off that Colonel Codazzi omitted assigning it to the republic in those maps which he got up by order of the government.

When the property of anything is proved by legal instruments, it matters not how far it is situated. If it is true, as is doubtless the fact, that Isla de Aves was incorporated into the captain-generalship of Caraccas, the question is then at an end.

The legitimacy of Venezuela's right is corroborated by the fact that the only nation which, by reason of proximity, could have claimed Isla de Aves, is France, by alleging that on the invasion of Guadaloupe in 1635, she also meant to take possession of it—and yet France has not undertaken such a pretension—which, let it be said in passing, would be less strange than that of the American citizens, who ground it upon the untenable assertion of the abandonment of the islet in question.

The omission of Colonel Codazzi is no proof at all. True it is, that his labors were the result of the special commission intrusted to him by the legislative power, who remunerated his services in an appropriate manner.

Howbeit, it does not follow that his work is strictly official, and much less that it has been approved of as every way perfect and exact by the government of Venezuela.

It would indeed be exceedingly strange to lay aside that documental proof which clears off the pending controversy, in order to make it dependent upon the insignificant and unforeseen accident of the imperceptible point of an islet, at that time worthless in all respects, being omitted in some maps.

We have it then that Isla de Aves, being included in the captain-generalship of Venezuela at the time of the emancipation from Spain, became an integral part of Colombia. This republic being dissolved in 1830, Venezuela constituted herself into an independent nation, comprising all the territory of the aforesaid captain-generalship. It was so declared by her fundamental constitution and in the treaty of peace and recognition between Venezuela and H. C. M., who, in article second, "recognizes the republic of Venezuela as a free, sovereign, and independent nation, composed of the provinces and territories expressed in her constitution and other subsequent laws, and also of any other territories or islands to which she may be entitled."

PROPOSITION THIRD.

Isla de Aves never abandoned, derelict.—In order to overthrow the specious grounds of the claim in all the branches of its argumentation, let it be supposed for a moment that Venezuela did not succeed Spain in her rights over Isla de Aves. The conclusion that the islet was not under possession in July, 1854, is not thus the more logical nor legitimate.

Hence, it is not possible to imagine there is in the Carribean Sea, already so well known and explored, a foot of land unoccupied by some nation.

Isla de Aves, then, if not the property of Venezuela, should belong to Spain, as has been shown in proposition first. But Spain has not claimed Isla de Aves as her own, nor has France nor England claimed it as annexed to any of their respective colonies. Does it follow, then, that it stood abandoned at the time mentioned? No; because, supposing that to be the case, there would yet be an opening for the pretensions of Holland with regard to the island.

It would not be consistent with the wisdom which distinguishes the government of the United States in its administration, nor with the principles of justice which guide its conduct, independent of the indestructible proofs of rightful property presented by Venezuela, to give more importance to the mere allegations of two or three American citizens, who, for the sake of speculation, maintain the abandonment of Isla de Aves, than to the assertion of two sovereign nations, who, although differing about the property, both agree upon the substantial point that Isla de Aves has never been derelict.

PROPOSITION FOURTH.

Isla de Aves derelict, Venezuela the first occupant.—In order to carry the gracious concessions to their ultimate expression, let it be supposed that Isla de Aves were absolutely abandoned—in a condition to receive primary occupation.

Even on this false supposition, the citizens of the United States who made their way into Isla de Aves in 1854 could not be deemed the proprietors of said island.

The United States legation has in no manner whatever demanded the island for the nation. She has never maintained that it is their property—the reason why she has not insisted upon its evacuation and delivery. She solely and exclusively demands pecuniary indemnification. What title does she invoke? Merely previous occupation by American citizens.

Well, then, on the supposition assumed, it is undeniable that the occupation by Venezuela should prevail against that of the American citizens, and should also produce the legal effects of which the occupation by private individuals is not susceptible, looked upon by international law as rash and preposterous the moment one man presumes alone to arrogate to himself an exclusive right over some territory, in order to constitute himself into a monarch without subjects.

The parties claiming have given proofs that they are conscious of the injury done to their pretensions by that well-received doctrine when they endeavor to demonstrate the contrary in their "Memoranda of the case for the State Department," laying down principles at variance with the rights acquired by nations, and forcing the interpretation of those already recognized in their enlightened practice; but in the midst of the false doctrine diffused in their document there always shines through the true one, as, for instance, in the following passage:

"Discovery by private citizens vests rights in the United States. It is entirely immaterial whether such discoverer is a private citizen or subject or a commissioned officer of a State. The same rights in either case vest in the State to which he belongs. (Vattel only refers to discoverers furnished with a commission from their sovereign, and this was the British argument in the Oregon case.")

But the most convincing proof that the claimants did not trust to the force of their demonstrations is furnished by the bill (*ad hoc*) which they submitted to the consideration of Congress with the object of declaring the rights "of American citizens who may discover and occupy derelict guano islands," &c.

The following are presented as foundations:

"Whereas the rights of the first discoverer of any island, key, or rock not appertaining to any State by contiguity, unless followed and perfected by continued possession and actual occupation thereof, becomes extinguished, and therefrom, or upon the abandonment of such possession, subsequent discoverers may take possession of and occupy such derelict island:

"And whereas, also, such subsequent discovery, possession, and occupation, whether by a commissioned officer of the United States or by a citizen thereof not in the public service, doth cause to inure to and vest in the federal government of the United States the plenary right of sovereignty or eminent domain over and to the same, unless expressly declined by the Executive or the Congress of the United States:

"And whereas, also, said discovery and possession and occupation by such citizen vest in such citizen the right to possess such island, key, or rock, and exercise the ownership thereof and of all that may be found thereon exclusively against all States and persons whatsoever except the government of the United States aforesaid, which has full power to restrain or regulate such exercise, and to limit such exercise by law:

"And whereas, to allow commissioned officers or others in the public service of the United States to acquire such individual rights by such discovery whilst engaged in the fulfillment of their public duties might be prejudicial to the public interest:

"And whereas, also, in such cases of discovery by private citizens, they should be protected in their said rights by the federal government, therefore, be it enacted," &c.

The conceptions contained in the above clearly show that the propositions contrary to those they involve are those generally received, and for this reason it was the pretension of the claimants to destroy them by a legislative act sanctioned expressly for the case.

It is idle to say that such insane principles as those set down in the clauses of the project could be sanctioned by the Congress of the Union. They were rejected.

It has been demonstrated that the claimant's clandestine expedition from the United States, not having discovered Isla de Aves, nor having taken possession of the same by an express commission from the nation, could not acquire a title of property worthy of respect by other nations, and therefore lack the right to any legitimate protection on the part of the federal government.

PROPOSITION FIFTH.

The government of the United States has recognized the sovereignty of Venezuela over Isla de Aves.—Nothing more eloquent than the facts relating to this point, which have been set forth in chronological order.

It follows, therefore, that the legation of the United States then regarded Isla de Aves as the property of Venezuela, so as to ask for the usufruct thereof in favor of the Wallace assignees, and now looks upon it as the property of American citizens, in order to support and confirm the present claim for indemnification.

Such is the delicate, not to say false position in which the government of the United States has been placed by the acts of Mr. Eames.

It is worth while to examine how he has attempted to extricate himself from the dilemma.

It is important to bear in mind that in December, 1854, occurred the act originating the present controversy, and also that the government of Venezuela leased the island to Mr. Wallace. The Pickrell claim originated in September, 1855.

Well, then, Mr. Eames, in his note of March 31, 1857, says to Senor Gutierrez:

"Both the government of the United States and the undersigned distinctly and affirmatively refused all manner of sanction to that contract, in so far as it related to the Island of Aves in question; and this refusal of all such sanction was officially made known to the government of Venezuela by the undersigned in his immediate notification to the government of Venezuela in the month of March, 1855, of the claim of these claimants for full indemnification for their unlawful expulsion in consequence of that contract from the Island of Aves."

The first conception in the preceding paragraph seeks to establish that it belonged to Mr. Eames to sanction the Wallace contract. Such intervention, indeed, was altogether inconsistent with the nature of the case from the outset.

As to the immediate notification, the government of Venezuela replied in its note of 31st October ultimo, as follows:

"It is not correct that Mr. Eames has clearly and affirmatively refused to sanction the contract in so far as it relates to Isla de Aves, although in 1855 he alluded, while in conversation with the secretary of foreign affairs, Senor Aranda, to the claim which some individuals residing thereon endeavored to establish."

This conversation took place about the latter part of March, 1855, and the same official note from Mr. Eames to Mr. Marcy, April 26, 1855—the first upon the subject—goes to show that the aforesaid conference was not intended solely, distinctly, and affirmatively to refuse the sanction of the Wallace contract, but to acquire data for officially grounding the Shelton claim.

"I had learned most of these facts when, in the last days of last month, (March,) shortly after the receipt of your instruction, I brought the matter to the attention of this government. I preferred to do this first in conversation, for I have heard something to the effect that the Americans on the island had, upon the arrival of the Venezuelan vessels there, signed a contract, &c.

"I therefore, in a personal interview, placed before the Minister of Foreign Relations as distinctly as possible the main facts of the case, as presented in your instruction and the accompanying paper, expressing my astonishment at the course pursued by Venezuela, and stating my expectation that the wrong would be at once recognized and repaired."

"In reply the minister at once and very confidently denied that any wrong had been intended or done, and that any reparation could be properly claimed. He insisted, &c."

"I expressed strongly my dissent from his opinion, &c.

"I told him I was aware of the Wallis (Wallace) contract, and also aware that Venezuela had inserted a clause plainly showing a consciousness that the island was not hers, by refusing to guaranty the privilege she conceded. [Mr. Eames seems to forget the pretensions of Holland, of which he speaks in this same note.] I added * * * He rejoined * * * I said, as we parted, that I very much regretted to find so wide a difference of opinion between us upon a matter which, as it stood before me, appeared so serious. But I felt, as I left him, well assured that, anticipating a discussion in writing, he considered he had an impregnable case against the claim, and was reserving his fire.

"Soon afterwards, and while I was still seeking to ascertain the exact nature of admissions which I should have to encounter in prosecuting the reclamations of the claimants, there was put into my hand by a merchant here a paper which purported to be a copy of an agreement entered into and signed at the Island of Aves, &c,"

After the month of April, 1855, up to September of the same year, Mr. Eames made no exertion whatever, either verbally or in writing, about the claim now before the government of Venezuela, as shown by the following paragraph extracted from the aforesaid note which Mr. Eames addressed to Senor Gutierrez, March 31, 1857.

"These two notes of the 24th of September, 1855, (memorandum,) and of the 8th of March, 1855, (in opposition to the claim of Holland,) were repeatedly referred to by the undersigned in his note of the 20th of December last, and such having been from the first, and up to the present time, the recorded and steadily maintained position of the undersigned and of the government of the United States as to the rights and claims of the present claimants, &c."

It follows, therefore, that during the first seven months elapsed after the armed occupation of Isla de Aves by Venezuela, Mr. Eames, having in view the introduction of the Shelton claim, made no kind of reservation, either verbally or in writing, concerning the Wallace contract.

In September, 1855, arose the claim of Pickrell, the agent for the Wallace assignees. It is now incumbent on the government of Venezuela to show that—

☞ The American minister on the occasion referred to, did not, as he has since alleged, except Isla de Aves from the claim which he indorsed, and therefore did acknowledge the sovereignty of Venezuela over said island.

Mr. Eames has attempted to prove the express exception by the following words of his memorandum, dated September 24, 1855:

"After this preliminary reference, and having previously presented to his excellency the agent of the company, the undersigned proceeded officially to make known to his excellency what he had previously declared to the minister of his excellency's government, that in rendering his good offices in aid of the purposes of the agent of the company to secure their rights as the assignees of the Wallace contract, the undersigned was emphatically instructed to forbear from saying or doing anything which could in the slightest degree affect or impair the claim against the Venezuelan government for full reparation on the part of those American citizens whom Venezuela had found in the possession of the Aves Island in December last. The undersigned explained, therefore, fully and clearly to his excellency that all which he might say or do in aid of the agent of the company must be understood with this express reservation: That the Aves claim was a wholly separate matter in no way to be compromised or affected by any arrangement which might be made in respect to the rights under the Wallace contract, or by any aid which the undersigned might render in bringing about such an arrangement."

Substantially what do these words mean? "I countenance the Pickrell claim, protesting that I do not renounce the right to support afterwards the Shelton claim." Such protest or reservation, far from excepting Isla de Aves, far from making both claims consistent, shows a deliberate purpose to slight the conflict involved by both, and therefore does not relieve the government of the United States from the delicate position in which it has been placed by its exacting, in favor of certain American citizens, compliance with a contract which presupposes Venezuela as the sovereign over Isla de Aves, and by afterwards refusing to acknowledge the same sovereignty, in order to demand indemnification in favor of other American citizens.

Mr. Eames further states in his note of the 31st of March, that the Pickrell contract "omitted all mention of the Aves in the article guarantying the usufruct of the guano islands of the republic to the assignees of that contract, and afterwards, in another article, specified the Aves apparently with the object of relieving Venezuela from liability to those assignees, in the event that her possession and use of it, for her own profit, should in view of this claim, or for any other reason, terminate."

This allegation is *contra producentem*, that is, contrary to what it is designed to prove. The demonstration is very easy. What really occurred in the Pickrell contract was, that although Isla de Aves was not specified in article first, it being comprised in the other guano islands of the republic, it was, notwithstanding, distinctly mentioned in article fifth, in order to relieve Venezuela from any liability to the Philadelphia company, in the eventual case of a cession in any arrangements with Holland. Mr. Eames alleges that the reservation had in view not the claim of Holland, but that of Shelton, which he had then in contemplation. So, then, such forced conjecture involves the same object as the true cause of the reservation; it supposes, likewise, the including of Isla de Aves in the Pickrell contract, and therefore this admission, through the interference of the American legation, implies the recognition of Venezuela's sovereignty over the island.

In order to obviate such a conflict, Mr. Eames, in September, 1855, had at his command two alternatives equally reasonable, but also equally unadapted, owing to the peculiar circumstances in which he found himself with regard to the opposing claimants.

One was, to support the Pickrell claim to the express exclusion of Isla de Aves.

But Mr. Eames could not act in such a manner, for the powerful reason that the very nature of the Philadelphia enterprise made the exception impossible. The fact has been above established, that the Pickrell protest referred specially to the guano from Isla de Aves. If Mr. Eames had attempted to except it at the time, Mr. Pickrell would not have consented to it, because the labors of the company being confined to Isla de Aves, the claim would have proved of no effectual benefit. This is confirmed by the fact of the Philadelphia company having resumed the exportation of guano from Isla de Aves, as soon as Mr. Pickrell renewed the Wallace contract.

The other was, to accumulate the two claims, so as afterwards to dispose of them at the will of the parties with opposing rights.

So it was proposed by his excellency, the President of Venezuela, in the conference alluded to in Mr. Eames's memorandum, 24th September; but the United States legation refused to adopt the measure.

"In reply to a remark from his excellency, expressing his preference that the claim in regard to the previous occupation of the Aves Island should, if possible, be disposed of in any arrangement which might be made with the agent of the company, the undersigned answered, as he had before answered to his excellency's minister upon the same point, that any such disposition of the Aves claim was wholly impossible, not only by reason of the entirely distinct character of the two subjects, and of the duty of the undersigned to treat them separately, but also by reason of the fact that the undersigned was not yet fully in possession of all the information requisite for the due adjustment of the Aves claim."

What is, however, most strange in the incidental question bearing upon the fact of Mr. Eames's excepting or not Isla de Aves in the Pickrell contract of 29th September, it is that the inclusion is proved by the confession of Mr. Eames himself in his note of March 8, 1856, to Señor Gutierrez, opposing the cession of Isla de Aves demanded by Holland:

"The undersigned, in this connection, deems it his duty further to state that he has in his possession a copy of a contract entered into on the 29th of September last, between the government of Venezuela and John F. Pickrell, a citizen of the United States, conveying to the said contractor and his associates certain exclusive privileges in the guano islands of Venezuela, in which contract the undersigned perceives that the Island of Aves, in question, is specified under certain conditions and stipulations therein set forth."

True it is that Mr. Eames, in the same note, March 8, undoubtedly perceiving the force of such confession extorted from him by the truth of the fact, sought to invalidate it by these words: "The undersigned, in view of that reservation, now abstains from giving any manner of sanction to the insertion of the Aves Island in that contract."

But such declaration is of no use when contrasted with a fixed fact. The whole of the learned world agrees upon this maxim: "*Protestatio contra factum nihil revelat.*" So that the proof is utterly useless when the fact protested against cannot be supported under any other head than that of renunciation. Facts, says Mr. Troplong, must be stronger than vain words.

It follows, from what is above set forth in the premises, that Venezuela, as the possessor and owner of Isla de Aves, ceded her usufruct thereof to the American citizen, Mr. Wallace, in December, 1854; that the United States legation at Caraccas, whether in March, 1855, when officially informed of the claim being presented at Washington by Shelton and associates, or even afterwards, did not transmit to the government of Venezuela any determination on the part of the American Cabinet, objecting to the lessees of the guano islands of the republic to continue in the enjoyment of the benefit of Isla de Aves, because of its being deemed the property of other American citizens; and that far from doing so, this very legation strongly interfered on the Pickrell question, in order to retain the usufruct of the island for the Wallace assignees.

The government of Venezuela, relying upon these facts, holds that her sovereignty over Isla de Aves has been recognized by the government of the United States by acts of unequivocal significance, leaving no room whatsoever for further protest.

PROPOSITION SIXTH.

Irresponsibility of Venezuela.—This is a conclusion which naturally follows from the facts and reasonings already established.

First. If Isla de Aves is the property of Venezuela, as has been proved by strong titles and acts of the complaining government itself, the American citizens, by invading it in 1854, committed an act of filibusterism.

The fact of their being even the first to discover guano thereon, did not vest them with the right to make themselves masters of the accessions, which nobody can deny, belongs to the owner of the territory.

However, they acknowledge the fact of their having been found on the island in December, with vessels ready to load guano, and of their having, previous to the above date, already extracted therefrom a considerable quantity of the article. So, then, Venezuela should have regarded them as pirates taken by surprise, or in *flagrante delicto*.

Their peaceful expulsion, far from making it an act of violence to merit indemnification, is one of condescension and kindness which the United States ought undoubtedly to acknowledge.

Second. If Isla de Aves is not the property of Venezuela, it must needs belong to Holland, who claims it.

The acts exercised thereon by American citizens, do not for this reason change their character. They are no less filibustering and piratical, the islet belonging to Venezuela, than they would be were it the property of Holland. As such, the Venezuelan navy had a right to expel them from the territory of a friendly nation.

On the supposition alluded to, the claimants have not the least right to demand indemnification from Venezuela, just as Walker and his followers could have no right to demand indemnification from Spain if one of her admirals had assumed the position of Commodore Paulding in the late events at Punta Arenas.

On the supposition under consideration, Venezuela would have violated the territory of Holland, and this nation would have been the one to resent the injury done; but the pirates could not have acquired the right to demand indemnification from Venezuela, for the same reason that the United States will never award reparation to the invader of Nicaragua, notwithstanding its being officially established that a commander of the national navy violated a foreign territory in order to succeed in the capturing of the filibusters.

The present administration of the United States government, which has assumed so strong a position on account of the Paulding-Walker affair, cannot fail to recognize the identity of the two cases. At least, it may be so presumed in view of the sound principles professed by the American press, which sustains the predominant policy of the ruling administration. We have only to substitute, in the present international claim alluded to, the agents of the case, in order to manifest the justice of Venezuela, sustained by the Committee of Foreign Relations of the Senate, and by the "Washington Union" of January 31.

"'The South' is compelled to dissent from both the premises and the conclusion of the able report of Mr. Mason, of the Senate Committee of Foreign Relations in the Paulding-Walker case. 'The South,' after stating the position of the committee that the affair of the arrest (expulsion) only concerns the government of the United States and the government of Nicaragua, (the government of Venezuela and the government of Holland,) exclaims with some enthusiasm: 'What! is not reparation due the individuals who are the victims of an act of legal violence and unwarrantable usurpation?' 'The South' (the attorney of the claimants) is sufficiently conversant with the principles of law, to understand that a party detected in the violation of statutes may not invoke the civil arm of government to put him right. If General Walker (Shelton party) set on foot a military (filibuster) expedition against the State of Nicaragua, (the Dutch Isla de Aves,) in contempt of our laws, it would be a monstrous perversion of well defined legal practice to yield to his demands of restitution and redress. If the expedition referred to left our shores illegally, General Walker and his men in connection therewith, (the invaders of Isla de Aves,) can never be treated as citizens having the right to claim the protection of the government. They are tainted with wrong. Nor can we agree with 'The South' (attorney of the claimants) that natural sovereignty is such an unappeasable organ, as to be incapable of determining the extent of its own wrongs, and of deciding upon the manner of their redress. If the sovereignty of Nicaragua (Holland) has been violated by us, (Venezuela,) we insist that Nicaragua (Holland) shall at least have the right to say how much, if any, she is injured, and what will satisfy her. We go so far as to maintain, in opposition to 'The South,' that it is clearly the right of any nation to consent to the military occupation of its soil by another," &c.

Third. Finally, if Isla de Aves was derelict in July, 1854. Venezuela, by occupying it, has not incurred any liability towards the American citizens whom she found there in December of the same year.

International law authorized Venezuela to do so, as has been shown above.

Besides, the American claimants themselves freely consented to the occupation by Venezuela, in the following document:

"Domingo Dias, captain of a ship-of-war, and second chief of the Venezuelan navy, and commissioned by the supreme government of the republic to watch the desert Antilles that belong to it in the Carribbean sea, has agreed, subject to the approbation of my government, that Messrs. Charles H. Lang, (agent of the company of Lang and Delano, of Boston,) and Nathan P. Gibbs, (agent of that of Sampson, Tappan & P. S. Shelton, also of Boston,) whom I have found extracting guano from this island, may:

"1. Continue to load the vessels that are actually taking in cargo.

"2. They may continue to load until the arrival of the company with whom the government has entered into contracts, or until the arrival of the approbation or disapprobation of the supreme government.

"3. And we, Charles H. Lang and Nathan P. Gibbs, engage to lend the aid that the garrison of the island may require.

"4. And to that effect we place our pieces of artillery and armament at the orders and under the Venezuelan flag, to which the island belongs; and,

"5. I, Dias, second chief of the Venezuelan navy, do order the commanders of men-of-war cruising in the Antilles, to respect the concession until the supreme government may dispose otherwise.

"NATHAN P. GIBBS.
"CHARLES H. LANG,
"*Agent for Lang & Delano, Boston.*
"DOMINGO DIAS.

"ISLAND OF AVES, [to windward,]
"*December* 13, 1854."

It now becomes proper to make mention of this incident, which proves the last assertion. As is already apparent, however favorable for Venezuela, her government has not required it for the justification of her conduct in the claim.

The agent for the two Boston houses acknowledged, in the above quoted document, the legitimacy of Venezuela's authority over Isla de Aves. The moment they thought of a lucrative claim upon that republic, the first thing to which they ought to have called the attention of their government, if they had actually been wronged, or deceived, in the act in question, was the existence of the permit of December 13. So remarkable an incident could not have been overlooked, through forgetfulness, in a claim the justice of which depended precisely upon the value that might be attached to that document.

However, it will be seen that Shelton and associates did not think of the exception of fraud and violence, until the American legation found itself unexpectedly stopped in its proceedings by the permit of December 13, 1854.

The claimants laid the case before the government of the United States, January 15, 1855, without mentioning the incident operating against them. This is the manner in which it was discovered by Mr. Eames, and the impression it made on him. The following are paragraphs from his note to Mr. Marcy, dated at Caraccas, April 26, 1855, in which he goes on to relate what had occurred after his interview with the secretary of foreign relations, about the latter part of March, as has been stated above:

"Soon afterwards, and while I was still seeking to ascertain the cxact nature of the admission, which I should have to encounter in prosecuting the reclamation of the claimants, there was put in my hands, by a merchant here, a paper which purported to be a copy of an agreement entered into and signed at the Island of Aves, on the 13th of December last." * * * * "Upon comparing this paper with the documents accompanying your instruction, which purported to invoke your interposition upon a full narration of the very events in which this paper forms so material a portion, the first inclination of my mind was either to doubt its genuineness, or the accuracy of the copy in my hands. I therefore took an early opportunity to have another interview with Mr. Aranda, in which I informed him that I had what purported to be a copy of one of the papers in the case, which, at this stage of the business, I wished to compare with the original. He at once assented, though he could not understand how a copy should have got out, and at a subsequent day, placed the papers in my hands for examination. I found the original there, to all appearance an authentic paper, and upon comparison, my copy proved to be exact. I then asked Mr. Aranda if he was satisfied of the genuineness of the original, and he replied that there could not be a doubt of it.

"With these facts before me, I find myself unable to resist the conviction that the case of the claimants is clothed by this paper with a character very different from that in which they brought it to your notice, and upon which your instruction was framed. If the case was one of a conflicting claim between the two governments to the eminent domain of the Aves, this agreement I should consider of no force whatever. But the case being a reclamation of private citizens for indemnity and restoration, I cannot avoid the conclusion that the claimants themselves have, by this act of their agents, if left unexplained, greatly embarrassed their government in its successful prosecution. At all events, there can be no doubt that the agreement of the claimants is regarded by the Venezuelan government as an effectual bar to any claim for indemnity by them or in their behalf.

"In this state of facts, I deem it proper to refer this new matter in the case to the department, in order to learn the view which you take of its bearing upon the further prosecution of the claim. I am the more induced to adopt this course because, considering the date of this agreement, I see no reason to doubt that it was known to the claimants when they presented their case to you on the 15th of January last, and I cannot understand what is their justification for not then bringing it to your attention, with whatever explanation of it might be in their power. It is proper to add, however, that I have of course made no admission whatever to this government as to the paper or the operation of it, and that when I receive your views of it, and of the case as affected by it, I shall be prepared to carry your instructions at once into effect."

When the claimants found themselves overwhelmed by a proof so decidedly against them, they then conceived the plan of making it void by launching a gross imputation upon an unblemished and honorable Venezuelan chieftain. They have not dared to deny their own signatures; they have only endeavored to make believe that force and fraud were used for the purpose of obtaining their acquiescence.

Force and fraud! Two actions which never go together, because the nature of each by itself excludes the other. The claimants, however, maintain that force and fraud intervened in the permit in question.

It is important to bear in mind the two versions suggested by the above mentioned incident.

The version of the Venezuelan government is:

That Colonel Dias, on the 13th of December, landed in Isla de Aves without any opposition, either by words or deeds, on the part of the American citizens there found; that at their request and entreaty the permit referred to was conceded; and that by various attentions shown the Venezuelans, did the Americans appear to be pleased and obliged by the act of compliance of the Venezuelan commissioner.

The claimants's version, supported by the United States legation at Caraccas, is:

That they did verbally oppose the occupation of the island by Venezuela; that, in fact, they did not do it, although with a superior force to that effect, with the view of avoiding extremities; and that the two agents for the Boston houses signed the document as well to prevent the use of force, as because of their ignorance that the permit in Spanish contained the recognition of Venezuela's title over the Isla de Aves.

The party for Shelton and associates has endeavored to prove his allegation, summoning various witnesses connected with the two Isla de Aves expeditions, some to declare before a justice of the peace in Boston, and others before a notary public in New York.

The government of Venezuela has repelled the false allegation by declarations from the commanders and officers who occupied the island on the 13th of December, 1854, all of which were taken at the office of the secretary of war, in the presence of Mr. Sanford, Shelton's agent, at Caraccas.

Which of the two versions is the true one? If the contending governments recognized one superior judge to weigh the proofs adduced by both parties, that of Venezuela would unquestionably be sustained by the following reasons, which, being the principal ones, are drawn from the whole of the testimony:

There was no fraud, first, because Mr. Lang, one of the two American agents, is very well acquainted with the Spanish language; second, because the permit, before Mr. Gibbs, the other agent, had signed it, was interpreted for him by Lang himself, and by Commander Cotarro, of the Venezuela navy.

There was no violence, first, because the document was signed when there were but three Venezuelan officers on shore; second, because even had the whole of the detachment and crew on board the schooner landed, the numerical superiority on the filibuster's side made fear impossible, even in men not so strong and resolute as they represented themselves in their declarations; and third, because these very invaders themselves, although obliged to prove such imaginary violence, have not ventured to mention any act of compulsion, death, wounds, or even blows.

The superior judge, supposed in the case, would have seen, as already stated, that fraud and violence are actions excluding each other from their very nature; that the very counduct of the American signers, such as is represented by their own declarations, before the act, during the act, and after the act of the permit, compels common sense to reject the allegation; and he must finally have seen that the proof, proceeding from a written document against the signers thereof, is always conclusive, since, by their own allegations, no legislation could invalidate it.

Yet Venezuela and the United States, equally independent, equally sovereign, do not recognize any superior judge impartially to weigh the proofs adduced. It belongs, therefore, to their respective governments to fulfill that delicate function, guided only by principles of justice.

The government of Venezuela, with a perfect knowledge of the case, has advanced its views on the question; they are very evident; they have herein been set forth, and clear it is that it could not be possible to enunciate them with stronger foundation.

The government of the United States must now, in its turn, express its opinion. Presided over as it is by a theoretically and practically just administration, Venezuela has a right to expect from it a disregard for the alleged exception of fraud and violence, not only in consideration of the reasons already given, but also because in the obtaining of the testimony presented by the claimants, there have been omitted all the tutelar formalities to insure credibility of the witnesses, as those connected with the case have never been brought to trial by judicial proceedings, nor have in their favor the guarantee of public examination.

All these guarantees were obtained by the evidence which the government of the United States presented to Great Britain in the recent question about recruiting; and yet when Lord Clarendon, in the name of his government, disregarded it on the ground of not being satisfactory, the Secretary of State, Mr. Marcy, did not arrogate to himself the right to judge alone, and on his own authority, of the value of the testimony presented, notwithstanding its having been obtained in a public formal trial, and corroborated with very important documents; but thought himself in duty bound to declare, in his note of 13th of October, 1855, to the American plenipotentiary in London, that:

"Should her Britannic Majesty's government see fit to disclose any specific objection to the mode by which the evidence has been obtained, or attempt in any other way to impeach it, this government will then feel called on to vindicate its course, and show its ability to sustain its charges by evidence to which no just exception can be taken."

How could, then, the government of Venezuela expect, in the controverted case, that the United States, disregarding such sacred forms, should deliberately sustain extra-judicial declarations of interested witnesses, too suspicious to the effect of exacting undue indemnification from a whole nation? Such a proceeding would present a repugnant contrast with that required by the ordinary course of the Union and of all other civilized nations, to condemn a single individual in a trial involving comparatively insignificant pecuniary interests.

In an international question, therefore, in which much more transcendental interests are concerned, the government of the United States will require for, the purpose of its conviction, what it is known is required in weighing the proofs of contradictory testimony; not only the preponderance of proofs, so that the one against the defendant will palpably exceed the one in his favor, but the full and satisfactory evidence; that is, such a degree of proof as will leave no reasonable doubt with regard to truth.

This evidence, thus qualified, is what the claimants have not presented, so as to destroy the value of the permit of December 13, and consequently, even in the denied admission of Isla de Aves being deemed derelict, there would be no ground left for the required liability of Venezuela.

The above statement of the justification of Venezuela would not be complete did it not further evidence that Mr. Eames had erroneously informed the cabinet of Washington that the cabinet of Caraccas had willfully retarded the consideration of this affair, whereas, by the official acts of both cabinets, quite the contrary is shown.

In March, 1855, Mr. Eames received from Mr. Marcy the first official note on the subject. In the same month, and in April following, he procured two interviews with the Secretary of Foreign Relations for the purpose of obtaining information. Afterwards he had occasion to mention the intended claim on the Pickrell question, (September, 1855,) and on that of Holland, (March, 1856.) The last declarations which the claimants tried, when they thought of annulling the permit of 13th December, were rendered in April, 1856. This last incident shows that Mr. Eames could not have introduced the claim into the cabinet of Caraccas before the 20th of December, 1856.

If, as it has been pretended, the claim was presented in the conversation of March, 1855, without any documentary evidence to sustain it, it is now about three years since it was initiated; but, even in such an inadmissible case, the discussion could only have taken place on the 20th December, 1856, when Mr. Eames presented his written demand. All the time, therefore, that the protected citizens required for obtaining their proofs against the permit of the 15th December is attributed to procrastination on the part of Venezuela.

In one way or the other, the truth is, that the discussion did not commence until the 20th December, 1856. The government of Venezuela contested the claim, repudiating it in a note of the 27th February, 1857. On the 31st March, Mr. Eames insisted in an extensive note, accompanied with the evidence of the claimants; and, without allowing time for the examination thereof, arrogated to himself the right of terminating the discussion, scarcely yet opened between two equal States that maintain and cultivate the most friendly relations with each other.

And what was his subsequent course of procedure? He still persists in denying to Venezuela the necessary time to collect such evidence in the case as was required to oppose that presented by Shelton and his associates. He pays no attention to the official citation served on him for the taking thereof, pretending, thereby, it may be presumed to put out of question those facts of fraud and violence which, for the first time, opposed the permit of December 13th; and, finally, having obtained permission from his government to return to his country, he ostentatiously demanded his passports, leaving it to be inferred as the result of the pending question, and as placing the relations of the two countries in a state full of perils.

The government of Venezuela, nevertheless, firm in its purpose to maintain its dignity, did not abandon its unquestionable right. Although engaged at the time with the sessions of Congress, and occupied by important public business, it lost no time in collecting the mass of facts that were necessary to answer directly to the cabinet of Washington, as was done in its reasonable note of October 31st ultimo, and to fix the solution of the question at this capital, sending to that effect the undersigned envoy extraordinary and minister plenipotentiary.

M. DE BRICENO.

WASHINGTON CITY, *March* 1, 1858.

Mr. Sanford to Mr. Cass.

BREVOORT HOUSE, NEW YORK,
April 13, 1858.

SIR: In letters to the department in July and August last, and repeatedly previously, I urged upon it the importance of having presented *in extenso* to the Venezuelan government a statement of the injuries and damages sustained by the claimants in the Aves case, verified by authenticated copies of all the proofs, depositions, and documents presented by them, a part of which have been unaccountably withheld by our minister at Caraccas, and of making a direct demand, a letter of request, upon Venezuela.

The unworthy and dishonorable quibbling and delays of that government, since that time, must have convinced you of the utter uselessness of future correspondence with such people, question of dignity apart.

The Monagas government has finally had justice done to it; its profligacy, crimes, and robberies belong to history. While I confidently hope from the respectability of the members of the new government that an era of honesty and justice commences there, I think it highly important that it should not be given any warrant for making the excuse of laboring under a misapprehension as to the definitive views and decision of our government on the subject of the Aves outrage.

I have read the pamphlet, recently issued, to the public (in violation of all diplomatic usage) by Dr. Briceno, special envoy to this country of the Monagas government. It is of a piece with the lofty annunciations in the Charleston newspapers, caused to be put in by himself on arriving in this country, of his rank, and of the objects of his mission, and teeming with gross misrepresentations of the facts of the case, and also of similar pronunciamentos of himself and the Monagas government on this claim, furnished to reporters, and upon which Mr. Shelton has already addressed the department, and to whose letter I refer you. With respect to the various issues as to veracity and honorable conduct made by the Monagas government directly with Mr. Eames, certainly the claimants have little to do, except in so far as they may affect their just rights and interests.

They cannot conceive it can prejudice them, especially in view of the fact, to which they call your attention, that as early as 1855 and 1856, I, as the representative of these claimants, in formal and separate communications, addressed as well to the then President and Secretary of State of the United States, forewarned them that such course would be taken by the Venezuelan government.

If the accusations of the Venezuelan government be true to the extent set forth in Dr. Briceno's pamphlet, in the last report of the minister of foreign relations of the Monagas government to the Venezuelan Congress, and in the letter of that minister to you, the case would seem to have but one parallel in the annals of diplomatic history—that of Lord Clives's "red-paper treaty" with Messrs. Jaffier and Omichund, in the East Indies, and which was so universally execrated by the civilized world. I cannot conceive it possible that the United States will allow its minister to be placed in such disgraceful position by the Monagas government, without requiring the most explicit and unexceptionable proofs of their accusations, or a retraction and prompt apology. Nor can I conceive it will pass unnoticed the means adopted to give these accusations publicity. I have felt ashamed and humiliated as an American citizen that such a publication as that issued by Dr. Briceno, the special envoy extraordinary and minister plenipotentiary of a foreign government, should have been made under the very eaves of the State Department, impugning and soiling the honor of my country—a pamphlet transmitted to the different governments of the world, as I have reason to know—sent to every member of Congress, and sought to be published in leading American newspapers, and that it should pass a single day unrebuked by his peremptory dismissal, as Washington served Genet, and General Taylor served Poussin, for their impudence.

But with all this the claimants have no interest beyond that of all other American citizens. If every word said on behalf of the Venezuelan government against Mr. Eames were true, the claimants insist, as they have from 1855 up to this date, that their rights and interests should not be compromised by any dereliction of duty on his part. On the contrary, if, for illustration, we can imagine the facts are as the Monagas government and Dr. Briceno state, the complicity—for it is notorious that they had personal and pecuniary interest in the guano contracts with the Philadelphia company, of members of the Monagas administration, in the tortious course they impute to Mr. Eames, and that they now urge the circumstances to screen themselves from the demands of justice—is as clear as the sun at noon day, and the considerations that the claimants have thus been prejudiced and delayed for three years by the remissness and improper conduct of the agent of their government, without any fault of their own, it seems to me should be an incentive to the more vigorous prosecution of their rights hereafter by the United States government. The claimants have a full confidence such would be the case. Years ago the claimants were reproved by the department for suggesting that such defenses were anticipated on the part of Venezuela, and the depositions of Captain Gibbs and the other witnesses at Aves, in 1854, prove that Dias boasted of the combination of powerful and political influence in Venezuela and the United States interested in sustaining him.

But with reference to the further conduct of their case, the claimants would again urge upon the department, not merely the propriety, but the imperative necessity, if anything is expected to be done in this case, of supplying forthwith one defect (alluded to in Dr. Briceno's pamphlet) which exists in it, caused by Mr. Eames's failure to furnish the Venezuelan government with the several depositions, documents, and proofs forwarded to him, duly exemplified for that purpose. Whether peaceful reprisals are resorted to or not, whilst the 34th article of the treaty of 1836 is in force, this should have been done. Venezuela, it is in the opinion of legal counsel, has the right under the treaty to ask for it, even though our government may decide to resort to some other mode of redress than reprisals. It is too much for me to ask of the department to require Mr. Eames by explicit instructions to forthwith deliver copies to the Venezuelan government of every deposition, document, and other proof transmitted to him in this case, not previously delivered by him *in extenso*, and to furnish the department with the proof thereof. With respect to Gibbs's deposition, it was presented mutilated, and a material part was omitted by Mr. Eames, the most important and extended deposition of Captain Wheeler, those of McCabe, Thornell, and others, are still retained in the archives of the legation—all important and all obtained with great trouble and at no inconsiderable cost.

If Dr. Briceno is sent home simultaneously with such instructions, and renewal of the peremptory demand for adjustment, which Mr. Eames has not yet presented to the Venezuelan government, or a letter of request be sent at the same time to that government direct, as a letter of request under the law of nations must be, I have some little hope that by the end of this year matters may approach something like the "commencement of the end!"

I have great confidence in the new government; I know some of the members of it personally, and they are high-toned, honorable men, deservedly respected by the country, and as yet unacquainted with official circumlocution; but I think it important that their sense of justice should be appealed to while it is fresh.

In view of the nearly approaching end of the session of Congress, and of the extraordinary, unjust, trifling and dishonorable course of the government of Venezuela in this matter, it appears to me that an intimation from the Executive to Congress that a law clothing the former with more plenary powers to enforce justice against that government than some suppose it possesses without such law, would not fail to be responded to by Congress. Of course no action would be had under such law if the new government of Venezuela act with more justice and honor than its predecessors. Of this I have stated that I had hopes, and would further say that Dr. Briceno was in Venezuela opposed to the Monagas administration, and being committed as he is by his pamphlet against the just settlement of this claim, it is possible that his representations to the new government on his return home may have an injurious influence.

I have the honor to be, with great respect, your most obedient servant,

H. S. SANFORD.

Hon. LEWIS CASS,
Secretary of State.

Mr. Briceno to Mr. Cass.

[Translation.]

LEGATION EXTRAORDINARY OF VENEZUELA TO THE UNITED STATES,
Washington, April 25, 1858.

EXCELLENT SIR: It has come to my notice that the government of the United States has seen with dissatisfaction that without its previous knowledge publication has been made of the memorial which I had the honor to transmit to your excellency with my dispatch of the 17th instant.

Under this impression, imbued with the constant desires which actuate my government to preserve the strictest relations of friendship with the government of the United States, and moved by sentiments whose loftiness I trust your excellency will not do less than recognize, I hasten to declare that it causes me pain that my mode of proceeding can have given just cause of complaint to the government of your excellency, for there has not been on my part the slightest intention to forget for a single instant the courteous demeanor or the respect which two friendly governments owe to each other.

With sentiments of distinguished consideration, I subscribe myself your excellency's obedient servant,

M. DE BRICENO.

His Excellency GENERAL CASS, *&c.*

Mr. Cass to Mr. Briceno.

DEPARTMENT OF STATE,
Washington, April 27, 1858.

SIR: I have had the honor to receive your communication of the 25th instant, in which you express your regret that your conduct in publishing your late memoir concerning the Aves negotiation without the previous knowledge of this department had given just cause of complaint to the government of the United States, and your assurance that the publication was made without the least intention of disregarding the respect due from the representative of a friendly power to this government.

It is quite true that the publication of the memoir in question was observed by the President with great surprise, but he is relieved from the necessity of expressing any further opinion upon that proceeding by the frank explanation and assurance which are contained in your note.

The undersigned avails himself of this occasion to offer to Mr. de Briceno a renewed assurance of his very high consideration.

LEWIS CASS.

Señor Don MANUEL DE BRICENO, *&c.*

Mr. Cass to Venezuelan Minister of Foreign Relationz.

DEPARTMENT OF STATE,
Washington, May 10, 1858.

SIR: The departure of Mr. de Briceno, late special envoy from the government of Venezuela, without having accomplished, during his residence here, any adjustment of the Aves Island reclamation, which was understood to be the particular object of his mission, devolves upon me the duty of communicating to your excellency the reply which is due to the note of Señor Jacinto Gutierrez to this department of the 31st October last, in respect to that claim.

Notwithstanding the mature consideration given to that note, as well as to the explanations and statements of Mr. de Briceno, the result has been only to confirm the views of this government in relation to the liability of Venezuela to make reparation for the wrongs our citizens have sustained. Your excellency will receive herewith copies of the correspondence which has passed between this department and Mr. de Briceno, which will inform you of the precise condition of the claim. A list of the inclosures is subjoined.

The case is now, by direction of the President, referred back to the government of Venezuela, in the expectation that the present enlightened and patriotic administration of that republic will not fail to coöperate in the speedy and harmonious termination of a question which has already encountered too much delay, and embarrassed too long the relations of both republics. If the instruction of this department to the Minister of the United States in Caraccas of the 31st August last, a copy of which was placed in the hands of Mr. Briceno, who doubtless communicated it to his government, has not been carried into effect, it has been partly because of the hopeful results looked for from the special mission of Mr. Briceno, and, since the change of government, partly from the anticipation entertained of an early settlement of the case by the existing authorities of Venezuela.

The minister of the United States will be fully instructed to communicate with your excellency on this subject, and I repeat the confident belief of the President that, the question of liability being admitted, there will be no serious difficulty in arranging the details of a satisfactory adjustment either at Caraccas or Washington.

I avail myself, &c.,

LEWIS CASS.

His Ex'cy THE MINISTER FOR FOREIGN RELATIONS,
Of the Republic of Venezuela.

List of Inclosures.

A.—Mr. Cass to Mr. de Briceno—February 22, 1858.
B.—Mr. Briceno to Mr. Cass—February 24, 1858.
C.—Mr. Cass to Mr. Briceno—February 26, 1858.
D.—Mr. Briceno to Mr. Cass—February 27, 1858.
E.—Mr. Cass to Mr. Briceno—March 4, 1858.
F.—Mr. Briceno to Mr. Cass—March 8, 1858.
G.—Same to same—April 7, 1858.
H.—Same to same—April 25, 1858.
I.—Mr. Cass to Mr. Briceno—April 27, 1858.

Mr. Cass to Mr. Eames.

No. 60.] DEPARTMENT OF STATE,
Washington, May 10, 1858.

SIR: Herewith I transmit an open letter addressed to the minister of relations of Venezuela, covering copies of the correspondence, which has passed between the department and Mr. Briceno, the special minister from Venezuela, in relation to the Aves Island claim of Shelton and others, the settlement of which was understood to be the principal object of Mr. Briceno's mission. From these papers, which you are requested to deliver, you will perceive that no perceptible advance has been made towards an adjustment of the claim referred to. In receiving the special minister from Venezuela as an act of courtesy due to a friendly State, it was far from the expectation of the President that this government would be invited to proceed to a discussion of the Aves Island question *ab initio*, instead of receiving propositions for an equitable adjustment of the claims involved, upon the grounds which for three years the United States have maintained in respect to the liability of Venezuela to atone for the grievous wrong done to our citizens and our flag.

It was not without surprise, then, that this government received Mr. Gutierrez's note of 31st October last, which elaborately defended Venezuela's title to the Aves Island, and denied to the claimants any indemnification for all their losses and damages.

Due consideration, however, has been given to the arguments and statements of Mr. Gutierrez, not merely upon their own merits, but in the light of the verbal conferences held with Mr. Briceno; but this renewed consideration of the subject has not, in any degree, modified the previous views of this government with reference to the Aves claim. The President perceives no reason for changing a decision which was only arrived at after sufficient investigation.

You will perceive from the papers transmitted, that before Mr. Briceno received the notice of his recall, he found it necessary to make an explanation to the department of his conduct in publishing a memoir upon the subject of the "Aves" case, which was manifestly a violation of diplomatic usage, and not in accordance with that respect which is due to the United States from the representative of a friendly power. This explanation was received with the greater satisfaction because it was believed that the course of Mr. Briceno was without authority from his government, and because it was not desired to do anything which might embarrass the new administration which had just been organized in Venezuela. Mr. Briceno accordingly was granted an audience of leave in the usual manner.

In reference to the "Aves" case, which was the chief subject of the special mission, there are reasons for supposing that the juncture is not unpropitious to the final and satisfactory removal of it from the prominence which has necessarily been given to it to the exclusion, in a considerable degree, of other interesting matters connected with our relations with Venezuela. One of these reasons is found in the character of the administration now controlling that republic; another, and more weighty one perhaps, is drawn from the intimation conveyed to you by Mr. Urrutia, in his note of the 24th March, accompanying your No. 48, that the withdrawal of the Venezuelan legation from the United States was justified partly by considerations of economy, and partly because "there will be no difficulty in continuing in (Caraccas) the discussion of the same business which is now being considered by the cabinet at Washington in relation to Venezuela."

In communicating the accompanying note to the minister of foreign relations, you will avail yourself of the opportunity to affirm to the government of Venezuela the expectation of the President therein expressed, which it is earnestly hoped may meet with a cordial and prompt response from the present authorities of that republic. If the liability of Venezuela be admitted, (as I trust it will,) it is presumed that no serious difficulty will be encountered in fixing the amount of indemnification.

Mr. Sanford, the agent of Messrs. Shelton & Co., has expressed an earnest wish that all the evidence transmitted to the legation in support of this claim, should be formally presented to the Venezuelan government, in order that there may be no question as to the fidelity with which the strict letter of the thirty-fourth article of the treaty of 1836 with Venezuela has been observed, preliminary to the resort to the remedy of reprisals contemplated therein. If there has been any omission in this respect, as to the presentation of the proofs forwarded, you will forthwith supply it; but, in doing so, you must have it distinctly understood by the Venezuelan government that the presentation of these proofs is only made from abundant caution, in order that there may be no cavil respecting the legality of ulterior measures, if, unfortunately, it should be found necessary to resort to them for the purpose of obtaining that justice which has been otherwise sought in vain.

You are at liberty to retain copies of the accompanying documents for the files of the legation.

Your dispatches to No. 48 (two of that number) inclusive, have been received.

I am, sir, your obedient servant,

LEWIS CASS.

CHARLES EAMES, Esq.,
&c., &c., &c.

Mr. Eames to Mr. Cass.

No. 55.] LEGATION OF THE UNITED STATES,
Caraccas, May 13, 1858.

SIR: With reference to my dispatch, No. 48, under date of 25th March last, in which I transmitted to the department the note of the then Minister of Foreign Relations of this government, informing me of its withdrawal of the special mission of Mr. Briceno, charged with Aves Island negotiation, and intimating the opinion then, as I informed the department, concurred in by me, that this new government having entered upon an era of reformation in the public policy of this country, would be ably now with more facility to adjust with this legation that question and other questions between the two governments in a manner favorable to the continuance of the good understanding existing between them. I have the honor now, in confirmation of the views then expressed by me, to transmit inclosed to the department, in copy and translation, a note addressed to me under date of yesterday by the new Minister of Foreign Relations, Mr. Toro.

The last dispatch received by me from the department, in relation to the Aves Island reclamation, is your No. 58, of 15th December last, which was crossed by the special mission of Mr. Briceno, who proceeded to the United States on the 9th of that month. From facts within my knowledge, I think, in an authentic shape, it would seem that his mission has not resulted in the satisfactory settlement of the question, and may have been brought to a close by his own course in the conduct of it, even before his recall by this government was received in Washington.

I suppose that instructions on the subject to this legation may be expected without much delay, and it is my purpose, meantime, to do what I prudently can do under the circumstances with this government to facilitate a prompt and satisfactory conclusion of the business.

With the highest respect and consideration, I have the honor to be your obedient servant,

CHARLES EAMES.

Hon. LEWIS CASS,
Secretary of State.

[Translation.]

Republic of Venezuela.

DEPARTMENT OF FOREIGN RELATIONS,
Caraccas, May 12, 1858.

The legations of Venezuela in the United States having been withdrawn by reason of the motives, which care was taken to communicate to Mr. Eames in the note of the 23d of March, the government has not ceased to preserve the most friendly sentiments towards that of the great American republic and its enlightened people, and in the absence of those organs, it fulfills its desires to cultivate the good understanding between the two countries through the Señor Minister Resident whom the undersigned now addresses. Doubtless, the sympathies so spontaneously manifested by Mr. Eames respecting the marvellous transformation just witnessed by him, and judged with the sound discrimination which distinguishes him, will have been already communicated to the American cabinet, and will find there the echo with which all the friends of liberty and of justice, without distinction of country, have responded to the noble efforts and rapid triumph of the holiest of causes. Mr. Eames has been able already to observe and appreciate the effects of the salutary change which has been accomplished for the welfare of the Venezuelan nation, and naturally, also, in promotion of the relations of friendship, of commerce, and of ideas which the republic ought and desires to confirm with other nations, and very especially with those of analogous institutions, and which, like the United States, by their power, greatness, and prosperity, excite general emulation.

Therefore, the provisional government being animated by these favorable dispositions, it is to be hoped that a similar spirit presiding on both sides in the discussion of the matters now pending between the two countries, these matters will not be an obstacle capable of opposing the fulfillment of loyal purposes.

The undersigned renews to Mr. Eames the assurances of his distinguished consideration.

F. TORO.

Hon. CHARLES EAMES,
Minister Resident of the United States.

Mr. Sanford to Mr. Cass.

WASHINGTON, *May* 22, 1858.

SIR: I feel a deep interest, as I have a right to feel, in the success of the recently established government in the republic of Venezuela, the result of the overthrow of the infamous Monagas and those combined with him. I feel such interest because I have confidence in the integrity of those who overthrew Monagas, and who are now in power; and because, also, I felt personally the injustice and utter want of principle of Monagas, Giuseppi, Guiterrez & Co.

Recent occurrences, if they be true, as detailed in late publications in newspapers of New York and elsewhere, seem to me to be of a character deserving the attention of the federal government of the United States. I inclose some of these publications, and I feel that I have a right as an American citizen, having charge, as agent, of important interests of American citizens in Venezuela, and depending, in in some degree, upon the action of those in power in that country, to invoke the attention of the department to the transactions detailed in these publications.

It cannot be questioned that the law of nations casts around the representative of a foreign country and his family, and those who are, *bona fide*, his suite or domestics, an immunity from arrest, and a like immunity for his residence from domiciliary or police invasions. Yet it is a monstrous and unnecessary abuse of such privilege, and a prostitution of the wise and beneficent principles of the law of nations, to allow such residence to be made the sanctuary for political or other criminals of the country to which such representative is accredited. These are instances of unquestioned authority to be found in the books of international law, showing that the most enlightened nations have maintained and enforced the principle that those attached to a legation, and even the foreign representative himself, in certain cases of heinous, flagrant, and atrocious crimes, are themselves not exempt from arrest, trial, and punishment by the laws of the country in which they are committed. And it is right; for it is not to be presumed that any just government, influenced by proper principles of self respect, and its own dignity and honor, would interpose the ægis of embassadorial privilege to shield such criminal, whatever his rank, if the proof of his guilt was manifest and notorious.

As to abuse of right of asylums, there are three instances related as occurring in the years 1745, 1765, and 1770, (see Moser Versuch, iv., 299, ff. 26–36; Beyträge, iv., 212; Bynkershoeck, F. L., xxi.,) of the seizure by the Venetian government of fugitives from justice who had sought asylums at the residence of foreign ministers. One was from the hotel of the French embassador, who, refusing to give up the refugees, the Senate sent troops and cannon to storm the house. The States of Holland have demanded the surrender of a fugitive who had taken refuge in the house of the English resident. (Bynk., F. L., xxi.) The Duke of Ripperden was seized in the house of the English ambassador at Madrid in 1726. (See Vattel, iv., § 119; Marten's *Causes Celêbres* 1, 5 Cause, p. 174.) In 1747, a Swedish merchant named Springer took refuge in the hotel of the Swedish embassador at Stockholm, and the embassador, yielding to force, finally gave him up. (Marten's *Causes Celêbres*, 1, 10 Cause, p. 326.) Pinheiro Ferrera says, (vol. 2, p. 196,) that if the embassador refuse to give up a fugitive from justice seeking asylum, and force be required to seize him, the embassador should be sent out of the country, care being first taken to secure the fugitive.

A case in point, with respect to members of an embassador's household, is that of Pantaleon de La, a brother of the Portuguese embassador to England, who had committed murder in the London exchange, Cromwell, then lord protector, had him seized at the house of his brother, and he was tried, condemned, and executed.

The immunity of an embassador is founded upon the principle, that whilst he is embassador, his acts are presumed to be the acts of his government, and done under its authority; and it cannot be possible that any decent government can be presumed to authorize its functionaries to perpetrate a felony, or other infamous crime, such as larceny, rape, murder; and no one doubts that for conspiracy, aiding and abetting treasonable practices against the government to which he is accredited, such government can proceed, as with other conspirators and traitors, against such embassadors. There are numerous cases on this subject. As to immunities of ministers, the following are recollected:

A celebrated case is that of Baron de Görtz, minister of Charles XII of Sweden, arrested for conspiracy against England, by the Dutch authorities of the Hague, in 1717, on the demand of England. The Swedish minister at London was also put under arrest by the English government. (Marten's *Causes Celebres*, 1, 75.) Mareville, French minister at Milan, was executed for murder. (9 Wicque, 1, 847. Flossan, *dip. fran.* 1, 364.) An embassador in Portugal, and a Venitian embassador at Milan, were put to death for adultery. (Bynk., F. L. XVIII.) And in our own history, Kosseloff, consul general of Russia, was tried and punished for rape.

Applying these principles to the recent occurrences in Venezuela, it seems to me that the course of the foreign legations there, in seeking to protect the infamous Monagas and his associates from arrest and prosecution, and just punishment for their crimes against their country and its laws, is without parallel in the annals of diplomatic history; and if the minister of the United States at Caraccas had not been participant in such unexampled course, deserves the notice of the federal government of the United States, in the exercise of the appropriate function of every free government as common conservator of the laws of nations.

The partisan interference of the foreign diplomats at Caraccas in the domestic political disputes of that country, cannot be justified upon any sound principles. The laws of nations demand that all interference in the local affairs of the country to which a minister is accredited, should be confined to regular diplomatic action for the maintenance and protection of the legitimate interest of his own country, (and the spirit and policy of our neutrality laws are in accordance with this principle,) and such of his fellow citizens or subjects as may be entitled to such protection. It is true, that some governments have not censured their representatives for interposing the shield of embassadorial immunity, from motives of humanity, for the protection of the weak and timid against the violence of popular fury, or the rancor of blind and vindictive persecution; but no case has occurred in which any respectable government has sanctioned proceedings like those that have recently occurred at Caraccas. The present emperor of the French, and also Napoleon I, have maintained the doctrine that international comity demanded that a friendly State should not allow the residence of alien conspirators against its own State within its jurisdiction, and where they were holding conspiracies against the government to which they owed allegiance, but should yield them up on the demand of said government, or subject them to criminal prosecution and punishment for such conspiracies; and very recently, the British government so far acquiesced (whatever may have been the influences) as to institute prosecutions against Bernard, Allsop, and others, concerned in the Orsini conspiracy and homicides.

But this reference is made merely in illustration of general doctrines, and it is not supposed that the precise rules allowed to govern in the case mentioned, or those principles so strongly maintained by the popular press of Great Britain against these doctrines, and which led to the overthrow of Lord Palmerston's ministry, either control or have any close analogy to a case of attempted embassadorial immunity of criminals, whether political or not, within the jurisdiction of the State where the crime was committed, and the laws of which had been violated. The cases are radically different, and whilst a liberal government may well refuse to grant the extradition of political offenders, or others, accused of offenses merely *malum prohibitum*, and not crimes *malum in re*, of which persons are accused who have taken refuge in their country, by the foreign State, (and such is the policy, and has been the uniform course of the United States,) yet it is carrying such doctrine a great deal too far, and further than is warranted by the laws of nations, to say that whilst they are in the country whose laws they have infringed, another government shall make itself the arbiter between the accused and his accusers, disregarding the laws of the country, and this justified solely upon the excuse of a sympathy for the unfortunate or overthrown, which may be often false, and is ever voluntary and gratuitous.

Now what do we see in the recent occurrences at Caraccas? What justification, even upon the ground of sympathy, is there for the course of the foreign legations there? For ten years Monagas and his family have been in the possession of usurped power, maintained by force, connected with the most atrocious murders, himself and those combined with him, mostly his family and connections, by corruptions and by a series of barefaced pillagings of the public treasury and oppressions of the people, have grasped millions of the public money for their private gain, large sums of which have been sent abroad; and, in the meantime, though totally disregarding the rights of other nations, their citizens and subjects committing flagrant spoliations upon them, (in one of which cases, as the department is aware, I am the agent to obtain redress,) utterly neglecting and withholding all just reparation. As to the Aves Island outrage, it is notorious that it originated in a private speculation, in which the person then occupying the position of Venezuelan minister of foreign affairs under Monagas, Simon Planas, and other public functionaries in that country, were parties.

Can such criminals justly claim the sympathy or even the slightest commiseration, if, at last, their oppressed countrymen, driven to desperation by their tyrannous and criminal courses, should arouse themselves, shake off the yoke they have borne, and drive their oppressors from the official power they have prostituted and abused?

In this case the people were successful in their efforts to establish a just and honest government. On the 15th day of March Monagas was constrained to resign. General Castro's government was organized, then became, and from that time continued to be, the established *de facto* government of the republic of Venezuela. Monagas acquiesced in and—though this was not necessary to give rightful authority to the new government—sanctioned its existence. The established principle to govern the conduct of the diplomatic representative of the United States of America in such case, is strongly exemplified in the memorable instance of the expulsion of Charles X and the accession of Louis Philippe to the throne of France, by the course of Mr. Rives, our minister there; and later, by the course of Mr. Rush, in the last named monarch's expulsion, and the inauguration of the temporary French republic; and still later, in the overthrow of the republic and the inauguration of the present empire, which last incident it was my fortune to witness as a functionary of our legation there; and upon being advised of which change, the government of the United States expressly instructed Mr. Rives to regard the government *de facto* as the rightful government.

In the recent case in Venezuela, General Castro having the government reins placed in his hands, was not the result of a merely temporary ebullition of popular feeling. Every foreign representative in Venezuela was well apprised of the universally extended popular sentiment in that country in favor of the overthrow of Monagas and the organization of a new government. Such was the remarkable unanimity of the popular voice on this subject, that the unparalleled spectacle is exhibited of the revolution being entirely successful, without the necessity of shedding a drop of blood, though large bodies of armed citizens were engaged in it. Monagas himself and his partisans, cowed under his convictions on this point, yielded up immediately office and power.

After the abnegation by Monagas of his office, made to the Congress of the republic then in session, and of which resignation the foreign representatives in Caraccas were apprised, he was escorted by them, or a portion of them, to the residence of the French chargé d'affaires, and placed therein as an asylum, with Giuseppi, his son-in-law, Gutierrez, his minister of foreign relations, and others in a like category, and the flags of the different foreign legations, that of the United States included, hung out from the house to prevent ingress by the new authorities into it.

Immediately thereafter, General Castro's government was organized and established, and recognized by the foreign representatives there as the government *de facto*, and subsequently the almost unanimous voice of the republic hath confirmed its authority.

After it was thus organized, the new government decided that the public interests and public justice demanded the arrest for trial of the persons above named for their numerous crimes whilst in power, and if convicted, that they should be compelled to disgorge their ill-gotten plunder, a portion of which had also extended over it, as above described, the embassadorial immunity, or alleged privilege of asylum.

The publications inclosed, if true, exhibit the ridiculous spectacle subsequently occurring of the British flag being spread as a carpet at the threshold of the French legation, and the British representative, himself under the protection of a generous ally, the Gallic eagle, daring the Venezuelan officers of justice to tread upon it to arrest the criminal with his plunder secreted in the house behind it, at the price of arousing the dread ire of the British lion! Whether this spectacle should be assigned to the category of farce or tragedy some future dramatist of Venezuela may decide.

Now, sir, I think the impartial judgment of every sensible and well informed man may be safely appealed to for the decision that upon no principle either of humanity or just philanthropy any of these representatives, or all of them together, had any more right to act thus with reference to Monagas and the others accused with him who are sought to be brought before the courts of justice of Venezuela for the violation of their laws, than they would have had to attempt by like means to shield a murderer, a highwayman, or one who had committed rape, theft, or arson in Caraccas.

The book upon the laws of nations that would sanction such extent of the embassadorial immunity has not yet been written. And again: the excuse preferred for the course of the foreign representatives at Caraccas, in sheltering Monagas and his associates—that they were political offenders—(if the principle of the impropriety of such representatives interfering in, and meddling with, the local, domestic, and political disputes of the country to which they are accredited, be respected)—but enhances the degree of their outrage upon Venezuela, and their violation of the law of nations. But the case does not end here. If the second publication inclosed to you be true, the still further extraordinary and inexcusable course is pursued of the foreign representatives uniting as a party on one side, and exerting the moral constraint that it may well be supposed they, professing to act for powerful States, would exert upon the minister of a newly formed Venezuelan government, itself comparatively weak and powerless at that juncture, and constraining him to hold a formal conference and negotiation with them respecting the disposition of the protected criminals, and of which conference and negotiation a diplomatic protocol was written before they would consent that the laws of Venezuela should be executed by the courts of Venezuela upon those owing allegiance to it, amenable to them for their misdeeds; and more, that they should then venture to exact a stipulation from him for the Venezuelan government for the benefit of the alleged criminals that they should go free from the country. It is true, as I have been glad to learn since, that General Castro and the other members of the government have disavowed the act and discharged the minister who signed the protocol.

I ask you, sir, if Count de Sartiges, Baron de Stoeckl, or Lord Napier should receive into their residences at Washington any of the persons who participated in the tumults at the mayor's election in this city some months since, and which resulted in the death or several persons, or if they attempted to shield a murderer or other felon from the action of our courts or authorities by an alleged embassadorial immunity of such residence and the secretion of the criminal therein, whether the government of the United States would tolerate for a moment such course? I will go further, and ask if a public officer should violate the sub-treasury law, and misappropriate public money to his own use, and thus under such law should become a criminal, and upon dismissal or resignation of his office should run to the residence of either of the very respectable diplomats named, whether the flags of Russia, France, or England, laid in triple folds on the steps of such residence to stop the ingress of a police office to arrest the criminal, would not be kicked out of the way or trampled upon by such officer, whichever mode might be supposed to manifest the most contempt for such presumptious interference? And I confidently ask, whither, in such case, the federal government would not sustain such officer?

If the position I maintain be not true; if the extravagant pretensions of the diplomatic representatives in Venezuela be allowed; then I ask, what is there that prevents a foreign minister at Washington, if he can inveigle an American citizen, male or female into his house, from holding him or her in perpetual duress and imprisonment there, in defiance of a writ of *habeas corpus?* It is no answer to say that a foreign minister who would thus act would be dismissed *instanter*, for, by the law of nations, even upon such dismissal, whatever the privileges and immunities that attach to his person and suite continue till he has had time to return home.

I think that upon a careful review of the circumstances which have occurred in Venezuela, the President and yourself will be satisfied that the opinion expressed in the commencement of this communication of their deserving the pointed notice of the federal government, will be concurred in; and I trust you will regard the facts I have stated as to my position and interests and feeling as a full apology for calling your attention to the subject. The principles with reference to this alleged right of asylum should be laid down distinctly to the American representatives abroad, and especially to those accredited to the Hispano-American republics south of us. In those States the residences of the foreign representatives, in case of revolution, seem to have been regarded for many years as a kind of political *alsatia* for all the unfortunate political rogues, when they have to give place like Pharaoh's fat kine, to lean political kine of the same character. I do not mean this last allusion to apply to the new Venezuelan functionaries, several of whom I know personally, and who are men of unblemished character, but the allusion is just with respect to Mexico and the States of Central America and others. The laughable idea seems to have obtained in these States that the house of a foreign minister was covered with a sanctified halo, like the holy altar of the Temple of Jerusalem, from the horns of which the criminal could not be wrested—with the additional privilege, however, of feeding freely at the expense of the minister while using his house as a sanctuary. All the doors and windows of the Temple of Janus seem now to be open; war rages in China, India, Mexico, Peru, Chili, and Europe is a smothered volcano. Ere long the ill-feeling so manifestly existing between England and France may result in hostilities, which event would cause the still unquenched fires of revolution on the continent to burst forth with a violence exceeding any former efforts of the people to change their governments. I need not assay to impress on the government of the United States the sound policy of the representatives being so instructed as to enable them to allow the alleged right of asylum in their residence, or the protection of the American flag only in proper cases to be stated by their own government.

With respect to the Hispano-American republics, the effects of such course would be most salutary. It would tend to make their public functionaries less unscrupulous as to crime, to which the certainty of impunity under the present practice is an incentive. It would tend to make the government more stable and respectable. It would add to the weight of our representatives in those States, by ridding them of the reproach of intermeddling and taking sides in the domestic concerns of such States—for there are instances of their having been accused of plotting with those in power; and instances have occurred, when a revolutionary party, under the excitement of such belief of intermeddling, as in the case of Mr. Poinsett, in Mexico, in 1826, have committed violations of admitted diplomatic immunities, and insulted the American flag.

"Mind your own business," is Dr. Franklin's own motto as to individuals and States. It is especially with respect to diplomats one of true wisdom and sound policy, and the interests of his country are never compromitted by sticking to it.

Lest I may be thought to be violating this maxim myself, I would add, as an additional reason for this communication from a private citizen, that heretofore while in the service of the government of the United States, the changes I have witnessed in the political governments of the countries where I was, produced by revolutionary action, deeply impressed me with the importance of the subject.

I have the honor to be, with great respect, your most obedient servant,

H. S. SANFORD.

Hon. LEWIS CASS,
Secretary of State.

Mr. Eames to Mr. Cass.

No. 59.] LEGATION OF THE UNITED STATES,
Caraccas, July 7, 1858.

SIR: I have the honor to acknowledge the receipt on the 11th ultimo of your dispatch of 10th May last, (which should be numbered 60,) in relation to the "Aves" Island claim, inclosing an open letter on that subject of the same date, addressed by the Department of State to the Department of Foreign Relations of this government, and covering copies of your correspondence with Señor De Briceno.

I have the honor now to transmit to the department further correspondence between this legation and this government in relation to that claim, being copy of my note to the Minister of Foreign Relations, under date of 21st ultimo, with copy and translation of his reply, under date of 1st instant, and copy of my note to him, under date of 3d instant.

By these papers the department will perceive that your open letter, with its inclosures, was delivered to the Minister of Foreign Relations on the 14th ultimo, and accompanied by the oral explanations suggested in your instruction, that the claim has been further urged by me in my note of the 21st ultimo, and that, in his reply of the 1st instant, the Minister of Foreign Relations, recognizing the propriety of reparation in the case, has announced the intention of this government to conclude an equitable settlement of the claim with the least possible delay. This result of the protracted controversy on the point of liability in this case is adverted to in my note to the minister under date of 3d instant, in a sense of satisfaction in which, I do not doubt, the department will participate.

By reference to my note of 21st ultimo it will, also, be perceived that I have transmitted to this government all the papers forwarded to this legation by the department, with its No. 37, of 14th August, 1856. This dispatch, as appears by my No. 40, to the department, was first received by me, in duplicate, on the 23d of October last, after my return from Washington, and between that time and the reception of your dispatch of 10th May last; the position and course of the "Aves" negotiation did not appear to offer me any suitable opportunity for the presentation of further proofs in the case.

The expressions of Mr. Flerrera in his note to me of 1st instant, in connection with those used by Messrs. Urrutia and Toro in their notes to me of 24th March and 12th May last, transmitted respectively with my Nos. 48 and 55, lead me to the conclusion that this government proposes to adjust the details of the indemnification in the "Aves" case with this legation; and taking into consideration your No. 58, of 15th December last, your correspondence with Mr. Briceno and your dispatch of 10th May last. I suppose such to be, also, the unchanged view of the department. In, therefore, proceeding with that business, I shall bear in mind the views of the department as indicated in its No. 58, of 15th December last, and its Nos. 46 and 50, of 3d February and 3d April, 1857, and their respective inclosures. Deeming it probable, especially from some of the expressions in your No. 58, that a further communication in regard to the details of the requisite reparation in the case, may be soon addressed to this legation by the department, I respectfully invite your attention to the suggestions contained in the closing paragraph of my No. 22, of October 9, 1856, in my No. 30, of January 7, 1857, and especially to the plan of adjustment indicated at the close of my note of December 20, 1856, to Mr. Gutierrez, which was transmitted to the department with my No. 30. This general idea of a satisfactory method of adjustment in the case was adopted by me after mature consideration of its equities, and understanding it to be in substantial conformity with the views of the department, as hitherto made known to me, I see no reason why it should not be now regarded as right and convenient.

Your dispatch* of the 10th May last is the latest received.

I have the honor to be, with the highest respect and consideration, your obedient servant,

CHARLES EAMES.

Hon. LEWIS CASS,
Secretary of State.

LEGATION OF THE UNITED STATES,
Caraccas, June 21, 1858.

SIR: The undersigned, minister resident of the United States, has had the honor, on the 14th instant, to place in the hands of the honorable minister of foreign relations of Venezuela, an open letter under date of the 10th ultimo, with specified inclosures, addressed through this legation, by the Department of State of the United States to the Department of Foreign Relations of this republic. This important paper, communicating to the Venezuelan government the failure of its late envoy extraordinary and minister plenipotentiary, Señor de Briceno, to accomplish any adjustment of the "Aves" Island reclamation, which was the special object of his mission, and setting forth, in a renewed and most formal manner, the definitive views adopted by the government of the United States, after due examination, and by subsequent mature consideration fully confirmed, as to the undoubted liability of Venezuela to make reparation for the losses and injuries sustained in that case by citizens of the United States, expresses in earnest terms the confident hope and expectation of his excellency, the President of the United States, that the case being thus referred back to the Venezuelan government, and the undersigned being fully instructed to communicate with it on the subject, the present enlightened and patriotic administration of Venezuela will not fail to coöperate in the speedy and harmonious termination of the question which has too long embarrassed the relations of the two republics, and that, the liability of Venezuela in the case being admitted, there will be no serious difficulty in arranging the details of a satisfactory adjustment.

These views and expectations of the government of the United States, the undersigned, under his recent instructions, has already had the honor to affirm and urge upon the attention of the government of this republic, in personal interviews with its minister of foreign relations, from whom he has been gratified to understand in reply that the Venezuelan government, recognizing the high and controlling motives of public policy, which require at this time the prompt and equitable adjustment of this case, proposes now, in that view, to give to it immediate and continuous consideration.

In this connection, and in compliance with recent instructions from his government, the undersigned has now the honor to present here-

---

* Erroneously numbered 58, I have numbered it, as it should be, 60, and request that the same correction be made on the records of the department to avoid confusion in referring to it.

with to the government of Venezuela, copies of certain additional testimony and correspondence in this case, as transmitted to this legation by the Department of State, in which their originals, furnished by the claimants, are on file. In presenting, however, these papers, a list of which is subjoined, the undersigned, in obedience to special instructions to that effect, makes fully known to the government of Venezuela that the presentation is made only from abundant caution, in order that there may be no doubt nor dispute that the strict letter of the thirty-fourth article of the treaty of 1836, and all other legal obligations have been fully and exactly complied with, both by the claimants and by their government, in view of the contingency, not now, it is hoped, to be expected, of ulterior measures unfortunately becoming necessary for the purpose of obtaining, in conformity with law, in this case, the justice otherwise sought in vain.

Notwithstanding the several conferences in which the undersigned has recently had the honor to press orally the present urgent aspect of this "Aves" Island reclamation on the consideration of the government of Venezuela, he cannot close this note without reiterating to the honorable minister of foreign relations, and through him to his excellency the Chief of the State, the profound conviction felt by the undersigned, that in view of the origin, character, and history of this reclamation, and especially of the attitude in which it is now presented, the weightiest considerations of justice and public policy imperatively demand that, without loss of time, the undersigned be authorized to assure his government that it is received by the new administration in Venezuela upon the basis of an admitted claim, and that in such character its details of indemnification shall have consideration and fair and and equitable adjustment with the least practicable delay.

The undersigned avails himself with pleasure of this first opportunity to offer Hon. Señor Flerrera, minister of foreign relations, the assurance of his very distinguished consideration.

CHARLES EAMES.

Hon. MIGUEL FLERRERA,
Minister of Foreign Relations.

List of accompanying papers.

A.—H. S. Sanford to Secretary of State—May 9, 1856, with specified inclosures.

B.—H. S. Sanford to Secretary of State—May 10, 1856, with specified inclosures.

C.—Deposition (printed) of John McCabe.

D.—H. S. Sanford to Secretary of State—July 15, 1856.

E.—P. S. Shelton and Sampson & Tappan to Secretary of State—July 21, 1856.

[Translation.]

Republic of Venezuela.

DEPARTMENT OF FOREIGN RELATIONS,
Caraccas, July 1, 1858.

The undersigned, minister of foreign relations of Venezuela, had the honor to receive the note and documents addressed to him by the honorable minister resident of the United States, under date of 21st ultimo, in relation to the Aves Island question.

Although accidentally and very recently charged with this department, the undersigned, by reason of the interest which that subject deserves from the government, has sedulously endeavored to acquaint himself with it in all its details by the study of the record, already voluminous, which has been formed out of what has already taken place in regard to it up to the present time. Not having been able yet to accomplish this purpose so completely as he desires, the undersigned might well defer to another opportunity the consideration of the matter with Mr. Eames, and this much more, considering that the provisional character of the government, the dangers now threatening the internal and external peace of the country, the mass of labor and business rendered necessary by the meeting of the national convention, and all the other difficulties which attend the actual situation, would abundantly justify such delay. But so favorable is the deposition of his excellency the Chief of the State towards the North American republic, and so ardent in his desire that everything should disappear from its relations with Venezuela which could operate to their prejudice or thwart his purpose of consolidating more and more the friendship of the two countries, that he has authorized the undersigned to waive those inconveniences in favor of this consideration. With this purpose, his excellency has directed the undersigned to make known to Mr. Eames his desire to terminate, by an equitable adjustment, the question in relation to the Island of Aves now pending before the government of Venezuela in the form of a reclamation by the government of the United States. His excellency flatters himself that this communication and the further communication that he is ready to devote his attention to the settlement of the demand as soon as the pressing occupations of the moment permit him to do so, will be viewed by Mr. Eames, and also by his government, as indisputable proof of the spirit which animates the government of Venezuela, and of the sincerity which it is striving to overcome the obstacles which oppose the amelioration of its relations with the United States.

The undersigned renews to Mr. Eames the assurance of his distinguished consideration.

MIGUEL FLERRERA.

Hon. MINISTER RESIDENT OF THE UNITED STATES.

LEGATION OF THE UNITED STATES,
Caraccas, July 3, 1858.

SIR: The undersigned, minister resident of the United States, has had the honor to receive the note, under date of 1st instant, of the honorable minister of foreign relations of Venezuela, making known the purpose of the Venezuelan government to terminate, by an equitable adjustment, the Aves Island reclamation, which has been so long pending between the two governments, and announcing that his excellency the chief of the republic, in view of his strong desire to maintain the most friendly relations with the United States, is prepared to carry into effect the settlement of that claim as soon as the urgent and indispensable occupations of present moment can permit.

This determination in relation to the Aves case will be immediately communicated to the government of the United States, by which the undersigned does not doubt it will be duly appreciated, not only as a proof of friendly dispositions, but also as offering, in the promptness with which it has been reached and manifested by the existing government of Venezuela an indication of a wise and just public policy, which is in highly satisfactory contrast with the difficulty and delay so unfortunately encountered under other circumstances in the adjustment of this claim.

As in the concurring judgment of the two governments, nothing now remains to be done in this case but to examine and regulate the details of a fair and equitable indemnification to the claimants, and as this legation is now prepared to proceed with that business, it is hoped and expected that the reclamation may very soon be definitively adjusted in a satisfactory manner.

The undersigned renews to Hon. Mr. Flerrera the assurance of his distinguished consideration.

CHARLES EAMES.

Hon. MIGUEL FLERRERA,
Minister of Foreign Relations.

Mr. Cass to Mr. Sanford.

DEPARTMENT OF STATE,
Washington, July 31, 1858.

SIR: The department received yesterday dispatches from Mr. Eames, one of which relates to the probable adjustment of the Aves Island claim at an early day.

An extract from one of these, (7th instant,) and a translation of a note to which it refers, are herewith inclosed to you, as the representative of the principal claimants, in order that you may be apprised of the favorable disposition of the government of Venezuela, and adopt such measures as the interests of your principals may seem to require.

As it is understood that the successor of Mr. Eames will not leave for his post before the close of the coming month of August, the department would be pleased to know whether the claimants have any further statements to make in respect to the final settlement of the case, and whether they would prefer that Mr. Eames should be instructed to proceed to an arrangement or that it should be deferred until the arrival of Mr. Turpin at Caraccas.

I am, sir, &c.,

LEWIS CASS.

HENRY S. SANFORD, Esq., *New York*.

Mr. Appleton to Mr. Turpin.

No. 3.]

DEPARTMENT OF STATE,
Washington, August 24, 1858.

SIR: The papers herewith furnished you, and those which you will doubtless find at your legation, will afford you full information as to the circumstances and present position of the Aves Island case. The spoliation and outrage at this island occurred in December, 1854, and from that time to this the government of the United States has steadily insisted that Venezuela should repair injury to our citizens which had been done under authority of the Venezuelan government. Proofs were offered of the extent of this injury, and in the case at least of Messrs. Shelton & Co., these were as full and explicit as they were promptly furnished. The 34th article of the treaty between the United States and Venezuela had thus been complied with, and the way prepared for employing the remedy which that article contemplates. Yet when the present authorities of Venezuela entered upon their duties, the just claim of the United States in behalf of its citizens who had been injured by the Aves Island outrage, had been neither adjusted nor acknowledged to exist. This was a condition of affairs which could not be suffered to continue. It was impossible that the government of the United States could permit its flag to be insulted and its citizens wronged, as they were insulted and wronged in the case referred to, without insisting upon reasonable redress, and, if necessary, pursuing that redress by force. It has not been unmindful, however, of the difficulties which have existed in Venezuela in respect to its political affairs, nor of the embarrassments which necessarily surrounded the existing authorities of Venezuela when they were called to the management of their government. A certain delay was unavoidable from these considerations, but the United States had great confidence that the new government of Venezuela would lose no time in terminating this delay and doing justice to those claimants who had been so seriously injured by the proceedings of Venezuela, and so long deprived of their rightful reparation. The dispatch of Mr. Herrera, minister of foreign relations, inclosed with that of Mr. Eames of the 7th ultimo, has a tendency, I am glad to say, to justify this hope.

The department does not find in it, however, that full and unequivocal admission of liability which it had a right to expect; yet from the friendly assurances of Mr. Herrera, from his declaration that the government of Venezuela desires "to terminate by an equitable adjustment the question in relation to the Aves now pending" before that government; and, from the testimony of Mr. Eames on the subject, this government is not disposed to doubt that the dispatch of Mr. Herrera was intended as a compliance with its previous demand in dispatch No. 53, and as an acknowledgment of the just liability of Venezuela to make good the losses which accrued to the American citizens by their eviction from Aves Island in 1854.

In this view of the case, nothing now remains but to adjust the question of damages. These were undoubtedly very great, and a full description of them will be found in your legation, and has doubtless been furnished to Venezuela. The view taken of them by the Venezuelan authorities is not known, because upon this branch of the subject no discussion whatever has been had. Upon many of the items there can be no difference of opinion; and there can be no doubt, either, of the general rule that Venezuela is bound to repair the injury which she inflicted. Her admission of liability implies a withdrawal of her claim to the island and its guano, but the parties cannot be required now to receive back the island after they have been driven away from it and their business destroyed, but are entitled to reasonable damages for its loss. It is understood, moreover, that a large quantity of guano has been removed from it since their eviction, and this department is not informed whether the island is now in possession by Venezuela, so that its surrender would be possible. If it can be returned, the parties interested may be willing, possibly, to receive it, in a spirit of compromise, and thus to reduce the amount of their claims. Indeed, this has been already stated to the department by the agent of the principal claimants. You will find inclosed the copy of a letter from Mr. Sanford to the Secretary of State, dated the 10th instant, which will put you in possession of his views on this subject. The claim of P. S. Shelton & Co., as presented in the printed statement now at Caraccas, and supported by a large amount of testimony, amounts in the aggregate to $650,000.

In view of the present condition of Venezuela, and for the sake of a speedy adjustment, they offer, as a compromise, to accept for their entire claim the sum of $150,000, United States currency, with interest at seven per cent., payable at such times as the Venezuelan government may agree with you therefor, to be secured by convention of the government of Venezuela similar to those negotiated by Mr. Steele, at Caraccas, on the 8th May, 1852, and 1st June, 1853, relating to claims—a copy of which you will find in the archives of the legation. This proceeds upon the condition that Venezuela is to relinquish to them the possession which they previously had of the island, but without, of course, any guarantee by Venezuela of their rights on the island as against any other government. This offer is made, you will observe, in a spirit of compromise; and should it be rejected, it will not diminish the right of Messrs. Shelton & Co. to insist upon the payment of their entire claim.

. Undoubtedly a compromise would be accepted also by Messrs. Lang & Delano, the other claimants in the case; and it is hoped that the department may be able to write you explicitly on this subject by the next packet to Venezuela. The greater injury seems, from the testimony now before the department, to have been done to Messrs. Shelton & Co., and hence they have been usually mentioned in the dispatches as the principal claimants.

You will lose no time, after your official recognition at Caraccas, in recalling the attention of the Venezuelan government to this Aves Island claim, in order that it may be promptly adjusted. The government of the United States will not allow itself to believe that this adjustment will be further procrastinated by the government of Venezuela. It is quite time that the case was at an end; and in justice to itself and its citizens, this government cannot permit it now to be unnecessarily delayed. You will be frank in stating these views to the proper authorities at Caraccas, and you will inform them that your government expects in return an early and explicit reply. It is hoped that the spirit of compromise which is manifested in the offer of Messrs. Shelton & Co., will be met by a similar spirit on the part of Venezuela, and that their claim may be thus terminated without further loss of time. In that event, you will have no difficulty in arranging the details of the adjustment in conformity with the plan proposed.

I am, sir, your obedient servant,

JOHN APPLETON,
Acting Secretary of State.

EDWARD A. TURPIN, Esq.,
&c., &c., &c.

Inclosures.

Aves Island document No. 64.
H. S. Sanford to Secretary of State, 8th and 10th August, 1858.

Messrs. Cotting and Lang to Mr. Cass.

BOSTON, *August* 31, 1858.

SIR: We have had some conversation with Mr. Sanford, attorney of P. S. Shelton and Sampson & Tappan, in the "Aves Island" claim, who informs us that it is important that the State Department be advised immediately of our views as to what we would take as a compromise of our claim against Venezuela. We therefore say that we will accept the sum of $50,000, United States currency, as a compromise, to be paid in monthly installments, as may be agreed on with our minister at "Caraccas," with 7 (seven) per cent. annual interest till paid. With respect to the claim of Wheelwright & Cobb, dependent upon us, we will cheefully (at the final settlement) yield such amount for false freight as you may decide to be just. We have this day given H. S. Sanford, Esq., our full power of attorney to act for us in this matter, and any arrangement he may make will be satisfactory to us; our power of attorney to Henry H. French being revoked. We will send you in a few days such proofs of the detail of our damage as we may be able to collect.

Mr. Sanford will doubtless inform the department that he has agreed to give us the benefit of the papers he has filed in behalf of P. S. Shelton and Sampson & Tappan.

We are, very respectfully, your obedient servants,

CHAS. U. COTTING,
Executor.
JOHN H. B. LANG.

Hon. LEWIS CASS,
Secretary of State.

Mr. Cass to Mr. Turpin.

No. 6.]

DEPARTMENT OF STATE,
Washington, September 3, 1858.

SIR: Herewith I transmit the copy of a letter of the 31st ultimo, from the representatives of Lang & Delano, who are claimants against Venezuela for their eviction from the Aves Island in 1853, by which you will learn their willingness to accept fifty thousand dollars ($50,000) as the minimum basis of compromise with that government, out of which, however, they bind themselves to satisfy the claim of Wheelwright & Cobb, who, from the first presentation of the subject, have likewise claimed indemnity.

This arrangement will enable you to present the Aves Island claim to the government of Venezuela for settlement as an entirety. It reduces the amount of indemnity from over a million of dollars to $200,000, and it is confidently expected that you will be enabled to announce, in your earliest communication from Caraccas after receipt of this dispatch, the final adjustment of the matter upon the terms proposed.

I am, sir, your obedient servant,

LEWIS CASS.

E. A. TURPIN, Esq.,
&c., &c., &c.

Mr. Sanford to Mr. Cass.

NEW YORK, *September* 8, 1858.

SIR: Since the departure of Mr. Turpin some circumstances have occurred in relation to the claims of Messrs. Shelton & Co. and Messrs. Lang & Delano & Co., of which I have advised you in my letter of 2d instant. Conforming to the earnest desire of the department in making which I understood it was influenced by considerations of friendly feeling towards the republic of Venezuela, involved as it now is in foreign and domestic difficulties, I have striven with the claimants, as their agent, to reduce their claim to the lowest possible amount that would reimburse them for their actual losses sustained in cash, without reference to hypothetical or consequential damages. Mr. Shelton, desirous to accede to the wishes of the department, has consequently, though reluctantly, agreed to compromise the Shelton claim for one hundred and fifty thousand dollars ($150,000) and the relinquishment of the Island. The other claimants, Lang & Delano, for themselves and Wheelwright & Cobb, have agreed upon the minimum sum of fifty thousand dollars ($50,000) in full of all their demand for damages, and Shelton & Co. have agreed in consequence to hold them to no liability growing out of their occupation of the island.

Mr. Turpin, I am informed by your letter of the 4th instant, has been advised of this arrangement, and instructed accordingly.

I deem it proper, as the attorney of all the claimants, to say that it seems to me that the liberal course pursued by the claimants in agreeing to this compromise submitted to the Venezuelan government should be presented forcibly to that government by yourself, and that the sum be indicated as the *ultimatum*, to be responded to without further evasion or delay, and as dispensing with the necessity for the procuring of further or additional proofs.

If accepted, the sum of $200,000 is *in solido,* without reference to details, items, or particulars, or relinquishment of the claim to the Isle, as a compromise merely of the whole claim, and not to be construed as an admission that they do not justly amount to more. If refused, and the parties are put to the necessity of procuring further proofs and incurring further expense and trouble, the offer, as stated when first made, is not to prejudice claimants against the recovery of whatsoever amounts they may show their just damages, direct and consequential, to be.

The friendly feelings of the government and of the American people towards Venezuela, struggling as she is with foreign and domestic difficulties, have, as before stated, had overruling influence in inducing the claimants to agree to this compromise. They desire to accede to the views of the department, and they trust that it will appreciate their course by urging, as suggested, upon Venezuela to accede to the proposition so made, with a view to take away any cause of difficulty between the two governments, and which the State department has been so instrumental in effecting.

I have the honor to be, with great respect, your obedient servant,

H. S. SANFORD,
Attorney for claimants.

Hon. LEWIS CASS,
Secretary of State.

Mr. Cass to Mr. Turpin.

No. 7.] DEPARTMENT OF STATE,
Washington, September 15, 1858.

SIR: I inclose the copy of a letter addressed to the department on the 8th instant by Henry S. Sanford, Esq., in relation to the Aves Island claim. Mr. Sanford has presented, with much force, considerations which should induce Venezuela to accept the basis of compromise offered by the claimants without further discussion or delay, and he has justly referred to the earnest wishes of this department that such an arrangement might be made among the claimants as would reduce the amount of the reclamation to the lowest sum consistent with the simple indemnification of absolute losses. This government is not insensible to the difficulties of a foreign and domestic nature with which Venezuela has been and is still entangled; and while it has forborne a resort to peremptory measures of redress, it has, on the other hand, represented to the claimants the propriety of large sacrifices, in order to avoid even the appearance of a want of sympathy for the embarrassed condition of the republic. They have deferred to this view, and have proposed a *minimum*, which Venezuela, weighing all the circumstances of the case, should cheerfully accept. You will accordingly, in pressing the claim, signify to the Venezuelan government the anticipations which we cherish that the adoption of this compromise will speedily remove any occasion of further dispute or embarrassment in the relations of the two countries.

I am, sir, your obedient servant,

LEWIS CASS.

EDWARD A. TURPIN, Esq., *&c.*

Mr. Appleton to Mr. Sanford.

DEPARTMENT OF STATE,
Washington, September 27, 1858.

SIR: Although, as you are aware, the department has notified Mr. Turpin of the compromise which has been effected among the several claimants against Venezuela in the Aves Island case, and has instructed him to press an early adjustment of the claim upon the terms indicated in your letters of the 2d and 8th instant, it is deemed proper to apprise you, as the legal attorney of Messrs. Lang & Delano, that in the contingency of the rejection by Venezuela of the arrangement you have proposed, there is no such proof in the department of the actual losses sustained by your principals as would enable it properly to present their claim to the consideration of the government of Venezuela.

The papers you have filed in support of the claim of Mr. Shelton and others, the benefit of which by virtue of your agreement with the other parties they are permitted to enjoy, substantiate the preliminary facts of discovery, occupation, and eviction, but do not prove the items of actual loss alleged by Lang & Delano. Should your offer of a settlement with Venezuela *"in solido"* be rejected, these proofs will be equally applicable in establishing the basis of their claim as that of Shelton; but they cannot supply the deficiency above referred to.

On the 21st June, 1855, Land & Delano filed the affidavit of George McGeorge, which proves the lading of the brig Comery with guano, her return to the United States, and the sending out of the ship Kentucky with twenty-one laborers to the Aves Island; and among the papers filed by you is an affidavit which estimates the value of Lang & Delano's buildings and materials on the island. This, it is believed, is the only specific proof furnished by them or by their agents of their actual expenses incurred, although in January, 1856, they present the items of a claim amounting to $647,910.

You will perceive the propriety, in the contingency referred to, of having these items supported by proofs in those cases which are susceptible of being so verified.

I am, sir, &c.,

JOHN APPLETON,
Assistant Secretary.

HENRY S. SANFORD, Esq., *New York.*

Mr. Turpin to Mr. Cass.

No. 4.]

LEGATION OF THE UNITED STATES,
Caraccas, October 23, 1858.

SIR: With reference to your dispatches Nos. 3, 6, and 7, with their respective inclosures, relative to the "Aves Island" reclamation, I have now the honor to transmit to the department, in copy, a note on that subject, addressed by me, in pursuance of your instructions, to the minister of foreign relations, under date of 17th instant.

The restriction by the claimants of their demand to a simple indemnification for their "actual, positive losses," and the exclusion by the department of "hypothetical and consequential damages," as expressed in your dispatches and in their inclosures, will, I trust, contribute very much to the prompt and equitable settlement of the reclamation by this government; and deeming this result to be of high importance, not only to the interests of the claimants, but also to the successful prosecution of the other business of the legation, so long embarrassed by the prosecution of this claim, I have striven, in my note to Mr. Sanojo, so to present the basis of compromise proposed by the claimants as to show in the strongest light its claims to a favorable reception.

Your No. 3 refers to the fact that the amount and mode of indemnification have not yet been at all discussed between the two governments, and though some of the expressions in your No. 7 may possibly be regarded as having a tendency to authorize me to present, as a minimum or ultimatum, the compromise offered by the claimants, I have thought it more in conformity with the usual practice in such cases, and with the probable wishes of the department, to reserve that point in my first note to this government on the subject, and while recommending strongly the proposed basis of adjustment, to hold myself free to obey your future instructions as to making it an ultimatum.

An inspection of the papers in the case presented to the department by the claimants, and forwarded to this legation, has confirmed me in this conclusion.

In a communication to the department, transmitted to this legation in dispatch No. 37, under date of February 20, 1856, Messrs. Shelton, and Sampson & Tappan stated their actual positive losses, exclusive of the guano on the island, which by the present proposition is to be relinquished to them, at $28,500; $20,000 of this sum being for false freights, &c., and $8,500 for fixtures and other property. In their subsequent communication to the department, by their attorney, Mr. Sanford, which was transmitted to my predecessor in dispatch No. 46, under date of February 3, 1857, they raised the amount claimed for such actual losses to about $50,000, by adding $16,300 to the sum claimed for false freights, &c., and $6,100 to the sum claimed for fixtures, &c. But by inspection of this second statement, the department will see, I think, that the $16,300 so added, is made up of those hypothetical and consequential damages which are now expressly relinquished.

As to the actual losses of Lang & Delano, there is as yet no proof nor voucher in this legation, and all the information I have on that subject is derived from the recent communication of Mr. Sanford to the department, dated August 10th last, and transmitted to me in your No. 3, which fixes their damages at a maximum of $10,000, and takes an unfavorable view of their right to recover at all. Similar views were expressed by Messrs. Shelton & Co., in the paper transmitted with No. 37, of the Department, to my predecessor; and these papers are now, by previous request of the claimants, expressed through the department, in the hands of this government.

Earnestly solicitous as I am, on every account, to bring this business without delay to a conclusion as favorable as possible to the interests of the claimants, I have thought it my duty thus respectfully to lay before the department the doubts and difficulties which embarrass me, as at present advised, in making an ultimatum of a proposition, claiming, besides the relinquishment of the island, the sum of $150,000 for Shelton, Sampson & Tappan, and $50,000 for Lang & Delano.

The general impression prevailing here, and referred to in previous dispatches to the department, as derived from the fact that the "Aves" was one of the first of the guano islands abandoned as not worth working, is also, I think the department will perceive, a serious difficulty to contend with. I trust, however, that the claimants will as soon as possible, furnish me with the means of counteracting this impression, or at least of replying to it conclusively, if, as I think it not unlikely, it shall hereafter be urged by this government as a reason for a further abatement of their present demand.

I have the honor to be, your obedient servant,

E. A. TURPIN.

Hon. LEWIS CASS,
Secretary of State.

LEGATION OF THE UNITED STATES,
Caraccas, October 17, 1858.

SIR: The undersigned, minister resident of the United States, has the honor, in obedience to the special instructions from his government to that effect, now to bring to the renewed attention of the honorable minister of foreign relations, and through him to that of his government, the existing urgent attitude of the Aves Island reclamation, with a view to that prompt and final settlement of the claim which the government of the United States regards as imperatively necessary.

The note of 1st of July last, addressed to the predecessor of the undersigned in this legation by the then honorable minister of foreign relations, made known upon rendered reasons "the determination of the government of Venezuela to terminate by means of an equitable adjustment the question pending in relation to the Aves Island" between the two governments; and added the assurance that "the settlement of the claim" should, without delay, be the subject of special and effectual attention.

This prompt and frank acknowledgment by the new government of the liability and of the purpose of Venezuela equitably to indemnify the claimants in the Aves case, leaving, as it does, in the concurring judgments of the two governments, nothing more now to be done in that case but to adjust the question of the amount and manner of such equitable indemnification has, the undersigned is prepared to state, produced a favorable impression upon the government of the United States, and in consequence of that impression, and taking into view the serious difficulties with which the government of Venezuela has for some time past been compelled to struggle, the government of the United States has made special efforts to facilitate the prompt and final adjustment of the claim upon principles of equity and in a spirit of liberal compromise.

The claim as at present presented before the government of the United States, belongs to quite a number of different individuals. The printed statement herewith inclosed shows that three of them—Messrs. Shelton, Sampson, and Tappan—claim damages to the amount of $650,000, United States currency, and they specify the items of their claim. The claims of all the other claimants in the case, as made known to the government of the United States, raise the total amount up to $1,000,000. By the efforts of the government of the United States, made in the motives referred to, these claimants have been induced to unite all their claims in one entirety, and adopting the principle of restricting their claims to the actual positive losses inflicted upon them, excluding all hypothetical and consequential damages, they have, in a spirit of compromise, and as a basis of an equitable settlement, offered to receive in full satisfaction for their whole claim the sum of $200,000, United States currency, at such times of payment and with such interest as may be stipulated between the two governments. This great reduction by the claimants of their demand down to one fifth part of its original amount upon the principle of restricting their claim to their absolute actual losses only, is approved by the government of the United States. This basis of compromise is offered upon the distinct understanding that the government of Venezuela will hereafter make no opposition whatsoever to the unmolested usufruct by the claimants of the guano on the island of Aves. And it must be further understood, that if this compromise, as offered by the claimants, should be rejected, it will not diminish their right to insist upon the payment of their entire claim.

The undersigned is further instructed to state to the government of Venezuela, that the government of the United States, in justice to itself and to its citizens, cannot consent that the final adjustment of this claim shall now be unnecessarily delayed; on the contrary, it will not allow itself to believe that such an adjustment will be further procrastinated by the government of Venezuela.

The claimants, deferring to the views of their government recommending the propriety of a large sacrifice on their part, in order to avoid even the appearance of want of sympathy with the embarrassed condition of Venezuela, have proposed a compromise which, the republic weighing all the circumstances of the case, should, in the judgment of the United States, cheerfully accept; and the undersigned, therefore, in pursuance of his instructions, announces to the Venezuelan government the anticipation cherished by the government of the United States that the early adoption of this compromise, avoiding the minute and tedious examination and further proof of actual losses which will otherwise be necessary, will speedily remove any occasion of further embarrassment in the relations of the two countries.

The undersigned renews to Hon. Mr. Sanojo the assurance of his distinguished consideration.

E. A. TURPIN.

Hon. LUIS SANOJO,
Minister of Foreign Relations.

Mr. Turpin to Mr. Cass.

No 7.]

LEGATION OF THE UNITED STATES,
Caraccas, December 1, 1858.

SIR: In conformity with instructions from the department on the 17th September last, I addressed a note to the Minister of Foreign Relations of this government on the subject of the Aves Island case, on the basis of admitted liability, presenting the reclamation as an entirety, and offering a compromise for the whole at the sum of $200,000 United States currency, and the restoration of the island to the claimants. That note I transmitted to the department with my No. 4, under date of October 23.

I herewith transmit the reply of the honorable Minister of Foreign Relations, in copy, to that note. The department will perceive that in the anticipated necessity of special conferences, the honorable minister invites me to come on to Valencia, where the provisional government temporarily resides, and to bring on with me all the documents and proofs bearing on the question, that the executive power may judge of the equity of the prosecution.

Had the whole reclamation been in the condition of that of the claimants Shelton & Co., I would have accepted the invitation, but, in view of the fact that one fourth of the compromise so offered was based upon a claim—that of Lang & Delano—in support of which but little proof had been offered, and in relation to which, indeed, documents inclosed in the department's No. 37, bearing adversely on this claim of Lang & Delano had been placed in the hands of this government by my predecessor, together with a knowledge of the fact that a part of this $50,000 offered to be accepted by Lang & Delano was for $15,000 claimed by Wheelwright & Cobb for false freight on one voyage of a single vessel, nearly five times as much as was charged by any other vessel on the same account between the same ports, I concluded that perhaps it would be prudent to await the views of the department after the receipt of my No. 4, by which time also, in all probability, the provissional government would have returned to Caraccas.

With the highest respect, I have the honor to be, your obedient servant,

E. A. TURPIN.

Hon. Lewis Cass,
Secretary of State.

P. S.—Inclosed copy of Mr. Sanojo's reply to my note of 17th October, translated.

[Translation.]

Republic of Venezuela.

Department of Foreign Relations.
Valencia, October 27, 1858.

The secretary of foreign relations has had the honor to present to the executive power the note dated 7th instant, in which the minister resident of the United States of America proposes to this government to fix at $200,000 in money of that country the reclamation relative to the Aves Island, and his excellency the chief of the State has determined that the following shall be communicated to Mr. Turpin:

The republic has offered to terminate by an equitable adjustment the question of the Island of Aves, for reasons which were set forth in the note of 1st July last to the predecessor of Mr. Turpin. It is now that for the first time in the course of this old business is indicated the amount of the indemnification which is claimed. Heretofore nothing more has been sought than the admission of the national responsibility, and the equity of the proposition of the claimants cannot be judged of by the note of Mr. Turpin and the accounts of the claimants which accompany it.

As this matter will make certain conferences necessary, it appears to the undersigned that the better means of advancing it would be that Mr. Turpin would be pleased to come on to this place, where the government resides, bringing with him all the documents and proofs on which the claim is sustained, the examination of which would place the executive power in a position to appreciate the nature of the proposed agreement.

The undersigned reiterates to Sen. Turpin the assurances, &c.

LUIS SANOJO.

Hon. Sen. E. A. TURPIN,
Minister Resident of the United States.

Mr. Sanford to Mr. Cass.

WASHINGTON, *December* 9, 1858.

SIR: I have lately had several conferences with a gentleman of high official position in Venezuela, who has just arrived from that country, and represents, as he informs me, and as I have no doubt he does, the views of the Venezuelan government with respect to the Aves claim.

The result of these conferences has been the conviction on my part, founded on his assurances, that a prompt settlement can only be made with that government by still further concessions on the part of the claimants, and that the embarrassments created by an insidious enemy, would, otherwise, be taken advantage of to create still further delay and difficulty.

We have named the sum of $200,000 as the least that would indemnify us for the actual losses sustained, and we are very reluctant to make any reduction in a sum which we have regarded as a minimum. Still, so anxious are we to have this long pending difficulty settled, and so desirous not to stand in the way of the renewal of the most friendly and cordial relations between the two countries, that I have determined, consulting the best interests of the claimants, exposed as they are to further delay as beforesaid, to accept a further reduction if offered by the government of Venezuela, on condition of immediate settlement.

As the national convention, which must ratify, to make binding on Venezuela, such settlement, will probably adjourn early in February, it is possible that, in order to expedite this business, I, or some other person, may proceed to Venezuela to represent the claimants.

I have therefore respectfully to request that Mr. Turpin be instructed to proceed immediately to the seat of government at Valencia to terminate this negotiation, and that he be authorized to accept, on behalf of the government, such further compromise as he and the representative of the claimants may mutually agree upon, or as he may be authorized by their attorney or representative to make.

With regard to the relinquishment of the isle to us, the desire was expressed by the person referred to, that the subject be left for a short time pending, in order not to embarrass the negotiations now progressing with Holland with reference to the title to "Aves." To this we assent; it being clearly understood that Shelton & Co. do not relinquish their claim to the isle, nor compromise it in any way, but insist upon their right to be restored to their previous possession, or to be indemnified by Venezuela in default of such restoration.

For the event, however, of a sum to be agreed by the government of Venezuela to Shelton & Co., for their relinquishment of all rights and title of the claimants to the isle, I have also to request that Mr. Turpin be instructed to make formal relinquishment of the same to Venezuela.

I have the honor to be, very respectfully, your obedient servant,

H. S. SANFORD.

Hon. LEWIS CASS,
Secretary of State.

Mr. Cass to Mr. Turpin.

No. 12.] DEPARTMENT OF STATE,
Washington, December 10, 1858.

SIR: Inclosed herewith you will receive a copy of a communication dated December 9, 1858, from Mr. H. S. Sanford, the agent of Messrs. Shelton & Co., and Messrs. Lang & Delano, on the subject of the Aves claim. It appears from this communication that there is reason to believe that the Venezuelan government is disposed to make a prompt and final adjustment of this claim, provided the parties interested will consent to such an adjustment upon the terms indicated in Mr. Sanford's letter. Of course this government has no desire to intervene against any settlement which may be satisfactory to the claimants, and not inconsistent with the rights and honor of the United States. Inasmuch as Venezuela is understood to have acknowledged the wrong which it committed in the eviction of our citizens from the island, and its consequent liability to make reparation, there is no good reason why the United States should not permit the parties aggrieved to accept any terms of adjustment which may be satisfactory to them. It is quite time, moreover, that the controversy was settled, and if it can be adjusted peaceably and speedily, this should be a source of gratification to the governments and people of both countries.

You will repair to Valencia immediately upon the receipt of this dispatch, and place yourself in communication with the government there on this subject. If you find that an adjustment is practicable, upon terms satisfactory to the claimants, you will lose no time in bringing it to a conclusion, without awaiting any further instructions from the department. When a compromise is to be made, there need be no question, of course concerning proofs and details; but you will not permit the idea to be entertained by Venezuela that the disposition of the claimants to compromise their claims grows out of any doubt, either on their part or on that of their government, of its entire validity or of their perfect ability to maintain it. They are weary, however, with delay, and prefer to abate a portion of their rights rather than endure a still longer procrastination, or be instrumental, in any way, in producing a rupture in the friendly relations of two republics which ought always to be on the best terms with each other. Keeping this view of the subject in mind, it is hoped that under the new aspect of the case presented by Mr. Sanford's letter, you may be able to terminate this troublesome controversy without further delay.

I am, sir, your obedient servant,

LEWIS CASS.

EDWARD A. TURPIN, Esq., *&c.*

Mr. Sanford to Mr. Cass.

WASHINGTON, *January* 14, 1859.

SIR: I have the honor to transmit herewith—

First. A revised statement of the claim of Lang & Delano for their losses sustained by reason of their expulsion from Aves Isle in December, 1854.

Second. The depositions of George McGeorge, Charles H. Lang, Captain Samuel Herrick, Captain James Phinney, George Wood Rice, Isaac R. Mills, Nathan N. Bridge, and John H. B. Lang.

Third. Duplicates of the above depositions with the exception of that of Captain Herrick.

Fourth. The original charter parties of the vessels named in the statement having been driven away or restrained from loading at Aves by the Venezuelan forces, as detailed in said statement and the depositions. These papers, with the exception of the duplicate depositions, I desire to have filed in the department for reference in the case of Lang & Delano.

And I have to request that a copy of this statement of claim, the duplicate depositions, and a copy of that of Captain Herrick be forwarded immediately to our minister at Valencia, with instructions to present them without delay to the government of Venezuala, as completing the testimony in this claim.

I would call the attention of the department to these depositions as fully substantiating every item of damage set forth in the accompanying statement; and if found satisfactory to the department, as I cannot doubt they will be, I have further to request that Mr. Turpin be instructed so to inform the minister of foreign relations of Venezuela.

Notwithstanding statements to the contrary insidiously made to those in authority in Venezuela, the deposition of Captain Gibbs, and other witnesses for Shelton & Co., are, so far as they go, confirmatory of the evidence given by Lang & Delano with respect to their losses. The only items specified in the former, were for estimated damages for loss of fixtures, provisions, utensils, &c., by Lang & Delano, which Captain Gibbs and others thought not to exceed $10,000 in amount. This is what is claimed by Lang & Delano, and what is proved to have been the amount of loss under that head. As to false freights and other losses, those depositions say nothing precisely; and had they contained estimates of them, they could have been but matters of opinion subject to verification by the testimony of those having positive and accurate knowledge on those points. The presentation of the accompanying depositions to the government of Venezuela will dissipate, I feel certain, the doubts which it has been sought to excite on the ground that there were discrepancies in these claims.

And, in this connection, I would respectfully ask to be informed whether it be true that the late minister of the United States at Caraccas had, prior to quitting that mission, communicated to the Venezuelan government any papers bearing on these claims other than the proofs which (at the request of claimants, and upon their complaint that he had withheld a portion of their proof and given another mutilated portion to that government) he had been directed forthwith to present it.

I have been informed that sundry letters written to the Department of State by Shelton & Co., or their attorney and counsel, in opposition to the pretensions of other claimants, and which I suppose to have been communicated to our legation at Caraccas for its information, had been placed in the hands of the Venezuelan government to the prejudice of these claimants, and had caused embarrassment in the prosecution of the claim. I should regret to learn that this had been done by an agent of the government, which, I conceive, could not have authorized any act to the prejudice of interests of our citizens confided to it, and I would respectfully ask to be informed whether, if it be true that such papers have been communicated to the Venezuelan government, it has been done with the sanction of the department.

I have the honor to be, very respectfully, your obedient servant,

H. S. SANFORD.

Hon. LEWIS CASS,
Secretary of State.

Mr. Appleton to Mr. Turpin.

No. 13.]

DEPARTMENT OF STATE,
Washington, January 22, 1859.

SIR: Herewith you will receive a series of documents transmitted to the department by Mr. Sanford, as attorney for Lang & Delano, in support of the claim against Venezuela, which, as you allege in your No. 7, was so deficient in proof that you had felt constrained to decline the invitation of the government to proceed to Valencia for the purpose of entering upon an investigation of the Aves claim, with a view of deciding upon the equity of the compromise offered by the claimants to the Venezuelan government.

Mr. Sanford, having been apprised of the lack of proofs complained of, has lost no time in supplying the needed documents, which the department regards as satisfactorily sustaining their accompanying detailed statement of losses, and which you will lose no time in laying before the government, unless, as is hoped may be the case, you may already have succeeded in procuring the adjustment of the claim upon the terms of the proposed compromise.

No. 7, above referred to, is the last dispatch received from you.

I am, sir, your obedient servant,

JOHN APPLETON,
Assistant Secretary.

EDWARD TURPIN, Esq.,
&c., &c., &c.

List of Inclosures.

A.—H. S. Sanford to Secretary of State—January 14, 1859.
B.—Detailed statement of Lang & Delano's claim.
C.—George McGeorge's affidavit.
D.—Charles H. Lang's affidavit.
E.—L. Herrick's affidavit.
F.—George Wood Rice's affidavit.
G.—Isaac B. Mills's affidavit.
H.—N. N. Bridge's affidavit.
I.—John H. B. Lang's affidavit.
K.—James H. Phinney's affidavit.

Mr. Cass to Mr. Turpin.

No. 14.]

DEPARTMENT OF STATE,
Washington, February 7, 1859.

SIR: At the request of Mr. Sanford I inclose herewith an attested copy of the deposition of Captain Charles Penfield in support of the claim of Lang & Delano, and to be considered in connection with the proofs forwarded with the last dispatch to you, since the date of which no communications have been received from you.

I am, sir, your obedient servant,

LEWIS CASS.

E. A. TURPIN, Esq.,
&c., &c., &c.

Mr. Turpin to Mr. Cass.

No. 10.]

LEGATION OF THE UNITED STATES,
Caraccas, February 8, 1859.

SIR: I have the honor to acknowledge the receipt, on the 3d January ultimo, of the department's No. 12, (previous numbers also received,) together with its accompanying inclosure of a copy of a communication to the department from Mr. H. S. Sanford, attorney of the Aves Island claimants against the government of Venezuela for losses and damages resulting from the eviction of their agents and employés from said island by the forces of Venezuela in the year 1854.

In compliance with the instructions contained therein, I left Caraccas the ensuing day for Valencia, and on the 14th of the same month succeeded in effecting an agreement with the government of Venezuela, a copy of which I herewith transmit, the conditions being almost indentical with the expressed wishes of the claimants, the only departures therefrom being in the inability to obtain from this government the alternative condition of recurrence to the custom-houses of the republic in case of the failure of punctual payments. This condition was suggested, not insisted on by the claimants, and the new administration, regarding it as derogatory to the dignity of the nation, had determined not to admit it hereafter. The other departure has been in a small extension in time of the payments to be made the first year, but as the amount is on interest, and the whole sum being still made payable within the period prescribed by the claimants, viz: six years, it was not deemed by me to be a matter of sufficient importance as to compensate for the risk of delaying the conclusion of the agreement to a later day in the session of the national convention, then preparing for its very early dissolution, since effected, on the 3d of this present month. On the other hand, I have obtained for the claimants interest on the whole amount of the indemnity, to commence on the first day of January instead of from the date of signing the convention, as instructed—say, on the 14th ultimo—in dispensing with the necessity of proof in the case of Lang & Delano, and also in the complete and final settlement of the question of property and relinquishment of the island, without the necessity of a formal reference to the government of the United States, which might have involved the necessity of a ratification by the Senate of the United States, thus delaying the first payments for a year or eighteen months.

In its approval the convention exacted as a condition indispensable that the interest accruing should be computed at simple, not compound rate, and it was further agreed that the last clause in the third article (included in the brackets in the copy) should be "not approved."

In reference to the sum to be accepted in lieu of the relinquishment of the island by Venezuela, the attorney for the claimants, in a confidential letter to me, had referred me to a gentleman of this city who was authorized by him to admit of a certain sum; that gentleman, Señor José M. Rojas, has communicated the same to me in writing, and his letter is filed in the archives of this legation. At the particular request of the secretary of foreign relations, this sum of $10,000 was incorporated in the agreement generally, in the gross sum of the indemnification, and not mentioned as the specific equivalent for the relinquishment of the island.

This question of the Island of Aves has attracted more than usual attention in Venezuela, and President Monagas, in his message to Congress in 1856, communicated a report of the secretary of foreign relations, in which the question was treated in a very decidedly Venezuelan point of view, being, indeed, very nearly identical with the publication made in the United States on the subject by Señor Briceno, then minister plenipotentiary of Venezuela near the government of the United States. This had given so very decided a bias to the public mind here, that it was not without considerable difficulty that the approbation of the national convention was obtained, and, at one period of the discussion, I had very serious apprehensions of being able to obtain it. I remained in Valencia, however, until it was finally done, and I trust that this question, by the present agreement, has been settled to the satisfaction of the government of the United States and of the claimants. Of this I feel quite confident, that the very highest amount and the very best terms for the claimants compatible with the amicable relations of the two governments have been obtained.

Since writing the above I have received a note, under date of 4th instant, from honorable Minister of Foreign Relations, recapitulating the conditions, above alluded to, of the approval of the Aves Island agreement and desiring the expression of my consent thereto in writing, which note, in copy and translation, I herewith transmit, together with my reply of this date to the same.

With the highest respect and consideration, I have the honor to be your obedient servant,

E. A. TURPIN.

Hon. LEWIS CASS,
Secretary of State.

List of accompanying inclosures.

No. 1.—Aves Island agreement.
No. 2.—Sanojo's note, February 4, and translation.
No. 3.—My reply to same, date February 8.

The undersigned, Edward A. Turpin, minister resident of the United States of America, and Luis Sanojo, secretary of state of the department of foreign relations of the government of Venezuela, being duly authorized to form an equitable agreement for the satisfaction of the damages and losses sustained by Philo S. Shelton, Sampson & Tappan, and Lang & Delano, in consequence of the eviction of their agents and employés from the Aves Island, by the forces of Venezuela, have agreed upon the following articles:

ARTICLE 1. The government of Venezuela obliges itself to pay to the government of the United States, or to its minister resident in Venezuela, the gross sum of one hundred and thirty thousand dollars, United States currency, ($130,000,) of which said sum one hundred and five thousand dollars ($105,000) are in liquidation of the claims of Shelton, Sampson & Tappan, and are to be distributed among themselves, and the residue, that is to say, twenty-five thousand dollars, ($25,000,) is in liquidation of the claim of Lang & Delano.

Article 2. The said sum of one hundred and thirty thousand dollars shall be paid in the following terms :.

Year	Date	For Shelton, Sampson & Tappan.		For Lang & Delano.	
1859.	June 1	$2,500			
	August 1	2,500			
	October 1	2,500			
	December 1	2,500			
			$10,000		
1860.	June 30	$7,500		$2,000	
	December 31	7,500		2,000	
			$15,000		$4,000
1861.	June 30	$10,000		$2,000	
	December 31	10,000		2,000	
			$20,000		$4,000
1862.	June 30	$10,000		$2,500	
	December 31	10,000		2,500	
			$20,000		$5,000
1863.	June 30	$10,000		$3,000	
	December 31	10,000		3,000	
			$20,000		$6,000
1864.	June 30	$10,000		$3,000	
	December 31	10,000		3,000	
			$20,000		$6,000
			$105,000		$25,000

Interest at the rate of five per cent. per annum shall be paid on the gross amount of indemnity, commencing on the first day of this present month, January, 1859, and being added to the several installments as they fall due, the interest being always computed on the amount of indemnity remaining unpaid at the time of the payment of the several installments.

Article 3. In consideration of the above agreement and indemnification, the government of the United States, and the individuals in whose behalf they have been made, agree to desist from all further reclamation [for] the Island of Aves, [abandoning to the republic of Venezuela whatever rights might pertain to them.]

Article 4. This agreement shall be submitted to present national convention, and in case it should not be ratified by it before the closing of the present session, then it shall be considered null and void.

E. A. TURPIN.
LUIS SANOJO.

Valencia, *January* 14, 1859.

[Translation.]

Republic of Venezuela.

DEPARTMENT OE FOREIGN RELATIONS,
Valencia, February 4, 1859.

SIR: I have the honor to inform you that the national convention has approved, on the first of this month, the agreement respecting the Island of Aves concluded with you, suppressing, in the third article, the second part, running thus: "abandoning to the republic of Venezuela whatever rights might pertain to them," together with the notice that the interest stipulated in the second article shall be always simple, and shall be only paid successively upon the capital unpaid.

Will you be pleased to state to this department whether, notwithstanding the said suppression, you will consent to the agreement?

I avail myself, &c.,

LUIS SANOJO.

Hon. E. A. TURPIN,
Minister Resident of United States.

LEGATION OF THE UNITED STATES,
Caraccas, February 8, 1859.

SIR: The undersigned, minister resident of the United States, has the honor to acknowledge the receipt of the note of the honorable minister of foreign relations, under date of 4th instant, in which the honorable minister informs the undersigned that the national convention had approved, on the 1st instant, the agreement respecting the Island of Aves concluded between the honorable minister of foreign relations and the undersigned, in Valencia, on the 14th of January last, suppressing, in the third article, the second part, reading thus: "abandoning to the republic of Venezuela whatever rights that might pertain to them," together with the notification "that the interest stipulated in the second article should always be simple, and be only paid successively upon the unpaid capital," and desiring the undersigned to state whether, notwithstanding such suppression, he still consented to the same; to which the undersigned briefly replies that he does.

The undersigned avails himself of this occasion of expressing to the Hon. Mr. Sanojo his sentiments of distinguished consideration.

E. A. TURPIN.

Hon. LUIS SANOJO,
Minister of Foreign Relations.

Mr. Appleton to Mr. Sanford.

DEPARTMENT OF STATE,
Washington, March 4, 1859.

SIR: Herewith I communicate to you as the attorney and representative of the claimants, a copy of a dispatch dated the 8th ultimo, and of its inclosures just received from our minister in Venezuela.

These papers inform the department of the final settlement of the claims growing out of the eviction from the Aves Island, by the armed forces of Venezuela, of the agents and employés of Messrs. Philo S. Shelton, Sampson & Tappan, and Lang & Delano, in 1854. Although there is a material abatement by the terms of the convention from the sum last named by this department to Mr. Turpin, as insisted on by the claimants, it is inferred from his dispatch that the arrangement will be satisfactory, since it appears to be in general conformity with certain powers and concessions granted by you for the purpose of facilitating the more speedy adjustment of the claims.

I am, sir, &c.,

JOHN APPLETON,
Assistant Secretary.

H. S. SANFORD, Esq.,
Brevoort House, New York.

Mr. Sanford to Mr. Appleton.

DERBY, CONNECTICUT, *April* 8, 1859.

SIR: Having received from you by your letter of 4th ultimo an official notification "of the final settlement of the claims growing out of the eviction from Aves Island, by the armed forces of Venezuela, of the agents and employés of Messrs. Philo S. Shelton, and Sampson & Tappan, and of Lang & Delano, in 1854," by the conclusion of a convention for the payment of $130,000 in yearly installments, payable from one to five years, it is meet that I should address you this letter in reply thereto.

And, in the first place, your inference is correct that Mr. Turpin acquiesced in this large abatement of the minimum sum, mentioned in the instructions of the department to him, with my assent as attorney for the claimants. I was induced to yield this assent, not only because I was willing to make a sacrifice of a portion of our just demands to avoid further trouble to my own government, but also because these claims had been in no little degree embarrassed and prejudiced by the action, prior to 1858, of the then American minister at Caraccas, which I was apprehensive would occasion further procrastination and difficulty if our full rightful demands were insisted upon.

The spoliation and eviction occurred in December, 1854. The

claimants, immediately on being advised of it, in January, 1855, made earnest representations to the federal government, and asked for its interposition to procure redress. In seeking this redress, the claimants soon found that they had not merely the Venezuelan government to encounter; a powerful combination of speculators in Philadelphia, New York, and Baltimore, known as "the Philadelphia Guano Company," composed of many persons in those cities possessed of reputed large pecuniary means, and at that time wielding no little political influence, it was soon seen, was by far our most formidable antagonist; and for the reason that its efforts to circumvent the payment of our just demands were chiefly exerted, and its influence most injuriously felt at Washington and upon the United States minister at Caraccas. This company claimed Aves Island under a conditional purchase from Venezuela made by contract with the Monagas administration on the 25th December, 1854, (based upon a previous understanding as to the eviction,) after the claimants had been six months in possession, though those conditions were not fulfilled, and the bills of exchange, the consideration of the sale, (called the "Wallace contract,") were protested, and the contract subsequently, in July, 1855, declared null and void by the Venezuelan government on account thereof, the same opposition to our just claims continued from the same parties. In relation to the "Wallace contract," Mr. Eames, in a dispatch dated April 6, 1856, gives its details, and adds: "I have permitted myself to go into these details in this dispatch, by reason of the expressed wish of the department that I should sift the nature of the transaction, and the motives which induced this government to occupy the Aves. There is, in my judgment, ground to believe that the act of occupation took place as a necessary condition precedent to the drawing of the drafts. The occupation took place on the 13th of December, just in time to be known here on the day when the contract was signed; that is, the 21st of the same month, the drafts being drawn and delivered four days afterwards." And he further says, "it is currently reported that high official men here, then in power, were to share in the profits of the contract. No fact has come to my knowledge which makes this statement improbable." And in September, 1855, the contract was renewed through the zealous and extraordinary interposition of the American minister, (indicating that the United States government took a great interest in its revival,) and this Island of Aves in terms included in it, with express exemption of guarantee of title by Venezuela; and this last contract, called the "Pickrell contract," was so procured by the active "good offices" of the American minister, ostensibly in compliance with a suggestion contained in a dispatch dated June 20, 1855, from Mr. Marcy, then Secretary of State; but it is considered in flagrant violation of the explicit instruction of Mr. Marcy "to forbear to do or say anything in favor of the Philadelphia company which will in any way affect the (our) claim," which the same dispatch informed the minister our government intended to enforce.

Mr. Eames seemed from the outset not merely indisposed to do anything to advance and sustain the claim, but the claimants then thought, and have seen no reason to change their opinion, that he was hostile to it, and interested, in feeling or otherwise, in favor of the Philadelphia speculators. It was not strange, therefore, that no copy of the "Pickrell contract," containing the provision in regard to Aves Island, was communicated to the department by him until February 22, 1856, and then only until Mr. Marcy, in his dispatch of December 24, 1855, somewhat significantly remarked to that official, in acknowledging the receipt of the dispatch advising of the consummation of the contract, "a copy of the contract itself, however, would have been acceptable to the department, especially as we are orally informed that, despite the reservation [Mr. Marcy evidently supposing it contained such reservation] of the rights and claims of those citizens of the United States who were ousted from Aves Island by a Venezuelan vessel-of-war, guano from that island has been recently brought to this country by vessels in the service of the company who are a party to the contract."

So unjust and annoying was the course of the American minister in reference to the claim, that, December 24, 1855, the claimants felt constrained to address a communication to the President, a duplicate of which was transmitted to the State Department, referring to that course as affording just ground for serious complaint, which letter, on the files of the department, it is important should be preserved, as it may be material hereafter, to vindicate the truth of history. The letter of Mr. Marcy to Mr. Eames of February 20, 1856, in relation to this complaint, it is not considered necessary to comment upon. Mr. Marcy, doubtless, at that time, entertained the opinion there expressed. And here it is proper to advert to the fact, that a most remarkable contradiction appears in the official accounts spread upon the records of this government and that of Venezuela, in relation to the mode and manner in which the "good offices" of the American minister in favor of the "Pickrell contract" were rendered, and in relation to the inclusion of Aves Island in that contract. In Mr. Eames's dispatch of February 12, 1856, forwarding the "Pickrell contract" by which the department was first apprised of such inclusion, Mr. Eames makes these singular statements: "Although I could, of course, claim no authority to prescribe the form of the contract, yet I do not doubt that the avoidance by this government of any reference to the Aves Island in the article granting the privilege, and the subsequent exception and limitation introduced with reference to that island were, in part, if not mainly, caused by my explicit and emphatic reservation of all the rights and claims of its prior American occupants, and by my declaration that those claims would, without doubt, in my judgment, be energetically sustained by the government of the United States." And in a previous dispatch of October 15, 1855, he states "I not only, in compliance with your instructions, reserved in the most clear and emphatic manner all rights and claims of the American citizens who were found in possession of the Aves Island by the Venezuelan authorities on the 13th of December, but I took care also to put on record my reiterated declaration that no act or word of mine in rendering my good offices in aid of the rights and interests represented by Mr. Pickrell should be considered as in any way affecting or impairing the anterior claim of those citizens to full reparation, in regard to which anterior claim I repeated to his excellency my confident conviction that it would be effectually sustained by the government of the United States.'' And with the same dispatch he incloses a note dated September 4, 1855, to Señor Aranda, Venezuelan minister of foreign relations, referred to as his ''protest'' in question, and which purports to be the substance of the observations which he then recently ''had the honor to address to his excellency the President of the republic in the presence of the honorable minister of foreign relations and of Hacienda, in an audience solicited by him for the purpose of making known to the government of Venezuela the views of the government of the United States in relation to what may be called the question of the guano islands.'' The representations in this note are remarkably inconsistent with, and contradictory to, those made in the official reports of the minister of foreign relations and Hacienda to the Venezuelan Congress, and which are filed in the department, and those in the dispatch of Señor Gutierrez to General Cass, brought by Dr. Briceno, special minister to the United States, and those in the pamphlet so exceptionably published in this country by that official, and indeed throughout all the Venezuelan correspondence. Extended and particular comment upon the irreconcilable statements made in these documents, would give unprofitable length to this communication, and the subject is a disagreeable one, for a perusal of those documents will show that a direct issue is made, the result of which depends wholly upon the veracity of the different statements by Mr. Eames on the one hand, and the several ministers of President Monagas's administration, present at the audience, on the other. These claimants then thought, and still think, that a sincere earnestness on the part of our minister, in obedience to the instructions of the department, would have excluded from the ''Pickrell contract'' all mention of Aves Isle, or, if mentioned, would have caused an express reservation of our rights in terms that could not have been misunderstood or disputed, and that at the same time he could even with more facility and greater advantage have secured to the Philadelphia Guano Company under it all they sought for with respect to the other guano islands. And especially are they confirmed in this opinion by the representations of Venezuelan authorities that the original draft of the ''Pickrell contract,'' including the Aves Island, was made or dictated by Mr. Eames himself without reservation of our rights, and that among his chief arguments used to the Venezuelan government to obtain its acquiescence was, that refusal so to revive the contract would imperil the friendly relations between the two governments.

The claimants attach importance to these facts, because, as the records of the department will show, the transfer of the possession of Aves Isle by the Venezuelan government to the Philadelphia Guano Company thus obtained was seriously detrimental if not totally destructive to their interests in the isle, and to their claim for indemnity beyond damages and actual losses resulting from the spoliation and eviction, and the Venezuelan authorities continually referred to it as an admission by the United States of the title of Venezuela to the isle. The Philadelphia Guano Company, under their most nefarious and iniquitous contract, procured in a great measure by the representation that eminent and influential political personages in this country were interested in the company, forthwith commenced, as the evidence on file shows, the abstraction of guano from the isle in large quantities under this very contract. (See Mr. Marcy's letter above quoted and correspondence respecting J. J. Keefe's advertisement.) It is proper here to note that Mr. Eames was absent from Caraccas when the "Wallace contract" was made in December, 1854. It is the "Pickrell contract," made in September, 1855, in effect continuing the grant to the Philadelphia Guano Company to which the last foregoing remarks and the letter to the President above referred to more particularly apply. And the files also show that it was in vain the claimants sought to invoke the permission of the department to institute proceedings in chancery against that company to prevent such abstraction; and that, in fact, their request made to the department to be allowed so to do was answered by the intimation that such course on our part would absolve the department from any obligation to press our claims further against Venezuela. These circumstances have been weighty in their influence upon the case throughout, and superadded to others, have, in a great degree, led to the compromise of our just demand below what our actual losses in fact were.

In the very outset of this case the American minister seems to have been somewhat anxious to find objection to our claim, and that it was indeed of not much importance; for in his dispatch of April 26, 1855, to the State Department he incloses to Mr. Marcy a copy of the famous military capitulation of the island by Gibbs and Lang, and states that it is regarded by the Venezuelan government as an effectual bar to any claim for indemnity and expenses, and the opinion that it will greatly embarrass its successful prosecution. Mr. Marcy, overlooking the fact that the same paper had been communicated to the department by claimants as one of the most cogent and strong items of proof in support of their claim, called the attention of claimants to it, and to this opinion of Mr. Eames as a difficulty to be obviated. In reply to this communication the claimants addressed a somewhat lengthy communication to Mr. Marcy under date of June 20, 1855, in which the circumstances connected with this capitulation and its true legal character and effect in the case are fully exposed, and showing that it was an important item of proof in favor of claimants. After the receipt of that letter, the claimants heard no more objections either from the department or from Mr. Eames based upon the capitulation. This alleged "effectual bar" was not merely overcome, but the instrument became a formidable weapon for claimants in the case. Notwithstanding all that Mr. Eames wrote to the department about his protests and reservations and the like, such seemed to have been his opinion of the case and his subsequent course at Caraccas in relation to it that, as it is stated again and again by the Venezuelan government, the first formal reclamation to it by him was not made until December 20, 1856, two years after the outrage! The files of the department show this fact to be asserted by the Venezuelan government. Wearied by the course of those whose duty it was to aid them, and despairing of favorable success from such aid, on the 19th April, 1856, the claimants addressed a memorial to Congress, which is to be found in Ex. Doc. 25, Senate, third session, Thirty-fourth Congress, p. 35, and accompanying which was a draft for a law, (to be found ib. page 93,) the substance of which was enacted by Congress, August 18, and which act has been highly important and beneficial to the country and to those American citizens engaged in the guano trade, although the written memorial to the President and State Department of the claimants who were thus iustrumental in procuring that act to be allowed to avail themselves of its provisions in reference to Aves Isle never received any reply or even notice from the late administration.

The only result of the memorial to Congress, beneficial to claimants, was the public exposition of their claim to the country by the printing of those of the documents communicated January 12, 1857, to the Senate by the State Department, in answer to the resolution of the 4th August and 9th January preceding; and, also, of the more important documents laid by memorialists before the Senate, amongst which was the printed brief in this case, (see page 38, &c., ib.,) in which the facts and law are fully discussed; and, also, copies of depositions and other proofs in the case, not communicated by the Department of State.

It is believed that the publication of these documents awakened the people of this country to the importance, in reference to the commercial and agricultural interests, not merely of the guano trade, but of the subject generally in respect of our national rights, and the rules of international law governing such cases, and of which the law passed at the instance of these claimants was merely the recognition and exponent, and which, it will be observed, was by the action primarily of the legislative department merely.

And I deem it not presumptuous on my part to further remark, that the publication by me of a *brochure* of thirty-four pages a short time afterwards, as an exposition of the law of "special reprisals" as a peaceful remedy under the *jus gentium*, applicable to this very case as a means of redress for our injuries, and which was printed for circulation before Congress, has, also, not been without beneficial effect in forming a just and correct public opinion on that subject, which will be salutary upon the course of this government if it is acted upon and carried out, as it should be, in all similar cases. I do not hesitate to avow the opinion, without any reference to the present administration, that one of the strongest reasons demanding the recognition and practice of the law of "special reprisals," and the passage of an act of Congress regulating such practice similar to that suggested with the pamphlet and printed, (copies of both are inclosed herewith,) is, that claimants would not be left to the mercy of ignorant, lazy, inefficient, perverse, and ill-disposed and unpatriotic, and perchance, drunken or corrupt diplomatic officials, and of those disposed to protect them. It would make the *lettre de requête*, and the "special writ of reprisal," as it is termed by Lord Chief Justice Campbell in his "Lives of the Lord Chancellors of England," (vol. 1, page 205,) "a judicial process." To this process the subject is entitled "of right," as is laid down in Molloy and other authorities, and its being granted is not to be controlled, except in extraordinary cases, by those "considerations of prudence and expediency which, waiving strict right, often influence the intercourse between nations." Stephens, in his Commentaries, states that the English statutes on this subject "have in some respect armed the subject with powers to impel the prerogative by directing the ministers of the crown to issue letters of marque and reprisal upon due demand," &c. Such law by Congress would prevent annoyance to the department by the presentation of unfounded claims. It would rid it of its voluminous correspondence on such subjects, and which, without assiduous and deep research into the facts and law, is apt to be superficial and inconclusive. The Executive would not, as now in every case, labor under the embarrassment caused by the knowledge that the consent of Congress must be obtained in such case for the employment of coercive means, and the consequent restraint from the use of suggestions that such means would be resorted to, even in the most flagrant cases. The idea of this great principle having become "obsolete" is perfectly absurd. Principles never die. It becomes this republican constitutional government to maintain that principle which, it may well be imagined, arbitrary and despotic governments find it their interest to bury. It would refer each case to judicial examination primarily, or, at least, before definite action by the department in most cases would be necessary, and then its action could not well be erroneous, as, the notorious Gibson case is an example, it may now sometimes be. It would save the necessity of special missions to obtain indemnity, of Greytown expeditions, of Paraguayan expeditions, and such like proceedings; for such law would arm the Executive in each case with the means, naval and military, of redress, and make it his bounden duty to use them, and that, too, without apprehension of impeachment for violation of the Constitution. How completely would such law invest the President with such power, (nay, "impel" him,) to fulfill the duty of giving redress to our citizens in such cases of spoliation as that which occurred a few days since in Nicaragua, and this, too, without form of war, and by a process which, under the law of nations, is held to be peaceful, and not a *casus belli;* but, on the contrary, a preventive of war.

But *revenons à nos moutons!* The only paper ever presented by the American minister to the Venezuelan government that can be characterized as partaking the character of an argument in support of the claim, was a communication of the 21st March, 1857, being a verbose dissertation or essay upon the ancient geographical jurisdiction of the captain generalcy of Caraccas, and of the Republic of Venezuela after it, which, however interesting to a historical reader, had but trifling bearing in the case, insomuch as the question pending was not one of geographical jurisdiction but was one of derelict, and dependent upon first and continued actual possession and occupation. The discussion invited by that communication was, in fact, calculated to protract the decision of the case, and to divert attention from the true legitimate points in issue, and which had been fully presented and discussed in the printed brief of claimants filed in the State Department long preceding, and a copy of which had been communicated by the department, and which the minister should have followed in any discussion of the case by him. The claimants understood their own case quite as well as he did. The voluminously extended note was more an ingenious mean of making it appear that he was strenuous in his exertions in behalf of the claim, and to conceal his previous remissness, than a sincere effort to redeem that remissness. And it is not alone in the circumstances before referred to that the claimants have found embarrassment to exist causing delay, and also causing difficulties in relation to the amount claimed. Until July last, that functionary had not presented the full proofs of the case transmitted to him April 25 and August 14, 1856, and February 3, 1857, by the department, and then only when explicitly instructed by the department forthwith to fulfill that duty, in doing which, he seems to have taken pains to communicate to the Venezuelan government papers not proofs in support of any portion of the claims, and which he must have known were not intended to be communicated to that government, and in relation to which he could not have been ignorant that their effect would be highly mischievous to a portion of the claims, as has, in fact, been stated by his successor. In one of the first dispatches of Mr. Turpin, the prejudicial effect of this act to the claim of Lang & Delano is expressly adverted to as having caused him embarrassment, and was expressly mentioned by me in a communication to the department, January 14, 1859, confirming thus the expediency of the request I felt constrained, in the interests of my principals, to make to this department, July —, that the further conduct of this case be withdrawn from Mr. Eames, and further action by the department be suspended until a new minister could be sent out.

Other courses of the same minister could be referred to exhibing inimical feeling to this claim, or, at least, an absence of official interest in its prosecution, and also laxity in regard to those proper exertions which, if they had been made by him, would have effected more than two years ago, a settlement of it to more advantage than has now been made. It is a sorry consolation to the claimants, that peradventure the explosion and insolvency of the Philadelphia Guano Company may have prevented the reaping any pecuniary profit in return.

This recital is thus made so particular to explain to the department why it is that the claimants consented to reduce their claims to an aggregate so much below the amount before insisted, (and which it would seem from your letter has caused some surprise to the department,) and to exonerate themselves from any suspicion of having originally presented an unfounded or exaggerated demand, or beyond what was rightfully due them, and it is presumed that it explains and justifies their course fully. This has been its sole object.

Turning from further consideration of these features of the case, I take pleasure in performing for the claimants the duty they owe to you, who have had especial charge in the conduct of this case, to the venerable Secretary of State, and to the President, and likewise to Mr. Turpin, and I could with sincerity, were it proper, add other gentlemen in your department subordinate to yourself, to place full acknowledgments on record of the energy, ability, promptness, and proper American spirit manifested since the advent of the present administration in the prosecution of this claim to its successful termination.

In a private letter to me, dated December 12, 1856, written by Mr.

Marcy, in reply to one of complaint on account of the procrastination of this case, he observes, referring to the difficulty experienced by our government in obtaining justice from the Hispano-American republics, that during his connection with President Pierce's administration, but one or two cases of claims of our citizens against those States had been brought to a settlement.

The recent report by the State Department of unsettled claims, made to the Senate in response to its resolution, is a sad verification of his remark. And the spectacle thereby presented of this great and powerful Confederacy calmly and tamely having submitted, not only year after year but decade after decade, to the most outrageous spoliations upon the rights of its citizens, and the plunder of their property, especially by some of the insignificant mulatto States south of us, several of whom seem to be impudent in comparative ratio to their insignificance, is disgraceful to our country. I have rejoiced, since March 4, 1857, that those who have charge of the government have displayed so praiseworthy an emulation to redeem the honor of our flag, sullied in this case by the neglect of their predecessors, and to afford that just protection of person and property which every citizen of these States may rightfully claim as his due. If the administration would only press upon Congress and secure the passage of the act before alluded to, authorizing summary and peaceful "special reprisals" as I have before sought to enforce, I would feel that an effectual guarantee would be afforded the rights of our citizens not dependent upon what is too often circumlocutory diplomacy. This claim being settled, I have no personal interest in the passage of such law beyond that possessed by every American citizen, unless, indeed, Venezuela should fail to comply with its convention, when such peaceful remedy would be an effectual and sure resort without a declaration of war, and without being dependent upon the caprice or whim or tardiness, and what not, of those who may administer the government when the installments become due.

At the hazard of extending this communication, I deem it proper to reiterate that I am prompted in making it by a sense of justice towards this administration, and of the duty I owe to myself of explaining why it is that these claimants, after preferring a demand for so large an amount, have acquiesced in receiving such a comparatively small sum as $130,000. No consideration in reference to the ability of Venezuela to pay the whole amount as stipulated has influenced it, nor any want of confidence in the honor and integrity of the present government of the country. It is true the Venezuelan government just being, as it were, newly established, is at present laboring under some financial difficulties and embarrassments, but the people and country are rich and prosperous, and its present rulers are honorable and just men. Considerations of friendly feeling towards them, and a desire to remove as far as was in my power, even by concessions of right, every obstacle to the restoration of the *entente cordiale* between them and my own country, have not been without influence; but I repeat that the position of the case created by the circumstances before referred to has been the controlling motive for such compromise. I am aware that this compromise has been a great sacrifice to the claimants. P. S. Shelton was allowed by it but $10,000 for the island and guano on it at the time of the eviction. Thousands upon thousands of tons have since December, 1854, been taken from the island by the Philadelphia Guano Company and others, and within the last few weeks numerous cargoes from that isle have arrived at different ports of the United States, and at this moment large parties of citizens of the United States are located upon it engaged in gathering guano and shipping it for sale. And I have no question that the estimate of the value of the island made by Commander de Horsey, R. N., in his report to the British admiralty, that the island was worth "one and a half million pounds sterling," (Ex. Doc., page 93,) before cited, was not exaggerated, and that the claimants could justly have increased their claim to more than ten times the amount originally preferred. We consider that P. S. Shelton's claim to the island, contradistinguished from that for actual losses and damages, had been so muddled, embarrassed, and prejudiced by the circumstances we have referred to, (perhaps because it was deemed "hopeless,") and also that the value of the island had been so much lessened by the abstraction of the guano, that we in a measure deemed it best to forego our claim except for actual losses. It is my deliberate conviction that if we had had no minister in Caraccas prior to Mr. Turpin's going there the claimants would have obtained, and earlier, a sum much nearer justice and right than that allowed by the recent convention.

I must believe that you will find in the propriety induced by a proper self-respect, and also my respect for the department of explaining my motives for this compromise a full apology if not entire justification for everything contained in this letter. I am convinced that you will be satisfied that this only could be my motive, as I have before stated, for the references in it to the course in this case by the late minister, and which, you will perceive, were necessary for a full explanation and exposition of the subject.

I have the honor to be, with great respect, your most obedient servant,

H. S. SANFORD.

Hon. JOHN APPLETON,
Assistant Secretary of State.

DERBY, CONNECTICUT,
October 17, 1859.

SIR: Permit me to call the official attention of the President, and to solicit yours also, to the position of the convention made by Mr. Turpin with the government of Venezuela in January last, and which was adopted and passed by the national convention of that country after the three discussions provided by law, and was ratified and confirmed by the President of Venezuela, and delivered to Mr. Turpin.

You will find this convention does not contain any clause respecting its ratification by the President and Senate of the United States, Mr. Turpin seeming to entertain the opinion that such formal approval by the President, by the advice and consent of the Senate, was unnecessary, on the ground that it was a mere convention or agreement, and not a formal treaty.

In the first place, I am satisfied that there is no difference between a convention and a treaty. The constitutional clause vesting the treaty-making power with the President and Senate, and requiring the "advice and consent" of the latter in all cases to make the exercise of such power valid and binding, cannot be evaded by styling the result of such exercise a "convention," an "agreement," or an "arrangement," instead of using the constitutional term "treaty." This wise constitutional provision reaches and covers all such cases just as much as if the terms of the compact or arrangement commenced with the formula: "In the name of the most holy and indivisible Trinity," and the like, and if it contained at the end the prescribed formula as to the *modus operandi* of ratification. A convention is not the act of the government of the United States without the concurrence of both President and Senate. The President is not the government, and, *à fortiori*, the United States minister at Caraccas is not the government of the United States; but *quoad*, the exercise of the treaty-making power, the Senate, and not a majority merely, but two thirds of the Senate must unite and consent to constitute and represent the government of the United States to make such arrangement constitutionally valid and binding. Until it is so consummated and perfected, such convention, arrangement, or agreement is inchoate and imperfect, not executed by the United States according to constitutional requisition, it is a merely one-sided promise, not accepted or agreed to by the other party in the fulfillment of its constitutional powers in the only way and form that such powers can be exercised. Now, this very convention contains a release by the United States to Venezuela of the claim involved upon payment of the sums stipulated. It cannot be said that the government of the United States has as yet constitutionally agreed to such release; and ratification by the President and Senate is indispensable to the perfection of that clause as well as the other portions of the treaty; and if such ratification is not made, Venezuela may hereafter quibble in respect to the payment upon the ground that it has not received such release from the government of the United States in constitutional and binding form.

I do not urge the argument that this loose mode of perfecting treaties between nations (originating in the fact that despotic monarchs possess plenary powers to make such arrangements without the assent of any third estate in the government) is inappropriate and inapplicable to a republican constitutional government, where the functions, authority, and powers of the respective branches of the government are delegated, prescribed, and limited by the Constitution itself; and that the attempt by one branch of the government to exercise such powers without the concurrence of the coördinate branch of the government, to whom with it, jointly, those powers were delegated, would be an usurpation; for I am satisfied it requires no suggestion from me to enable you to perceive the force of such argument.

I would respectfully ask, therefore, that Mr. Turpin be instructed forthwith to transmit to the department the original convention in his possession, to the end that it may be approved by the President and may be laid before the Senate at an early period of next session, for the constitutional advice and consent of that body for its ratification. The claimants are entirely satisfied that such ratification would be given at once, and if not, it is important that they should know the precise legal and constitutional ground on which their just claim rests, and be enabled at an early period to ask for the institution of measures that shall probably be consummated in constitutional form.

If not improper, I would like that you indicate to me the probable course of the Executive on this point, as it will materially affect the worth of the claim in which I am deeply interested.

I shall probably leave the country in a few days, to be away some months, and it is important to me to know what course will probably be taken on this subject.

I have the honor to be, very respectfully, your most obedient servant,

H. S. SANFORD.

Hon. LEWIS CASS,
Secretary of State.

DEPARTMENT OF STATE,
Washington, October 22, 1859.

SIR: I have to acknowledge the receipt of your communication of the 17th instant, inviting the attention of the Executive and of this department to the expediency of submitting to the Senate, for its formal approval, the convention negotiated by Mr. Turpin with the government of Venezuela, in January last, in relation to the Aves Island claim of Messrs. Shelton and others.

In reply, I have to inform you that it has not been the practice of the government to submit to the Senate conventions providing for the adjustment of private claims, unless such a course is indicated in the instrument itself. It does not appear, from an examination of Mr. Turpin's convention, that any ratification or approval of it on the part of the United States is contemplated. But the want of such ratification on the part of this government, does not prevent recourse to that formality at any future period, should it be deemed expedient; nor does it in any respect weaken or invalidate the binding effect of the convention upon Venezuela. Indeed, the good faith of the government of that republic having been pledged to the provisions of the convention, by the ratification of the proper authorities, there would be no more hesitation on the part of this government to enforce its stipulations, should it become necessary, than if the instrument had been ratified by the United States as well as Venezuela.

In order, however, that the rights of the parties interested may be properly guarded, Mr. Turpin has been instructed to forward to this department the original convention signed by him, as well as an authenticated copy of the acts of ratification and confirmation by the Venezuelan authorities.

I am, sir, your obedient servant,

LEWIS CASS.

HENRY S. SANFORD, Esq.,
Derby, Connecticut.

www.ingramcontent.com/pod-product-compliance
Lightning Source LLC
LaVergne TN
LVHW020932110826
845150LV00004B/842

9781425552732